Imperial power and popular politics

In this series of interconnected studies Rajnarayan Chandavarkar offers a powerful revisionist analysis of the relationship between class and politics in India between the Mutiny and Independence. Dr Chandavarkar rejects the 'Orientalist' view of Indian social and economic development as unique and exceptional, which calls for explanations specific to its culture, and reasserts the critical role of the working classes in shaping the pattern of Indian capitalist development. He demonstrates the inadequacy of 'culture' as a dominant tool of historical analysis, especially as manifested in those recent subaltern studies which have focused upon colonial discourse to the almost complete exclusion of the material things. An underlying and recurrent theme of the book is how perceptions of power shaped alignments of class and influenced changing definitions of social identity. The book ranges widely across the social and political history of the working classes in India, examining the character of trade unions, the political culture of the working class neighbourhoods, the nature of violence and policing, popular responses to the moral panic of the plague epidemic and the Gandhian inflection of nationalist rhetoric. Dr Chandavarkar's analysis of political discourse, community structure and class relations in industrializing India has major implications, and *Imperial power and popular politics* offers one of the most sustained and sophisticated critiques yet made of both Marxist and functionalist narratives of industrialization. In their stead Dr Chandavarkar emphasizes the fluidity and flexibility of the relationships between discourse and power, language and political practice, and in the work's concluding chapter he offers an alternative schematic view of the process of class formation in India, within the context of 'world capitalism'.

Sustained in argument and elegant in exposition, this book represents a major contribution not only to the history of the Indian working classes, but to the history of industrial capitalism and colonialism as a whole. *Imperial power and popular politics* will be essential reading for all scholars and students of recent political, economic and social history, social theory, and cultural and colonial studies.

Imperial power and popular politics

Class, resistance and the state in India, c. 1850–1950

Rajnarayan Chandavarkar

Trinity College, Cambridge

CAMBRIDGE
UNIVERSITY PRESS

PUBLISHED BY THE PRESS SYNDICATE OF THE UNIVERSITY OF CAMBRIDGE
The Pitt Building, Trumpington Street, Cambridge CB2 1RP, United
Kingdom

CAMBRIDGE UNIVERSITY PRESS
The Edinburgh Building, Cambridge CB2 2RU, United Kingdom
40 West 20th Street, New York, NY 10011-4211, USA
10 Stamford Road, Oakleigh, Melbourne 3166, Australia

First published 1998

Printed in the United Kingdom at the University Press, Cambridge

Typeset in Plantin 10/12 pt [VN]

A catalogue record for this book is available from the British Library

Library of Congress cataloguing in publication data

Chandavarkar, Rajnarayan.
Imperial power and popular politics: Class, resistance
and the state in India, *c.* 1850–1950 / Rajnarayan Shamrao Chandavarkar.
   p.   cm.
Includes bibliographical references and index.
ISBN 0 521 59234 8 (hb). – ISBN 0 521 59692 0 (pb)
1. Capitalism – India – History – 19th century.   2. Capitalism –
India – History – 20th century.   3. Working class – India – History –
19th century.   4. Working class – India – History – 20th century.
5. Social classes – India – History – 19th century.   6. Social classes –
India – History – 20th century.   7. Imperialism – History.   I. Title.
HC433.C445   1998
330.12'2'0954 – dc21   97–8911 CIP

ISBN 0 521 59234 8 hardback
ISBN 0 521 59692 0 paperback

For Jennifer

Contents

Acknowledgements

This book is part of a wider enquiry into the social history of capitalism in India with which I have been engaged. It develops suggestions offered in *The Origins of Industrial Capitalism in India: Business Strategies and the Working Classes in Bombay, 1900–1940* (Cambridge University Press, 1994), seeks to open up fresh lines of enquiry and raises questions, some of which I hope to pursue in a further study of working-class politics in Bombay in the early twentieth century.

The research for this book has been generously supported by the Master and Fellows of Trinity College, Cambridge; the Managers of the Smuts Memorial Fund; and the General Board of the University of Cambridge. For facilitating this research, I am indebted to the custodians, archivists, librarians and staff of various institutions: of the Maharashtra State Archives, the Mumbai Marathi Grantha Sangrahalaya and the Bhau Daji Lad Museum in Bombay; of the record rooms of the Bombay Millowners' Association, the Commissioner of Police, Bombay, and the Deputy Inspector-General, Criminal Investigation Department, Maharashtra; the Gokhale Institute of Politics and Economics, Pune; the National Archives of India and the Nehru Memorial Museum and Library in New Delhi; the Asiatic Society of Calcutta; the Oriental and India Office Collections at the British Library in London; and in Cambridge, the University Library and the Centre of South Asian Studies, whose Secretary-Librarian, Lionel Carter, has once again been unfailingly helpful.

Chapters 2, 4 and 7 have been previously published: chapter 2 appeared in *Modern Asian Studies*, 19:3 (July 1985) in a special issue which reviewed the *Cambridge Economic History of India*; chapter 4 in *Modern Asian Studies*, 15:3 (July 1981), in a special issue, entitled *Power, Profit and Politics: Essays on Imperialism, Nationalism and Change in Twentieth Century India, 18701940*, edited by C. J. Baker, G. Johnson and A. Seal; and chapter 7 in P. Slack and T. Ranger (eds.), *Epidemic and Ideas: Essays on the Historical Perceptions of Pestilence* (Cambridge University Press,

1994). I thank the editors and publishers for their permission to reproduce those chapters.

Most of the chapters of this book have been presented, in part or whole,
at seminars in Cambridge, Oxford, Hull, London, Amsterdam, Boston,
and at Dartmouth College, New Hampshire, Trinity College, Hartford,
Connecticut, the Nehru Memorial Museum and Library in New Delhi,
the Department of History, Calcutta University, and the Centre for
Studies in Social Sciences in Calcutta. I am grateful to those who participated and thus forced me to re-think and re-cast my ideas. Tony
Giddens, Tapan Raychaudhuri, Gareth Stedman Jones and John Saville
read an earlier draft of this book and provided comments and encouragement. Many friends, students and colleagues have, through their scholarship, or in conversation and argument, helped to shape this work. It is a
particular pleasure to thank for their friendship and support in numberless ways Arup Banerji, Subho Basu, Chris Bayly, Joya Chatterji, Orlando
Figes, Nandini Gooptu, Douglas Haynes, Gordon Johnson, Anil Seal,
Samita Sen, Sunita Thakur, Hari Vasudevan and David Washbrook.
There are few ideas in the following pages which I have not rehearsed with
Jennifer Davis, whose insight, patience and understanding has made this
book, and much else besides, possible.

Abbreviations

AICC	All-India Congress Committee
AITUC	All-India Trade Union Congress
ATLA	Ahmedabad Textile Labour Association
BDEC	Bombay Disturbances Enquiry Committee
BMOA	Bombay Millowners' Association
BPP SAI	*Bombay Presidency Police, Secret Abstracts of Intelligence*
BRIC	Bombay Riots Inquiry Committee
BSEC	Bombay Strike Enquiry Committee
BTLU	Bombay Textile Labour Union
CEHI	*The Cambridge Economic History of India*
CPI	Communist Party of India
CWMG	*The Collected Works of Mahatma Gandhi*
GOB	Government of Bombay
GOI	Government of India
IESHR	*Indian Economic and Social History Review*
ILO	International Labour Organization
ITB	Indian Tariff Board
JAS	*Journal of Asian Studies*
MAS	*Modern Asian Studies*
MCC	Proceedings of the Meerut Conspiracy Case
MSA	Maharashtra State Archives, Bombay
NAI	National Archives of India, New Delhi
NMML	Nehru Memorial Museum and Library, New Delhi
OIOC	Oriental and India Office Collections, British Library, London
PP	*Parliamentary Papers*
PRO	Public Record Office, London
PWD	Public Works Department
RCLI	*Royal Commission on Labour in India*
TLIC	Textile Labour Inquiry Committee

Glossary

adivasi	original inhabitants; denotes 'scheduled tribes' under the Indian constitution
ahimsa	non-violence
akhada	gymnasium; meeting place; residence of religious mendicants
badmash	hooligan
bania	trader, moneylender, grain dealer; also a caste name
bhadralok	gentle-folk; refers mainly to higher caste and literate groups in Bengal
charkha	spinning wheel
chawl	tenement
dacoit	bandit; robber who uses violence and operates in gangs
dada	literally, 'elder brother'; used to describe a neighbourhood tough
dalit	oppressed; 'untouchable' caste
ganja	cannabis
Ganpati	another name for the Hindu god Ganesh
garibi hatao	abolish poverty; Congress Party slogan in the early 1970s
goonda	hooligan, thug
hakim	physician
halalkhore	sweeper who removed refuse and excreta from houses and streets
hartal	strike, cessation of work or trade dispute
havildar	constable
jamat	council of a caste, neighbourhood or sect
khaddar	coarse, home-spun cloth
kotwal	police or legal official
lathi	stick, bludgeon
mahajan	merchants' guild, assembly, association
majur	labourer
malik	patron, proprietor, boss

maulvi	Muslim priest or learned man
mela	festival; company of dancers taking part in a festival
mofussil	the provinces or hinterland
moholla	neighbourhood, quarter of a town
panchayat	council or tribunal, typically consisting of five people
patel	village official, headman
sadhu	Hindu ascetic; holy man with saintly qualities
sangh	association, organization
saraf, shroff	banker, money-changer
satyagraha	truth-force; a term used by Gandhi for his technique of passive resistance
seth	wealthy financier; merchant; head of trade guild
shuddhi	ritual of purification, movement for conversion of Muslims to Hinduism
sirdar, sardar	foreman, labour contractor, jobber
swadeshi	product of the nation; goods made in India
swaraj	self-rule
tabut	shrine; a model of the tomb of Husain at Kerbala which is carried in procession during a festival
talimkhana	gymnasium
taluka	an administrative unit below the level of the district
taluqdar	landlord, especially in north India
tamasha	show or entertainment; folk theatre
tanzeem	organization; specifically organization for Muslim unity
toli	gang of men who levied contributions from shopkeepers for Mohurran or other festivals
ugarani	the collection of money which is considered to be due
vaidya	physician, especially in the Ayurvedic tradition
waaz	sermon or discourse preached in a mosque
wadi	quarter or neighbourhood of a town
zamindar	landowner

1 Introduction

This book investigates the interplay between class relations and political discourse in late nineteenth- and early twentieth-century India. It seeks to develop and elaborate lines of enquiry which I had begun to pursue in earlier work on the social history of capitalism in India.[1] This work had suggested that the history of capitalism and of the working class in India could most fruitfully be investigated, not as an exception – neither as a case of 'pre-capitalist' development nor as a product of a peculiar and unique 'Indian culture'[2] – but firmly in relation to what are deemed to be the 'rules' or expectations of sociological discourse. An old, persistent and frequently re-activated 'Orientalist' tradition has long encouraged historians to deem Indian society an exception to every rule of social (and historical) explanation. In no aspect of the study of Indian society has this assumption of exceptionalism been more resolutely embedded and more subtly manifested than the investigation of the working classes. Yet to assume the exceptionalism of Indian society is to obscure and distort its character and to deepen its more intractable conundrums. Opened to the logics of explanation deployed elsewhere, its history offers a significant vantage point from which the theoretical apparatus of social analysis, conventional explanations and analytical expectations – developed primarily in relation to the unique historical experience of Britain – may be interrogated, re-assessed and revised. This book proceeds, therefore, in a spirit contrary to Kipling's maxim.

The principal aim of this book is to ground the investigation of social conflict and power relations in late nineteenth- and early twentieth-century India more firmly in their political (and intellectual) context.

---

[1] Especially in Rajnarayan Chandavarkar, 'Workers' Politics and the Mill Districts in Bombay Between the Wars', *MAS*, 15:3 (1981), special issue, *Profit, Power and Politics: Imperialism, Nationalism and Change in India, 1870–1940*, edited by Christopher Baker, Gordon Johnson and Anil Seal (reprinted below as ch. 4), and *The Origins of Industrial Capitalism in India: Business Strategies and the Working Classes in Bombay, 1900–1940* (Cambridge, 1994).

[2] This argument has been most explicitly restated by Dipesh Chakrabarty, *Rethinking Working Class History: Bengal, 1890–1940* (Delhi, 1989).

While the following chapters traverse the quotidian realms of society and culture, their aim is to retrieve the significance of politics from the solvents of 'popular culture' and 'everyday life' within which it has too often been submerged. The contention of this book is that the form and meaning of social relations, and not least the forms of knowledge, or the discourses by which they are constituted, are determined by political conflict and defined by the outcome of power relations. It is concerned, therefore, with how forces of resistance perceive dominant groups and institutions and how agencies of control imagine, define and sometimes actively respond to problems of order, how perceptions of interests and identities at particular moments can facilitate alignments of power which cut across class, and how political conflict and debate can lead, within a particular historical conjuncture, to the definition of class.

Furthermore, an attempt is made in this book to scrutinize the nature and meaning of certain concepts, which are central and recurrent in the subject – most extensively, 'industrialization', 'violence', 'crime', 'nationalism', 'world capitalism', and inevitably, of course, 'class' – and, in particular, to examine their construction within a given historical context. This scrutiny is primarily historical, not philosophical, in approach. The nature of these concepts is examined in their engagement with the historical evidence, frequently the awkwardness of the evidence with which scholarship, built on the conventional discourse of the social sciences, is copiously presented in the Indian archives and libraries. The conceptual and interpretative problems addressed in this book are not exhaustive and no attempt is made to provide or disinter a list of 'keywords'. Nor is this discussion offered as a methodological exercise, which has almost always given pleasure to those who attempt it strictly in proportion to the pain it causes to those upon whom it is inflicted.

However, close attention of this sort to the conceptual vocabulary of the historian, and its relationship to the meaning of these concepts in contemporary politics, does, indeed, serve a methodological purpose. It is, of course, a commonplace, often repeated, that the history of the powerless and the poor comes to us primarily in the voice, and perceptions, of their rulers and exploiters. Some historians have suggested that a path may be cut through such difficulties by reading the sources 'against the grain'. Others have taken the implication of this dictum a step further and recommended that we should read the sources for their 'silences', by shifting the emphasis from the text to its marginalia or even its omissions.[3]

---

[3] In Indian historiography, these exhortations have most frequently emanated from the so-called 'subaltern' historians. R. Guha (ed.), *Subaltern Studies*, vols. I–VI (Delhi, 1982–89); P. Chatterjee and G. Pandey (eds.), *Subaltern Studies* vol. VII (Delhi, 1992); D. Arnold and D. Hardiman (eds.), *Subaltern Studies*, vol. VIII (Delhi, 1994); S. Amin and D. Chakrabarty (eds.), *Subaltern Studies*, vol. XI (Delhi, 1996).

Of course, to some extent, and with varying degrees of success, these 'methods' have long been deployed by even the most conventional historians. But the effects of spelling out the habit of an art into a methodological doctrine have not always been fruitful, least of all, ironically, in the hands of its advocates. To effectively transcend the discourse of the colonial rulers and the dominant classes, historians would not only have to read their sources 'against the grain' but also subject their own texts to the same vigorous and self-conscious process of deconstruction. Otherwise, despite their intention to provide a subversive reading, historians were liable, especially, for instance, in their analysis of violence, crime and popular culture, to replicate the assumptions and prejudices of the dominant discourse. Moreover, the strategy of reading the sources for their 'silences' and 'absences', of pouring over the record for what it does not contain, has sometimes served to blunt the sensitivity of historians to, perhaps dull their curiosity for, what they actually can and do tell us and to distract them from fully exploring the uses to which they may be put.

In earlier work, I had suggested that the pattern of capitalist development in India had been shaped largely by the role of the working classes. Business strategies and entrepreneurial choice in early twentieth-century India had been determined by the struggle to control and discipline labour. The social responses and political action of workers, both within and beyond the workplace, often defined the options available to capital.[4] Although historians and anthropologists have paid close attention, in studies of Indian capitalism, to trade and commerce, merchants and entrepreneurship, burghers and bazaars, they have continued to neglect the history of the working classes. In the light of the historiographical traditions and practices which have dominated the study of colonial India, this is not, perhaps, wholly surprising. It was not simply that, until recently, historians have largely focused their attention on governance and upon elites, but, more crucially, that the contours of the subject came to be mapped in relation to the process of imperial conquest and consolidation. The historical narrative of Indian society in the colonial period has turned upon the relationships and events which facilitated or impeded the entrenchment of British rule: conquest and mutiny, revenue extraction and judicial administration, rural organization and village society, indigenous tradition and customary practice, collaboration and nationalism, changing strategies to retain the empire and sacral conflicts which were deemed to have driven the partition of India. If Indian historiography could not fully escape the rigours of colonial knowledge, it was at least in part because the dominant categories of historical investi-

---

[4] Chandavarkar, *The Origins of Industrial Capitalism*.

gation emerged as an adjunct of the colonial task of managing and controlling Indian society.

In this historical narrative, the problem of labour, and the social formation of the working classes, remained no more than a minor, indeed, marginal motif. The clash between imperialism and nationalism provided the organizing principle of research in Indian history. Questions which could not be contained within these polarities were simply excluded. Even economic historians primarily debated the counter-factual question of whether British rule had modernized or retarded the Indian economy. Social history appeared to consist less of the study of the history of Indian society than of evaluating the extent of the 'Westernization' and 'modernization' of 'indigenous' society under the impact of colonialism. In this investigation of 'indigenous' tradition, scholars concentrated upon what were seen as its unique and exceptional features and embarked, accordingly, upon a cultural anthropology of the past. At a more general level, historians investigating particular social groups often took their unitary character for granted. Castes, religious and regional groups, occupations and even loosely banded social classes were readily hypostatized. Moreover, since Indian society was deemed to be essentially 'agrarian' and 'traditional', their attention was directed towards land revenue policies, 'the mode of production' in Indian agriculture or the rise of the rich peasant. Such a historiographical context, marked by its emphasis on magnates and elites, its consideration of governance at the expense of social process, its Orientalist attraction to the uniqueness of 'Indian culture', was scarcely conducive to the study of the urban working classes or, indeed, labour in general.

Yet when historians addressed the subject of the working classes, they did not always serve to liberate it from the dead-weight of traditional historiographical practice. Until recently, the focus of enquiry has rested upon the functionalist question of the role of labour in economic development: whether it could be recruited, trained and organized sufficiently to serve the needs of Indian industry. The recruitment and adaptation of workers, and the mechanisms for their control and discipline in the factories, provided the core around which research in Indian (and perhaps, much colonial) labour history has developed.[5] Similarly, studies of

[5] C. A. Myers, *Labour Problems in the Industrialization of India* (Cambridge, Mass., 1958), M. D. Morris, *The Emergence of an Industrial Labour Force in India: A Study of the Bombay Cotton Mills, 1854–1947* (Berkeley and Los Angeles, 1965); D. Mazumdar, 'Labour Supply in Early Industrialization: The Case of the Bombay Textile Industry', *Economic History Review*, second series, 26:3 (August 1973), 477–96; B. Misra, 'Factory Labour During the Early Years of Industrialisation: An Appraisal in the Light of the Indian Factory Commission 1890', *IESHR*, 12:3 (1975) 203–28; C. P. Simmons, 'Recruiting and Organizing an Industrial Labour Force in Colonial India: The Case of the Coal

the labour movement have, in different ways, turned upon how far and with what consequences, modern trade unions (and modern methods of management and collective bargaining) could replace the traditional leaders and practices of the working classes.[6] These lines of enquiry emanated from and embraced diverse traditions of scholarship, including those which were hostile to their functionalist inheritance. Frequently, the working classes have been represented in terms of 'cultural' characteristics attributed to particular economic categories or occupational states of being – 'migrant workers', 'the urban poor', 'landless labour' or 'factory operatives' – which in turn were overlaid with expectations produced by 'cultural' definition – of caste and religion, for instance – and generated by the discourse within which Indian society as a whole was objectified and characterized. In other words, historians 'read off' the attitudes, mentalities and social consciousness of these social groups from the categories within which they lumped them. In this way, the working classes entered Indian history over-burdened with the historians' or social scientists' expectations and, indeed, their tautologies. This has only made it seem more crucial to scrutinize both the language of historical analysis as well as the vocabulary of contemporary political discourse.

If historians of the Indian working classes thus approached their inquiries within the limits imposed either by the universalist teleologies of the

Mining Industry c.1880–1939', *IESHR*, 13:4 (1976), 455–85; R. Das Gupta, 'Factory Labour in Eastern India: Sources of Supply, 1855–1946: Some Preliminary Findings', *IESHR*, 13:3 (1976), 277–328; L. Chakravarthy, 'Emergence of an Industrial Labour Force in a Dual Economy – British India 1880–1920', *IESHR* 15:3 (1978), 249–327; R. Newman, 'Social Factors in the Recruitment of the Bombay Millhands', in K. N. Chaudhuri and C. J. Dewey (eds.), *Economy and Society: Essays in Indian Economy and Society* (Delhi, 1979); P. S. Gupta, 'Notes on the Origin and Structuring of the Industrial Labour Force in India – 1880 to 1920', in R. S. Sharma, (ed. with V. Jha), *Indian Society: Historical Probings: In Memory of D. D. Kosambi* (New Delhi, 1979), pp. 414–34; R. Newman, *Workers and Unions in Bombay 1918–1929: A Study of Organisation in the Cotton Mills* (Canberra, 1981); Chitra Joshi, 'Kanpur Textile Labour: Some Structural Features of Formative Years', *Economic and Political Weekly*, 16:44–6, (November 1981), special issue, 1823–38; Chitra Joshi, 'Bonds of Community, Ties of Religion: Kanpur Textile Workers in the Early Twentieth Century', *IESHR*, 22:3 (1985), 251–80; D. Arnold, 'Industrial Violence in Colonial India', Comparative *Studies in Society and History*, 22:2 (1980), 234–55; D. Chakrabarty, 'On Deifying and Defying Authority: Managers and Workers in the Jute Mills of Bengal, circa 1890–1940', *Past and Present*, 100 (August 1983), 124–46; Chakrabarty, *Rethinking Working-Class History*; Marina Carter, *Servants, Sirdars and Settlers: Indians in Mauritius, 1834–1874* (Delhi, 1995); I. J. Kerr, *Building the Railways of the Raj, 1850–1900* (Delhi, 1995), especially chs. 4–6.
[6] Morris, *The Emergence of an Industrial Labour Force*; Newman, *Workers and Unions in Bombay*; D. Kooiman, 'Jobbers and the Emergence of Trade Unions in Bombay City', *International Review of Social History*, 22:3 (1977), 313–28; E. A. Ramaswamy, *The Worker and His Union: A Study in South India* (New Delhi, 1977); Arnold, 'Industrial Violence in Colonial India', 234–55; E. D. Murphy, *Unions in Conflict: A Comparative Study of Four South Indian Textile Centres 1918–1939* (New Delhi, 1981); Chakrabarty, *Rethinking Working Class History*.

social sciences, derived from both functionalism and Marxism, or alternatively, by the exceptionalism generated by an Orientalist and colonial discourse, they were also influenced by trends in British and European historiography. Here, the history of the working classes had long been studied as the history of the labour movement, and then, increasingly, the social conditions and social and cultural practices of its constituent groups. From nineteenth-century socialism, historians of the 'Western' working classes inherited the assumption that economic development determined the character of labour, its social organization and political consciousness. The pattern and pace of industrialization, it was supposed, shaped the character of the social struggle and its political forms. The notion of the stages of industrialization yielded a matching evolutionary scheme of the stages of class consciousness. The history and development of the labour movement was, thus, assumed to constitute the prelude to the rise and triumph of socialism. In this way, the history of the working class came to be studied as an inseparable part of the rise of socialism. For some, the point of interest in studying the history of the labour movement was to investigate how its historic mission, the achievement of socialism, could be advanced or even realized and to track its progress. For others, its interest lay in discovering how the antagonisms and conflicts embodied by the labour movement could be managed, contained and defused. More significant than these differences, which sometimes generated fierce debate, was the fact that their shared teleology defined the scope of historical inquiry.

The effect of this teleology upon the interpretations of the working classes in general have been severely limiting, but in the case of India, in particular, they proved especially damaging. Economic backwardness, in this reasoning, made the very notion of a working class unthinkable, just as the peculiar cultural institutions of India seemed to place it in a special category of its own. The nature of the labour force, shaped by a low level of industrialization, could not be expected to develop a class consciousness or a socialist politics. Moreover, if the weight of the factory proletariat in a predominantly peasant economy was small, and its political potential correspondingly weak, the history of the working class appeared unimportant, or at any rate it became increasingly difficult to identify and assess its significance. So if the Indian working classes constituted either the antecedents of Western society or a special and unique case, its history was unlikely to release materials for thinking about class formation and class consciousness more generally.[7] Most crucially, this teleology im-

---

[7] It is ironical, therefore, that at least one recent attempt at 'rethinking working-class history' on the strength of the Indian 'case' has been predicated wholly and insistently on its cultural exceptionalism (and economic backwardness). Chakrabarty, *Rethinking Working Class History*.

posed upon the working classes an arbitrary and misleadingly narrow definition as an industrial labour force. In this sense, the industrial labour force was abstracted from its connections with other categories of labour who were proletarianized in nineteenth- and twentieth-century India by similar social processes and who were increasingly being subjected to the dominance of mercantile and industrial capital.

It was also implicit in this teleological view that industrialization constituted a universal, serial, technological process through which every society passed at an appropriate level of development. The nature of the Indian working class, it seemed, could scarcely be understood outside the context of the fact that the Indian economy was passing through an 'early stage' of industrialization. By making Indian society coeval with Britain (or Europe) in a previous and not its contemporaneous epoch,[8] scholars took the first major steps towards entrenching the myth of Indian exceptionalism or, alternatively, the parallel notion that the Indian case was a defective variant of the West.

In *The Origins of Industrial Capitalism*, I had sought to retrieve and delineate the wider context within which the working classes formed in India. The links between factory workers, casual labour and various streams of rural migrants, I had argued, were sufficiently intimate to strain the rigid definition of the 'working classes' as an 'industrial labour force' to the point of obliteration. This book seeks to develop the argument that the history of the working classes can only be grasped fully in the light of the powerful connections, which were established in the process of their social formation, between factory proletarians, casual workers, rural migrants, agrarian labour, artisans, 'tribals' and dalits. The Indian working class was largely composed of rural migrants who retained close connections with their village base. Indeed, they often migrated to earn the wages which would enable them to retain their village holdings, and as a result, they were frequently more militant in defending their jobs and earnings in the workplace. If the working classes were thus firmly rooted in the countryside, there was no clear line of demarcation between factory hands and the casual poor. No clear distinction can be sustained between them in their attitudes to work and politics, their lifestyles and job preferences, their response to the law and their propensity to violence. Yet, tautologically, these imputed behavioural characteristics have often provided the means of distinguishing between 'the casual poor' and 'the respectable working classes'. As an analytical concept and a heuristic category, the working class were never very clearly demarcated from 'the peasant' or 'the casual poor'.[9] Indeed, recruits to 'the working class' in India encompassed very diverse social formations, as tribals were inden-

---

[8] J. Fabian, *Time and the Other: How Anthropology Makes Its Object* (New York, 1983).
[9] Chandavarkar, *The Origins of Industrial Capitalism*, chs. 3, 4 and 5.

tured for the tea gardens or recruited for the coal mines, and dalits and landless peasants sought work as field labourers at harvest time or migrated to nearby towns for employment in the trades or the 'service sector'. Factory hands, who were deemed to constitute the working class in the narrowest and most traditional sense, could necessarily be described by several other labels. The conventional definition of 'the working class' in terms of an urban factory proletariat appeared particularly limited when it was measured against the historical evidence of labour force formation in late nineteenth- and twentieth-century India. Ironically, the commonplace that the working class derived its identity primarily from the relations of production – more specifically, from the factory and the production line – has held firm at the very moment at which 'the factory system' itself, in its most developed Fordist form, was finally being dissolved.

If, on conventional expectations, the very notion of a working class in India appeared unthinkable, a detailed investigation of workers' politics in Bombay between the wars suggested that these conventions may have to be revised. For Bombay not only witnessed a scale of industrial and political action which was rarely replicated in conditions of 'advanced capitalism' but workers' struggles, at particular historical conjunctures, disclosed a fiercely held 'class consciousness'. This exploration of the nature of workers' politics in Bombay, originally published in 1981, is reprinted below as chapter 4. The remaining chapters in this volume address problems and seek to develop perspectives which had first emerged in that essay.

The more closely 'the Indian case' was examined the more it cast into doubt the evolutionary assumptions which had held the subject together. Significantly, it became apparent that it was impossible to understand the central issues of labour force formation in the cotton mills without grasping its intricate, if inextricable, connections with the social organization of the neighbourhood. These connections between workplace and neighbourhood were vital not only to the recruitment and control of labour, but, as the mill committees of 1928–29 showed, also to the organization and conduct of collective action. The investigation of the history of the working class, it seemed, had been unduly restricted by its narrow and exclusive focus upon the workplace.

The investigation of the interplay between the social relations of the workplace and the social organization of the neighbourhood had numerous implications for our understanding of class formation. First, it was customarily supposed that it was the caste, kinship and religious loyalties of workers which constituted an insuperable obstacle to the growth of class consciousness. Until further industrialization dissolved these 'primordial ties', class consciousness would not develop. Yet it was precisely within the social organization of the neighbourhood that the solidarities of collective action were forged and their informing ideologies shaped. Second, the neighbourhood was not only an arena in which the political solidarities of the working classes were forged, but also the site in which its differences and divisions were seen to become manifest. From the vantage point of the neighbourhood, the segmentation of the labour market as well as the rivalries of the workplace were laid bare. The aggregation of workers within the factory or the mill did not necessarily sharpen their sense of common interest; indeed, it could serve to expose the whole spectrum of their differences. Third, as the workers' politics were defined in terms of the inter-relationship between the spheres of workplace and neighbourhood, so their development could be more fully explained in terms of the playing out of diverse sets of power relations rather than simply as an effect of their relationship to the means of production. Social consciousness and social being were shaped in a political domain, extending from the daily social relations of workplace and neighbourhood to more public conflicts and confrontations with the state. The political consciousness of the working classes appeared to be shaped crucially by their experience of, and their relationship with, the state. Their solidarities were not the natural outcome of popular culture or a reflex of the specific character of production relations, but, rather, they were politically constituted, and as such they were contingent, sometimes transient and even evanescent. The politics of the working classes had therefore to be situated in the wider context of the social and political alignments which shaped them. In studies of the bubonic plague epidemic and the discourse of violence in workers' politics, strategies of policing and law enforcement and the appeal of the Congress among the urban working classes, I have sought, therefore, to investigate the power relations, entailed, described and determined by these alignments, and the distorting prisms through which the state and the dominant classes and those who challenged and resisted them viewed each other.

From this perspective, the working class could not be grasped as a unitary formation, with a real essence and a single homogeneous identity. Its social formation was the outcome of processes and relationships which were contingent; it encompassed identities which were varied, conflicting and labile. The social groups which comprised the working class could be disassembled by diverse and contradictory criteria into numerous fragments, variously constituted. Their broadly similar relationship to the means of production did not yield objective interests in common, overriding their sectionalism. If sectional difference, based on gender and occupation, caste and kinship, religion and ideology, came to be negotiated into alliances and unities at specific historical conjunctures, then it became yet more pressing to explain why these solidarities could be forged at all. Perceptions of mutual interests, indeed the language for their description, were the product of a specific intellectual and political context. Similarly, the interests of these elements which made up the working class depended upon, and were defined within, specific historical circumstances, which were themselves constantly in flux. As they changed, they served to redefine the interests of their constituent social groups and to reconstitute their social identities. The sectionalism of the working classes was integral to the process of its social formation; it was not the product of its unique culture or its backward economy. As historians of the Western working classes paid closer attention to the competing and conflicting identities of ethnicity and religion, kinship and gender, neighbourhood and nation, they began to focus attention upon the very issues which had led them previously to regard the Indian case as unique and exceptional in the first place. Yet to describe these divisions within the working class as a process of sectionalism is to lend a certain coherence to its 'sections' and the interests which made them up, as if they were impervious to change and resistant to further decomposition and reconstitution in a different form under changed circumstances. In fact, if the formation of the working classes is seen as primarily a political process, contingent upon given historical conditions, it should follow that its constituent elements could equally plausibly be defined in terms of several other social identities.

Once the significance of the relationship between workplace and neighbourhood for class formation and the economy of labour had been admitted, it severely undermined the commonplace that the working class discovered its identity exclusively, or even primarily, at the point of production. Nor could the connection between the level of economic development and the nature of social conflict and the forms of their political expression be readily taken for granted. Yet it was precisely the belief that there was an immediate and intimate analytical connection between the economic history of the labour movement and its political expressions which had long underpinned Whiggish and diffusionist notions of industrialization.

If these evolutionary assumptions about class formation could not easily be sustained, it became clear that conventional models of industrialization as a social process would have to be re-examined. The definition of the working class in terms of a factory proletariat seemed intimately related to an understanding of industrialization as a serial, technologically determined process which lay beyond the realm of social choice or political conflict. Such a definition could only be justified by, and, indeed, it may be reduced to a usage of, modernization theory. To challenge this usage is also to demand the rethinking of the social meaning of its informing process: 'industrialization'. Chapter 2 – first published as an essay in

1985 – represented an initial attempt to undertake this task. It challenged the assumption, shared by Marxists and functionalists alike, that industrialization constituted a unilinear process, which shaped society inevitably in a single direction. Indeed, it seemed as if scholarly disputations between Marxists and functionalists about the nature of industrialization and its social consequences had served to bring them closer together and to consolidate and entrench the assumptions they shared. Accordingly, the starting point of chapter 2 was a growing scepticism about the received wisdom that industrial development in India was the outcome of a process of technological diffusion set in motion by the industrial revolution in Western Europe and, indeed, that economic (or industrial) development would lead inevitably to large-scale factory production.

It had become increasingly apparent that evolutionary assumptions about the nature of industrialization had entailed a significant interpretative cost for Indian economic history. For these assumptions were derived from and served to entrench a normative ideal of the nature and course of industrialization. In turn, it led historians to abstract large-scale industry from its wider economic and political context. It drew us towards a heroic view of entrepreneurs, as if they carried single-handedly the burdens of risk and the challenge of innovation, and struggled to raise the economy above the inescapable constraints which held it captive. Most crucially, perhaps, the implicit assumption that technology constituted a neutral force blinded historians to the extent to which workers turned it into the site of conflicts over its use and, correspondingly, to the impact of labour upon the pattern of industrial development.

Yet, on closer scrutiny, industrialization did not follow a unilinear path. Its outcome was neither inevitable nor inscribed into its origins. The development of large-scale industry in India was neither simply the result of the visionary genius of entrepreneurs driven to innovate and invest in the newest and best technology, nor were its limitations the consequence of their 'mercantile' and speculative attitudes or rent-seeking motives. Nor could it be supposed that large-scale industry alone pointed the way to the future or represented the only source of dynamism in the economy. As Christopher Baker's study of Tamil Nadu had shown, the handloom-weaving industry had disclosed a remarkable ability to adapt and survive, expand and innovate.[10] But this did not represent an exceptional case.

[10] C. J. Baker, *An Indian Rural Economy: The Tamil Nad Countryside 1880–1950* (Oxford, 1984), ch. 5. Later work has strengthened this picture. See Tirthankar Roy, *Artisans and Industrialization: Indian Weaving in the Twentieth Century* (Delhi, 1993); D. Haynes, 'The Dynamics of Continuity in Indian Domestic Industry: *Jari* Manufacture in Surat, 1900–1947', *IESHR*, 23:2 (1986), 128–49 and D. Haynes, 'From Merchant Capital to Weavers' Capital: The Slow Transformation of Artisanal Production in the Bombay Presidency, 1900–1950', unpublished paper.

Moreover, industrial expansion was sometimes facilitated by improvisation with old, even obsolete, machinery, the effective manipulation of raw materials and the intensive exploitation of cheap labour. Capitalist strategies were frequently and in crucial ways determined by workers' initiatives to defend their jobs and wage levels and to retain some measure of control over their own labour. The path of industrialization in India was strewn with conflicts and contradictions which often altered its course and determined its patterns of development.

To a large extent, diffusionist assumptions about the nature of industrialization and evolutionary schemata of its course had held together the conventional narrative structure of labour history. If, in a radical interpretation, the labour movement signified the emergence of working-class consciousness, whose further development was manifested in the rise of socialism, in a more conservative, functionalist variant, more industrialization provided the scope, sometimes even the incentive, for labour to adapt to its imperatives and abandon spontaneous resistance for formal collective bargaining. In chapter 3, this book examines the nature of the labour movement while seeking to divest it of such evolutionary and diffusionist assumptions about the character of industrialization. It argues that the nature of trade union organization and the pattern of industrial action were neither the product of an 'early stage of industrialization' nor a reflex of the 'pre-industrial' or 'pre-capitalist' mentalities of the workers. Of course, the sectionalism of the working class often made it difficult to form trade unions or to forge wider political solidarities. But this sectionalism was neither unique to the Indian working class, nor simply generated by its cultural particularities. It was frequently developed by industrialization. It emanated from the division of labour and the organization of work. It remained, indeed, inherent to the process of labour force formation. Politicians, employers and the state often played upon these sectional differences and served at times to accentuate them. We cannot take for granted that the aggregation of workers in factories led them naturally to perceive their interests as uniform.

To recognize that the solidarity of the working class was by no means immanent in the unfolding of industrialization or capitalism was to direct attention to the question of why trade unions formed in the first place. Workers' resistance did not necessarily lead to its consolidation in trade union organization. Trade unions often appeared to be no more than a lofty title for a strike committee. When they formed, they were often ephemeral to the dynamic of working-class action. Conversely, trade union weakness coexisted alongside the solidarities which workers sometimes forged and the determined struggles they waged to defend their collective interests. No simple connections can be made between social

consciousness, trade union organization and political action. The formation and growth of trade unions did not necessarily reflect the nature of
working-class consciousness. On the contrary, the characteristics of the
labour movement, often represented as symptomatic of a pre-industrial
society, were the product of the political context in which they took
shape. How the nature of trade union organization and the forms of
industrial action were shaped by this political context, fashioned by the
policies of employers and the state, provides the substance of this chapter.

This argument has a wider relevance for explanations of the origins and
growth of labour movements. If the weakness of trade unions reflected
not the 'pre-industrial' nature of the workforce but the intolerance of the
employers, the growth of a labour movement may be best explained by
identifying the conditions in which, as the outcome of the complex
relations between workers, trade unions and governments, the employers
and the state manifest a willingness to tolerate workers' combinations.
The readiness of capitalists to tolerate workers' combinations has often
depended upon political pressure exerted by workers' struggles at the
level of the state and the wider perception of the attendant threat to the
social order. If labour movements constituted neither the natural corollary to capitalist development nor the expression of an immanent social
consciousness, their formation calls for a political explanation and, in
particular, the examination of their changing relation to the state.

The implications of this hypothesis are here sketched schematically and
cannot be developed in a study of this kind. They call for a more
comprehensive and comparative treatment of labour movements. However, chapters 5 to 8 follow some of its suggestions of an approach to the
analysis of class and power. In 'Workers' politics', I had suggested that
the social and political alignments of the working-class neighbourhoods
reached out to wider arenas of politics, encompassing the colonial state
and political organization at various levels. The working-class neighbourhoods of Bombay did not yield a natural propensity to class solidarity.
Nonetheless, the working classes were able at times to forge impressive
solidarities out of a social context riven by conflicts and antagonisms,
competing and diverse interests and cultural and economic sectionalism.
But these solidarities could not be reduced to a common denominator of
popular culture or interpreted as the realization of class interests. Within
the working-class neighbourhoods, political organization and action was
constituted by the play of power relations and their reciprocities, between
jobbers and workers, landlords and tenants, creditors and debtors, all
manner of patrons and clients, as much as between the state, employers
and the working classes. The political consciousness of the working
classes formed in relation to the state and the public discourse stimulated

by its interventions and the political negotiation around them. It is to this political discourse and the play of power relations in shaping the alignments of class, its broken solidarities as well as its fundamental differences, that this book turns in chapters 5 to 8, addressing the discourse and practice of violence, methods of policing and law enforcement, the plague panic of the 1890s and 1900s and the response of the working classes to the protean languages of Indian nationalism.

The central concern of these chapters is to examine the relationship between discourse and power, language and political practice. They examine how particular social groups were defined and categorized in political rhetoric and public discourse. The fixity which these definitions were attributed in public discourse was frequently belied by the flexibility of their usage, which could change according to their context. Nonetheless, the definition of social groups, and their accompanying characterization, sometimes had large consequences – which the colonial state developed with energy and enthusiasm – for the policies of government. Similarly, the colonial state and its agents played a prominent role in shaping this rhetoric, especially in relation to violence, crime and disease. But the purposes of the colonial state would not have been served if they had not also been embedded in, and even influenced by, a wider political discourse in which diverse elements of Indian society shared. The process by which social groups were so defined and characterized in public discourse also created and developed political alignments and shaped social antagonisms which cut across class and caste, gender and community, religion and nation and sometimes reconstituted these old principles of social division.

Chapter 5 elucidates and analyses a colonial discourse about working-class violence. But this was a discourse in which Indian elites also participated; at particular junctures, it could encompass diverse elements of Indian society, including some working-class groups as well. Later historians, sometimes in quest of 'the mind' of the working classes, have often unwittingly taken over and replicated this discourse and sometimes even elevated it into grand explanatory frameworks and transcendent sociological truths.[11] Contemporary observers, like the scholars who followed them, attributed a particular propensity to violence to specific groups within the working class: the casual poor, the rural migrant, the insufficiently proletarianized. Where contemporaries sometimes spoke from fear and sought to employ characterizations of violence to justify particu-

---

[11] D. Arnold, 'Industrial Violence in Colonial India'; Chakrabarty, 'On Deifying and Defying Authority', 127; Chakrabarty, *Rethinking Working Class History*; Joshi, 'Bonds of Community, Ties of Religion', 261–3; V. Das (ed.), *Mirrors of Violence: Communities, Riots and Survivors in South Asia* (Delhi, 1990).

lar lines of policy or forms of state action, some historians have tended to valorize subaltern violence. Ironically, historians who valorized the violence of the urban poor have often replicated the colonial construction of the roughness of the lower orders.

Chapter 5 sets the spurious analytical precision with which scholars have conceptualized violence in relation to the ambiguities of its classification and its social meanings. The colonial state and its agents were often able to exploit the ambiguities inherent in the very concept of violence to create a wider consensus for some of their harshest and most repressive policies. How this was effected in practice may be seen in the way in which measures were put together to repress the communist leaders of the Bombay Girni Kamgar Union after the general strike of 1928, culminating in the tragic, if somewhat laborious, drama of the Meerut Conspiracy Case. Like its republican successor, the colonial state was often able to evoke widespread support for its acquisition of repressive powers when it was able to demonstrate the need to use them against particular and 'deviant' social groups which it defined into existence: most commonly, 'goondas', the 'floating population' of large cities, the casual poor, or 'anti-social elements' in the current phrase. It is particularly striking that those who styled themselves as 'respectable' frequently ascribed the blame for communal riots – and readily continue so to do – to those whom they perceived as 'rough'. Such representations of the urban poor may be taken historically to reflect the aspiration of Indian elites to subordinate and control labour and, in the long run, to cheapen its cost. Colonial rule enabled Indian elites to realize this aspiration; half a century of independence has enlarged their freedom and power to consolidate and extend their control yet further.

In the following chapter, this book turns to the most obvious, ubiquitous and public instrument of this control. Chapter 6 investigates the mechanisms and techniques of urban policing in Bombay in the late nineteenth and early twentieth centuries. In particular, it seek to situate the police and their methods of operation more firmly within the context of the social organization of the neighbourhood. Administrative and institutional histories of the police, however, have often tended to present it as a monolithic force and to exaggerate its discipline and its responsiveness to central command.[12] As a result, they have tended to overlook the extent to which the police in their quotidian functions were exposed to

[12] Percival Griffiths, *To Guard My People: The History of the Indian Police* (London, 1971); A. Gupta, *The Police in British India, 1861–1947* (Delhi, 1979); D. Arnold, *Police Power and Colonial Rule: Madras, 1859–1947* (Delhi, 1986); P. Robb, 'The Ordering of Rural India: The Policing of Nineteenth Century Bengal and Bihar', in D. M. Anderson and D. Killingray (eds.), *Policing the Empire: Government, Authority and Control, 1830–1940* (Manchester, 1991), pp. 126–50.

the negotiation of power relations in the street and the neighbourhood. The police often became a valuable resource in the earthy battles fought for control and dominance within the neighbourhood. Moreover, individual connections between policemen and residents, sometimes based on caste, kinship and village, allowed the working classes to enlist their help and their protection. Around the police, their strategies and their interventions in the neighbourhood, shifting patterns of alliance and antagonisms between various contending elements formed and fractured.

Attention to the quotidian dimension of policing illuminates a paradox which lies at the heart of the colonial autocracy. British rule in India was an oriental despotism which rested on force. The British developed through the police and the army, what often appeared to be a formidable apparatus of control and repression; yet they sometimes appeared to deploy this sanction of physical force with a constraint and economy which was not always evident in Britain.[13] Conversely, while the police often appeared to be constrained by significant organizational and structural weaknesses, they also sometimes revealed an ability to respond to the threat of disorder with a ruthless brutality which would not always have been contemplated elsewhere. Chapter 6 tries to resolve these conundrums by examining strategies for the maintenance of order from the perspective of everyday policing. It analyses the assumptions of the agencies of the colonial state which informed their perception of the threat of violence and drove them at times to respond on a scale which rendered the distinction between 'minimum' and 'maximum' force meaningless. As a result, the colonial state seemed to threaten its subjects less but killed them more often in India than it did in its own heartland in Britain. As the colonial state passed under the greater influence of Indian elites in the 1930s, however, it acquired an increasingly repressive demeanour. As they gained leverage upon the instruments of repression, Indian propertied elites saw no reason to desist from using them to control and discipline labour more effectively, whether in the towns or the countryside. The Congress ministries which took office under provincial autonomy between 1937 and 1939, erstwhile protagonists of non-violent satyagraha and civil disobedience, sometimes swiftly and enthusiastically slid their mailed fists into the velvet gloves of their British predecessors. In this sense, the growing willingness of the Indian state since Independence to appropriate large executive powers, repress its opponents and under-

---

[13] V. A. C. Gatrell, 'Crime, Authority and the Policeman State, 1750–1950', in F. M. L. Thompson (ed.), *The Cambridge Social History of Britain, 1750–1950* (Cambridge, 1988), pp. 243–310; K. Jeffrey and P. Hennessey, *States of Emergency: British Governments and Strikebreaking since 1919* (London, 1983); Jane Morgan, *Conflict and Order: The Police and Labour Disputes in England and Wales, 1900–1939* (Oxford, 1987).

mine civil liberties should not surprise us. It was firmly embedded in the habits of statecraft which the republican regime inherited – more than democracy, a British legacy for which Indian elites had quickly shown enthusiasm in the colonial period.

From everyday policing, this book turns to the plague epidemic of the 1890s. Chapter 7 takes a further step away from the conventional arenas of politics to examine the interplay between power and discourse, class and resistance in the construction of the bubonic plague epidemic of the 1890s and 1900s. The case of the plague epidemic provides further illustration of the process by which different elements in Indian society sought to define themselves within public discourse and to negotiate alignments and accommodations with each other, sometimes cutting across divisions of caste, religion and class.

Popular responses to the epidemic have sometimes been interpreted in strongly Orientalist terms, as the inevitable clash between Western rationality and Eastern superstition, and as an expression of an indigenous popular culture.[14] Yet these interpretations, or preconceptions, are inadequately supported by the evidence. We can neither discern a single homogeneous popular response to the plague, nor can the popular reaction be clearly distinguished from the official and the elite. Rather, the diagnosis of bubonic plague unleashed a moral panic which engulfed medical experts and research scientists, colonial officials and Indian elites, plague administrators and the victims of the plague 'measures' alike. To investigate how the epidemic came to be constructed seemed to allow a way around the sterile dichotomies of East and West, science and superstition, rationality and rumour which had enveloped the subject. Moreover, it was clear that the epidemic could not be seen as a single, integrated phenomenon, which was experienced in the same way by all, but signified different things to different people. For this reason, it seemed necessary to examine the specific political conjuncture in which the epidemic was constructed. The political construction of the epidemic in the late 1890s was the outcome of the interaction between its disparate and numerous constituent elements: for instance, colonial perceptions of Indian society, medical and scientific rivalries, the policies devised to combat the plague and the manner of their implementation, and the response and resistance of its victims. The popular response to the epidemic was neither culturally specific nor irrational and pre-scientific.

[14] D. Arnold, 'Touching the Body: Perspectives on the Indian Plague, 1896–1900', in Guha (ed.), *Subaltern Studies*, vol. V, pp. 55–90; reprinted in D. Arnold, *Colonizing the Body: State Medicine and Epidemic Disease in Nineteenth Century India* (Berkeley and Los Angeles, 1993), ch. 5; Ira Klein, 'Plague, Policy and Popular Unrest in British India', *MAS*, 22:4 (1988), 723–55.

Rather, it reflected the reluctance of the oppressed to place their faith fully either in the draconian, panic-stricken measures or to believe the assurances of their authoritarian oppressors. Indeed, in the manner of its construction, the plague epidemic of the 1890s in India disclosed remarkable similarities with the onset of the AIDS epidemic in San Francisco in the 1980s.[15]

Chapter 8 examines how public discourse could serve not merely to constitute social groups within a particular historical conjuncture, but also to facilitate political alliances between them. Since these 'social groups', so-called, could scarcely be dissolved into irreducible units, their constitution may be taken to reflect the outcome of the process by which alliances were negotiated and took shape around a wider political discourse. The focus of this chapter rests upon the popular appeal of nationalism in its 'mass phase' in the final decades of British rule. Its aim is to explore, and to seek to explain, the nature of the popular response to the Congress. Conventionally, historians have either treated popular participation in nationalist agitations as a function of elite rivalries or of a diffusionist process of mobilization by which the 'masses', more or less undifferentiated, are brought into the political domain by their leaders seeking to extend the basis of their support. Alternatively, they have stressed the autonomy of subaltern politics. In either case, these approaches have made it difficult to grasp the relationship between the Congress and its fluctuating and fractious following.

In chapter 8, it is argued that an understanding of the nature of the popular following evoked by the Congress, which neither wholly displaces it onto elite rivalries nor collapses into the pitfalls of mobilization, would have to turn upon the extent to which its political programme provided diverse groups with the means of comprehending their own social and political situation as well as suggesting realistic means by which they could transform it.[16] To this end, the chapter focuses upon Gandhi's rhetoric about the working classes and sets it in relation to their social and political struggles, particularly in Ahmedabad in the late 1910s and early 1920s. It is neither intended to suggest that the working classes may be attributed a fixed social and political identity nor that the Congress espoused a single, consistent political programme, let alone that they articulated it in a univocal rhetoric. Nonetheless, Gandhi's distinctive language increasingly inflected the rhetoric and programme of the Con-

[15] Randy Shilts, *And the Band Played On. Politics, People and the Aids Epidemic* (London, 1988).

[16] It draws here upon the seminal essay by G. Stedman Jones, 'Rethinking Chartism', in G. Stedman Jones, *The Languages of Class: Studies in English Working Class History, 1832–1982* (Cambridge, 1983), pp. 90–178.

gress. For this reason, I seek to examine the imaginative possibilities which Gandhi's rhetoric offered workers' politics and the limitations which it imposed upon them. In addition, the chapter argues that the popular interpretation of the rhetoric and programme of the Congress would also depend upon how its often varied and inconsistent political interventions were perceived by the working classes. Accordingly, this chapter investigates how the changing character of the Congress in the last decades of colonial rule affected its ability and its willingness to represent the working classes and their discontents. Conversely, it examines the constraints within which workers' combinations struggled to emerge and the relationships which they sought to forge with politicians and publicists. It is in this context that the often guarded response of the Congress to the motley and evanescent trade unions which formed and collapsed in this period should be situated. For the Congress, the task of reconciling the differences among its diverse constituents posed insuperable problems to identifying themselves as the champions of the workers' (or any sectional) interests. Finally, this chapter examines the nature of working-class nationalism and, more generally, sets the rhetoric of the Congress in relation to the sectionalism, whether of class or caste, language or religion, gender or region, of its putative followers.

Chapters 5 to 8, therefore, pick up in various ways and develop a critique of the concept of popular culture and its usage by historians of the subcontinent and, indeed, elsewhere, which was suggested by the investigation of the working-class neighbourhoods in chapter 4. Notions of working-class culture emerged from attempts by social historians to retrieve from the vitality of civil society the oppositional practices and traditions of resistance among the working classes. For those who concluded that class and class consciousness could only be found in their real form in advanced capitalist societies, 'culture', especially 'popular culture' provided an alternative to 'class consciousness' and offered a looser category for the discussion of the ideologies and political actions of workers in the context of economic backwardness. Not only did the concept take for granted, thereby, the evolutionary assumptions which had circumscribed the scope of Indian working-class history but, more crucially, perhaps, the use of the term has been riddled with contradictions and conceptual confusions. The concept has enabled historians to attend to the agency and initiative of the working classes, both within the political and the social sphere. However, assumptions about the cultural characteristics of the working classes have often informed conclusions about their attitudes to work and politics, as if their choices were governed by a logic consistently beyond their control. While it may appear that culture would enable historians to identify diversity, it has far more often nudged us towards an assumption of social homogeneity. For if we acknowledge the diversity of customs, values and social practices of a given social group, how could they be reduced to the single common denominator of culture? In view of the variations of local context, and the tensions and antagonisms by which it is constituted, it is often merely the assumption of the existence of a 'popular culture' which enables historians to pull across the often fundamental differences of perception, social being and discourse, the unity and homogeneity of a 'popular culture'. In addition, the use of the term has often concealed, or at any rate failed adequately to address, significant methodological difficulties. For the delineation of 'popular culture', historians have often depended, not surprisingly in the Indian case, upon the perceptions and characterizations of elite observers, frequently of functionaries, publicists and journalists. Moreover, historians who have employed the term have sometimes eschewed social and economic explanation, sometimes even inquiry into the material world, as unduly deterministic; yet, they have often inferred the values and attitudes of social groups from their modes of existence. The notion of a 'pre-capitalist' or, indeed, a 'bourgeois' culture remains inescapably deterministic.[17] Indeed, such inferences overlook the obvious cultural fact that the circumstances are rare in which most people, and especially subordinate groups, can give free expression to their cultural preferences. The notion of culture was the product of imperial expansion which brought Europeans into contact with exotic peoples. It has subsequently provided a method of ordering, disciplining and bringing within a rational discourse these perceptions of the exotic. The working classes and the poor, whether in the 'North' or the 'South', it would appear, have often remained as exotic to the scholar in his attic in either hemisphere as the European conquistadors and seafarers found the people they encountered and colonized.

The final chapter seeks to bring together the leading themes and arguments of this book. It offers a schematic view of the historical and social formation of the working classes in India and seeks to situate it within the context of 'world capitalism'. At the same time, it interrogates the concept of 'the capitalist world economy' and the explanatory framework of dependency theory from the historical perspective of the Indian subcontinent. In so doing, it stresses the argument that the formation and reproduction of an industrial labour force was integral to the historical processes which shaped diverse forms of labour use in the Indian economy in the nineteenth and twentieth centuries. It also attempts to situate the history of indigenous capitalism in its global and colonial setting, not

[17] Notably, for instance, in the highly charged polemic against determinism offered by Chakrabarty, *Rethinking Working Class History*.

to track its steady 'incorporation' into the capitalist world economy, but rather to recover more fully the subcontinental context and history of capitalist development. The subordination of indigenous to international and metropolitan capitalists, mediated and directed, as it was, by colonial power, shaped both the patterns of capitalist and industrial development in India as well as the forms of labour exploitation.

For historians of India, over the past decade, the tidal waves of intellectual fashion (slightly delayed in this case) have threatened to sweep away the study of the material world and to leave in its wake a bleaker landscape of deconstruction and textual exegesis. Historians have been led on this terrain towards a preoccupation with a close reading of texts, with the construction of colonial policy, with the often Eurocentric question of colonial discourse which is taken to have influenced and encompassed Indian representations of themselves and, inevitably perhaps, given the human condition, with gazing into the mirror of historiography. This is a landscape which has been increasingly denuded of the investigation of the social and material world, and especially of the struggles waged by the subaltern classes.[18] Its preoccupation with colonial discourse, having promised to expose the Eurocentricity of post-colonial scholarship, has often served to entrench it. Those who focus upon colonial discourse have been led to practise a 'Eurocentricity' of their own. Close attention to how colonial society constructed Indian society has encouraged a preoccupation with the intellectual foundations of colonialism while the history of Indian society is faded into the background. Overly concerned with how colonial discourse and its hegemonized agents represented their subjects, and seeking to liberate themselves from this discursive trap, scholars, rather like colonial ideologues, have increasingly assumed the mantle of representing the native.

Few today would deny the intimate connections which bind knowledge and power in a single nexus. Nor would many scholars be astonished any longer by the suggestion that knowledge about Indian society and its past was produced in relation to the harsh facts of imperial dominance. The recognition that the truth about the past did not lie in a finite archival record waiting to be extracted by scholars, able to discover it by the use of more objective and 'scientific' methods, somehow untrammelled by 'political' bias, may have appeared as a revelation to literary critics and social scientists, but it was unlikely, even before Said or even Foucault, to surprise historians, who had necessarily been forced to grapple with the

---

[18] This trend is most readily visible in the recent volumes of *Subaltern Studies* (especially in vols. V–VII), the fruits of a project which dedicated itself to the study of the 'subaltern classes', to restoring them to the pages of history, and therein retrieving them from the margins and the footnotes to the main text.

unremitting awkwardness of archival evidence. The appreciation that knowledge, the definition of its scope and manner of its creation, was imbricated in the imperatives of its political context was integral to the historian's craft. Even the most positivistically minded historians – and their tribe has been populous – acknowledged that their findings were contingent and that their interpretations, in offering no more than one version of the past, only served to locate them in relation to their sources, the historiography in general and its wider intellectual context.

Nevertheless, with the systematic and lucid exposition of Orientalism, historians of India lost their nerve and found a theory. If colonial discourse was constituted by, and provided an expression of, imperial domination and control, Indian society and its past appeared simply as its product and its consequence. The motor of history appeared to lie in the hegemonic colonial discourse and its construction of India. Accordingly, historians now concentrated their attention upon the study of colonial discourse, the processes by which it was constituted, its manifold constructions of India – its people, its social institutions, its body politic and its intellectual and cultural history – as the object of its knowledge and its power. Textual exegesis cast its lengthening shadow over social being. Human agency seemed to be yet another delusion fostered by the Enlightenment. Authors, like actors, were necessarily marginalized within, sometimes vaporized from, the historical account. The material world was merely the final distortion reflected by the hall of mirrors which historical research seemed to represent. Necessarily, then, scholars have tended to examine the mirrors minutely and ignore the object whose image it refracts.

The effects and implication of this reasoning have, of course, been deeply conservative. If we refuse to acknowledge the materiality of the social world, we could not possibly change it. Its deficiencies, injustices and oppressions must seem quite as illusory as the social world and the process of its refraction. To acknowledge the intimate connections between power and knowledge, and their effect in delineating, even defining, the materiality of the social world is not to deny its existence. More than some of his disciples and imitators, Edward Said allowed for the distinction between the material world and its representation in public discourse. For 'the lives, histories and customs' of the Orient, he noted, 'have a brute reality obviously greater than anything that can be said about them in the West'.[19] The historian's task in studying the material world is perhaps to create and enter the space between this level of 'brute reality' and the discourse which is generated by, and relates to it, whether in India or the West.

[19] E. Said, *Orientalism* (New York, 1978), p. 5.

By averting their gaze from the material world, while focusing upon its representation and, more generally, its configuration as knowledge, historians have often served to replicate colonial representations of the material world and the assumptions upon which they were built. Nowhere has this more consistently been the case than in the investigation of the working classes, or indeed, peasants and the rural poor. For colonial discourse in India, as elsewhere, was largely a discourse about labour. The British in India were concerned to put Indians to work in the interests of their larger imperial purposes. The colonial project was characterized, primarily, by the struggle to acquire closer control over labour, to cheapen its costs and to subordinate it more fully to the disciplines of capitalism. In important ways, the Orientalist construction of India described the displacement of the colonial construction of its labour problem onto the field its discourse defined as culture.

Colonial ideologues and entrepreneurs built their image of labour upon the assumption that Indian society was traditional, static and timeless. To a large extent, what colonial discourse identified as traditional about Indian society in the nineteenth century was its own creation as it sought to harness local resources to its global imperial purposes. In this discourse, Indian tradition was constituted by the village community, the caste system and the agrarian character of the economy. The village community was portrayed as immutable and harmonious, composed of primarily subsistence, yet interdependent, cultivators who understood and observed their mutual obligations.[20] Intimately associated with the village community was the representation of 'the caste system' as an integral aspect of religion rather than as a mechanism by which rulers could obtain and exercise control over the whole being of the labourer, not simply the fruits of his labour.[21] In colonial discourse, the caste

---

[20] H. S. Maine, *Village Communities in the East and West* (London, 1871); B. H. Baden-Powell, *The Indian Village Community* (London, 1896). On the impact of the characterization of the village community on land revenue policies and land tenure, see E. Stokes, *The English Utilitarians and India* (Oxford, 1959). See also, Louis Dumont, 'The Village Community from Munro to Maine', *Contributions to Indian Sociology*, 9 (December, 1965), 67–89. On colonial constructions of the village community, see Clive Dewey, 'Images of the Village Community: A Study in Anglo-Indian Ideology' *MAS*, 6:3 (1972), 291–328; for a more systematic analysis of its relationship to a wider Orientalist discourse, see R. Inden, *Imagining India* (Oxford, 1991).

[21] J. Breman, *Beyond Patronage and Exploitation: Changing Agrarian Relations in South Gujarat* (Delhi, 1993); G. Prakash, *Bonded Histories: Genealogies of Labor Servitude in Colonial India* (Cambridge, 1990); N. Bhattacharya, 'Agricultural Labour and Production: Central and South-East Punjab, 1870–1940', in K. N. Raj, N. Bhattacharya, S. Guha and S. Padhi (eds.), *Essays on the Commercialization of Indian Agriculture* (Delhi, 1985); J. Banaji, 'Capitalist Domination and the Small Peasantry: Deccan Districts in the Late Nineteenth Century', *Economic and Political Weekly*, 12: 33–4 (1977), special number, 1375–1404. For an argument in favour of a political interpretation of caste, see N. Dirks, *The Hollow Crown: Ethnohistory of an Indian Little Kingdom* (Cambridge, 1987); see also Inden, *Imagining India*, ch. 2.

system, perceived as the defining moral code of Indian society, and the village community, served to explain why the essence of its civilization might cohere and survive unchanged in the face of political turmoil and revolution. What underpinned the immutable village community and the caste system in colonial discourse was a stagnant agricultural economy, characterized by smallholding, self-sufficient cultivators, highly resistant to the rationality of the market. Of course, colonial discourse concealed, at any rate it did not register, its own active role in creating the traditional and stagnant agricultural economy which it was able to identify by the end of the nineteenth century.[22]

The colonial discourse about labour came to be shaped by this representation of the traditional character of Indian society. It sought to deny labour's modernity. Within its terms, the traditional trappings of caste, religion and village community rendered labour immune, or even antithetical, to capitalist rationality. This was, however, a discourse riddled with contradictions. For instance, it took for granted that, even as the structural stagnation of the agrarian economy made a growing number of smallholding families dependent upon wages, it would be difficult to loosen labour from the moorings of the village community.[23] If labour was

---

[22] E. Stokes, *The Peasant and the Raj: Studies in Agrarian Society and Peasant Rebellion in Colonial India* (Cambridge, 1978); D. A. Washbrook, 'Law, State and Agrarian Society in Colonial India', *MAS,* 15:3 (1981), special issue, *Profit, Power and Politics: Essays on Imperialism, Nationalism and Change in Twentieth Century India,* edited by C. Baker, G. Johnson and A. Seal, pp. 649–721; Banaji, 'Capitalist Domination'; N. Bhattacharya, 'Lenders and Debtors: Punjab Countryside, 1880–1940', *Studies in History,* new series, 1:2 (1985), 305–42; S. Guha, *The Agrarian Economy of the Bombay Deccan, 1818–1941* (Delhi, 1986).

[23] Hence, the volume of complaints from entrepreneurs and some officials about the scarcity (and high cost) of labour, especially until the first world war. Statements about the scarcity of labour are to be found extensively in the annual reports of various employers' associations – especially the Bombay Millowners' Association (BMOA) and the Indian Jute Mill Employers' Association – trade journals, like the *Indian Textile Journal,* and various public enquiries into the conditions of labour since the late nineteenth century, especially *The Report of the Indian Factory Labour Commission* (Simla, 1908), vol. I – but they were disputed by B. Foley, *Report on Labour in Bengal* (Calcutta, 1906). See also *Report of the Indian Factory Commission, Appointed in September 1890, under the Orders of His Excellency, the Governor-General-in-Council, with Proceedings and Appendices* (Calcutta, 1890). They were also expressed in the official histories of the jute and cotton textile industries; see D. R. Wallace, *The Romance of Jute* (Calcutta, 1909) and S. D. Mehta, *The Cotton Mills of India, 1854–1954* (Bombay, 1954). The evidence on labour supply is closely examined in Morris, *The Emergence of an Industrial Labour Force,* ch. 4 and in Das Gupta, 'Factory Labour in Eastern India'. See also Simmons, 'Recruiting and Organizing an Industrial Labour Force'. I have examined the implications of labour migration and the nature of the rural connections of urban workers in Chandavarkar, *The Origins of Industrial Capitalism,* ch. 4. For a valuable study of the implications of labour migration in Bengal, particularly for gender relations, see Samita Sen, 'Women Workers in the Bengal Jute Industry, 1890–1940: Migration, Motherhood and Militancy', unpublished Ph.D. thesis, University of Cambridge, 1992, chs. 1 and 2.

difficult to obtain, colonial capitalists and officials recognized that it would have to be bought out.[24] But to pay them more than skill and aptitude deserved was incompatible with the need for cheap labour so crucial to the gimcrack production regimes which colonial expansion brought to India and whose development it stimulated.[25] Yet if labour was not easily mobilized, colonial officials and entrepreneurs nonetheless feared that, once it was set free, it would prove restless and unrestrained, elusive of control and impossible to discipline. Indentured servitude, 'a new system of slavery' developed under the colonial aegis to replace the old after its abolition in 1834,[26] was, like the jobber system, devised to prise labour out of the village community as well as to pin it down to the mines, plantations and factories.[27] But by the 1920s, as employers grew increasingly resentful of the extent to which they had been cut out of their own systems of labour control and recruitment, colonial discourse, adopting the high moral ground, came to focus upon the abuses and evils of the jobber system.[28]

It was assumed that workers had to be pinned down in this way because

[24] This argument was explicitly made in Mazumdar, 'Labour Supply in Early Industrialization'. For a critique, see Newman, 'Social Factors in the Recruitment of the Bombay Millhands', and Chandavarkar, *The Origins of Industrial Capitalism*, pp. 307–26. Employers, of course, frequently complained about high wages while officials sometimes expressed concern at the intense exploitation of labour, not least because it gave Indian employers an advantage over metropolitan rivals. This latter concern provided an important motive for passing factory legislation to regulate the hours and conditions of work. For an account of the official discourse, see D. Chakrabarty, 'Conditions for Knowledge of Working-Class Conditions: Employers, Government and the Jute Workers of Calcutta' in R. Guha (ed.), *Subaltern Studies*, vol. II (Delhi, 1983), pp. 259–310.

[25] Especially in the extractive and plantation industries of the nineteenth century: indigo, tea and coal. This style of frontier capitalism which emerged in the wake of colonial expansion conditioned entrepreneurial attitudes, business strategies and patterns of labour deployment and discipline in most other industries in the twentieth century in significant ways. For an overview of the evolution of this style of frontier capitalism, see C. J. Baker, 'Economic Reorganization and the Slump in South and South-east Asia', *Comparative Studies in Society and History*, 23:3 (1981), 325–49.

[26] H. Tinker, *A New System of Slavery: The Export of Indian Labour Overseas, 1830–1920* (Oxford, 1974); Brij Lal, 'Kunti's Cry: Indentured Women on Fiji's Plantations', *Indian Economic and Social History Review*, 22:2 (1985), 55–71; E. Valentine Daniel, H. Bernstein and T. Brass (eds.), *Plantations, Proletarians and Peasants in Colonial Asia* (London, 1992); Carter, *Servants, Sirdars and Settlers*; J. Breman, *Taming the Coolie Beast: Plantation Society and the Colonial Order in Southeast Asia* (Delhi, 1989); P. Ramasamy, *Plantation Labour, Unions, Capital and the State in Peninsular Malaysia* (Kuala Lumpur, 1994).

[27] Recruitment, like the question of labour supply, has provided the organizing principle of research in Indian (perhaps much colonial) labour history. In view of its significance in colonial discourse, this is perhaps not surprising; but it may be taken as yet another indication of the extent to which colonial discourse has been unwittingly replicated in Indian historiography.

[28] Chandavarkar, *The Origins of Industrial Capitalism*, pp. 99–109, 195–200, 295–307.

they would not honour their contracts. Labour's failure to honour its contracts, indeed its inability to understand the very concept, was inextricably related to the fact it had to be mobilized out of a society which inhabited a previous, not the contemporary bourgeois epoch. From this characterization of Indian labour as pre-modern followed the conclusion that it lacked skill, except, that is, skills which were hereditary and genealogical and associated with caste, but which were not always or easily transposed to the industrial setting. The notion that skill was relative, contingent and often politically defined was not entertained in this discourse about labour. Nor was the considerable ingenuity and constant improvisation demanded of workers, and frequently observed, allowed to qualify the axiom that Indian workers possessed low absolute levels of skill.[29]

Colonial discourse represented workers as primarily 'agriculturists at heart', despite the fact that, as landless labourers, dalits, tribals, artisans and so on, they were drawn from diverse occupational strata. Their peasant character was invoked to explain what was perceived as their casual attitude to work, their restless search for casual and temporary employment wherever it may be found and their lack of commitment to the industrial setting.[30] It was supposed, nonetheless, that workers were greedy for cash, motivated by the desire to earn as much as possible as quickly as they could, in order to return to the land. This supposition could scarcely be reconciled, however, with the notion that they were unable to hold down a job for any length of time and that they moved restlessly in search of casual employment.[31] While this portrayal of workers betrayed colonial capitalist anxieties about wage competition and

[29] Ironically, this dependence upon skilful improvisation was necessitated by low levels of investment, especially in technological change. Historians have largely neglected the detailed investigation of the labour process and the social relations of the workplace but this has not prevented them adopting the characterizations of the colonial discourse. Assumptions both about 'the pre-capitalist culture' of the Indian labour force and its lack of skill are central to Dipesh Chakrabarty's portrayal of jute mill labour in Bengal; see Chakrabarty, *Rethinking Working-Class History*. For an alternative view of Bengal jute mill labour, see Sen, 'Women Workers'; S. Basu, 'Workers' Politics in Bengal, 1890–1929: Mill-Towns, Strikes and Nationalist Agitations', unpublished Ph.D. thesis, University of Cambridge, 1994.

[30] See *Report of the Indian Factory Labour Commission*, vol. I; *Report of the RCLI* (London, 1931), which both dismissed the view of workers as peasants in proletarian guise and then espoused it. For a discussion of the representation of migrant labour, see Chandavarkar, *The Origins of Industrial Capitalism*, ch. 4.

[31] The detailed examination of the urban labour market does not bear out the notions that casual labour sought out temporary work wherever it was to be found or that a clear distinction can be made between the attitudes to work of casual labour and factory proletarians. See Chandavarkar, *The Origins of Industrial Capitalism*, ch. 3. On Bengal, see Basu, 'Workers' Politics in Bengal'.

labour mobility, it also had the self-serving virtue of implying that they were paid enough to accumulate and repatriate substantial savings to their village base.[32]

On the other hand, a recurrent theme of colonial discourse, running in an opposite direction, was that workers did not respond to incentives, whether in the form of increased wages or improved conditions. Higher wages, it was assumed, would only induce workers to withdraw their labour and retire, clutching their savings, into the traditional recesses of the village community. This argument, arising out of the assumption of the pre-modern and pre-capitalist culture of Indian workers, had been most explicitly set out by Max Weber in his treatise on *The Religion of India*:

The workers want to earn some money quickly in order to establish themselves independently. An increase in wage rate does not mean for them an incentive for more work or a higher standard of living, but the reverse. They then take longer holidays because they can afford to do so, or their wives decorate themselves with ornaments. To stay away from work as one pleases is recognized as a matter of course, and the worker retires with his meagre savings to his home town as soon as possible. 'Discipline' in the European sense is an unknown idea to him.[33]

This ignorance of, or aversion to, discipline in 'the European sense' suggested, in this discourse, why labour could not easily be organized either for work or for politics. Their peasant character, forged by the hierarchies of caste, rendered them tolerant and acquiescent, but it also accounted for their propensity to violence, lightning strikes and spasmodic protests.[34] Employers and managers held fast to the belief that their workers were ordinarily content and had no 'real' grievances. Labour unrest was inevitably the result of the baneful influence of outside agitators, although why contented workers should be seduced by the blandishments of troublemakers was never fully explained. If workers lacked the discipline to adapt to the rhythms of industrial capitalism, they could scarcely acquire it swiftly for the purposes of collective bargaining or trade union organization.[35] Indeed, it seemed obvious to conclude that workers who belonged to an older and not necessarily better age and for whom, therefore, the concept of contract remained alien and mysterious, could scarcely be expected to negotiate collectively, formulate strictly

[32] Employers and colonial officials, thus, paid particular attention to the extent to which workers remitted their savings to their villages and historians have similarly made much of the limited evidence so far available on the issue.
[33] Max Weber, *The Religion of India*, translated by H. H. Gerth and D. Martindale (Glencoe, Ill., 1958), p. 114.   [34] See ch. 5 below.
[35] These issues are examined in greater detail in ch. 3 below.

reasonable demands or display the discipline to stick to bargains struck with their employers.[36]

It was precisely because these supposedly pre-industrial workers, rural migrants, seemingly half-peasant and half-proletarian, could not be relied upon to operate within the domain of reason that they were perceived, in this view, to be quite so threatening. Not only could they be easily worked up into 'a state of excitement' about wages and working conditions, but their material grievances were readily turned against government. Similarly, it was thought that their resentments and grievances could find frenzied expression in their caste prejudices and religious fanaticism, always liable to result, or so it seemed, in violence and bloodshed. Moreover, colonial officials took it for granted that unless these discontents were contained or resolved immediately they could in an instant develop into a massive political conflagration beyond the ability of the state to control. Since their political action could rarely be traced back to, let alone contained within, the domain of reason, workers appeared, in this discourse, to inhabit a very narrow spectrum between passivity and fanatical fury. The imperative for immediate and effective action to contain their threat seemed at times, therefore, to legitimize measures of repression, whose brutality was disproportionate to the threat they sought to contain, just as an acute awareness of the vulnerability of the colonial state, when faced with mass revolt, and the futility of ruling India by force, sometimes imposed constraints upon its uninhibited use.

For all the contradictions and confusions which marked the colonial construction of its 'labour problem', the latter's significance for the colonial project was enormous. Consequently, colonial discourse about labour extended naturally towards, and encompassed, just as it was informed by, its characterization of 'traditional Indian culture'. Following in the footsteps of Foucault and Said, often with a rather heavy tread, ponderously in quest of theory, historians increasingly concerned with colonial discourse and its production of Indian society have concentrated single-mindedly upon what it constituted as 'culture'. When they have sought to investigate the history of Indian society, they have increasingly focused upon colonial discourse to the exclusion of the material world which it represented, and as a result, perhaps, tended to replicate the axioms and premises of the colonial discourse sometimes as readily as an innocent, even uncritical, reading of the archival record might produce. The contradictions which proliferate in the colonial discourse suggest not only the difficulties encountered by colonial rulers and the dominant

---

[36] The lack of a notion of contract in the pre-capitalist culture of the working classes has recently been offered as one reason for the weakness of trade unions by Chakrabarty, *Rethinking Working Class History*.

classes in maintaining control over labour but also those entailed in grasping and reconstituting the social world which it inhabits. The injunction 'to read the sources against the grain' has been so often repeated, not least because of its poetic and mystical ring, that it has come to be something of a cliché. To read against the grain the sources predominantly produced by colonial rulers and the dominant classes is to read the discourse for its contradictions and through its contradictions to interrogate its construction of the material world. The following chapters traverse the discursive space between the material world and its varied representations, not merely to register the available evidence about the former, but also to strip it of at least some of the mythologies narrated by the colonial discourse.

2   Industrialization in India before 1947: conventional approaches and alternative perspectives

Models of industrialization and social change, whether Marxist or functionalist, have been derived largely from the historical experience of Western Europe and, especially, of Britain. Social theories came to be constructed upon a specific reading of a particular, and in some respects, unique, historical development. These theories or models, now deep-seated in our historiographical consciousness, increasingly offer yard-sticks against which industrial development elsewhere in the world is measured. On closer examination, universal postulates thus derived have appeared to generate a large number of special cases. Vast expanses of the globe are seemingly littered with cases of arrested development or examples of frustrated bourgeois revolutions.

Since the study of the rise of industrialism, the central problem of sociology, has hinged on so specific a historical example, it is not surprising that in spite of fundamental differences of intellectual traditions, conceptual frameworks and political values, diverse models of economic development and industrialization have been built upon essentially similar assumptions. Of course, these models have often been criticized in their parts, but they have scarcely been rejected as a whole and while historians may disclaim some of the assumptions upon which they are based, these continue to be pervasive in the analysis of economic development both in the West and the Third World. This essay sets out these shared assumptions, common to Marxism and functionalism alike, about the character of industrialization as a social process. Since they have left their imprint firmly upon the investigation of Indian industrialization and economic development, this essay will attempt to set these assumptions against the approaches and arguments which they have generated in the specific case of India. To do so may not only indicate the inadequacy of the latter, but may also serve to highlight the limitations which these assumptions have imposed upon empirical research and historical interpretation. Finally, this essay will offer some alternative perspectives on, and draw attention to, some neglected questions in the history of Indian industrialization.

The historical example of India offers a particularly helpful perspective upon prevailing models of industrialization. For one thing, in conventional terms, India was substantially on the road to industrialism from the mid-nineteenth century onwards without perhaps ever having quite reached its destination. This would suggest that either we should understand industrialization in India (and other similar examples) as a special case requiring a special model of its own or that existing models may be in need of revision. Furthermore, the history of industrialization in the West is taken primarily to mean the evolution of factory from craft industry, generally presupposing the prior development of a market economy, the social differentiation of the peasantry and changing legal and social structures. In India, all these forces were working together at the same time; and if some showed signs of acceleration in the late nineteenth century, their development usually had long historical roots, pre-dating the imposition of colonial rule. In other words, no simple evolutionary schemata of social change and economic development can be readily applied to the Indian evidence.

I

For functionalist writers, industrialization constituted a serial process through which society would duly pass at an appropriate stage of development. The roads towards a fully industrialized society were many, but the outcome was invariably the same: 'industrialism . . . that which the industrialization process inherently tends to create'.[1] This 'process' was guided by an underlying 'logic',[2] by the 'imperatives of industrialization' which 'cause the industrializing élites to overcome certain constraints and to achieve certain objectives which are the same in all societies undergoing transformation'.[3] The signposts of this transformation were characteristically an advanced level of technology, large-scale enterprise and the

---

[1] C. Kerr, F. H. Harbison, J. T. Dunlop and C. A. Myers, *Industrialism and Industrial Man: The Problems of Labour and Management in Economic Growth* (London, 1962), p. 33; C. Kerr and A. Seigel, 'The Structuring of the Labour Force in Industrial Society', *Industrial and Labour Relations Review*, 8:2 (1955), 151–68; B. E. Hoselitz and W. E. Moore (eds.), *Industrialization and Society* (Paris, 1963); W. E. Moore and A. S. Feldman (eds.), *Labour Commitment and Social Change in Developing Areas* (New York, 1960); N. J. Smelser, *Social Change and the Industrial Revolution* (London, 1959) and *Theory of Collective Behaviour* (New York, 1963).   [2] Kerr *et al.*, *Industrialism and Industrial Man*, p. 17.
[3] C. Kerr, F. H. Harbison, J. T. Dunlop and C. A. Myers, 'Industrialism and Industrial Man', *International Labour Review*, 82:3 (1960), p. 238.

formation of a consensus of values governed by goals unknown in 'traditional society'.

If the direction of change from traditional society to industrialism was universal, its tendency was too strong to be resisted and its outcome inevitable.[4] Industrialism worked ceaselessly upon a static, passive traditional order. The society and its constituent elements, moulded by the inexorable advance of industrialism, was as clay in its hands:

Industrialization redesigns and restructures its human raw materials, whatever the source. Thus, the development of an industrial work force necessarily involves the destruction of old ways of life and the acceptance of the new imperatives of the industrial work community.[5]

Whereas 'dynamic elites' initiated industrialization, chose its route and shaped its forms, workers, like other traditional groups, were 'in the end malleable'. Indeed, 'man is everywhere adaptable to the industrial system'.[6] Of course, the process of 'his metamorphosis gives rise to many forms of protest' but these reflect his maladjustment and 'partial commitment' to the industrial setting. With further industrial development, the worker is reconciled to his machine, and 'incipient protest is moderated, channelled and redirected', so as to 'conform and contribute to the strategy of the industrializing elites'. Labour resistance, in this view, is irrational and atavistic: a doomed attempt to stem the tide of history. For the most part, however, as workers adapt to the industrial setting, protest inherently tends to disappear, or at least to be harnessed ultimately to the larger imperatives of industrialism.

Similar assumptions informed the perspectives of a number of labour economists, development specialists and Parsonian sociologists. For many economists and sociologists, writing in the 1950s, the 'developed' countries revealed to the underdeveloped the image of their own possible future: 'social and political models' characterized by full employment, universal adult suffrage and the welfare state. Higher per capita incomes were recognized as an essential pre-condition for the achievement of these goals. This made economic growth measured in terms of national income highly desirable.[7]

At the same time, historians of the industrial revolution in Britain set

[4] Ibid., 241; Kerr et al., Industrialism and Industrial Man, p. 47.
[5] Kerr et al., 'Industrialism and Industrial Man', 246.   [6] Ibid., 245–6.
[7] Beneath this desire lurked a different rationale. Development in this sense possessed other advantages, apart from higher per capita incomes. It might help to thwart the communist menace. It would prevent potential markets, raw materials and investment opportunities from being dragged behind the Iron Curtain. It would more positively open up these resources to the West, particularly if per capita incomes rose. For a brief but perceptive discussion, see D. Seers, 'The Birth, Life and Death of Development Economics', Development and Change, 10:4 (1979), 707–19.

out to examine the 'historical experience of economic development'.[8] 'The identification of the advantages in any one' of the advanced industrial economies, it was supposed, could be 'of value to those other countries which still seem bereft of a good hand of cards'.[9] If 'the central fact of economic development is rapid capital accumulation', as W. A. Lewis declared, its 'central problem' was to investigate how a given society raised its level of saving and investment from '4 or 5 per cent of its national income or less' to '12 to 15 per cent or more'.[10] Ironically, 'this hypothesis was derived from the empirical study of twentieth-century underdeveloped countries, and especially from the case of India'.[11] If the industrial revolution in Britain was to serve increasingly as a model against which industrial development in India could be counterposed, the fine carvings of that model had originally been made upon Indian stone. When this emphasis upon capital accumulation, large-scale industry, entrepreneurial initiative and transformative lead sectors established a firm grip on Indian economic history, the circle had begun to go back on itself.[12]

But there was a deeper sense in which the history of the industrial revolution in Britain came to acquire the status of a universal model.[13] This related not simply to identifying the circumstances of 'take-off', nor even to the analysis of the social and economic pre-conditions of industrial development, but more fundamentally to a conception of the underlying social processes of industrialization. Thus, David Landes, in his classic study of European industrialization, defined an industrial revolution as:

[8] H. J. Habakkuk, 'The Historical Experience of Economic Development', in E. A. G. Robinson (ed.), *Problems in Economic Development* (London, 1965), pp. 112–38. For a recent historiographical survey of the industrial revolution in Britain which shows how this approach came into vogue among economic historians in the 1950s, see D. Cannadine, 'The Present and the Past in the English Industrial Revolution, 1880–1980', *Past and Present*, 103 (May 1984), 131–71.

[9] E. L. Jones (ed.), *Agricultural and Economic Growth in England 1650–1815* (London, 1967), p. 2. See especially, W. W. Rostow, *The Stages of Economic Growth: A Non-Communist Manifesto* (Cambridge, 1960), p. 139 and *passim*.

[10] W. A. Lewis, 'Economic Development with Unlimited Supplies of Labour', *The Manchester School of Economic and Social Studies*, 22:2 (1954), 155.

[11] F. Crouzet, 'An Essay in Historiography', in Crouzet, *Capital Formation in the Industrial Revolution* (London, 1972), p. 11.

[12] A. K. Bagchi, *Private Investment in India, 1900–1939* (Cambridge, 1972); R. K. Ray, *Industrialization in India: Growth and Conflict in the Private Corporate Sector, 1914–1947* (Delhi, 1979); M. D. Morris, 'The Growth of Large-Scale Industry', in D. Kumar (ed.), *CEHI*, vol. II: *1750–c. 1970* (Cambridge, 1983), pp. 553–676.

[13] Of course, the industrialization of the 'latecomers' has sometimes acquired the status of a model in its own right. However, in terms of the social process of industrialization, it has usually borne a strong resemblance to the original British model. For a useful summary, see R. C. Trebilcock, *The Industrialization of the Continental Powers, 1750–1914* (New York, 1981), pp. 1–21.

that complex of technological innovations which, by substituting machines for human skill and inanimate power for human and animal force, brings about a shift from handicraft to manufacture, and, by so doing, gives birth to a modern economy. In this sense, the industrial revolution has already transformed a number of countries, though in unequal degree; other societies are in the throes of change; the turn of still others is yet to come.

It gives rise to novel forms of industrial organization, characteristically the factory. The factory constituted something 'more than just a larger work unit. It was a system of production', which over time created a 'new breed of worker'.[14] In this light, industrialization is taken to constitute an autonomous force, determined by a neutral technology, whose 'imperatives' and 'inherent tendencies' appear to lie beyond the realm of social choice or political control, and which acts to shape society inevitably in a single direction. It is not intended to suggest that there were no differences of approach between the numerous writers in various fields who investigated the 'transition to industrialism'.[15] Rather, what needs to be emphasized is that in spite of specific differences, these assumptions about the character of industrialization as a social process came to be shared by a remarkably wide range of scholars.

These assumptions, often implicit, have influenced the study of industrialization in three ways. First, by postulating a unilinear direction of change, they have trained our sights upon 'large-scale industry', as constituting the lead sector of the economy, and have obscured not only our understanding of other centres of dynamism and stagnation within it, but also of their role in determining the structure of the economy as a whole. It has enabled, indeed sometimes depended upon, arbitrary definitions of 'large-scale industry' or the so-called formal sector. Above all, it has often led to the identification of the general problem of economic backwardness almost exclusively with the specific question of industrial failure.

Second, the crude distinction made between pre-industrial and industrial societies frequently fails to advance our understanding of the former or even its transition to the latter. Pre-industrial societies are often taken to be predominantly agrarian societies in which large-scale industry has not been established. They are thus lumped together irrespective of their levels of technology, economic activity or social organization. In this perspective, the mainsprings of dynamism and change within pre-indus-

---

[14] D. S. Landes, *The Unbound Prometheus: Technological Change and Industrial Development in Western Europe from 1750 to the Present* (Cambridge, 1969), pp. 1–2.

[15] For a recent exposition of different sociological traditions, stemming originally from the work of Marx, Durkheim and Weber, see P. Abrams, *Historical Sociology* (London, 1983), pp. 19–146.

trial society are obscured. Similarly, models of industrializing societies often provide no means of differentiating between them, even as they operate at greatly differing economic levels. Consequently, they have generated endless false analogies between fundamentally different societies and inspired scores of meaningless computations of industrial achievement. Thus, in 1914, we are told, India boasted 'the world's largest jute manufacturing industry, the fourth and fifth largest cotton textile industry (depending on what is being measured), and the third largest railway network'.[16] By 1945, India was said to be 'the tenth largest producer of manufactured goods in the world'.[17]

Third, these models frequently postulate a simple and direct relationship between the levels of industrialization and the pattern of social response. Thus, while the early stages of industrialization are characterized by spontaneous and volatile working-class behaviour, further development, it is often supposed, leads to the formation of trade unions, the emergence of 'group protest' and the more ready acceptance of formal collective bargaining; or alternatively to the 'secular decline of protest', for more industrialization means less labour resistance.[18] Conversely, prior assumptions about the forms of social action supposedly appropriate to a given stage of industrial development have shaped and perhaps limited historical analysis of the nature of working-class politics.

To a remarkable extent, various forms of Marxist analysis have borne a strong resemblance to functionalist sociology. Like the functionalist models, Marxist theory built upon the English experience of industrialization. Classical Marxism, like later functionalism, appeared to take for granted that 'underdeveloped' or 'backward' societies operated at some original stage of development.[19] Of the various modes of production, capitalism alone was expansive, relentlessly progressive and inherently generative of further economic development. As new regions, 'even the most barbarian nations', in Marx's Darwinian language, are pulled into the orbit of capitalism, they are liberated from the deadening impulses of pre-capitalist modes of production. Classical Marxism, like later func-

---

[16] Morris, 'Large-Scale Industry', 553.

[17] B. R. Tomlinson, *The Political Economy of the Raj: The Economics of Decolonization in India* (London, 1979), p. 31; see also Ray, *Industrialization in India*, pp. 14–21.

[18] Kerr *et al.*, *Industrialism and Industrial Man*, pp. 193–223; C. Kerr, 'Changing Social Structures', in Moore and Feldman (eds.), *Labour Commitment and Social Change*, pp. 348–59.

[19] For a recent restatement of the classical Marxist case, see Bill Warren, *Imperialism – The Pioneer of Capitalism* (London, 1980). See also, A. Brewer, *Marxist Theories of Imperialism: A Critical Survey* (London, 1980), especially, pp. 27–127, 286–94.

tionalism, assumed that capitalism, like industrialism, would duly be achieved in underdeveloped countries.[20]

Of course, the thrust of 'dependency theory' postulating that capitalism systematically prevented the development of productive forces in 'satellite' economies has been precisely to attack some of these evolutionary assumptions.[21] Where optimists projected a model in which expanding trade and the growth of a market economy would produce cumulative economic development, dependency theorists envisaged the same processes 'enforcing the rise of economic backwardness'. In pursuing their 'intention to negate the optimistic model of economic advance derived from Adam Smith', as Brenner pointed out, 'they have ended up by erecting an alternative theory of capitalist development which is, in its central aspects, the mirror image of the "progressist" thesis they wish to surpass'.[22]

Within the Marxist tradition, the focus has rested on the progression from pre-capitalist to capitalist modes of production. Anticipating a single direction of change, their theoretical expectations have sometimes encouraged historians to examine the past for the first signs of capitalism, the development of the factory system or the dawn of class consciousness. It has often led to the explanation of facts and events which belie theoretical expectations in terms of the survival of old modes of production, arcane social forms or traditional ideologies. And it has sometimes allowed Marxist historians and sociologists to accept too readily the determining character of production relations and it has nudged them, even as they asserted the power of human agency, towards an understanding of the economic sphere,

as an alien force existing outside them [individuals], of the origin and ends of which they are ignorant, which they cannot control, which on the contrary, passes

[20] However, Marx himself did not rule out the possibility that under certain circumstances, capitalism might not effectively breach pre-capitalist modes of production. 'The obstacles presented by the internal solidity and organization of pre-capitalist national modes of production to the corrosive influences of commerce', he observed, 'are strikingly illustrated in the intercourse of the English with India and China'. Karl Marx, *Capital*, vol. III (New York, 1967), pp. 333–4, cited by R. Brenner, 'The Origins of Capitalist Development: A Critique of Neo-Smithian Marxism', *New Left Review*, 104 (July–August 1977), 26, fn. 2.

[21] P. Baran, *The Political Economy of Growth* (New York, 1957); A. Frank, *Capitalism and Underdevelopment in Latin America: Historical Studies of Chile and Brazil* (New York, 1967). For a sympathetic critique which developed these arguments in fresh directions, see Bob Sutcliffe, 'Imperialism and Industrialisation in the Third World', in Roger Owen and Bob Sutcliffe (eds.), *Studies in the Theory of Imperialism* (London, 1972), pp. 171–92; see also Brewer, *Marxist Theories of Imperialism*, pp. 158–81, 286–94. For a more searching critique, see Brenner, 'Origins of Capitalist Development', 25–94.

[22] Brenner, 'Origins of Capitalist Development', 27.

through a peculiar series of phases and stages independent of the will and action of men.[23]

Not surprisingly, Marxist theories of industrialization and class formation have often nestled under the carapace of modernization theory. The linear development of the capitalist mode of production was to be witnessed in the progressive evolution of the market economy, increasing bourgeois dominance, the expropriation and pauperization of the peasantry, the growth of a proletariat and, finally, the emergence of capitalist industry. The 'factory system' was the characteristic – in some senses, the defining – feature of the new social order. It was from the emphasis upon the transition from 'manufacture' to 'modern industry', from the 'formal' to the 'real subsumption of labour to capital' that the development of the factory system acquired its centrality in the Marxian tradition.[24] This process also served to create for Marxists what Landes was to call 'a new breed of worker'.

The development of capitalist industrialization, it was assumed, tends to increase the homogeneity of the working class. By concentrating workers into larger masses, the factory system helps to weld the working class into a greater unity. Workers increasingly form trade unions, join political parties and finally effect revolutions. The burden of labour history, as a result, has been to explain, in a number of cases, why sectionalism persisted within the working classes and why they so often remained such reluctant revolutionaries. Yet if the assumption that the working class contained within itself an innate propensity for unity was set aside, the problem itself would disappear.

For Marxists, as for functionalists, the nature of social consciousness was directly related to the level of industrialization. Of course, the fundamental difference lay in the Marxist expectation that protest, far from registering a tendency to decline, would be raised to new unprecedented levels of intensity and action. But in relation to the nature of industrialization and the forms of social change, which are assumed to cause this protest, Marxists have often arrived, albeit by a different route, at the same destination as functionalist social scientists with whom they have long been locked in academic and political dispute.

The broad acres of these shared assumptions may have narrowed the

---

[23] K. Marx and F. Engels, *The German Ideology* (London, 1965 edn), p. 54, cited by Abrams, *Historical Sociology*, p. 38. Of course, this notion of the autonomy of the relations of production was least evident, if not at times contradicted, in their historical writings.

[24] Etienne Balibar, 'Basic Concepts of Historical Materialism', in L. Althusser and E. Balibar, *Reading Capital* (London, 1970). For an attempt to develop these concepts in historical analysis, see G. Stedman Jones, 'Class Struggle and the Industrial Revolution', *New Left Review*, 90 (1975), 35–69. See also, G. Stedman Jones, *The Languages of Class: Studies in English Working Class History, 1832–1982* (Cambridge, 1983), pp. 1–24.

scope of historical enquiry and limited the development of social theory. This essay will next examine in the specific case of Indian industrialization how these assumptions were translated into the medium of historical research and attempt to explore their interpretative cost.

II

Just as economic historians of the West have made it their task to explain why France and Germany took several decades to emulate the technological innovations of Britain,[25] the history of Indian industrialization is counterposed to the example of Western Europe. Industrialization, in this conception, was a process of technological diffusion, inaugurated by the invention of the steam engine and the spinning jenny in Britain which spread incompletely in various ways, and at different times, over the rest of the world. 'Industrial development in India' could thus be seen as 'part of the very broad movement which had its origins in Western Europe'.[26] Yet 'before the more productive technology of the industrializing West could become something other than a casual and accidental feature of the Indian landscape', it was clear, in this view, that Indian society would have to begin to resemble Western Europe on the verge of industrialization.[27]

How ready, then, was India to embark upon industrialization? The question, although a nodal point around which historical research is organized, is characteristically posed with chronological vagueness. In one view, the necessary pre-conditions simply did not exist. Capital was scarce and immobile. The quality of labour was poor, even if its quantity was abundant. Technology was simple, static and backward.[28] There was no 'formal structure of public and private facilities that minimizes uncertainty', no futures markets, no 'insurance devices', no dependable 'flows of statistical and other information'.[29] Furthermore, 'the culture' was not 'preoccupied in any systematic way with the increase of man's control

---

[25] 'In view of the enormous economic superiority of these innovations', wrote Landes, 'one would expect the rest to have followed automatically. To understand why it did not . . . is to understand not only a good part of the history of these countries, but also something of the problem of economic development in general'. Landes, *Unbound Prometheus*, p. 126. But if we did not 'expect' the rest to follow 'automatically', the question itself would not arise. See also S. Pollard, *Peaceful Conquest: The Industrialization of Europe, 1760–1970* (Oxford, 1981).   [26] Morris, 'Large-Scale Industry', 553.   [27] *Ibid*.

[28] *Ibid*., 558–63. Morris argues that the backward technology of iron manufacture restricted the industry's output in the eighteenth century, but that the civilization, of course, generally adjusted to the limited supply of iron by using it very sparingly (*ibid*., 560–1). But the increased demand did not produce technological innovation. In other words, backward technology limited the supply of iron, which was therefore used sparingly. But technology remained backward because demand was small enough to be absorbed through adjustments in the application of labour.   [29] *Ibid*., 555–6.

over his material environment',[30] while 'a scientific approach to technology was virtually non-existent'.[31] Such propositions have been sanctified by repetition but detailed scrutiny has more often highlighted their weaknesses than their strengths.[32] In contrast, others have argued that the appropriate circumstances for industrial development did not exist because they were systematically destroyed by colonial rule.[33] Some recent research on the eighteenth century has served to suggest that whatever the direction in which the economy had been developing, it was distorted and diverted into less fruitful channels by the impact of colonial rule.[34] Whatever the disagreement, the method of approach to a counter-factual question has necessarily taken on a counter-factual tone.

But if Indian society in the eighteenth and nineteenth centuries lacked 'not only an extensive array of basic social, political and economic preconditions but also the development of an institutionalized capacity to solve new problems that continually emerged in the process of change',[35] it must be presumed that these conditions existed somewhere else at the inception of industrialization. It might be salutary to ask where this was so. In his classic account of the development of the British economy, Eric Hobsbawm wrote:[36]

the technological problems of the early Industrial Revolution were fairly simple. They required no class of men with specialized scientific qualifications . . . Most of the new technical inventions and productive establishments could be started on a small scale, and expanded piecemeal by successive addition. That is to say, they required little initial investment, and their expansion could be financed out of accumulated profits. Industrial development was within the capacities of a multiplicity of small entrepreneurs and skilled traditional artisans.

The factors which are now identified as the 'pre-conditions' of economic development have more often turned out to be the consequences rather

[30] *Ibid.*, 562–3.   [31] *Ibid.*, 562.
[32] On the initiatives of traditional merchants, see C. A. Bayly, 'Indian Merchants in a "Traditional" Setting: Benares, 1780–1830', in C. J. Dewey and A. G. Hopkins (eds.), *The Imperial Impact: Studies in the Economic History of Africa and India* (London, 1978), pp. 171–93; on technology, see I. Habib, 'The Technology and Economy of Mughal India', *IESHR*, 17:1 (1980), 1–34; on the dynamism of the commercial economy in eighteenth-century South India and its subsequent decline, see D. A. Washbrook, 'Some Notes in Market Relations and the Development of the Economy in South India, *c.* 1750–1850', paper presented to the Second Anglo-Dutch Workshop on Comparative Colonial History, Leiden, September 1981.
[33] The best statement of this case is to be found in Bagchi, *Private Investment*; see also, A. K. Bagchi, 'Foreign Capital and Economic Development in India: A Schematic View', in K. Gough and Hari P. Sharma, *Imperialism and Revolution in South Asia* (New York and London, 1973), pp. 43–76.
[34] F. Perlin, 'Proto-Industrialization in South Asia', *Past and Present*, 98 (February 1983), 30–95.   [35] Morris, 'Large-Scale Industry', 558.
[36] E. J. Hobsbawm, *Industry and Empire* (London, 1968), p. 39.

than the causes of growth.[37] We know most often that the pre-conditions existed only because we also know that development had subsequently occurred. In any case, accounts which counterpose the history of Indian industrialization against the historical experience of eighteenth-century Britain and Western Europe overlook the crucial fact that the tasks of industrialization were becoming by the late nineteenth century increasingly complex and expensive.

If industrialization was, indeed, a technologically determined process which spread outwards from late eighteenth-century Europe, how did this 'diffusion' occur? In the existing literature, it is generally supposed to have been the consequence of India's relationship with the West largely through the medium of trade and fortified subsequently by formal colonialism. Technological diffusion occurred, in this view, through the 'great presidency towns' or 'colonial port cities': Bombay and Calcutta, centres of an expanding import and export trade, of finance and banking, and of course, of consumption. From the 1850s onwards, 'the first substantial manifestations of modern industrialism' became discernible.[38] Once set in motion, the movement along the path to industrialism was apparently only forward. Although 'large-scale industry', presumably mass production and the factory system, did not spread easily across the economy as a whole 'the pace of its extension within specific sectors was reasonably brisk'.[39]

As soon as entrepreneurs recognized 'the commercial possibilities of local factory production', and 'the opportunities must have seemed very obvious',[40] they embarked upon industrialization. Once begun, the process continued through functional necessity. As their interests came to rest upon large-scale industries, so entrepreneurs were committed to technological advance and optimal efficiency. Faced with market fluctuations or intense competition, entrepreneurs either altered their product or else attempted 'to diversify and upgrade the quality of their output'.[41] Sometimes, they attempted to suppress wage costs. Sometimes, and with varying degrees of success, they attempted to take cover in sheltered markets. But, in the long run, the only answer lay in 'technical and administrative reorganization'; from this 'purgation', their industries emerged healthier and more efficient. This linear view of industrialization

---

[37] 'There is scarcely one of these pre-conditions', Habakkuk had observed nearly twenty years ago, 'which cannot be shown to have been absent in the case of some acknowledged case of growth. Indeed, it is not difficult to cite cases where the absence of what is commonly regarded as a pre-condition proved to be a positive stimulus to growth.' Habakkuk, 'Historical Experience', pp. 118–19.
[38] Morris, 'Large-Scale Industry', 566.   [39] Ibid., 553.   [40] Ibid., 574.
[41] Ibid., 617.

has led to an almost exclusive concern with a few major industries, and among them a concentration upon its most important centres.[42]

In this perspective, entrepreneurs are perceived as the decisive force in the process of industrialization. Marxists have focused upon their agency in the development of capitalism and upon the frustration of their economic interests as the catalyst in the emergence of nationalist movements. The emphasis in neo-classical and functionalist arguments has rested variously, in the case of apologists for empire, seeking to minimize the destructive effects of colonial rule upon the Indian economy, upon the failure of businessmen to take their chances, or alternatively, in a nationalist argument, upon the daring and brilliance with which they manipulated limited resources to maximum advantage. For Morris, the 'economy' itself appears to have been constituted by 'actual entrepreneurial choices'. The decisions of private businessmen determined 'the allocation of resources' in the economy as a whole; they also serve to 'explain' why 'the scope of industrial development [was] restricted'.[43] But the effect of this argument is simply to reformulate the question. For if 'the range of alternative profit-making opportunities . . . explains the rate at which businessmen invested',[44] what determined those opportunities in the first place?

Yet, despite the central role thus allocated to the entrepreneur, there are, apart from various hagiographical lives, few studies of individual firms or of entrepreneurial development.[45] Historians who place the entrepreneur at the heart of their story of the rise of industry have sometimes neglected to examine how businessmen made their choices or indeed how far their intentions were translated into achievement.

Existing interpretations of the course of industrial development in India, based upon models of apparently successful industrialization elsewhere, have taken over pervasive assumptions about the nature of industrialization: that it was a technologically determined process beyond the realm of social choice; that it was a serial process whose imperatives were similar in each case; that it was inevitably and inexorably progressive; that, flowing from the West, it constituted the only dynamic force acting upon a passive 'indigenous' economy. The result has been the develop-

---

[42] In dealing with the development of the cotton textile industry, for instance, Morris focuses exclusively upon Bombay despite the fact that it constituted 'a diminishing part of a still-expanding industry' in the inter-war period. *Ibid.*, 617, 572–83, 603–5, 616–24.

[43] *Ibid.*, 554.   [44] *Ibid.*

[45] However, on the early colonial period, see C. A. Bayly, *Rulers, Townsmen and Bazaars: North Indian Society in the Age of British Expansion* (Cambridge, 1983), pp. 369–426; and A. Siddiqi, 'The Business World of Jamsetji Jejeebhoy', *IESHR*, 19:3 and 4 (1982), 301–24; and for the nineteenth and twentieth century, see T. Timberg, *The Marwaris: From Traders to Industrialists* (New Delhi, 1978), and D. Tripathi, *The Dynamics of a Tradition: Kasturbhai Lalbhai and His Entrepreneurship* (New Delhi, 1981).

ment of a Whig historiography of industrialization whose unflinching focus is the so-called lead sector of the economy, and which faithfully chronicles the continuing discovery and application of increasingly efficient, 'rational' and modern methods of production. In this perspective, the role of supposedly backward sectors in determining the structure of the economy as a whole is obscured. Moreover, in this view, industrialization is ripped out of its historical context. The influence of the agrarian economy, the role of the colonial state, the effects of international capitalism, or the impact of labour is often neglected; at best their interplay in the process of economic development broadly defined receives cursory attention.[46]

These teleological approaches to industrialization have informed and shaped the wider field of Indian economic history. First, it has helped to create a hiatus in the historiography of the Indian economy in the early colonial period. Whereas historians of the seventeenth and early eighteenth centuries, like those of the later nineteenth and twentieth centuries, address themselves to substantive economic issues – agriculture, trade and markets; the growth of towns and industries; workers and capitalists – the investigation of the early colonial economy is largely evacuated in favour of guiding themes such as the expansion of British power and the development of land revenue systems.[47] The economic history of colonial India is thus generally commenced only from the mid-nineteenth century onwards. It is at this point that historians discern the first signs of modern industrialism, bringing in its wake a period of quickening social change. 'To describe the processes at work', explained one historian, speaking for many, 'one turns to words like "anglicization", "modernization", "secularization".'[48] Now the historian can trek along the familiar path to industrialism. The 'historical experience of economic development' can now be applied to the study of India's past; the way is cleared for the history of Indian industrial development to be counterposed to the experience of Western Europe. The past appears increasingly in the image of the present.

[46] Ray, *Industrialization in India*. Ray's synthesizing history of industrialization combines an interesting treatment of the colonial state with an almost total neglect of labour or indeed the wider economic context. Morris, 'Large-Scale Industry', touches upon the role of labour but finds its impact minimal.

[47] So much so that one of the most valuable studies of 'agrarian relations' and land revenue systems in the early colonial period was able to disclaim 'a full discussion of prices, productivity, cropping patterns and the like'. T. R. Metcalf, *Land, Landlords and the British Raj: Northern India in the Nineteenth Century* (Berkeley and Los Angeles, 1979), p. xii. For a recent attempt at integration, see Bayly, *Rulers, Townsmen and Bazaars*.

[48] R. Jeffrey, *The Decline of Nayar Dominance* (Brighton, 1976), p. xiv. To this armoury, we might also add the generic 'Westernization'. It is significant that in these approaches social change is represented by essentialist cultural descriptions.

Furthermore, the concern of economic historians, their attention attracted to when and how 'modernization' came to India, has been to explain why industrialization failed to transform the Indian economy and its corollary, why the so-called pre-conditions were missing. The result has been a primarily counter-factual history. Since the possibility and prospects for economic development are so closely associated with the growth of large-scale industry, it is not surprising that the general problem of the backwardness of the Indian economy and the more specific issue of the slow rate of industrialization not only seem to warrant the same explanation but at times even appear to be identical. The diffusionist approach has contributed to the identification of industrialization as the focal point not only for assessments of the prospects for economic development in India but also for explanations of its failure in the colonial period. Similar 'causes' are held to account for both underdevelopment and the limited extent of industrialization. The result is often to perpetuate an inherent tautology in such reasoning. If economic backwardness, reflected by the absence of 'pre-conditions', is held to explain the modest scale of industrialization, economic backwardness itself is explained in terms of the failure of industrialization. Since at least the late nineteenth century, writers on the subject have invited us to choose between colonial rule and the Indian social structure as the main cause of economic backwardness. These options have provided the organizing principles for the bulk of the research and writing in the economic history of colonial India. But a specifically historical analysis of social and economic change in India may be better served by declining this choice and exploring more fully the interplay between them.

III

The teleological perspective has concentrated attention on 'large-scale industry' as the lead sector at the expense of other supposedly backward activities, on the triumphs of enterprise while neglecting the nature of business failures, on the role of entrepreneurs as catalysts in economic development while assuming that labour and other social groups were passive factors moulded and shaped by the autonomous imperatives of industrialization. By examining the categories thus used in the investigation of industrialization, it is possible to allow alternative emphases and perspectives to emerge. It is the intention of this essay to suggest that our focus may usefully be shifted from large-scale industry to the economy as a whole, not as an autonomous entity subject to the mysterious workings of the laws of supply and demand, but as it was constituted by production conditions, by the relationship between town and country, by the agency of social classes, by the political presence of the colonial state, and by the larger context of the world economy. There is no reason to assume that the outcome of economic development was pre-determined or that it would inevitably lead to the factory and the production line. Rather, at every step, it was the interaction of a whole constellation of social forces, whose tensions and antagonisms and conflicts were articulated within a context conditioned by the world economy as well as by the political priorities of the colonial state, that determined the sometimes wayward direction of change. Measured against the ideal types of social theory and Whig history, industrial development and social change, both in the West and the Third World, have registered a remarkable propensity to go their own way.

If large-scale industry has been commonly accepted as the apex of universal models of social change, historians have only identified the phenomenon with considerable unease. Large-scale industries often produced the same products as small-scale workshops. Frequently, they followed similar production strategies, regulating their levels of output according to market fluctuations rather than to stock. Patterns of labour use, intensive, yet flexible and casual in deployment, were common to both the formal and the informal sectors. The labour process was often minutely subdivided in small workshops. Factories were sometimes no more than ramshackle sheds cheaply put together, using simple, often hand-driven machinery. Some traders combined the factory system with 'putting out' to workers who worked on the premises.[49] The advance of mechanization often took eccentric routes. Whereas electro-plating processes were replacing the wood block in many small workshops in Bombay by the early twentieth century, the large silk mills followed traditional practices of stamping designs by hand.[50] The characteristics of the capital market which restricted businessmen to small industrial units also served to narrow the freedom of action of millowners and factory magnates.[51] Despite the confidence which the firm commanded among investors all over India, Tata Iron and Steel Company could raise capital for its Greater Extensions programme in the 1920s only at the expense of granting 'their leading creditor, F. E. Dinshaw a permanent share of their managing agency commission'.[52] A similar arrangement in the coal mining industry placed N. C. Sircar on the road to bankruptcy which led finally to Benares.[53]

---

[49] Chandavarkar, *The Origins of Industrial Capitalism*, pp. 76–94.
[50] C. G. H. Fawcett, *A Monograph on Dyes and Dyeing in the Bombay Presidency* (Bombay, 1896), p. 38.
[51] For the case of the cotton textile industry in Bombay, see Chandavarkar, *The Origins of Industrial Capitalism*, pp. 44–71, 279–95.   [52] Ray, *Industrialization in India*, pp. 27–8.
[53] C. P. Simmons, 'Indigenous Enterprise in the Indian Coal Mining Industry, 1835–1939', *IESHR*, 13:2 (1976), 193–5.

Ultimately, it would seem, the only factor which distinguished large-scale industries from small-scale industries was their size.[54] It is not surprising that faced with such tautology recent historians of industrialization have been unsure of which industries to include in their accounts: for instance, Ray's account of 'private investment in specific industries' left out jute, perhaps the most important of them all, and Morris's chapter in the *Cambridge Economic History of India* took no cognizance of coal mining.[55]

If the destination of such linear development is uncertain, the route itself on closer scrutiny appears meandering. Factory industry was not the only source of dynamism in the economy. Seemingly archaic forms of enterprise not only survived but sometimes even expanded over considerable periods of time. This point may be illustrated with reference to handicraft industries.

Most historians broadly agree that handicraft production declined in nineteenth-century India but that its decline proceeded unevenly, affecting different regions at different times and to varying degrees.[56] Although historians may dispute how far the process of dissolution went, there is widespread agreement about its general trend. For some historians, this process of dissolution was inevitable, 'a world-wide development affecting different countries at different times' and 'as integral a part of the Industrial Revolution as the coming of the factory system'.[57] For Morris, too, the products of textile mills, foreign and especially Indian, ruined the handloom-weaving industry, but its death, if inevitable, was slow and protracted.[58]

In the case of cotton, the broad outlines of the story are familiar. The import of Lancashire yarn and cloth undermined handicraft spinning and, to a lesser extent, weaving in the early nineteenth century. The major

---

[54] In their recent study of the Bombay labour market, Joshi and Joshi discovered that their 'family of criteria' for distinguishing between the organized and unorganized sector could not 'easily be used for empirical investigation' and resorted instead to 'the size of the establishment' as the only workable criterion. See H. Joshi and V. Joshi, *Surplus Labour and the City: A Study of Bombay* (Delhi, 1976), pp. 46–7.

[55] Ray, *Industrialization in India*; Morris, 'Large-Scale Industry'.

[56] A. K. Bagchi, 'De-Industrialization in Gangetic Bihar, 1809–1901', in B. De (ed.), *Essays in Honour of Professor S. C. Sarkar* (Delhi, 1976), pp. 499–522; A. K. Bagchi, 'De-Industrialization in India in the Nineteenth Century: Some Theoretical Implications', *Journal of Development Studies*, 12:2 (1976), 135–64; Morris, 'Large-Scale Industry', 668–76; M. J. Twomey, 'Employment in Nineteenth Century Indian Textiles', *Explorations in Economic History*, 20:1 (1983), 37–57; G. Pandey, 'Economic Dislocation in Nineteenth-Century Eastern Uttar Pradesh: Some Implications of the Decline of Artisanal Industry in Colonial India', in P. Robb (ed.), *Rural South Asia: Linkages, Change and Development* (London, 1983), pp. 89–129; M. Vicziany, 'The De-Industrialization of India in the Nineteenth Century: A Methodological Critique of Amiya Kumar Bagchi', *IESHR*, 16:2 (1979), 105–46; A. K. Bagchi, 'A Reply', *IESHR*, 16:2 (1979), 147–61.

[57] D. Thorner and A. Thorner, *Land and Labour in India* (Bombay, 1962), p. 70.

[58] Morris, 'Large-Scale Industry', 670–1.

centres of the traditional industry in Bengal and the Gangetic Valley were the worst affected. But by producing durable coarse cloth for local markets and to a lesser extent fine goods and fancy designs which ordinary power looms could not handle, parts of the handloom-weaving industry survived until the late nineteenth century. Then the expansion of the Indian cotton textile industry finally spelt its doom.

Baker's study of the handloom-weaving industry in Tamil Nadu shows how far its development ran counter to the apparent all-Indian trend.[59] The handloom-weaving industry in Tamil Nadu began to expand in the late nineteenth century, precisely when it should have gone into decline in the face of growing competition from Indian mills. In fact, the handloom sector grew faster than factory industry and by 1939 supplied 60 per cent of the market for cloth in the Madras Presidency. This expansion was based in part on the home market but exports to South-East Asia and the Persian Gulf quadrupled between the late 1880s and 1920s. Production was organized through various forms of putting out. While many families looked upon the manufacture of coarse cloth 'as a form of social security', they required working capital and the problems of marketing cloth were sufficiently complex to require specialized knowledge. Precisely because many families turned to handloom-weaving when the local economy was depressed, there was a continuous risk of overproduction and the demand for and supply of both labour and cloth had to be carefully coordinated. Moreover, little value was added in the process of production so that those who were stranded with stocks when the price of yarn was falling might easily be ruined.

Between the wars, the internal economy of Tamil Nadu, like other regions, was subject to violent fluctuations of prices and demand arising largely from its relationship with the international economy. The cost of production for handloom workers, as well as the price of cloth, tied to unstable agricultural prices, were highly vulnerable to international fluctuations. The effects of these conditions were registered in a growing emphasis among handloom capitalists upon coarse goods, an increasing concentration of control over working capital in the industry, the development of 'larger and more loosely organized production systems' or the emergence of 'large putting-out networks', and a shift in the location of the industry towards the towns.

It is not clear how far master-weavers or 'independent' weavers were involved in the marketing of their own goods. But they faced obvious disadvantages in dealing with such unstable markets. Large merchants,

[59] C. J. Baker, *An Indian Rural Economy, 1880–1955*, pp. 393–413. On the growth of weaving workshops in the Deccan, see N. M. Joshi, *Urban Handicrafts of the Bombay Deccan* (Poona, 1936).

on the other hand, could simply by cutting off supplies of working capital to their weavers reduce the output of cloth. Since they operated wider marketing and production networks, they were also better placed to identify and to respond to changes in price or demand. Yet these tendencies towards concentration did not mark a shift towards the factory system. On the contrary, market fluctuations made capitalists even more reluctant 'to commit themselves to regular working and expenditure on plant'.[60]

This instability did, however, encourage the handloom capitalists to diversify their interests, buying land, trading in mill-made piecegoods, investing in the film industry. The decline of the export trade in fine goods had undermined the master weavers, engaged in luxury production, and circumscribed the 'independence' of the skilled 'independent' weavers from the traditional weaving communities. Many of them turned to the coarse goods trade, inflated its labour supply and probably accentuated its instability. As the number of weavers producing coarse cloth increased, their incomes fell and the extent of regular employment available declined. Many were forced to seek work elsewhere, turning to agricultural labour or service employment in the towns. Consequently, 'the industry was becoming more part-time than permanent'. By the 1940s it was already being deserted, and this rather than factory competition alone may account for its decline after 1948.[61] But there were other underlying pressures: especially the interplay between the international and the internal economy, and the political priorities of the colonial state which prevented it from mediating the impact of international fluctuations upon the internal economy and which in fact led to the adoption of fiscal, monetary, tariff and financial policies which aggravated their effects.[62]

The case of handloom-weaving in Tamil Nadu suggests that non-factory forms of production organization were capable not only of adaptation and survival in the face of factory competition, but also of dynamism, expansion and technical and organizational innovation. Nor can this dynamism be viewed simply as the preliminary stage to the development of the factory. And it is by no means the only such example. In jute, too, 'the handicraft sector expanded rather substantially between the late 1830s and about 1880'.[63] Similarly, for much of the colonial period, Indian capital in the coal mining industry was 'typically confined to

[60] Baker, *An Indian Rural Economy*, p. 404.   [61] *Ibid.*, pp. 402–13.
[62] *Ibid.*, ch. 2; Tomlinson, *Political Economy*, ch. 2.
[63] Morris, 'Large-Scale Industry', 567. For the case of sugar, see S. Amin, *Sugarcane and Sugar in Gorakhpur: An Inquiry into Peasant Production for Capitalist Enterprise in Colonial India* (Delhi, 1984).

small-scale individual or family proprietorships mining second class . . .
coal from very shallow depths'.[64] Nevertheless, operating on this basis,
several firms survived with remarkable success over surprisingly long
periods.[65] The factory system and large-scale production were not the
invariable outcome of industrial development.

If by focusing upon large-scale industry, teleological perspectives have
tended to overlook handicraft production and apparently archaic forms of
enterprise, they have also concentrated attention on what are readily
perceived as the successes of industrialization and this has led to the
neglect of the failures. It is almost customary for historians to preface
their accounts of industrial development with passing reference to the
first attempts which failed, before hurrying on to chronicle the triumphs
of those which succeeded. It may appear perverse to suggest that the
history of industrialization may be usefully approached through the ventures that failed. Yet business failures frequently occurred as a consequence of the very constraints which also inhibited the firms that succeeded and which established the limits within which all were forced to
work.

The first jute mill was established in 1855 by George Acland, formerly
a coffee planter in Ceylon. Despite his 'considerable experience in South
Asia', his 'sense of foreign markets' and his supposedly special knowledge
of 'how to organize Indian labour', 'the firm was never very successful'.[66]
The other four mills established by 1866, however, were 'supposed to
have been very profitable'. But this did not encourage a rush of entries
and the industry began to expand significantly only in the later 1870s.[67] In
coal mining, too, triumphant Indian entrepreneurs, like business failures,
were similarly, though not perhaps equally, starved of capital. In the coal
mining industry, capital was not so much progressively 'Indianized' as
'Europeanized'. Coal mining was initiated by Dwarkanath Tagore in the
1830s but the collapse of his firm in 1847 marked the beginning of
European ascendancy in the industry, and in the decades which followed,
Indian entrepreneurs were increasingly squeezed into the least profitable
sectors of the industry.[68]

Early attempts by the East India Company and by European investors
to launch iron and steel production failed largely because they were

[64] Simmons, 'Indigenous Enterprise', 200, 189–217.
[65] In Japan, handlooms locked the cotton mills out of the domestic market until the 1920s
and 1930s. For a general survey of the literature on Japanese industrialization which
places it in a comparative context, see B. R. Tomlinson, 'Writing History Sideways:
Lessons for Indian Economic Historians from Meiji Japan', *MAS*, 19:3 (1985), 669–98.
[66] Morris, 'Large-Scale Industry', 567.   [67] *Ibid.*
[68] Simmons, 'Indigenous Enterprise', 200, 189–217. B. B. Kling, *Partner in Empire: Dwarkanath Tagore and the Age of Enterprise in Eastern India* (Calcutta, 1981), pp. 73–121.

undercapitalized and because they could not effectively adapt technology to existing factor costs and to the size of the market. But the same problems inhibited subsequent attempts. The Bengal Iron Works Company collapsed through undercapitalization in 1879. The failure of the steel project initiated in 1906 by its reincarnation, the Bengal Iron and Steel Company, was also in part due to the fact that it was 'grossly undercapitalized'. Even the redoubtable Tata family encountered serious difficulties in raising capital.[69] Their survival has commonly been put down to the business acumen and entrepreneurial skill of J. N. Tata and his descendants. But other factors also contributed to their success. In particular, the inroads made by Belgian steel into the Indian market as well as the lessons of the first world war – that it was as well to add an ordnance base to the oriental barrack – increased the readiness of the colonial state, whatever the modesty of its ambitions or the limited efficacy of its policies, to assist the enterprise.[70]

The first attempts at establishing cotton mills in Bombay failed because the entrepreneurs had 'difficulty mobilizing capital'.[71] Yet maintaining the supply of fixed as well as working capital remained a perennial problem for the Bombay millowners throughout the history of the industry. Millowners with established reputations, who had gained the confidence of the public investor and who rarely had serious difficulties in raising capital, were liable to be hoist with their own petard. Their ease of access to funds encouraged a tendency towards overextension and resulted in some spectacular failures: Dwarkadas Dharamsey in 1909; Greaves Cotton and Company, which managed the largest group of mills in the city, in 1915; Narottam Morarji in 1929; Currimbhoy Ebrahim, who owned roughly 15 per cent of the industry's capacity, in 1933. The high cost of fixed capital as well as their dependence upon the changeable money market for their working costs led the millowners who survived to adopt flexible production strategies, geared to the maintenance of their turnover, averse to holding stocks, deploying sizeable proportions of casual labour and regulating production according to demand.[72]

Among the various constraints within which entrepreneurs operated, and which led to the collapse of some, the lack of capital was prominent.

[69] Morris, 'Large-Scale Industry', 583–92.
[70] Ray, *Industrialization*, pp. 74–93; Bagchi, *Private Investment*, pp. 291–331; D. M. Wagle, 'Imperial Preference and the Indian Steel Industry', *Economic History Review*, 34:1 (1981), 120–31.
[71] Morris, 'Large-Scale Industry', 574. But Morris suggests a few lines later that the first mills 'were not exceptionally costly ventures by local standards' and fairly easy to establish. *Ibid.*, 574–5.
[72] These arguments are further elaborated in Chandavarkar, *The Origins of Industrial Capitalism*, pp. 67–71.

Yet this did not signify an absolute scarcity of supply. It was rather the case that capital was most easily raised in small pools, by entrepreneurs whose fame and fortune were already legendary, for whose enterprises the markets were already proven and the risks well known. This is not to return by a different route to old notions about the shyness of capital. Attention to the nature of business failures should alert us, on the contrary, to the highly adventurous spirit of much investment, and serve to emphasize the magnitude of risk which it entailed.

The evidence is increasingly conclusive that whereas most early Indian ventures failed, European initiatives succeeded: in the coal mines,[73] the jute mills[74] and the cotton textile industry of Madras.[75] This was primarily because European entrepreneurs enjoyed easier access to and, therefore, a greater command of capital while their connections with banks and managing agencies facilitated its mobilization. On the other hand, their Indian counterparts had to rely primarily upon their kinsmen, caste fellows and acquaintances. Yet by deploying their own connections of kin, caste and friendship, European entrepreneurs were able, under certain conditions, critically to disadvantage their Indian rivals.[76] A closer examination of business failures also provides a context within which the nature and quality of entrepreneurship may be assessed. If the causes of failures also dogged the survivors in their moments of triumph, there is no reason to identify the collapse of firms necessarily with inferior entrepreneurial skill. Rather, failures served as a reminder that entrepreneurs did not inevitably overcome the difficulties they faced.

In this perspective, it is possible to assess entrepreneurial responses as well as to establish how they might be compared. Historians have continued to address this problem primarily in terms of community. Morris, for instance, registers 'the different responses by various Indian groups and of natives in contrast to foreigners'.[77] Reluctance to break into large-scale industry in a particular instance suggests to him the timidity of capital or the lack of enterprise among local business communities. Since he finds no 'obvious barriers' to entry by Indians to the jute industry, their absence signifies to Morris 'the passivity of Indian capital'. He concludes that Bengali businessmen were primarily 'small investors and rentiers' rather than 'aggressive entrepreneurs'.[78] By contrast, 'the aggressive and

[73] Simmons, 'Indigenous Enterprise'.
[74] Bagchi, *Private Investment*, pp. 157–217, 262–90.
[75] Baker, *An Indian Rural Economy*, pp. 339–42.
[76] Bagchi, *Private Investment*, pp. 165–70. See also, O. Goswami, 'Collaboration and Conflict: European and Indian Capitalists and the Jute Economy of Bengal, 1919–1939'. *IESHR*, 19:2 (1982), 141–79; B. R. Tomlinson, 'Colonial Firms and the Decline of Colonialism in Eastern India, 1914–1947', *MAS*, 15:3 (1981), 455–86.
[77] Morris 'Large-Scale Industry', 557.   [78] *Ibid.*, 568–70.

successful merchants' of Bombay were quick to seize their chances.[79] If 'it cost no more and probably somewhat less to set up a jute mill than to open a cotton mill in Bombay at the same time . . . why was native capital [in Calcutta] so timid?'[80] But if the Bengali entrepreneur was backward in jute, how should we explain his initiatives in coal, under increasingly adverse conditions?[81] And in any case, what are we to make of the early failures to promote iron and steel making? For over one hundred years, efforts by 'Europeans responding to the needs of Europeans', with the help of a modest quotient of official support and encouragement, ended in catastrophe. The question of whether European capital, apparently the most dynamic agency in the Indian economy, was timid has scarcely arisen in this line of argument. Yet in the case of iron and steel one (presumably, crucial) cause of failure was that 'even successful charcoal iron operation required a shift to much larger-scale techniques than were ever contemplated'.[82]

Morris's own evidence suggests that the problem of entrepreneurial response posed in terms of community is not very helpful. For conversely, the successful penetration of Marwari entrepreneurs into the jute industry in the 1920s and 1930s, like Parsi enterprise in the founding of the Bombay cotton textile industry, is attributed by Morris not to any innate business acumen but to their firmly established base as traders which enabled them to invest effectively in industry.[83] On such evidence, differences in entrepreneurial responses, it would seem, are better explained in terms of given economic contexts rather than what are perceived to be the immutable characteristics of particular business communities. Indeed, these communities themselves are often arbitrarily defined, referring interchangeably to different categories of identity – to race ('European', 'native'), religion (Parsi, Jain), region (Bengali, Marwari, Gujarati) and caste (bania). Any single capitalist from any one of these 'communal' groups might also be defined in terms of other particular attributes. To approach the problem of differential entrepreneurial response in terms of community is to assume that these diverse kinds of communities possessed an internal coherence, and it has usually led no further than the discovery that entrepreneurs of any single community, however defined, often had as much or as little in common with each other as they had with the members of any other group. A more promising way forward lies in examining the pattern of entrepreneurial response as a whole, for by establishing what was general to businessmen, operating at different

[79] *Ibid.*, 574.   [80] *Ibid.*, 570.   [81] Simmons, 'Indigenous Enterprise'.
[82] *Ibid.*, 585. How far does the notion of 'timidity' explain why European capital, having come to dominate export-oriented industries, remained reluctant to explore the possibilities of the domestic market?   [83] *Ibid.*, 580–1, 615–16.

levels, we might be better placed to identify what was specific to any particular community: how religion or caste, race or region influenced their decisions and shaped their actions. This approach may have a general bearing upon the study of the interactions between different communities in their various and changing forms.

IV

Even if we were to view the process of industrialization through the prism of entrepreneurial choice, an investigation of the conditions under which businessmen made their decisions, what they perceived to be their options and why they made certain choices rather than others at particular moments of time, may well reveal that the direction of change, far from being unilinear or uniformly progressive, was determined by ceaseless improvisations, which, in turn, pulled the economy several ways at once. It was not the case that Indian businessmen, having recognized the commercial possibilities of factory production, relentlessly adopted 'the more productive technology of the industrializing West'.[84] The development of industry can be viewed differently. Whatever the difficulties of raising funds in a highly imperfect capital market, entrepreneurs who become known and whose firms appeared to prosper swiftly attracted eager investors.[85] This was the moment for most businessmen to diversify. Factory production was one possible outcome of this process of diversification. But far from being either a necessary or an inevitable consequence, it was in most circumstances an unlikely one. There is little reason either to suppose that its inherent tendency pointed in the direction of continuous technological advance or to assume that it would reach its culmination in the production line. This process of diversification into factory production and the strategies of entrepreneurs for further industrial development and technological advance can be illuminated by looking more closely at the case of the cotton textile industry.

Entrepreneurial strategies which apparently led to the establishment of factory industry were not always consistently expansive. The shift from trade to industry has sometimes been portrayed as an obvious, indeed logical progression. Exposed to the agencies of the colonial trade and international capitalism, it appeared to be merely a matter of time before cotton merchants, involved in the export of raw materials and the import of manufactured goods, would adopt modern techniques, import machinery and produce yarn and cloth on their own account.[86] It is more

---

[84] Morris, 'Large-Scale Industry', 553.
[85] Chandavarkar, *The Origins of Industrial Capitalism*, pp. 67–71, 243–4, 285–95.
[86] Morris, 'Large-Scale Industry', 573–5.

likely, however, that investment in industry was the response of some merchants to and, in general, a reflection of, their subordination in the export trade in raw cotton.

As Vicziany has shown, a series of innovations in the organization of the cotton trade in the 1860s reduced the previously generous margin of risk in the export trade, but because their use presupposed a considerable command of capital they accentuated the differentiation between the large-scale exporters, in whose hands business came to be increasingly concentrated, and the merchants who operated on a small scale.[87] These innovations combined with the growing importance of Liverpool and European markets for Indian raw cotton to work strongly in favour of the large European agency houses. Indian merchants subordinated in the export trade began to invest their capital in spinning mills. By investing in industry, the large cotton traders gained considerable flexibility in their operations. They could buy raw cotton when prices were low and sell when prices rose. If the cotton trade remained depressed, they could switch stocks intended for export to the manufacture of yarn. Rather than build warehouses to store their cotton and await the next failure of the American crop or an increased demand among Chinese spinners, they could deploy their stock of cotton according to its optimal short-term use, adjust their operations to the uncertainties of the market and adapt to the severe competition in both trade and manufacture.

This relationship between the trade and industry which entailed investment in the latter to hedge the uncertainties of the former, was to become an enduring characteristic within the industry. Cotton brokers and piecegoods dealers, indeed entrepreneurs of all kinds, seeking to diversify their commercial interests, provided the thrust behind the expansion of the number of entrepreneurs in the industry. Subsequently, spinning mills periodically left stranded by the fluctuations of the yarn market diversified into weaving to consume the surplus yarn which they could not sell.[88] Even the 'aggressive and successful merchants'[89] of Bombay were not motivated by the urge to embark upon a process of cumulative technological development, but rather by an anxiety to hedge their bets, to diversify and survive. The apparently revolutionary process of industrialization was thus launched with limited liability.

Entrepreneurial initiatives in the Ahmedabad cotton textile industry

[87] M. Vicziany, 'Bombay Merchants and Structural Changes in the Export Community, 1850 to 1880', in K. N. Chaudhuri and C. J. Dewey (eds.), *Economy and Society: Essays in Indian Economic and Social History* (Delhi, 1979), pp. 163–96.
[88] Chandavarkar, *The Origins of Industrial Capitalism*, pp. 61–71, 244–51.
[89] Morris, 'Large-Scale Industry', 574.

were not nurtured in foreign trade, shaped by European influence or inspired by the English example. Ahmedabad had been an important commercial and manufacturing centre since the sixteenth century.[90] The town's long-developing commercial institutions, its merchant mahajans and sarafi networks, provided the basis for industrial development.[91] The severance of their role as bankers to pre-colonial states and armies, the growing competition of the Bombay firms in the raw cotton trade, the decline of the opium trade, the advent and competition of the English exchange banks were by the mid-nineteenth century combining to limit the opportunities for local traders and bankers. Their response was to seek a share of the profits in textile production. By investing in spinning yarn for the sizeable local handloom industry, local merchants were simply diversifying their interests and many continued to regard their trading and banking activities as the most vital to the business concerns of their family. Moreover, the development and structure of the textile industry continued to be intimately connected with the structure of indigenous banking and commercial mahajans in the town. Some of the first mills were built by the most prominent and prosperous merchants. Not only were mill-managing agencies and sarafi firms sometimes owned by the same family, but there was also considerable inter-investment between them. Mills invested their surplus funds with shroffs, while in return for their loans, the latter were often given a share in the managing agency commission. Shroffs organized and often supplied the short-term deposits upon which the Ahmedabad mills were dependent for the bulk of their fixed capital.[92]

These financial practices, which government agencies, academic experts and tariff boards found rather primly 'to be open to grave objection',[93] also gave the Ahmedabad mills a number of advantages. Capital could be mobilized by the Ahmedabad mills at some of the lowest interest

---

[90] D. Tripathi and M. J. Mehta, 'The Nagarsheth of Ahmedabad: The History of an Urban Institution in a Gujarati City', *Proceedings of the Indian History Congress* (1978?), pp. 481–96; K. Gillion, *Ahmedabad: A Study in Indian Urban History* (Berkeley and Los Angeles, 1968), pp. 11–36.

[91] Gillion, *Ahmedabad*, pp. 37–104; Tripathi, *The Dynamics of a Tradition*; M. J. Mehta, *The Ahmedabad Cotton Textile Industry: Genesis and Growth* (Ahmedabad, 1982). For a critical appraisal of the books by Tripathi and Mehta, and some valuable comments on the Ahmedabad case, see Rajat Kanta Ray, 'Pedhis and Mills: The Historical Integration of the Formal and Informal Sectors in the Economy of Ahmedabad', *IESHR*, 19:3 and 4 (1982), 387–96.

[92] In the early 1930s, it was estimated that 39 per cent of the total capital of the Ahmedabad mills was drawn from public deposits. *Report of the Indian Central Banking Enquiry Committee, Majority Report* (Calcutta, 1931), vol. I, part i, p. 278; *Report of the ITB, 1932* (Calcutta, 1932), pp. 82–4.

[93] *Report of the ITB*, vol. I: *Report* (Calcutta, 1927), p. 90.

rates in the country.[94] Whereas most mills in India had to borrow a significant proportion of their working capital from indigenous bankers and the money market, their special connection with the shroffs often served to protect the Ahmedabad millowners from the vagaries of a volatile capital market. By comparison, the practices of the joint-stock banks remained far too rigid, conservative and inflexible adequately to serve the needs of industry.[95] Although, during the depression, capital was more reluctantly mobilized, and interest rates rose in Ahmedabad in the early 1930s, the industry did not suffer the massive withdrawal of public deposits experienced by Bombay.[96] Thus in 1932, the Tariff Board had to recognize that 'in practice, the Ahmedabad mills have seldom experienced any difficulty during the past 30 or 40 years owing to the bulk of their fixed capital being composed of deposits' and was, therefore, led to admit that, 'it seems to have effectively stood the test of time'.[97]

Moreover, the Ahmedabad shroffs did not merely act as bankers to the millowners, but frequently had interests in the purchase of raw cotton and the selling of piecegoods. Piecegoods dealers in the domestic market often encountered problems mobilizing funds, in contrast to the importers of foreign manufactures who were more freely financed by the exchange banks. It is probable that the interconnections between indigenous bankers and the piecegoods dealers relieved some of these difficulties and they help to explain in part why the Ahmedabad mills were more oriented towards the domestic market for piecegoods, able to establish a firmer grip upon it in the 1910s and 1920s, and to remain more alert to the specific patterns of demand within it. More immune to the progressive influences of the West than their rivals in Bombay, the Ahmedabad millowners, whatever their arcane styles of management or traditional connections, were also considered more progressive and innovative in the management of their industry: they produced finer varieties of goods, competing with imports and of a quality comparable with the best of Bombay's efforts; they exploited more skilfully the possibilities of the domestic market; managed their mills more closely and more prudently; and were more ready to renew their plant and replace old machinery.[98]

The development of the cotton textile industry provides a useful vantage point from which to observe the options which entrepreneurs perceived and the choices which they made. Cotton textiles constituted

[94] *Gazetteer of the Bombay Presidency*, vol. IV: *Ahmedabad* (Bombay, 1879), p. 68.
[95] *Report of the ITB, 1927*, vol. I, pp. 90–2.
[96] S. D. Mehta, *The Cotton Mills of India, 1854–1954* (Bombay, 1954), p. 178.
[97] *Report of the ITB, 1932*, p. 84.
[98] Several official reports and contemporary observers commented on the more progressive and efficient management of the Ahmedabad mills, but it was most extensively treated in the *Report of the ITB, 1927*, vol. I, *passim*.

India's most important industry and in conventional terms formed the lead sector of the economy. Superficially, at least, it appeared to illustrate perfectly the thesis that industrialization was an autonomous process of technological diffusion. In the nineteenth century, Indian cotton mills 'confronted the most important, the most internationally aggressive and politically most powerful industry in Britain'.[99] In the face of this formidable competition, the Indian textile industry expanded. The Bombay mills, equipped by Platt's machines, built to Lancashire's designs, staffed by British technicians, were able to compete effectively with the metropolitan industry in particular markets. Subsequently, as these techniques were diffused throughout the subcontinent, up-country centres of production challenged Bombay's dominance in the domestic market. As the technological innovations of the industrial revolution spread across the globe, India's turn it would appear had arrived. On a closer examination, however, a different picture of the development of the cotton textile industry begins to emerge. It was not so much the continuous application of new techniques which characterized the growth of the industry in India as much as relentless improvisation in the use of old machinery, the manipulation of raw materials and the exploitation of cheap labour.

Three distinct phases of expansion characterized the development of the cotton textile industry. The first spurt of growth, centred in Bombay, in the 1870s and 1880s, was based upon the penetration of the Chinese market at the expense of British industry.[100] Capital, in retreat from the adverse competitive conditions in the export trade in raw cotton, now sought to exploit Bombay's comparative advantage in labour costs, its access to abundant sources of short-stapled cotton, and its relative proximity to the market, in order to produce low-count yarn for handloom-weavers in China more cheaply than Lancashire.[101]

The later nineteenth and early twentieth centuries witnessed steady, if gradual growth and the dispersal of the industry, diluting its early concentration at Bombay. In Ahmedabad, capital diverted from the lucrative trading and banking activities of the late eighteenth and early nineteenth centuries was gradually attracted to the spinning mills to supply the needs of the town's sizeable handloom industry, especially for the lower and medium counts of yarn.[102] Capital stepped forward with caution: the

[99] Morris, 'Large-Scale Industry', 573.
[100] Bagchi, *Private Investment*, pp. 229–37; Mehta, *The Cotton Mills of India*, pp. 40–63; S. M. Rutnagur (ed.), *Bombay Industries: Cotton Textiles* (Bombay, 1927).
[101] Manchester Chamber of Commerce, *Bombay and Lancashire Cotton Spinning Enquiry: Minutes and Evidence* (Manchester, 1888); Bagchi, *Private Investment*, pp. 229–37; Morris, 'Large-Scale Industry', 572–83; Mehta, *Cotton Mills*, pp. 40–63. D. A. Farnie, *The English Cotton Industry and the World Market, 1815–96* (Oxford, 1979), pp. 81–134.
[102] Gillion, *Ahmedabad*, pp. 74–104; Mehta, *The Ahmedabad Cotton Textile Industry*. In

mills in Ahmedabad remained much smaller than those in Bombay and their growth was much slower. Although the first mill was built in 1861 by Ranchodlal Chotalal, who had lost his job in the government service for allegedly accepting a generous bribe,[103] there were by the early 1890s only nine mills working in Ahmedabad. Then, between 1896 and 1899, in a period of famine, agrarian crisis and considerable difficulty for their Bombay counterparts, the number of mills in Ahmedabad doubled.[104] In part, this was because mills which were projected in more prosperous times had been able to commence operations only after the downturn. But their survival in the late 1890s and early 1900s suggests also that the demand from the local handloom industry was far from saturated[105] and, further, that the scarcities of the late nineteenth century and the late 1890s in particular had increased income disparities in the countryside, thus shoring up the purchasing power of some consumers.[106] Between 1906 and 1911, there was a further spurt of growth in the industry when in response to economic recovery and the opportunities provided by the Swadeshi movement and the boycott of foreign cloth, the weaving capacity of the Ahmedabad mills was doubled.[107] This period also witnessed a dramatic expansion of looms in Bombay, reflecting the efforts of its millowners to adapt to the increasingly effective competition of the Japanese mills and of local spinners in the Chinese market.[108] The output of the new looms was biased towards coarse and medium varieties of piece-goods which were less exposed to the competition of Lancashire's imports.

The dispersal of the industry reached far beyond Ahmedabad. The new mills mainly produced low-count yarn and in a few cases coarse cloth as well, intended largely for local consumption, using cheap labour and local supplies of raw cotton.[109] These factors prompted mill-building in Sholapur, an important centre of the handloom industry, situated in proximity to the cotton tracts of the Deccan. Similarly, in Kanpur, investment in industry was a response to the demand for cheap low-count mill-made yarn among local handloom-weavers and was further stimu-

1900, there were 10,000 weavers operating in Ahmedabad and as late as 1914 there were said to be 1,000 looms in the town, see Gillion, *Ahmedabad*, pp. 47–9.
[103] S. M. Edwardes, *Memoir of Rao Bahadur Ranchodlal Chotalal* (Exeter, 1920); Gillion, *Ahmedabad*, pp. 81–5.   [104] Gillion, *Ahmedabad*, p. 88, fn. 16.
[105] Tripathi, *Dynamics of a Tradition*, pp. 45–50; Gillion, *Ahmedabad*, pp. 46–50.
[106] N. Charlesworth, 'Rich Peasants and Poor Peasants in late Nineteenth Century Maharashtra', in C. J. Dewey and A. G. Hopkins (eds.), *The Imperial Impact: Studies in the Economic History of Africa and India* (London, 1978), pp. 97–113; C. N. Bates, 'The Nature of Social Change: The Kheda District, 1818–1918', *MAS*, 15:4 (1981), 771–821.   [107] Bagchi, *Private Investment*, p. 234, table 7.4.
[108] Bombay Millowners' Association, *Annual Reports*; Bagchi, *Private Investment*, p. 234, table 7.4.
[109] M. M. Mehta, *Structure of Indian Industries* (Bombay, 1955), pp. 163–73.

lated by the needs of the British Indian Army stationed in the local cantonment.[110] Such expansion was not simply a function of the restless quest by capital for yet more productive sources of investment but the outcome of its adaptation to specific types of demand and often fairly localized production conditions. Since labour and raw materials constituted the largest share of the cost of production, these up-country mills were able to undercut Bombay and Ahmedabad in the coarser varieties and poorer qualities especially in the local market. Their increasing competitiveness was not based upon the use of machines newer and better than those used in Bombay and Ahmedabad but upon second-hand machinery which had sometimes been scrapped by their older rivals.

This pattern of location, geared to sources of cheap raw material and labour and to centres of proven demand, was reflected in the geography of the cotton textile industry in India. By the mid-1920s, cotton mills came to be widely scattered throughout the country, outside Bombay and Ahmedabad. Out of the twenty-three Indian states and British provinces which contained cotton mills eighteen had fewer than ten mills, five had no more than a single mill, and only two – the United Provinces and the Bombay Presidency – had more than twenty. Half the mills in the UP were concentrated in Kanpur, the rest being widely dispersed, and out of the twenty-four mills in the Bombay Presidency, outside Bombay and Ahmedabad, fifteen were divided equally between Sholapur, Surat and Broach while the remaining nine were thinly spread across the rest of the Presidency.[111]

A third spurt of growth occurred in the 1930s. Indian industry held its own under the initial impact of the depression and then began to expand in the middle years of the decade.[112] Whereas the early growth of the

[110] Bayly, *Rulers, Townsmen and Bazaars*, pp. 440–9; *Report of the Indian Industrial Commission, 1916–18* (Calcutta, 1918), pp. 28–9.
[111] *Report of the ITB, 1927*, vol. I, pp. 25–6.
[112] Tomlinson, *Political Economy*, pp. 31–4. Of course, in several respects this expansion betrayed a rather fragile character. It took the form of import substitution in a period in which the purchasing power of the peasantry was declining. It was not accompanied by rising investment in new plant and machinery. It was facilitated by a range of contingent factors and special circumstances: tariff protection which, though not wholly effective, helped the growing centres rather more than Bombay for whom in large measure it had been designed; the disruption of international trade and the decline of Lancashire in particular; and the outbreak of war which rescued the industry when it had appeared to reach the limits of import substitution by the late 1930s. The difficulties underlying this spurt of growth was also demonstrated in the acute problems faced in the 1950s by many of the new centres of textile production which emerged in this period. For an insight into the demand for cotton textiles, see Bagchi, *Private Investment*, pp. 237–53; on machinery imports, *ibid.*, tables 7.10 and 7.11, pp. 258–9, and R. Kirk and C. P. Simmons, 'Lancashire and the Equipping of Indian Cotton Mills: A Study of Textile Machinery and Supply, 1854–1939', in K. Ballhatchet and D. Taylor (eds.), *Changing South Asia: Economy and Society* (London, 1984), pp. 169–81; on the relationship between town and

industry had been financed by the profits of the long-distance trade, both internal and international, the capital which financed the mill-building of the 1930s was primarily in retreat from the countryside, in the shadows of agrarian crises and the depression. Creditors who lent money on the condition that it be repaid in grain had to recover their loans when prices were falling and from clients who frequently could not afford to pay. As the value of land declined and the price of its products collapsed, the risks of default rose steeply and the means of hedging them disappeared. Under these conditions, as the terms of trade moved in favour of industry, rural capital migrated to the towns.[113]

Moreover, the trend towards the dispersal of the industry away from Bombay and Ahmedabad, which had already manifested itself in the late nineteenth and early twentieth centuries, was accentuated.[114] Mills were built once more in proximity to local markets and to sources of raw materials and to cheap and plentiful supplies of labour. The viability and competitiveness of these mills depended upon their ability to shelter in local markets for coarse goods where foreign competition was least effective. Moreover, in these lines of production the advantages of the up-country mills in cheaper labour and raw material costs could be made to count in competition with a struggling Bombay industry. Like the new mills of the earlier twentieth century, these mills were often equipped with second-hand plant and frequently with machinery scrapped by older mills which were either going bankrupt or were sufficiently successful and progressive to be retooling.

Historians are generally agreed and indeed have frequently reiterated that these mills were 'very often badly designed and badly managed' and characterized by 'ignorance of the best technical conditions on the part of entrepreneurs and their managers'.[115] Their owners and managers have invariably had a bad press. It is perhaps not their incompetence but their resourcefulness which deserves emphasis. They were not, it is true, concerned with achieving and maintaining what may theoretically have

country during depression, Tomlinson, *Political Economy*, ch. 2 and Baker, *An Indian Rural Economy, passim*; on tariffs, see B. Chatterji, 'The Political Economy of "Discriminating Protection": The Case of Textiles in the 1920s', *IESHR*, 20:3 (1983), 239–75, and Chatterji, 'Business and Politics in the 1930s: Lancashire and the Making of the Indo-British Trade Agreement', *MAS*, 15:3 (1981), 527–73; C. J. Dewey, 'The End of Imperialism of Free Trade: The Eclipse of the Lancashire Lobby and the Concession of Fiscal Autonomy to India', in Dewey and Hopkins (eds.), *The Imperial Impact*, pp. 35–67, and I. Drummond, *British Economic Policy and the Empire, 1919–1939* (London, 1972), ch. 4.
[113] C. J. Baker, 'Debt and Depression in Madras, 1929–1936', in Dewey and Hopkins (eds.), *Imperial Impact*, pp. 233–42; Baker, *An Indian Rural Economy, passim*: Tomlinson, *Political Economy*, ch. 2.
[114] Mehta, *Structure of Indian Industries*, pp. 164–73; *Report of the ITB, 1927*, vol. I, pp. 4–28, 100–23.   [115] Bagchi, *Private Investment*, p. 252.

constituted optimum levels of efficiency. On the other hand, their aim was simple: to maximize profits within the existing economic context; and in this aim they clearly succeeded in the short term.

Coimbatore, which expanded dramatically in the mid-1930s, symbolized most accurately the character of the industry's expansion in this period.[116] The Coimbatore mills benefited from a number of developments taking place in the regional economy: the expansion of local cotton cultivation, especially in the long-stapled Cambodian varieties, which supplied by the early 1930s about half the raw cotton requirements of South Indian mills, thus considerably cheapening its cost; the expansion of the local handloom industry which provided a ready market; the establishment of the Pykara hydro-electric project which offered a convenient and relatively cheap source of electricity; tariff policies designed to alleviate Bombay's ills served centres like Coimbatore perhaps rather better. Moreover, the Coimbatore mills were known to pay the lowest wages in the subcontinent and later in the decade, as they ran into difficulties, they sought to cut wages further.[117] The declining profitability of moneylending and the trade in agrarian produce released local capital for industrial investment, and the substantial cultivators and rural traders of the region, already deeply involved in the marketing of cotton, now sought the returns to be offered by the spinning of yarn.[118] This capital was used economically to establish small spinning mills largely with machinery scrapped by the large number of Bombay mills which were closing down in this period and the few who were seeking cautiously to replace parts of their old equipment. Indeed, by the 1930s, the Sassoon group of mills preferred to destroy rather than sell their discarded machinery for scrap lest the upstart millowners of Coimbatore bought them up and then used these to jostle Bombay out of the domestic market.[119]

Each phase of the industry's expansion since its earliest beginnings had been characterized not by the progressive adoption of newer and better techniques but rather by persistent adaptation to available markets, existing production conditions and changing economic constraints. Just as the Bombay mills had penetrated the Chinese market in the 1870s and 1880s by exploiting their advantage of cheap labour, proximity to suitable raw

[116] Baker, *An Indian Rural Economy*, pp. 339–72.
[117] A. Pearse, *The Cotton Industry of India: Being the Report of a Journey to India* (Manchester, 1930), pp. 105–13; B. Shiva Rao, *The Industrial Worker in India* (London, 1939), p. 121; E. A. Ramaswamy, *The Worker and His Union: A Study of South India* (Delhi, 1977), pp. 17–32; Baker, *An Indian Rural Economy*, pp. 361 ff.; E. D. Murphy, *Unions in Conflict: A Comparative Study of Four South Indian Textile Centres, 1918–1939* (New Delhi, 1981); E. Perlin, 'Eyes Without Sight: Education and Millworkers in South India, 1939–76', *IESHR*, 18:3 and 4 (1981), 263–86.   [118] Baker, *An Indian Rural Economy*, p. 353.
[119] Proceedings of the TLIC, Main Inquiry, Oral Evidence, Mr F. Stones, Managing Director, Sassoon Spinning and Weaving Company Limited, File 70, 3450–51, MSA.

materials and to the market, economizing as far as possible on the cost of machinery and using labour-intensive methods to produce cheap, coarse qualities, so the newer up-country centres commanded an increasing share of the domestic market at Bombay's expense largely by the same means.

In the 1920s and 1930s, rationalization became an increasingly prominent issue in the affairs of the cotton textile industry. Because the crisis of the industry in the inter-war period was largely localized in Bombay, the pressure to effect rationalization schemes impinged most directly upon its millowners. By the 1920s, Bombay had been ousted from the Chinese market, lost its competitive advantage in cheap labour costs to both Indian and Japanese rivals and found itself heavily committed to the production of low-count, coarse goods which were rapidly becoming saturated in the domestic market as a result of the expansion of the up-country mills.[120] The general strikes of 1924 and 1925 showed conclusively that direct wage cuts would be met with bitter and possibly damaging labour resistance and therefore offered no solution to Bombay's problems.[121] Tariff protection appeared to be only a slightly more promising remedy: keeping the Indian market open for Lancashire manufactures had been one of the most important ground rules of the colonial state and Indian millowners made painfully slow progress against this entrenched tradition.[122] In response to their demand for protection, the Tariff Board lectured the Bombay millowners on the need for them to put their own house in order before seeking the assistance of the state. The answer lay, they argued, in raising their efficiency and lowering their labour costs, in improved labour discipline and increased productivity, changed patterns of labour deployment, methods of management and composition of output, the adoption of a more rational financial and marketing structure, the replacement of old plant and the introduction of new machinery.[123] Every subsequent committee of enquiry, which enquired into the conditions of the industry, whether its brief was tariff protection or labour relations, commented upon the need for rationalization, assessed its progress and urged its speedy implementation. The millowners' commitment to technological advance was increasingly called into question and the terms on which they would undertake to revamp their methods and organization were now to be increasingly clarified.

[120] *Report of the ITB, 1927*, vol. I, pp. 100–8.
[121] *Ibid.*, pp. 133–4; for a narrative of these general strikes, see R. Newman, *Workers and Unions in Bombay, 1918–29: A Study of Organization in the Cotton Mills* (Canberra, 1981), pp. 142–8, 153–9.
[122] Chatterji, 'The Political Economy of "Discriminating Protection"'; and Dewey, 'The End of the Imperialism of Free Trade'.
[123] *Report of the ITB, 1927*, vol. I, pp. 124–67.

The Bombay millowners could claim with some justification to have diversified into higher counts and finer qualities, adjusted their production and sales more closely to the needs of the domestic market, and streamlined their labour force. But their achievements by the end of the 1930s remained remarkably modest. Rationalization, as one official report commented in 1940, 'has a wider and a narrower meaning' and 'improvements in labour productivity and efficiency' constituted 'one aspect of the latter sense'.[124] The Bombay millowners did not proceed far beyond this partial aspect of the narrow construction of its scope: the implementation of 'efficiency schemes' which involved increasing workloads and reducing the strength of the labour force. Weavers who worked two looms were now to be put in charge of three or four while single siders would mind both sides of the spinning frame. Yet even these efficiency schemes were far from sweeping. In the late 1930s, less than one-fifth of the weavers in the Bombay mills operated more than two looms and less than one-half of the siders worked two sides.[125] The millowners did not respond to their competitive situation or to official exhortations by consistently rationalizing the structure and organization of their industry or by effecting technological change.

The reasons for the weakness of the millowners' attempts to rationalize were complex and although no comprehensive discussion of them can be undertaken here,[126] the direction and emphasis of their response is readily demonstrated. The axiom that Indian entrepreneurs were highly speculative in business and inherently averse to innovation need not detain us. The argument which stresses the constraints imposed upon businessmen by the absence of a domestic capital goods industry is, if more prosaic, also more plausible. Of course, businessmen were inhibited by the depressed conditions of the trade. However, the positive changes which the Bombay mills did effect suggest that their owners did not entirely shrink from taking risks, and some millowners at least would not have found it impossible to raise capital for more far-reaching reform. We need to dig deeper than the absolute scarcity of capital for a more convincing explanation.

The supply of capital to the industry, the nature of its markets and the pattern of labour deployment within it interacted to dampen the millowners' enthusiasm for change. Most mills regulated their production according to the short-term fluctuations of the market. This business strategy arose, in part, from the dependence of most mills upon the money market for their working capital and sometimes a proportion of

[124] *Report of the TLIC*, vol. II: *Final Report* (Bombay, 1953), p. 183.
[125] *Ibid.*, p. 187, table 44.
[126] I discuss this issue at greater length in Chandavarkar, *The Origins of Industrial Capitalism*, pp. 271–77, 335–96.

their fixed costs as well. In these conditions, they sought to avoid the accumulation of stocks and to maintain a rapid turnover to pay their debts and to attract investment. Moreover, the Indian market was reputed to take the greatest variety of counts of yarn and types of piecegoods in the world.[127] In response, mills produced a bewildering range of counts of yarn and varieties of piecegoods, each of diverse qualities. The regulation of production to demand in these circumstances meant that carding machines, spinning frames and looms allocated to one type and quality of output often had to be turned swiftly to another. As the industry diversified its range of production, so these tendencies were exacerbated. Yet the cost-reducing effects of investment in machinery could only be fully realized if the flow and consistency of orders were maintained. For the millowners to remain alert to market fluctuations and to the varieties and specificities of taste was often incompatible with a commitment to vast outlays on plant and machinery. Far from responding to the unseen logic of industrialism or long-term technological imperatives, the millowners attempted to maximize their returns within the constraints which they encountered.

A further consideration which often had a more crucial bearing on the introduction of rationalization and reforms was the response of labour. The brunt of these changes was after all to be borne by the workforce in the form of greater workloads, higher unemployment and sometimes lower wages. In fact, reviewing the progress of the previous decade, Maloney, the Secretary of the Millowners' Association, observed that 'the main cause of slow progress' in the implementation of rationalization was not 'the lack of capital' but 'the opposition of the workers'. And as Fred Stones, Managing Director of the Sassoon group of mills added, 'progress is hampered very much by the fact that there are so many strikes, and it would be inadvisable to invest money in machinery in the circumstances'.[128] Changes in working conditions or wage rates, even those which resulted from short-term changes in the character of production, had always been liable to prompt industrial action. Attempts to increase workloads in 1927, which threatened jobs in general and the status and position of weavers especially, prompted industrial action, which culminated in the general strikes of 1928 and 1929. The strike of 1928 began in April and ended in October in a temporary truce which brought the millowners to the negotiating table.[129] The following six

---

[127] *Report of the ITB, 1927*, vol. I, p. 48.
[128] Proceedings of the TLIC, Main Inquiry, Oral Evidence, Representatives of the BMOA, File 57–A, p. 63, MSA.
[129] *Report of the Bombay Strike Enquiry Committee*, vol. I (Bombay, 1929); Newman, *Workers and Unions*, pp. 168–209; see also ch. 4 below.

months witnessed over seventy industrial disputes until in April 1929 another general strike was effected. This strike proved more difficult to sustain, but although it began to weaken in July, it did not end until September.[130] The question of rationalization once more had an important bearing upon the general strike of 1934.[131] The disruption of production which followed frequently undermined the competitive position of individual mills and, in the case of general strikes, the industry as a whole. Better by far in these circumstances, especially when their markets were in a slump, for the millowners to do the best they could within the limitations imposed upon them.

Industrialization was not simply a function of entrepreneurial choice. The impact of labour frequently deflected the course of industrialization and shaped its character. The actions of workers, rather than technological imperatives alone, frequently determined the options and thus the strategies of capitalists. Indeed, the response of capitalists to innovation in machinery or production patterns was guided by the general anxiety that changes in working conditions might provoke labour resistance and unsettle the delicate balances upon which industrial peace rested. Even the Ahmedabad millowners, widely believed to be more progressive than their rivals in Bombay, and supposedly blessed with a more docile labour force, were even more cautious in the introduction of rationalization and efficiency schemes. 'In spite of their eagerness to introduce efficiency measures', it was reported, 'they have not been able to do so on account of the determined opposition of the Textile Labour Association'.[132]

How far labour resistance shaped the attitude of the entrepreneurs towards the introduction of new technology was exemplified when the Bombay millowners, pressed to rationalize their industry, considered the adoption of the automatic loom from the late 1920s onwards. The Northrop loom required a larger capital outlay and suffered a higher rate of depreciation than the ordinary Lancashire loom. Moreover, stores and spare parts for the automatic loom were both relatively more expensive and less readily obtainable. This additional cost had to be made up, as the Tariff Board noted, by 'higher production, higher prices or a reduction in

---

[130] *Report of the Court of Enquiry into a Trade Dispute between Several Textile Mills and their Workmen* (Bombay, 1929); Newman, *Workers and Unions*, pp. 211–50; see also ch. 4 below.

[131] Labour Office, Bombay, *Wages and Unemployment in the Bombay Cotton Textile Industry* (Bombay, 1934).

[132] *Report of the TLIC*, vol. II, pp. 188–9. The constraints thus exercised by workers upon entrepreneurial choice have often been perceived as a reflection of their pre-industrial mentalities, dysfunctional to the industrial setting. However, entrepreneurs in Britain, at the height of its industrial 'maturity', similarly showed a propensity to shelter in traditional markets rather than effect fundamental changes which, while increasing their productivity and their competitiveness, also raised the spectre of industrial action.

labour costs'.[133] In the late 1920s and 1930s, there was little prospect of rising prices. Trial runs conducted in Bombay revealed that the automatic loom did not yield an appreciably higher output. Furthermore, the automatic loom required weft yarn of a higher quality and greater strength. In turn, this called for a better quality of raw cotton, improved mixings and preparation as well as the adoption of different techniques of winding, for the weft yarn had to be put onto special pirns. In 1927, these adjustments alone were estimated to increase the costs of production by seven pies in the pound, at a time when certain lines of Bombay's output were being undersold at the cost of production in the domestic market by Japanese mills.[134] Clearly, they would also have repercussions on the organization of the entire mill. It was scarcely economical to 'swing-off' the expensive Northrop loom as most mills did with regard to the ordinary loom. To supply the Northrop looms adequately, each process of production would have to be suitably adapted. Its adoption would require the lengthening and standardization of production runs throughout the mill, from the preparatory processes to the weaving sheds. Given their financial structures and their volatile market conditions, the millowners could scarcely transform their production patterns so thoroughly.

The viability of the automatic loom thus came to turn increasingly upon whether labour costs could be reduced. The millowners were reluctant to promulgate direct wage cuts which they expected would provoke industrial action. The possibility of reducing labour costs would depend therefore upon whether the number of looms allocated to each weaver could be increased. It was very apparent at the time, however, that 'it would be difficult to get weavers in Bombay to look after more than four looms'. Yet, even if the number of automatic looms per weaver was raised to six, it was thought that the ordinary loom would still be more economical.[135] In one of its nicer formulations, therefore, the Tariff Board concluded that 'in present conditions no solution of the problem presented by labour costs in Bombay lies in the introduction of the Northrop loom'.[136] Despite the recovery of the mid-1930s, a greater measure of protection and the extent of unemployment which created a reserve supply of labour, the millowners remained reluctant until the end of the decade to invest in the Northrop loom.[137] The future, as the millowners perceived it, lay with the Lancashire loom; and with perpetuating the existing state of affairs, while if possible and where necessary increasing the number of old looms tended by each weaver. The case of the automatic loom shows that while capital costs, low prices and

[133] *Report of the ITB, 1927,* vol. I, pp. 143–5.   [134] *Ibid.*   [135] *Ibid.*
[136] *Ibid.,* vol. I. p. 144.
[137] Proceedings of the TLIC, Main Inquiry, Oral evidence, BMOA, File 57–A, MSA.

foreign competition as well as fluctuations of quality and composition of output made for the lack of enthusiasm with which the Northrop was received in Bombay, the most significant factor was the difficulty of getting weavers to work a larger number of looms.

V

The assumption that industrialization was determined by its own inherent logic rather than by social choice has often led historians to take it for granted that capitalists were able consistently to create the labour force they sought. The technological imperatives of industrialization, in this view, determined the characteristics of the workforce. Labour is thus consigned to a peripheral role in the history of industrialization. But the formation of an industrial labour force, like the process of industrialization itself, cannot be adequately understood outside the context of the choices and actions of the workers themselves.

The bulk of the industrial labour force was composed of migrant workers recruited from varying distances. Yet crucially most workers attempted to retain their rural connections. This was in part the consequence of low wages and predominantly casual and uncertain conditions of employment. But it also reflected conscious choice. Rural smallholders migrated to the towns and factories in order to conserve their position in the village, to pay off their debts, to hold onto their land, and to retain their crop shares. Urban employment, they often discovered, afforded their families at the village base a readier access to cash, but it did not consistently facilitate social mobility. The indebtedness of industrial workers suggests that by utilizing their greater access to cash and credit, they simply transferred some part of the burden of debt borne by their family from the countryside to the towns. The maintenance of a rural base was essential to their strategies for subsistence in the industrial setting, and conversely, urban wage employment played a vital role in the reproduction of the family economy in the village. The formation of an industrial labour force was not simply a matter of 'raw novices' from the countryside who 'had to be converted into an army of disciplined mill hands, responsive to the general requirements of industrial work and to the special needs of the mills'.[138] Nor was the migrant status of industrial workers a reflection of the 'early stages of industrialization', or a passing phase in their progressive 'urbanization'. The formation of the labour force cannot be understood in terms of the smooth progression of peasants into proletarians. In the case of Bombay, workers have retained their

[138] M. D. Morris, *The Emergence of an Industrial Labour Force: A Study of the Bombay Cotton Mills, 1854–1947* (Berkeley and Los Angeles, 1965), p. 107.

rural connections through several vicissitudes since the beginnings of industrialization, over a century ago, until the present day. Far from being backward or passive or traditional or conservative in their political consciousness, migrant workers were active in the defence of their jobs, conditions and wage levels. In fact, urban proletarians, without an alternative source of support, however meagre, were more easily recruited to break strikes than those who possessed a rural base and village connections.[139]

Industrial workers not only maintained their rural ties but in many cases forged social networks and institutions of their own in the urban neighbourhoods. Through these neighbourhood connections, they found work, housing and credit. Landlords, grain dealers and moneylenders might extend credit to local residents in periods of unemployment, rural distress or indeed industrial action. Social connections of the neighbourhood were used to prevent some men usurping the jobs of others during strikes, sometimes by influence and sometimes with force. In these ways, the social organization of the neighbourhood had an important bearing upon the affairs of the workplace. It strengthened their bargaining power and often enabled them to resist the policies of employers more effectively.[140]

It is often supposed that the role of the jobber was created by employers not only to recruit rural migrants but to facilitate their adaptation to the industrial setting. But this process of adaptation was shaped to a large extent by the actions and autonomous organizations of rural migrants, not by the agency of the employers alone. Although the jobber has often been portrayed as a figure of awesome power, and the fulcrum of industrial relations, there were numerous alternative locations of power and patronage in the workplace and the neighbourhood with which the jobber was forced to negotiate and which severely narrowed his freedom of action. Subject to the pressures of both the management and the labour force, jobbers frequently found themselves inside the jaws of a nutcracker. It was by no means easy to maintain an adequate supply of labour in the face of short-term fluctuations of demand, to hire workers at short notice or lay them off according to need, and at the same time to prevent wages from rising and workers from combining. Indeed, the development of working-class politics in Bombay in the 1920s and 1930s led to the gradual erosion of the jobber's position. The state was now forced to fulfil some of the functions once left to the jobber: it intervened increasingly in the maintenance of labour discipline especially through a growing legislative machinery for the conciliation and arbitration of disputes and an

[139] Chandavarkar, *The Origins of Industrial Capitalism*, ch. 4.   [140] See ch. 4 below.

increasingly elaborate legal structure which defined the conditions for the conduct of strikes and the existence of trade unions.

The political organization and action of the working class was neither the natural consequence of their aggregation in large factories and cities, nor a direct reflection of the level of industrialization. The notion that the development of working-class consciousness and politics matched some inevitable process of its evolution from an essentially rural-based, casually employed immigrant labour force to the formation of a mature, industrial proletariat is not borne out by the Indian evidence. In Bombay city, workers were active in the defence of their interests from the earliest years of the cotton textile industry. Although no trade unions existed among them, they were always known by their employers as well as contemporary observers to be capable of combining to defend their wage levels.[141] At various times, especially in the early 1890s, 1901 and 1908, strikes affecting very large numbers of workers were sustained for considerable periods of time.[142] Although nearly one-third of the labour force in the cotton mills was employed on a casual basis,[143] the textile workers were able to mount eight general strikes between 1919 and 1940, which lasted longer than a month and in 1928–29 were sustained for the most part of one and a half years.[144] Indeed, dock workers who were hired almost exclusively on a daily basis at the dock gates and were generally more quiescent than textile workers effected a three-month strike in 1932.[145] The possession of a rural base, and the development and utilization of the social connections of the neighbourhood by the city's workers helps to explain why they were able repeatedly to mount and sustain long periods of industrial action in the 1920s and 1930s. The institutions which workers created and the more or less informal social connections which they forged remained a decisive influence on the politics of the workplace and exercised effective constraints on the ability of employers to create the labour force they wanted.

[141] *RCL, Foreign Report*, vol. II, *The Colonies and the Indian Empire*, Memorandum on the Labour Question in India, Evidence, Mr J. M. Campbell, Collector, Land Revenue, Excise and Opium, Bombay, *PP*, 1892, vol. XXXVI, p. 128.

[142] V. B. Karnik, *Strikes in India* (Bombay, 1967), pp. 3–56; Commissioner of Police, Bombay, to Secretary, GOB, Judicial Department, no. 10503–6–R, 27 August 1908, GOB, General Department, vol. 114 of 1908, reprinted in *Source Material for a History of the Freedom Movement in India* (*Collected from Bombay Government Records*), vol. II: *1885–1920* (Bombay, 1958), pp. 256–75.

[143] *RCL*, Evidence, Mr J. M. Campbell, Collector, Land Revenue, Customs, and Opium, Bombay to the Chief Secretary, Bombay, *PP*, 1892, vol. XXXVI, p. 129; Labour Office, Bombay, *Report on the Wages, Hours of Work and Conditions of Employment in the Textile Industries (Cotton, Silk, Wool and Hosiery) in the Bombay Presidency (including Sind), May 1934, General Wage Census, Part I – Perennial Factories, Third Report* (Bombay, 1937), p. 20.   [144] See ch. 4 below.

[145] Karnik, *Strikes*, pp. 265–6; R. P. Cholia, *Dock Labourers in Bombay* (Bombay, 1941).

VI

This essay has attempted to sketch an albeit ragged consensus of opinion that conceives industrialization as a neutral, technologically determined process, which, transcending social choice, shapes society in a single, inevitable direction. In this view, industrialization fashions labour in its own image; for some, even according to its needs. Its culmination is invariably large-scale enterprise, the factory system and the production line. It is characterized by an inherent tendency to increasing technical sophistication and efficiency. Historically, it is assumed to constitute a process of diffusion which, beginning in Britain, spread to Western Europe and the United States, and then unevenly and incompletely across the globe. For dependency theorists, the process was essentially the same, even if its effect in large parts of the world was the opposite: not development, but the development of underdevelopment.

These notions about the nature of industrialization have deeply in-fluenced studies of economic development in India. Economic historians of India have been concerned to explain why the perceived pre-conditions for industrialization did not exist in early nineteenth-century India, and why industrialization subsequently failed to transform the Indian econ-omy. Explanations have boiled down to a residual choice between the baneful effects of colonial rule or the timeless torpor of Indian society. In one view, general poverty, the dead-weight of tradition and social organ-ization that was weakly geared to the rationality of the market meant that the Indian economy would have remained torpid but for the benefits of colonial rule.[146] But if colonial rule had mobilized the Indian economy to the point where the first weak impulses of 'industrialism' began to mani-fest themselves, why did it not go further? Thus, in another view, the failure of the Indian economy is ascribed conversely to the nature of British rule. Both sets of arguments assume that external agencies, colo-nialism and the world economy constituted the only active element in the Indian situation, whether their force was exerted to plunder Indian re-sources or to mobilize them. This debate which originated in the late nineteenth century, has long petrified into dead-lock. Its resolution may lie less in choosing between these two positions than in more positively exploring the interplay between Indian social structures and colonial rule, between the internal and the external economy, though not as an unprob-lematic marriage between equals.

The counter-factual nature of this debate has arisen in part from an unilinear and evolutionary schemata of social and economic change

---

[146] For a version of this argument, see Morris, 'Large-Scale Industry', especially, 558–66.

against which the development of the Indian economy is measured. Recently, Irfan Habib has argued that while technology in Mughal India had been surpassed in sophistication by Western Europe and indeed was not necessarily following the latter's path of development, it was nevertheless dynamic and open to improvement and innovation.[147] The point may perhaps be generalized to the pattern of economic development as a whole. Typologies of social and economic change have necessarily drawn attention to sharp discontinuities. Historians who have sought to apply them to the past have had to reconcile the far subtler modulations of change and the long-term continuities in the social processes they encounter with the dramatic ruptures suggested by social theories and typologies of change. The growth and spread of commercialization in land, labour and produce, capital and credit, scarcely the creation of colonial rule alone, were slow and gradual processes, but did not develop in a single, unilinear direction.

In addition, the patterns of economic development at a national level, defined in correspondence with political boundaries and states, are liable to mask fundamentally diverse changes which manifest themselves at more local or regional levels. Recent studies of land tenure and agrarian social structure demonstrated how greatly production conditions could vary between localities of a fairly modest scale.[148] Areas of 'dynamism' sometimes developed into areas of 'enervation'[149] while changing circumstances, not necessarily directly related to the means of production, might facilitate buoyancy in apparently stagnant localities and the development of certain regions at the expense of others. Studies of national income have emphasized the 'vast disparities in regional income' in the eighteenth century and suggested that the fortunes of particular regions altered substantially during the period of colonial rule.[150] Similarly, Heston and Summers have identified as an essential problem of 'Indian economic history in the last century' the need 'to deal with the heterogeneous experience of very large regions with populations in tens of millions that have shown aggregate growth not so much lower than many individual countries, while at the same time dealing with several relatively stagnant regions'.[151] And regional studies of the Punjab have reinforced this

[147] Habib, 'Technology and Economy'.
[148] E. T. Stokes, *The Peasant and the Raj: Studies in Agrarian Society and Peasant Rebellion in Colonial India* (Cambridge, 1978).
[149] E. T. Stokes, 'Dynamism and Enervation in North Indian Agriculture: The Historical Dimension', in *ibid.*, pp. 228–42.
[150] D. Kumar and J. Krishnamurthy, 'Regional and International Economic Disparities since the Industrial Revolution: The Indian Evidence', in P. Bairoch and M. Levy-Leboyer (eds.), *Disparities in Economic Development Since the Industrial Revolution* (London, 1981), pp. 361–72.
[151] A. Heston and R. Summers, 'Comparative Indian Economic Growth: 1870 to 1970', *American Economic Review*, 70:2 (1980), 97.

point.[152] These studies serve to suggest that the nature of economic development will be illuminated by studying more closely the fate of regional economies: the different paths of economic change followed by them, the relationships between the diverse economic activities and social groups within them, and the effects of various factors, often contingent and political, in determining, altering and redirecting the lines of economic change.[153] This may help to offer a dynamic context of social and economic change within which industrialization and economic development may be placed.

This paper has attempted to argue that large-scale industry was neither the only source of dynamism within the economy nor the natural culmination of economic development. The path of industrial development was constructed by the interaction of various social forces. Its direction was the outcome of these conflicts and did not follow pre-determined lines or proceed towards a single, ultimate destination. The development of industry in India cannot be adequately understood as the manifestation of a progressive technological diffusion working outwards from Western Europe. Neither was industrialization the only agency of economic development, nor need large-scale industry be construed as its logical culmination, and, indeed, it is doubtful whether large-scale industry can usefully be placed in a distinct functional category of its own. On the one hand, seemingly traditional forms of industrial organization showed themselves able to survive, adapt and prosper within a given context. On the other hand, business strategies and methods of labour deployment followed in large factories often resembled the practices of small-scale enterprises in the informal sector. Finally, it is clear that the process of industrialization cannot be fully explained without reference to the crucial impact of labour upon its course and character. Notions of modernization have offered convenient categories and narrative schemes for understanding social change; yet far from working upon a passive social order, what are labelled forces of modernization have more usually been tied down and shaped by existing social institutions and supposedly traditional agencies.

If the burden of predominant approaches to the economic history of colonial India has been to produce a largely counter-factual problematic, the remedy cannot simply lie in a plea for a more positive historiography. For this line of advance has tended to offer accounts of the performance of the Indian economy, irrespective of the political fact of colonialism and without seeking to relate this economic performance to the nature of the

---

[152] C. J. Dewey, 'The Agricultural Output of an Indian Province: The Punjab, 1870–1940'. Paper read to the Economic History Seminar, Institute of Commonwealth Studies, London, 30 April 1973; Dewey, 'Some Consequences of Military Expenditure in British India: The Case of the Upper Sind Sagar Doab, 1849–1947', in C. Dewey (ed.), *Arrested Development in India: The Historical Dimension* (Delhi, 1988), pp. 93–169.
[153] The 'regional economy' before 1857 is examined in *CEHI*, vol. II, pp. 242–375.

colonial state and its wider imperial purposes or indeed to the international economy.[154] Thus, studies of British rule and the Indian economy inform us simply about the performance of the latter in the period no more than chronologically defined by the former.

To examine the interplay between Indian society and colonial rule, it will be essential to absorb more fully into the existing debate about the imperial impact two lines of enquiry which have already begun to emerge discretely in recent studies. First, existing arguments about the modernization or retardation of the Indian economy focus almost exclusively on the period after the mid-nineteenth century. Yet it is obvious that economic and social structures developing in the pre-colonial period established the historical context within which the colonial economy formed and within which its dynamic and expansive components emerged. Recent research has suggested that the world economy was beginning to impinge upon and influence the internal economic and political structure well before the imposition of formal colonial rule in the late eighteenth century.[155] Moreover, what Britain could achieve in India was determined to a large extent by the changing condition of the internal economy and its developing class structure.[156]

Second, it is becoming increasingly possible to relate the political priorities of the colonial state to the changing character of the Indian economy. The most common arguments about the effects of the colonial state on the Indian economy have usually concerned the way it acted to preserve and protect the economic interests of the metropolitan ruling class. But the colonial state was also vulnerable to the pressures which dominant classes in India could exert upon it. Moreover, under certain conditions, it subordinated particular, even powerful metropolitan interests to the claims of specific Indian groups. The balance of political power and the composition of economic interests within the metropolitan ruling classes was subject to change. In any case, 'intention' and conspiracy have

[154] For instance, the imperial dimension is played down in the judicious and positive account offered by N. Charlesworth, *British Rule and the Indian Economy, 1800–1914* (London, 1983).

[155] C. A. Bayly, 'Putting Together the Eighteenth Century in India: Trade, Money and the "Pre-Colonial" Political Order', paper presented to the Second Anglo-Dutch Workshop on Comparative Colonial History, September 1981; I. Habib, 'Monetary Systems and Prices', in T. Raychaudhuri and I. Habib (eds.), *CEHI*, vol. I (Cambridge, 1982), pp. 360–81; Perlin, 'Proto-Industrialization'; A. Hasan, 'The Silver Currency Output of the Mughal Empire and Prices in India in Sixteenth and Seventeenth Centuries', *IESHR*, 6:1 (1969), 85–116; J. F. Richards, 'Mughal State Finance and the Premodern World Economy', *Comparative Studies in Society and History*, 23:2 (1981), 285–308; K. N. Chaudhuri, *The Trading World of Asia and the English East India Company, 1660–1760* (London, 1978).

[156] D. A. Washbrook, 'Law, State and Agrarian Society in Colonial India', *MAS*, 15:3 (1981), 649–721.

sometimes in this line of argument been difficult to prove. On the other hand, it was also the case that India was ruled in the interests of Britain's global imperial system.[157] This fact alone served to shape the Indian economy in ways which were not conducive to growth: the burden of land revenue, especially in the early nineteenth century; the alignment of the colonial state with predominantly conservative social elements; the commitment to balanced budgets, to meeting the Home Charges and to guarantees on interest payments which governed the financial, fiscal and monetary policies of the state and whose effects were at times to squeeze the internal economy and severely damage commercial activity. The imperial impact was governed less by the specifically economic interests of the metropolitan ruling classes in Britain alone than by the changing political priorities of the colonial state.

[157] In the case of India, this point has been most extensively documented in Tomlinson, *Political Economy*, and his articles, 'India and the British Empire, 1880–1935', *IESHR*, 12:4 (1975), 339–80 and 'India and the British Empire, 1935–1947', *IESHR*, 13:3 (1976), 331–52.

3   Workers, trade unions and the state in colonial India

It is a commonplace that the period between 1917 and 1920 constituted a benchmark in the history of the Indian labour movement. Although more unions were formed, many of them remained ephemeral to the politics of the workplace. Their connections with the workforce were often tenuous. They usually arrived on the scene of a strike after it had begun and frequently failed to persuade workers to accept the settlements which they had negotiated. Some trade unions had about as much life as the letter-heads which they printed ostentatiously on their notepaper. Most of them existed as little more than a nucleus around which workers would gather in the course of a strike. When work was resumed, their membership dwindled rapidly and in many cases disappeared altogether. Trade unions existed often as a loose superstructure constructed over an active undergrowth of informal organization and seemingly spontaneous industrial action.

Conventionally, historians have understood the weakness of trade union organization and the supposed volatility of the workforce as responses characteristic of the early stages of industrialization.[1] Frequently, historians have postulated too simple and economistic a relationship between industrialization and labour protest. Industrialization has been widely portrayed as an independent force, determined by a neutral technology which lies beyond the realm of political control or social choice.[2] In this view, the level of industrialization has been closely associated with a particular pattern of working-class behaviour and consciousness. If the early stages of industrialization are characterized by volatility, further economic development is supposed to lead to the more ready acceptance

---

[1] The most recent and systematic exposition of this convention is Chakrabarty, *Rethinking Working Class History*. Most accounts of workers' politics, despite substantial differences of approach, have subscribed to this convention. For some examples see C. A. Myers, *Labour Problems in the Industrialization of India* (Cambridge, Mass., 1958); Morris, *The Emergence of an Industrial Labour Force in India*; Newman, *Workers and Unions in Bombay*; Arnold, 'Industrial Violence in Colonial India'; Murphy, *Unions in Conflict*; Joshi, 'Bonds of Community, Ties of Religion'.

[2] The interpretative costs of these perspectives are examined at length in ch. 2 above.

of formal collective bargaining. Within the terms of such reasoning, political maturity should properly be measured in yards of cloth or tons of rolling steel.

It would be tempting to fit the Indian case to this conventional wisdom were it not for what the Industrial Disputes Committee observed as 'the capacity of the operatives to remain on strike for considerable periods despite the lack of any visible organisation'.[3] This was exemplified in Bombay where general strikes occurred in 1908, 1919, 1920 and 1923 without the initiative of any effective trade union; in 1928 when both major unions were opposed to its occurrence; in 1934 and 1940, when the Girni Kamgar Union was unable to play any significant part in the daily relations of the workplace. All these strikes, except for 1908, lasted for at least a month; in 1928–29, they lasted for about twelve months in eighteen. These extensive, if informally organized, strikes were not confined to Bombay. They were witnessed in Ahmedabad in 1918, 1923, 1935 and 1937; in Sholapur in 1920, 1928, 1934 and 1937; in the Calcutta jute mills in 1929 and 1937; on various railways especially between 1928 and 1930; in Nagpur in 1934 and Coimbatore in 1938.[4]

Confronted by extensive evidence of sustained and prolonged industrial action, it is difficult to accept the common argument that the nature and dynamics of Indian trade unions simply reflected the level of consciousness among industrial workers. It is clear that for the beginnings of an explanation we will have to dig at deeper levels. We will have to avoid the assumption that the realization by workers of the utility and indeed necessity of formal trade union organization led simply to its being effected in reality or indeed that intention was unproblematically translated into achievement. We will also have to pursue the hypothesis that the terrain upon which the Indian working class, perhaps any working class, fought its battles was determined by its opponents and, therefore, their forms of action reflected not their level of consciousness, but the range of options available to them inside a particular economic and political conjuncture.

If, on the one hand, the nature of working-class politics was not merely a function of its adaptation to the industrial environment, the structural characteristics of the labour force, on the other hand, were not simply sculptured by neutral, technological forces. The politics of employers or the state often actively encouraged, indeed, developed, many of the supposedly pre-industrial characteristics of the workforce. In Calcutta in

---

[3] *Report of the Industrial Disputes Committee, 1922*, in *Labour Gazette*, 1:8 (April 1922), 24.
[4] Karnik, *Strikes in India*.

the 1890s and the 1900s[5] and in Bombay in the 1870s and 1890s[6] employers in the jute and cotton textile industries respectively attempted to diversify the social composition of the workforce by replacing local, urban labour with rural migrants. Their objective was not merely to meet their expanding labour needs but also to check the growth and intensification of labour unrest which occurred in the 1890s on a scale never before witnessed.

Similarly, in order to meet the often fluctuating demand for labour, employers devised systems of recruitment based on jobbers or sardars who ensured the presence of a full contingent of workers and were given considerable disciplinary powers at the workplace. In order to fulfil their diverse managerial tasks, jobbers as well as other supervisory officials had to operate through their caste, kinship, village and neighbourhood connections. It has commonly been assumed that the role of the jobber was to temper the cultural diversity of the working class as well as to mediate between managers and men, both linguistically and socially.[7] It is more likely that by having to recruit and more generally to operate along the lines of caste, kinship, neighbourhood and village that supervisors and jobbers accentuated the sectionalism of the workforce.[8]

Of course, the structural characteristics of the workforce influenced the nature of industrial action and trade union organization; but their relationship was neither uniform nor consistent. In Bombay, workers who maintained connections with their villages were often considered the most resilient during industrial disputes and more active in the defence of their interests than those who had severed their ties with the land.[9] Ahmedabad appeared to combine the most urbanized, proletarianized workforce with the most stable and sophisticated trade union in the country. Although the militant sections of the workforce were also the

[5] B. Foley, *Report on Labour in Bengal* (Calcutta, 1906), para 29; Das Gupta, 'Factory Labour in Eastern India'.
[6] *Report of the Indian Factory Commission, 1890* (Calcutta, 1890), *Annual Report of the BMOA, 1892*, pp. 11–12, 43–5, *ibid., 1896*, pp. 149–60, *ibid., 1897*, pp. 4–6; Morris, *The Emergence of an Industrial Labour Force*, pp. 54–6; Misra, 'Factory Labour During the Early Years of Industrialisation'; Mehta, *The Cotton Mills of India*.
[7] Newman, *Workers and Unions*, pp. 27–34 and *passim*; Newman, 'Social Factors in the Recruitment of the Bombay Millhands'; Mazumdar, 'Labour Supply in Early Industrialization'; Morris, *Industrial Labour Force*, chs. IV, V, VIII and IX; Das Gupta, 'Factory Labour in Eastern India'; Simmons, 'Recruiting and Organizing an Industrial Labour Force in Colonial India'; Chakrabarty, *Rethinking Working Class History*, pp. 95–114, and *passim*, especially chs. 5 and 6; Kooiman, 'Jobbers and the Emergence of Trade Unions in Bombay City'.
[8] In contemporary discourse, as well as some recent scholarship, it was assumed that jobbers were the product and expression of the caste, kinship and village ties which were taken to constitute Indian society and its tradition, as well as its working class.
[9] *RCLI, Evidence, Bombay Presidency (including Sind)* (London, 1931), Mr M. S. Bhumgara, vol. I, part i, p. 499; *BPP SAI*, 1928, no. 3, 21 January, para 61.

most urbanized, they remained the least integrated into the Ahmedabad Textile Labour Association.[10] Nagpur which recruited its labour locally was noted for its quiescence, but Sholapur, which did the same, at times appeared turbulent even insurrectionary in its politics.[11]

Although employers were to gain considerably at times from the sectionalism of the workforce, from caste and religious mentalities, from village, kinship and neighbourhood ties, it cannot be assumed that these acted only to restrict the possibilities of working-class politics. Indeed, caste and communal connections sometimes provided the basis for combination at the workplace. Thus, one of the earliest organizations of Bengal's jute mill operatives was Kazi Zahiruddin Ahmed's Mohammedan Association founded at Kankinara in 1895. It combined as its major preoccupations the employment of more Muslims in the jute mills and the renovation of mosques.[12] In Bombay, too, the Kamgar Hitwardhak Sabha which played an active role in the settlement of several industrial disputes in the 1910s and early 1920s was, primarily a welfare association for non-Brahmin workers.[13] Marathas from Ratnagiri were among the most ready participants in industrial action and their village and caste connections contributed to some of the networks upon which communist organization in Bombay was grounded.[14] Muslim weavers in Ahmedabad remained initially aloof and were increasingly alienated from the Gandhian Textile Labour Association, and by the 1930s they had formed their own communist Mill Mazdoor Sangh.[15] Its popularity among the city's workers was sufficient to cause deep concern in the Ahmedabad Textile Labour Association, and it is this factor, perhaps, rather than capitalist pressure upon the Congress, which explains the highly repressive policies of the Congress Ministry towards the commu-

[10] *RCLI, Evidence, Bombay Presidency*, vol. I, part i, pp. 287–9; S. Patel, *The Making of Industrial Relations: The Ahmedabad Textile Industry, 1918–1939* (Delhi, 1987); Mehta, *Cotton Mills*, pp. 277–86; Gillion, *Ahmedabad – A Study in Indian Urban History*; Salim Lakha, *Capitalism and Class in Colonial India: The Case of Ahmedabad* (New Delhi, 1988).

[11] GOB, Home (Special), File 550 (14) of 1933, File 543 (53) A of 1934 and File 550 (25) IV-A of 1938, MSA.

[12] D. Chakrabarty, 'Communal Riots and Labour: Bengal's Jute Mill Hands in the 1890s', *Past and Present*, 91 (May 1981), 140–69. For an interesting argument which shows that it would be folly to conclude that these apparently 'communal' forms of organization reflected a political consciousness governed by 'community' or the strength of traditional sentiments and primordial loyalties among workers, see Basu, 'Workers' Politics in Bengal, 1890–1929', pp. 117–51.

[13] *Labour Gazette*, 2:7 (March 1923), 26; 'The Kamgar Hitwardhak Sabha: A Brief Sketch', *Indian Textile Journal*, 29 (July 1919), 177–9 and *ibid.*, 29 (August 1919), 209–10. On the earlier and interesting case of Lokhande, see the recent study by Manohar Kadam, *Narayan Meghaji Lokhande: Bharatiya Kamgar Calvalliche Janak* (Bombay, 1995).

[14] MCC, Statements Made by the Accused, Non-Communist Series, Examination of S. H. Jhabvala, p. 756.   [15] GOB Home (Special), File 550 (25) III-A of 1938, MSA.

nist unions during its period in office under provincial autonomy between 1937 and 1939.[16]

In Kanpur, the communist revival of the mid 1930s, master-minded by the organizational genius of P. C. Joshi, stemmed from two sources. First, the existing Kanpur Mazdoor Sabha (KMS) which had been founded in 1919 was led largely by high-caste Hindus, some of whom had been connected with the Arya Samaj. Logically, the communists turned their attention to Muslim workers who had remained largely aloof from the KMS. Second, they attempted to breathe life into old mill committees and neighbourhood committees, and sometimes established new ones. Between 1936 and 1938 the old leadership of the KMS found that their base was moving beneath them, and following the general strike of 1938 the communist ascendancy in the union was complete.[17] In following this strategy, P. C. Joshi and the other communist trade union leaders in Kanpur embarked more systematically on a course which their counterparts in Bombay had discovered accidentally in the later 1920s. It is not intended to suggest that this style of organizing beyond the workplace was peculiar to the communists, but it is clear that in Bombay, and to a lesser extent in Sholapur and Kanpur, they performed it most effectively. The Bombay Textile Labour Union did not by any means stay out of this critical arena of labour politics and N. M. Joshi, who was in official circles for over two decades the most trusted spokesman for the 'labour interest', realized soon enough that his credibility in the councils of government could not be assured if he ignored, or even neglected, the men who cut a figure on the street corner.[18] The Congress organization in the working-class neighbourhoods of Bombay, during the non-violent days of civil disobedience, rested on the broad shoulders of the ex-jobber and neighbourhood boss, Keshav dada Borkar.[19] Ultimately, the most successful trade unions were those which intervened in the informal organizations of the working class, furrowed beneath the existing empires of street and neighbourhood and indeed resurrected their own. What needs to be examined are the factors which determined this style of trade union politics.

Clearly, the divisions of caste and kinship, occupational and neighbourhood cultures intensified tensions, encouraged factions and induced rivalries within unions. However, historians have frequently viewed the problem of trade union rivalries through the wrong end of the telescope.

[16] ATLA Papers, File 3, Part 2, microfilm copy, reel 9, NMML.
[17] S. M. Pandey, 'Ideological Conflict in the Kanpur Trade Union Movement: 1934–1945', *Indian Journal of Industrial Relations*, 3:2 (1967), 243–68.
[18] V. B. Karnik, *N. M. Joshi: Servant of India* (Bombay, 1972).
[19] Chandavarkar, *The Origins of Industrial Capitalism*, pp. 204–11. Also see below, ch. 4.

In this view, pre-industrial societies appear to be characterized by diverse forms of labour use while industrialization increases the homogeneity of the working classes. As workers are concentrated into larger masses, their interests are thought to become more uniform and their struggles are thought to acquire a common base. Historians have thus been constrained to explain in each case why workers did not perceive their interests as uniform and why political differences and rivalries persisted. In India, and as in other cases cast as defective variants of the Western model, pre-industrial survivals in the industrial context appear to explain everything. At the political level, labour history often takes the form of an epic romance in which heroic deeds are followed closely by internecine jealousy and villainous betrayal. However, if the tendency to hypostatize the working class or indeed the assumption that it contained within itself an inherent propensity towards unity was set aside, the problem itself would disappear.

If large-scale industrial production brought large masses of workers together, the sophistication of the division of labour meant that the impact of trade fluctuations or managerial policies were felt differentially throughout the workforce. Industrialization did not always reduce, in fact it often accentuated, competition between workers.[20] Trade union rivalries can only be fully understood in terms of this competition between workers over the supply of raw material or the quality of the machinery; at the level of the jobber system over the control of jobs, the maintenance of wage levels and the domination of neighbourhoods; and over power, at the sometimes autonomous level of politics itself. It would appear from this perspective that rivalry and competition rather than homogeneity were integral to the formation of a labour force and endemic to labour politics. To this extent, the supposedly pre-industrial characteristics of the workforce do not in themselves offer a sufficient explanation for working-class sectionalism and trade union rivalry. On the contrary, employers could bring cultural differences into the workplace and institutionalize them along the lines of the economic divisions created by industrialization.[21] In other words, these supposedly pre-industrial characteristics of the workforce were not epiphenomenal survivals but essential to the process of industrialization. If they informed the tensions and conflicts within trade unions, and could be manipulated by employers to circumscribe the bargaining power of their workers, they did not simply impede trade union growth and, indeed, their linkages could sometimes

---

[20] Chandavarkar, *The Origins of Industrial Capitalism*, chs. 7 and 8.
[21] GOB, Home (Special), File 344 of 1929, pp. 113–15, MSA, for an example of attempts to use Muslim workers to break a strike. See also G. D. Birla to P. Thakurdas, 4 May 1929, Thakurdas Papers, File 81 (II) of 1929, NMML.

be harnessed for organization as well as for action. The bargaining power of industrial workers was not determined by the neutral advance of technology alone, but rather by conflicts waged in order to control its use. These conflicts occurred, however, within an arena which was being defined by the policies of the employers and the state. This chapter will, therefore, turn to an examination of how these arenas were defined and how operating within them shaped the contours and determined the style of trade union politics.

In most industries, jobbers and similar supervisory ranks played a critical role in the maintenance of factory discipline. To some extent, disputes were resolved within the jobber's team or arbitrated upon by head jobbers and other supervisory personnel. When workers attempted to combine, they were as far as possible cajoled, persuaded, threatened or dismissed at these levels. When disputes escalated beyond these levels, employers could continue to manipulate the wage relationship, with its ultimate sanction of dismissal, in order to thwart combinations. As long as a significant proportion of jobbers and workers were not connected with a particular union, there was little need for an employer to deal with it; when it began to acquire any considerable influence among the workers, he could discipline or even dismiss some as a warning to the rest. If their resistance was too great, he could concede in the short term and then gradually begin to replace his employees. At the same time, by choosing whom he would negotiate with, the employer could decisively influence the larger alliances of trade union politics. On the other hand, the strength of a particular trade union in the city as a whole could make it a powerful influence dislocating the sensitive balances upon which labour control rested within an individual factory. As the communist Girni Kamgar Union began to assert its hegemony over the mill districts of Bombay in 1928–29, the Millowners' Association was forced to deal with it at the level of the industry while individual owners could not prevent its intervention at the level of the mill.[22] In general, however, workers who participated in trade union activity were likely to be victimized, discriminated against in the distribution of raw materials or allocation of machinery and unlikely to be promoted.[23]

Employers also sometimes used forms of espionage, systems of political intelligence and even physical force to combat the threat of combination. The Sassoon group of mills in Bombay had an extensive organization for coercion led by one Milton Kubes who styled himself 'a well-known boxer' and claimed to have 'my own secret service'.[24] And indeed he did. Babaji Rane, giving evidence before the Court of Enquiry investigating

[22] See below, ch. 4.   [23] Chandavarkar, *The Origins of Industrial Capitalism*, pp. 403–4.
[24] BRIC, 1929, Oral Evidence, Milton Kubes, File 5, pp. 241–3, MSA.

the 1929 general strike, described himself as a 'a CID man in the Sassoon mills' and said that Kubes was the head of the CID department. Rane himself was an ex-policeman. His job was to take a squad of ten or twelve others to communist meetings, sometimes disguised he said with false moustaches, and armed with a spring which he described as 'a small thing when folded but it can be stretched out and can be used for attacking others'. Their job was to listen to the speeches and 'report to the masters', to bring back any handbills which were issued and 'to create some trouble in the meeting and to see that it was broken up'. Rane was later dismissed by the Sassoon group because he said having had to attend all their meetings and listen to their speeches, he had decided that 'the Red Flag Union was a very good union'.[25] Physical force was more frequently employed against pickets or ordinary workers, occasionally against union leaders. N. G. Ramaswamy's meteoric career as the leader of the Congress Socialist Textile Worker's Union in Coimbatore was brought to a swift conclusion when he was crippled by the assaults upon him, and died as a result of his injuries at the age of thirty-one in 1943.[26]

In an overstocked labour market, industrial action necessarily placed jobs in jeopardy. Faced with a strike, employers often simply dismissed the strikers. Between the wars, workers' militancy made this more difficult for employers and managers to effect as a matter of course in Bombay, for instance, than it was in Ahmedabad, despite its model Textile Labour Association.[27] Unless workers effected a strike, it was often the case that their grievances were not seriously considered by the management; but if they were unable to effect a fairly complete strike, they stood little chance of negotiating their demands with the management, let alone achieving any concessions. If the mood of the workers was too determined and the strike too complete, and especially if the market was in slump, an employer could lock them out until they were harassed by their landlords and their creditors to return or, alternatively, until he was able to organize a new set of jobbers and workers to replace them. When an employer wanted to end a strike quickly, his best bet was to keep production going, essentially by recruiting blacklegs, driving them into the factory and working as many machines as possible. As soon as some workers returned, the danger of losing their jobs often brought several others back to the workplace. The effect of this reaction once set in motion could overcome a sizeable section of the workforce. The employer was then placed in a position from which he could dictate the terms and the time at which the mill would be reopened. At times, and with varying

[25] Proceedings of the Court of Enquiry, 1929, File 5, MSA.
[26] Ramaswamy, *The Worker and His Union*, pp. 17–32.
[27] *Labour Gazette*, Monthly Report on Industrial Disputes, *passim*.

degrees of success, employers were able to call upon the assistance of the state – which could extend, for instance, to providing a police escort to help them take blacklegs into the workplace,[28] sometimes to arrest and prosecute 'agitators', most dramatically, of course, in the Meerut Conspiracy Case, and, periodically, 'to restore order'.

The formidable obstacles to combination are illustrated in a report by the moderate labour leader, B. Shiva Rao, highly respected in official circles, on the difficulties he faced in forming trade unions at Madurai, Tuticorin and Koilpatti. At Madurai and Tuticorin, he reported, the time-keeper had instructed the jobbers 'to attend the meeting I addressed and take down the names of those present'. At Tuticorin,

the Police Circle Inspector and Sub-Inspector stood right in front of me while I was speaking, and it was only when I referred to the prominence of the police at the meeting that they thought it better to move aside and sit down.

Prior to the meeting, a procession in Shiva Rao's 'honour' was organized. It passed the mill gates after 5.30 p.m.; the time-keeper had the gates shut 'until the procession had passed safely beyond the mill gate' and 'everyone was warned that, if he or she attended the meeting there would be punishment'. In Koilpatti, a large majority of the workers lived in quarters provided free of rent by the employers. To enter the premises, it was necessary to pass the house of the head clerk

who apparently is a sort of a watch man. So the movements of any outsiders enquiring into the conditions of the workers are noted. The workers are afraid . . . lest they should be turned out of the mill and simultaneously ejected from their quarters.

His tour of these southern textile towns, not surprisingly, proved a failure. 'The workers are so frightened and coerced,' he wrote plaintively,

that they will not come to a meeting until after dark. I am trying to establish a Trade Union at every centre but the influence of the employer is very strong. The police seem to be on his side, and labour is so plentiful that the workers are afraid of being penalized.

It is possible that in the smaller towns the employers were better placed to exercise such extreme coercion, and that the police were more nervous of the consequences of 'agitation'. When employers attempted to establish their presence in the working-class neighbourhoods of Bombay or the jute mill towns of Calcutta, in this way, as indeed they did, they met with a more fierce and consistent opposition than might have been possible in Koilpatti.[29]

[28] *Times of India*, 8 August 1929.
[29] 'Report by B. Shiva Rao on his visit to Madurai, Tuticorin and Koilpatti to organize Trade Unions', N. M. Joshi Papers, File 36, NMML.

It is scarcely surprising that under these conditions employers were able to prevent workers' combinations from gaining a permanent foothold in the workplace. Since the earliest days of industry, workers had to seek the assistance of agents outside the workplace for the provision of necessary, usually legal, services and, because of the costs of industrial action, to intervene on their behalf, to seek redress for their grievances and, as a corollary, to negotiate and conduct strikes. There is some evidence to suggest that operatives of the Baranagar jute factory in the Calcutta area turned to the law courts as early as the 1860s and 1870s to recover overdue wages and in one case to sue an assistant manager for assault.[30] Similar cases were filed by Bombay's workers in the small causes courts and police courts of the city. By the early twentieth century, pleaders' offices proliferated in the mill districts of the city. Some of them operated under what the commissioner of police described as 'various high-sounding titles such as "Labourers' Union", "Millhands' Association", etc.'.[31] They provided the base upon which Tilak built his following in the 1900s and upon which the Home Rule League arose in the 1910s. In these offices, leave notices were written, grievances received and petitions against unfair dismissal or ill-treatment by superiors were drafted. Occasionally, the most successful pleaders intervened in disputes and attempted to negotiate settlements. Nothing was as good for business or guaranteed to attract custom as the successful negotiation and settlement of a strike.

Between the wars, the legal and administrative structure which impinged upon the working class became more obtrusive and elaborate, creating new arenas in which pleaders and politicians were better equipped to act than the jobbers and workers themselves. Of course, this provided a spur to the formation of trade unions.[32] However, the professionalization of trade unions did not transform their role in industrial relations. They continued to provide workers with social and legal services and receive and seek redress for their grievances. Their success continued to depend largely upon their own entrepreneurial initiative. Workers might seek their favours, often as a last resort. But if they were to swell their clientele or expand their constituencies, they had to find a more effective way of making their presence felt in the workplace.

By the early 1920s, partly in response to the wave of strikes between 1918 and 1922 which affected most parts of the country, some employers

[30] D. Chakrabarty, 'Sasipada Bannerjee: A Study in the Nature of the First Contact of the Bengal Bhadralok with the Working Class of Bengal', *Indian Historical Review*, 2:2 (1976) 339–64.
[31] General Department Order no. 3253/62 – Confidential, 15 May 1917, Bombay Confidential Proceedings, 1917, vol. 25, p. 15, OIOC.
[32] *RCLI, Evidence, Bombay Presidency*, GOB, 'Conditions of Industrial Labour in the Bombay Presidency', vol. I, part i, p. 104.

and, more especially, colonial officials were beginning to talk about the establishment of what they called 'genuine' and 'healthy' trade unions.[33] Their intention was not necessarily to float 'company unions'; rather the underlying calculation was that the institutionalization of workers' combinations would constrain their propensity to effect lightning and spontaneous strikes, which seemed to lack leadership and offered no possibility of mediation until relations had broken down completely. Certainly from 1920 onwards, the Government of India began to nominate a labour representative to the Central Legislative Assembly. Throughout the inter-war period, the positions within legislative assemblies and government councils, the political rewards available to the representatives of labour within the state, were increasing.

The extension of the franchise made the labour vote increasingly difficult to ignore. The Ahmedabad Textile Labour Association played a critical role in the city's municipal politics.[34] Similarly in Calcutta, white-collar employees, transport workers and self-employed groups like rickshaw pullers, blacksmiths and cart and carriage drivers – workers who were most directly affected by the municipal administration – were among the most formally organized workers in the early 1920s, while several self-styled trade union leaders, from C. R. Das to Surendra Nath Mallik, were prominent municipal and provincial politicians.[35] From 1928, four seats were reserved for representatives of labour in the Bombay Municipal Corporation.[36] Similarly, more nominated and later elected seats became available to labour leaders in the provincial legislature.

In themselves, these rewards were not sufficient to support numberless political careers. It is not intended to suggest that these developments alone explain why publicists grew more interested in the cause of labour.

[33] Bombay Confidential Proceedings, Judicial, November 1920, vol. 53, pp. 467–84, OIOC; GOI, Home Poll (B), April 1920, Proc. no. 189, NAI; GOI, Home Poll (B), December 1920, Proc. no. 264, NAI; GOI, Home Poll (B), December 1920, File 291, NAI; GOI, Home Poll (B), December 1920, File 306, NAI; *Report of the Industrial Disputes Committee*; Chakrabarty, 'Conditions for Knowledge of Working-Class Conditions'.

[34] ATLA Papers, File 2, Part 2, microfilm copy, reel 10, NMML. Patel, *The Making of Industrial Relations*, pp. 86–92; see below, ch. 8.

[35] R. K. Ray, *Urban Roots of Indian Nationalism: Pressure Groups and Conflict of Interests in Calcutta City Politics 1875–1939* (New Delhi, 1979), pp. 83–98. Basu, 'Workers' Politics in Bengal, 1890–1929', ch. 5; Siddhartha Guha Ray, 'Tramworkers of Calcutta: Some Reflections on their Unionisation and Political Experience', *Social Scientist*, 156 (May 1986), 15–32; Partho Datta, 'Strikes in the Greater Calcutta Region, 1918–1924', *IESHR*, 30:1 (1993), 57–84; Ira Mitra, 'Growth of Trade Union Consciousness among Jute Mill Workers, 1920–40', *Economic and Political Weekly*, 16:44–6 (November 1981), special number, esp. 1840–1; Sanat Bose, 'Industrial Unrest and the Growth of Labour Unions in Bengal, 1920–1924', *Economic and Political Weekly*, 16:44–6 (November 1981), special number, 1849–60.

[36] *RCLI, Evidence, Bombay Presidency*, GOB, Vol. I, part i, 145–6; *Bombay 1928–29: A Review of the Administration of the Presidency* (Bombay, 1930), pp. 24–5.

However, it is also true that their effect was to create the space for some trade unionists to establish a certain legitimacy as respectable spokesmen and representatives of the labour interest. They might thus be called in by employers to settle disputes; they could hope to be consulted by officials on matters of policy; their influence in the councils of government and the confidence they commanded with employers made them useful allies for jobbers, workers and the lesser leaders of the neighbourhood. In practice, this position was difficult to achieve and sometimes impossible to main-tain. At times, their credentials were challenged by the employers and the state. At others, their pretensions were rejected by their constituents. More permanently, they were subjected to the competition of rivals. To establish themselves as important spokesmen for labour, politicians had to organize and control as many unions as possible. Thus, a few individ-uals in the labour movement controlled a vast number of unions. N. M. Joshi was the general secretary of the All-India Trade Union Congress until the split in 1929 and was president or treasurer of twelve other Bombay unions. Until he was imprisoned in the Meerut Conspiracy Case, S. H. Jhabvala was connected with at least twenty unions.[37] In the later 1930s, P. K. K. Sarma was an office-bearer in thirty-seven unions in Madras.[38] The list of multiple office-holding in trade unions could be considerably extended both in Bombay and elsewhere. The largest unions were often built upon extensive, if sometimes uncertain, alliances. Thus Jhabvala said of N. M. Joshi, 'He appointed me as an office-bearer in one of his unions and I appointed him as one in mine', and of another oligarch of Bombay labour, F. J. Ginwalla (who was himself connected with thirteen local unions), 'We had a constitutional understanding that we would nominate each other wherever we thought it necessary to do anywhere and at any time.'[39]

By controlling an extensive network which spread itself across several trades, these men acquired important advantages in the conduct of indus-trial disputes. They could prevent casual workers in one trade being hired to break a strike in another and crucially they could command greater financial resources. These advantages were manifested most often on a local scale, but in the mid-1920s, N. M. Joshi was inundated with requests from all over India for a share in the funds, collected by and donated to the All-India Trade Union Congress.[40] His response was to

---

[37] *RCLI, Evidence, Bombay Presidency*, GOB, 'Conditions of Industrial Labour', vol. I, part i, p. 112.

[38] D. Arnold, 'Labour Relations in a South India Sugar Factory 1937–39', *Social Scientist*, 65 (December 1977), 16–33.

[39] *Proceedings of the MCC*, Statements Made by the Accused, Non-Communist Series, S. H. Jhabvala, pp. 731, 788.

[40] N. M. Joshi Papers, Files 23, 36, 37, NMML. These files indicate the wide range of unions with which Joshi became involved.

send small sums to those applicants who could prove their need. But the bulk of this money appears to have been used to provide rations and relief to the Bombay millworkers during the 1928 general strike.[41]

Although a few individuals came to dominate the trade union movement at this level, beneath them lay a closely woven web of alignments which ultimately held them captive. The number of unions they controlled was no reflection of their influence among the workers. Several trade unionists found it difficult to enlist members, mainly because of the tenuous connection of such organizations with the daily problems of the workplace. Moreover, attempts to organize workers earned the suspicion of employers, while at the same time the conduct of industrial action intensified their dilemma. If they supported a strike, they earned the displeasure of the employers and probably the state. If they remained aloof, their paper empires could be swept aside by the militancy of the workers or the intervention of more adventurous rivals. Thus, N. M. Joshi's Bombay Textile Labour Union was pulled by the momentum of industrial action into the general strike of 1928. With better-established political connections and more to lose from possible failure, Joshi advocated caution. On the other hand, the isolated communists of the Bombay Labour Group calculated that to lead a strike when the mood of the millworkers was militant offered an invaluable opportunity to establish contacts and extend organization among them.[42] During the course of the strike, the communists were able to burrow beneath the foundations of the Bombay Textile Labour Union and emerged as the dominant force in the city's labour movement.

The Ahmedabad Textile Labour Association, usually portrayed as exceptional to the general pattern of trade union development, was bedevilled by rather similar problems. More strikes occurred without its authority than with its leadership and strikes were frequently accompanied by the dismissal and replacement of strikers. It exercised little influence with the most skilled and most militant section of the workforce, the weavers, who tended to organize outside the union. However, the machinery for the arbitration of disputes which Gandhi had persuaded the Ahmedabad millowners to accept in 1923 institutionalized the Textile Labour Association as the main and most effective channel through which workers could express their grievances.[43] But the millowners tended to ignore this machinery and preferred the freedom to make separate settlements, outside the existing institutions of arbitration.

---

[41] The accounts of the Joint Mill Strike Committee in Bombay during the 1928 general strike are to be found in N. M. Joshi Papers, Files 47 and 48, NMML.

[42] See below, ch. 4.

[43] Patel, *The Making of Industrial Relations*, pp. 31–63.

Labour policy became the cause of open schism within the Ahmedabad Millowners' Association, while at the same time the arbitration machinery threatened to break down and take away with it much of the union's organization.[44]

For those trade unions whose existence was not underwritten by the relative tolerance of the employers or the state, there was little alternative but to generate their connections through action.[45] They were forced to pursue strategies of confrontation. Thus, they had to meddle in the daily disputes of the workplace, be willing to take up even minor grievances and, above all, to demonstrate their ability to secure favourable settlements for their members. This was by no means easy to achieve. The costs of industrial action were high and militant workers always a target for retrenchment or dismissal. The wider the union's base, the less individual employers could isolate it at the workplace; yet such a base could only be built up across an industry or an industrial centre by intervening relentlessly at the level of the individual workplace. However, at certain times, such a strategy of confrontation enabled trade unions to escalate out of the repressive structure of industrial relations. By intervening in minor strikes, confined to individual departments and mills, these outriders of the trade union movement were able to generate sufficient momentum for large-scale action. Necessarily, they established themselves most successfully during general strikes. Moreover, in relation to their rivals, they had a further advantage. Since most workers' combinations were effectively excluded from the workplace, trade unions which intervened energetically in minor disputes and assiduously aired workers' grievances, were able to forge closer and more direct connections with the workplace. Excluded from the workplace, these unions often paid closer attention to building up connections in the neighbourhood than some of their counterparts. They were able to use these connections to prevent blacklegs usurping the jobs of strikers, to persuade grain merchants to extend credit to their members, and in various ways to sustain industrial action despite the overwhelming obstacles it encountered.

In the aftermath of the 1928 general strike, the Girni Kamgar Union was able to formalize these connections, built up through industrial action, both in the neighbourhood and in the workplace, through their union centres and mill committees.[46] The repressive onslaught upon the union and its allies and supporters, orchestrated by the employers and the

---

[44] G. L. Nanda to S. G. Banker, 23 March 1933, ATLA Papers, File 40, pp. 77–83, microfilm copy, reel no. 1, NMML. These issues are more extensively treated in ch. 8, below. See also Patel, *The Making of Industrial Relations.*   [45] See below, ch. 4.
[46] *Proceedings of the MCC*, Statement submitted by S. A. Dange, pp. 2498–557. See ch. 4 below.

state, which followed the next general strike in 1929 swept these institutions away. But between 1932 and 1934, the Girni Kamgar Union once more asserted itself through minor strikes which breathed life into these old, withering linkages and culminated in the general strike of 1934.[47] For trade unions like the Girni Kamgar Union, faced with exclusion at the level of the individual mill, lacking the goodwill of the employers, and sometimes subjected to repression by the state, it was clear that they could not consolidate through patronage the linkages forged in action. To function as a trade union at all, they had often to adopt a stance of continued opposition to the employers and the state. In this way, the structure of repression which trade unions were forced to confront impelled them towards increasing and sometimes frenetic activism simply in order to survive.

Trade union leaders who adopted this interventionist style were in the late 1920s known to the jute millworkers of Bengal as 'the strike babus'.[48] Moni Singh, the veteran communist leader of Bengal, and subsequently chairman of the Communist Party of Bangladesh, has left us an instructive, if somewhat surreal, account of their political style.[49] Having accepted 'the contention' of the time that 'the workers were the most revolutionary class', Moni Singh left for Calcutta in 1926 'to start work among them'. Almost as if he was enacting the fondest fantasies which intelligence officers entertained about 'Bolsheviks', he set up an office on Clive Street 'with the name, Oriental Trading', presumably as a front for what he hoped would be his revolutionary activities. His primary 'objective', of course, was 'to find out how one could join the working-class movement'. Here he was at first thwarted. Although he met a number of 'communist-minded' activists, Moni Singh 'could find no opportunity to participate in the workers' movement'. Then 'one day in 1928', two whole years later, comrades Gopen Chakraborty and Dharani Goswami came to his house to announce 'a tremendous opportunity to get involved in the workers' movement'. K. C. Mitra, once a railway clerk, now a sadhu, and known as Jatadhari Babu in deference to his matted hair, had organized a strike in the Railway workshop at Lilooah. Moni Singh 'rushed' with his comrades to the Lilooah Railway Union Office and arrived the following day. 'Just then a non-Bengali worker came and asked in Hindi' for Jatadhari Babu. The millhands of the Keshoram Cotton Mills in Metiaburuz had gone on strike and, said the worker, they wanted him to represent them. 'Jatadhari

---

[47] GOB, Home (Special), Files 543 (48), 543 (48) K, 543 (48) L, 543 (48) J, 543 (48) E, MSA.
[48] Mitra, 'Trade Union Consciousness among Jute Mill Workers', p. 1841.
[49] Moni Singh, *Life is a Struggle*, tr. Mrs Karuna Banerjee (New Delhi, 1988), pp. 17 ff. I am grateful to Subho Basu for drawing this passage to my attention.

was not in the office at the time.' Jatadhari Babu was a 'reformist' and Moni Singh and his comrades were scarcely that. Undaunted and now fretting for action, they presented themselves to 'the non-Bengali' weaver, Rehman, as the sadhu's followers, offered on these false pretences to help in his absence, and accordingly accompanied him to the mill.

Metiaburuz was quite far from that place. We three arrived there. The workers were very happy to see us. Most of the workers in the Keshoram Mills were non-Bengali, people from Bihar and UP. The workers began to explain to us in chaste Urdu, why they had gone on strike. It was a language we did not know. Neither did we have any experience of textile mills. Gopen Da had a smattering of Hindi. Even he failed to understand much. Seeing our blank looks, the workers realized that we could follow nothing. They said, 'Come to the Secretary Sahib'. Though called secretary, he was actually the manager. The manager was an educated Marwari gentleman, young in age. We considered it better to see the manager, because we could not understand the problem at all . . . We told him we were nationalist activists. We had come to find out the cause of the strike in the mill. The secretary welcomed us and asked us to sit down.

The point he made was that previously the weavers used to be paid by the weight . . . Now they would be paid by the yard. This system is followed all over the world. The Birlas were noble people. They could not possibly harm the workers. The workers were fools, they had gone on strike without understanding anything. Though we had no knowledge about these things, we came to a conclusion on the basis of our principle that the bourgeoisie could never do anything good for the workers. On this basis, we argued blindly. For we did not have the least idea about wages in a mill.[50]

Subsequently, posing as 'a nationalist activist', Moni Singh sought out the weaving master at the Bangalaxmi Mill at Serampore to seek guidance on the intricacies of the various methods of wage calculation. Fortified by this knowledge, he returned to Metiaburuz where he set up a union and 'within a few months' had acquired 'a working knowledge of Hindi and Urdu'.[51] Of course, it is not intended to suggest that the radicals were alone in encountering the problems created for publicists by the social and linguistic gulf which separated them from the workers, but rather it is important to recognize that to secure a foothold at the workplace, when they were excluded from it, trade unionists often required considerable resources of inventiveness, imagination and ingenuity.

The changing arenas of labour politics also helped to facilitate strategies of confrontation. Increasingly, in the inter-war period, employers' associations became necessary instruments in attempts to influence government fiscal, monetary and financial policies. During the slump of the early 1920s and the early 1930s some centralized attempts, only partially

[50] Ibid., pp. 21–2.   [51] Ibid., p. 24.

successful, were made to control production, maintain price levels and sometimes to reduce competition.[52] However, in the cotton textile industry as much as in jute, the conditions and character of production as well as the methods and objectives of labour management varied considerably from mill to mill. Necessarily, individual mill managements remained wary of the centralizing initiatives of their employers' association. It cannot be said that employers' associations successfully centralized the power to formulate and enforce policies across each industry. However, it is clear that individual mill managements were more closely affected by the policies of their associations in the inter-war period than they were before 1914. As policies were formulated for the entire industry, labour responded at the same level. This facilitated the generalization of disputes, which in turn opened the door to the more adventurous strategies of some trade unions. Unlike Bombay, Calcutta was relatively free of general strikes. Yet the general strikes in the jute industry in 1929 and 1937 followed policies regarding increased hours of work in the case of the former, and rationalization in the case of the latter, formulated not by individual employers but by the Indian Jute Mills' Association for the industry as a whole.[53] In Bombay, the general strike of 1928 became general when it was clear that rationalization schemes introduced in particular mills had begun to spread throughout the industry and when it was recognized that resistance at the level of the individual mill had failed to halt their progress.[54] It was frequently at moments of extensive, industry-wide action that trade unions like the Girni Kamgar Union were able to establish themselves or retrieve their position in labour politics.

This argument which differentiates between two fairly general styles of

[52] A. K. Bagchi, *Private Investment in India 1900–1939* (Cambridge, 1972), chs. 6, 7 and 8; On the cotton textile industry, see Chandavarkar, *The Origins of Industrial Capitalism*, pp. 239–396; on the jute industry, see O. Goswami, *Industry, Trade and Peasant Society: The Jute Economy of Eastern India, 1900–1947* (Delhi, 1991); O. Goswami, 'Sahibs, Babus and Banias: Changes in Industrial Control in Eastern India, 1918–1950', *JAS*, 48:2 (1989), 289–309; Goswami, 'Collaboration and Conflict'; O. Goswami, 'Then Came the Marwaris: Some Aspects of the Changes in the Pattern of Industrial Control in Eastern India', *IESHR*, 22:3 (1985), 225–49; and Chakrabarty, *Rethinking Working Class History*, ch. 1.

[53] P. Saha, *History of the Working Class Movement in Bengal* (New Delhi, 1978), pp. 114–31, 148–70; Karnik, *Strikes*, pp. 234–48, 284–6; on the 1929 general strike, see Basu, 'Workers' Politics in Bengal, 1890–1929', ch. 6, esp. pp. 208–21; Chakrabarty, *Rethinking Working Class History*, pp. 196–205; O. Goswami, 'Multiple Images: Jute Mill Strikes of 1929 and 1937 Seen Through Other's Eyes', *MAS*, 21:3 (1987), 547–83.

[54] Proceedings of the BSEC, vol. I, pp. 71–2, MSA. On the nature of rationalization and attempts to implement it, see Chandavarkar, *The Origins of Industrial Capitalism*, pp. 335–96; and Rajnarayan Chandavarkar, 'Workers' Resistance and the Rationalization of Work in Bombay between the Wars', in D. Haynes and G. Prakash (eds.), *Contesting Power: Resistance and Everyday Social Relations in South Asia* (Berkeley and Los Angeles, 1991), pp. 109–44.

trade union politics needs to be qualified. Of course, no simple distinction between strategies of patronage and confrontation are tenable. Trade unions which restricted their dealings to the councils of state and the offices of the managers discovered that the promise of future concessions or the lure of patronage were not enough to hold their organization together, let alone allay immediate grievances. Similarly, the linkages of direct action had to be consolidated. There was little point in effecting industrial action if it secured no concession or merely invited repression. It was crucial for all unions, excluded from the workplace, to maintain their connections with it. The crux of the matter lay in getting the minor as well as the major grievances of the workers settled. As one labour leader pointed out, 'If workers find that the Union does not function properly with the Millowners' Association, and that their legitimate grievances are not redressed then naturally their influence goes down.'[55] At some point or other, company unions had to support a strike and yet try to protect their favoured status, while the most radical unions had to face the dilemma of how to reflect the militancy of their members without permitting it to go too far. Thus the Girni Kamgar Union, too, floundered at times between conciliation and opposition. Despite the hostility of the Congress Government of 1937–9, it seemed reluctant to initiate industrial action. After 1942, it performed a major holding operation on working-class politics. By 1947, its support had declined as a result and its dominant position in the industry was soon eclipsed.[56]

If the structure of dominance and control at work decisively influenced the nature of trade union activity, it also shaped the forms of action. Certain issues, under existing conditions of labour management, could only be confronted through general strikes which encompassed an entire industry and which admirably suited a militant style of trade union politics. However, historians have sometimes taken the frequency of lightning strikes and what they perceived as the riotous, even 'violent' nature of industrial action to be characteristic of labour politics in the early stages of industrialization.[57] It is difficult to reconcile this picture of primordial consciousness with the more sophisticated political consciousness manifested in the extended, well-organized general strikes by the same workers in the same centres of industry. Once again, the beginnings of a more plausible explanation will rest in the considerable risks which

[55] Proceedings of the Court of Enquiry, File 6, R. R. Bakhale, MSA; see also *RCLI, Evidence, Bombay Presidency*, The Bombay Textile Labour Union, vol. I, part i, pp. 352–56.
[56] Fortnightly Reports, 1937–47, L/P + J/5/163, OIOC; GOB Home (Special), File 543 (13) B (3) of 1940, 543 (13) B (4) of 1941–3, 543 (13) B (5) of 1943–5, MSA.
[57] For instance, Arnold, 'Industrial Violence'; Chakrabarty, 'On Deifying and Defying Authority'. See ch. 5 below.

industrial action entailed. In view of the powerful constraints upon the initiation and conduct of industrial action, for workers to warn their employers in advance that they would strike was also to allow the latter the time and opportunity to subvert industrial action and dismiss its protagonists. As R. R. Bakhale, a moderate trade union leader who was never throughout his long and illustrious career willingly involved in leading a strike, informed a Court of Enquiry in 1929, there was often no time for workers to notify the employers of their intention to strike. 'The conditions in the textile industry are such', said Bakhale, referring to the widespread opposition among employers to trade union organization, 'that lightning strikes, whatever they may be, are inevitable.'[58] Indeed, the definition of lightning strikes – 'whatever they may be' as Bakhale put it – was often the subject of debate and in a sense the object of struggle between employers, trade unions and workers. Wild-cat strikes, then, were not an expression of uninhibited spontaneity; more frequently, they entailed strategic calculation.

This element of calculation did not relate simply to wages and working conditions. The forms which strikes sometimes took suggest that they were staged as an appeal to a higher level of authority.[59] Lightning strikes, when workers stopped their machines and assembled briefly in the mill compound in protest against their treatment by a supervisor, could be designed to invite the intervention of the manager; the daily processions and mass rallies during general strikes not only maintained morale but more widely asserted the importance of their cause; when strikers stoned mill after mill in order to close them down, this was in part a response to blacklegging and the risks consequent upon a partial stoppage, but it sometimes also drove officials to persuade employers to negotiate. Certainly, the forms of struggle as they developed and changed deserve investigation. It is possible that forms of collective action manifested in particular social contexts emerged from and evolved out of an older experience of struggle. In any event, the spectacular, and sometimes riotous, character of industrial action was in part adapted to the audience for which it was performed. Faced with the determined opposition of factory managers, workers sought thereby to attract the notice of the employer and more usually the state in order to have their grievances heard and redressed. The colonial state did not by any means constitute only the audience in the theatre of industrial relations. It frequently intervened as an active participant; occasionally, it performed the leading role. For one thing what began as a dispute between employers and workers could rapidly acquire a public dimension. When workers left their

[58] Proceedings of the Court of Enquiry, 1929, R. R. Bakhale, File 7, MSA.
[59] See below, ch. 4.

factories and impinged upon the social spaces of the street, they were often quickly perceived to represent a considerable threat to the social order.[60]

Since the nineteenth century, the police had intervened and sometimes even arbitrated in industrial disputes.[61] Well into the twentieth century, even as negotiations were conducted at more centralized levels of the administration, the police continued to act at more discrete levels, dissuading workers in their chawls from joining a union, attending a meeting or striking. They might even attempt to persuade shopkeepers to withhold their credit to strikers.[62] More overtly, they intervened only to the detriment of the workers' interest where earlier they may occasionally have defended it. At times, police action defeated pickets and protected or aided blacklegs and often contributed to the suppression of their demands and destruction of their organizations. Although police action did not constitute as much of a permanent and structural obstacle to trade union development as the policies of employers, changes in police practice did affect the way in which the working class came to perceive the state and decisively influenced the development of their political consciousness.[63]

The presence of the state also began to be felt in the growing body of legislation which governed industrial relations. Laws were passed to compel the registration of trade unions, thus opening their books to official scrutiny, to install procedures for the conciliation and arbitration of disputes and to require from workers notice of their intention to strike, thereby differentiating between legal and illegal stoppages, while providing employers with the opportunity of subverting industrial action before it was effected. From the mid-1930s, a series of measures were taken which were applicable specifically to Bombay and designed to isolate the communist Girni Kamgar Union further from its members and sympathizers in the mills.[64] The Trade Disputes Act of 1934 made provision for the appointment of a government Labour Officer whose function would be to receive workers' grievances and seek to remedy them and thus, while addressing the avoidable causes of popular discontent, they could encroach upon, and even, perhaps, usurp the traditional role of the trade union.[65] Later, in 1938, the Congress Ministry in Bombay passed further

---

[60] See ch. 5 below.
[61] S. M. Edwardes, *The Bombay City Police – A Historical Sketch 1672–1916* (London, 1923). See ch. 6 below.
[62] *RCLI, Evidence, Madras Presidency*, B. Shiva Rao, vol. VII, part ii, p. 202.
[63] See below, ch. 4.
[64] Note by Home Member, 16 May 1934, GOB Home (Special), File 543 (48) L, p. 26, MSA; *BMOA Annual Report 1934*, pp. 22–4.
[65] A. W. Pryde, 'The Work of the Labour Office', in C. Manshardt (ed.), *Some Social Services of the Government of Bombay* (Bombay, 1937).

legislation which made conciliation compulsory and stipulated that trade unions, to be representative, had to count among their members a quarter of the workforce.[66] It also laid down elaborate procedures of notice, negotiation, conciliation and arbitration as necessary stages preceding a strike and thus robbed the workers of any advantage they may have gained from determining the timing of a strike. Further legislation in 1946 was passed to encourage the development of a single union for each industry, on conditions which favoured the Congress trade union, the Rashtriya Mill Mazdoor Sangh.[67] Of course, it is not intended to suggest that legislative fiat alone could undermine the Girni Kamgar Union after 1938 but there can be little doubt that this spate of measures served to severely narrow its freedom of manoeuvre.

Outside Bombay, industrial disputes legislation was less marked by this heavily repressive character. For the most part, and in Bombay perhaps at least until 1940, and arguably even later, the manipulation of, as well as the control exercised through, the wage relationship was a more persistent and formidable obstacle to combination than the laws of the state. Moreover, the colonial state was not committed to the unilateral repression of industrial workers,[68] however nervous it may have been of the development of class struggle within the context of nationalist agitation. On the contrary, there are signs that in the aftermath of the civil disobedience movement, the Government of India, reassured that Indian business interests would hold Congress radicalism in check, began to court labour's friendship and initiate some protective legislation, even to the detriment of Indian business interests.[69] Labour in its turn could now be encouraged to step forward as colonial collaborators. The legacy of these initiatives was witnessed in the first phase of provincial autonomy until the Congress began in 1938 to set the process in reverse.

These sometimes insuperable obstacles which workers faced in forming a trade union, establishing its presence at the workplace and coordinating its activities across an industry even in the same locality provides an indication of the scale of the problems which engulfed attempts to create a national framework for trade union organization.[70] If at the level

[66] GOB Home (Special), Files 550 (24) of 1938, 550 (25) III A, MSA; ATLA Papers, File 3, part 2, microfilm copy reel 9, NMML; AITUC Papers, File 59, NMML.
[67] Morris, *Industrial Labour Force*, pp. 193–5; R. C. James, 'Trade Union Democracy: Indian Textiles', *The Western Political Quarterly*, 11:3 (1958), 566–72.
[68] This assumption is widely made: for an example, see Arnold, 'Industrial Violence'.
[69] The signs were to be found in the greater willingness of the state to countenance limited welfare legislation, see *Labour Gazette*, 16:10 (June 1937) 760–3; *ibid.*, 16:11 (July 1937), 846–50; *ibid.*, 16:12 (August, 1937), 926–37. The anxieties of the Bombay millowners in this respect can be followed in the Minute Books of the Committee of the BMOA, 1934–8, Office of the BMOA.
[70] N. M. Joshi, *The Trade Union Movement in India* (Poona, 1927).

of particular industries and cities, trade unions operated at one level removed from the workplace, at the national level they rarely, if ever, became effective bargaining agents. The All-India Trade Union Congress was formed in 1920 in order to elect delegates to represent Indian labour at the International Labour Conference.[71] Five years later, the president of the AITUC described his own role in the trade union movement as 'nugatory'.[72] This self-deprecation was unwarranted since scarcely anything more positive could be said about the organization over which he presided. In the mid-1920s, it functioned around the redoubtable figure of N. M. Joshi, principally as a treasury to which real unions brought their begging bowls.[73] The attempt by the communists to capture the AITUC in the late 1920s enlivened its politics. Following the collapse of the Bombay Textile Labour Union, N. M. Joshi attempted to come to terms with V. V. Giri and B. Shiva Rao, 'moderates' or 'reformists' concerned largely with South Indian labour, in a bid to outflank the communists in the AITUC.[74] The culmination of these manoeuvres was that the AITUC split at its Nagpur session in 1929, when Joshi, Giri and their friends left to form a rival Indian Trades Union Federation.[75] Significantly, the issue which split the AITUC was to which international federation it should affiliate, despite the fact that its national existence was largely fictional. Thus, in 1928 and 1929, the AITUC witnessed some excitement. However, even at this period of its greatest activity, its president, Jawaharlal Nehru, complained that the job bored him. He wrote to D. B. Kulkarni, the rival candidate for the presidency at the previous Trade Union Congress, to tell him that he had not wanted to take up the office. 'Owing to my absence' [at the Jharia Congress], he confessed, 'I was elected and later I did not know how to get out of it . . . I am glad however that my period in office is coming to an end.'[76] After this brief flurry, the national unions settled down to a further period of inactivity. In 1932, the secretary of the newly formed Trade Union Federation reported that the organization had not found it possible 'to concentrate much of our time to questions directly connected with the working class', let alone 'to give

---

[71] *AITUC – Fifty Years On: Documents*, introduction by S. A. Dange (AITUC, New Delhi 1973), vol. I.
[72] C. F. Andrews to N. M. Joshi, 18 September 1925, AITUC Papers, File I, NMML.
[73] N. M. Joshi Papers, Files 2, 6, 13, 14, 15, 21, 25, 30, 31, 33; AITUC Papers, File I, NMML.
[74] B. Shiva Rao to R. R. Bakhale, 10 February 1929, N. M. Joshi Papers, File 36, NMML; see also V. V. Giri, *My Life and Times*, vol. I (Delhi, 1976), pp. 67–8, 46–75.
[75] AICC Papers, File 12 of 1929, NMML; B. Shiva Rao, *The Industrial Worker in India* (London, 1939) pp. 149–77; C. Revri, *The Indian Trade Union Movement: An Outline History 1880–1947* (New Delhi, 1972), pp. 115–71.
[76] J. Nehru to D. B. Kulkarni, 10 September 1929, AICC Papers, File 16 of 1929, p. 113, NMML.

direct help to the affiliated unions when they had been engaged in struggles against their employers'.[77]

By the late 1930s, attempts were being made to patch up the differences of the previous decade.[78] To a large extent, these developments at the national level were responses to local imperatives. If the split in 1929 can be explained largely in terms of the trade union rivalries in Bombay city, the attempts at unity in the later 1930s were the result of the repression of the communists, the expectations aroused by the prospect of gains to be made from the newly elected Congress Government and, finally, the wisdom, indeed necessity, of all trade unions in Bombay to close their ranks against the threat of the passing of the 1938 Industrial Disputes Bill. It was only after the 1950s that trade unions acquired a national framework, but this was in part the outcome of their close connections with political parties and their considerable importance for elections, for the first time based on universal franchise.

The Congress Party, which may have taken a more active role in creating such a national framework, remained for the most part aloof from trade union politics. It never regretted its connections with the Ahmedabad Textile Labour Association (ATLA); in fact it guarded these connections jealously, never allowing the ATLA to join up with any of the national federations.[79] Yet having developed strong and intimate links with the ATLA, it neither wanted nor sought any further trade union affiliations. To associate too closely with a particular class interest was for the Congress to sacrifice other more powerful groups which coalesced within it and to surrender its claim to solely represent the nation as a whole.[80] As Nehru wrote when he presided over the AITUC, 'Of course, everyone knows that the Congress is not a labour organization . . . To expect it to act as a pure labour organization is a mistake. The National Congress is a large body comprising all manner of people.'[81] In the 1930s, the Congress Socialist Party professed a more direct interest in the working class and played a more active role in trade union organization.[82] But their activities were conducted, not as organic parts of the national

---

[77] Quoted by Revri, *Indian Trade Union Movement*, pp. 195–6.

[78] N. M. Joshi Papers, File 75; AICC Papers, File LI/1935 and PL-2/1938; AITUC Papers, Files 59 and 60, NMML.

[79] Anasuya Sarabhai to General Secretary, Textile Labour Union, Bombay, 21 April 1927, N. M. Joshi Papers, File 32, p. 75, NMML; P. P. Lakshman, *Congress and the Labour Movement in India* (Congress Economic and Political Studies, no. 3, Economic and Political Research Department, All-India Congress Committee, Allahabad, 1947).

[80] See ch. 8 below.

[81] J. Nehru to D. B. Kulkarni, 10 September 1929, AICC Papers, File 16 of 1929, pp. 111–13, NMML.

[82] GOB Home (Special), Files 800 (75) A to 800 (75) A VII of 1938–42 (7 files); File 800 (75) AB of 1935 and File 800 (75) D-(I) of 1938, MSA.

body, but, in their private capacity, as one group among the 'all manner of people' which the Congress comprised. Consequently, by the mid-1930s, organizing and representing labour had become a specialist activity for politicians and publicists.[83]

Labour organizations did not officially participate in the Congress agitations of the early 1920s, early 1930s or early 1940s. Gandhi and the Congress sometimes actively discouraged workers from entering the lists. But the workers did not always follow their leaders' bidding, least of all in Ahmedabad, and even in Bombay industrial workers, with varying degrees of enthusiasm at different times, participated in the nationalist agitations.[84] The depth and character of working-class nationalism is not easily assessed. Its particular social meaning, in the context of the highly localized political experience of workers, is difficult to determine. Clearly, this nationalism did not arise out of commitment to a territorial principle or even from the concern that the interests of the Indian people were homogeneous. It was probably fed by the racial conflicts between European or Eurasian foremen and Indian workers on the railways.[85] It appears to have been more marked in Bengal where capital was overwhelmingly dominated by Europeans and the jute mills were both owned and managed by them.[86] The increasing realization that the colonial state in the 1920s and 1930s was hostile and repressive in its attitude to labour politics encouraged workers to identify with movements apparently directed against it.[87] Conversely, the increasingly vociferous nationalist campaigns also helped workers to crystallize their antagonism towards the state and thereby to identify their own solidarities.

The weakness of trade union organization in India has often been attributed to 'the early stages of industrialization' and the 'pre-capitalist mentalities' of the workers. But it would be difficult to make sense, within these evolutionary terms, of the impressive solidarities which workers forged at the same time or the fiercely disputed and protracted strikes

[83] See ch. 8 below.
[84] Patel, *The Making of Industrial Relations*; see ch. 8 below, where these issues are addressed more fully.
[85] Arnold, 'Industrial Violence'; Lajpat Jagga, 'Colonial Railwaymen and British Rule: A Probe into Railway Labour Agitation in India, 1919–1922', in B. Chandra (ed.), *The Indian Left: Critical Appraisals* (New Delhi, 1983), pp. 103–45; *Proceedings of the MCC*, Defence Statement, K. N. Joglekar, pp. 1766–965.
[86] Chakrabarty, *Rethinking Working Class History*, ch. 5; Bagchi, *Private Investment in India*, ch. 8; Tomlinson, 'Colonial Firms and the Decline of Colonialism in Eastern India'; Basu, 'Workers' Politics in Bengal, 1890–1929', ch. 3. On Kanpur, Chitra Joshi, 'Worker Protest, Managerial Authority and Labour Organization: Kanpur Textile Industry', NMML, Occasional Papers on History and Society, no. 27 (1985), pp. 10–11; Zoe Yolland, *Boxwallahs: The British in Cawnpore, 1857–1901* (Norwich, 1994).
[87] This argument is elaborated in ch. 4 below; see also Chandavarkar, *The Origins of Industrial Capitalism*, especially ch. 9.

which they repeatedly sustained. The nature of the labour movement in India cannot be deduced either by measuring the level of industrialization or by the divination of a particular social consciousness. Rather, its growth and its limitations were shaped by the political conditions of its development.

The formation of trade unions and their methods of operation can most fully be grasped in relation to the formidable obstacles to combination. The fragility of trade union organizations, their tendency to collapse and disappear as suddenly as they formed, and their failure to entrench themselves within the framework of industrial relations were largely the consequence of the sustained attempts by employers to repress them at the point of production. The apparent volatility of strikers, their seeming propensity to take 'lightning' action and the violence which sometimes occurred between strikers and blacklegs were often symptoms of the repression of labour organization. It is not intended to suggest that the emergence of trade unions would have directed workers towards apparently more 'responsible' forms of negotiation and bargaining but rather that the repression by the employers infused the politics of the workplace, in every aspect, with the imminent possibility of 'violence'. As employers sought to repress workers' combination, sometimes with the calculated support and sometimes the unwitting complicity of the state, they began to define the arenas within which labour resistance took shape. In turn, having to operate within these arenas shaped the nature of trade union organization and forms of action. Undermined within the workplace by the sustained hostility of the employers, workers' combinations had to draw sustenance from the social relations of the neighbourhood. Frequently dismissed when they expressed their own grievances, workers had to seek the intervention of 'outsiders', intermediaries and political agents. Denied the means of negotiating with their employers, workers and their representatives were sometimes forced to adopt a strategy of confrontation which imposed its own pattern of labour relations and collective bargaining. Indeed, the militancy and volatility of the workforce often became a means of insuring against the considerable sanctions imposed upon strikers. Conversely, if trade union weakness belied the solidarities which workers forged, their industrial and political action did not necessarily find enduring expression in trade union organization. The formation of trade unions offers no index of the nature of working-class consciousness. No simple, direct and necessary relationship linked consciousness, organization and action.

The history of the labour movement in India has commonly been treated as a special case, which was unlikely, precisely because of its economic backwardness and its cultural peculiarities, to release materials for thinking more generally about class formation and consciousness. In fact, the development of the labour movement in India suggests that the origins and development of trade unions in general calls for a political, rather than a specifically social or cultural, explanation. The development of trade unions was largely conditioned by, perhaps dependent upon, the willingness of employers and the state to tolerate them. It neither signified the development of a particular stage of class consciousness nor did it anticipate the rise of socialism. The quotient of capitalist tolerance for labour organization has usually been determined by the outcome of the changing relations between workers, trade unions and the state. Significantly, it has depended upon the political leverage which workers were able to gain upon state power, and thereby, through political pressure and negotiation, to raise the threshold of capitalist tolerance. States have been opened up to a measure of working-class influence when the coalition of interests by which they are constituted has recognized the need to expand and diversify their social bases in order to secure their dominance, sometimes by widening the franchise and extending the representation they afford to the working classes within the institutions of the state. Of course, it is the threat of industrial and political action which has, most commonly, forced this recognition upon ruling elites. Conversely, as the working classes have consolidated their position within the alliances which constituted the state, so workers' struggles and their institutional and political forms have been able to exercise greater leverage upon it. In this sense, the growth of trade unions and the development of labour movements may be more plausibly explained in terms of the stake which the working classes were allowed in the nation and the political entitlements which they were able to wrest from the state rather than the languages of capitalism and class alone.

4   Workers' politics and the mill districts in Bombay between the wars

Between the wars, the development of a labour movement in Bombay reflected a growing polarization in social and political relations in the city. This period, which saw an intensification of social conflict, also witnessed changes in the character of industrial action. Until 1914, strikes in the cotton industry were largely confined to particular departments and mills; increasingly, after the war, they were coordinated across the industry as a whole. Rising prices and unprecedented profits which accompanied the post-war boom led to the demand for higher wages supported by two general strikes. In the mid-1920s, as the industry's markets slumped, attempts to cut wages were once again strongly resisted. With a slight improvement in their fortunes in the later 1920s, the millowners introduced 'rationalization' schemes; for the workforce this meant more work, less wages and higher chances of unemployment. Between April 1928 and September 1929, two general strikes crippled the industry for about eleven months, and the extension of these schemes and a further round of wage cuts led to another strike wave in 1933–34. Apart from several one-day closures, eight general strikes occurred in the industry between 1919 and 1940. The impact of this militancy was felt not only in other occupations in Bombay but also in other industrial centres, such as Sholapur and Ahmedabad. As Bombay became the scene of militant working-class action in India, its labour movement, under communist leadership since 1928, acquired an explicitly political direction.

Yet even as strikes were coordinated across several mills, no stable trade union growth occurred until the mid-1920s; subsequently, the unions remained weak, vulnerable and often ineffective. To some contemporaries, this suggested the existence of concealed sources of leadership within the working-class communities;[1] to most, it indicated the

---

[1] After the 1919 general strike, the Government of Bombay believed that 'while the workers had no accepted leaders' the conduct of the dispute 'appeared to indicate the probability of some controlling organisation'. J. Crerar, Secretary to GOB, to Secretary to GOI, Home, Delhi, 7/15 February 1919, in Bombay Confidential Proceedings, vol. 46, 1919, OIOC. This riddle of leadership bemused the *Bombay Chronicle*, too, in 1924 when it

malign intervention of the political agitator. More recently, our historiographical common sense has been overtaken by such notions as the political immaturity and rural passivity of Bombay's workers. Historians have
thus been concerned with the 'survival' of the 'pre-industrial' characteristics of the workforce, rather than their rationality within an industrial
context. The traditional loyalties of the working class, in this view, obstructed the development of 'modern' trade unions. These accounts have
assumed that the development of labour politics in Bombay can best be
understood in the light of existing models of an 'early' factory labour
force. In the context of the Bombay textile industry, this remains a
problematic assumption. It is not satisfactory either to portray a factory
labour force which had been in existence for about half a century by 1918[2]
as if it was in a 'nascent' state of formation, or to analyse its history as if it
were in transition towards the product of another historical experience, or
indeed to measure its development against some universal paradigm of
'class'.

It is perhaps by focusing too exclusively on the sphere of the workplace,
by confining their model of social consciousness to what was reflected by
trade union development, that historians have overlooked the extent to
which workers were active in the making of their own politics. The
dynamic of labour politics in the inter-war years, in one view, was the
struggle between politicians, attempting to mobilize labour, and their
traditional leaders, the jobbers in the cotton mills.[3] The motive force
behind labour militancy is thus located outside the realm which workers
controlled: their political (and moral) choices, it would appear, were
consistently being made by others. In such a view, the history of the
working class becomes interchangeable with the history of their leaders,
trade unions and political parties. As a result, the impact of labour
militancy upon the development of labour politics in Bombay between
the wars has been neglected; instead, the emphasis has rested upon the
role of the nationalist and communist agitator and the role of the jobber,
the agent of labour recruitment and control.

However, the weakness of trade union organizations did not prevent
Bombay's workers from mounting an effective and sustained defence of

commented: 'it is absurd to suppose that the men are lacking in leadership . . . it is clear
that there is good sound leadership among them somewhere'. *Bombay Chronicle*, 21
February 1924.

[2] The first cotton mill was built in 1856, see Morris, *The Emergence of an Industrial Labour
Force*, p. 17.

[3] R. Newman, 'Labour Organisation in the Bombay Cotton Mills, 1918–1929', unpublished D. Phil. thesis, University of Sussex, 1970; Kooiman, 'Jobbers and the Emergence
of Trade Unions'. Morris attributes the growth of labour militancy to 'the role of the
middle-class intellectual appearing in his first full-blown opposition to British rule', in
Industrial Labour Force, p. 180.

their own interests. To understand the development of the perceptions and actions of Bombay's workers, therefore, we need to examine not only the social relationships of the workplace but particularly the context in which workers lived outside it. Since the earliest inquiries into the conditions of factory labour in Bombay, the interconnection between the spheres of workplace and neighbourhood have been frequently mentioned; but its implications for industrial politics have surprisingly remained neglected.

Customarily, the heterogeneity and cultural sectionalism of the working class is identified with the neighbourhood; yet in Bombay it provided an indispensable base for industrial action. Far from being herded peacefully by their jobbers and neighbourhood 'leaders', workers often acted to constrain them. The momentum of industrial action was not merely provided by men of prominence; sometimes it was maintained against them. Without organization and action in the neighbourhood, it is doubtful whether the general strikes could have been sustained. At the same time, the conduct of industrial action in the public arena of the street and the neighbourhood necessarily generalized the disputes of the workplace, at times brought workers into conflict with the state and created an explicitly political dimension for their struggle. While it would be misleading to portray Bombay's workers as a 'revolutionary proletariat' or indeed to play down the important tensions and antagonisms between them, it is in terms of the political culture of the working-class neighbourhoods that the scale of industrial action and the ascendancy of the communities can be explained.

I

From the late nineteenth century, a distinctly working-class district began to emerge in Bombay. Already in the 1850s, an official investigator had noticed the growing social and cultural distance between the mass of the population and 'the educated and more influential classes (whether Native or European) of our community'. 'The principal acquaintance of these [influential] classes with the Native Town', he wrote, 'is generally formed by traversing the Kalbadevee or Girgaum bazaar roads, in going from the country to the Fort, or from the Fort into the country; and of all the densely peopled districts lying *behind* these great thoroughfares, they generally know as little as they do of the interior of Africa.'[4] The inception of industry added a further dimension to the city's social geography. An overwhelming majority of the common mills came to be situated in the

[4] H. Coneybeare, *Report on the Sanitary State and Requirements of Bombay*, Selections from the records of the Bombay Government, new series, vol. XI, (Bombay, 1855), p. 2.

three wards to the north of the old 'native town'. Increasingly the working classes, fairly evenly dispersed in the native town of the mid-nineteenth century, crowded into this area. By 1925, 90 per cent of the millworkers lived within fifteen minutes' walking distance of their place of work.[5] To its inhabitants, this area came to be known as Girangaon, literally the mill village. As the labour movement gathered momentum between the wars, Girangaon ceased to be a mere geographical entity; rather it came to represent an active political terrain.

The physical structure of the working-class neighbourhoods imparted a certain public quality to its social life. The landscape of the mill district was dominated by ramshackle, jerry-built chawls packed closely into the land between municipal thoroughfares. A survey conducted in 1921 discovered that 27 per cent of the population in Parel and 33 per cent in Umerkhadi lived in rooms containing six or more persons.[6] Another investigation conducted in the mid-1930s found over 35 per cent of families of 'untouchable' workers sharing a single room with at least one other family, while over 63 per cent lived in a single room.[7] 'Every sixth person in the city', it was reported in 1939, 'lives in conditions which are prohibited even by the existing antiquated law'.[8] The extent of over-crowding brought about by high rents, housing shortages and low wages meant that the inhabitants of the chawl spilled over into the courtyard of the wadi and the street.

The importance of the street did not derive simply from the fact that men lived on it. Street life imparted its momentum to leisure and politics as well; the working classes actively organized on the street. Thus, street entertainers or the more 'organized' tamasha players constituted the working man's theatre. The street corner offered a meeting place. Liquor shops frequently drew their customers and gymnasiums their members from particular neighbourhoods.[9] Social investigators continue to be bemused that, when asked to give 'an account of their leisure time activities', the vast majority of workers 'could not be specific and

---

[5] *Labour Gazette*, 4: 7 (March 1925), 745–7. This survey was based on a sample of 1,349 male and 715 female millhands.

[6] J. Sandilands, 'The Health of the Bombay Workers', *Labour Gazette*, 1:2 (October 1921), 14–16.

[7] G. R. Pradhan, 'The Untouchable Workers of Bombay City,' unpublished M.A. thesis, University of Bombay, 1936.

[8] *Report of the Rent Enquiry Committee*, vol. I (Bombay, 1939), p. 9. The committee noted pertinently that the minimum space required by the Bombay Jail Manual for a prisoner was double that which was stipulated as permissible under the Bombay Municipal Act of 1888. It also reported that 256,379 people lived in rooms occupied by six or more persons and 15,490 lived in rooms with at least twenty others, see pp. 7–9.

[9] For a description of the social life of the mill districts in this period, see Parvatibai Bhor, *Eka Rannaraginichi Hakikat*, as told to Padmakar Chitale (Bombay, 1977).

said that they pass time roaming, which they consider a mode of relaxation'.[10]

The pleaders' offices, which proliferated along the streets of the mill district during the 1910s, were focal points of organization in industrial and political action; some also became important centres of social activity. 'There is a constant stream of millhands to these offices', noted the police commissioner in 1914, 'which in the evening especially become a regular "rendez-vous". Here the millhand gets in touch with the Brahmans or Marathas, who read the vernacular newspapers to them, and not infrequently incite them to go on strike.'[11] With the 'professionalization' of trade unionism in the 1920s, the methods of recruitment and publicity continued to be reminiscent of the modes of the street entertainer. S. H. Jhabvala, admittedly one of the most 'professional' publicists of labour's cause, and an official of nearly twenty unions in 1929, thus described his own recruiting drive:

I would stand at the end of the street when the factories were whistled off and would cry 'Ye who are fallen and miserable, come ye here and I shall help you out of the slough of distress'. A few letters were scribbled on behalf of the distressed individuals, posted by me to their employers and God helps those who help themselves, strange enough a couple of them were solved, and the poor illiterate flocks thought that I was a good instrument for the redress of their evil lot . . . Often I ventured to take a yellow-robed saint with me who attracted a larger crowd. Mr Ginwalla managed to pay him eight annas per day, because he rolled in wealth and had no issue. He [the saint] sang Mahratta songs and I afterwards gave a dose of unionism . . . The result was that in a short time flocks of people, man [sic], women and children anxiously waited for me to hear some of their grievances and to get them solved.[12]

In its contrasting political style, the communist Girni Kamgar Union sustained the political momentum of the working-class neighbourhoods by holding regular processions and public meetings – at times, these were an almost daily occurrence. Their public commemorations of notable events in the socialist tradition – from the birth of Marx to the death of Parashuram Jadhav, a worker killed in police firing during the 1928 strike in Bombay – were sometimes well attended, and at all times contributed to the pageantry of political activity.

Although these forms of social behaviour can be identified with the neighbourhood, they cannot be considered in isolation from the context of work. The separation of workplace and neighbourhood was more

[10] K. Patel, *Rural Labour in Industrial Bombay* (Bombay, 1963), p. 150.
[11] General Department, Order no. 3253/62–Confl; 15 May 1917, in Bombay Confidential Proceedings (1917), vol. 25, p. 15, OIOC.
[12] *Proceedings of the MCC*, statement by S. H. Jhabvala, vol. II, non-communist series, pp. 786–7. The fact that the Bible – as Jhabvala told the Meerut court – was 'one of my daily readings' perhaps explains his prose style.

evident in the cotton textile industry than, for instance, in the smaller artisanal workshops;[13] yet in the textile industry as well these two social spheres were inextricably connected. Nowhere is this to be seen more clearly than in the role of the jobber, who straddled the boundaries between workplace and neighbourhood. Usually promoted from the shopfloor, the jobber was delegated vast powers over the workforce. So as to enable him to discipline labour effectively, management allowed him considerable discretion in the employment and dismissal of workers – the ultimate weapons of labour control. In return, the millowners expected their jobbers to keep production going: in other words, to maintain an adequate supply of labour, to resolve disputes between workers and to ensure industrial peace. The execution of these functions was complicated by the fact that the day-to-day demand for labour varied, partly because of absenteeism and partly in response to market fluctuations, which determined the counts of yarn to be spun or the type of cloth to be woven and thereby governed the amount of labour required by management. Each mill employed a sizeable proportion of its workers on a casual, daily basis. Across the industry as a whole, this was estimated at 28 per cent of the average daily employment.[14] So every jobber had to maintain connections with potential badli or 'substitute' labourers to meet fluctuations in the daily demand for labour.

It was, therefore, integral to the jobber's managerial functions that he should acquire and maintain connections outside the workplace. To recruit and discipline workers 'with success', recorded the *Gazetteer*, the jobber is 'bound to have a following of men and boys who usually live in the same neighbourhood and often in the same chawl as himself'.[15] Burnett Hurst, in his study of the condition of wage-earners in Bombay in the 1920s, observed that the jobber 'endeavours to acquire an influence over his friends and acquaintances who live in the same or neighbouring chawls. He lends them money, advises them on family affairs and arbitrates in disputes. When labour is required, he uses the influence so gained and is generally successful in procuring hands.'[16] Later evidence, however, suggests that this picture of close neighbourhood control must

---

[13] For the organization of the handloom-weaving workshops in the city see R. E. Enthoven, *The Cotton Fabrics of the Bombay Presidency* (Bombay, 1897). The separation of workplace and neighbourhood in the mill district also had its physical aspect. The mill compounds resembled fortresses in the mill district, protected by high walls, iron gates and sentries equipped with lathis.

[14] Labour Office, Bombay, *General Wage Census, Part I; the Perennial Factories: Report on the Wages, Hours of Work, and Conditions of Industry in the Textile Industries (Cotton, Silk, Wool and Hosiery) in the Bombay Presidency (including Sind), May 1934* (Bombay, 1937), p. 20.

[15] *Gazetteer of Bombay City and Island*, compiled by S. M. Edwardes, 3 vols. (Bombay, 1909), vol. I, p. 493.

[16] A. R. Burnett-Hurst, *Labour and Housing in Bombay: A Study in the Economic Conditions of the Wage-Earning Classes in Bombay* (London, 1925), pp. 46–7.

be modified. Jobbers did not always live in the same chawls as their workers, and workers from a single mill did not usually live together.[17] There can be little doubt, however, that the jobber's power within the workplace rested upon his connections outside, and that at least some jobbers actively invested in the development of a following and a network of power and influence. What Ambalal Sarabhai said of the jobber in Ahmedabad could equally apply to Bombay: 'He becomes a jobber if he has friends and relatives in important positions in the mills and is also a favourite of the head of the department; the chances of his becoming a jobber entirely on his own merit are very few.'[18]

Not all jobbers sought to build these connections; but few could ignore them altogether. They attempted to establish themselves at influential points within the material structure of the neighbourhood. Frequently, they acted as rent collectors, sub-lessors and occasionally even as landlords. They sometimes helped to organize the khanavalis or boarding houses which catered specially for groups of single workers. They also lent money on their own account and more often guaranteed loans. Indeed, loans guaranteed by a jobber could be obtained at discounted rates of interest.[19] They sometimes ran liquor shops and gymnasiums, and were often active in the organization of religious ceremonies and festivals. Their authority at the workplace and the influence they acquired outside made them valuable members of chawl committees and caste panchayats as well as useful allies for politicians at various levels. These high-flying connections, deriving from their position at work, in turn enhanced their value within the neighbourhood. This range of activities did not, however, simply establish the jobber as a provider. His services to the community as well as his disciplinary function at the workplace placed him in a situation of potential conflict with the workers.

For the millowners, in turn, the jobber's connections outside the workplace increased his value as an agent of discipline. These connections were usually based on the caste, kinship and village ties of the jobber. Recruitment through the jobber ensured that the cultural diversity of the workers was brought into the workplace; consequently, the jobber served as an impressive bulwark against combination and provided

---

[17] BDEC, oral evidence, Dhaku Janu Lad, pp. 103–5; Mathura Kuber, p. 499, Daji Sakharam, p. 507 and several others in GOB, Home (Special), File 550 (25) III B of 1938, MSA. Such evidence should modify the widely accepted picture of the jobber's awesome *personal* control, which has tended to neglect the institutional basis of his power.

[18] *RCLI, Evidence, Bombay Presidency (including Sind), 1929–31* (London, 1931), vol. I, pt I, pt i, written evidence, Seth Ambalal Sarabhai, Ahmedabad Manufacturing and Calico Printing Co. Ltd, p. 277.

[19] Proceedings of the Bombay Provincial Banking Enquiry Committee, 1929–31, File 12 c, Replies to the questionnaire . . . submitted by the Currimbhoy Ebrahim Workmen's Institute, MSA.

a useful mechanism for strike-breaking. Significantly, it was when working-class militancy began to complicate the jobber's task of disciplining labour that the millowners grew concerned about the efficiency of his role in production and in the mid-1930s took steps to modify their methods of recruitment.

Workplace and neighbourhood were brought into relation with each other not only by the methods of labour recruitment but also by the uncertain conditions of employment. Periods of unemployment and chronic underemployment were commonly experienced by many mill-workers, and even the 'permanent' jobs, which were held in high esteem, offered little security. Not surprisingly, workers organized outside the workplace to hedge against their narrow and fluctuating margins of survival. These informal welfare systems, or arrangements for mutual assistance, were based on their immediate social connections. Not only did migration occur within these connections of caste, kin and village, but workers also relied upon them to find work and housing, and turned to them in periods of distress. For instance, groups of single male workers, often from the same village, would rent a room together. As residents left, their friends and relatives who had moved to the city were also given a share.[20] This practice has inspired thought about its anthropological significance: the re-creation of villages within the city or the recourse to traditional ways of life. However, it probably bears a simpler explanation: that this was an obvious response to housing shortages and high rents.

In 1936, one social investigator noted 'the fact that distant relations, with a view to finding a job in Bombay, come and live with their relatives here'. But he also suggested the double-sidedness of this dependency when he reported that workers 'find it very difficult to pay the rent . . . and therefore . . . they keep sub-tenants . . . People cannot generally afford to have one room per family'.[21] Such arrangements fulfilled a reciprocal need: newly-arrived migrants had a place to stay and contacts through which to find work; the more established residents were able to meet their living costs, renew their rural ties, fulfil family obligations and even extend their sphere of influence in the city. The importance of these social arrangements was reflected by the fact that, as far as housing was concerned, 'the neighbourhood of persons of one's own circle is sought'.[22] It is the political consequences of these interconnections between workplace and neighbourhood that the rest of this essay will explore.

---

[20] See Patel, *Rural Labour in Industrial Bombay*, p. 72. The most noted example of such organization was the 'clubs' established among the Goanese in Bombay. They were financed by subscription and operated as a welfare system, giving preference to the unemployed among them, see *RCLI, Evidence*, vol. I, part i, The Bombay Seamen's Union, p. 293.   [21] Pradhan, 'The Untouchable Workers', pp. 7–12.
[22] *Report of the Rent Enquiry Committee*, vol. I, p. 20.

II

If the social patterns of the neighbourhood cannot be abstracted from their material context, nor can they be portrayed as if they were devoid of political conflict. Not only in devising strategies for living but also in industrial and political action, workers had to act across the boundaries of workplace and neighbourhood. As spheres of social action, workplace and neighbourhood are frequently assumed to exert opposite pressures on the development of workers' perceptions and actions. At the workplace, it is said, economic factors assert their primacy in the conflict between capital and labour and the lines of class antagonism are clearly drawn. The social patterns of the neighbourhood, on the other hand, are cast in the image of villages transplanted to the city: here, workers appear to be the prisoners of their traditional loyalties. Yet time and again the urban neighbourhoods belied this image and the mill district became a militant and, at times, even an insurrectionary centre.

The image of the urban neighbourhood as composed of villages ruled by their headmen derived its plausibility from the informal welfare systems operating in Bombay. Undoubtedly, these welfare systems created opportunities for some people to establish themselves as patrons and providers. But it would be misleading to portray their power as if it ran in a single direction. A closer examination of these relationships between neighbourhood 'leaders' and their 'followers' suggests the limits of political command and indicates the social basis for collective action.

The jobber, the dada or neighbourhood boss, the grain dealer, the landlord, the moneylender, each acquired an impressive degree of influence in the course of their daily commerce. Yet few neighbourhood patrons were able to escape the constraints imposed upon them by the social and political demands of their clients. Their continued command of resources depended on their ability to fulfil the moral and material expectations of the neighbourhood. For instance, if the jobber's position at the workplace was based, as we have seen, on his influence within the political and economic structure of the neighbourhood, he was also constrained by this interdependence. Since his strength derived from the social and commercial ties he established with his workers, he had to remain receptive to their needs and responsive to their demands. It was when his patronage was extended to the wider organization of credit, housing and recreation that it was exposed to greater competition from rival jobbers as well as other neighbourhood patrons. Landlords, moneylenders, brothel-keepers and grain dealers no less than workers could choose between jobbers. The interdependence of his position within the workplace and the neighbourhood meant that a jobber had to extend as far as possible the ambit of his control, unavoidably weakening his own lines of defence. Like all neighbourhood patrons, he had to compete not only for clients but also for the favour of those more powerful than himself, from employers and trade unions to politicians and minor officials.[23]

By virtue of their place within the credit structure of the neighbourhood, shopkeepers and grain dealers also commanded considerable influence and some became desirable political allies.[24] In their case, too, their ability to do favours for people from their neighbourhood was central to their own business interests. Often, they were pressed to finance various social and political activities from festivals to strikes. The expenditure involved was sometimes considerable. For instance, it was reputed that, during Mohurram, mohollas spent between Rs 100 and Rs 400 to erect a tabut and carry it out in procession. Every street where a tabut was being prepared would also arrange for a maulvi to deliver the waaz up to the tenth day of the month. For his description over five nights of the martyrdom of Husain, the maulvi was paid between Rs 30 and Rs 100. These expenses were met – as was common to all religious observances – by the subscription of local residents. During Mohurram, it was said, 'youths preceded by drummers and clarionet players, wander through the streets, laying all the shopkeepers under contribution for subscriptions'.[25] Often these shopkeepers were non-Muslims. The shopkeepers had paid their dues – often, no doubt, with reluctance – because it was expected that they would. The relationship was more one of obligation than of enforcement. It was only when the arrangements of the ugarani, the

---

[23] Of course these relationships were not stagnant. Between the wars, the jobber's authority at the workplace diminished. This was partly because the growth of labour militancy made it increasingly difficult for him to reconcile the demands of his men with the imperatives of management. As the jobber's influence at work declined, it became more necessary and, at the same time, more difficult for him to entrench himself within the neighbourhoods. It was probably the case that, by the late 1930s, the jobber's position became less crucial to political and commercial advance in the neighbourhood. The extent of the jobber's decline should not, however, be exaggerated. In the mid-1930s, the Bombay Millowners' Association, in response to the declining efficacy of the jobber, introduced schemes to revamp the system of labour recruitment and control in the industry. However, individual mill managements remained the jobber's last defender. At the level of the individual mill, the jobber still retained his uses for management. Ineffective in countering industry-wide action, the jobber attempted to entrench himself in the neighbourhood in order to dominate more completely the politics of the particular mill. At this level, BMOA schemes to control the jobber met with considerable initial resistance from some of its own members. For a summary of the BMOA schemes to control badli hiring and the jobber system in general see the *Report of the Textile Labour Inquiry Committee*, vol. II: *Final Report* (Bombay, 1953), pp. 337–50; BMOA, *Annual Report* (1935), pp. 27–9 and BMOA, *Annual Report* (1936), pp. 37–40.

[24] BDEC, oral evidence, Ravji Devakram in GOB, HD (Special), File 550 (25) IIIB of 1938, pp. 277–9, MSA.   [25] *Gazetteer of Bombay City and Island*, vol. I, p. 185.

collection of funds for the tabut levied by each moholla, broke down that its operation became evident to the state. For this reason the violence of the arrangement was most noticeable to the police commissioner who wrote in 1911 that the money was 'extorted – there is no other word for it – from Marwadi and Bania merchants, who are threatened with physical injury unless they subscribe liberally'.[26]

The first decade of the twentieth century was a sensitive period for the conduct of the Mohurram festival.[27] As the state intervened in this sphere, local shopkeepers discovered the language in which they could complain about the payments they had hitherto been obliged to make. The desire of the city police to intervene could find justification in the 'extortion' of which shopkeepers complained; at the same time, this gave the shop-keepers the means by which they could rid themselves of the burden imposed by these enforced payments. These complexities – and especially the expectations of the neighbourhood – can be illustrated by the outcome of a complaint lodged by some Marwadi merchants at Pydhoni police station that they were being harassed and assaulted by Muslims of the Bengalpura Moholla. When the police warned the 'leaders' of the moholla not to continue these extortions, 'this was treated as a grievance and Latiff himself had the impertinence to come to the Head Police Office and complain that "the police were not assisting the collection of funds".'[28]

A similar picture of service, obligation and reciprocity emerges from the role which shopkeepers played in the conduct of strikes. Without their long-term credit, the general strikes which lasted between a month and six months would not have been possible. During the 1919 general strike, for instance, even as the millworkers were out in the streets, most of the shops in the mill areas remained open.[29] This was at an early stage of the strike. Prolonged strikes often placed immense pressure on local credit arrangements. During the general strike of 1928, which lasted six months, workers had to turn to their lenders of last resort, reputed to charge the highest rates of interest: the Pathans. The Pathans' attempts to recover their loans was one important reason for the communal riots of February 1929.[30] During the general strike of 1940, the *Bombay Chronicle*

---

[26] Commissioner of Police, Bombay to Secretary, Judicial Department, Bombay, No. 545–C, 20 January 1911, reprinted in S. M. Edwardes, *The Bombay City Police*, Appendix, p. 198. Edwardes' account of Mohurram related largely to areas of the city outside the mill district. But some of these relationships described for these areas were equally applicable to the mill district.

[27] See J. Masselos, 'Power in the Bombay "Moholla" 1904–1915: An Initial Exploration into the World of the Indian Urban Muslim', *South Asia*, 6 (1976), 75–95.

[28] Edwardes, *Bombay City Police*, Appendix, p. 198.

[29] *Bombay Chronicle*, 13 January 1919.

[30] *Police Report on the Riots in Bombay, February 1929* (Bombay, 1929); *Report of the Bombay Riots Inquiry Committee* (Bombay, 1929).

reported that the cheap grain shops, offered to workers when they demanded an increased dearness-of-food allowance following the price rises which accompanied the outbreak of war, were unacceptable because they 'cut away the credit which workers had so far been enjoying with other grain merchants. In times of disputes between workers and employers, Bania grain dealers allow credit to workers to the extent of five or six months.'[31] These were vital connections; even in times of industrial and political peace they could not be ignored; in moments of conflict, they were indispensable.

If the local shopkeeper was a figure of considerable importance, it was crucial to cultivate his protection and his patronage. For shopkeepers it was their ability to fulfil these functions that defined their local importance and drew them into more exalted political connections. During the one-day strike of 7 November 1938, Tukaram Laxman, determined to go to work, turned to the bidi or tobacco shop, when he was stopped by strikers: 'I requested the bidi shopkeeper to send me to work. I said "Mama, anyhow see that I get to work. Then the Bidiwalla asked the [presumably his] motor driver who was nearby to take me to my mill".'[32] On the same day, however, several grain shops were 'looted'. Baijnath Bahadur complained that strikers entered the shop in which he worked, removed the gunny cloth covering the grain, ate the grain and ran away.[33] The police commissioner described the looting of a shop near the Worli Chawls in similar terms: 'The shopkeepers were arguing with these people. The crowd seemed to treat the whole affair as a joke. They would just pick up a handful of grain and throw it.'[34] The apparent festivity with which these shops were looted concealed the underlying tensions in the relationship between shopkeepers and the residents of the neighbourhood.

The dada – essentially, a title for a neighbourhood leader – fascinated and repulsed contemporary observers. For the dominant classes of the city the dada symbolized the 'roughness' of industrial politics. Burnett Hurst described the 'dada' as 'a hooligan, who lives by intimidation. He is both lazy and dangerous.'[35] In public discourse, neither the employers' nor the workers' organizations cared to be connected with the world of the dada even though they operated within it. Anti-communists used the term to describe the following of communist unions; communists used it to signify strike-breakers. During the investigations which followed the

[31] *Bombay Chronicle*, 7 February 1940.
[32] BDEC, evidence of Tukaram Laxman, in GOB, Home (Special), File 550 (25) III B of 1938, p. 517, MSA.
[33] BDEC, evidence, Baijnath Bahadur in *ibid.*, p. 639.
[34] BDEC, evidence, W. R. G. Smith, Commissioner of Police, Bombay, in *ibid.*, p. 1049.
[35] Burnett-Hurst, *Labour and Housing in Bombay*, p. 49.

communal riots of 1929, Hindu and Muslim witnesses used the term in connection with the rival, rather than their own community.[36] In fact, 'dada' was a term of respect. Although, in public, everybody tried to dissociate themselves from 'dadas', as one trade unionist pointed out, 'I know personally that Dadas like to be called Dadas.'[37]

The dada was not a special kind of working man. Several workers established themselves as dadas by participating in crucial neighbour-hood activities such as the running of gymnasiums or rent collection. In the course of their activities, the dadas became, as V. H. Joshi, an official of the Girni Kamgar Union put it, 'agents dealing in working people'.[38] The metaphor is instructive of the dada's vulnerability to the ultimate sanctions of neighbourhood politics: social and, in reality, commercial boycott. If the dada was 'an agent dealing in working people', he could not alienate his clientele. This was why 'the dadas left to themselves cannot harm a mass of people'.[39] For this reason dadas could be engaged against strikers least during periods of solidarity and most when they were in some ways least needed, at times of working-class vulnerability.

The scale of a dada's activities was determined by his social connec-tions and the base from which he was able to operate. Some, like Keshav dada Borkar, dominated the whole area of Ghorapdeo for several dec-ades; others were small men, neither recognized nor respected in the next chawl. In a sense, dada was properly a reputation rather than a status – a reputation for physical prowess or for getting things done. The dada, said Balubhai Desai, 'is a person who has got this reputation of controlling the hooligans by rendering services to the hooligans and protecting them, giving grain to them and really of course controlling them . . . some of these Dadas are rich'.[40] Their ability to exert this control depended upon their facility in providing such services. They did not always fight them-selves, but they could mobilize men to do their fighting and in any case their leadership depended upon the belief that they were capable of fighting. In order to protect their followers they had to have the means to pay surety for those of their men who were arrested 'and help in any other way they can'. It was only 'in that way they collect the hooligans'.[41] To build and maintain a following a dada needed influential friends and patrons; but to catch the eye of the great, let alone achieve a following, he needed to cut a figure on the street corner and in the chawl. Such prominence was often achieved through the leadership of a gymnasium.

[36] BRIC, oral evidence, Balubhai Desai, File 8, and A. R. Dimitimkar and S. Nabiullah, File 7, MSA.
[37] BRIC, oral evidence, G. L. Kandalkar and V. H. Joshi, p. 71, MSA.   [38] Ibid., p. 69.
[39] Ibid., p. 61.   [40] BRIC, oral evidence, Balubhai T. Desai, File 8, pp. 29–31, MSA.
[41] Ibid., p. 29.

These gymnasiums, where wrestling contests were held and where men trained in stick play, proliferated in the mill district. Their cultural and political role will be examined later in this essay. What must be stressed here is that they formed an important part of the dada's domain. It was here that dadas served their apprenticeship and it was through these gymnasiums that they often built their reputations. According to V. B. Karnik, the prominent trade union leader of the 1930s,

every gymnasium used to have, say, two dozen or three dozen or sometimes even a much bigger number of students and those students were under the control of the gymnasium – that is the dada who taught at the gymnasium. And that dada could utilise his students in any way that he liked . . . Every party tried to get the support of one dada or the other.[42]

The extent to which workplace and neighbourhood overlapped and the roles of jobber and dada could be combined was indicated by Dhaku Janu Lad, a jobber in the Bombay Cotton Mill. He had been prevented from going to work during the one-day strike of 7 November 1938. His less prominent brother had, however, managed to enter the mill. Because his brother had not returned when the first shift should have ended, Dhaku Janu walked to the mill to see whether he needed help. Crowds of strikers who had failed to stop some workers entering the mills, now decided to prevent them from leaving instead. The police might escort the workers out of the workplace, but they could not extend this service to their doorsteps. For this reason, it was unsafe for the workers to leave the mill. When Dhaku Janu approached the mill gates, 'those who were working in the mill went up to the Manager as soon as they recognised me'. The manager sought the help of the police to escort the workers out of the mill, and Dhaku Janu Lad took two separate groups of workers to their rooms.[43] The provision of this kind of service was among the most crucial demands made upon dadas and jobbers. They acted as informal guardians of a public order and morality which they interpreted, sometimes arbitrarily, and enforced without an excess of decorum.

The material conditions which made informal welfare organization necessary for most workers also created nodes of power and influence in the neighbourhood. The struggles waged around the jobber, the grain dealer and the dada indicate the reciprocity of these power relations. As people got together to meet their social needs, their actions defined the extent, and the limits, of social control. It is important to turn from the institutional basis of dominance in the neighbourhood – arising from its

[42] Interview, V. B. Karnik, April 1979.
[43] BDEC, evidence, Dhaku Janu Lad, GOB, Home (Special), File 550 (25) III B of 1938, pp. 103–17, MSA.

material structure – to the patterns of association which occurred within them. The collectivities fostered by the conduct of religious festivals, especially in the earlier twentieth century, and the gymnasiums of the mill district reveal how social behaviour itself provided a basis for political mobilization.

The relationship between these collectivities and politics is difficult to determine. Of course, the fact that men were brought together to crack a pot during the Gokulashtami, carrying Ganpati to the sea or dance with the toli bands at Mohurram did not mean that they could then be frogmarched into politics. The observance of some religious occasions, such as the Ganpati festival, had an explicitly political content and others, like Mohurram during the early years of the twentieth century, began to reflect social antagonisms, invited the intervention of the state and were dragged into the public domain.[44]

The associations which emerged in the conduct of religious observances became the focal points of community sentiment and rivalry. The internal structure and organization of the melas – the companies of dancers at Gokulashtami – provide further insight into the complex interplay between leaders and followers. Participation in a mela sometimes depended upon the payment of an entrance fee, a monthly subscription and contributions to the general expenses of the mela. Before being admitted to the mela, each entrant had to take an oath in which he swore not to divulge its secrets to any other mela and not to join its opposing or rival party even if he severed his connections with his own. Group loyalty was a central feature of these melas. The leader of the mela was afforded considerable respect, usually being a man of some local prominence, and it was expected that the members of the mela would remain strictly obedient to him. But the leader had to manage the mela, protect its interests and was held personally responsible for making all the necessary arrangements on the day. His continued leadership depended upon satisfying his team.[45]

In their organization, leadership and group loyalties, these associations resembled street or neighbourhood gangs. As one observer of the toli bands which danced at Mohurram wrote:

Each street has its own band to parade the various quarters of the city and fight with bands of rival streets. If the rivalry is good humoured, little harm accrues; but if, as is sometimes the case, feelings of real resentments are cherished, heads are apt to be broken and the leaders find themselves consigned to the care of the police.[46]

[44] See R. I. Cashman, *The Myth of the Lokamanya: Tilak and Mass Politics in Maharashtra* (Berkeley and Los Angeles, 1975), pp. 75–97; Masselos, 'Power in the Bombay "Moholla",' 75–95.   [45] K. Raghunathji, *The Hindu Temples of Bombay* (Bombay, 1900).

[46] Cited by the *Gazetteer of Bombay City and Island*, vol. I, pp. 187–8.

The dynamic of neighbourhood competition on such occasions lay in the reputation which neighbourhood leaders, especially the dadas who led these gangs, were seeking to gain or conserve. These rivalries were part of the permanent social relationships of the neighbourhood, not the product of spectacular occasions alone.

Like the great festivals, the gymnasium was an important, albeit less public, focus of working-class culture. The akhada or gymnasium was not necessarily a place which the 'respectable' abjured. Sir Purshottamadas Thakurdas announced proudly that he had trained at one in his youth and that he now sent his grandson to an akhada. Balubhai Desai, the Congress politician, claimed in 1929 that he still attended an akhada. It was, however, he added, an akhada only for 'decently behaving gentlemen', and he chose it because it was the only gymnasium in Bombay with machines 'for reducing fat which I am taking advantage of'. A more common feature of gymnasiums, however, was lathi-play. Those who trained in akhadas thus acquired a special skill. Balubhai Desai applauded its use as a form of self-defence. 'A lathi', he said, 'can give you protection if you are surrounded even by 50 people and you can escape unscathed.'[47] But akhadas were not associated with physical culture or self-defence alone. Young men, brought together at a gymnasium, skilled at fighting and trained in the use of lathis, had considerable potential for political mobilization, and frequently provided a basis for neighbourhood action. As social centres, gymnasiums could also become focal points of political organization. According to the moderate labour leader, Syed Munawar, 'akhadas and teashops were the rendezvous of riff raffs and hooligans . . . those were the best places for them to meet'.[48] During the communal riots of 1929, they were again identified as sources for the organization of violence. Indeed, one witness argued that the Muslims had been put at a disadvantage in the riots by the decline of the Muslim dada 'since the Mohurram taboot processions in Bombay were stopped more than 15 years ago, and since the closing of the Muslim talimkhanas'.[49]

Gymnasiums were also pulled into industrial action, on both sides, by strikers and management alike. Some workers, by virtue of being dadas, could deploy the gymnasium members in support of a strike, while the management recruited strike-breakers from their ranks. The role of the gymnasiums in political mobilization is more easily identified than the part they played in industrial action. Political pamphlets and the reported speeches of strike leaders often claimed that gymnasiums were being used in strike-breaking. But it is extremely difficult to document the relationship between gymnasiums and mill managements. Obviously, strike-

[47] BRIC, oral evidence, Balubhai T. Desai, File 8, pp. 69–71, MSA.
[48] Ibid., oral evidence, Syed Munawar, File 3, p. 279.
[49] Ibid., oral evidence, A. R. Dimtimkar and S. Nabiullah, p. 271.

breaking could offer gymnasiums a means of earning an income; the greater their income the better equipped they would be in relation to other gymnasiums, the more effective in attracting members and perhaps the more successful in the contests arranged between them. It is easy to see that strike-breaking could become an activity essential to the success of some gymnasiums. From the point of view of the jobbers or the management, importing the hired strength of a gymnasium to settle scores on the shopfloor was not always advisable, nor often necessary. It was only when the employer 'became desperate and wanted to see that the mill started again', when he felt he had exhausted all other options, according to V. B. Karnik, the Royist labour leader,

that he would get hold of a dada and recruit some strike-breakers . . . it all depended upon the market; if there was demand for cloth then he was anxious to re-open the mill; if there was no demand for cloth then he was not so keen; if the mill remained closed for a week or ten days or even a month it did not matter to him.[50]

There is as yet little available evidence on the organization and working of gymnasiums. Such evidence as exists suggests that the organization of some gymnasiums could be extremely elaborate. For instance, the Hanuman Vyayam Shalla was found in 1912 by a certain Narayan Rao. By 1928 it claimed branches in parts of the city as dispersed as Vajreshwari, on the outskirts of Bombay in the neighbouring Thana district, and Bhoiwada in the heart of the mill district, apart from its headquarters in Prabhadevi. In January 1928 it acted as host to a contest between fifty other gymnasiums from all over Bombay. This particular occasion involved over 150 wrestling bouts and the collection amounted to over Rs 2,500. It was likely that a lot of money would pass through gymnasiums; no doubt competition for their control could be fierce. Elections were held to decide the constitution of the committee. Gymnasiums sometimes even advertised their elections in the Marathi press, notifying their members of the time and place at which they would be held, and announcing how they could establish their qualification to vote. The candidates were sometimes men of considerable importance. In the case of the Shri Samarth Vyayam Mandir, the nationalist campaigner, Dr N. D. Savarkar, offered himself as a candidate.[51]

It was as much a mark of prestige for gymnasiums, as it was for chawl committees and neighbourhood leaders, to be able to invite eminent people to their great occasions. When the Hanuman Vyayam Shalla held its contest in January 1928 it invited S. K. Bole, founder of the Kamgar Hitvardhak Sabha and, in 1928, vice-president of the Bombay Textile

[50] Interview, V. B. Karnik, April 1979.   [51] *Nava Kal*, 6 January 1928.

Labour Union, to preside at the function. S. K. Bole, it was reported, gave the gymnasium a handsome donation.[52] Because of their obvious importance in political mobilization, politicians and trade unionists did not treat such connections lightly. Indeed, their political relevance enabled gymnasiums and their dadas to form alliances at exalted levels, which, in turn, then became an important factor in their position within the neighbourhood.

The tensions and conflicts within the working class were most obviously manifested in the neighbourhood; but here, too, the solidarities of labour politics were forged. Political experience in this arena was formed, in part, by the struggle to constrain and at times direct neighbourhood leaders. Power and control in the neighbourhood entailed a set of shifting relationships in which dominance was achieved and limited through negotiation, manoeuvre and sometimes violence. As the neighbourhood was increasingly brought into the sphere of industrial and public politics as well, it shaped the development of the political consciousness and political action of the working class.

III

Social relationships in the neighbourhood increasingly impinged upon industrial politics. This was partly because material conditions limited the possibility of organization at the workplace. In an overstocked labour market, employers were well placed to defeat workers' combinations and at times even exclude them from the workplace.[53] Consequently, if workers were to demand better conditions, fight wage cuts or protect employment levels, it was imperative that they organize in the neighbourhood as well. The arcane procedures and legal niceties of collective bargaining were never far removed from the baser negotiations of the street.

In dealing with labour unrest, mill managements employed the usual forms of repression, as well as some novel ones. Workers who participated in trade union activity were less likely to be promoted to more responsible and lucrative posts. They were obvious candidates for retrenchment after an industrial dispute or during a recession. They were also vulnerable to discrimination in the allocation of machinery or the distribution of raw materials. As the Social Service League pointed out, 'Complaints about victimization of workmen taking a prominent part in the trade union

---

[52] Ibid.
[53] One mill manager told B. Shiva Rao, 'For every one who goes out of this gate there are nine more waiting outside who would be grateful for the wages I am paying.' Shiva Rao, *The Industrial Worker in India*, p. 55.

movement are frequently heard.'[54] Trade unions – particularly those which did not meet with the employers' approval – could neither collect subscriptions nor hold their meetings in the vicinity of the workplace. By choosing with whom they would negotiate, by choosing between rival unions or factions, employers could deal with their most favoured workers and thus strengthen the organizations they approved of while attempting to destroy those they considered dangerous. Such action was by no means confined to the textile industry; however, both within and outside it, these measures were most effective when the conditions of employment were casual and the level of skill low.

Significantly, although the millowners failed to combine across the industry in order to control production when their markets slumped,[55] they were able to coordinate impressively in dealing with industrial action. As early as 1893, the millowners had circulated the names of strikers among themselves.[56] As conflict in the textile industry intensified between the wars, their efforts grew more vigorous. By the mid-1920s the Sassoon group, for instance, was employing agents to spy upon the meetings and organization of their workers as well as to take down and translate such speeches as were made.[57] Each mill had in its Watch and Ward department its own organized force for coercion. The superintendent of the Watch and Ward department at the Sassoon mills was 'a well known boxer' called Milton Kubes. When asked how he had collected the speeches he claimed to have done in 1928, Kubes said, 'I have got my own secret service'.[58] The millowners were also able to mobilize their own brigades for political action. In opposition to the Red Flag Union, it was said, the millowners 'post their own pickets, publish leaflets, handbills and keep watch and ward inspectors'. The object of the pickets 'is to help the loyalist workers to go to work . . . and to see that they are not molested . . They simply move around in the chawls, post themselves as pickets in front of the mill gates, and advise willing workers to go to work and if any of their workers are molested they go to their rescue.'[59] To organize such pickets, millowners relied upon their jobbers either to mobilize the support of their workers against the strike or to encourage anti-strike alliances in the neighbourhood. By the mid-1930s, they had become more systematic in keeping an eye on trade union activities, reporting on workers'

[54] *RCLI, Evidence, Bombay Presidency*, vol. I, part i, written evidence, The Social Service League, p. 445.
[55] Dissatisfaction in this regard was often expressed in the speeches of the chairmen of the Bombay Millowners' Association at their annual general meetings; see, for instance, BMOA, *Annual Report*, 1934, Chairman's speech, p. ii.
[56] BMOA, *Annual Report*, 1893, p. 16.
[57] BRIC, oral evidence, Milton Kubes, File 5, pp. 241–3, MSA.   [58] *Ibid.*, p. 201.
[59] *Ibid.*, oral evidence, Syed Munawar, File 3, p. 269.

meetings and sharing information with each other. Indeed, this political intelligence was embodied in the monthly report of the labour officer of the Bombay Millowners' Association to its committee. It was also made available to the police as well as to official inquiries into strikes, disturbances and seditious conspiracies, and seems to have been treated largely as unproblematic evidence.[60]

In addition, the millowners were increasingly able to call upon the assistance of the state. Fearful of the infiltration of class struggle into nationalist agitation and concerned at the spread of support for the communists among Bombay's workers in the late 1920s, the provincial government grew increasingly ready to intervene in industrial disputes. From the late 1920s, the government constructed a legal framework for the conduct and settlement of disputes, sent more police to the mill gates during strikes to restrict picketing and control 'intimidation', and prosecuted the communist leaders of the labour movement more readily for incitement or conspiracy. The presence of the state was most evident, however, in the form of the police when they supervised pickets or escorted blacklegs to work. Introducing the Prevention of Intimidation Bill in 1929, the Home Member of the Bombay Government recalled his memories of the general strike of that year for the benefit of the Legislative Council:

One of the most remarkable sights it has ever been my fortune to view was a long procession headed by mounted police, followed by foot police and then by a hollow square with women workers in the middle and the workmen around them on all sides. The procession was wound up by more armed police and another party of mounted police. As they marched along the road, the street corners and points regarded as dangerous were guarded by still more police. Day after day these men and women were thus escorted to their work and away from it in complete security. These measures continued so long as they were necessary. As the number of men at work increased and the danger of their being overawed by strikers decreased the police precautions were gradually relaxed.[61]

These were formidable obstacles against which to conduct a strike; they could scarcely leave the forms of industrial action, let alone its possibility, unaffected.

This structure of dominance within industrial relations, ranging from the economic sanctions available to employers at the workplace to the political means of repression outside, was often sufficient to smother any sustained resistance from the workers. For one thing, industrial action necessarily placed jobs in jeopardy. Moreover, unless workers were able

---

[60] BDEC, evidence, extracts from the monthly reports of the Labour Office, BMOA, in GOB Home (Special), File 550 (25) III of 1938, pp. 173–245, MSA.
[61] *Times of India*, 8 August 1929.

to effect a fairly complete strike, they stood little chance of negotiating their demands with management, let alone achieving any concessions. When the state intervened, workers were placed under greater pressure to devise means by which they could prevent their jobs being usurped by 'blackleg' labour. It shifted the focus of action to the neighbourhood where social pressure as well as force could be deployed to maintain an offensive. Workers' combinations, excluded from the workplace, were forced to act in the social arena outside. The disputes of the workplace were brought into the street. Patterns of association developed in the neighbourhood were integrated into the conduct of industrial action. Managements were, at times, also active in forging anti-strike alliances in the neighbourhood, but unless workers had been able to constrain and immobilize these alliances, they would have been able to offer little effective resistance. As the neighbourhood itself became an arena of industrial conflict, workers used their social connection outside the workplace in two ways: first, as a material base and second, for varying degrees of direct action.

Neighbourhood social connections, indispensable to the daily life of workers, influenced the possibilities of their collective action. How long workers could remain on strike was governed by the extent to which they could draw upon the material resources of the neighbourhood and especially upon the credit they were able to mobilize. If through participation in a strike a worker risked his job, his willingness to strike would to some extent be influenced by his chances of finding another job, and for this he depended upon his neighbourhood connections. Industrial action sometimes even brought into play the rural connections of the workers. M. S. Bhumgara, formerly manager of the Khatau Makanji Mills, explained in 1931 that it was upon workers who had lost all connections with the land that 'the millowners generally depend to break the strike as these people have no home to return to and hence they are the worst sufferers at such times'.[62] Those workers who could fall back upon their village connections were often the most resilient in industrial action.[63] Migrants with strong rural connections were expected to be less concerned, perhaps even less conscious of their economic interests in the city than urban proletarians with nowhere else to turn. In this case, however, it would appear that migrants with the strongest rural connections could also be the most conscious of their 'urban' interests and most active in their defence.

[62] RCLI, Evidence, Bombay Presidency, vol. I, part i, written evidence, Mr M. S. Bhumgara, p. 499.
[63] In January 1928, during the strike wave which finally launched the general strike, the police observed: 'The strikers were determined not to work the new system and are gradually leaving for the native places by the coasting steamers and trains after receiving their wages'. BPP SAI, 1928, no. 3, 21 January, para. 61.

Strikers, trade unions and the political parties also had to rely upon the pressure which they could bring to bear upon the community as a whole in confronting strike-breakers. Their actions were based partly on their own strength of numbers, partly on the alliances which they could effect within the structure of neighbourhood power and partly on their ability to publicize and thereby discredit workers and jobbers, dadas and gymnasiums involved in strike-breaking. It was sometimes said of the communist-led Girni Kamgar Union that it hired 'mavalis and bad-mashes', literally 'roughs', to stop workers crossing the picket lines or to 'intimidate' blacklegs in their chawls.[64] But most unions did not have money for such enterprises. They were probably most capable of hiring dadas when their membership figures rose dramatically and their sub-scriptions permitted them a few luxuries, as for example during some general strikes. Yet at such times, the militant mood of the workers was often enough to enable them to dispense with these extravagances. On the other hand, as V. B. Karnik put it, if 'usually it was the strikers themselves who used to take the lead in organising this type of defence' against organized blacklegs, 'sometimes some of the strikers may them-selves be dadas'.[65]

One of the achievements of organization – especially the extensive organization which the communists were able to build up after 1928 – was that unions could deal with dadas in an attempt to contain their hostility or negotiate their support. From 1928, the Girni Kamgar Union maintained a list of dadas in the mill district and invited workers to contribute to it.[66] *Kranti*, the union's official organ, published the names of 'loyal' workers, which meant their jobbers and escorts as well.[67] Workers, too, were involved in making the identities of strike-breakers public, and, indeed, moral outrage was repeatedly expressed at their deeds at meetings and through leaflets. For instance, the residents of a wadi sometimes held public meetings at which local dadas were forced to explain and justify their actions. Blacklegs were often brought to strike meetings and humiliated. On 31 May 1928, two blacklegs were arrested by workers and brought, their faces blackened with soot, to Nagu Sayaji's Wadi, the communist stronghold in Prabhadevi. There, the communist leader, S. A. Dange, lectured them on the treachery which blacklegging involved. Dange was later arrested for his part in this episode, but was released on bail when the two workers failed to pick him out in an identity parade.[68]

[64] BRIC, oral evidence, S. K. Bole, File 3, p. 217, MSA.
[65] Interview, V. B. Karnik, April, 1979.
[66] BRIC, oral evidence, G. L. Kandalkar and V. H. Joshi, File 16, p. 71, MSA.
[67] *Ibid.*, S. K. Bole, File 3, p. 247.
[68] *Proceedings of the MCC*, statement by S. A. Dange, pp. 2447–8.

Often, strike-breakers suffered social boycotts. Their names, particularly those of collaborationist head jobbers, were read out at strike meetings. Indeed, during the general strike of 1940, these lists of names were sent in with so much enthusiasm that it embarrassed the leadership. The secretary of the Council of Action for the conduct of the strike, R. S. Nimbkar, had to advise speakers not to read out these names as they were not always correct and 'were sent sometimes on account of personal grudge'.[69] Men and women going to their mills were taunted. Strikers would, it was said, call out to somebody on his way to a mill: 'He is a *malik*'s son, that is why he is going so faithfully to work.' Such action, said Kandalkar, presenting hostile evidence against the communists who had jockeyed him out of power by the late 1930s, 'no doubt caused some embarrassment to the workers who were going in for work . . . being put to shame in the presence of their brother workmen naturally annoyed them.'[70] That moral pressure could be effective emphasizes the ambiguity inherent in the behaviour of some 'blacklegs'. Although the effect of working during a strike was clearly to contribute to its defeat, it would be misleading to assume that when workers crossed the picket lines they simply signified total opposition to industrial action, or revealed thereby an undeveloped social consciousness. Several contradictory pressures, both moral and material, for as well as against action, operated throughout the conduct of a strike, and governed workers' options. Indeed, it was for this reason that moral pressure, which often entailed some degree of physical coercion as well, could be effective at all: it found an ideological resonance in the public morality of the neighbourhood.

At the same time, moral pressure and public embarrassment, however effective, were not always enough. Throughout the 1930s, communist leaflets highlighted the causes of unemployment and argued the case for an identity of interest in the long term between the jobless and the workers in an attempt to deter 'blacklegs', while maintaining a steady, moralizing attack against 'blacklegging'.[71] Notions of morality and justice – or more clearly injustice – infused the most direct and physical forms of public pressure. At a meeting called to propagate the one-day strike of 1938, Lalji Pendse said that 'some goondas have beaten our volunteers' and called upon those children of workers who trained at gymnasiums to 'teach a good lesson to these dadas'.[72] Towards the last stages of the 1940

[69] Commissioner of Police, Bombay, Daily Report, 6 April 1940, in GOB, Home (Special), File 550 (23) C-I of 1940, p. 83, MSA.
[70] BDEC, evidence, Girni Kamgar Union, Bombay (Kandalkar) in GOB, Home (Special), File 550 (25) III of 1938, p. 431, MSA.
[71] See leaflets collected in GOB, Home (Special), File 543 (46) of 1934 and 543 (46) pt I of 1934, MSA.
[72] BDEC, confidential statement submitted by the Bombay Millowners' Association in GOB Home (Special), File 550 III of 1938, p. 315, MSA.

general strike, the Council of Action of the Bombay Provincial Trades Union Congress had to deal with the exertions of Mane Master. At a meeting on 31 March 1940 a communist worker, Khaire, said that,

Mane Master was defaming the Marathas and blackening the face of the Great Shivaji by conducting on the one hand the Shivaji Gymnasium at Bhoiwada and on the other hand trying to break the strike. This Mane Master who was a member of the Maratha League had blackened the face of the Marathas and was himself a blot on Maratha society and as such they should break his legs.[73]

It was sometimes necessary as well as possible for strikers actively to picket particular neighbourhoods, road junctions and even inside their chawls. For instance, during the 1938 strikes Madanpura was picketed so effectively that the Simplex Mill reported that its 'jobbers complained that they were not allowed to leave the moholla'. The experience of the Simplex Mill was by no means exceptional; workers from the New Great Eastern Mills, who lived in Kamathipura, and from the Madhavji Dharamsi Mills suffered a similar fate.[74] The efficacy of such action depended upon the particular political circumstances of each neighbourhood. As S. K. Patil, the brain behind Congress organization in Bombay city in the 1930s and general secretary of the Bombay Provincial Congress Committee, explained it, not all strikes or meetings could be broken:

the breaking activities can succeed only in certain areas. Even in the labour area, there are spheres of influence. If you go to a sphere other than your own, it is easier for them to break up a meeting, because they have a larger following round about. That is not possible everywhere.[75]

The fact that several mills of the Sassoon group continued to work on 7 November 1938 was attributed to perhaps the most significant dada in Bombay between the wars, and a Congressman, Keshav Borkar, 'The peculiarity about those mills', said deputy commissioner of police, U'ren,

is that they are in the area which is looked after by Keshav Borkar. He was naturally against the strike . . . It is quite obvious that by virtue of the fact that he holds sway in that area, the Red Flag Union did not think that they could get much success there . . . The mere fact that he was the headman of that area, I think, was sufficient for the Red Flag volunteers not to bother with that area.[76]

---

[73] Commissioner of Police, Bombay, Daily Reports, 1 April 1940, in GOB, Home (Special), File 550 (23) C-I of 1940, p. 21, MSA.
[74] BDEC, confidential statement submitted by the BMOA, Annexe B-I in GOB, Home (Special), File 550 (25) III of 1938, pp. 317–43, MSA.
[75] BDEC, oral evidence, S. K. Patil in GOB, Home (Special), File 550 (25) III B of 1938, p. 401, MSA.
[76] BDEC, oral evidence, Mr U'ren, Deputy Police Commissioner in *ibid.*, pp. 681–3.

The balance of power in the streets was clearly a crucial factor in determining the geography, and sometimes even the possibility, of political action.

Another common response to the structure of control which workers had to face was to impose pressure at the most vulnerable point of most strikes: the jobber. In 1928, strike-breaking jobbers were hounded out of their neighbourhoods. S. D. Saklatwalla of the Tata group of mills informed the Fawcett Committee that one jobber had 'to change his place of residence twice because they [workers] once found that he had entered the mill and . . . they were therefore persecuting him. He said he changed his residence although he had to pay increased rent.'[77] In one case reported in 1938, Jaysingrao Bajirao, a head jobber of the winding department related how during the one-day strike of 7 November, workers waited in batches of ten to twenty until 11 p.m. at night 'in order to assault me if I ventured to go out of the mill gate'.[78]

It was because workers were often most effective in political action beyond the workplace that the millowners preferred the state to intervene in the conduct rather than the settlement of strikes: for instance by deploying the police to prevent picketing not only at the mill gates but also in the neighbourhood.[79] Ten years later, the millowners continued to argue a similar case: but more explicitly and with increased vehemence. During general strikes, 'the collection of crowds in streets and thoroughfares near the mills should certainly be prevented', urged the Bombay Millowners' Association, 'as otherwise free access by employees to their place of employment becomes impossible'. Such access was a necessary pre-condition for taking blacklegs into the workplace and maintaining production. Preferably, they argued, pickets 'should be confined to peaceful conversational persuasion and they should not be permitted to shout slogans or use abusive language or better still they should not be allowed to speak at all'. They were particularly emphatic that picketing at the workers' 'place of residence' should be made a criminal offence, for 'it is precisely this type of picketing that is most desirable to prevent'.[80]

The intimidation of 'ordinary workers' by 'strikers' often explained to the millowners as well as the Home Department why political agitators and their allies were able to shut down their mills. Clearly, intimidation by itself did not explain the solidarity of a strike, as, for instance, the

[77] Proceedings of the BSEC, 1928–29, vol. I, p. 121, MSA.
[78] BDEC, oral evidence, Jaysingrao Bajirao in GOB, Home (Special), File 550 (25) III B of 1938, p. 553; see also the evidence of Dhaku Janu Lad, p. 105, MSA.
[79] *BMOA, Annual Report* (1928), Chairman's speech, AGM, p. iii.
[80] BDEC, BMOA answers to the questionnaire in GOB, Home (Special), File 550 (25) III of 1938 pp. 141–5, MSA.

Bombay Millowners' Association believed it did;[81] at the same time without 'intimidation' it was impossible at times to conduct a strike. In public discourse, intimidation simply meant that union bullies threatened to beat those who went to work. Undoubtedly, the sanction of physical force lay behind most forms of 'political' pressure in the neighbourhood. But intimidation was not conducted only by such 'professional' groups. It was more usual for workers who favoured a strike to act in their own chawls to prevent their fellow residents from going to work. Since their own jobs were in the balance, it is unlikely that their actions needed to be instigated or organized for them. One jobber described the working methods of those who canvassed for the 1938 strike: 'Usually five or ten men are real workers, they approach people but these five or ten people are followed by a large crowd.'[82] When union bullies acted successfully in their self-conscious role as bullies, they appear to have done so with the aid and approval of the chawl.

As intimidation became a subject for public debate, workers began to use it to their own advantage. One millowner told the Bombay Riots Inquiry Committee, 'I have had certain talks with groups of work people, and I have questioned them: "Why don't you come forward and report these people [who intimidate] to the police?" They say "if we do so, we are marked men".'[83] However, there was an underside to the picture presented by the employers and the state. As N. M. Joshi argued, workers used intimidation as an excuse to remain on strike. 'It may be that there was intimidation on your part', he told S. D. Saklatwalla, during their negotiations after the 1928 strike, 'and so the men could not tell you the truth.'[84] Similarly, K. F. Nariman, the populist Congress leader, pointed out that the intimidation of which workers claimed to be the victims was often fictional. 'Sometimes what happens is this', said Nariman,

The millhands do not want to go to work for reasons which they believe exist. When somebody on behalf of the millowners asks them 'Why don't you go?' they have not got the courage to say that they do not want to come [to work]. They say that they are intimidated and so we [sic] do not come. They narrate their grievances to the Union. If anybody who commands their confidence asks them the question they would narrate their grievances.[85]

By pleading intimidation as their excuse for industrial action, workers attempted to establish their bona fides as loyal employees and thus to ensure they were given back their jobs.

[81] *BMOA, Annual Report* (1928), Chairman's speech, AGM, pp. v–vii; *BMOA, Annual Report* (1933), Chairman's speech, AGM, p. v.
[82] BDEC, oral evidence, Dhaku Janu Lad, in GOB, Home (Special), File 550 (25) III B of 1938, p. 105, MSA.   [83] BRIC, oral evidence, J. Addyman, File I, p. 85, MSA.
[84] Proceedings of the BSEC, vol. I, p. 122, MSA.
[85] BRIC, oral evidence, K. F. Nariman, File 6, p. 89, MSA.

We have already seen that workers could exert some pressure on their jobbers in a variety of ways and it was by no means customary for the culmination to be violent. Although there was no positively definable point at which the jobber's position would be entirely rejected, it was essential for him to bend with the political temper of the mill district, to know when he should act with the workers and when he should act against them. It was particularly in the face of mass action, effectively orchestrated by a powerful trade union, and extending to more than a single mill, that the limits of a jobber's power were exposed, and that employers appeared vulnerable without the physical potency of the state. In periods of working-class solidarity, the jobber's opposition or his participation in victimization could lead to the desertion of his men, moral opprobrium from the community and the severance of the social and commercial ties upon which his position rested. At such times, working-class action to neutralize hostile neighbourhood alliances of all kinds was most successful. It is not intended to suggest that the ability of Bombay's workers to resist their employers or shackle their neighbourhood leaders was by any means equal or uniform. Their place within the material as well as the muscular structure of the neighbourhood registered differences between workers; some were plainly better equipped than others to absorb or counter their antagonists. Nor can it be said that there was any linear development in the balance of power between the 'forces' for or against the labour movement, let alone that these forces in their entirety remained consistently on either side of the divide. Clearly, the success of the Girni Kamgar Union enabled it in 1928 and 1934 decisively to alter the existing political balances of the neighbourhood, and it was probably the case that working-class action was in general most effective when the union was able both to protect workers at the mill and coordinate their action in the neighbourhood.

The permanent social relations of the workplace, and of the industry, pushed strikes which began within the limits of the workplace into the wider arena of the neighbourhood. As workers attempted to cope with the limits which this structure of control imposed upon them, paradoxically their actions acquired an important political edge. Conventionally, we should consider a strike as a form of industrial or even political action, as an event which related directly to the workplace and concerned particular groups of workers. However, as industrial action was forced into the public sphere, into the streets and neighbourhoods, the effects of industrial disputes were generalized. In this wider context, the parochial disputes of a mill or a group of mills were placed before the mill district as a whole. By being placed in the wider arena of the working-class neighbourhoods, each individual strike became an essential part of the collective experience of Bombay's workers. As a result, the apparently limited nature of industrial disputes became essential to the process by which the social experience and the social consciousness of the working class as a whole were forged.

IV

It has already been argued that the social exchange of the neighbourhoods shaped the perceptions of Bombay's workers and influenced the forms of industrial action. But its ramifications were wider still. It exercised an important influence upon the character of workers' politics in the public domain. From the late 1920s onwards, the communist-led Girni Kamgar Union became the dominant force in the politics of the mill district. Not only was the GKU the only union to achieve a more or less permanent presence in industrial politics but it also led every general strike in the industry after 1928. Throughout much of this period, it was subjected to considerable repression by the state. In the early 1930s, the Bombay Millowners' Association withdrew its recognition of the union; in 1934, along with other communist organizations it was declared illegal. As a result, the Girni Kamgar Union was at times incapacitated. But it was a measure of its achievement that although it was subjected to severe repression and its members to victimization and disfavour, it was repeatedly able to re-assert its ascendancy. 'Had it not been for certain measures', the police commissioner admitted in 1935, referring to the Meerut arrests and the passing of such repressive legislation as the Criminal Law Amendment Act and the Bombay Special Emergency Powers Act, 'the communists would no doubt have become a positive danger by this time.' For, although its activities 'have been paralysed to a great extent by the internment of active communists . . . [and] they have comparatively few leaders and organisers . . . the subterranean activities of the Communists are not effectively kept in check by the measures adopted by the Government from time to time'.[86] As late as 1940, Bombay was still considered the 'nerve centre of Communist agitation in India'.[87] Not only did the communists survive this repression, but they also succeeded in creating an active political tradition: in the 1930s, their office became a landmark in the mill district and rival unions competed to adopt the name of the Girni Kamgar Union.[88]

The spread of support for the communists reflected changes that were

---

[86] Commissioner of Police, Bombay, to Secretary, GOB, Home (Special), Secret no. 3757 B, 8 August 1935, in GOB, Home (Special), File 543 (77) of 1935, p. 77, MSA.
[87] Departmental note in GOB, Home (Special), File 543 (42) of 1940, p. 16, MSA.
[88] During the 1930s, three unions adopted this name.

occurring within the political culture of the working-class neighbour-hoods, changes which were the outcome of growing conflicts, both in the workplace and outside. In the process, tensions within the working class and between millworkers were exposed. It is not intended to suggest that the intervention of the communists heralded the dawn of working-class unity. However, it is also clear that from the late 1920s onwards, an impressive community of political sentiment formed around the commu-nists. As Syed Munawar, the 'moderate' trade union leader, said in 1929, 'Communist principles have captured the minds of textile workers to a great extent in the Parel area.'[89] For the millworkers in particular, the Girni Kamgar Union created the possibility of a sustained political ex-pression.

The place which the communists came to occupy in the mill district was partly the result of the nature of their intervention in industrial politics. It has already been argued that material conditions as well as the employer's policies made workers' combinations vulnerable at the work-place. This meant that trade unions had to maintain an effective presence in the neighbourhood; at the same time, it also meant that they were excluded from the area of the daily social relations of the workplace and forced to operate often at a level removed from the thrust of working-class action.

The tension between trade union organization at the level of the individual mill and at the level of the whole industry was crucial to the determination of the politics of the textile industry. The system of labour control based upon the jobber worked best at the most parochial level. At this level, what mattered was the extent to which jobbers, acting within the context of the neighbourhood as a whole, were able to resist or incorporate pressures from the workforce. At this level, too, trade unions were most easily rendered ineffective. As long as a significant proportion of jobbers and workers were not connected with a particular union, there was little need for the employer to recognize its existence, and even when a trade union acquired any considerable influence amongst his workers, an employer could discipline or at worst dismiss some of them as a warning to the rest. It was at a more general level that trade unions operated, making alliances with jobbers and then representing their case to management, to the Millowners' Association and to government when necessary. Significantly, the first trade unions in Bombay were essentially pleaders' offices where grievances were heard and services, such as the writing of leave notices and the drafting of petitions, were provided.[90] Yet, to operate successfully at this more general level, it was obviously essen-tial to establish more than an ephemeral presence at the workplace.

[89] BRIC, oral evidence, Syed Munawar, File 3, p. 267, MSA.
[90] See Confidential Proceedings of the GOB, 1917, vol. 25, pp. 15–19, OIOC.

The major problem which trade unions faced was their inability to act at both levels. Most trade unions were constrained by this intermediary position. As intermediaries who built upon their jobber and neighbourhood connections, they were better placed to mediate in the workers' disputes than to lead them. Trade unions, like the Kamgar Hitwardhak Sabha, the Social Service League and the Bombay Textile Labour Union (BTLU) never became company unions, but nor were they free to champion the workers' cause. Following the momentum of workers' action could bring them directly into conflict with jobbers and other neighbourhood patrons. It could also invoke the displeasure of the state and of the employers, whose benevolence and trust was vital to their political survival. For it was their influence in ruling circles which made these unions valuable allies for the workers and the lesser leaders of the neighbourhood. 'Had the millowners been a little more sympathetic towards the Union', the representatives of the BTLU mused upon the fate of their own organization, 'the success it had achieved would have been more substantial and the Union would not have required to go through the agonies it went through after the 1928 strike.' It was 'only recently', the union argued in the aftermath of the communist-led strikes of 1928 and 1929, 'when an undesirable element has entered the trade union fold that the employers have begun to talk in terms of sympathy towards the unions'.[91] Their political alliances inhibited them in advancing the workers' interests and thereby also restricted their membership. At least, by force of habit, these unions were better placed to act as advocates when they had no clients than as spokesmen when they had no audience.

Not only their material interests but also their conception of their own role in relation to workers limited the efficacy of their leadership. Organizations like the Kamgar Hitwardhak Sabha and the Social Service League were concerned mainly with social work and the 'uplift' of the poor. They were, as the Labour Office reported, less trade unions than 'associations for the welfare of their members'.[92] Their aim was to rescue workers from the depths of ignorance. In response to low wages, they suggested more education; as a solution to bad housing conditions, they tried to teach workers hygiene; faced with poverty they advocated thrift. Their strength lay in speaking on behalf of the poor; in active struggle, they often disintegrated.

It is against this background that the intervention of the communists in the labour movement in 1927–28 was significant. It marked a radical

[91] *RCLI, Evidence*, vol. I, part i, written evidence, the Bombay Textile Labour Union, p. 353. The outcome of these agonies was that by 1931 the union's membership figure stood at 56 and was to fall further to 20 in 1938; see *Labour Gazette*, 'Principal Trade Unions in the Bombay Presidency', *passim*.
[92] *Labour Gazette*, 2:7 (March 1923), p. 26.

transformation in the style and content of trade union leadership. The communists entered the labour movement in 1927 through the Girni Kamgar Mahamandal, a trade union founded and organized by jobbers and mill clerks during the 1924 general strike. Since 1927, rationalization schemes had been introduced into certain mills. Although their object was efficiency, these schemes increased workloads, created the possibility of greater unemployment and induced among the millworkers 'a genuine fear of less wages'.[93] As strikes followed these changes in work practices from mill to mill, it became apparent that individual resistance, however determined, was doomed. As N. M. Joshi put it later, 'a strike in one mill does not and will not succeed. If there is discontent on a large scale there must be a general strike. Then only the grievances have some chance of being redressed.'[94] Between August 1927 and April 1928, strikes occurred in twenty-four mills.[95] Under the impact of this political determination among the workers, the leadership of the labour movement vacillated.

The only significant pressure in favour of a general strike came from the communists; but they were still incapable of carrying the Girni Kamgar Mahamandal with them. To lead a strike when the workers' mood was militant offered the communists an invaluable opportunity of establishing organization among the workers. Moreover, unlike the other unions, the communists of the Bombay Labour Group had two advantages. First, they attributed a positive value to industrial action, for larger purposes than the immediate conflict, in developing the political and revolutionary consciousness of the working class. At the same time, their enthusiasm was not as yet weighed down by neighbourhood or even jobber connections which they would have to defend. The Girni Kamgar Mahamandal and the Bombay Textile Labour Union, on the other hand, with more established political connections were hesitant to risk their linkages in a strike liable to fail. As the strike wave spread across the mill district, both groups were faced with the danger of being outflanked by the communists. Tensions between the two rival courses of action dominated the affairs of both these unions. By March 1928, the Girni Kamgar Mahamandal divided and one of its founders, Mayekar, was expelled in a dispute over the control of funds.[96] 'What happened in this strike', as Dange said later, 'was that the rank and file was forcing the lead on the organisation.'[97] This general strike lasted for six months. The intensity of

[93] Departmental note in GOB, Home (Special), File 543 (10) E Pt D of 1929, p. 25, MSA.
[94] Proceedings of the BSEC, vol. I, p. 71, MSA.
[95] *Proceedings of the MCC*, statement submitted by S. A. Dange, pp. 2413–15.
[96] *Proceedings of the MCC*, examination of Arjun A. Alwe, p. 961; *BPP SAI*, 1928, no. 20, 19 May, para. 793; GOB, Home (Special), File 543 (18) C of 1928, MSA.
[97] *Proceedings of the MCC*, statement submitted by S. A. Dange, p. 2424.

class consciousness which was expressed in the period was never perhaps to be repeated.

The linkages which were forged in this strike placed the communists firmly in control of the GKM and enabled them to dominate trade union politics. They were now forced to confront the problems posed by the structure of industrial relations. The initiative taken by the communist leadership in reflecting working-class militancy enabled them to establish their political presence at the level of the industry as a whole. To consolidate this support, it was imperative for the Girni Kamgar Union, as it was now called, to penetrate the level of the individual mill. This was precisely what occurred in the following months. The general strike of 1928 had ended on the basis of an agreement that the rationalization schemes would not be extended until the committee of inquiry appointed to investigate the dispute had reported. Between October 1928 and March 1929, seventy-one lightning strikes occurred as millworkers resisted victimization or zealously ensured that the agreement was not breached. The Girni Kamgar Union's intervention in these disputes had, as Dange put it, a 'magical' effect upon organization.[98] On 30 September 1928, the Girni Kamgar Union had a membership of 324; by the end of that year, they boasted 54,000 members.[99] The organizational achievement of this period was the mill committees which sprang up throughout the industry. Workers from each department elected representatives to the mill committee. At the same time, the Girni Kamgar Union opened several centres within the mill area for the enrolment of members and the collection of subscriptions, but especially to establish and extend connections with the workers of their neighbourhoods. These centres supervised the work of mill committees in their area. The members of a mill committee would contact their centre as soon as a dispute arose in their department or their mill. Each centre elected a committee, which in turn elected a managing committee for the union as a whole and to whose decisions it remained subordinate. The committee of each centre was elected by the most effective unit of the union machine: the mill committee.[100]

The representatives elected onto the mill committee were responsible for the organizational tasks of the union in their department. They enrolled members and collected subscriptions; they acted as watchdogs of the workers' interests; they formulated grievances and approached management to negotiate settlements; and if this brought them no joy,

---

[98] *Ibid.*, p. 2507.
[99] 'Report of the Court of Inquiry into a Trade Dispute Between Several Textile Mills and their Workmen', 1929, p. 11, MSA.
[100] See BRIC, oral evidence, Milton Kubes, File 5, pp. 209–13, MSA; see also *Proceedings of the MCC*, statement submitted by S. A. Dange, pp. 2498–537.

they approached the union, or more frequently in practice, proceeded to strike. In this way, they brought the union to that microcosmic level of the individual mill and department from which it had so effectively been excluded in the past. While it was their ability to intervene at this micro-cosmic level which enabled the Girni Kamgar Union to gain such formidable support and create such an extensive organization, it was precisely their strength across the industry as a whole which prevented the mill-owners from excluding them from the politics of the workplace. 'We are helpless', complained Sir Manmohandas Ramji in 1929. 'If we dismiss a man who is a member of that union, the question of victimization comes in, and we create a strike. If today my mill is working partially and I suspect a man who belongs to that union and try to dismiss him, there will be a strike next morning.'[101] The strength of the Girni Kamgar Union across the industry enabled it to protect its members as well as advance their interests at the level of the mill.

The mill committees linked, and operated at the junction of the work-place, the neighbourhood, the mill and the trade union headquarters. But the mill committees of 1928–29 did more than this – they also became 'parallel organs of supervision and control' in rivalry with the jobber and constraining his freedom of action. In 1928–29, they sometimes seemed to give substance to Dange's claim that the Girni Kamgar Union 'over-threw the power of the jobbers and the head jobbers'.[102] Through the mill committees, workers gained access to the union offices. The result was to give meaning to the union as an alternative source of patronage, extending from the workplace and the neighbourhood to the union head-quarters, which operated at a level well beyond the jobber's reach. Their presence forced jobbers to choose between making an alliance with the union to preserve their position with the workers and risk managerial disfavour, or else to ally with the management to break the mill commit-tee and isolate the union. As the union penetrated the workplace, it brought new complexities to bear upon the jobber's function of labour control.

However much the mill committees checked the jobber's power in the short term, it did not, contrary to Dange's claim, overthrow him.[103] At times the union leadership even found itself attempting to defend the jobber against the opposition of workers. At a public meeting to elect the mill committee for the Kohinoor Mill, on 24 November 1928, one section of the workers pressed for the exclusion of the head jobber of the weaving department and his six men. Dange and Alwe advocated re-straint: they argued that it would not be practical to exclude men of

[101] BRIC, oral evidence, Sir M. M. Ramji, File 2, p. 367, MSA.
[102] *Proceedings of the MCC*, statement submitted by S. A. Dange, p. 2514.   [103] *Ibid.*

influence, especially those who had the backing of their department. They suggested a compromise in the form of a resolution to warn that those who opposed the majority opinion of the mill committee or ignored union policies would be removed.[104] To attack the jobber, it was clear, the union would have to proceed with care. In the short term, it was arguably sufficient and perhaps only possible, to constrain him. The mill committee could not overthrow the jobber; but their failure meant that as the union's position across the industry weakened, the jobbers were able to re-assert themselves.

In 1929, the Girni Kamgar Union, by leading another general strike, built upon the momentum established in the previous year and then exhausted it. Already, the arrests and imprisonment of its most important leaders created chaos in the union's organization. In 1930, G. L. Kandalkar, its new president, declared his support for the Congress and carried an important section of the union into the nationalist fold. In the face of growing unemployment in the industry, the millworkers' militancy was seemingly diluted. As the overarching trade union organization grew weaker, its relationship with the mill committees grew more tenuous. The weakening of the bond between the mill committee and the union or a decline in the activism of the union made it easier for the jobber to turn the mill committee into yet another institution around which to consolidate his power. However, where they survived, mill committees formed a core of shopfloor organization, through which the Girni Kamgar Union could rehabilitate itself.

To some extent, the organizational basis of 1928–29 was revived during the strike wave of 1933–34; moreover, it was diversified and extended more formally to the neighbourhood. The Millowners' Association emphasized the vital role of the union's chawl committees in the conduct of the general strike of 1934.[105] In December 1937, the police noted the fact that the organization of the union integrated both workplace and neighbourhood. 'They have gone to great trouble', it was reported, 'to establish "communist cells" in mills and industrial concerns, and in addition they have appointed Chawl Committees to influence the workers still further.'[106] Although the communists could not re-create their achievement of 1928–29, these changes enabled them to absorb the growing repressive pressures at the workplace and, at the same time, to maintain their presence in the neighbourhood.

---

[104] *Proceedings of the MCC*, vol. X, Marathi Exhibits, Girni Kamgar Union Minute Book, Public Meetings, pp. 6–7.

[105] BDEC, evidence, extract from monthly report of the Labour Officer, BMOA, August 1935, in GOB, Home (Special), File 550 (25) III, of 1938, p. 181, MSA.

[106] GOB, Home (Special), File 546 (13) B (1) of 1937–38, p. 7, MSA.

The re-assertion of the communist ascendancy out of the doldrums of the early 1930s occurred through industrial action, in the strike wave of 1933–34. This militancy forced choices upon workers, jobbers as well as other trade unions. In 1934, when the communists attempted to persuade the Council of Action, composed of the representatives of several unions, to support a general strike, 'quasi-communists such as Alwe and Abdul Majid felt they had to come in or be pushed aside' and the Royists 'in order not to lose such influence with the workers as they had, felt impelled to join in and pose as communists'.[107] That the communists were able to exert such pressure on the other unions in 1934 suggests the extent of their recovery. That they recovered at all was due to the powerful base and the political sympathy they had created in 1928–29.

It was probably their stance of continued opposition to the employers and the state which established for the communists their place within the political culture of the neighbourhood. The communists came to be identified as the only political group untainted by their association with the state, for instance by nominations to provincial and central legislatures, to royal commissions, and even to ILO conferences. This enabled the communists to present themselves as the one political group in the labour movement which acted in the interests of the working class alone. When asked why the Girni Kamgar Mahamandal had permitted the communists to enter and work in the union although it had recently rejected the leadership of the 'outsiders' of the Bombay Textile Labour Union, Arjun Alwe, President of the GKM, replied: 'we believed to be true the fellow-feeling which they exhibited towards the workers'.[108] After 1928, the communists' exertions in the workplace and neighbourhood served to confirm, at least for some workers, this assessment.

Between the wars, the state intervened increasingly in the working-class neighbourhoods. The effect of this intervention was not universally to antagonize workers. Legislation was passed to protect trade unions and govern working conditions, to grant maternity benefits and to provide compensation for injuries and even to ensure the prompt payment of wages. The police were known to arbitrate in labour disputes and occasionally even to ensure the payment of overdue wages.[109] In practice, however, there was little life in the new legislation; and the police, the most immediate point of contact between workers and the state, appeared increasingly as the most organized of the repressive forces which con-

[107] W. R. G. Smith, Commisioner of Police, to R. M. Maxwell, Secretary, GOB, Home (Special), no. 3035 L, 20 June 1935, in GOB, Home (Special), File 543 (48) L, pp. 99–101, MSA.
[108] *Proceedings of the MCC*, examination of Arjun A. Alwe, 12 August 1931, p. 972.
[109] See, for instance, Edwardes, *Bombay City Police*, Appendix, p. 197.

fronted the working class. Indeed, police action during strikes defeated pickets and aided blacklegs and in the process contributed to the suppression of workers' demands and the destruction of their organizations.

Moreover, as conflicts between national and imperial interests were increasingly articulated in the political domain, they helped to clarify the relationship between the workers and the state. During and immediately after the first world war, the living conditions of most workers, characterized by rising prices, high rents and general scarcities, worsened considerably. Grain prices rose almost immediately after the war began, and the government had to take active measures to prevent food riots. The opening of labour camps in Dadar in 1917 and the work of military recruiting officers led to considerable tension within the working-class neighbourhoods of Bombay.[110] The impact of the first world war upon workers was to reveal to them that the Indian economy was 'now influenced by international factors'.[111] Imperialism signified another force which governed their conditions of life but over which they had no control. Several factors clarified these perceptions. First, the millowners were closely identified with the social rituals of a foreign ruling class. Second, the nationalist campaigns of 1917–22 stirred people's minds and involved a racial self-assertion. It could affect the way in which workers related to their Anglo-Indian and Parsi supervisors who were closely associated with the British rulers. Third, the economic campaigns of their employers also sharpened the lines of conflict between Indian workers and an imperial state. Indeed, at certain points, the state appeared to be the cause of their worsening economic conditions and of their industry's problems.

Although the millowners were perceived by the workers as being socially associated with this ruling imperial culture, their attempts to confront the long-term depression in the industry's fortunes brought them into conflict with the state. When the Government of India refused to abolish the excise duty on Indian mill production, the Bombay millowners cut wages by 11.5 per cent. This wage cut led to a general strike. Indeed, when in the face of the threat of prolonged working-class action, the Government abolished the excise duty, the millowners rescinded the wage cut. Similar connections between the economic policies of the colonial state and the worsening conditions of the industry and its workers were made by the capitalist class during its currency campaign of 1927–28. Within the labour movement it appeared as if both the

---

[110] 'Statement relating to the disturbances in the City of Bombay in April 1919', in Bombay Confidential Proceedings, 1920, vol. 53, pp. 13–27, OIOC; 'A Report from the Commissioner of Police, Bombay to the Government of Bombay Concerning Political Developments before and during 1919', in Curry Papers, Box IV, item nos. 54 and 55, Centre of South Asian Studies, Cambridge; *BPP SAI*, 1917, no. 29, 21 July, para. 794.
[111] *Proceedings of the MCC*, statement submitted by S. A. Dange, p. 2404.

Government of India and the capitalists were arguing opposite cases while professing the interests of the working class, and that both posed as the guardians of labour in order to promote their own particular interests. It was said that while the government's case for a higher exchange ratio rested upon the contention that a lower ratio would depreciate wages and lead to serious strikes, the capitalists argued that in order to function at the higher ratio they would be forced to reduce wages.

It was not merely at one remove that workers were forced into confrontation with the state. Their economic struggles also brought them into political arenas. In the immediate post-war period, a pattern of resistance and surrender to wage demands had established itself. Its consequence was to make the power of combination and the effectiveness of industrial action increasingly clear. During the 1920s, as the millowners organized across the industry to influence the policies of the state, their Association began to affect the management of individual mills. As the level of the individual mill and the industry were integrated, workers, too, had to act across the industry to press their demands. As strike activity occurred on a larger scale, negotiations were conducted at more elevated levels. The mill manager no longer conducted the case for the management alone; the centralizing initiatives of the Millowners' Association became increasingly important. The state intervened less through the office of the police commissioner and increasingly from Government House. The mutuality of workers' interests became more evident and their conflicts with the state occurred at new levels. A general strike, a matter of industrial politics, could entail visible forms of class confrontation: from the police escorting blacklegs across the picket lines to the work of an arbitration court headed by a High Court judge or a civil servant, whose rulings were perceived to be unjust.

To a large extent, the political experience of the working class was constituted in relation to the state; this relationship in turn influenced the development of their political consciousness. For instance, the police impinged upon the conduct of a strike in various ways. During the general strike of 1928, police reporters attended workers' meetings; policemen supervised pickets at the mill gates and attempts were made to restrict their number to two;[112] and when picketing was carried into the neighbourhoods, the police presence extended to the chawls as well. At a meeting at the communist stronghold of Nagu Sayaji's Wadi in Parel on 1 June 1928, according to the police reporter's account, Dange reminded his audience, 'the police have no right to come to your room without a warrant . . . Even if he comes in the room with uniform but is not armed

---

[112] *Ibid.*, pp. 2438–9; BRIC, oral evidence, K. F. Nariman, p. 87, MSA.

with a warrant, you can consider him a thief . . . You must protect your own chawl.'[113] The opinion was being more readily expressed that, in general, the police had shown greater solicitude for the millowners than for the strikers.[114] For many people, the police came to represent not the guardians of the law but the long arm of tyranny. 'Many things are not reported to the police out of fear', said one observer, who also noted that 'Hindus . . . always avoid to go to the courts and police.'[115]

The Borkar riot which occurred on 11 December 1928 in support of the communist leaders, two months after the general strike had officially ended, showed how in a single moment the levels of neighbourhood and industrial and public politics could be combined. The origins of the riot dated back to the split within the old Girni Kamgar Mahamandal in March 1928, when Mayekar was expelled from the union. Finding his old bases of support being pulled away from under him, Mayekar came to lean upon his friendship with Keshav dada Borkar, gymnasium owner and neighbourhood boss of Ghorapdeo. Borkar's terrain at Ghorapdeo became Mayekar's last refuge. Throughout 1928 Mayekar, now isolated within the labour movement, opposed the communists with the help of Borkar, and attempted on several occasions to break up their meetings. 'For six months and more', reported Horniman's *Indian National Herald*, 'the leaders of the communist-led Girni Kamgar Union were repeatedly disturbed by his unwelcome presence which at once acted as a disintegrating factor on one section of the workers and an infuriating phenomenon on the other.'[116] The effect of Mayekar's intervention 'through his friend Borkar',[117] at several communist meetings was interpreted very differently by left-wing sympathizers and by the police. While the police commissioner reported that frequent complaints were received that they were 'seeking to stir up trouble at the communist meetings . . . but no serious clash occurred',[118] the *Indian National Herald*'s version was that the communist leaders 'went to the length of even dissolving crowded meetings', to avoid confrontation. Indeed, at practically every meeting the leaders exhorted the men to remain restrained in the face of provocation.[119] If the Mayekar–Borkar alliance had been able to create a riot, this would have provided the police with the kind of opportunity they sought

[113] GOB, Home (Special), File 543 (18) C of 1928, MSA.

[114] BRIC, oral evidence, W. T. Halai, File 5, p. 81, MSA.

[115] BRIC, oral evidence, Dr P. G. Solanki, File 6, p. 165; see also, oral evidence, G. L. Kandalkar and V. H. Joshi of the Girni Kamgar Union, File 16, pp. 65–7, MSA.

[116] *Indian National Herald*, 7 December 1928.

[117] Letter, Commissioner of Police, Bombay, to Secretary, GOB, Home, Bombay no. 5395 L, 13 December 1928, in GOB, Home (Poll), File 265 of 1928, MSA.   [118] *Ibid.*

[119] *Indian National Herald*, 7 December 1928. Mayekar, claimed the paper, only 'masquerades as a labour leader and is, in fact, alleged to be an agent of the Criminal Investigation Department'.

to take further repressive action. During the strike, Mirajkar had told a strikers' meeting at Kalachowki on 2 August 1928 that:

our strength lies in unity and peace. On Monday attempts are [sic] made to disturb our peace with the use of lathis. If they use their lathis we can also retaliate in the same way; but as we want to win the struggle, we must keep peace. If we disturb peace, lathis and guns will be used and under that threat they will try to put men into the mills. But our men are firm and they already know the knavery of the millowners. They [strikers] have already resolved not to fall prey to the hirelings of the millowners.[120]

On 11 December 1928, a message was received at the Girni Kamgar Union office, calling for their assistance in connection with a dispute at the David Sassoon Spinning and Manufacturing Mill at Ghorapdeo – the heart of Borkar's territory. The communist leader R. S. Nimbkar, P. T. Tamhanekar, Govind Kasale and a few others who went to investigate found the complaint to be false. As they left the mill, Nimbkar and his associates were set upon and attacked by Keshav Borkar and a gang of about twenty men. Complaints lodged at the local police station, however, 'of course failed to trace the assailants'.[121] The following morning workers from the David Sassoon, Morarji Gokuldas, Moon and Shapurji Broacha mills did not resume work, out of sympathy for their bruised leaders. At a meeting of the Girni Kamgar Union at Poibavdi that morning, Kasale, who had taken the brunt of the attack, displayed his wounds. Clearly the temper of the meeting was highly charged. Plain-clothes policemen in the crowd were identified and assaulted.[122] Within minutes, about 500 workers set off towards Borkar's house, 'with the intention presumably of settling accounts with him. He got intimation of their advance and left his house.'[123] By the time the crowd reached Borkar's house they were estimated to be more than three thousand strong. The contents of his house were pulled onto the street and a bonfire was lit. His furniture and cooking utensils were damaged; the house was ransacked, the tiles on his roof were removed and thrown away; his gymnasium was wrecked.[124]

As the morning wore on, mill after mill was brought out on strike by workers who gathered at the gates and stoned the premises until those who had remained inside the mill were locked out by the management. The

[120] GOB, Home (Special), File 543 (18) C of 1928, MSA.
[121] Proceedings of the MCC, statement submitted by S. A. Dange, p. 2522.
[122] Telegram, police commissioner to Secretary, GOB, Home (Special), no. 5368 L, 12 December 1928, in GOB Home (Poll), File 265 of 1928, MSA.
[123] Letter, Police Commissioner to Secretary, GOB, Home, Bombay no. 5395 L, 13 December 1928, in ibid., pp. 41–5.
[124] Report of H. C. Stokes, Inspector, Byculla Police Station, D. Division in ibid., pp. 13–15; Times of India, 21 December 1928.

police were alerted and brought into action: the result was riot. By the time Inspector Klein of Bhoiwada Police Station met the crowd on Suparibagh Road, they were, according to him, armed with sticks, bamboos, iron rods, gymnastic paraphernalia and 'obviously bent on mischief'. With a small force and awaiting reinforcements, the police attempted to stop this crowd by throwing a cordon across the road. The result was that the police were routed. Crowds appeared from every direction and hemmed the police in on all sides, while 'stones were also being thrown from the rooms and windows of the neighbouring houses'. When Klein fired with his revolver, the crowd 'held back slightly but came on with renewed vigour'. The constables began to climb into the police lorry and Klein failed to 'force them to stand fast'.[125] His deputy was set upon by the crowd and badly beaten. Klein was forced to take refuge in a nearby building while 'the mob furiously attacked the house from outside'.[126] The police lorry had to be chased by Superintendent Spiers, who noticed it hurtling away from the action.[127] Spiers returned to the scene of action, fired into the crowd, 'drove the rioters helter-skelter off the roads', and rescued the brave if battered Klein.[128] However, several features of this riot must be noted. First, the nature of the police intervention had the opposite effect to what was intended: for instance, the attempt to stop the crowd with an ineffective cordon at first, and later by the show of a pistol, and an attempt by some constables to snatch away the red flag which some workers were carrying aggravated the situation.[129] Second, five workers died in the riot, four of them from bullet wounds. 'We must put an end to the idea prevailing in police circles', one newspaper reporter wrote indignantly, 'that human life is so cheap that it can be wantonly destroyed on the slightest provocation.'[130] However, it must be taken as an indication of popular anger and determination that the crowd withstood considerable police firing and returned to counter-attack, 'with renewed vigour'. Third, the 'mob' on the streets was neither undifferentiated nor, in its response, exceptional to working-class sentiment. As the police commissioner noted, 'I am told by the officers that the stones were being hurled not only by the rioters on the road, but by millhands who were in the rooms of houses adjoining the road. These stones could not have been obtained on the road itself and it appears to me that the strikers were out

[125] Report by Inspector Klein, Bhoiwada Police Station to Superintendent of Police, E. Division, Bombay in GOB, Home (Poll), File 265 of 1928, pp. 21–5, MSA.
[126] Letter, Commissioner of Police, Bombay, to Secretary, GOB, Home, Bombay no. 5395 L, 13 December 1928, in *ibid.*, pp. 41–5.
[127] Report by W. D. R. Spiers, Superintendent, E. Division, in *ibid.*, pp. 27–31.
[128] Letter, Commissioner of Police, Bombay, to Secretary, GOB, Home, Bombay no. 5395 L, 13 December 1928 in *ibid.*, pp. 41–5.
[129] *Indian National Herald*, 7 December 1928.   [130] *Ibid.*

yesterday for mischief and had brought the stones with them.'[131] Yet the scene of action – Suparibagh Road – was one of the main thoroughfares through the mill district. If we are to believe that 'this strike was mainly brought about by those (communist) leaders and was done very secretly and in a well organized way', we must also believe that this conspiracy involved a vast proportion of the Bombay working class. Significantly, what began as an expression of protest on an impressive scale against the anti-union activities of Borkar and his men, culminated in a full-scale battle with the police.

While it was by supporting the militant tendencies within the neighbourhood, and through their apparent refusal to collaborate with employers and the state that the communists staked their claim to be the party of the working class, this claim was not always accepted. In the early 1930s, for instance, their refusal to associate with the Congress and their attempts to lead their constituents – exhausted by the strikes of 1928–29 and faced with the threat of unemployment – into battle once more cost the communists membership, neighbourhood allies as well as political sympathy. The support for the communists was not a simple fusion of shared antagonism towards the capitalist class and the state. Clearly, the Girni Kamgar Union brought to trade union politics a fresh concept of the conduct of working-class politics, and in contrast to the condescension of the vacuous sermons of improvement of the early labour organizations, a new concern with the daily issues of working-class life.[132] These departures in trade union leadership arose, in a sense, from necessity. Faced with exclusion at the level of the individual mill, the communists lacked the resources – essentially the good will of the state and the employers – to renew their linkages through patronage. To function as a trade union at all, the Girni Kamgar Union had to intervene energetically in the disputes of individual mills and build up enough support across the industry to prevent the employers from disregarding them. In one sense, the price of survival itself was militancy. However, this brought them into immediate conflict with the state. The conduct of a strike, which required organization and action in the neighbourhood, carried workers into public forms of confrontation and shaped their political consciousness.

[131] Letter, Commissioner of Police, Bombay, to Secretary, GOB, Home, Bombay no. 5395 L, 13 December 1928, in GOB, Home (Poll), File 265 of 1928, p. 45, MSA.
[132] Their leaflets, fly-sheets and public meetings dealt with such questions as jobber tyranny, methods of wage calculations, the shortcomings of 'efficiency' schemes which increased workloads without improving machinery, the use of the rotation of shifts to weed out troublesome workers and the causes of unemployment. See, for instance, the communist fly-sheets and leaflets collected in GOB, Home (Special), File 543 (46) of 1934 and File 543 (46) Pt 1 of 1934, MSA.

V

'In recent times', K. F. Nariman was to say in 1929, 'a new spirit of organization and class consciousness has come into existence among our labouring classes.'[133] But it is difficult to estimate the impact of this class consciousness upon other competing social identities amongst Bombay's workers. It would be misleading to suggest that the response of Bombay's workers to the growth of industrial action and the communist ascendancy in labour politics was in any sense uniform. The possibilities of action varied with their village connections, their position in the neighbourhood and their bargaining power in the workplace. For instance, weavers, working in the most profitable and rapidly growing sector of the industry, and protected by their level of skill, formed the most militant section of the workforce; while Mahars who manned the unskilled jobs in spinning departments or north Indian workers, whose lines of supply from their villages were weak, were more easily contained. The predominant cultural influence within the labour movement was exercised by Marathas from Ratnagiri and Satara. 'Labour activity in Bombay', Jhabvala was to say, considering his isolation, 'is largely Mahratta in its nature. The leaders must be conversant firstly with the Mahratta language, secondly with Mahratta habits of life and with a good deal of social outlook upon life that is Mahratta partly in its character.'[134] On the other hand, after 1929, Muslim workers were probably increasingly alienated from the labour movement in Bombay, partly no doubt as a consequence of increasing communal tension within national politics.

Many of these cultural differences were developed into political conflicts and sectarian rivalries by the actions of the employers and the state. As we have seen, the jobber system operated along the lines of these cultural divisions; it not only facilitated strike-breaking but also could, if necessary, enable employers to replace one group of workers with those of another caste or religion. Indeed, the communal riots of 1929 began during a strike when Hindu workers tried to stop Muslims from going to work.[135] It is probable that industrialization, far from dissolving caste, strengthened its bonds. The cotton textile industry did not depend upon the perpetuation of these bonds, but it profited greatly from their use. Caste should, therefore, be seen less as a cultural condition whose

---

[133] *Times of India*, 8 August 1929.

[134] *Proceedings of the MCC*, statements made by the accused, non-communist series, examination of S. H. Jhabvala, p. 756. This comment must also be read in the light that Jhabvala by his own admission 'knew very little Mahratti' and was, when he spoke these words, apparently isolated within the labour movement.

[135] Memorandum by Director of Information, GOB, 3 May 1929 in GOB, Home (Poll), File 344 of 1929, pp. 113–15, MSA.

primacy was being challenged by the emergence of 'class' than another important tension embedded within a class context.

This essay has attempted to depict a network of social relationships out of which the working-class experience was formed. It was in the neighbourhood that the classic picture of the Indian working class, bound immutably by their changeless past, their powerless present and their hopeless future was most apparent. Yet the neighbourhood, which was integral to the relationships of the workplace, became an important base for industrial and political action. It was here, where tensions within the working class were played out, that the solidarities of class also received their most public expression.

5   Workers, violence and the colonial state: representation, repression and resistance

I

That Indian workers were prone to spontaneous and violent action was a commonplace among policemen, civil servants and employers. This perception was not confined to colonial rulers or Indian elites alone. It expressed and informed the anxieties of wide sections of the population. As rural migrants, illiterate and uneducated, devoid of factory experience, short of commitment to the industrial setting, apparently lacking in proletarian maturity, Indian workers were deemed to be inherently rough and volatile. They were believed to be acquiescent and incapable of organization, but easily provoked, liable to violent outbursts and particularly vulnerable to the blandishments of political agitators. Their volatility was often perceived as a function of their pre-industrial character. Such workers, it was supposed, could not readily form, or sustain, trade unions, and their inability to organize only reinforced, in this view, their tendency to express their grievances through violence.

Observers commented on the frequency of lightning strikes. Trivial grievances, they noted, led to immediate closures. Employers complained that workers often went on strike without formulating their grievances and after the strike had begun would put forward several and extravagant claims. Strikes, it was said, were maintained by threat, intimidation and assaults upon 'loyal workers'. Trade unions that formed usually failed to formulate demands or negotiate concessions and, if they did, they could rarely persuade their members to accept any settlements they might achieve.[1] As a result, trade unions proved incapable of channelling workers' grievances into organized and disciplined expression. In any case, in this view, rural migrants were incapable of organization. The circularity of this reasoning captured one of the numerous contradictions that beset the colonial discourse about labour: their rural and pre-industrial mentalities rendered workers too volatile to form trade unions, but

---

[1] *Report of the Industrial Disputes Committee, 1922*, in *Labour Gazette*, 1:8 (April 1922), 24.

143

the weakness of trade unions explained why they remained volatile.[2] If the pre-industrial culture and rural mentalities of workers, in this discourse, predisposed them to violence, it was also supposed that their backwardness rendered them the innocent prey of political agitators who, for their own particular purposes, were able to manipulate, incite and provoke their followers to act in ways which damaged the long-term interests of both labour and capital. This perception of their volatility in politics was intimately related to the parallel notion of their immunity to factory discipline. Workers who were reluctant to commit themselves to regular employment could hardly be expected to submit themselves to the constraints of collective bargaining or political organization.

The truisms of contemporaries have now been enshrined as the dogma of historians. If contemporary observers often put forward this picture of spontaneous and spasmodic actions, later historians have done little to disturb it. An impressively wide range of scholars, employing different methods and pursuing diverse, even conflicting, objectives, appear to agree that Indian workers were given to sudden outbursts of violence and have taken over intact the contemporary characterizations of their roughness and brutality. Morris D. Morris explained 'the violent and catastrophic behaviour' of Bombay's millworkers in terms of the fact that their unrest manifested itself before 'strong trade unionism could give that militancy any sense of direction and discipline'.[3] For the most part, 'their sullen frustration could only express itself in seething discontent and a susceptibility to strike at the slightest provocation. Whenever articulate leadership appeared to kindle the spark, protest could burst out in an industry-wide conflagration'.[4] Thus, 'in the tumultuous, fear-ridden and violent atmosphere of the mills', it was plain to see 'the ease with which the operatives could fall under the Communist influence and be turned into a revolutionary political force threatening the very fabric of the established social order'.[5] According to Richard Newman, 'the typical manifestation of discontent in the Bombay mills was . . . a lightning strike, unpredictable, short-lived and unsuccessful'.[6] This pattern of industrial action 'arose out of the millhand's lack of commitment to industrial life', for in view of his attachment to his village base, 'he seldom felt it necessary to fight for reforms in his urban environment'.[7] A. D. D. Gordon found the city's labour force 'highly volatile', 'highly suggestible' and 'subject to periodic bouts of riots'.[8]

---

[2] This contradiction in the colonial discourse is unwittingly replicated in Arnold, 'Industrial Violence in Colonial India'.
[3] Morris, *The Emergence of an Industrial Labour Force in India*, pp. 185–6.
[4] *Ibid.*, p. 207.   [5] *Ibid.*, pp. 185–6.
[6] Newman, *Workers and Unions in Bombay*, p. 68.   [7] *Ibid.*, p. 67.
[8] A. D. D. Gordon, *Businessmen and Politics: Rising Nationalism and a Modernising Economy in Bombay, 1918–1933* (New Delhi, 1978), p. 45.

These characterizations of working-class politics were not confined to Bombay. Dipesh Chakrabarty provided a gloss on the complaints of mill managers, caught in troubled times, and the strike reports of police commissioners, when he observed that 'working-class protest in the Calcutta jute mills was frequently marked by a strong degree of physical violence or personal vengeance'.[9] For him, the propensity of workers to violence was both a symptom and a consequence of India's 'hierarchical, pre-capitalist culture'. On the other hand, communal violence was the hallmark of the rural migrant. In the 'sudden emphasis placed by mill-hands on communal issues' in the 1890s, Chakrabarty discerned the influence of 'an "immigrant mind" at work'.[10] In late nineteenth-century Madras, according to David Washbrook, 'Factory hands, in the difficult state of assimilation into an urban proletariat . . . could be drawn into violent demonstration, without much difficulty or particular cause.'[11] According to Chitra Joshi, violence and crime were a characteristic of early twentieth-century Kanpur's 'large population of casual poor', most-ly 'migrants from the neighbouring villages', a 'marginally employed sub-proletariat', a volatile 'class of desperate people with dashed hopes', many of whom 'were apparently willing to do anything for a few annas'. Although they were to be distinguished from the industrial workers, 'the lives of these people were closely interwoven with those of the workers' and 'the milieu' of 'the worker immigrants' was 'one where street fights, assaults and murders were familiar occurrences'.[12] In a similar portrayal of the undifferentiated roughness of the migrant poor, Gyanendra Pandey observed that Kanpur, 'the fastest-growing city in the province and easily the most over-crowded', substantially 'covered with slums' and inhabited largely by 'recent migrants', was by 1930 'noted for its volatil-ity':

It had more than its fair share of the *goonda* and *badmash* groups which abound in any large Indian city today and are often in the pay of wealthy men and willing to perform any service for the money. Some of them engaged in cocaine smuggling, trade and gambling, and readily took to other criminal activities.[13]

Similarly, Veena Das has sought to explain collective violence in present-day South Asia in terms of

[9] Chakrabarty, 'On Deifying and Defying Authority', 127; Chakrabarty, *Rethinking Working Class History*, ch. 5.
[10] Chakrabarty, 'Communal Riots and Labour', 145, 148–9. For a similar recourse to 'thugs', 'goondas' and 'criminals' in explanation of communal riots, see Das (ed.), *Mirrors of Violence*.
[11] D. A. Washbrook, *The Emergence of Provincial Politics: The Madras Presidency, 1870–1920* (Cambridge, 1976), p. 249.
[12] Joshi, 'Bonds of Community, Ties of Religion', 261–3.
[13] G. Pandey, *The Ascendancy of the Congress in Uttar Pradesh, 1926–1934: A Study in Imperfect Mobilization* (Delhi, 1978), pp. 131–2.

the large number of new migrants who live on the margins of the city . . .
Generally, such migrants constitute the floating populations which become potential recruiting ground for the underworld activities of smuggling, drug-ped-
dling and hired assassination . . . The inhabitants of these slums . . . become a
human resource for conducting the underlife of political parties . . .

. . . the unorganized labour sector [which] provides personnel for smuggling
drugs, weapons, [sic] and the crowds and processions for various political parties –
is also responsible for providing the personnel that can be mobilized into a hostile
crowd.[14]

In perhaps the most explicit statement of the case, David Arnold has
argued that 'industrial violence' was 'a common and persistent feature of
labour relations in colonial India'. The crucial problem for analysis, he
tells us, is what 'disposed workers to express themselves through violent
rather than peaceful means'.[15] This violent disposition of Indian workers
is attributed to a tradition of violence among the rural poor, which they
carried with them into the towns and factories; 'the strength and persist-
ence of pre-industrial forms of protest' among workers at 'an early stage
of industrialization'; and the failure of trade unions to develop – in a
circular argument – partly because of the migrant and pre-industrial
character of the workforce, and partly because of 'the colonial and racial
context of industrial labour'.[16] Obstructed from forming trade unions,
industrial workers, primarily rural migrants, resorted to the kind of behaviour they innately knew best: 'by default they clung to their violent
traditions'.[17] Violence is, thus, taken to be the behavioural attribute of a

[14] Veena Das, 'Introduction: Communities, Riots and Survivors: The South Asian Experience', in Das (ed.), *Mirrors of Violence*, pp. 12–13.
[15] Arnold, 'Industrial Violence in Colonial India', 235.
[16] *Ibid.* What Arnold has called 'the peculiar colonial and racial context' of Indian industry
is offered by him, along with the migrant character of the labour force and the failure of
trade unions to develop, as three factors which explain workers' disposition to violence.
Having first ascribed industrial violence to the nature of the labour force, he asserts later
that 'colonialism and racism were the *basic* [emphasis added] causes of the high level of
industrial violence in India'. These are large categories and they proliferate confusion.
After 1947, when managerial and minor supervisory ranks in all industries had been
Indianized, there was, according to Arnold, no great diminution of violence. Arnold
attempts to resolve this paradox by arguing that 'the Indian state apparatus, especially the
police, and Indian and international managers of the post- independence period . . . have
made their own attitudes towards labour that formerly characterised colonial India'
(255). So what, we might well ask, was either racial or colonial, about these attitudes
towards labour? Similarly, Chakrabarty has argued that 'the authority of the mill manager
[in the Bengal jute mills] was bolstered up by his position as a member of the ruling race'.
But, he confesses, 'in some respects one also cannot help noticing the essentially Indian
nature of this authority'. This finally led Chakrabarty to explain that 'the word colonial is
meant here to include what was indigenous to Indian society'. Chakrabarty, 'On Deifying
and Defying', 132–3; and Chakrabarty, *Rethinking Working Class History*, p. 166.
[17] Arnold, 'Industrial Violence in Colonial India', 254, 236–42; for a more nuanced
statement of a similar position, see Chakrabarty, *Rethinking Working Class History* and
Chakrabarty, 'Communal Riots and Labour'. In any case, the constellation of forces

particular social group – in this case, a group as large, diffuse and heterogeneous as the Indian rural poor – and, as a corollary, the cultural inheritance of the urban working classes. Their propensity to violence, it would seem, was inherent, even natural, to their being.[18]

These perceptions of the violence of the rural poor, the 'marginally-employed sub-proletariat' of the towns and industrial workers at the early stages of industrialization have been given a transcendent theoretical status by Ranajit Guha who wrote in his manifesto for *Subaltern Studies*:

Elite mobilization tended to be relatively more legalistic and constitutionalist in orientation, subaltern mobilization relatively more violent. The former was, on the whole, more cautious and controlled, the latter more spontaneous.[19]

This uninhibited spontaneity and violence formed, according to Guha, whatever its actual social context or manifestation, 'the paradigm of peasant insurgency'. Colonial officials would not have joined in praise of the rebellious spirit or the celebration of its propensity to violence but they would scarcely have quarrelled with this portrayal of the roughness and brutality of the poor and they would almost certainly have shared its condescension.

These characterizations of, and explanations for, workers' violence in India have been inseparably intertwined with assumptions about the nature and consequences of social transformation and the behavioural attributes of particular social groups. The disposition of Indian workers to industrial violence is thus closely related to their rural origins, their status as casual labour and their incomplete adaptation to the industrial setting. In some accounts, it is readily, indeed explicitly, extended to a perception of the ease with which 'marginal' proletarians may be recruited to criminal, communal or political violence.

Such characterizations of working-class violence have not been limited to the historiography of India. They have been shared by scholars working

which disciplined workers at the point of production devastated their attempts at combination more consistently, if less visibly, than police action against strikers or the prosecution of trade union activists. It should not be assumed that the struggle to form trade unions was waged solely or even primarily in relation to and against the colonial state. See ch. 3 above. For the specific case of the Bombay textile industry, see Chandavarkar, *The Origins of Industrial Capitalism*, chs. 7 and 8.

[18] So the 'popular culture' of the rural poor and the urban working classes, of which this violent disposition is deemed to be a part, turns out to be little more than an assumption about 'the nature' of the rural poor who inhabit it. At best, it would appear that the attempt to bury one myth about the Indian rural poor – their passivity – has resulted in the resurrection of another, culturally specific stereotype of their violence. It is perhaps salutary to recall that images of peasant brutality, like those of rural idiocy, are the product of post-industrial culture.

[19] R. Guha, 'On Some Aspects of the Historiography of Colonial India', in Guha (ed.), *Subaltern Studies*, vol. I, pp. 4–5.

on diverse regions and within divergent and conflicting intellectual traditions. The assumption that the level and incidence of violence in society provides an index for measuring the extent and direction of social change is rooted in a venerable functionalist tradition. Similar assumptions have informed Marxist accounts of the evolution of forms of protest from 'primitive rebellion' and 'everyday forms of resistance' to revolutionary action, from primordial, through reformist and trade union, to revolutionary socialist consciousness.[20] Just as workers who are insufficiently assimilated to the factory are seen in functionalist accounts as being the most volatile, so in the Marxist variant, the perpetrators of violence, disorder and even crime are to be found among the insufficiently proletarianized: the casual poor, the rural migrant, the lumpen-proletariat.[21] Not only do these arguments derive changes in political style or even consciousness from changes in the structure of the economy, sometimes, more crudely, from quantitative shifts in the extent of industrialization, but they also portray the development of working-class politics in terms of a general progression from spasmodic and spontaneous violence to organized and disciplined action.[22] Sometimes, this shift is portrayed in terms of the advance of civilization. Thus, for instance, Lawrence Stone discerned in early modern England the 'slow, downward drift of less violent cultural norms' as polite manners gradually diffused from 'intellectuals, lawyers, nobles and bourgeois' to the 'violence-prone poor'.[23]

[20] E. J. Hobsbawm, *Primitive Rebels: Studies in Archaic Forms of Social Movement in the 19th and 20th Centuries* (Manchester, 1959); James Scott, *Weapons of the Weak: Everyday Forms of Peasant Resistance* (New Haven, 1985); James Scott and B. J. T. Kerkvliet (eds.), *Everyday Forms of Peasant Resistance in South-east Asia* (London, 1986).

[21] S. Hall, C. Critcher, T. Jefferson, J. Clarke and B. Roberts, *Policing the Crisis: Mugging, the State and Law and Order* (London, 1978).

[22] C. Tilly. 'The Changing Place of Collective Violence', in M. Richter (ed.), *Essays in Theory and History: Approaches to the Social Sciences* (Cambridge, Mass., 1970), pp. 139–64. For Charles Tilly, for instance, modernization transformed 'local food riots' and other 'scattered' and 'sporadic' protest into 'organised demonstrations, bloody strikes and sophisticated attempts at revolution' and revealed in 'urban rebellion' 'increasing signs of durable formal, politically active working class organisation'. See also Charles Tilly, Louise Tilly and Richard Tilly *The Rebellious Century, 1830–1930* (London, 1975); a similar approach is followed in Dick Geary, *European Labour Protest* (London, 1981). It is not surprising, perhaps, that Arnold was to find it 'possible to see' in early twentieth-century South India the same transformation which Tilly has described for Europe (Arnold, 'Industrial Violence', 241). The notion that endemic violence characterizes societies in the process of transition to modern capitalist (or industrial) societies has been so deeply entrenched that one scholar set out to prove that early modern England was less violent than other contemporary societies were, in order to clinch the argument that it had already, by the seventeenth century, passed through this period of transition. Had it not done so, so the reasoning goes, seventeenth-century England would have witnessed endemic violence. A. Macfarlane, *The Justice and the Mare's Ale: Law and Disorder in Seventeenth Century England* (Oxford, 1981).

[23] L. Stone, 'Interpersonal Violence in English Society, 1300–1980', *Past and Present*, 101 (1983), 29–30. Stone draws primarily upon T. R. Gurr, 'Historical Trends in Violent

Yet, it would seem, this diffusion of manners ground to a halt in the face of Irish immigration to nineteenth-century England and of Afro-Caribbeans in the mid-twentieth.[24] In recent times, the investigation of popular politics has been considerably advanced by the scrutiny to which historians have increasingly subjected the meaning and usages of terms like 'the mob', 'the crowd', 'riot' and more recently, 'crime'. Yet historians have continued to conceptualize 'violence' in unexamined ways.

Contemporary observers, as well as later historians, have often lumped together and conflated diverse forms of behaviour under the category of violence. Yet, as this chapter will argue, violence does not constitute a single, readily defined phenomenon. Indeed, the category has amounted to little more than a misleading label for disparate actions and has subsumed forms of behaviour with only the most tenuous similarities. It can scarcely, therefore, be offered as a problem for analysis in itself or accepted as an organizing concept for social investigation. By failing to differentiate between different kinds of violent acts, and the specific contexts in which they arose, historians in quest of the 'popular culture' of the urban poor have – like contemporaries, seeking to discipline and control them more effectively – generated a paradigm of their roughness and brutality and, thereby, often unwittingly, have replicated the colonial discourse. But the problems posed by its conceptualization are not always made easier by breaking it down into its specific parts. Industrial violence, for instance, has included various and fundamentally different forms of action, from lightning strikes to industrial sabotage, from situations of potential violence to active clashes between strikers and blacklegs or, indeed, the police; and sometimes, significantly, the threat or even the perception of the threat of violence. 'Criminal', 'collective' or 'crowd' violence have signified acts as diverse as those lumped together as industrial violence and have offered categories no more coherent for social analysis. To dispute the validity of the category or the coherence of the phenomenon of violence is to question the very possi-

---

Crime: A Critical Review of the Evidence', *Crime and Justice: An Annual Review of Research*, 3 (1981), 295–353. For Gurr, early modern Englishmen 'were easily provoked to violent anger, and were unrestrained in the brutality with which they attacked their opponents'. *Ibid.*, p. 307, quoted by Stone, 'Interpersonal Violence', 25. See also J. A. Sharpe, 'The History of Violence in England: Some Observations', and L. Stone, 'A Rejoinder', in *Past and Present*, 108 (1985), 206–15; and J. M. Beattie, *Crime and the Courts in England, 1660–1800* (Oxford, 1986), pp. 132–9, especially pp. 136–8; J. S. Cockburn, 'Patterns of Violence in English Society: Homicide in Kent, 1560–1985', *Past and Present*, 130 (February 1991), 70–106.
[24] For the parallels in the portrayals of the roughness of the casual poor, especially Irish and blacks in London in the nineteenth and twentieth centuries, see Jennifer Davis, 'From Rookeries to Communities: Race, Poverty and Policing in London, 1850–1985', *History Workshop Journal*, 27 (spring 1989), 66–85.

bility of a general explanation for patterns of behaviour which are identified as violent.

But the argument can be pushed further. The reporting of violence has largely determined how the evidence of its occurrence is recorded and its significance evaluated. Whether workers were believed to be either peaceful or violent in disposition reflected more accurately the perceptions of the observers than the behaviour of the actors. These perceptions did not reflect reality; in fact they frequently distorted it. The social phenomenon of violence, and its conceptualization, was a construct of public discourse and private anxieties. That industrial and political action in India, as elsewhere, sometimes took violent forms is not at issue. Rather, the emphasis in this chapter will rest upon how and why perceptions of violence came to be constructed. The roughness and violence of the working classes and the urban poor, in the dominant discourse, was the necessary attribute of a social group, which the ruling classes and the state were concerned to discipline, whose resistance they were anxious to break and whose political movements they were determined to repress.

This chapter attempts to delineate the ideological and political processes by which a discourse about the roughness and violence of the working classes came to be constructed and the portentous political consequences to which it gave rise. It first examines more closely the opacity of the term 'violence' and the ambiguities which were inherent in its use. Their effect has often been to proliferate confusion rather than to facilitate clarity in historical and sociological analysis. It then proceeds to analyse how a discourse about the violence of the working classes came to be constructed in the context of an increasingly militant labour movement and the particular social groups which came to be characterized in its terms. Characterizations of working-class violence reflected widespread anxieties about the social order. In the context of the 1928 and 1929 general strikes in Bombay, led by the communist Girni Kamgar Union, they enabled the colonial state to legitimize its interventions to contain and repress the industrial and political action of the working classes and, in particular, facilitated and seemingly justified the use of a criminal conspiracy case to destroy their leadership. The language of violence was not merely fashioned by the colonial state and ruling elites as a blunt instrument of repression; rather, its political significance derived from the fact that large sections of the population subscribed to its usages. Crucially, in the late 1920s, this language of violence appeared so plausible to so many people not simply because of the general strikes or an apprehension of the red menace but specifically because of their experience of communal riots in the city in February and May 1929.

II

The meanings, indeed usages, of violence have never been unproblematic. Although the term implies physical assault and the use of physical force, it is also used in situations which do not necessarily involve actual violence. It could denote the threat of violence or the awareness, in a particular moment of social action, of the possibility of its occurrence. At times, it has meant little more than the generalized and random perception of the roughness of the lower orders, or the threat posed by particular social groups. The criminal charge of personal assault includes the possession of an offensive weapon or simply threatening or disorderly behaviour. Obviously, the threat of violence might obviate the need to use it. But the threat of violence itself is often no more than the subjective perception of its possible use; and it is only in the context of specific circumstances that it becomes possible to appreciate and sometimes not even then, the shifting threshold at which violence is deemed necessary or its threat perceived as such by the actors involved.[25] The term 'violence' crept into public discourse in India with the full force of these ambiguities.

The scope of these ambiguities is most fully appreciated in the light of particular situations of conflict. For instance, industrial sabotage did not necessarily mean the physical destruction of machinery; it was used to describe non-violent actions by which the workforce impeded the attainment of maximum levels of production. Attempts by workers to retain some control over their own labour, or at best, their refusal to surrender complete control over it, could from a different vantage point appear as the unruly defiance of the imperatives of factory discipline. At one level, the perception of industrial violence, like the practice of industrial action, arose out of the permanent antagonisms of the workplace; at another level, its perception was governed by the confidence of the ruling classes in their dominance and of the colonial state in the fragile alliances upon which it rested – in other words, in their ability to control and discipline the dangerous 'lower orders'.

For instance, in one account,[26] evidence for the 'combustibility' and the violent disposition of Indian industrial workers has been drawn largely from the case of the South India Railway strike of 1928. In this case, the response of the railway authorities as well as the government to the strike lays bare the ideological and political processes by which the discourse of industrial violence and its perception as an attribute peculiar to the working class came to be constructed. Since the railways were deemed a

---

[25] See the illuminating discussion in R. Williams, *Keywords: A Vocabulary of Culture and Society* (London, 1976), pp. 278–9.   [26] Arnold, 'Industrial Violence'.

public utility industry, strikes which affected them were always likely to invite stern repressive action. But, in addition, this strike occurred at an extremely sensitive moment marked by widespread labour unrest, the Bardoli Satyagraha, and the arrival of the Simon Commission which promised the renewal of widespread political agitation. The Government of India, anxious to keep their lines of communication open, were concerned to bring the strike to a swift and satisfactory conclusion. This strike was classified under the general rubric of 'unlawful and violent movements', and the district magistrates of Madras Presidency were directed 'to be on the lookout for inflammatory speeches or other incitements to violence'.[27] It should not surprise us that magistrates, policemen and functionaries instructed 'to be on the lookout' for 'violence', should have reported the strike in these terms. In this way, categories were created, a vocabulary supplied and conditions generated for the definition, reporting and characterization of industrial action, or the conduct of an ordinary trade dispute, in terms of violence. If the meaning of violence is ambiguous, its attribution to particular social groups by scholars has, to some extent, arisen from an innocent and surface reading of the available evidence.

An implicit but fundamental assumption in the analysis of violence as a social phenomenon is that the level and incidence of violence in one society at a particular time was higher than in another. Otherwise, it would scarcely warrant interest or explanation. But the basis for such comparison is beset with numerous methodological problems. Historians of violence have often had to rely on extremely impressionistic evidence. Significantly, for instance, those who have argued that Indian industrial workers were disposed to violence have not produced convincing evidence to support their claim. Such evidence is, of course, extremely elusive, not simply because, as one historian recently complained, 'detailed and quantitative comparisons would be difficult to compile',[28] but because once collected they would have limited value for social and historical analysis. Whether particular incidents were labelled 'violent' would be conditioned by the sensitivity of the state to the problems of public order. The manner in which they were reported to the police, to magistrates or to labour commissioners would affect the way they were recorded. The perception of the observer – often in the case of industrial politics, that of policemen and employers – would establish the difference between a 'street brawl' and 'industrial violence', between 'picketing' and 'criminal intimidation', even perhaps between an 'affray' and a 'riot'.[29]

[27] Fortnightly Report for the second half of July 1928, Madras; Political, Simla to Acting Chief Secretary, GOB, F.8/XX/28, 1 September 1928, in GOB, Home (Special), File 543 (10) D Part A of 1928, MSA.   [28] Arnold, 'Industrial Violence'.
[29] For an interesting discussion of the subjective bias which vitiates the quality of criminal

For assessments of the nature, extent and frequency of violence, we are still to a large extent dependent upon the observations and perceptions of officials and policemen, and sometimes, when they were its object, of propertied elites, employers and their agents. As Richard Cobb showed long ago, the reporting of violence and social protest is often distorted by the specificities of police practice; sometimes, it helped to create the social phenomenon.[30] By focusing exclusively upon violence, abstracted from the specificities of its context, historians have become the prisoners of the assumptions and self-image of the rulers and their agents.[31]

Since the meaning of the term embraced such a wide range of events, both violent and non-violent, from cases of physical assault to prognoses about the possibility of violence, it signified different things to different people and it was subject to varying interpretations by the same observers under different circumstances. This point is usefully illustrated by juxtaposing two starkly conflicting descriptions, by comparably placed observers, of the same event: the 'riots' and strikes in Bombay which followed the trial and conviction of the nationalist leader, Bal Gangadhar Tilak in 1908. According to police commissioner, H. G. Gell, Tilak's 'sympathisers and friends' attempted 'to stir up the feelings of the people against Government' between 24 June when he was arrested and 22 July when he was convicted. Even before the commencement of the trial on 13 July, 'one thing' was 'pretty clear' to Gell:

and that was that either at the trial or after it large bodies of mill-hands would attempt to make demonstrations at or near the High Court, and that, if allowed to assemble in any great masses, they might become disorderly and cause a great deal of damage not only to property but also to life.[32]

statistics, see J. Ditton, *Controlology: Beyond the New Criminology* (London, 1979); and J. Davis, 'The Garrotting Panic of 1862: A Moral Panic and the Creation of a Criminal Class in Victorian England', in V. A. C. Gatrell, B. Lenman and G. Parker (eds.), *Crime and the Law: The Social History of Crime in Western Europe since 1500* (London, 1980), pp. 190–213.

[30] Richard Cobb, *The Police and the People: French Popular Protest, 1789–1820* (Oxford, 1970).

[31] At times the price is the abdication of reason. Thus, one historian, having considered the problems of using police evidence, concluded, 'Though one-sided and exaggerated, this evidence is convincing due to its range, depth and detail'. S. Henningham, 'The Contribution of Limited Violence to the Bihar Civil Disobedience Movement', *South Asia*, new series, 2:1 and 2 (1979), 60.

[32] Commissioner of Police, Bombay to Secretary, GOB, Judicial, 27 August 1908, in GOB, General, vol. CXIV of 1908, MSA. Reprinted in *Sources for the History of the Freedom Movement*, vol. II, pp. 256–75. On the political context of the Tilak riots, see Cashman, *The Myth of the Lokamanya*; I. M. Reisner and N. M. Goldberg (eds.), *Tilak and the Struggle for Indian Freedom* (New Delhi, 1966); G. Johnson, *Provincial Politics and Indian Nationalism: Bombay and the Indian National Congress, 1880–1915* (Cambridge, 1973); and Shashi Bhushan Upadhyaya, 'Cotton Mill Workers in Bombay, 1875 to 1918: Conditions of Work and Life', *Economic and Political Weekly*, Review of Political Economy (28 July 1990), PE-87–PE-99.

To the police commissioner, the potency of this threat, should it be realized, seemed devastating. He estimated that the eighty-five mills in the city employed some 100,000 hands, 'of which at least 50,000 must be able-bodied'.[33] 'Anyone able to enlist the sympathy of so large a number of men', he proceeded, 'must occupy a powerful position and if intent on disorder, can practically set all authority at defiance'. It was true, he observed, that at present the millworkers 'had no organisation, no leader, no common object and no weapons other than stones'. However, there was little reason to be sanguine about the future.

If a combined movement against Government can ever be effected, then we may expect that there will be organisation, a leader, a common object, and there will be weapons, such as pickaxe, hatchets, crowbars, bludgeons, etc. . . . The object will be the destruction of Europeans, Government buildings, offices, the Railways, the tramways, the telegraph lines, etc., looting of shops, European for choice, and possibly the burning of mills belonging to Europeans. The area over which they will operate will be the 23 square miles of Bombay and the numbers engaged will be 50 or 60 thousand able-bodied millhands plus such of the population as are inimical to British Rule.

The police force, in the mind of its chief, would be 'incapable of resisting and, if possible, nipping in the bud, such an outbreak'. Furthermore, he did not believe 'that it would be possible to strengthen the police in such a manner as to deal with a combined movement which lasted for any considerable time'. In the face of such an onslaught, the imperial state would be powerless.[34] It was rare, indeed, for the 'thin red line' of the British empire to be so clearly exposed or, indeed, the nature of its physical presence in India, watchful, weary and for ever on its nerve-ends, to be so fully articulated.

S. M. Edwardes, civil servant and historian of Bombay city, writing at the same time as Gell and, indeed, soon to succeed him as the city's police commissioner, saw the same situation in a fundamentally different light. What particularly struck Edwardes about the Tilak riots of 1908 was how

remarkable was the quaint juxtaposition during the height of the riots of seething disorder and the quiet prosecution of their daily avocations by the bulk of the people . . . At Jacob's Circle there was a great display of military and magisterial strength . . . All the pomp and circumstance of Law and Order were represented there and there could scarcely have been a greater display of armed force, more secret consultations, more wild dashes hither and thither, more troubled parley-

[33] It is not clear whether the police commissioner was here counting two hands per able body or providing unwitting comment on the conditions under which the millworkers lived and laboured.
[34] Commissioner of Police, Bombay to Secretary, GOB, Judicial, 27 August 1908, in GOB, General, vol. CXIV of 1908, MSA; *Sources for the History of the Freedom Movement*, vol. II, pp. 256–75.

ing, if the entire city north of Jacob's Circle had been in flames. And yet behind it and around it the daily life of the people moved forward in its accustomed channels.[35]

This startling contrast between the description of the same riot by the police commissioner and his immediate successor may serve to highlight the nature of British paranoia in India but it exemplifies in particular the extent to which the subjective perception of violence determined its definition.

The ambiguities which marked the use of the term arose in part from the failure both among contemporaries and later historians to differentiate between particular cases of violence. This failure to distinguish between different forms of action involving violence, to specify their protagonists or to delineate the actual context in which they developed has not only resulted in the elision of qualitatively different kinds of events and social actions but it has also made it extremely difficult to probe their social meaning or indeed to assess their significance.[36] Incidents which entailed some violence in the industrial setting are lumped together to constitute 'industrial violence', qualitatively different forms of action are conflated and each instance contributes cumulatively to the general picture of working-class volatility. Yet the more closely particular cases of industrial violence are examined, the less they appear to have in common with each other. Indeed, the social meaning of discrete acts of violence in the industrial setting are often too diverse to permit analysis under the same label. The extent to which industrial violence has become a catch-all term for that whole area of industrial politics which is excluded by formal collective bargaining and organized trade union activity is indicated by the fact that even wild-cat strikes – a feature of industrial relations everywhere and not necessarily violent – have been considered in much of the work on Indian labour as integral to the special phenomenon of industrial violence.[37] These ambiguities inherent in the definition and analysis of violence illustrate the fact that in moments of collective action, violent and non-violent forms of behaviour are often intimately intermeshed and indeed extremely difficult to distinguish. As a result, forms of

[35] S. M. Edwardes, *The By-ways of Bombay* (Bombay, 1912), pp. 135–6.
[36] Nor, indeed, have historians offered a satisfactory working definition of the phenomenon which they attempt to investigate. The result, of course, is proliferating confusion. Thus, one historian defined violence during the civil disobedience movement as 'the use (or threatened use) of physical force against people and property: it incorporated sabotage, intimidation, physical assault and also social boycott' (see Henningham, 'The Contribution of Limited Violence', p. 60). It is plain to see that many of these forms of action were in fact non-violent. It also discloses how difficult it is to establish when 'violence' really is violence.
[37] Most explicitly, again, in Arnold, 'Industrial Violence'; see also Morris, *Industrial Labour Force*, pp. 178–97.

collective action which were essentially non-violent were often represented in public discourse in terms of their supposed violence. If this interchangeability arose from the ambiguities integral to the discursive character of violence, it has only served to accentuate the problems inherent in its definition.

III

The ambiguity and exceptional elasticity of the term 'violence', which has made it elusive and confusing to scholars prone to invest it with a heuristic status, has endowed it with a powerful, sometimes explosive significance in public discourse. This elasticity meant that it could be put to varied, diverse and even conflicting uses. But it would be misleading to construe its use in a purely instrumentalist fashion. Labelling individuals or whole social groups as 'violent' might presuppose the manipulative or, at least, a partial, reading of the evidence and it could serve to justify measures taken by the state for their closer control. However, this labelling, indeed the partial reading of the facts, in themselves, reflected and expressed deepseated social anxieties and tensions as much as they were instrumental in the strategies by which the state, its constitutive elements and its agencies, sought to establish their dominance and control.

To appreciate the role of violence in the language of politics, it is necessary to examine how these characterizations of working-class violence came to be constructed. To this end, this chapter will focus upon the particular context of Bombay's working classes and examine the implications of this construction of the threat of working-class violence for the struggles waged by them in the 1920s and 1930s. Necessarily, the nature of working-class political action varied with the particularities of local social, economic and political conditions. Nevertheless, Bombay's workers provided the paradigm by which Indian industrial workers came to be judged as typically spontaneous, volatile and spasmodic in their political response.[38]

Working-class violence was frequently portrayed by contemporary observers – policemen, civil servants, employers, journalists – in non-specific, exaggerated and generalized terms and frequently they attributed arbitrary causes and random consequences to the phenomenon. As social and political tensions mounted, statements about the violence and the roughness of the lower orders grew wilder and more irrational. Disparate

---

[38] Ironically, Bombay was also sometimes taken in the colonial discourse (as well as by later scholarship) to approximate to what was deemed, for India, a relatively advanced state of industrialization, and, therefore, considered more likely to yield formal trade union organization.

forms of threatening behaviour came to be inextricably linked. This discourse of violence, the assumptions upon which it was built, and the connections which it made, reflected not so much real social behaviour as the threat which the ruling elites perceived to their control and dominance, at one level, and to their person and property, at another. Indeed, how generously the ambit of working-class politics could be drawn around its supposed violence is easily illustrated. 'The outstanding feature of the year', the Government of Bombay reported, referring to 1921–22,

was the large increase in serious crime, especially in violent and other crime against the person and property. Among the reasons to which this increase may by attributed were the general contempt for law and order fostered by the Non-Cooperation movement, the pre-occupations of the police with political agitation and its resulting activities, a general spread of unrest in the industrial world and the withdrawal of a large number of police from their normal duties in connection with the two Royal Visits.[39]

The official mind perceived a seamless web of connections inexorably linking industrial unrest with nationalist agitation, which combined to foster 'a general contempt for law and order' and to create diversionary pressures upon the police, and which was likely to culminate in 'violent and other crime against the person and property'.

Such anxieties about the city's working classes were sharpened by the momentum of industrial action witnessed in Bombay in the 1920s. The general strike of 1928, which lasted for six months and brought the millowners to the negotiating table on nearly equal terms, was followed by several months of lightning strikes, culminating in another general strike in April 1929. Significantly, during these strikes the labour movement came to be dominated by the communist Girni Kamgar Union. Now already deepening anxieties sometimes acquired the dimensions of a panic, especially among the millowners, merchants and professional middle classes as well as among some officials. These anxieties increasingly focused upon the potential for violence among the working classes. The full depth and force of this panic cannot be documented here. However, its most tangible results were to be seen in a rash of repressive legislation, in at least three public enquiries which functioned at times like a public trial of the communist Girni Kamgar Union, and above all in the Meerut Conspiracy Case. The effects of this repression were to be felt in the labour movement throughout the 1930s and the 1940s.

These repressive measures were motivated by the special terror which the threat of communism held for the official mind. But colonial officials

[39] *Bombay 1921–22: A Review of the Administration of the Presidency* (Bombay, 1923), p. 20.

could not always afford to give free expression to their darkest fears. These measures could not have been effected without a more general consensus built around anxieties about the threat of working-class violence. But these initiatives had more modest beginnings: in a widespread official anxiety about working-class militancy in general and the success of the communist-led Girni Kamgar Union in particular. 'The respect for authority' noted a senior civil servant in January 1929,

which has hitherto kept the worker in this country in order, has been so grievously weakened during recent years, that they are only ready to accept the lurid hopes held out by the communists that, if only they combine to overthrow capitalism and the Government, they must succeed and the result will be a millennium for themselves.[40]

When another general strike seemed imminent, a few months later, in April 1929, another official advocated the banning of workers' meetings on the grounds that recent experience had established beyond doubt that 'Millhands' meetings *inevitably* led to the strike becoming general . . . and the communistic teachings result in disturbances and murder.'[41]

But this deepseated trepidation about the 'general contempt for law and order' or the consequences of 'the grievous weakening' of a traditional 'respect for authority' was not, of course, confined to officials alone. It was shared by large sections of the city's elites. In December 1928, Mr T. Watts, the superintendent of the Currimbhoy group of mills complained to Dange, then the general secretary of the Girni Kamgar Union, that five workers in the roving and the weaving departments of the Currimbhoy Mill had been leaving their machines in order to recruit members for the Girni Kamgar Union. They had been, he complained, 'neglecting their own work and moving about in other departments. I beg to bring to your notice that this attitude of the men causes excitement which leads to lightning strikes, riots and bloodshed, etc.'[42] Barely two weeks later, J. H. Roebuck, an employee of the Kastoorchand Mills, wrote to Duff Cooper, the member of parliament for his native constituency, Oldham, urging him to use his influence to persuade the colonial authorities to take tougher measures to control the red menace. 'No officer in any mill', he wrote, 'is sure of coming away without serious injury to himself any day of the week, for the labour [*sic*] is entirely out of

---

[40] Note by Secretary, GOB, General 23/1/29 in GOB Home (Special), File 543 (18) K of 1929, p. 21, MSA.
[41] Note by H. F. Knight, Secretary, GOB, Home (Special) n.d. (probably late April 1929), in GOB, Home (Special), File 543 (10) E Part D of 1929, pp. 15–17, MSA.
[42] T. Watts to S. A. Dange, 31 December 1928, Proceedings of the Court of Enquiry into a Trade Dispute between several Textile Mills and their Workmen, 1929, File 23, Exhibit 1/40, MSA.

hand and cannot be controlled . . . The attitude of the workers inside the mill is one of open defiance.' The workers prevented the mill officers from attending to the maintenance or repair of the machinery, he complained, and when this resulted in a loss of production, they would nonetheless demand full pay,

otherwise they stop the mill and stopping the mill means – a howling mob who in many cases don't hesitate to pick up Iron bars, lathis and various other things with the intention to smash up something or somebody, & the preaching of the leaders of these men has led them to believe that any capitalist or officer in the employ of the capitalist is a fit and proper person to vent their indignation on.[43]

While the millowners were convinced in 1928–29 that they were fight-ing a last-ditch battle to preserve order and discipline in the mills, and exerted considerable pressure for the state to act forcefully against the labour movement, the official mind had for some time shown an urgency to take decisive measures against the spectre of communism. In the light of the peculiar intensity of the struggles of 1928–29, the fears and anxie-ties of the state – its imperative to preserve the thin crust of order so essential to its rule – now found a wider resonance. These perceptions of the potential of the working class for political violence began to dovetail with more widely held notions of the roughness of the city's poor. These notions of roughness arose in part from the social distance which separ-ated classes and castes, religious communities and linguistic groups. But sections of the working classes also, and not only the city's magnates looking down from a great height, subscribed to similar perceptions of their peers. Hindus and Muslims believed the dadas of the rival commu-nities to be particularly sinister. Marathas feared the Mahars. The Ghatis from Satara, the Bhayyas, as North Indian migrants were derisively known and Julaha Muslims were believed to be wild, rough, exceptionally strong, with a particular taste for fighting.[44] The working-class claim to respectability, as Kanhoba, the old stalwart in Mama Varerkar's classic novel of the Bombay cotton mills, *Dhavta Dhota*, typified, was grounded firmly upon the perception of the roughness of others.

Particularly crucial to public discourse, and increasingly influential in shaping policy, was the belief held especially firmly by those who did not inhabit them, that the working-class neighbourhoods were characterized

---

[43] J. H. Roebuck to Duff Cooper, 18 January 1929, Private Office Papers, L/PO/1/23(i), pp. 84–7, OIOC. The mill officers in Bombay, Roebuck reminded Duff Cooper, were 'practically all Lancashire and Yorkshire men' (presumably of those who were 'Euro-peans') and several were from Oldham. Duff Cooper, aware that he would, sooner or later, have to face his own howling mobs at the hustings, took the matter sufficiently seriously to approach the Secretary of State and the Viceroy.

[44] See also G. Pandey, *The Construction of Communalism in Colonial North India* (Delhi, 1992), ch. 3.

by their roughness. Here, it was thought, the badmash and the mavali ruled the streets. These men were typically idle, unemployed and mischievous. They were believed to hang around the street corners or frequent the akhadas and teashops which, according to one labour leader, 'was the best place for them to meet'.[45] They were said to be as easily recruited to break strikes as to man picket lines. They provided agitational fodder for trade unions as well as the Congress politicians. Their baneful influence was found to be prominently manifested in the communal riots which sometimes consumed the city. Similarly, to their activities was frequently attributed the disorder which sometimes erupted in the conduct of religious festivals. According to one newspaper, the toli bands of Mohurram imparted to this religious observance the character of 'a saturnalia of not only the Muhammadans but of all the roughs of Bombay of all creeds'.[46] As a result of their presence, according to another observer, 'heads are apt to be broken'.[47] 'The tolis', thundered the police commissioner in 1908,

are irreligious rascality let loose for five days and nights to play intolerable mischief in the streets and terrorize the peaceful householder . . . the only unobjectionable feature of the ten days of the celebration are the nightly Waaz or religious discourse by chosen preachers. But unfortunately these are little patronised by those to whom they would do most good, namely the bad characters in the tolis.[48]

Above all, the most commonly identified characteristics of the roughs were that they were rural migrants and that they were unemployed. 'While I am referring to hooligans', H. D. Nanavaty explained, 'I do not refer to the mill hands. I am referring to the people who have got no ostensible means of livelihood.'[49] The labour leader, R. S. Asavale, explained that 'bad characters turn out to be bad characters on account of unemployment. When people get no work they resort to a bad life to maintain themselves.'[50] One newspaper editorial argued that the cause of the social and political unrest in Bombay was the existence of a class of

men without any definite occupation who are always ready to join any quarrel in the chance of securing some loot. Going to jail has no terror for them as not a few of them are old jail-birds. The existence in Bombay of this class is a constant menace to peace and prosperity. Government may well consider the means of reducing to a minimum the number of such hooligans.[51]

The connection between unemployment and political action was

[45] Proceedings of the BRIC, 1929, oral evidence, Syed Munawar, File 3, p. 279, MSA.
[46] *Bombay Gazette*, 25 February 1907. Quoted in Masselos, 'Power in the Bombay Moholla', 82.
[47] *Gazetteer of Bombay City and Island* (Bombay, 1909), vol. I, pp. 185–6.
[48] Edwardes, *The Bombay City Police*, Appendix.
[49] Proceedings of the BRIC, 1929, oral evidence, H. D. Nanavaty, File 6, p. 301, MSA.
[50] *Ibid.*, oral evidence, R. S. Asavale, File 3, p. 83.   [51] *Indian Daily Mail*, 7 May 1929.

simple enough, not because the condition was a cause for discontent, but because by making men idle, it left them free to get into mischief. According to the leading merchant and millowner, Lalji Naranji, during periods of public 'disorder', 'hooligans take advantage of such troubles and . . . live upon such troubles'.[52] Similarly, to the labour leader, Syed Munawar, hooligans were mostly 'unemployed and unemployable' – except, presumably, for hooliganism.[53] The fact that 'hooliganism' could thus become a field for entrepreneurial activity and a source of employment only sharpened the concern of the state for the social and political organization which lay beyond its ken. Behind every form of political activity it was increasingly to see the monstrous hand of the unemployed. Similarly, the view was also aired in official circles that 'the majority of bad characters' were rural migrants and gave rise to the happy suggestion that 'on the threat or outbreak of disturbances all Badmashes should be rounded up or deported out of Bombay'.[54]

In this discourse, the working classes were portrayed in terms of a dichotomy between the respectable and the rough, the conscientious and the criminal, stable, loyal and settled workers as against the idle and dangerous who were always ready to support lightning strikes, irrespective of whether they had a particular grievance. A distinctive semi-criminal class of hooligans and roughs came increasingly to be linked with the mounting political tensions of the 1920s and 1930s. It was a short step to heaping upon them the invariable responsibility for political violence. The Commissioner of Police, Bombay, used precisely this argument when he wrote in 1926,

when political, industrial or communal unrest culminates in disorder on a large scale in a big city, it is not generally speaking the ordinary resident with a home and an occupation who keep the police and the military busy. It is the riff-raff, the scum of the city that gives the trouble. The habitual criminals and the casual criminals who are kept in some sort of control in normal times and can commit crime only by stealth, swarm to the surface and taking advantage of the excitement and panic, openly burn and loot and murder and cause incalculable damage to the city. These are the people whom it is the duty of the police to get under complete control in normal times, and in proportion as the police are successful in putting the criminal in jail and ridding the city by other means of undesirables so will their labours be lightened in times of disorder.[55]

The fact that the police were so easily overstretched was an argument in favour of expanding the force and spending a larger share of the govern-

---

[52] Proceedings of the BRIC, 1929, oral evidence, Lalji Naranji, File 6, p. 11, MSA.
[53] *Ibid.*, oral evidence, Syed Munawar, File 3, p. 279.
[54] Secretary, BRIC, GOB, Home to P. E. Percival, Chairman, BRIC, Karachi, 5 June 1929, Proceedings of the BRIC, 1929, File B, MSA.
[55] Commissioner of Police, Bombay, to Secretary, GOB, Home, File 12305/7, 9 December 1926; *ibid.*, File 6779/239, 27 June 1929 in Proceedings of the BRIC, 1929, File B, MSA.

ment's revenues upon it. If 'the scum of the city', who were ordinarily 'kept in some sort of control in normal times' could be brought 'under complete control' by an expanded police force better able to identify, jail or deport them, they would not be able to 'swarm to the surface' in times of disorder and 'cause incalculable damage to the city'.

In practice, of course, these distinctions were impossible to maintain. About one-third of the city's mill workforce, the most organized sector of the labour market, consisted of casual labour, hired daily at the mill gates. For those sections of the workforce considered 'permanent', conditions of employment were not much more secure. Managerial practices relating to dismissals were notoriously arbitrary. Rules governing leave and absenteeism were not standardized, sometimes not even stipulated. The casual and uncertain conditions of employment were integral to the shared experience of Bombay's working class.[56]

Similarly, the facility with which those who had pretensions to respectability referred to 'bad characters' belied the difficulties of separating them from the good ones. Indeed, the police maintained a list of 'bad characters' just as they drew up a register of criminal tribes.[57] This sometimes led people to believe that most 'bad characters' were known to the police and to criticize them for not putting their knowledge to good effect. In practice, this supposed knowledge was remarkably thin on the ground while improved lists of bad characters were by their nature unattainable. Indeed, it was by working from a position not of imperfect knowledge, but relative, and often absolute ignorance, that the police succeeded in creating, or perhaps, more accurately, in reinforcing their own image of a class of 'bad characters'. How this occurred was revealed when the police responded to the communal riots of February and May 1929 by what they described as 'rounding up' the bad characters. Their methods were simple. Sometimes assisted by the army they would surround a particular wadi or neighbourhood, cover possible exits, enter the chawls and arrest anybody they thought looked suspicious. Those who were arrested were then jailed in a block of unoccupied government-built chawls at Worli.

At the same time, the Government of Bombay was pressing for the introduction of legislation, modelled on the Goonda Act in Bengal, to enable the police commissioner to intern or deport 'bad characters' for up to a year. As these hapless 'bad characters' were being rounded up, the Home Secretary suggested that the police be 'instructed to get information as to the birth-places of persons in Worli for it could strengthen the case [for a Goonda Act] if it could be shown that the majority of bad hats

[56] Chandavarkar *The Origins of Industrial Capitalism*, esp. pp. 72–122.
[57] See ch. 6 below.

in Bombay are immigrants'.[58] The statistics which relate to the 'bad characters' reflect nothing more than the random manner of their arrest. As many migrants from outside the Bombay Presidency as migrants from its constituent districts were found among those arrested. Overall, the ratio of Bombay men to outsiders reflected the relative proportions in the city as a whole. Nevertheless, the Home Member saw in these figures 'strong evidence' to support the argument that bad characters had emigrated to Bombay and therefore to justify the legislation he sought to 'extern' them. The general figures for arrest and conviction are similarly revealing. More prisoners were discharged for want of evidence than were brought before the magistrates. By July, five months after the first riots, only about a third of the prisoners against whom charges could be made had in fact been tried and almost as many were discharged as were convicted. There was only one instance of a man arrested and released in February who was arrested again in May.[59] No doubt these figures suggested to the police the salutary effect which the rounding up of bad characters in February had upon them in May and confirmed their prejudice that magistrates were unwilling to convict in cases with political overtones. In an alternative, more literal, reading, however, they neither lend credence to the belief that there existed in Bombay a distinctive class of habitual 'bad characters' who swarmed to the surface in periods of disorder, nor justify the confidence of Bombay's respectable citizens that the police knew their roughs. Nevertheless, the rounding up of 'bad characters' was a dramatic operation. As the testimony of several witnesses before the Bombay Riots Inquiry Committee in 1929 indicated, it conveyed or confirmed the impression not only that a distinct class of bad characters existed but also that they were already known to the police.[60] The notion that there existed a distinct class of semi-criminal 'bad characters' within the working class was sanctified by police measures. This loosely defined and easily generalized notion of the social threat which it harboured was, in the context of increasing working-class militancy, to prove increasingly convenient for the colonial state.

IV

The general strikes of 1928–29 established beyond doubt that Bombay's millworkers were capable of concerted and sustained action. It also

[58] Note by Secretary, GOB, Home (Special) 7/5/29, in GOB Home (Special), File 543 (10) E Part G of 1929, pp. 12–13, MSA.
[59] P. A. Kelly, Commissioner of Police, Bombay to E. W. Trotman, Secretary, GOB Home (Special), File 3968/A/122, 16 July 1929, in GOB Home (Special), File 543 (10) E Part G of 1929, p. 73, MSA.   [60] Proceedings of the BRIC, 1929, Files 1–17, MSA.

became clear that a coterie of communist leaders had gained a powerful following in the working-class neighbourhoods. Since 1917, the British had been apprehensive of the Soviet threat to imperial interests as a whole. By the mid-1920s, the Government of India was becoming fearful that 'the immense power of mass action' had been recognized by 'nationalist intellectuals of advanced views' and that even 'communism had begun to earn appreciative comment in quarters which could not be dismissed as irresponsible'.[61] The events of 1928–29 brought these general anxieties into sharper focus.

There were now several reasons for the government to act swiftly. The communists were recognized as a 'serious menace' in Bombay city. They dominated the city's Congress organization. Without their efforts, it was readily acknowledged, the Simon Commission boycott in the city would have been a dismal failure. More crucially, it was feared the recent success of the communists might result in the intensification of agrarian agitation and, as one official noted, 'the danger is really far more serious among the agriculturists than among the industrial workers'.[62] As yet, however, the influence of the communists outside Bombay was insignificant. So if the state was to intervene at all, it was advisable for it to act immediately – certainly before the communists had established a stronger presence in the countryside – in order to detach them from the momentum of nationalist politics. It was with an easily comprehended urgency, therefore, that the Home Secretary in Bombay stressed in January 1929 'that all questions regarding the industrial situation in Bombay are now subordinate to the need for stopping the spread of communism'.[63]

However, to declare war on the communists was not necessarily to acquire the means of waging it. To act against a significant focus of political opposition – and in Bombay city, the communists commanded considerable popular support – the colonial state required some measure of public sympathy. The blessings of the millowners for repressive measures against the Girni Kamgar Union were not difficult to obtain. Indeed, it was partly at their insistence that the Government of Bombay had begun to consider seriously the possibility of a concerted campaign against the communists and to take soundings from New Delhi to assess its reactions. The provincial government also derived some strength from the widespread prejudice – among the city's professional and commercial

---

[61] Note: 'A Review of Recent Communist Activities in India', in GOI Home 7/7/37 Poll, p. 3, NAI.

[62] Note, Secretary, GOB, General, 23/1/29, in GOB Home (Special), File 543 (18) K of 1929, p. 22, MSA.

[63] Note, Secretary, GOB Home (Special), 23/1/29, in *ibid.*, p. 17.

classes and expressed in several newspaper columns – about the roughness of the working-class neighbourhoods. But it was, nonetheless, imperative that the government, in attempting to preserve the public order, should not appear to intervene on one side of what was, after all, a trade dispute. In addition, government intervention to repress 'industrial unrest fomented by the communists' was bound to be ineffective unless it was accompanied by a strategy to contain their political challenge. To complicate matters further, as colonial officials in Bombay readily recognized, the millworkers had 'genuine grievances' and unless these were resolved their discontents were unlikely to evaporate.[64] For, as the police commissioner pointed out, 'no legislative measures can prevent discontented workmen from following extremist leaders'.[65]

It should not be assumed that the colonial state was monolithic or that it took a single or even always a steady view. Nothing was more likely to open up differences within it, at various levels of government, than the attempt to undertake an elaborate and concerted campaign of repression. It was not enough that the Government of Bombay had begun to perceive an opportunity to destroy the communists before their influence acquired more menacing proportions. It was essential for Bombay to obtain the support and concurrence of the Government of India. This was at times to prove somewhat more difficult. If the provincial government had determined upon the need for repressive action, this was by no means self-evident to the Government of India. Indeed, it required more vigorous justification in New Delhi, which was distanced from the complexities of the problems of local control, sensitive to its possible repercussions in national politics and answerable to political criticism in England. As early as June 1928, the Government of Bombay had begun seeking New Delhi's views on the prosecution of the communists.[66] The Government of India took away some of the provincial government's impetus by suggesting that the best means of dealing with the communists was to institute a conspiracy case against all the major communist leaders in the country, and not just against the Bombay men. They were advised that a conspiracy case under the Indian Penal Code offered a better chance of success than either prosecution for incitement to violence, which could not, after all, 'be taken seriously' when the general strike of 1928 had been

[64] See, for instance, GOB, Home (Special), Departmental Note, 21 December 1928, in GOB, Home (Special), File 543 (18) G of 1928, MSA.
[65] 'Notes on a Conversation with Mr Kelly, Commissioner of Police, Bombay, on 4 June 1929', by H. G. Haig, 4 June 1929, in GOI, Home (Poll), 303/1929 & KW's I and II, p. 2, NAI.
[66] GOB, Home (Special) File 543 (18) K of 1929, MSA; GOI, Home (Poll) 303/1929, NAI.

'carried on peacefully' for five and a half months,[67] or the acquisition of special legislative powers by the provincial government, for instance, to deport 'goondas' from the Presidency and communists from British India and to prevent 'intimidation'. Accordingly, the Government of India deputed a special officer to collect, examine and report on available material bearing on a conspiracy charge and instructed all provincial governments to 'look up evidence with a view to considering the possibility' of prosecution.[68] As late as January 1929, New Delhi, having taken the matter out of Bombay's hands, was unwilling to commit itself to such a prosecution. As the communist threat in Bombay seemed more menacing and the provincial government's enquiries grew more urgent, the Government of India prevaricated and vacillated and its replies became increasingly evasive.

For the colonial state there were several complicating factors to be taken into account. In principle, as one senior official noted in consideration of a bill to deport communists, the Government of India did not want to be seen to be 'endeavouring to take power over those who may merely hold extreme opinions.'[69] There was also the fear of failure. Government officials were clear that 'no case should be instituted unless we are practically certain of a conviction'.[70] The researches of the special officer had soon yielded the alarming insight that the 'big conspiracy case', as officials now began to refer to it, 'would have to be of a very elaborate and comprehensive character'. The realization had dawned that 'the amount of material to be collected and tested' before the decision to prosecute could be taken was 'very great'.[71] The Government of Bombay had a different explanation for New Delhi's prevarication. At an early stage of the official conspiracy to prosecute the communists, the Government of India had decided to institute the case either in the United Provinces or in the Punjab, but, at any rate, not in Bombay.[72] The 'unofficial reason' for the delay in instituting the case, the Home Secretary in Bombay informed the police commissioner, was that 'no other

---

[67] Note by Secretary, GOB, Home (Special), 21 December 1928, in GOB, Home (Special), File 543 (18) G of 1928, p. 61, MSA.
[68] Note by H. G. Haig, Secretary, GOI, Home, 8 November 1928, in GOI, Home (Poll), File F/18/VII/28, NAI; Secretary GOB, Home (Special), to Commissioner of Police, Bombay, 21 August 1928, in GOB, Home (Special), File 543 (18) A of 1928, MSA.
[69] Note by H. G. Haig, Secretary, GOI, Home, 12 July 1928, in GOI, Home (Poll), File F/18/VII/28, NAI.
[70] Note by H. G. Haig, Secretary, GOI, Home, 3 October 1928, in GOI, Home (Poll), File F/18/VII/28, and Keep-Withs I–IX, NAI.
[71] Note by H. G. Haig, Secretary, GOI, Home, 8 November 1928, in GOI, Home (Poll), File F/18/VII/28, NAI.
[72] Secretary, GOB, Home (Special), to Commissioner of Police, Bombay, 21 August 1928, in GOB, Home (Special), File 543 (18) A of 1928, p. 5, MSA.

provincial Government' – that is other than Bombay – 'is willing for the case to be run in its territory, and such a case if put before a Bombay High Court for trial by jury would end in acquittal on account of the political leanings of the jury men'.[73]

In November 1928, New Delhi had decided to keep their special officer at his labours until the end of March 1929 and did not expect 'to be in a position to decide whether the case should be launched until some time in May'.[74] Meanwhile, the situation had, if anything, become more difficult and complicated for the millowners and the provincial government's anxieties had scarcely been allayed. After the general strike had ended in October 1928, scores of strikes occurred in individual mills over the following two months. In many cases, the millowners had been forced to accede to the workers' demands. In February 1929, a communal riot, which began with the millworkers attacking Pathan moneylenders, raged through the city. Some officials in the provincial government grew increasingly impatient with their colleagues in New Delhi. Cases of assault in the mills – two of which resulted in deaths – quickened the panic, increased their sense of urgency and afforced their desire for swift and decisive action.

The Bombay Government now considered invoking regulations framed in 1827 which would enable them 'to place under personal restraint individuals against whom there may not be sufficient grounds to institute any judicial proceedings'.[75] It was anticipated, however, that 'the Government of India, having no real idea of the conditions in Bombay will probably object on the grounds of injury to political or labour susceptibilities', despite the fact that, as the Home Secretary urged, 'the situation is now too serious for these considerations to have weight'.[76] To overcome these scruples about 'political or labour susceptibilities' and, at the same time, to gain a wider basis of support, it was necessary to demonstrate that the consequences of the communist presence went beyond any simply political question. The role of the communists in working-class politics, it was recognized, could best be presented in terms of their incitement of 'overt crimes of violence'. Their objection to the communists, the Government of Bombay accordingly claimed, was not 'political' but rather that 'their activities endanger the lives of the public'. Both the Government of India and a wide section of public opinion could be expected to sympathize with arguments about the imminent disinteg-

[73] Note by Secretary, GOB, Home (Special), 21 December 1928, in GOB, Home (Special), File 543 (18) G of 1928, p. 69, MSA.
[74] Note by H. G. Haig, Secretary, GOI, Home, 8 November 1928, in GOI, Home (Poll), File F/18/VII/28, NAI.
[75] Home (Special), Note 8/1/29 in GOB Home (Special), File 543 (18) K of 1929, p. 5, MSA.   [76] Note by Secretary, GOB, Home (Special), 23/1/29, in *ibid.*, p. 18.

ration of the social order and the threat of violence to life and property. Furthermore, the Government of Bombay recognized that, as soon as the anxiety that the city was being overwhelmed by an atmosphere of 'riot and assassination' lessened, public opinion might even oppose the prosecution of the communist leaders, the repression of political opponents of the Raj and the infringement of what were, in any case, rather fragile civil liberties. On the other hand, public discussions of violence, the intimidation of 'loyal workers' by strikers and the communist menace in general provided an excellent basis for the Government of Bombay to claim with force the need to extend by legislation their own executive and police powers. It was in this context that the belief that the Indian working class was disposed to violence acquired new and explicit political meaning.

Nevertheless, the Government of Bombay remained consistently short of evidence to substantiate their claim that the millworkers were prone to violence, especially at the behest of communist leaders. In January 1929, three Pathan watchmen of the New China Mills at Sewri were assaulted and killed. The police made over a hundred arrests and then released about seventy-five millworkers. The remainder who were charged were members of the Girni Kamgar Union's mill committee. The Government of Bombay concluded that 'the recent murderous outrages . . . are the clear result . . . of these communist speeches' and contemplated the prosecution of the leaders for incitement to violence. But they foresaw two difficulties: first, 'that there was practically no violence during the general mill strike' of 1928 and second, 'that there is nothing to show that the present outrages are not disapprobated by the communist leaders'.[77] Their legal advice was even more unequivocal. Not only was there no evidence to connect the speeches of the leaders to the Pathan murders, the legal department doubted 'very much if it will be possible to establish such a connection'.[78] Indeed, the Home Secretary took sufficient note of this advice to inform the Bombay Millowners' Association – in flat contradiction to the spirit of his own jottings on the file – that 'the fact that the general mill strike endured for $5\frac{1}{2}$ months with only one serious collision between the strikers and the police testifies to the good sense and the good temper of the majority of the workmen' and declared that he had found 'no sign that speeches, however mischievous in intention, are bearing fruit in violence'.[79]

When a kidnapping scare implicating Pathans and fights between

[77] Note, Home (Special), 23/1/29, GOB Home (Special), File 543 (18) I of 1929, p. 4, MSA.
[78] Note by the Remembrances of Legal Affairs, *ibid.*, p. 11, MSA.
[79] Secretary, GOB, Home (Special), to Secretary, Bombay Millowners' Association, 26 January 1929, in GOB, Home (Special), File 543 (18) G of 1928, p. 95, MSA.

millworkers and Pathan blacklegs and moneylenders developed into a communal riot, in February 1929, the provincial government informed Delhi that 'it is commonly believed that the kidnapping scare was deliberately organized by communists to intimidate Pathan workmen and promote disorder' but admitted that 'evidence sufficient for a court of law' was not available.[80] The Home Secretary added in a separate note that

the recent murder of Pathans has indicated to other labour – e.g. Pathan to join up with the Communist unions or be forced out of Bombay ... Unless prompt steps are taken to deal with Communist propaganda further labour disturbances in Bombay are inevitable in the near future and these may, as the present riots, develop into serious communal trouble or may be anti-Government.[81]

The Home Secretary's laborious memorandum is another seminal document of official paranoia, but it is by no means an exceptional statement of the case. In the event, it was not forwarded to New Delhi, partly because the Home Member had been led to warn his secretary that the Government of Bombay would be well advised 'to mention only briefly the theories and suspicions regarding the communist connection with the recent disturbances, which are when all is said and done, rather debatable ground'.[82] Nonetheless, provincial pressure on Delhi to act was mounting. Certainly, the special officer's researches speeded up and the Government of India, having decided to proceed with their case, ordered the arrest of thirty-six communist leaders on 20 March 1929 to be tried at Meerut for conspiring to overthrow the King-Emperor.

The Meerut arrests had dramatic consequences in Bombay. They deepened the sense of grievance, which had been building up among the millworkers since the end of the general strike in October 1928, that the millowners had been nibbling away at piece rates, altering the conditions of work and victimizing members of the Girni Kamgar Union, even as negotiations between the joint mill strike committee and the Millowners' Association proceeded before the Fawcett Committee. On 26 April 1929, more than a month after the arrests, the Girni Kamgar Union called upon the workers to strike. Two days earlier, the union had agreed that the workers should enter the mills as usual and then stop work and leave together during the mid-day recess. The police commissioner was especially impressed that 'this programme was carried out in a perfectly peaceful way and with remarkable unanimity, something like 80 per cent of the men after leaving the mills at mid-day declining to return'.[83] If the

---

[80] Telegram, GOB Home to GOI Home, 6 February 1929 in GOB Home (Special), File 543 (18) K of 1929, p. 27, MSA.   [81] Draft letter to GOI, Home, in *ibid.*, p. 35.
[82] Note by Home Member, 5 March 1929, *ibid.*, p. 49.
[83] 'Notes on a Conversation with Mr Kelly, Commissioner of Police, Bombay, 4 June 1929', by H. G. Haig, 4 June 1929, in GOI Home Poll 303/1929, pp. 1–2, NAI.

millowners and colonial officials alike were alarmed, they were probably no more surprised than the leaders of the Girni Kamgar Union by this show of solidarity. As the colonial state grew more concerned to contain the threat of labour, the Millowners' Association determined 'to break the Girni Kamgar Union . . . and they are, therefore, prepared to fight to a finish'.[84] The discourse of violence, and the gathering panic about the consequences of the strike and general disorder, now strengthened the millowners' position. They argued forcefully, and with steadily growing confidence that they would secure the sympathy of the colonial state, that the workers' solidarity had been sustained by intimidation and that the government should adopt legislative measures to prevent its occurrence. Colonial officials, always prepared to take the opportunity to widen the powers at their command, and themselves perturbed by the red menace in their midst, gradually joined in the cacophonous discourse of violence.

Indeed, how consciously the language of violence could be deployed for political purposes now became increasingly evident. On 4 June 1929, the Commissioner of Police was sceptical of the millowners' claim that the continuance of the general strike was the result of the intimidation practised by the Girni Kamgar Union.[85] He was not, he declared, 'disposed to think that intimidation plays the important part which the millowners attribute to it'. Indeed, picketing was of 'a perfectly peaceful character' and was in any case 'rendered ineffective by the counter-picketing introduced by the millowners which has turned picketing rather into a matter of ridicule'. By the end of May, it had seemed as if the strike was petering out. On 24 May, only seven mills were still closed and four days later, only two mills were not working, and these for reasons unconnected with the strike. On 6 June, after the workers received their wages, however, the strike intensified: seventeen mills closed and over 30,000 workers stopped work. Within the next fortnight, the Government of Bombay completely reversed its earlier position. Portraying the industrial situation as if intimidation was practised by the Girni Kamgar Union 'with gradually increasing frequency in the streets and in or near the chawls', the Government of Bombay sought an ordinance from New Delhi to make 'intimidation' a cognizable offence, to be dealt with by direct executive action. The matter, they argued, was much too urgent for them to draft and debate a piece of legislation. New Delhi, alarmed at Bombay's volte-face, refused the ordinance and insisted that the provin-

---

[84] J. F. Gennings, Director of Information and Labour Intelligence, Labour Office, Bombay to Deputy Secretary, GOI, Industries and Labour, Simla, 18 May 1929, in GOI, Home Poll, 10/10/1930 & KW, p. 24, NAI.

[85] 'Notes on a Conversation with Mr Kelly, Commissioner of Police, Bombay, on 4 June 1929', by H. G. Haig, GOI, Home Poll, File 303/1929, NAI.

cial government face its legislative council but could scarcely now advise against the measure itself.[86]

To some extent, this radical shift in the provincial government's thinking reflected what the Home Secretary in Delhi had observed as an 'uncertainty of outlook' on the part of its officers and their inability to take 'a definite and consistent line of policy in dealing with a situation which is admittedly most complicated'. Indeed, colonial officials in Bombay had divided – and vacillated – between the view that the labour leaders, especially the communists, were to blame for the strikes and that the millowners had been clumsy and cack-handed in dealing with their workers, thus provoking 'the maximum of opposition'.[87] The Government of Bombay had found it difficult to take a steady view. But now there were also some more substantive considerations to focus the attentions of the official mind. The long period of acute social conflict which Bombay had witnessed since April 1928 had placed the police force under considerable strain. By the middle of 1929, the police commissioner regarded 'the prospect of these conditions continuing indefinitely' rather nervously. On the one hand, he feared that 'a large number of [police] men have a good deal of sympathy with the strikers'; on the other hand, the police were 'constantly being badgered by the millowners and by Bombay public opinion for not stopping conditions over which they really have no power'.[88] Cumulatively, it was feared, this served to undermine the morale of the police force. Moreover, the general strike of 1929 was a divisive conflict, unlike the industrial action of the previous year. In its initial stages, Bombay's Home Secretary had warned: 'So long as the strike is not general and complete, violence may be expected.'[89] This formulation described quite persuasively the character and timing of violence during strikes. Certainly, the divisions among the workers manifested themselves in a flow of complaints about intimidation. Some of these were lodged with the police; many were reported to the mill authorities who passed them on to the police. The nature of the complaints reveal that this 'intimidation' was not always violent. Frequently, they consisted of 'threat', 'abuse', 'obstruction' and even 'theft of clothes'. For the most part the alleged perpetrators as well as the complainants were described in collective nouns: for instance, 'mawalis' or 'union volunteers', in the case of the former, or 'the millhands of the Bombay Industrial Mill' in the case

[86] GOI Home Poll 303/1929, NAI; Telegram, Home, Simla to Bombay, Poona, 2 July 1929 in GOB, Home (Special), File 543 (10) E Part G of 1929, pp. 105–7, MSA.
[87] 'Summary', by H. G. Haig, 11 June 1929 in GOI, Home (Poll), File 303/1929 & KW's I and II, pp. 5–6, NAI.
[88] 'Notes on a Conversation with Mr Kelly', by H. G. Haig, 4 June 1929 in GOI, Home (Poll) File 303/1929, p. 2, NAI.
[89] Note by Secretary, GOB, Home (Special), 29 April 1929 in GOB, Home (Special), File 543 (10) E Part D of 1929, p. 28, MSA.

of the latter.[90] Nonetheless such evidence of 'intimidation', construed synonymously with violence, helped to increase the pressure among diverse groups for repressive measures by the police.

By June 1929, the colonial state had discovered a growing confidence as it moved against the massed ranks of militant workers. The Meerut arrests had scarcely raised a howl of protest that the limited freedoms of the Indian people were being trampled and no more than a murmur of complaint from the Congress leaders. On the contrary, 'there is a very strong and growing feeling in the city' the police commissioner observed, 'that drastic and very early action is necessary to deal with the communists who are responsible for the mill strike'.[91] Without a certain confidence in the strength of this feeling, the colonial officials would have found it much harder to act against the strikers. What informed this feeling was the generalization of the perception that the strikes, 'fomented' by the communist and other mischievous labour leaders, had created an atmosphere of violence and disorder. Ironically, it was less the declaration of a second communist-led general strike in April 1929 than the communal riots which occurred first in February and then in May which acted to generalize and entrench this perception.

V

It is not intended to suggest that the millowners and civil servants orchestrated a discourse of violence simply in order to repress an increasingly militant labour movement. Rather, the fact that images of the roughness and violence of the working classes were so widely accepted enabled the millowners to impose their particular interpretation upon the strikes of 1928 and 1929 and, further, to prevail upon the colonial state to act quite so explicitly in their own interests. While subscribing to this discourse, the millowners as well as the state were able to serve their own different purposes. What led a wide range of people in the city, and outside, to so deeply fear impending disorder and violence and to acquiesce in the appropriation of large repressive powers by the state was the nature of the communal riots as a social experience.

Bombay's residents, especially its elites, had prided themselves on the pluralist traditions of the city and the cross-communal basis of its politics and they were startled by the scale and ferocity of the riots.[92] Both riots

[90] 'Statement of Cases of Intimidation in Connection with the Mill Strike from 26 April 1929 to 11 July 1929, reported to the Mill Authorities', in GOB, Home (Special), File 543 (10) E-(BB) of 1929, pp. 71–85, MSA.

[91] Commissioner of Police, Bombay to Secretary, GOB, Home (Special), 11 June 1929, in GOB, Home (Special), File 543 (10) E-(BB) of 1929, p. 3, MSA.

[92] No communal riots on this scale had occurred since 1893 and it is probable that only a small minority, in this city of migrants, had experienced them.

had been sparked off by conflicts which arose out of labour disputes. In February, Pathans had been hired by the employers to break the strike at the oil refinery at Sewri. Yet the hiring of Pathans as blacklegs had occurred against the background of widespread antagonism towards, and fear of them in Bombay. During the strike of 1928 and its aftermath, millworkers had borrowed extensively from Pathan moneylenders, who were alone in their willingness to lend to destitute strikers. For this service, they charged what were seen as exorbitant rates of interest and they were believed to be exceptionally brutal and ruthless in the recovery of their loans. This combination of fear and loathing, exclusion and exploitation came together in February to make the Pathans the target of working-class violence. In May, conflicts between some, predominantly, Hindu strikers and largely Muslim non-strikers, and attempts by millowners to recruit Muslims to keep their looms and spindles running, developed into a widespread communal riot. In both cases, the riots soon spread out of the mill districts and into the central parts of the island and as they did so the participation of millworkers in them declined. There was some evidence to suggest that the labour leaders and especially the communists exhorted the workers not to be drawn into the communal violence. But none of this shook the growing conviction that the riots were the inevitable outcome of a process set in motion by the trouble-making communists. The Bombay Riots Inquiry Committee, which met in June 1929 and took evidence, in its investigation of the causes of the violence, concluded that the underlying cause was 'the speeches of extremist labour agitators from May 1928'.[93] Yet those who read the transcripts of the oral evidence deposed before the committee are likely to find little to substantiate the claim – apart from the repetition of the claim itself – that communism or the manipulation and intrigues of its political advocates caused the violence.[94] In fact, rather, more powerful and complex factors were at work.

Remarkably, it was these communal riots, rather than prolonged strikes or the apparently sweeping successes of the communists, which persuaded many residents of Bombay – and not merely its elites – that the colonial government should acquire fresh and sweeping repressive powers and deploy them forcefully against the city's millworkers. The impact of the communal riots on the public perceptions of violence and the social order is perhaps best explained in terms of their nature, as a period of social conflict. However potent the threat of working-class violence had seemed during the general strike of 1928, it had in fact passed without violence. The communal riots entailed real and murderous violence on an extensive scale and the violence they manifested was

[93] *Report of the Bombay Riots Inquiry Committee* (Bombay, 1929), pp. 4–5, 7.
[94] The proceedings of the BRIC are preserved in the MSA, Bombay.

apparently without economy. In February as well as May, there were relatively few confrontations between hostile crowds.[95] For the most part, the violence consisted of assaults on passers-by who had wandered into a strange neighbourhood. Everybody, it seemed, was at risk and nobody could anticipate who might turn upon whom. At another level, whatever their aversion to the violence around them, everybody was implicated either as potential victims or as potential aggressors. Millowners and merchants, landlords and shopkeepers, seeking to protect their premises could only do so by the same means as those who threatened them. The respectable, concerned to secure their neighbourhoods, had no option but to adopt the methods of the rough. This state of fear and anticipation of violence could in its own right generate further violence. During the riots, agencies which ordinarily maintained order appeared ineffective or were perceived to be partial and tainted by the conflict. Above all, few could make sense of the riots. They appeared inexplicable and irrational. Since everyday social and commercial exchange did not disclose clearly demarcated communities, but close connections across boundaries now so clearly drawn, it was difficult to make sense of the polarization of the city between putative, if improbable, units of Hindus, on the one side, and Muslims, on the other.

Under these circumstances, anxieties about 'the other', fortified by social prejudices harboured in ordinary times, now acquired an awesome and menacing shape. The difficulty was that 'the other' now became everybody else. The rich feared the poor; Hindus and Muslims feared each other; women feared men; everybody feared 'the hooligan'. Indeed, the responsibility for the violence was displaced onto 'the hooligan'. 'The worst offenders', it was reported, 'have been hooligans who haunt the bye-ways and who stab or hit and then run for safety into a maze of houses and gullies'.[96] The hooligan became the universal embodiment of 'the other'. His methods appeared to encapsulate the random and arbitrary nature of the assaults associated with the riots. His presence allowed those who aspired to respectability to absolve themselves from responsibility for the violence and to dissociate themselves from its brutality. For those who lived through the riots, the hooligan provided an explanation for the inexplicable, a rationalization of the seemingly irrational, a semblance of sense where nonsense abounded. If for most people this polarization by religious community made no sense in the pattern of their daily social relations, blaming those they perceived as marginalized, poorly integrated, semi-criminal desperate groups allowed them to grasp the extraordinary events of the riots, and to reconcile the communalization

[95] GOB Home (Special), File 348 Part II of 1929; GOB Home (Poll), File 344 of 1929; *Report of the BRIC*; Proceedings of the BRIC, MSA.   [96] *Times of India*, 6 May 1929.

which accompanied them with the syncretism of daily life. Finally, and quintessentially, 'the hooligan' personified the collapse of order. It was not simply that 'hooligans' were believed to 'swarm to the surface' during the riots, but more significantly, that the violence could not be confined to the domain of 'the hooligan'. As the riots spread, 'completely disorganizing business and traffic throughout the city',[97] they threatened to sweep up everybody in their embrace. None were spared from the threat of violence. Bombay's inhabitants tracked 'the steady progress of the city towards chaos' and were bewildered and frightened by 'the atmosphere of anarchy' which prevailed.[98]

It was in this 'atmosphere of anarchy' that the need for the forceful intervention of the state seemed imperative in the most unlikely quarters. Thus, even the nationalist *Bombay Chronicle* observed that 'it would be disastrous' if the city were to 'become a prey to hooliganism on the slightest of pretexts' and reminded its readers, and the colonial state, that 'the most important function of a modern Government is to prevent the outbreak of lawlessness'.[99] The roots of this state of anarchy could be traced back to the two general strikes, the preaching of the communists and the spreading contempt for law and order which they were believed to have fostered. To those who had once been sceptical about the colonial state's tilting at the windmill of the red menace or had cast a knowing eye over the millowners' agenda, the discourse of violence – and the connections which it forged between disorder, hooliganism, working-class roughness, strikes, communists and communal riots – began to appear less improbable, sometimes even rather plausible. Public opinion in India – by no means confined to the propertied elites alone – was willing to endow the colonial state with repressive powers, which it was at times reluctant to acquire itself. Yet these repressive powers would not only undermine the liberties of its subjects but, once in place, could thereafter be used against opponents of the state, and, potentially, therefore, under changed circumstances, against those who now pressed for the adoption of the most draconian measures.

This representation of working-class politics in terms of its essential roughness and violence served to justify repressive action, whether in the streets, or in policies formulated in the secretariat or in powers assumed by the state and codified in the legislatures. As this representation of the working class became increasingly pervasive, various interests sought to deploy this discourse to their advantage. The police argued the case for greater resources. Millowners wanted the state to help them to discipline their recalcitrant workforce and destroy the influence of the communists.

---

[97] *Ibid.*   [98] *Ibid.*   [99] *Bombay Chronicle*, 6 May 1929.

Labour leaders sought to displace their more radical rivals. Indeed, the Gandhian conquest of violence signified at one level the attempt by Congressmen to control, not merely to lead, their followers. Colonial officials could, within the terms of this discourse, try to justify the appropriation of greater powers to wield against threats to the social order and, indeed, their own future. Throughout the 1930s, measures broadly taken against labour organizations were justified in terms of the potential for working-class violence. This vocabulary was not specific to the vernacular of the British in India; it was also deployed by the provincial ministries of the Congress in the late 1930s as well by the governments of independent India after 1947. It reflected social anxieties no less real for being so loosely formulated. Indeed, it was precisely this looseness of definition that imbued the discourse of violence with considerable political value for the colonial state and for its various shifting groups of collaborators. The power and resilience of violence in public discourse derived from its lack of definition and especially its elasticity of meaning. It was this elasticity of meaning which facilitated the creation of a vocabulary which carried a resonance for diverse social groups. The perception of the threat of violence – particularly by the working classes, or groups among them – could for this reason be widely shared, even among those groups who were vulnerable to being characterized in its terms. Characterizations of working-class violence, now so enthusiastically taken over by historians, were integral to the dubiously moral economy of the ruling classes in colonial India.

VI

The notion that the working classes, or particular groups among them, were inherently predisposed to violence arose from the prejudices of the dominant classes about the roughness of the lower orders. But it was also integral to a wider discourse. Frequently, characterizations of the violence and roughness of the working classes, often devised by employers, policemen and civil servants, prepared the ground for pushing forward policies which particular interests desired. Beneath their cognitive surface lay a crucial, if unwarranted, shift from the observation of particular acts of 'disorder' to the definition of violence as a quality innate to the working class. It is misleading, therefore, to displace these characterizations onto the 'realities' of working-class life and working-class politics.

This discourse of violence tended to generalize rather than to specify its meaning. Thus, the consideration of industrial violence came to be inextricably linked with, sometimes it was merged into, criminal, revolutionary or even communal violence or, more broadly, a pervasive contempt for authority. Frequently, the causes of 'industrial violence' came to be identified with, indeed embodied in, the very same groups – marginal elements, casual labourers, rural migrants – who were perceived to have a particular predisposition to criminal and violent behaviour. The identification of the casual poor or the rural migrant with criminality and violence has reflected police practice rather more accurately than it has described their behaviour. Because they were perceived as dangerous and criminal, they – or groups within them – were policed more closely and became more vulnerable to arrest. Once they were drawn into the criminal justice system, their presence afforced the perception of their character-type as criminal. In this way, the perception that they were prone to crime and violence preceded the behaviour of any individuals defined as belonging to this stratum and was then affirmed by selective policing. To complete the circle of perception and practice, this affirmation of their roughness and criminality then served to legitimize policies directed specifically to control them.

The identification of these social groups with violence has developed from the assumption widely, sometimes implicitly, made in the social sciences that endemic violence characterizes societies in the process of transition to modern, industrial capitalism. By this ahistorical, normative, evolutionary scheme of social change, apparently applicable to all societies at all times, it followed that workers in the early stages of industrialization were characteristically volatile; that communalism could appear as a survival from a previous epoch characterized by a sacral conception of the polity and the public domain; and that the violence and criminality of the urban poor signified the archaic remnant of pre-bourgeois attitudes among the working classes. The notion that violence is endemic in societies in the process of transition to modern industrialism has led to its identification in the Indian case as the characteristic of social groups affected, but also marginalized, by that process of transition: early industrial workers, inadequately assimilated to the factory; the urban poor; rural migrants in the industrial setting. Yet in India – and, of course, not only in India – the 'casual poor' and rural migrants were not marginal to the economy or the social order, but, rather, were integral to the processes by which these were constituted and reproduced.

If violence is taken to be integral to the culture of the poor and the character-types of whole social groups, its practice is thus abstracted from the particular social and political circumstances in which it occurs. The claim that their propensity to violence is inherent to the culture and social character of particular groups suggests that it exists independently of the wider context, even if that context is invoked to explain it. On the other hand, if violence is to be explained as a function of social transformation, then its investigation would direct our attention to the political and economic context of change rather than the symptoms to which, it is suggested, it gave rise.

Violence, both actual and potential, has been in all societies a powerful instrument for the negotiation of power relations, whether for the maintenance of control or the organization and conduct of protest. In India, it acquired a special dimension. The final sanction for the maintenance and perpetuation of imperial rule was necessarily physical force. But the colonial state could not afford to use it freely. It lacked the financial resources or even the military might to rule so vast and turbulent a land by force. To attempt to do so was always likely to necessitate the sacrifice of other more crucial imperial priorities.

One solution to this problem was to ignore it or, at any rate, to throw a hastily constructed facade of order across deeper levels of social conflict. The perpetuation of colonial rule depended to a large extent upon the effectiveness of local structures of control. But there was nothing stagnant about the social relationships underlying these structures. At these levels, the dadas, the street gangs, the retainers who might throw their holds or wield their lathis in the interests of the local boss could as easily turn against him. This was why when the existing relationships of power in local society were undermined or existing structures of dominance effectively challenged, they threatened to take away with them much of the facade of order behind which the Raj nestled. Social control has always been more easily theorized than enforced.

Unlike the post-colonial state, which has proved more willing than its predecessor to turn its cannons on its opponents, colonial rulers did not possess sufficiently powerful social and cultural ties by which to negotiate social tensions or maintain order. They could neither easily legitimize the use of force nor justify their own policies of repression. Yet the weakness of their cultural hegemony and their lack of social influence meant that they were repeatedly thrown back upon the use of force, repressive laws or even extra-legal coercion. The further the colonial state intervened in areas of social conflict in order to maintain intact this facade of order, whether against non-violent satyagrahis or more fearsome strikers in the industrial setting, the more fundamentally were its weaknesses exposed. It is hardly surprising, therefore, that the colonial state remained so sensitive to the threat and the possibilities of violence.

At the same time, in the last decades of British rule, the colonial state was brought increasingly under Indian control. Indeed, Indian elites were now more easily able to deploy the power of the state to maintain their dominance. As the colonial state became more and more Indian, so it lost more of its scruples about the political susceptibilities of its subjects and showed a growing willingness to repress strikes with greater ferocity. The political conjuncture of 1928–29 in Bombay illustrates how Indian elites gained from colonial rule the political power to control and exploit labour more intensively. Colonialism in India might, in this light, be defined, in one of its characteristic aspects, as the process by which labour was cheapened and more fully subordinated to capital, both indigenous and imperial.

6 Police and public order in Bombay, 1880–1947

I

British rule in India was characteristically autocratic and repressive. It could at times be brutal and violent. The rhetoric of civil liberties and individual freedoms decorated its claims to legitimacy but, in practice, these considerations occupied a lowly place in its order of priorities. In a history characterized by annexation and conquest and by the maintenance of dominion by force, it is not surprising that the organization and activities of the police should be taken to reflect the authoritarian nature of colonial rule. For some, it has appeared to be 'expressive of the very nature of colonial rule in India'.[1]

By focusing upon the administration and organization of the police, historians have often tended to foster the supposition that it constituted a monolithic force.[2] However, this organizational perspective has made it difficult to resolve apparent contradictions in the nature of colonial policing and sometimes served to proliferate confusion. Thus, in one account, the police appeared to constitute the most effective and powerful instrument of colonial repression, but they were also found to be 'often inadequate to meet the major crises of rural control'. On the one hand, 'the coercive strength and disposition of the colonial police' was said to be nourished by colonial and racist ideology; on the other hand, we are told that 'India's colonial regime fell short of being a police state' or a 'society ruled through fear' because of 'Britain's own political culture' whose innate liberalism served as a check upon unbridled despotism. Colonial and racist attitudes, presumably not drawn from 'Britain's own political culture', underlay the violence of the state, yet, largely, 'the police alignment was with the propertied classes and not merely the ruling race'. Thus, the police have been portrayed as the main force of a colonial state

[1] Arnold, *Police Power and Colonial Rule*, p. 235.
[2] Percival Griffiths, *To Guard My People: The History of the Indian Police* (London, 1971); A. Gupta, *The Police in British India, 1861–1947* (New Delhi, 1979); Arnold, *Police Power and Colonial Rule*; Robb, 'The Ordering of Rural India'.

which was both hegemonic and vulnerable; characterized as coercive yet found to be ineffectual; motivated by racism yet restrained by an inherent metropolitan liberalism; allied closely with Indian propertied elites and yet the bludgeon of the ruling race.[3]

This chapter will suggest that generalizations about the nature of policing should rest most securely upon the investigation of its daily operations rather than its administrative design or its organizational form. Accordingly, it will focus upon what might be described as 'everyday policing'. Its aim is to place police methods of operation in relation to the social organization of the neighbourhoods in Bombay city in the late nineteenth and early twentieth centuries. The daily operations of the police were determined by the financial and political constraints within which they developed. At this quotidian level, the police were integral to the processes by which power relations were negotiated in the street and the neighbourhood, and thus constituted an important element in the formation and consolidation of local power. Their actions influenced, as, indeed, they came to be moulded by, patterns of local dominance. Furthermore, at lesser levels, albeit less systematically, the working classes, too, could draw upon, appropriate and deploy their personal and social caste and kinship connections with the police. As the police became embedded within the social and political networks of the neighbourhood, they operated less as simply an instrument of social control, but proved more responsive to influences which were relatively autonomous of their own internal structure of command. In this light, and viewed through the prism of their daily operations, the police, far from being monolithic, appear to have been responsive to varied and often conflicting sets of social pressures.

It is not intended to suggest that we should replace the notion that the police were indiscriminately repressive with the notion that they were uniformly benign. In Bombay, as elsewhere, the police lacked the political and financial resources to control and discipline the working classes as a whole. The conventional and pragmatic response of the police has been to proceed selectively. Some elements among the poor and the working classes, singled out for particular attention, must have experienced the police as a particularly brutal and violent force. But if the police were open to recruitment by diverse groups within the urban neighbourhoods, they could not fulfil their disciplinary, even coercive, function systematically. On the contrary, their selective interventions were probably often experienced as somewhat arbitrary, but they would have seemed no less oppressive and no more limited for being less systematic. If the police

[3] Arnold, *Police Power and Colonial Rule:*, pp. 147, 230, 233, 235.

lacked the political and financial resources to set out to control and discipline the working classes as a whole, they also found it difficult to proceed more selectively by identifying particular social groups as the targets of their actions. For the task of establishing a general and uniformly applicable consensus about the particular social groups to be discriminatingly identified as the proper objects of policing often proved beyond the capacity of the colonial state in India. From the perspective of everyday policing, it would seem implausible to portray the police as simply and unproblematically the enforcers of social control designed by the colonial state and its collaborators or to suppose that they were able consistently to give practical effect to the intentions of the official mind. Indeed, frequently, their methods of operation undermined and contradicted the most carefully devised blueprints of the colonial state.

Two further considerations embedded the police more deeply within the social organization of the neighbourhood. First, in India the police force had military origins. Its primary concern was to police those who had been subjugated, to facilitate the collection of revenue and to ensure the free movement of goods. After the 1860s, when a uniform police system was put in place, the police understanding of its own role, and its perception of crime and the social order, was coloured by its military antecedents. The police were liable, therefore, to understand crime primarily in terms of rebellion and disorder, public and political security, rather than simply in terms of law-breaking and the security of property and the person. Of course, no police force could set itself the task of rooting out crime wherever it was to be found, with any realistic expectation of accomplishing it. On the contrary, police activity, and the operation of the criminal justice system as a whole, often served to define and indeed, therefore, to create crime. The more conscientiously the police set out to abolish crime, the more likely it was to both become aware of it, generate fresh categories of offences and criminalize old patterns of behaviour. The operations of the police imparted to the notion of public security an explicitly, and narrowly, political meaning. For this reason, it neither sought to intervene energetically nor to disturb too greatly the practices by which offences against person and property were handled within informal social networks or local power structures. Of course, the police everywhere have relied to varying degrees upon the collaboration of local residents. Its consequence in India was that propertied elites, merchants and industrialists and local magnates, created their own private arrangements for protection and policing. For this reason, too, the scope and the daily practices of the police, and their apparent ambiguities and contradictions, need to be situated within the context of the social relations of the neighbourhood.

Second, although the colonial state increasingly assumed that the maintenance of public order was ordinarily the duty of the police, troops were frequently summoned to deal with 'local disturbances'. Significantly, public order policing in India, even after the 1860s, was largely conducted by the army. When the police were called upon to deal with 'local disturbances', their strategies were largely shaped by their own relationship to the social organization of the neighbourhood. It was at this quotidian level that the parameters within which the police approached larger and more dramatic problems of public order were defined. Senior police officers recognized the value of establishing close connections with the informal social networks of the neighbourhood, both to detect crime and to protect the public order. But such connections only served to heighten their anxieties about the quality of the discipline of their rank and file. Frequently, faced with 'a local disturbance', the police felt they were unable to cope and that they were in danger of being overrun by the 'mob'. They required the army to stand by and strengthen their nerve and sometimes to intervene and restore order. The armed force which the colonial state could command was formidable and when it perceived a serious threat to its security, it unleashed it with a ruthless, sometimes murderous, brutality. Its sanction and its power were essential to the maintenance and perpetuation of British rule. Yet the British sometimes appeared unable to deploy it to repress their opponents. The British in India did not, they could not, constitute an army of occupation. Had they attempted to so style themselves, the armed force at their disposal would have seemed woefully inadequate.[4] In any case, they did not rule India for its own sake; their purposes were global and imperial and extended beyond the limits of political dominion. For the historian, therefore, the central problem in the policing of colonial India is how to match the repressive power of the state to the fragility of its control. It was primarily because the police established these connections within the neighbourhood, remained open, however unwittingly, to its influences, and sought to maintain public order through these alliances, that they were able to postpone for a time having to bear the ultimate cost of their most brutal repressive efforts. Thus, the supposedly 'coercive disposition' of the police force and its repressive practices were inextricably connected to the nature of its daily operations in the street and the neighbourhood. Accordingly, this chapter will first set out the constraints within which the police operated in Bombay; it will proceed to ask how these constraints

[4] Thus, in 1938, there was one British soldier to every 88 square miles of the territory and for every 20,000 inhabitants of the subcontinent. 'The British Element in Internal Security Troops', Appendix E to Annex 2, CID 198–D, CAB 6/6, PRO, cited by D. Omissi, *The Sepoy and the Raj: The Indian Army, 1860–1940* (London, 1994), p. 212.

influenced police practice; and, finally, it will examine how this dimension of everyday policing shaped their strategies for the maintenance of public order.

II

If the colonial police were, as they have sometimes been described, the most effective instrument of state repression, it is striking that India was far more sparsely policed than England. Both in personnel and resources, the thin blue line was very thin indeed. The Bombay Presidency had one of the most centralized administrations in India and, in per capita terms, its police force was perhaps the strongest in the subcontinent. Although the Presidency, excluding the 'native states', was in land area more than twice the size of England and Wales, the strength of its police force engaged on what were called 'station duties' in the early twentieth century was slightly over a third of that deployed in England and Wales. While in England and Wales there was a policeman for every 772 people in the first decade of the twentieth century, the Bombay Presidency, at the time, raised a ratio of one policeman for 1,360 people. The level of expenditure on the police force presents a similar contrast. The total cost of the police in England and Wales was estimated at £99 9s per man per annum; in Bombay, it amounted to slightly more than £12.[5] These statistics for the Presidency as a whole included Sind, the laboratory of Sir Charles Napier's early experiments and the model for police organization in India, where the density of policemen was the highest in the subcontinent.[6] As a result, they also conceal the sparseness of policemen in the districts of the Konkan, South Gujarat and Karnataka, where their ratio to the population varied between 1,100 and 1,300, without allowing for those who were not engaged on 'station duties'.[7]

Over large parts of the Indian countryside there was no police presence

[5] E. C. Cox, *Police and Crime in India* (London, 1910), pp. 125–27. These figures according to Cox date from 'three or four years ago': *ibid.*, p. 125.
[6] According to Hunter, there was a policeman for every 336 people in Karachi and for every 367 people in Thar and Parkar in Sind in 1890. W. W. Hunter, *Bombay, 1885 to 1890: A Study in Indian Administration* (London, 1892), p. 426. By 1930, there was a policeman for every 820 people in the Bombay Presidency while there was one for every 64 people in Sind. Calculated from J. C. Curry, *The Indian Police* (London, 1932), Appendix, p. 347.
[7] Hunter, *Bombay, 1885 to 1890*, p. 426. Policemen not engaged on station duties included 'a large number of men employed on the guarding of a multitude of Government treasuries, the escort of Government treasure, the personal escort of officers, the guarding of jails, and of railway trains, stations, and goods-sheds, together with other quasi-military and miscellaneous duties none of which are required of the police in England'. Cox, *Police and Crime in India*, p. 126. These men were excluded from the calculations which Cox made of the ratio of policemen per head of population in India and England, but Hunter's calculations do not appear to have allowed for them.

at all. Villages were omitted from the administrative design of the police force. The basic unit of the District Police was the subdivisional outpost which lightly supervised the works of the village watch, ostensibly conducted by the hereditary servants of the village community, an institution always more active in the sociological imagination of the official mind than it was in rural society. When it was effective, the village watch was to a large extent the strong arm of its headmen or, more broadly, its dominant families. According to Edmund Cox, the village watch in the Bombay Presidency was 'for the most part an elegant fiction'. It usually consisted of 'a rabble of over a dozen nondescripts', who rarely 'use the powers that have been conferred upon them' and 'so far from assisting the more disciplined guardians of the peace, they are actually at the bottom of much concerted crime'.[8]

The Bombay City Police was organized separately from the provincial force, with its own commissioner on the model of the Metropolitan Police in London. It might be supposed that a large and growing commercial and industrial centre like Bombay city, with a significant European presence, would be more closely policed. Yet its police force was half the strength of Calcutta and considerably weaker than London. In 1885, it was reported, 'the strength of the Police available to meet all demands is considerably less in number than in 1865', its responsibilities were increasing and their range widening. The result was 'a cruel over-working of the Police'. Policemen were expected to be on duty for 14 to 17 hours 'on alternate nights and for 2 consecutive months'. In addition, following their spell of duty, they were expected to attend the courts or the commissioner's office to discharge particular cases. The lowest grade of constable received in pay about two-thirds of the average millworker's wage and perhaps as much as the unskilled and lowest paid occupations in the cotton textile industry. Since it was 'impossible to obtain efficient men in any way suited to make policemen', the commissioner could not afford to be too particular about whom he recruited. The height for entry was lowered to 5 feet 4 inches and the minimum chest measurements to increasingly modest levels.[9] The situation had not changed appreciably by the early twentieth century. 'I have had at times', confessed one police officer in 1910, 'to enlist men who had not come up to the standard'.[10] The Bombay City Police were not a prepossessing force. However much the commissioner may have yearned for the fine strapping specimens of the martial races, his men were characteristically diminutive and not infrequently consumptive. What they lacked in muscle they did not make

[8] Cox, *Police and Crime in India*, pp. 254, 258 and 256.
[9] *Annual Report on the Police in the Town and Island of Bombay for 1884* (Bombay, 1885), pp. 13–15.   [10] Cox, *Police and Crime in India*, pp. 144–5.

up with arms. In the 1880s, the police force had forty swords between them while the remainder were given batons.[11] In the following decades, a larger component of the force was armed, usually with muskets, which were as likely to damage the marksman as his mark. It was only in the 1920s, after the Amritsar massacre and growing financial constraints forced some reconsideration of the role of the army in quelling civil disorder, that an armed police reserve was developed and it was only during the second world war that it was significantly expanded.[12] The organizational weaknesses of the police should not lead us to the conclusion that the police were complacent about the task they faced in Bombay. Indeed, as one senior policeman in Bombay put it in the 1930s, the city and the Presidency capitals

act as magnets to attract the most hardened criminals of all the criminal classes of Asia. They have incredible underworlds, sordid, inflammable and incurable . . . The mawalis of Bombay are men who live by trading in every kind of human vice: chicanery, fraud, drugs, women, murder, the whole gamut of evil.[13]

These disadvantages were compounded by another: the city's residents showed little enthusiasm for serving in the force. Senior police officers expressed a preference for recruiting those who were 'natives of the district in which they are required to serve', for 'knowledge of the language, customs and geography of the district' was 'very essential' for the effective discharge of their duties. However, as one officer noted in 1910, 'local recruitment is not . . . always possible'.[14] In 1913, the Government of Bombay complained, 'Great difficulty is reported to have been experienced in finding sufficient men to bring the force up to its sanctioned strength.'[15] In other words, the city police could not attract enough recruits to spend the money they were allocated. 'Were it not for the steady flow of Marathas from Ratnagiri', it was reported in 1913, 'there would be a constant and serious shortage of constables'. Special recruiting parties sent into the Deccan 'met with little or no success'. The 'Pardeshi' (literally, foreign) Hindus from North India showed a decreasing interest in employment in the police force largely due 'to the prospect of higher wages without the trouble of discipline' elsewhere. The decrease

[11] *Annual Report on the Police in the Town and Island of Bombay for 1884*, pp. 13–15.
[12] Bombay Confidential Proceedings, Home Department, January, 1921, vol. 62, OIOC; on the development of the armed police in Madras, see D. Arnold, 'The Armed Police and Colonial Rule in South India, 1914–1947', *MAS*, 11:1 (1977), 101–25; on the expansion of the armed police during the second world war, see Gupta, *The Police in British India*, p. 547, see also pp. 492–563.   [13] Curry, *The Indian Police*, p. 49.
[14] Cox, *Police and Crime in India*, p. 143.
[15] Judicial Dept. Circular, 14 July 1914 in *Annual Report on the Police in the City of Bombay, 1913*.

in Pardeshi applications was not in itself entirely reason for regret. For, in the view of the authorities, 'the Pardeshi makes a much less satisfactory policeman than the recruit from the Bombay Presidency, for apart from his other failings he is in the first instance less educated and he exhibits a tendency to become somewhat invertebrate and melancholic under the depressing effects of the Bombay monsoon'.[16] In fact, all over India, 'Pardeshis' entered the police force in profusion. 'They generally possess considerable physical strength', Edmund Cox declared,

they are proverbially honest and faithful, but their brain-power is very limited . . . they are well-fitted [sic] for guards and escorts. For the work of the unarmed police such men are entirely unsuitable. They usually know nothing of the language of the countries other than their own. They have no friends or interests among the people and are useless for the purposes of investigation.[17]

Conversely, Marathas from Ratnagiri often had too many friends and interests among the people to police them reliably and consistently according to the commands of their senior officers. Distaste for employment in the police force remained significant in the 1920s. The Deccan Marathas, it was observed, were still 'not so enamoured of service in the police', while now even Hindu migrants from North India sought out alternative employment when the opportunity arose. Only Muslims from the Bombay Presidency as well as from North India, along with Marathas from Ratnagiri, were more readily recruited into the police force.

In addition, there was a substantial turnover of policemen every year roughly at the rate of about 10 per cent. This prompted the suspicion that 'agriculturalists from the Konkan and elsewhere are merely making use of the Police Department for tiding over a few months of the year when they might otherwise be idle'. However, further investigation satisfied the police that this was not the case because 'enlistments and resignations are distributed fairly equally over different months of the year'.[18] In fact, a large proportion of the city's working class retained their rural connections but sought more or less permanent work in Bombay. However, the maintenance of their village connections demanded considerable flexibility to move between town and country, sometimes at short notice, often for varying periods of time, while retaining a lien on their jobs in Bombay.[19] Certainly, the strategies to preserve their stake in the village often proved incompatible with the maintenance of police discipline. The fact that recruitment and resignation were distributed evenly throughout the

[16] *Annual Report on the Police, 1913*, p. 16.   [17] Cox, *Police and Crime in India*, pp. 143–4.
[18] *Annual Report on the Police, 1922*, p. 22.
[19] See Chandavarkar, *The Origins of Industrial Capitalism*, ch. 4.

year need not necessarily rule out the possibility that the rural interests of policemen propelled the rate of turnover among constables.

The low wages of the lowest ranks of the force did not serve to attract recruits. Further disincentives were 'to be found in the unpleasant conditions in which recruits have to live owing to shortage of housing accommodation and in the large number of vacancies which results in duties being often imposed on recruits in the first months of their service from which they should be exempt'.[20] Periodically, in the 1920s and to a lesser extent in the 1930s, the police found themselves unable to operate even at the inadequate strength sanctioned by provincial government budgets.[21] The building of 'police lines' and barracks, and the housing of constables in military-style barracks has often been interpreted as a reflection of a colonial style of policing but it was primarily a pragmatic response to the difficulties of recruiting a police force. The provision of housing in Bombay was a necessary inducement to attract recruits and essential for the survival of poorly paid constables. As long as the police force was undermanned, and women were not generally recruited to serve in this period, it was difficult to weed out recruits who 'did not show good promise during their training' or more generally 'to enforce a higher standard of discipline' within the police force as a whole.[22]

Nor did the police become progressively more effective. The value of stolen property reported to the police amounted to about 4 annas per capita in the 1880s and rose to under 6 annas in 1908 or roughly the average daily wage of millworkers. By inflating their valuations, the police were able to raise this figure to 12 annas in 1910, but were unable to sustain this figure during the decade and it was not until the early 1920s that their estimates amounted to 2 rupees.[23] It would be reasonable to assume that a significant proportion of this property was probably stolen from the vast majority who paid no taxes and exercised no control over municipal expenditure. Since law-breaking cost the city's elites so little, they saw no reason why law enforcement should cost them more.

Significantly, between 1865 and 1907, the Government of Bombay tried to hive off the police charges for the city onto the Municipal Corporation. The distribution of this expenditure between the local and provincial levels of the state was 'a perennial source of friction between Government and Corporation'.[24] The successive financial crises which

[20] *Annual Report on the Police, 1922*, p. 29.
[21] P. J. Thomas, *The Growth of Federal Finance in India* (London, 1939), p. 518.
[22] *Annual Report on the Police, 1924*, p. 32.   [23] *Annual Reports on the Police, passim.*
[24] R. P. Masani, *The Evolution of Local Self-Government in Bombay* (Oxford, 1929), p. 329.

the Government of India faced in the 1860s had encouraged it to devolve responsibility for matters such as the police and sanitation, which were marginal to Britain's global imperial interests, to municipalities and district councils constituted by the wider representation and election of Indian interests. This was known as local self-government, which in view of its supposed educative value enabled the colonial state to do good by doing well. Local elites could thus carry the political costs and garner the profits of taxing and spending around the parish pump. In 1865, the whole cost of the city's police was thrown upon the Municipal Corporation and although the provincial government was persuaded to contribute to these charges later in the decade, it simply and suddenly stopped payment in 1873. Although the principle of the provincial government's contribution was restored through the arbitration of the Government of India, the burden which each body would bear remained a matter of dispute until 1907, with the Government of Bombay reducing its investment at every opportunity. The parsimony of the provincial government persisted into the 1920s and 1930s. Although the total expenditure of the Government of Bombay increased gradually in the 1920s, the budget allocated to the police declined while both fell together in the 1930s. Expenditure on the police declined from about 13 per cent of the provincial budget in 1921–22 to 11 per cent in 1929–30 and although it increased in the wake of civil disobedience, it still accounted for 11 per cent in 1939–40.[25]

Various attempts were made from the late nineteenth century onwards to re-organize the police force and increase its efficiency. But their effects were by no means dramatic. Among the many shortcomings of the city's police force, the reformers identified 'the absence of any proper record of complaints and investigations' and that 'the station is constantly left for several hours' without officers 'capable of recording a complaint properly and commencing enquiries'.[26] In fact, it was said, 'the Governor-in-Council has reason to believe that there has been a tendency in the past to discourage the lodging of complaints of petty thefts'.[27] In the late nineteenth century, these conditions had invariably led the Government of Bombay to the happy conclusion that the city was populated by peaceable and law-abiding people. In 1875, the Government of Bombay compared crime statistics for Bombay and Calcutta and without allowing for the more intensive policing of the latter or for

[25] Calculated from Thomas, *The Growth of Federal Finance*, p. 518.
[26] *Annual Report on the Police, 1909*, p. 9.
[27] Circular, Under Secretary, Judicial, GOB to Commissioner of Police, Bombay etc., 2 September 1910, in *ibid.*, p. 1.

under-reporting, applauded the moral character and peace-loving nature of its inhabitants.[28]

Although they continued to regard the volume of crime as 'a natural consequence of the general weakness of the administration',[29] the Judicial Department of the Government of Bombay anticipated by 1910 that improved methods of reporting or, at least, an end to the practice of actively discouraging people from lodging complaints, would lead to an increase in crime rates.[30] There was, indeed, an immediate increase in recorded crime. This increase, explained the police commissioner,' was the result of 'various changes which have taken place in the police force' serving to increase facilities for the reporting and detection of crime'. However, 'the rapid increase in genuine reported crime which had been a marked feature in the previous three years in Bombay City', it was noted in 1914, 'suffered a check' for causes 'the nature of which is obscure'.[31] Indeed, whether station officers had continued the old habit of discouraging people from lodging complaints or simply manifested 'the desire to burke cases in order to show good statistical results'[32] was not given public consideration even if it caused private anxiety within the Judicial Department or the police commissioner's office. Two decades later, the tendency to prevent cases being 'burked' by policemen who were 'unwilling to register crime which [they] had little or no hope of detecting' had by no means abated.[33] Yet victims were no more willing to report crimes than the police appeared ready to register them. One police officer bravely offered 'very rough estimates based upon experience' of unreported crime: 2–3 per cent of murders and between 10 and 40 per cent of reported burglaries and thefts were 'concealed'.[34] But the 'dark figure' of crime is by its very nature unknowable. Indeed, if the real volume of crime is determined largely by the way in which the machinery of criminal

[28] Statement of the State of Crime in Bombay and Calcutta, 17 June 1875, GOB, Judicial, 1875, vol. CDLXXXVII, p. 117, MSA. In 1884, there was a policeman for every 227 residents in Calcutta and every 507 residents in Bombay. *Annual Report on the Police, 1884*, p. 13. In 1930, Calcutta had a policeman for every 188 inhabitants, while Bombay had one for every 265. Calculated from Curry, *The Indian Police*, Appendix, p. 347. A more recent attempt to calculate crime rates in Bengal showed that 'major crimes', whether violent or property offences, declined in the last quarter of the nineteenth century and that their frequency per capita was lower than other provinces. This finding led its author to conclude, in the spirit of the Government of Bombay in 1875, that 'the population of Bengal was less crime-prone and that the criminal administration in Bengal was more effective in terms of crime prevention'. A Mukherjee, 'Crime and Criminals in Nineteenth Century Bengal (1861–1904)', *IESHR*, 21:2 (1984), pp. 166–7, 160–2.
[29] Edwardes, *Bombay City Police*, p. 4.
[30] Under Secretary, Judicial, GOB to Commissioner of Police, 2 September 1910, in *Annual Report on the Police, 1909*, p. 1.
[31] *Annual Report on the Police, 1913*, Judicial Dept. Circular, 14 July 1914, p. 1.
[32] *Annual Report on the Police, 1911*, p. 2.   [33] Curry, *The Indian Police*, p. 184.
[34] *Ibid.*, pp. 184–5.

justice bears down upon social exchange, the 'dark figure' is merely an illusion. The low rates of crime and the modest value of property stolen may suggest that the policeman's experience cannot serve as a reliable guide to the extent of under-reporting. But they also bear testimony to the reluctance of people consistently to seek redress formally through the police.

III

The shortcomings of the police force, its financial and numerical weakness, its lack of discipline and organization combined with the general reluctance to seek redress through the formal structure of the police and the courts to ensure that the overwhelming majority resorted most commonly to informal sanctions for the settlement of disputes. This fact was in turn to shape the methods and strategies of policing, whether in relation to the detection of crime or the maintenance of public order. The nature of these informal sanctions varied enormously according to the nature of the conflict and its protagonists. The locations of power within the working-class neighbourhoods were diffuse, fluid and subject to intense rivalry and conflict. Landlords, moneylenders and grain dealers, jobbers and labour contractors, caste panchayats and chawl and wadi (residents') committees, each provided a forum around which disputes were conducted, sometimes settled, and social relationships were negotiated, challenged and defined. Dadas, literally elder brothers, were men who had acquired a particular reputation for toughness, sometimes precisely by asserting their own public role through the enforcement of justice and the protection of their friends, neighbours and clients.[35]

Jobbers and dadas, akhadas, the melas and tolis, the 'volunteer' corps and neighbourhood gangs were often lumped together inside a notional culture of roughness. But informal sanctions were by no means either the preserve of neighbourhood roughs nor the prerogative of neighbourhood magnates. Contemporaries, and later historians and anthropologists, often perceived the social organization of the urban neighbourhoods in the language of rural description. Dadas or jobbers were portrayed as village headmen. The social organization of the neighbourhood appeared to be reconstituted forms of caste and kinship ties. But these are highly misleading counters of description; none of them more so than the insistence upon a clear demarcation between the rough and the respectable. To emphasize the importance of informal sanctions is not to imply that urban society was cohesive, harmonious or consensual. Nor should the

---

[35] See ch. 4 above.

operation of informal sanctions be interpreted as the rule of the patrons and magnates of the urban neighbourhoods or its social organization and institutions as the instruments of social control and hegemony. In fact, magnates were constrained by the demands of reciprocity; their power was contested and limited by their rivals; honouring their clients often narrowed the patron's freedom of manoeuvre.[36]

Colonial officials often tried to invest those they perceived as neighbourhood leaders with power and influence which they never possessed. Sometimes, this was because they picked their leaders badly. More usually, it represented the forlorn attempt by policemen, magistrates and civil servants to place their faith in any existing structure of power which might maintain order. If they did not enquire too closely how it was maintained, they might not have to care whether it was preserved.

Nonetheless, the official mind which explained political action in terms of incitement or mobilization by leaders and publicists also put its faith in more responsible patrons and magnates for the restoration of order. During the Mohurram riots of 1908 between rival sects of Muslims, one observer complained, 'there are no regular leaders with whom those in authority can communicate, nor any recognized heads who possess a real influence to whom the processionists owe allegiance'.[37] Similarly, during the general strikes of 1919 and the early 1920s, the absence, sometimes the evanescence, of trade unions led officials and other observers to wonder how large-scale action by workers could be coordinated and orchestrated without the existence of 'some controlling organization'[38] or some 'good sound leadership among them somewhere'.[39] Leadership within the working-class neighbourhoods appeared heavily concealed and one of the functions of the CID was increasingly to ferret it out.

Yet even when apparently accredited leaders were found, their influence seemed to be in doubt. When disputes over cow slaughter during Bakri-ld appeared to heighten 'communal' tensions between Hindus and Muslims in 1944, the police commissioner approached the leaders of Madanpura but discovered in time that 'these so-called leaders have very little standing and less authority over the Muslims who live in this area'. When he called a meeting of 'respectable, influential Muslim leaders', he found that 'They all with one voice admitted that they had no control and no influence with the Muslims who reside in Nagpada and Madanpura.'[40] The assumption underlying these expectations was that Indian society

[36] *Ibid.*
[37] *Times of India*, 15 February 1908. Masselos, 'Power in the Bombay Moholla 1904–15'.
[38] Secretary, GOB, Home to Secretary, GOI, Home, 7/15 February 1919, Bombay Confidential Proceedings, vol. 46, 1919, OIOC.
[39] *Bombay Chronicle*, 21 February 1924.
[40] Note by Commissioner of Police, 3 November 1944, GOB, Home (Special), File 1002 (1), 1893–1945, p. 257, MSA.

was mediated by culturally specific social forms and institutions which regulated its functions, resolved its disputes and restored its harmony. The task of colonial rulers was then to identify these locations of power and influence and operate through them.[41] In this way, public order was founded upon shifting sands. It was maintained in spite of, and not because of, the strategies so elaborately and feverishly devised by the official mind for the purpose.

Moreover, the respectable operated through agencies which they readily assigned to a culture of roughness. The magnates who joined in the condemnation of Mohurram as a 'saturnalia of not only the Mahomedans but of all the roughs of Bombay of all creeds'[42] frequently financed the celebrations of the moholla. Similarly grain dealers, shopkeepers and landlords played a prominent role in the organization of the Ganpati or Gokulashtami melas, themselves often little more than street gangs embellished in a new guise. Landlords hired rent collectors; creditors sometimes recovered dues by force or the threat of force; lawyers employed touts; mill managers recruited jobbers and street corner bosses to combat pickets or destroy workers' combinations. When millowners were particularly determined to re-open their mills during strikes, for instance in times of buoyant demand when orders were flowing in and prices rising, or when they could not afford to have their assets locked up in protracted disputes, they often turned to akhadas or gymnasiums in order to recruit, escort and protect blacklegs.[43]

E. D. Sassoon and Company were the managing agents for the largest group of mills in Bombay. They had a reputation for managing the best, the most efficient, progressive and innovative mills and, indeed, for being considerate and far-sighted employers of labour. Yet, as we have seen,[44] they appointed as the head of their 'watch and ward department' a Eurasian ex-boxing champion called Milton Kubes and as the communists gained ascendancy among the millworkers in the late 1920s, the most prominent anti-communist boss of Bombay, Keshav dada Borkar, under the portentous title of 'Superintendent of Labour'. Kubes liked to boast that he commanded his own squad of spies and enforcers, who attended workers' meetings, took down speeches, collected handbills and strikers' pamphlets and, when it proved possible, simply disrupted the proceedings. The speeches collected by Kubes were made available to the

---

[41] If there is a colonial dimension to the policing of contemporary Britain, as Brogden has suggested, it may perhaps be located in the hypothesization of 'community leaders' and the ceaseless quest for 'spokesmen' of the ethnic minorities. Their language and approach may suggest how far the official mind in Britain has imagined the colonization of Brixton, Brick Lane, Handsworth and Toxteth. See M. Brogden, 'The Emergence of the Police: the Colonial Dimension', *British Journal of Criminology* (1987), 4–14.

[42] *Bombay Gazette*, 25 February 1907, cited by Masselos, 'Power in the Bombay Moholla', p. 82.   [43] See ch. 4 above.   [44] See ch. 5 above.

police and used as evidence in the prosecutions of trade union activists for incitement and notably of the communist leaders in the Meerut Conspiracy Case. Kubes attended meetings, 'to get an idea of the atmosphere that is brought about by the speeches' and although, as he confessed, 'I know Marathi but little, I can get a sense of what they say'.[45] His ignorance of the language did not apparently impede his collection of evidence. Similar problems arose in relation to the evidence presented against the communists by the police in the Meerut Conspiracy Case. The problem in this case arose because police reporters who knew Marathi often did not have a command of shorthand while those English or Eurasian reporters who learnt shorthand did not know the language.[46] This conundrum was finally resolved by the police and indeed the court by trusting God's Englishmen who having spent sufficient time in India were able to divine more accurately from the intonation and inflections of speech what was, in fact, being said.

Similarly, retailers and shopkeepers in the cotton, piecegoods and bullion markets often hired Pathan watchmen to guard their shops. Frequently, it was said, a head Pathan accompanied by ten or fifteen others would go around the shops offering to watch them for two rupees or more a piece. Each gang could keep watch for at least seventy or seventy-five shops. Bombay experienced a number of moral panics about 'the Pathan menace'. They were classified as 'a criminal tribe' in the early twentieth century.[47] In the city, they were believed to be rapacious moneylenders, charging exorbitant interest rates, recovering their dues through violence, taking away the wives of their debtors in cases of default or kidnapping children of both sexes for prostitution.[48] In 1923, the police assigned one officer and two constables 'for keeping watch over undesirable Pathans in the city' at the cost of over 6,000 rupees.[49] But they complained that their actions were neutralized by the kind of businessman who would write to the press to complain of the 'Pathan menace' while at the same time, employing a Pathan 'to look after his shops merely because he is afraid that if he does not, the Pathan will loot the shop'.[50] But Pathans were not alone in prospering from running such neighbourhood protection rackets. Gurkhas and 'Pardeshi' Hindus also

[45] Proceedings of the BRIC, oral evidence, File 10, p. 225, MSA.
[46] *Proceedings of the MCC, Statement by S. A. Dange, made in the court of R. L. Yorke, Esq., I. C. S., Additional Sessions Judge, Meerut, October 26, 1931, in the Case of King Emperor versus P. Spratt and Others*, pp. 2475, 2484–8.
[47] M. Kennedy, *Notes on the Criminal Classes in the Bombay Presidency* (Bombay, 1909).
[48] Proceedings of the Bombay Provincial Banking Enquiry Committee, Replies to the Questionnaire, Currimbhoy Ebrahim Workmen's Institute, File 12–C, MSA; *Times of India*, 9 February 1929; Proceedings of the BRIC, oral evidence, Lalji Naranji, File 4, p. 121; P. G. Solanki, File 6, p. 127 and sundry others, MSA.
[49] *Annual Report on the Police, 1922*, p. 52.   [50] *Ibid.*, p. 33.

attempted to develop their own beat and the competition between them was one of the factors underlying the Hindu–Muslim riots of February 1929.[51]

Similarly, informal tribunals were formed around caste and neighbourhood to resolve disputes and maintain order. They were sometimes constituted out of village connections. These tribunals frequently sat in judgement over the behaviour of local residents. Dadas and jobbers, strikers and blacklegs, moneylenders and rent collectors could be called upon to explain their behaviour or justify their actions and, at this level too, sanctions were deployed against those who failed to satisfy the neighbourhood tribunal, the caste panchayat or the chawl committee.[52] These institutions should not be perceived as the spontaneous expression of a popular culture, but the outcome of alliances and rivalries in the neighbourhood, and integral to the processes by which the distribution of local power was determined. There was nothing static about these local structures of power. It was within and around them that most of the functions of policing, the maintenance of order and the mediation of conflicts were conducted. Not only low expectations of the police, but also the vitality of neighbourhood organization explains, to a large extent, why few people lodged complaints with the police.

Significantly, the police often adopted means and methods which were indistinguishable from these agencies within the urban neighbourhood. In fact, they frequently depended upon alliances which they could make in the neighbourhoods in order to exert their influence within them. Frequently, too, the police were recruited by prominent figures in the neighbourhood to serve their parochial interests or to swing the balance of local power in their favour. Policemen thus constituted yet another resource in the politics of the neighbourhood. The structural weaknesses of police organization confined their activities to particular targets often chosen in consequence of more widespread anxieties about particular social groups. Similarly, their methods were dictated by contingencies and often by the nature of their alliances in the neighbourhood.

Paranoia was the hallmark of the colonial imagination. Consequently, great emphasis was laid on disguise and detection, subterfuge and surveillance to distil the popular mood, uncover the plots and rumours of the bazaar for which colonial officials had a particular weakness, and to discern the concealed sources of power, influence and community leadership. Hartley Kennedy was a police commissioner with a penchant for disguise and a particular hatred for bagatelle players, beggars and foreign pimps. He posted detectives at the docks to meet foreign steamships and,

---

[51] Proceedings of the BRIC, 1929, Sir M. M. Ramji, File 2, p. 337; Sir P. Klein, Commissioner of Police, Bombay, File 18, p. 167, MSA.   [52] See ch. 4 above.

according to one of his successors, to mark down 'every Jewish trafficker who showed his nose in Bombay'.[53] Kennedy's preference was to dress himself in purdah and 'thus altered', he was said 'to have wandered about the city after nightfall in company with one of his agents'. Unfortunately, an ankle injury had left him with a permanent limp, so that this Englishman in drag, hobbling around the city at night, was readily recognized as 'the lame Kennedy saheb' and was long afterwards remembered 'affectionately', it is said, by 'the old law-breakers and disreputables who recollect his efforts to bring them to book'.[54]

In various ways, the police were drawn into the social and political networks of the neighbourhood and, of course, the greater the emphasis on detection, the more dependent they became upon them. While operating within these networks, the police often found themselves imprisoned within their confines. The official historian of the Bombay city police was thus able to name a mere handful of detectives upon whom the success and failure of law enforcement depended. In the late nineteenth century, it was said, Mir Abdul Ali, 'wielded a degree of control over the badmashes of the City wholly disproportionate to his position as the superintendent of the safed kapdewale or the plain-clothes police'.[55] Similarly, in the 1920s and 1930s, Rao Bahadur Sabbaji Rao, Superintendent of the Criminal Investigation Department, was 'one of a few well-educated men' who had entered the force in the 1890s, had 'risen from the rank of Head Constable' and arrived at his post after more than three decades of experience with the police. The Rao Bahadur acquired a similarly legendary reputation. His particular gift was 'an almost uncanny sixth sense concerning receivers who were likely to be approached with property of different types'. Thus, following a major jewellery heist in the Fort in April 1928, the Rao Bahadur moved into action and 'warned the most likely receivers' that they might be approached with the stolen goods. Indeed, 'such was his reputation' that one of the receivers, visited by the robbers, 'detained them on some clever pretext and informed the formidable, if not quite clairvoyant, Sabbaji Rao.[56] Others appeared to have the almost magical quality of solving crimes 'to which at first there seemed to be no clue whatever'. Their particular, perhaps enabling gift, was 'to keep closely in touch by methods of their own with the more disreputable and dangerous section of the urban population'.[57]

Collaboration of this kind brought fame and increasingly sonorous titles to the policemen; but its fruits must also have been tasted by their agents and partners in the neighbourhood. Not only were the latter often allowed a free hand but the policeman concerned could be required to

[53] Edwardes, *Bombay City Police*, p. 115.   [54] *Ibid.*, p. 118.   [55] *Ibid.*, pp. 72–3.
[56] Curry, *The Indian Police*, pp. 169–70.   [57] Edwardes, *Bombay City Police*, pp. 72–3.

bring official authority and resources to bear decisively on the side of their allies in neighbourhood disputes. In some cases, it was said, the police commissioner used 'private agents of his own' to keep a check on the police and to accumulate supposedly 'an uncomfortably accurate knowledge of what was going on in various quarters of the city'.[58] Yet these same methods required on a more systematic scale, could leave the police in darkness, despite the fact, or perhaps because, they were so deeply embedded in the neighbourhood. After the strike which followed Tilak's trial and transportation in 1908, C. J. Stevenson-Moore, the Director of Criminal Intelligence concluded that 'the City Detective Department knows no more about the inner history of the business than my boot'. In fact, he continued,

I am compelled to say that the ignorance of the Bombay police as to the agency and methods used for engineering the strike is nothing short of appalling . . . Many of the constables live in the chauks from which some of the worst natives come. Yet no information. They are all Ratnagiri men together and of course in league; 75 per cent of the Bombay Police are Ratnagiri men.[59]

The police were often deeply implicated in the social and political arrangements of the neighbourhood. In the early twentieth century, when the 'Pathan menace' had first begun to grip the minds of the police and the public, the police commissioner identified four 'communities' among them, chose leaders for each and ceremonially invested them with turbans, swords and shawls as symbols of their authority as the head of their respective jamats. In 1929, when the Pathan riots led to a search for the redoubtable leaders of the community, only one was to be found: Khan Sahib Samad Khan, the sardar and patel of the Kohat Pathans, and especially those who were employed in the docks. The Khan Sahib told the Bombay Riot Inquiry Committee that the other three headmen had died, two of them nearly twenty years previously. They had not been replaced because the jamats 'never took the trouble to inform the commissioner of police of the death of their headmen'.[60] Perhaps the jamats had been dissolved and some Pathans had regrouped along different lines. Certainly, some Pathans had formed their own jamats and elected their own patels without reference to the government. Nonetheless, Samad Khan lamented the decline of the headman appointed by government, confessed that his authority was no longer what once it had been

[58] *Ibid.*, pp. 113–14.
[59] C. J. Stevenson-Moore, Offg. Director, Criminal Intelligence, to Sir Harold Stuart, Offg. Secretary, GOI, Home, 5 August 1908 in GOI, Home Poll (A), December 1908, nos. 149–69, NAI.
[60] Proceedings of the BRIC, 1929, oral evidence, Khan Sahib Samad Khan, File 2, p. 201, MSA.

and took the opportunity to press for its renewal through another ceremony, presumably with more turbans and shawls.[61] The police commissioner regarded these importunities rather coolly. This had not prevented him in the intervening period from seeking out putative leaders of the 'Pathan community' in order to gain their collaboration in allaying fears of their 'menace'. In 1924, the police commissioner had invited them 'to keep a strict check on new arrivals and to give me information of the presence of bad characters in the city with a view to their deportation. They agreed to do so: it remains to be seen if any good will come out of it.'[62] The kidnapping scare of 1929 and the 'Pathan hunt' by millworkers which followed does not suggest that the panic was contained. Yet in the late 1910s and early 1920s, the arbitrator in disputes between Pathans, whether between moneylenders, straying into each other's patch, or conflicts between dock workers and their sirdars, and their adviser in their relations with other groups and especially the police was an inspector in the CID and a fellow Pathan called Ubedullakhan.[63]

The police also intervened informally in the conduct of industrial disputes and were often drawn into communal conflicts. Sometimes, the police intervened at the highest levels to mediate labour disputes and effect settlements. Favours gained in one sphere could be encashed in another. About the Julaha weavers, 'an extremely illiterate and fanatical population', the police commissioner claimed in 1911, 'I have had something to do with them, in the matter of getting them re-employed after a strike and obtaining their backwages from their employers.' During Mohurram in 1911, he decided to realize 'the gratitude which they professed for this help' by sending for Badlu 'who lives in Madanpura and controls a tabut supported by the Julahi weavers of that locality' and persuading him to keep out of the way of rival Muslim moholla processions.[64] Similarly, during the 1919 general strike, the police commissioner, Vincent, repeatedly tried to discover spokesmen for the workers and engage them in negotiations with the employers, but failed to find leaders whose terms the workers were willing to accept.[65] 'Fatty' Vincent, as he was 'usually known in the service', had been born and brought up in Bombay, where his father had been a police commissioner before him, and had, according to one of his subordinates, 'an exceptionally good knowledge of Marathi'.

[61] *Ibid.*, pp. 187–205.   [62] *Annual Report on the Police, 1924*, p. 35.
[63] *Times of India*, 16 July 1917.
[64] Commissioner of Police, Bombay, to Secretary, GOB, Judicial, March 1911. Reprinted in Edwardes, *Bombay City Police*, Appendix A, pp. 196–7.
[65] Vincent's role as a mediator in the strike and its limitations are evident in newspaper reports in the *Bombay Chronicle* and *Times of India*, especially in the third week of January. For an account of the strike, see Newman, *Workers and Unions in Bombay*, pp. 120–30 and R. Kumar,' The Bombay Textile Strike, 1919', *IESHR*, 8:1(1971), 1–29.

To Vincent's 'close association with his Marathi-speaking ayah and the Maratha sepoys of the Police', during his childhood, was attributed not only his fluency of language but more especially

his command of colloquial expressions in common use among such people. The term 'colloquial expressions' embraces a wide variety of jests and other phrases which among us are regarded as indecent. This command of language was not without a useful effect when dealing with people like the mill-hands of Bombay.[66]

For Fatty Vincent, however, swapping smutty jokes, exchanging the choicest abuse or indulging in badinage with the workers, was not quite enough to secure a settlement of the strike.[67]

In this way, police commissioners sometimes imagined for themselves the role of the kotwals of the great Mughal cities. At lesser levels of the hierarchy, too, and within local police stations, deals were struck, favours sought and recovered and disputes settled between rival magnates or between employers and workers. For instance, in 1937, the police were actively involved in an industrial dispute in the tanneries of Dharavi and particularly in its trade union rivalries. The rivalry among Marava and Adi Dravida leather workers was not simply confined to the workplace or even the locality. It stretched back to Tinnevely district in Madras Presidency from where these workers had emigrated to Bombay and its ramifications extended to caste conflicts and personal feuds, which appeared to converge upon the figure of Moses Nallakhan or M. N. Moses as he styled himself. Moses invited S. V. Parulekar, the trade union leader, to form the Dharavi Tannery and Leather Workers' Union. Moses' attempt to call in the wider resources of trade unionism to alter the local balance of power in his favour and against his Marava enemies backfired when the tannery owners used this opportunity to replace his friends with his foes in their labour force and thus neutralize the threat of trade union activity. This only served to intensify the rivalry. At the outset, however, Moses was called to the police station and 'warned', and he was later charged with assault and intimidation. On the other hand, the police appeared to refuse to take action against the Maravas. In a petition to the Home Minister, Moses drew the conclusion that 'we are not getting justice because our opponents have got monetary assistance and money to spend to ruin us whereas we are poor and helpless people'. In February 1938, Moses complained to the police commissioner that although

[66] Curry Diaries, 'The Joy of Working', vol. II, pp. 55–7, Curry Papers, Box 1, Centre of South Asian Studies, Cambridge.
[67] However, it is clear that both Vincent and the Governor played an important role in persuading the millowners to make concessions and thus to bring the strike to an end. *Bombay Chronicle*, 20 January 1919; *Times of India*, 20 January 1919; *ibid.*, 21 January 1919; *ibid.*, 22 January 1919.

he had been assaulted by Ayyaswami Thevar and three others in the presence of a constable, the officer at Mahim police station disregarded his and the constable's evidence and in fact refused to record a statement from him. Subsequently, when one tannery owner informed Inspector Raje 'about his intention to effect a reduction in wages', the latter organized a police guard at the workplace, a response which may provide a clue to his earlier attitude to Moses.[68] Until the 1920s, the police intervened in the conciliation of disputes through the commissioner's office; in the following decades, the growing scale of industrial action drove such state intervention progressively to higher and more centralized levels within the provincial government. As the role of the police was focused, more formally and so less flexibly, upon the containment and regulation of industrial action, it came to be seen more clearly as a repressive force in workers' politics.[69]

Policemen active in the regulation of prostitutes often profited from them and some became involved to varying degrees in the organization and protection of brothels. To this end, they used their authority as policemen informally to gain the compliance of pimps and prostitutes, tailors and moneylenders and a variety of intermediaries involved in the trade. Sometimes they cuffed their collaborators into profitable, if unequal, partnerships. It was when the tensions between those involved escalated beyond the ability of the police officers to manage, contain or resolve them, or indeed, when police officers succeeded in making enemies of all their business partners, that their profitable rackets of protection and terror were brought to light.

Indeed, it was precisely such a breakdown of business arrangements in 1917 which uncovered a complex web of extortion and corruption in the police force, which seemed to lead to its highest levels. In April 1917, an internal enquiry into various allegations found that Inspector Favel 'had been guilty of systematically taking illegal gratifications from prostitutes and other persons with whom he came in contact officially'.[70] Barely, a year earlier, Inspector Favel had been awarded the King's Police Medal.[71]

---

[68] GOB, Home (Special), File 550 (23) A of 1937, MSA.   [69] See above chs. 3 and 4.
[70] F. A. M. Vincent, Commissioner of Police, Bombay to Secretary, GOB, Judicial, 6 April, 1917, Bombay Confidential Proceedings, Judicial Department, vol. 25, 1917, p. 95, OIOC.
[71] Statement of Mr D. Meyer of 23 Rampart Row before F. C. Griffith, Deputy Commissioner of Police, CID, 29 March 1917 in *ibid.*, p. 100. Indeed, as one Mr D. Meyer, a commission agent, who had fallen in love with Mary Fooks, a Russian prostitute, who worked under the inspector's protection, deposed before the police enquiry, Favel liked to boast that 'he was the only Jew in the Police who had won the medal'. In fact, Favel expressed the opinion that 'something ought to be done to celebrate it'. Since Favel had already threatened to deport Mary Fooks, Meyer recognizing that discretion was the better part of love, paid Rs 600 for a picnic at the Elephanta Caves in the inspector's honour.

During the war, Inspector Favel had been assigned the task of 'dealing with the large number of enemy and neutral aliens who have come under notice'. Indeed, the colonial state had attached considerable, perhaps excessive, importance to these duties. In this role, according to Vincent, the commissioner of police, Favel had become his 'right-hand man'.[72] Thus, the commissioner took the firm view that 'it would be highly impolitic publicly to disgrace' such an officer by instituting disciplinary procedures against him or prosecuting him.[73] His recommendation that Favel should be allow to resign and to return his medal was quickly adopted by the Government of Bombay.[74]

The police enquiry into Inspector Favel's activities focused primarily on his dealings with 'foreign prostitutes'. Mancharam Pitambar, a tailor, known to his friends as Barny, had followed his father into the trade as a dressmaker to the European prostitutes in Bombay, and on the strength of some seventeen years' experience was able to provide a recent history of the 'European' brothels.[75] Although his history went back to the turn of the century, it was in about 1909 that the European prostitutes had been placed 'under the direct supervision of Inspector Favel'.[76] At this time, the chief impresario of the white slave trade was a Russian Jew known as M. S. Toster, who acted as a broker 'between the police and the prostitutes' and as a sort of labour exchange for the women, facilitating their transfer between brothels and meeting and accommodating 'new arrivals', and helping to 'put them in touch with the Mistresses of the brothels'. Favel allied with his rival Maurice Finckelstein to ease Toster out of Bombay. Finckelstein now stood 'alone in his glory and wielded enormous power over the women, both girls and Mistresses'. In his moment of glory, however, Finckelstein 'had a quarrel with Inspector Favel' about 'the division of the money extorted from the prostitutes'. As Barny noted portentously, 'the bond between them had snapped'. Six

[72] F. A. M. Vincent, Commissioner of Police, Bombay to Secretary, GOB, Judicial, 6 April 1917, in *ibid.*, p. 95.   [73] *Ibid.*
[74] Secretary, GOB, Judicial, to Secretary, GOI, Home, 8 June 1917, in *ibid.*, p. 103. Indeed the Government of Bombay pointed out to New Delhi that after all 'there was very little difference between resignation in the circumstances disclosed in the case and dismissal'. It also suggested that a prosecution of Mr Favel was unlikely to stand, because of 'the low moral character of many of the witnesses' and because the evidence consisted of 'mere statements taken down by the police and the persons who made them, being equally guilty of giving illegal gratification are not likely to adhere to them, and so admit their guilt, in a witness box'.
[75] Statement of Mancharam Pitambar alias 'Barny', in *ibid.*, pp. 95–8. Barny claimed that 'by reason of my business dealings with these women, I got to know all intimately and I made myself useful to them by doing little odd jobs for them outside my more regular business'. Indeed, these 'business dealings' had turned him into something of a linguist. He had learned 'the languages most commonly spoken by these women, namely Yiddish, Italian, and a little German and also a smattering of French'. *Ibid.*, p. 95.
[76] *Ibid.*, p. 96.

months later, in about 1911, Finckelstein was deported. The deputy commissioner of police, in the Criminal Investigation Department at the time of his deportation was none other than Fatty Vincent.[77]

With the departure of Finckelstein, Favel had effectively become both the middleman and, in his police duties, the final receiver and enforcer in the web of extortion which had been spun around the brothels. As official anxieties about aliens mounted with the outbreak of war, Favel found that his duties afforded large and growing opportunities for profit. Favel routinely received presents from the pimps and prostitutes. He was paid for leading the women through the maze of regulations that governed their entry into and movement within the subcontinent. He expected to be rewarded for settling disputes within and between brothels. He charged 'a heavy commission', from both buyers and sellers, whenever a brothel changed hands and there appears to have been a rather bullish market for shares in them. The broker in these transactions was a Mrs Markovitch, who had no papers to prove her nationality,[78] and was consequently wholly at Favel's mercy. Favel took a cut of the proceeds of the annual ball, which Mrs Markovitch organized at the Balcon, the hotel of the European prostitutes, and which, it was said, made 'a good deal of money'.[79] Favel colluded with Mrs Markovitch and his former lover, Fritza, the mistress of No. 392 Falkland Road, to ensure that 'all fresh arrivals' went to the latter's house. As a result, 'Fritza's brothel flourishes with the number of girls while other brothels are starved'.[80] Needless to say, Favel also required free access to the brothels, although his visits, paid for by the mistress of the house, were, it was said, 'by no means as frequent as they used to be'. Nonetheless, these visits would make Fritza, who was still 'his very good friend', 'very angry and jealous'.[81]

The threat of deportation was the most powerful sanction which Favel could apply not only to extort money, but also to tighten his control over the pimps, prostitutes and mistresses. He liked to order the pimps to leave Bombay 'by the first available steamer' but 'on squaring Mr Favel they were permitted to stay on for a few weeks'. Pimps were, thus, expected 'to pay for the privilege of extending their stay in Bombay and for protection against executive action'.[82] The same sanction was used to release brothels from the protection of his own rivals, named by one 'mistress' as Mr Sloane and Mr Nolan (presumably police officers), and as Mlle Mina of No. 6 Grant Road found, to bring them more fully under his sway.[83] Similarly, the deportation as an enemy alien of Fritza's partner at No. 392

---

[77] *Ibid.*   [78] Statement of Mml. Margot, mistress of No. 6 Grant Road, in *ibid.*, p. 99.
[79] Statement of Mancharam Pitambar, alias Barny, in *ibid.,* p. 97.
[80] Statement of Mml. Margot, mistress of No. 6 Grant Road, in *ibid.,* p. 99.
[81] Statement of Mancharam Pitambar, alias Barny, in *ibid.,* p. 97.   [82] *Ibid.*, p.96.
[83] Statement of Mml. Mina, of No. 6 Grant Road, in *ibid.,* p. 101.

Falkland Road, Sophie Schlamp, a German subject, enabled Fritza to sell a half share in the brothel, realizing nearly 80 per cent on her original outlay in eight years[84] and to share the proceeds with Favel.[85] Having ostensibly sold her share in the brothel, Fritza continued to live in it. As the purchaser, Mlle Jennette, complained, Fritza still 'shares the profits with me',[86] and after a decent interval she even began 'trying to sell Sophie's share to me'.[87] When Mr D. Meyer, a commission agent, fell in love with Mary Fooks, 'a Russian girl', who worked at Fritza's brothel and 'desired to rescue her from the life she was leading', he became a soft target for Favel. The inspector used the threat of deportation to pull Mary Fooks back into the brothel and then over two years to extort some Rs 4,000 from Mr Meyer, until once again and once too often, Favel 'once more started to squeeze me'. Meyer decided this time that he 'had done quite enough for him and I had a row with him and broke with him'.[88]

Once Favel had acquired such extensive, virtually monopolistic powers in the trade, it was always going to require deft and dextrous management to hold his business interests together. Not surprisingly, Favel soon began to gather foes about him. His business partners had been kept in place almost exclusively by threat, coercion and humiliation. In time, even they became disgruntled. Before the war, Barny, his agent after Finckelstein's departure, believed that some 80 per cent of Favel's takings 'came through me and the balance directly from the "giver".'[89] But, 'since the outbreak of war' when Favel had acquired greater powers to supervise the movement of alien subjects, Favel's 'income from the prostitutes had increased considerably' and further, 'he now takes much more money direct than he used to take and less of it comes through me'. To make matters worse, Fritza added insult to penury: taking advantage of her relationship with Favel, she had 'no compunction in calling me "a bloody cooly".'[90] While Fritza remained loyal to Favel, she sometimes felt scorned and was often racked with jealousy.[91] Several mistresses resented the collusion of Favel, Mrs Markovitch and Fritza which starved them of business.[92] Favel's handling of Meyer, indeed, of the opportunity which he provided, suggests that he did not always know where and how to stop. Too many people, often too close to the police by virtue of their

[84] Statement of Mancharam Pitambar, alias Barny, in *ibid.*, p. 97; statement of Mrs Fritza Shalome alias Mme Fritza, in *ibid.*, p. 102.

[85] Statement of Mancharam Pitambar, alias Barny, in *ibid.*, p. 97.

[86] Statement of Jennette, mistress of 392 Falkland Road, in *ibid.*, p. 101. This ideal business arrangement for Fritza would presumably have been impossible to maintain without the protection of her partner. Statement of Mancharam Pitambar, alias Barny, in *ibid.*, p. 97.

[87] Statement of Jennette, mistress of No. 392 Falkland Road, in *ibid.*, p. 101.

[88] Statement of Mr D. Meyer of 23 Rampart Row, in *ibid.*, pp. 99–100.

[89] Statement of Mancharam Pitambar, alias Barny, in *ibid.*, p. 96.   [90] *Ibid.*, p. 97.

[91] *Ibid.*, p. 96.

[92] Statement of Mml. Margot, mistress of No. 6 Grant Road, in *ibid.*, p. 99.

livelihoods, and frequently dependent upon Favel's patronage, had, over the six years since Finckelstein's departure, accumulated too many scores to settle with Favel for his empire of extortion not to come unravelled.

In view of the range of their involvement in the social organization and political networks of the neighbourhood, it is not surprising that one of the perennial anxieties of senior officials in matters of public order policing was the discipline of the police force. 'In times of disturbance', S. M. Edwardes commented in reference to his own period as commissioner, the police 'often reaped a fair harvest of tips and presents from timorous townspeople who desired protection from mob violence, and also discovered in the aftermath of rioting an easy means of paying off old scores'.[93] These opportunities presented themselves most clearly when 'times of disturbance', whether communal riots or strikes or civil disobedience campaigns, were sustained over extensive periods. At the level of the neighbourhood, the police often appeared to operate as protection racketeers like the dadas whom they branded as rough and criminal or the groups of Pathans who watched the shops of the bazaar for a price and apparently on pain of looting them.

At a formal level, the strategies of the police, indeed the meditations of the official mind, merged law enforcement in relation to crime with the maintenance of public order. Committed to the theory that political movements were the result of the machinations of agitators misleading, manipulating or mobilizing the illiterate, the fanatical and, especially, the rough, it was easy to conclude that the stricter control of 'bad characters' or 'any tribe, gang or class addicted to the commission of non-bailable offences'[94] would remove some of the most combustible materials available to political troublemakers. Conversely, periods of public disorder, the police claimed, diverted their attention and allowed criminals the freedom and the opportunity to practise their craft without restraint.[95] Similarly, in 1926, the commissioner of police deployed the same argument to press the case for greater resources for his force. When there was 'disorder on a large scale', he argued, criminals who were 'kept in some sort of control in normal times' took 'advantage of the excitement and panic to openly burn, loot and murder and cause incalculable damage to the city'. To the extent that the police were effectively able to jail or deport 'undesirables' in 'normal times', they would be successful in maintaining the peace in periods of 'disorder'.[96]

[93] Edwardes, *Bombay City Police*, p. 183.   [94] Cox, *Police and Crime*, p. 205.
[95] *Bombay 1921–22: A Review of the Administration of the Presidency* (Bombay, 1923), p. 20.
[96] Commissioner of Police, Bombay to Secretary, GOB, Home, 9 December 1926, Copy in BRIC, 1929, File B, MSA.

Thus, whenever they wanted to clear the streets, for instance during the royal visit of 1911, the police simply jailed those whom they believed were hooligans or 'bad characters'. The Criminal Procedure Code allowed magistrates to require a person placed before them on suspicion by the police 'to show cause why he should not give security for good behaviour for a year'. But 'hardened malefactors' underwent a less stringent procedure and could be jailed if they failed to produce the security. Yet, as Edmund Cox pointed out, one 'remarkable feature' of the regulations was that a person could be proved to be 'an habitual offender . . . by evidence of general repute or otherwise'. In fact, 'it is easy in India', he observed, 'to obtain evidence of general repute that any person who has rendered himself in anyway unpopular is an habitual offender'.[97] In Bombay, however, the police placed few such cases before the magistrate, and most of them were either discharged or withdrawn. Only fifty people were placed before magistrates in Bombay in 1922 as compared with 902 in Calcutta.[98] This was attributed sometimes to the difficulty of obtaining evidence from the public who feared retaliation from 'badmashes' and at others, rather more weakly, to the fact that 'in the city there is not that knowledge of one's neighbour's affairs that is such a characteristic of village life'.[99] But the police did not, on the other hand, find it easy to convince magistrates. Until 1921, therefore, when he wished to round up hooligans, the commissioner of police, 'exercised his powers as a Magistrate and a Justice of the Peace and . . . used to have accused persons put up before himself as a Magistrate and to remand them into Jail or Police custody'. But the magistracy objected to this procedure and the Government of Bombay conceded the point and removed his magisterial powers. 'So now', the police commissioner observed, 'it is not so easy to deal with mawalis and such persons as it was then'.[100] But such legal difficulties did not lead them to abandon this strategy altogether.

The police, as we have noted, maintained a list of 'bad characters' but, in practice, this was hard to achieve. While drawing up a register, it was difficult to know whom to exclude; once compiled, it was no easy task to decide whom to strike off and when. 'I have often found the registers in the utmost confusion', noted one official, 'and still containing names of

---

[97] Cox, *Police and Crime*, pp. 108–9.
[98] *Annual Report on the Police, 1922*, p. 17. See Suranjan Das, 'The Goondas: Towards a Reconstruction of the Calcutta Underworlds through Police Records', *Economic and Political Weekly*, 29:44 (29 October 1994), pp. 2877–83.
[99] *Annual Report on the Police, 1923*, pp. 22–3.
[100] Proceedings of the BRIC, 1929, P. A. Kelly, Commissioner of Police, File 18, p. 207, MSA.

persons who have led an honest livelihood for years, or who have disappeared, or have long since died.'[101]

Although public discourse lent a certain authority to the term 'bad character', it was not always easy to identify him. In Bombay, as elsewhere, the police readily identified crime and disorder with the poor and especially the unemployed and the rural migrants.[102] But these categories covered the vast majority of the city's population. The overwhelming majority of the city's population – and, indeed, a significant proportion of police force – were rural migrants, who held on tenaciously to their rural base and returned regularly to their villages. Few workers enjoyed secure conditions of employment. Casual labour was used extensively both in the so-called formal as well as the informal sector and periodic unemployment was integral to the shared experience of the working classes. Moreover, identifying bad characters was often complicated by the confusion of stereotypes in public discourse. Thus, in the early twentieth century, while cotton millworkers from Ratnagiri were believed to be volatile and averse to punctuality and discipline, dock labourers from the Deccan and employed usually on a daily basis were portrayed as steady and sober, pliant and docile, loyal and obedient.[103]

Indeed, when the police decided to round up 'bad characters' during the communal riots of February and May 1929, and then undertook a sociological survey of their prisoners, their results, as we have seen, revealed nothing more than the random manner of their arrests.[104] The social profile of the prisoners bore a remarkable resemblance to a cross-section of the city's population. A senior police official was later to recall that the quarters which had been 'combed out' were 'notoriously criminal' and that the police had

arrested everyone known to them as having previous convictions and belonging to the apache type. . . . Most of them had previous convictions, sometimes half a dozen or more. Many criminals fled the city, and conditions gradually became normal.

During the combing-out process many of the hooligans came out of their houses without any trouble, when called out by police officers who knew them; other bolted like rabbits, only to find their earth stopped.

Indeed, 'one gang which made an ineffectual attempt at resisting' was 'a notorious lot of cut-throats known to the British police sergeants as "Jenny's gang", owing to the fact that they were controlled by a wicked old woman whose name sounded something like Jenny'.[105] Colourful

---

[101] Cox, *Police and Crime*, p. 205.   [102] See ch. 5 above.
[103] H. A. Talcherkar, 'Raghu, the Model Millhand: A Sketch', *Indian Social Reformer* (March 1908); Chandavarkar, *Origins of Industrial Capitalism*, ch. 4.
[104] See ch. 5 above.   [105] Curry, *The Indian Police*, pp. 180–1.

stories, many of them less enthralling than these, were no doubt frequent-ly retold in Bournemouth and Bath by the returning heroes of the empire. But there is no evidence to support the claim that 'combing-out' brought the riots to an end. The police may well have tried to round up the usual suspects, but there was in fact little evidence to connect them to the riots and most of those arrested were released after trial. Certainly, the police operation failed to lend credibility to the notion that 'bad characters' formed a discrete social group and belied the claim that the police knew who they were.[106] The drama of the police operations, indeed their claim of maintaining a register of 'bad characters', drew attention to the gulf between their grand claims and modest achievements in controlling crime and maintaining order.

IV

The police deployed the same methods in the political sphere which they developed in relation to crime, and frequently within very similar con-straints. To the official mind, Indian politics often appeared to be indis-tinguishable from a conspiracy. Political movements were mobilized by agitators who incited the credulous and manipulated the naive. Colonial officials believed that agitations could be prevented and riots averted in their early stages, but once they gained momentum, they could quickly spread beyond their control. Preventive measures entailed gaining access to what the official mind imagined were the whispered rumours of the bazaars. To find clues to the popular mood, to ascertain what was unknowable and often irrational, and to penetrate the political networks of the street and the neighbourhood, colonial officials believed they had to rely upon spies, informers and detectives. Political surveillance was given considerable importance but it scarcely yielded more satisfying results. From the early 1890s, the CID maintained a 'secret abstract' of political intelligence in which reports from every district were collected. But large parts of these abstracts consisted of extracts from newspapers or reports of speeches made at various public meetings and political conferences, including the annual session of the Indian National Congress, which were, especially at the time, readily available elsewhere. The CID also censored plays and proscribed books and confiscated those which were subsequently published. Some officers must have become very widely read. In 1910, for instance, they claimed to have scrutinized 297 plays, rejected six outright, but passed a further seven after some un-

---

[106] GOB, Home (Special), File 543 (10) E Part G of 1929, MSA.

doubtedly brisk and forthright alterations.[107] In addition, they kept a
watch on political agitators and foreigners arriving and departing at the
port. The secret abstracts testify to the fascinating bar gossip which
policemen picked up, but their accuracy cannot invariably be relied upon.
They also suggest that the surveillance of political agitators was far from
systematic and hardly a permanent obstacle to political organization and
action.

Frequently, the police were surprised by the onset of 'disturbances'. In
police reports, 'rioters' often appeared in a flash and disappeared without
a trace. Thus, after the communal riots which occurred over cow slaughter in 1893, the commissioner of police reported that although the police
had 'an inkling' of what was to come, when it happened 'the rioters spread
like a flash of lightning and in about an hour the whole of the Native
Town was in an uproar and fighting and looting was the order of the
day'.[108] It was perhaps an inherent characteristic of communal riots that
the patterns of violence, its perpetrators and their targets, often seemed
arbitrary and unpredictable to the police as much as to the city's inhabitants. But for all their efforts at surveillance and gathering intelligence, the
police appeared to know as little about the situations in which public
order had appeared to break down and sometimes to understand it less
than the residents of the neighbourhood. It was not unusual for the police
to be misled by their own intelligence.[109]

Following the mill strike of 1908, the CID confessed that they lacked
the means to watch and follow political agitators effectively and their
budgets were further being squeezed. Indeed, the commissioner of police
declared that he needed to double the strength of the CID to watch
'prominent political agitators'. Agitators revealed a remarkable tendency
to multiply, when they were closely watched, so that the work of the CID
had increased 'by several hundred per cent in the last few years'. Political
'suspects', as the commissioner of police pointed out, could arrive and
depart at twenty-one railway stations in the city. When they drove off in a
victoria carriage on arrival, the detective found it 'almost impossible to
keep them in view'. In addition, 'they invariably put up with friends in
large blocks of buildings which makes it very difficult to locate them for
some time'. To make matters worse, agitators who became conscious of
being watched by the Clouseaus of the plain-clothes police began to take

[107] *Annual Report on the Police, 1910*, p. 7. The impact of their actions upon the local theatre
has sadly passed unrecorded. In addition, the CID also took vigorous action to confis-
cate 21,154 proscribed books in the same year.
[108] Acting Commissioner of Police, Bombay, to Secretary, GOB, Judicial, 12 August 1893,
in GOB, Judicial, 1893, vol. 194, Compilation no. 948, Part I, p. 147, MSA.
[109] See, for instance, the case of the Bandra Observation Camp during the plague panic in
1898, in ch. 7 below, pp. 251–2.

precautions and thus proved yet more elusive.[110] As the Government of Bombay contemplated the problems of political surveillance, they grew increasingly elaborate and complicated. The Home Secretary agreed that it was advisable to employ a special force to shadow political agitators. In addition, the district and railway police should be instructed to exercise 'absolute watchfulness', he suggested, when agitators began their journey and to telegraph the 'known or possible place of destination' while sufficient men had to be detailed to shadow them 'en route' and after arrival.[111] Another senior official noted that it was vital to have enough men 'to keep a watch over each suspect's house, night and day and to watch the headquarter Railway Station as well as the two stations on either side'. It followed that watchers should be made 'thoroughly familiar with the personal appearance of all suspects' and it was essential to provide them with enough support so that local policemen were made available to relieve them at the destination as well as en route, in case 'suspects' made a switch.[112] On the verge of tying down the rickety apparatus of the police with their delusions, the Government of Bombay drew back. As they scrutinized their own plans, they began to realize that it would be impossible to provide enough men to watch all agitators. Instead, the Home Member suggested that the police ought to obtain 'information of any serious movements or plans' by 'employing private informers and rewarding them handsomely for all information of value'.[113] Needless to say, the police had their own network of informers. It is doubtful whether the Government of Bombay, if they had sought to formalize it, would have found the information they received about political movements and conspiracies worth the money they considered lavishing upon them.

Moreover, political agitators raised the same problems of procedure as 'bad characters'. It was difficult to gauge who should be watched and when some could be simply ignored. The consequences of their constraints were sometimes farcical. Kanchan Kumar, a stump orator during the mill strike of 1908, was kept under surveillance for eight years thereafter and, especially during the first world war, his movements were laboriously recorded in the Secret Abstracts of Intelligence. Kumar adopted numerous disguises, took on aliases and travelled sometimes as an ascetic, a holy man, sometimes as a peddler. By 1915, he was reported to be consuming $1\frac{1}{2}$ tolas of ganja daily. His aliases and increasingly exotic

[110] Commissioner of Police, Bombay to Secretary, GOB, Home (Special), 3 November 1908, in GOB, Home (Special), File 71 of 1908, pp. 25–7, MSA.
[111] Note by Secretary, GOB, Home (Special), 21 October 1908, in *ibid.*, pp. 32–5.
[112] Note by JAG, 6 November 1908, in *ibid.*, pp. 37–9.
[113] Home Member's Note, 24 November 1908, in *ibid.*, pp. 43–4.

disguises, his continuous flight from the police and his ceaseless movement across the subcontinent, his failure to hold down a steady job, his
increasingly voracious appetite for cannabis only served to confirm the
suspicion of police intelligence that he was dangerous and prone to crime
and that, indeed, in view of his past, the possibility that he may be
involved with a seditious conspiracy could scarcely be ruled out. When, in
1916, eight years after they first took an interest in him, the police,
bemused by his ingenious disguises, troubled perhaps by the several lines
which his aliases now took up in the secret abstract, finally hauled him in
for questioning, Kanchan Kumar complained about being pursued by the
police. As a result, he had been unable to secure or hold down a job. For
no sooner had he found a job, than the police would turn up to question
his employer and he would be sacked. To get away from the CID, he had
changed his name, moved to new places, even adopted disguises to throw
the police off his trail. He could no longer stay in the same town long
enough to find employment. His last resort, he said, was cannabis which
at least momentarily allowed him to lose himself.[114]

Undaunted, the police continued to develop their own methods of
surveillance. By 1910, an inter-provincial list of agitators was being
maintained to enable the CID to follow those who came to Bombay from
elsewhere in the Presidency.[115] Three years later, the Inspector General of
Police suggested an exchange of CID officers with other provinces so that
each could watch arrivals from their own jurisdiction.[116] The response
from Bengal provided little encouragement: while they were willing to
send staff to Bombay, they replied, they did not really need any officers in
exchange. In any case, Bengal extremists did not seem to communicate
with Bombay very much and 'there is no centre outside Calcutta which
the latter visit'.[117] By 1920, the commissioner of police seemed less than
satisfied with the style of operation of the CID. Their methods had
become outmoded. For, he noted, 'Political agitators nowadays do not
hide their light under a bushel. Publicity and advertisement are as the
breath of their nostrils and on them they chiefly rely for their success.'
Indeed, nothing showed how inappropriate their procedures had become, he observed, than the fact that at the height of the non-cooperation
campaign, neither Gandhi nor Vallabhai Patel appeared on the current
list of agitators.[118]

From 1919, special officers were detailed to report on Bolshevik activ-

---

[114] *BPP SAI*, 1914–16, *passim*.   [115] GOB, Home (Special), File 71 of 1908, MSA.
[116] Inspector General of Police, Bombay to Inspectors General of Police, Bengal, Central
Provinces and Punjab, 1 July 1913, in *ibid.*, p. 163.
[117] J. C. Cumming, Secretary, Government of Bengal, Home to C. C. Watson, Acting
Secretary, GOB, Political, 19 August 1913, in *ibid.*, pp. 181–2.
[118] Note by Commissioner of Police, Bombay, 24 December 1920, in *ibid.*, p. 241.

ities, but there were no communists to be found in India as yet. However, later in the 1920s, the political surveillance of communists proved easier to conduct than spying upon nationalists. The communists were self-defining, more exclusive and they had a smaller membership. They placed a considerable weight on propaganda, used a distinctive language and to a large extent operated openly. Their internal feuds also helped to make information more freely available to the police. The evidence presented for the prosecution in the Meerut Conspiracy Case conducted in the early 1930s shows how readily the coterie of communists who led the Girni Kamgar Union in Bombay were observed, how often their letters were intercepted and how easily, if not always reliably, their speeches were reported.

Police action has sometimes been portrayed as the greatest obstacle to the growth of trade unions. Its role in Bombay was rather more limited. In fact, workers' combinations were more consistently thwarted at the point of production.[119] However, the momentum of industrial action, and especially the scale of the general strikes, invited the increasingly robust intervention of the state and, necessarily, the police, in industrial disputes. From 1929 onwards, they tried to limit picketing at the mill gates to two people and found support in subsequent legislation for this measure. They sometimes escorted blacklegs to work, thus helping to keep the mills working when the employers were trying to break the strike. They arrested the leaders of the Girni Kamgar Union for the seditious tone of their speeches. In the general strike of 1934, police detectives were posted to maintain a watch over propaganda and picketing in the workers' chawls.[120] Although the Government of Bombay proclaimed its lofty intention on the eve of the strike 'to keep the ring clear for both parties', one newspaper quipped the following day, that 'the ring in Parel was so full of armed policemen that there was hardly any room left for the workers'.[121] Four days later, all meetings and processions were prohibited in the mill districts. In the next three weeks, in two stages, twenty-eight communists in the Joint Strike Committee were arrested under emergency powers legislation for 'abusing the liberty of speech'.[122] In the later 1930s, by its legislative initiatives as well as at times by police action, the provincial government continued to attack the communists of the Girni Kamgar Union.

The colonial state was reluctant to wage and sustain a war of attrition against a significant focus of political opposition. But in the case of the

[119] See ch. 3 above; also ch. 5.   [120] GOB, Home (Special), File 543 (48) of 1934, MSA.
[121] *Bombay Sentinel*, 24 April 1934.
[122] GOB, Home (Special), File 543 (48) of 1934, p. 115; GOB, Home (Special), File 543 (48) K of 1934, p. 5, MSA.

communists they could draw upon wider public sympathy. The mil-lowners had, of course, urged them to repress the communists since 1928. But the government also gained from the fear of the threat of communism among larger sections of the professional and commercial classes, local Congressmen, and even the press, all of whom more readily linked communism with their own perceptions and prejudices about the roughness of working-class neighbourhoods. If the communists could thus be isolated, the colonial state could attack them without incurring the risk of debilitating political costs. However, it was still necessary to distinguish between state intervention to preserve the rule of law and maintain public order, on the one hand, and to favour one side of an industrial dispute, on the other. For, in the long run, the future of colonialism would depend upon its ability to extend and diversify its social base and seek collaboration within the working class.

V

As the police strove to maintain public order in the early twentieth century, they encountered political action on an impressive scale. Bombay became the seat of an increasingly militant labour movement and the centre of mass nationalist agitation, and between 1929 and 1947 sporadic communal riots engulfed the city. In the light of the organizational weaknesses, the financial and political constraints and the strategic and operational shortcomings of the police, we might suppose that they would find it impossible to maintain public order under growing political pressure. In fact, the police accumulated and used the means of repression with growing readiness. Increasingly, in this period, and especially in the 1930s, the willingness of the police to swing their lathis and point their guns at antagonistic or disorderly crowds quickened. But it should not be supposed that the police were able to function as a consistent, systematic or sustained force for repression. Rather, their coercive character was unevenly, if sometimes rather violently, manifested.

Certainly, perennial anxieties within the higher echelons of the police about the rank and file surfaced under conditions of potential violence. Faced with the tasks of crowd control, the police could act with considerable brutality. Sometimes, police violence was indiscriminate and sometimes it emanated not from the humble havildar, whose discipline so often appeared suspect to his commanding officers, but from his superiors, often British and Eurasian, whom they trusted. Thus, for instance, the Home Member noted in exasperation that, during the civil disobedience movement, in September 1930, on polling day in the council elections, which were being boycotted by the Congress, there had been a flood of complaints that the 'police, Sergeants and sepoys alike, failed to distinguish between friend and foe . . . and even persons going to the Town Hall to record their vote were beaten with lathis'. It would have been reasonable to expect, the Home Member went on, that the police would be able to understand that people dressed in khaddar were against the government and those in 'European or old-style Indian clothes' were not, 'Yet after every fracas we hear of several (I nearly said "numerous") cases in which friendly persons have been indiscriminately beaten. And the Sergeants who ought to know better are said to be the culprits.'[123] The indiscriminate violence of the sergeants during civil disobedience suggests that the official mind had reason for concern about the brittle discipline of the force when it encountered protesters.

Within the higher ranks of the force, at least, there was probably considerable sympathy for the police commissioner's view, expressed in the immediate aftermath of the communal riots of 1929 that 'the only medicine for rioters was the bullet'.[124] But the police were not always free to translate these sentiments into action. The police opened fire more frequently and killed more people in India than would have been politically tenable in Britain, but they were often more reluctant to show force. On a conservative, if impressionistic, estimate the police and the army killed at least seventy-five people between 1919 and 1942 by shooting in order to disperse crowds of strikers, nationalist agitators or communal rioters. More than thirty people were killed in the first three days of the Quit India movement in August 1942 alone.[125] But it would be misleading to conclude that these deaths were simply a direct reflection of the colonial and racist view that Indian lives were cheap. In fact, senior police officers were often called upon to justify their use of force and they sometimes went to desperate, even absurd, extremes to explain the actions of their men. The absurdity of their explanations reflected less the confidence of colonial officials that whatever excuses they offered would be accepted, but rather anxiety and guilt born out of a desperate search for self-justification. During the communal riot of May 1929, soon after which the commissioner of police had expressed his view that rioters deserved to be shot, he reported an incident in which 500 strikers, supposedly Hindus, were said to have stoned a group of 200 Muslim workers in the Fazulbhoy Mill, who having been hired as blackleg labour, were being escorted to their homes by the police. Thirteen shots were

[123] Note by Home Member, Home Department, 26 September 1930 in GOB, Home (Special), File 750 (26) of 1930, p. 185, MSA.

[124] Proceedings of the BRIC, 1929, oral evidence, P. A. Kelly, File 18, MSA.

[125] GOB, Home (Special), File 1110 (6) - A (1) of 1942, MSA; GOI, Home Poll, File 3/15/43, NAI; Hutchins, *India's Revolution*, pp. 228–33.

fired 'to disperse the crowd and save the Mohammedans'. Two strikers received 'slight' injuries, one of them a bayonet wound to the head. But, as the commissioner pondered, there had been no bayonet charge. 'It appears', he concluded solemnly, 'that he [the striker] must have hit himself against the bayonet while running away'.[126] Nearly two years later, during the civil disobedience movement, an elderly woman, who had, along with others, mounted a picket outside the Municipal Corporation buildings, 'fainted' as the police attempted 'to disperse the crowd'. She later alleged that she had first been dealt a blow with a lathi to the stomach and then had been pushed also in the stomach with the end of a lathi. The first allegation, declared the commissioner briskly in the secrecy of the Home Department's file, was 'impossible' because no lathi blows were struck and the second was 'equally unlikely' because 'lathis were used horizontally against the backs of resisting women to push them along. It is possible that the woman may have in some way pressed herself against the end of one of these.'[127] Mercifully, there are no recorded instances in Bombay of miscreants hurling themselves in the path of a speeding bullet, though some no doubt suffered severe damage while resisting arrest.

When the police opened fire, they frequently justified their action by the claim that they were on the point of being overwhelmed. There was a real and pragmatic side to this perception and the anxieties it generated. Their numerical and organizational weakness meant that police pickets often found themselves surrounded, outnumbered and attacked. The police operated on the front line of crowd control. They were fully exposed to the 'mob' and brought directly into confrontation with it. Whether they patrolled the streets in small groups, formed pickets to defend a street corner or entrenched themselves in a police chowky, they became exposed targets in hostile situations. Significantly, when troops were called out, the army generally refused to adopt 'police methods' precisely because they would thereby be left exposed and vulnerable to attack.[128]

Moreover, their techniques of crowd control were never imaginative and often crude. Between the baton and the bullet, they often appeared to have no intermediate options available. In the early 1920s, the Bombay police developed a sufficient enthusiasm for technological innovation in

[126] Commissioner of Police, Bombay, to Secretary, GOB, Home (Special), Bombay, 15 May 1929, in GOB, Home (Special), File 348 Part II of 1929, p. 77, MSA.

[127] Note by Commissioner of Police, Bombay, undated (probably 23 February 1931) in GOB, Home (Special), File 750 (26) of 1930, pp. 217–21, MSA.

[128] GOI, Home Poll 33/12/32 and 21/6/33, NAI. See N. Narain, 'Co-option and Control: the Role of the Colonial Army in India, 1918–1947', unpublished Ph.D. thesis, University of Cambridge, 1993, ch. 6.

the form of 'lachrymatory gas bombs' to disperse crowds to seek the advice of Scotland Yard and the Philadelphia police. In 1922, the police officer who had been the commissioner of police two years earlier recalled that he had favoured their use during the general strike in Bombay but had been thwarted because the government feared that 'political capital would be made of the use of such a measure'. Their particular value lay in the potential they offered for dispersing crowds when otherwise the police would have to shoot, and thus risk causing 'irreparable damage to a great deal of very valuable machinery and very possibly the loss of a number of lives'. Lachrymatory bombs provided a means of dealing with 'rioters' 'more effectively and much more mercifully than any other'.[129]

However, the Government of Bombay continued to be apprehensive about its political consequences. To the provincial government's fear about 'political capital', New Delhi pointed out that if 'the use of poison gas at war' was unlawful, they could scarcely contemplate its use in peacetime. 'Although the gas itself is reported to be harmless', the Government of India noted, 'the nervous shock caused by it might result in death', for instance, they elaborated imaginatively, 'in the case of a man suffering from advanced heart disease', and then, 'the death would be attributed to the gas'.[130] More fundamentally, perhaps, colonial officials feared that the 'mob' might panic and set off a stampede resulting in casualties which would embarrass the government.[131] Indeed, the Bombay Municipal Corporation had at least after the event taken the view that it would have been preferable to use tear gas to disperse satyagrahis during the civil disobedience agitation than for the police to lay about them with lathis.[132] However, throughout the 1920s and 1930s, colonial officials held fast to the belief that tear gas was likely to induce panic and cause stampedes, that spectators and not just the trouble-makers would be affected, and even that 'the police were too stupid to avoid gassing themselves'.[133] The axiom that Indian mobs were unpredictable and excitable led the colonial state, until the 1940s, to regard firing their weapons as no less destructive and far more appropriate under Indian conditions. Tear gas was used sporadically in the middle and late 1930s, but it was not until the early 1940s that it was eventually accepted by officials and then used more extensively during the Quit India movement.[134]

[129] Note by Acting Inspector General of Police, Bombay Presidency, 25 April 1922 in GOB, Home (Special), File 610 of 1922, pp. 25–6, MSA.
[130] Secretary, GOI, Home (Political) to Secretary, GOB, Home (Special), 16 June 1922, in GOB, Home (Special), File 610 of 1922, pp. 31–3, MSA.
[131] GOI, Home Poll, 8/II/30 and 8/II/31, NAI.   [132] *Ibid.*, 8/II/31, NAI.
[133] Arnold, 'The Armed Police', p. 116.
[134] GOB, Home Department, Resolution No. 3766/2–V, 10 July 1941. in GOB, Home (Special), File 610 of 1922, MSA.

The representation of the mob in colonial discourse vitally influenced the response it evoked from the state and, in particular, it helps to explain why, when faced with it, the police often felt overwhelmed. Colonial discourse developed an elaborate aetiology of popular politics and especially of mass violence.[135] It has already been suggested that this discourse often treated Indian politics as a synonym for, and the outcome of, conspiracy, developed through incitement, rumour, propaganda and sedition and spread by unscrupulous agitators to credulous, illiterate and volatile masses, whose own responses fell outside the universe of reason. This combination of unscrupulous and irresponsible agitators and irrational and volatile people signified, in this discourse, the ever present and palpable threat that, in no more than an instant, tension could flicker into riot, mere discontent could erupt into an epidemic of violence, antagonisms could be inflamed into a major political conflagration. The inflammability of the people and their politics made it crucial that the colonial government should, for the sake of its own subjects as much as itself, maintain and strengthen public order and stamp out disturbances at the first sign of their appearance. Imperial prestige and the pride of the ruling race required that the colonial state should assert its control but, more crucially, officials recognized only too well how easily they could be swamped by the swelling tide of frenzied and fanatical natives. Their fanaticism was often expressed through violence; but sometimes it appeared to know no bounds. In June 1930, the Government of Bombay observed darkly that Gujarati traders in the city had been 'worked up', by 'the preaching of Gandhi and his followers', to 'a state of fanatical excitement in which they are prepared to suffer extreme violence while for the most part remaining non-violent. Their obstinacy makes them very difficult to deal with, while their non-violence renders forcible measures against them extremely unpleasant to those engaged in them.'[136]

Imperial prestige and the vulnerability of its agents were inextricably linked. This sense of their own vulnerability imposed powerful constraints upon the uninhibited expression of what the maintenance of their prestige demanded. At other times, imperial prestige spurred on the police to take actions which were often more extreme than the circumstances warranted. As the commissioner of police informed the Home Department in 1930, 'very restrained action by the police . . . only results in encouraging the dregs of the population to insult and jeer at the Police . . . I therefore propose to take more vigorous action in the future.'[137] If

[135] See ch. 5 above.
[136] Express Letter, Bombay Special, to Home, Simla, 4 June 1930, in GOB, Home (Special), File 750 (26) of 1930, p. 27, MSA.
[137] Commissioner of Police, Bombay, to Secretary, GOB, Home (Special), 1 December 1930, in *ibid.*, p. 215.

pride and weakness combined to require 'more vigorous action' by the police, the Bombay government, or New Delhi, or, perhaps especially, London, would sooner or later have to ask themselves how much vigour they could prudently permit. Vigorous action could create a wider sympathy for its victims and deepen and extend antagonism against the state. Such calculations continually racked the official mind. For instance, Congress processions during civil disobedience allowed British rule to be pilloried from the street, but they were non-violent. Any attempt to prohibit them 'would certainly provoke defiance' and the situation could well run out of control, although just how completely only the official mind could imagine:

A number of processions would begin in different parts of the City. Before long police would be unable to stop them and the military would have to be called in. Shooting on a large scale would be inevitable and elements of the population now quiet would join in in sympathy. Peace would only be restored after serious riots.[138]

The urgency which the colonial state felt about the need to maintain order at all times and to thwart any threat to it at the first opportunity arose from its perception of its subjects as volatile and fanatical as well as its own awareness of its weakness and vulnerability. These perceptions fed and developed the anxiety of the colonial state and its agents, especially the police, that they might be on the point of being overwhelmed. It also entrenched an intermittent tendency to restore order with excessive force. In other words, the weakness of the police arose in part from the fallibility of their assessment of the threat to the social order and of their judgement about the best means of reasserting control.

This tendency to feel overwhelmed and to restore what it perceived as order with excessive force was inherent to the statecraft of colonial rule and embedded in strategies of public order policing in India. As late as 1920, the Home Secretary reminded New Delhi that 'India possesses an internal frontier', which was marked by 'the relative instability of the social organism . . . the ease with which on skilful instigation all causes of popular discontent can be directed into courses directly hostile to the authority of Government [and] the growing tendency for political controversies to assume a racial and nationalist complexion'.[139] Similarly, J. C. Curry, a senior police officer in Bombay, observed how the inherent volatility and barely suppressed turbulence of Indian society threatened to expose the weaknesses of the British position in India. In India, various influences, 'racial, communal, criminal and traditional', fostered 'condi-

[138] Express Letter, Bombay Special to Home Simla, 4 June 1930, in *ibid.*, pp. 27–9.
[139] Secretary, GOB, Home, to Secretary, GOI, Army, 12 January 1921 in Bombay Confidential Proceedings, January 1921, vol. 62, p. 32, OIOC.

tions of public instability'. This meant that the police 'must be ever ready to suppress ebullitions of violence'.[140] The cotton mills of Bombay, in his view, 'never fail to find the crowds which become mobs, and the mobs which turn to frenzied slaying'.[141] It was imperative, therefore, for the police to establish control and impose order upon the crowd at the first opportunity. In India, it seemed, it was essential for the police and the state to act quickly and decisively. Thus, 'the first and last rule of conduct for all ranks', declared Curry, 'is to go straight for any trouble and deal with it before it becomes more serious. There can be no excuse for failing to learn of a small cloud low on the horizon which . . . may quickly obscure the sky.'[142] Yet dealing with the crowd required specialized knowledge and exceptional and particular skills in India. For

popular disturbances can often be prevented from coming to a head by tact and foresight on the part of officers who understand the various diverse peoples, and know when to use persuasion, how to appeal to the sense of honour innate in well-bred Indians, and when to hint at the presence of that power which, in the circumstances of India, must always be available, even if undisplayed and in reserve.[143]

The implications of the inherent instability and volatility of Indian society extended beyond police practice to embrace the law and the powers of the state which were necessary to contain it and, therefore, also circumscribe the freedom and autonomy of civil society. It was, after all, to perform precisely this essential function for its subjects that Britain ruled India. Indeed, Curry continued:

These circumstances render it compellingly necessary for authority to be armed with wide powers for which no need exists in other more homogeneous countries . . . No government, indigenous or foreign, autocratic or constitutional, can hope to administer such a country, unless its local officials have extensive legal powers and ultimately the backing of unlimited force.[144]

The Amritsar massacre in 1919 showed precisely where this line of reasoning was liable to lead. For General Dyer justified his decision to open fire at Jallianwalla Bagh in 1919 in terms which were familiar to the point of banality and, therefore, commanded an unquestioning authority within colonial discourse. Under his orders, 1,650 rounds of ammunition were fired for ten minutes by the army at a peaceful meeting, killing by the most modest calculation 379 people and wounding a further 1,200. He had been faced, he later told the Hunter Committee, with only two options: either to fulfil his 'very distasteful and horrible duty' of 'suppressing disorder' or else risk 'becoming responsible for all future bloodshed'.

[140] Curry, *The Indian Police*, p. 86.   [141] *Ibid.*, p. 99.   [142] *Ibid.*   [143] *Ibid.*, p. 86.
[144] *Ibid.*

In suppressing disorder, his task was not a matter of 'merely dispersing the crowd, but one of producing a sufficient moral effect, from a military point of view, not only on those who were present but more specially throughout the Punjab'. Under these circumstances, 'If I fired, I must fire with good effect, a small amount of firing would be an act of folly.' In the end, he had employed 'the least amount of firing which would produce the necessary moral and widespread effect it was my duty to produce'. Therefore, the force he employed could not by its very nature be excessive; it had no economy. As he put it, 'There could be no question of undue severity.'[145] In this way, colonial representations of the 'mob' justified the use of repressive measures which could not be contemplated elsewhere. Yet if colonial discourse facilitated and legitimized the most brutal repression, this did not mean that the state developed, let alone deployed, the means of coercion it may have deemed necessary. Indeed, until its demise, the colonial state remained particularly aware of its vulnerability to the threat of being suddenly overwhelmed by mass discontent.

VI

It was, in any case, primarily the army and not the police which provided the muscle to move the coercive apparatus of the colonial state. To a large extent, public order policing in India was conducted by the army. When officials perceived an imminent breakdown of public order, they summoned the army and deemed the military presence indispensable. Official discourse had enunciated the principle at least since 1860, affirmed by the Eden Commission in 1879 and repeated ever since that while 'the preservation of the public peace is the duty of the police', the function of the army was 'to suppress rebellion and to resist invasion'.[146] Yet, of course, it was difficult, if not impossible, to distinguish too neatly between disorder

[145] *Report of the Committee Appointed by the Government of India to Investigate the Disturbances in the Punjab etc. Parliamentary Papers, 1920,* vol. XIV, Cmd. 681, p. 1116; and *Disturbances in the Punjab, Statement by Brigadier-General R. E. H. Dyer, PP, 1920,* vol. XXXIV, Cmd. 771, especially pp. 686–90; see also D. Sayer, 'British Reactions to the Amritsar Massacre, 1919–1920', *Past and Present,* 131 (May 1991), 130–64. Yet, in Britain certainly, the question of 'undue severity' posed intractable problems for the military when it was called upon to provide aid to the civil authority. According to the Secretary of State for War in 1908, 'The law to my mind is clear that the soldier is in no different position from anybody else . . . an excess of force and an excess of display ought not to be used. The soldier is guilty of an offence if he uses that excess.' See *Report of the Select Committee on the Employment of the Military in Cases of Disturbances, 1908,* Examination of Rt. Hon. R. B. Haldane, *PP, 1908,* Cmd. 236, vol. VII, p. 387.

[146] Secretary, GOI, Army to Chief Secretary, GOB, 19 October 1920, Home Department (Confidential) Proceedings, Bombay Confidential Proceedings, January 1921, vol. 62, p. 19, OIOC.

and rebellion, let alone anticipate accurately when the former might develop into the latter. Moreover, for the British in India, the introduction of the police had occurred at a time when 'the pacification of the country and the introduction of a stable civil order were proceeding concurrently'.[147] As a result, no clear demarcation of function between the army and the police had seemed necessary or, indeed, been effected. At no stage in its development had the police been organized on a scale which presupposed that 'they should discharge the full extent of their duties',[148] as they had been defined by the Eden Commission, 'of preserving order, of protecting property and of quelling disturbances', let alone in the stricter terms of the requirement set out in the early 1920s, that they 'should be able to deal promptly and effectively with local disturbances without invoking the aid of the military'.[149] Indeed, as one official remarked in 1920, the ordinary, unarmed police were 'practically useless in the case of really violent disturbance', while the armed police force was 'entirely inadequate to put down serious disturbances'.[150] In practice, therefore, as officials knew only too well, it was upon 'the military authorities that the duty falls of seeing that efficient arrangements are made for internal security' and, as a result, far too frequently, 'regular troops were used for purely police purpose'.[151] Whereas officials believed the use of the army 'to deal with domestic disturbances' was in Britain and elsewhere in the empire, 'little more than a theoretical consideration', in colonial discourse, *the case of India is entirely different*. In India, troops were employed several times a year 'to prevent internal disorder and, if necessary, to quell it'.[152]

Although the troops were called out when the police felt overwhelmed, there was a general reluctance to use the military for police purposes. The extensive use of troops was an expensive method of ensuring public order and in the face of tightening budgets, the army resented the fact that such use constituted a charge upon the military estimates. The civilian employment of troops might diminish 'their general efficiency and fighting value' as a military force. 'It exposes them moreover to the machinations of agitators', as the Government of India observed. In addition, 'it must be remembered that among British soldiers of today there are many to whom military interference in trade disputes between employers and

---

[147] Secretary, GOB, Home, to Secretary, GOI, Army, 12 January 1921, in *ibid.*, p. 32.
[148] *Ibid.*
[149] Secretary, GOI, Army to Chief Secretary, GOB, 19 October 1920, in *ibid.*, p. 19.
[150] P. R. Cadell, Commissioner, Southern Division to Secretary, GOB, Home, 25 November 1920, in *ibid.*, p. 28.
[151] Secretary, GOI, Army to Chief Secretary, GOB, 19 October 1920, in *ibid.*, p. 19.
[152] *Report of the Indian Statutory Commission*, vol. I: *Survey* (London, 1930), p. 95.

employed is particularly repugnant'.[153] Yet, ironically, the Indian army was to become increasingly in the 1920s 'a force of screw-guns and mules',[154] now best suited, perhaps, to the task of combating non-violent satyagrahis and unarmed strikers. The frequent use of the army for public order policing between 1918 and the early 1920s, and especially perhaps the Amritsar massacre, led to a re-evaluation of its role in the maintenance of the Raj. The repeated use of troops against civilians with such brutal consequences could undermine its discipline and sap its strength.

If the army was to be used more sparingly, the obvious solution, in the early 1920s, was to strengthen the police and, in particular, its armed contingent. If the police were to be expected to maintain public order without the assistance of the army, however, its size would have to be expanded beyond the capacity of the state's coffers. The prospect of expanding the armed police brought a whole range of problems in its wake. If large forces of military police had to be stationed at what were deemed 'trouble-spots', they would incur enormous cost for the relatively rare occasions on which they would be required. Not only would it be difficult 'to provide sufficient men without an impossible burden of expenditure',[155] but the creation of 'a large idle body like this would also be an administrative difficulty and danger'.[156] The question of arming the police inevitably raised anxieties about the discipline of the force. If the mob were to disarm them, they could wreak havoc. The armed police might prove mutinous or they might be partisan in a dispute. They might take sides in a communal riot; they might sympathize with strikers when they were expected to discipline them; they might be persuaded by nationalist agitators to turn their guns on the government it was their duty to serve. The British most fully trusted 'European' officers and the suggestion that they should be marshalled in a mobile force to quell disorder was believed to merit serious consideration. But while the 'Europeanization' of the police force appealed to the primordial sentiments of some colonial officials, wiser counsels appreciated that it might have the effect of 'accentuating the racial question which is generally incidental to disturbances in present times' or 'of raising strong

[153] Secretary, GOI, Army Department to Chief Secretary, GOB, 19 October 1920, Bombay Confidential Proceedings, Home Department, January 1921, vol. 62, OIOC.
[154] J. Gallagher and A. Seal, 'Britain and India Between the Wars', *MAS,* 15:3 (1981), 403.
[155] P. R. Cadell, Commissioner, Southern Division to Secretary, GOB, Home, 25 November 1920, in Bombay Confidential Proceedings, Home Department, January 1921, vol. 62, p. 28, OIOC.
[156] J. Ghosal, Acting Commissioner, Northern Division, to Secretary, GOB, Home, 17 November, 1920, in *ibid.,* p. 25.

popular prejudice against the proposed force'.[157] Nor could a riot squad manned by Europeans be relied upon to be more effective. As one district magistrate observed, Indian police officers of higher ranks had been 'conspicuous for devotion to duty, courage and coolness'. They were, he added, 'better fitted to deal with mobs than such Europeans as would replace them because they know the people and their language more intimately and can gauge the consciousness of a situation more accurately'.[158]

Some troops were ordinarily stationed in Bombay. Their presence was deemed to be essential 'to prevent the serious consequences which would follow from civil disturbances' in what was after all a major metropolis and a political and commercial centre of vital imperial importance. These troops were sometimes alerted, even if they were not always 'called out' when officials perceived the threat of 'disturbances'. While the police and the army were most vociferously pilloried for their brutality during nationalist agitations, the deployment of the military was most readily justified in the case of communal riots. The often apparently random and unpredictable violence which characterized periods of communal riots swiftly alarmed wide sections of the city's inhabitants, whatever the degree of their complicity in their occurrence. They were quick to demand the use of troops to restore order and highly critical of both the government and the police for not calling out the army soon enough. Troops were called to the aid of the civil authorities most often in the case of communal riots. Indeed, 'the vast majority of the disturbances which call for the intervention of the military have a communal or religious complexion'.[159] For 'police forces, admirably organized as they are, cannot be expected in all cases to cope with the sudden and violent outburst of a mob driven frantic by religious frenzy'. So, in colonial discourse, the fact that Indians were not deemed to have fully entered the universe of reason – for 'India is a country in which the wildest and most improbable stories of outrage and insult spread with amazing rapidity' – served to justify the use of the military in civil disturbances, and more brutal repressive practices in general, which either could not be contemplated elsewhere or, at best, amounted to 'little more than a theoretical consideration'.[160]

Army units detailed for internal security duties consisted of a significant proportion of British troops. The Indian army in 1930 had a ratio of one British soldier for every two and a half Indian soldiers, but among

---

[157] Commissioner of Sind to Secretary, GOB, Home, 7 December 1920, in *ibid.*, p. 30.
[158] District Magistrate, Hyderabad, to Commissioner of Sind, 19 November 1920, in *ibid.*, p. 31.   [159] *Report of the Indian Statutory Commission*, vol. I, p. 95.   [160] *Ibid.*

troops allotted for internal security, 'a majority of British troops is employed', on average in the ratio of eight British soldiers to every seven Indians. In communal riots, the demand, as the Indian Statutory Commission noted, was overwhelmingly for the use of British troops who could be seen to have 'no bias, real or suspected by either side'.[161] Yet even when they could be seen to be tainted with 'bias', their presence was rather re-assuring to colonial officials. Thus, while the Government of Bombay readily acknowledged in 1920 'the serious disadvantages' entailed in 'the employment of troops in industrial and political disturbances', it was precisely 'the character of the political agitation at present being carried on, and the rapid development of the labour situation' which determined them to reject any attempt to restrict their option to invoke military aid when they considered it necessary.[162] If, in colonial discourse, no form of political action could be readily distinguished from sedition, it was folly to assume that labour disputes could simply be taken for what they were – disputes between employers and their employees. 'It is well known', as colonial officials often gravely told each other, 'how easily a mass of uneducated Indians ordinarily well-disposed towards Government can be excited against the authorities by a few firebrands.' Thus, colonial officials took it for granted that 'any unrest even of an economic character can be easily directed against the forces of law and order'. Moreover, in Bombay Presidency, it seemed that 'nearly all local disturbances . . . though often purporting to be connected with questions of pay and employment have been engineered by outsiders . . . prominently connected with agitation against government'.[163] In the context of the political turbulence witnessed in Bombay and the city's vital strategic, political and economic importance to imperial interests, and by comparison with the brutality of the military repression effected elsewhere, what is surprising is how rarely, not how extensively, troops were used. Although troops were kept in readiness during each of the general strikes, they were not by any means called out as a matter of course. They were alerted and mobilized more frequently during the nationalist agitations of the early 1920s and early 1930s, but on these occasions officials often appeared to invest the 'moral effect' of their proximity with greater significance than their active use. Nonetheless, between the two world wars, it was reported that 'the use of the Army for the purpose of

[161] *Ibid.*
[162] Secretary, GOB, Home to Secretary, GOI, Army, 12 January 1921 in Bombay Confidential Proceedings, vol. 62, pp. 32–4, OIOC.
[163] P. R. Cadell, Commissioner, Southern Division, to Secretary, GOB, Home, 25 November, 1920 in *ibid.*, p. 27.

maintaining or restoring internal order was increasing rather than diminishing'.[164]

To some extent, the increasingly frequent deployment of the army to restore order reflected the growing scale of social conflict and political action. In addition, organizational changes, arising in part from improved communications and the expansion of the railway network, made it possible to mobilize the army more easily. It could now be concentrated and garrisoned in larger units rather than dispersed in small outposts and it could, therefore, be deployed more quickly, more efficiently and even more flexibly. Thus, units of the field army could swiftly reinforce those assigned to internal security and fewer troops had to be tied down to the tasks of watch and ward.[165] Moreover, political reform and the devolution of ministerial power to elected politicians heightened British anxieties and contributed to their readiness to perceive the collapse of order and to summon the army. Accordingly, during the successive rounds of constitutional reform in the late 1910s and the mid 1930s, the British sought to maximize their control over the repressive apparatus of the colonial state, even as greater power was devolved to elected representatives.[166] The army remained suspicious, throughout this period of reform, that provincial governments invoked military aid more frequently and perhaps more often than was necessary, largely because they were reluctant to spend adequately on the maintenance and expansion of their police forces. So it seemed to the generals that while Indian politicians lost no opportunity to castigate the Government of India for its vast military expenditure, they took advantage of their growing power in the provinces to divert expenditure away from the vital needs of the police and of public security. But if the police were under-resourced, the army would have to be called out more often. In this way, the actions of Indian elected representatives served to increase the demands on the military estimates which they were themselves pressing to cut. As the repressive power of the colonial state was expanded, so the ranks of the police and the army not only continued to be staffed by Indians but their officer corps, especially in the case of the latter, underwent a process, however slow and halting, of Indianization. More crucially, however, increasing state repression coincided with increasing Indian control over the institutions and agencies of the state. In an important sense, the growing dependence upon the army for public order policing reflected the tendency of local elites, as they gained in-

[164] *Report of the Indian Statutory Commission*, vol. I, p. 95.

[165] Omissi, *The Sepoy and the Raj*, pp. 199–214; Narain, 'The Colonial Army in India, 1918–1947', ch. 6.

[166] Arnold, 'The Armed Police'; Omissi, *The Sepoy and the Raj*, pp. 194–231; Narain, 'The Colonial Army in India', ch. 6; S. P. Cohen, *The Indian Army: Its Contribution to the Development of the Indian Nation* (Berkeley, 1971).

creasing influence over the local and provincial machinery of the state, to deploy its resources to discipline and control labour, whether in the towns or the countryside. During the period of provincial autonomy, between 1937 and 1939, the Congress Ministry showed few inhibitions about taking repressive action and, sometimes, a suspiciously greater willingness to force strikers back to their machines under the muzzle of a gun, in Bombay as well as in Ahmedabad and Sholapur, than the preceding colonial regimes.[167] 'We had expected the Bombay Ministry to taboo the old bureaucratic violence', observed the *Congress Socialist* after the police had opened fire on the workers during the one-day strike of 7 November 1938, 'Our expectation has not been fulfilled.'[168]

VII

The system of policing which the British created in the mid-nineteenth century grew out of the need to separate its function from the revenue administration, on the one hand, and the military, on the other. The British had become increasingly aware that 'the preservation of the public peace' would require an agency which was less cumbersome and more flexible than the army. If the British were to assert the legitimacy of their rule, especially after 1857, beyond the claims of conquest and occupation, this agency would have to be more clearly subject to civil authority. In any case, the extensive and repeated use of the military for public order policing entailed the risk of overly exposing soldiers, especially Indian troops, to situations of political and social conflict, which could compromise their loyalty and undermine their discipline. In Britain, the police force had taken its modern shape in the mid-nineteenth century when the political order had been consolidated and ruling-class anxieties came to be focused primarily upon the protection of private property.[169] For the

[167] On the Bombay Trade Disputes Bill sponsored by the Congress, see GOB, Home (Special), File 550 (25) III-A of 1938; GOB, Home (Special), File 550 (24) of 1938; on the one-day strike to protest against the bill, see *Bombay Sentinel*, 7 November 1938 and *Times of India*, 8 November 1938; *Bombay Chronicle*, 8 November 1938. See also C. Markovits, *Indian Business and Nationalist Politics, 1931–39 The Indigenous Capitalist Class and the Rise of the Congress Party* (Cambridge, 1985), ch. 6; Sujata Patel, *The Making of Industrial Relations: The Ahmedabad Textile Industry, 1918–1939* (Delhi, 1987); on Madras, see E. D. Murphy, *Unions in Conflict: A Comparative Study of Four South Indian Textile Centres, 1918–1939* (New Delhi, 1981), pp. 148–219; on Jamshedpur, D. Simeon, *The Politics of Labour under Late Colonialism: Workers, Unions and the State in Chota Nagpur, 1928–1939* (New Delhi, 1995), chs. 7–9; V. Bahl, 'Attitude of the Indian National Congress Towards the Working Class Struggle in India, 1918–1947', in Kapil Kumar (ed.), *Congress and Classes: Nationalism, Workers and Peasants* (Delhi, 1988), pp. 1–33.   [168] *Congress Socialist*, 13 November 1938.
[169] C. Emsley, *Policing and Its Context, 1750–1870* (London, 1983); R. Reiner, *The Politics of the Police* (Brighton, 1985), ch. 1.

British in India, however, the political order seemed irremediably fragile and its social base inherently volatile. The function of the police was primarily to safeguard India's 'internal frontier' and to secure its political order rather than simply to detect or prevent crime. Yet ironically the police could not discharge this task without the assistance of the army, which in turn was organized and deployed to defend 'the internal frontier': 'to hold India against the Indians', as Kitchener discovered in 1905, rather than 'with regard to possible danger from outside'.[170] As a distinct police system was separated out from the army and institutionalized, the role which was delineated for it ensured that it never fully escaped its military origins.

This preoccupation with public order meant that the police left the prevention and detection of crime largely to be handled within local power structures. It also determined the definition and ordering of crime. Thus, for instance, it was the British attempt to establish their sway over large tracts of a mobile and strife-torn countryside which led to the invention of 'thuggee' in the 1830s.[171] Similarly, the criminalization of particular tribes and castes arose out of the need to pin down wandering cultivators, pastoralists, forest dwellers and itinerants, so that they could be taxed and policed more effectively.[172] 'Dacoity' became another catch-all category within which a wide range of 'crimes' could be lumped and diverse kinds of agrarian conflicts addressed.[173] Riots were no more easily definable than dacoity and no more easily counted. In fact, they were often mistaken for each other and each was sometimes subsumed within the other. Nonetheless, by the late nineteenth century, in some rural districts, as the magis-

---

[170] Kitchener to Roberts, 12 January 1903, Kitchener Papers, 30/57/29, PRO cited by Omissi, *The Sepoy and the Raj*, p. 206.

[171] See the excellent article by Stewart N Gordon, 'Scarf and Sword: Thugs, Marauders and State Formation in 18th Century Malwa', *IESHR*, 6:4 (1969), 403–29, especially 407–15; see also Radhika Singha, 'Providential Circumstances: The Thuggee Campaign of the 1830s and Legal Innovation', *MAS*, 27:1 (1993), 83–146.

[172] S. Nigam, 'Disciplining and Policing the Criminals by Birth, Part I: The Making of a Colonial Stereotype – the Criminal Tribes and Castes of North India', *IESHR*, 27:2 (1990), 131–64 and S. Nigam, 'Disciplining and Policing the Criminals by Birth, Part II: The Development of a Disciplinary System, 1871–1900', *ibid.*, 27:3 (1990), 257–87; M. Radhakrishna, 'The Criminal Tribes Act in the Madras Presidency: Implications for the Itinerant Trading Communities', *ibid.*, 26:3 (1989), 269–95; and M. Radhakrishna, 'Surveillance and Settlements under the Criminal Tribes Act in Madras', *ibid.*, 29:2 (1992), 171–98.

[173] However, see D. Arnold, 'Dacoity and Rural Crime in Madras, 1860–1940', *Journal of Peasant Studies*, 6:2 (1979), 140–67. For all the problems of arbitrary classification, Arnold concludes that dacoity can be taken to constitute a real, discrete and measurable activity rather than a function of the perceptions of the colonial rulers and their agencies of law enforcement. Thus, he notes, 'Although the crime statistics published by the police from 1863 were doubtless inaccurate . . . there is no reason to believe that the figures fail to show the general pattern of the incidence of dacoity.' *Ibid.*, p. 143.

trate of Saran noted, 'the most important offence with which the police have to deal . . . [is] rioting'.[174] In this instance, the police appear to have been managing disputes over land and rural resources between rival land controllers rather than the actions of the dispossessed against the dominant elites.[175] For the colonial state largely left rural magnates free to discipline and control their dependants and labourers, when they could, even if they were willing to bolster the efforts of rural elites when this proved necessary. Indeed, by the late nineteenth century, the criminalization of pastoralists, nomads and wandering groups may be seen to have extended to landholding elites and prosperous tenants the means and opportunities to exert considerably closer control over labour.[176]

This pattern of policing was produced by a force which, as Christopher Baker has observed, 'was useful in the rural areas only in an emergency and even then with mixed results'.[177] Yet in the cities, and Bombay was no exception, the police lacked resources, discipline and sometimes even manpower. To a very large extent, both in the towns and the countryside, Indian society relied upon informal systems of policing and conflict resolution. The structural and organizational weaknesses of the police in Bombay forced them to operate through alliances, networks and connections made within the neighbourhoods. Sometimes, these were alliances forged between the police and dominant elements within the neighbourhood. Sometimes, they were personal and kinship connections which could be put to use by the humble and powerless. The working classes could, therefore, sometimes use their connections with the force, however individual and personalized, to obtain protection, secure advantage or resolve conflicts. At a daily level, therefore, the police did not act monolithically as a force external to the working classes as a whole. Moreover, the rank and file of the police were sometimes responsive to social pressures within the neighbourhoods, irrespective of the internal structures of command within the force. It is not surprising, perhaps, that superior officers of the police remained concerned about the state of discipline among the subordinate staff. On the other hand, they also put their faith devoutly in the value of these street and neighbourhood connections for the detection of crime. In fact, their belief was belied by the

---

[174] 'Annual Crime Report for 1882', no. 346, 14 February 1883, Saran Collectorate, Faujdari Basta, cited by A. Yang, 'The Agrarian Origins of Crime: A Study of Riots in Saran District, India, 1886–1920', *Journal of Social History*, 13:2 (1979), 292.

[175] Yang, 'Agrarian Origins'; see also S. Freitag, 'Crime in the Social Order of Colonial North India', *MAS*, 25:2 (1991), 227–61; and S. Freitag, 'Collective Crime and Authority in North India', in A. Yang (ed.), *Crime and Criminality in British India* (Tucson, Ariz., 1985), pp. 140–63.

[176] Freitag, 'Crime in the Social Order'; Nigam, 'Disciplining and Policing the Criminals by Birth', Parts I and II.   [177] Baker, *An Indian Rural Economy*, p. 69.

criminal statistics. For the low rates of recorded crime suggest both a reluctance on the part of residents to report them and on the part of the police to record them. This reluctance only serves to afforce the suggestion that the prevention and detection of crime, as well as the meting out of punishment, remained throughout this period largely the preserve of the social networks of the neighbourhood.

The constraints under which the police functioned meant that they were only likely to be effective if they marginalized and concentrated upon selected targets. In this process of selection, they would necessarily have to rely upon a general consensus about which groups in society were especially prone to criminal activity and might constitute, therefore, the proper objects of policing. In the context of colonial India, this consensus proved particularly difficult to achieve. Of course, by enacting this principle of selection, the colonial state was able to create criminal tribes and castes. But while it might police them energetically, the criminal tribes were scarcely, by the late nineteenth century, a potent threat to the social order. To marginalize more substantial social groups was an intractable and often hazardous proposition. In particular localities and regions, it was sometimes possible to find a consensus which isolated and marginalized some social groups. But social groups which were marginalized in one area might be harder to isolate in another; indeed, they might even exercise some influence on the strategies for policing the public order. Among those who laid claims to respectability and sought to distance themselves from the rough, there were many for whom the experience of selective policing was never too remote. With the development of nationalist politics, a greater variety of people found a possible consensus about the strategies of policing and the definition of its proper objects unconvincing and untenable, in the light of their own experience, real or imagined, of the state. The intensification of communal conflict only made this consensus more difficult to achieve. By generating and developing a political vocabulary of sectarianism, the colonial state in fact foreclosed the possibility of creating a viable language of order. This was why it often found it difficult to satisfy the logic of its position by freely expressing its coercive disposition. The function of crime for the capitalist industrial state, we are sometimes told, was to regulate society more closely and to discipline and punish the working classes. The colonial state, however, was thrown back upon the more slippery alliances and political contingencies, in particular shifting alliances with its collaborators, to underwrite the social order.

The exigencies of public order policing, and especially situations of crowd control, exposed the weaknesses of the police and, indeed, laid bare their own sense of vulnerability. It was an essential characteristic of the Indian crowd, in colonial discourse, that unless it was quickly dispersed it would rapidly get out of control. Frequently, therefore, they tended to perceive the potential for crowd violence too readily and invoke military assistance. Yet, for all their sense of weakness, the police were sometimes ruthless and even brutal in their response to the crowd. In part, this use of excessive force may be seen as a symptom of panic, arising out of their awareness of their own weakness. But it also reflected what might be described as the statecraft of the police and was integral to their approach to the problems of public order. Assumptions about the cultural peculiarities of Indian society suggested that it could only properly be managed by methods, codes and knowledge which were specific to its culture. So the detection of crime acquired, in this context, a new and unusual meaning. Crime became an important part of the endeavour of colonial anthropology. Informers and spies became essential to unravelling the hidden meanings of the East. Policemen, civil servants and magistrates developed out of this quest for the culturally specific a whole ethnography of evil. While in reality crime went largely unreported and unrecorded, police reports and memoirs identified and described in painstaking detail crimes of savage brutality or extraordinary guile and cunning or those which reflected exotic customs and elaborate rituals. Of course, this was particularly the case with 'thuggee' and the criminal tribes and castes, whose supposed criminality was represented as an inheritance and a profession, inextricably connected to their lineage and genealogy;[178] but this search for the culturally specific infused the tone and language of the police reports in Bombay city as well. The mysteries of the Orient extended to criminal behaviour and demanded that colonial rulers fashioned culturally specific measures to control them.

Similarly, colonial discourse about popular politics began with the assumption that the populace lived beyond the realm of reason. Rumours, malicious information, skilful instigation were always liable to push a fanatical people over the edge of violence. This propensity only heightened the need for swift, firm and effective action to prevent a minor affray turning into a major riot or a local disturbance into widespread and uncontrollable rebellion. The speed of response by the police and the army always seemed crucial. Moreover, it was deemed that the efficacy of the police and the army in any single situation would determine its 'moral effect' upon potential 'miscreants' elsewhere. Colonial officials were often concerned that without the option of using extra-legal compulsion and unlimited force they could not be certain of maintaining order. Yet the imperative for immediate and effective action to impose control

---

[178] See, especially, Nigam, 'Disciplining and Policing the Criminals by Birth', Parts I and II; Gordon, 'Scarf and Sword'.

tended to obscure the distinction between minimum and maximum force. In addition, the social chasm which divided commanding officers of the police and the army from the crowds they sought to control also contributed towards this tendency to overreact. Frequently, they found it difficult to judge a situation accurately and tended to perceive the potential for violence rather too hastily.

The notion that 'the mass of uneducated' Indians could be easily worked into 'a state of excitement' which, because it pushed them outside the domain of reason, rendered them impossible to control, was compounded by another aspect of the way colonial rulers represented themselves and their subjects. The legitimacy of British rule in India was founded in this discourse upon the unfitness of Indians to govern themselves. While the purpose of their rule was, they claimed, to bring enlightenment and civilization to areas of darkness and to prepare Indians for eventual self-government, it was also incumbent upon the British, while educating their subjects, to discipline them with firmness and justice. Paternalist benevolence was inseparable from necessary punishment which, happily, in any case, redounded to the good of their subjects. Of course, paternalism had to be enlightened and from its lofty standpoint, the authoritarian excesses of colonial agents were harshly judged. Just as the moral progress of empire could be set against the crass notion of economic imperialism, so moral outrage at the lapses of colonial agents camouflaged the exploitative purposes of imperialism.[179] In this way, colonial discourse insisted not only upon the use of excessive force but deemed it essential for 'moral effect' and necessary for the good of its subjects. In this light, it becomes possible to see why the police and the army, for all their apparent weaknesses, sometimes responded to revolting and disorderly subjects with a ruthless and murderous brutality. It also becomes clear that Dyer's actions at Amritsar were not, in Churchill's characterization, 'an episode without precedent or parallel in the modern history of the British Empire . . . a monstrous event, an event which stands in sinister and singular isolation'[180] but, on the contrary, it was integral to and the outcome of the colonial conceptualization of and response to the problems of public order.

It is sometimes suggested that the autocratic nature of the colonial state in India was tempered by the liberal and democratic political culture of Britain. This is a romantic view and should be regarded with scepticism.

[179] For an excellent delineation of this discourse, see R. Robinson, 'Oxford in Imperial Historiography', in F. Madden and D. K. Fieldhouse (eds.), *Oxford and the Idea of the Commonwealth: Essays Presented to Sir Edgar Williams* (London, 1982), pp. 30–48.

[180] Quoted in Omissi, *The Sepoy and the Raj*, p. 218; see especially, Sayer, 'British Reactions to the Amritsar Massacre'.

For some social groups in Britain, like the casual poor and the Irish, the state must at times have appeared extremely authoritarian and oppressive.[181] Nor were the activities of troops and police in the Welsh coal fields in the early twentieth century or the Black and Tans in Ireland redolent of a political culture which honoured civil liberty above all else.[182] Similarly, the British state was able to respond to strikes with a ferocity it did not often attempt in India. When Clydeside workers struck in January 1919, 'infantry and tanks were rushed in, and machine gun posts set up in the City Chambers'. During the police strike in Liverpool in the same year, 'the army was sent in with bayonets fixed to keep the peace and a battleship was posted to the Mersey, no doubt to cow the masses'.[183] The scale of military mobilization during the general strike of 1926 in Britain, 'when the government responded with the full panoply of law enforcement, with police and special constables backed up by battalions of troops, many warships, and marines and thousands of civilian volunteers drawn from the loyalist middle class'[184] was never, in the course of a trade dispute, matched in India.[185]

The British in India showed no aversion to deploying their armed force with destructive effect when they believed that their position was under threat and when they feared the repercussions of their repression less than the consequences of disorder. The most violent campaigns waged by the army carried a large punitive, even retributive, content, effected as an example and a lesson to their subjects: in the aftermath of the Mutiny of 1857;[186] Jallianwalla Bagh and the repression which accompanied the Rowlatt satyagraha in the Punjab;[187] the suppression of the 'fanatical'

---

[181] Gatrell, 'Crime, Authority and the Policeman State', pp. 243–310; J. Davis, 'Jennings' Buildings and the Royal Borough: The Construction of an Underclass in mid-Victorian England', in D. Feldman and G. Stedman-Jones (eds.), *Metropolis: London, Histories and Representations since 1800* (London, 1989), pp. 21–40.

[182] P. Townshend, *The British Campaign in Ireland, 1919–1921: The Development of Political and Military Policies* (Oxford, 1975).

[183] K. Jeffrey and P. Hennessey, *States of Emergency: British Governments and Strikebreaking since 1919* (London, 1983), pp. 11–13.

[184] Jane Morgan, *Conflict and Order: The Police and Labour Disputes in England and Wales, 1900–1939* (Oxford, 1987), p. 25.

[185] The British, however, mobilized massive military power during the Quit India movement in 1942.

[186] W. H. Russell, *My Diary in India in the Year 1858–59*, 2 vols. (London, 1860); J. W. Kaye, *A History of the Sepoy War in India, 1857–58*, 3 vols. (London, 1864, 1870 and 1876); S. N. Sen. *Eighteen Fifty Seven* (New Delhi, 1957); P. C. Joshi (ed.), *Rebellion – 1857: A Symposium* (Delhi, 1957).

[187] *Report of the Committee Appointed by the Government of India to Investigate the Disturbances in the Punjab etc. PP*, 1920, Cmd. 681, vol. XIV; *Punjab Disturbances, 1919–20*, 2 vols., *Report of the Commissioners Appointed by the Punjab Sub-Committee of the Indian National Congress to Look into the Jallianwalla Bagh Massacre* (Delhi, 1976); Sayer, 'British Reactions to the Amritsar Massacre'; V. N. Datta, *Jallianwalla Bagh* (Ludhiana, 1969).

Mapillas in the early 1920s, which may have resulted in some ten thousand deaths;[188] the sustained military initiatives, supposedly against terrorism in Bengal in the early 1930s;[189] and the Quit India movement in 1942, when British military power was at its greatest and its mobilization for the maintenance of internal security was, indeed, formidable.[190] These military campaigns, part punitive, part repressive, were staged largely in areas where government was least firmly entrenched and the British were least confident of the stability of their collaborative base: Punjab, Malabar, Medinapur, eastern UP and north Bihar. In Bombay city, where British rule was more securely based, the colonial state did not embark on a sustained and generalized campaign of repression against their opponents in the same fashion. Nonetheless, it is significant that despite the strength of their collaborative alliances and the entrenchment of their rule, the police and the army often resorted to violence to preserve the public peace at a considerable cost to human life.

The imperial purpose in India was to deploy its resources in Britain's global interests, neither simply nor necessarily to maintain colonial rule. The time might come when dominion would have to be sacrificed to these larger imperial priorities. The fact that India was ruled in the global interests of British imperialism imposed a self-denying ordinance upon its Oriental Despotism. British rule had to preserve the public peace to enable the mobilization of Indian resources for its imperial purposes. But it could not secure its rule and mobilize resources without the collaboration of powerful Indian interests. So it was essential for the British to invest in and honour existing configurations of power in Indian society while trying to control, in the last resort, those domains of power which

[188] K. N. Panikkar, *Against Lord and State: Religion and Peasant Uprisings in Malabar, 1836–1921* (Delhi, 1989), p. 163, see also pp. 139–90; S. F. Dale, *Islamic Society on the South Asian Frontier: The Mappilas of Malabar, 1498–1922* (Oxford, 1980), pp. 179–218; C. Wood, 'Peasant Revolt: Interpretation of Moplah Violence in the Nineteenth and Twentieth Centuries', in C. J. Dewey and A. G. Hopkins (eds.), *The Imperial Impact: Studies in the Economic History of Africa and India* (London, 1978), pp. 132–51.

[189] GOI, *Terrorism in India, 1917–1936* (Simla, 1937); T. Sarkar, *Bengal 1928–34: The Politics of Protest* (Delhi, 1987); see also, for the wider political context of Bengal, Joya Chatterji, *Bengal Divided: Hindu Communalism and Partition, 1932–47* (Cambridge, 1994); for details of the military campaign in Bengal, see Omissi, *The Sepoy and the Raj*, pp. 223–5; and Narain, 'The Colonial Army in India', ch. 6.

[190] GOI, Home Poll, File 3/15/43; GOI, Home (Poll), File 3/52/43, NAI; P. N. Chopra (ed.), *Quit India Movement: British Secret Report* (Faridabad, 1976); F. Hutchins, *India's Revolution: Gandhi and the Quit India Movement* (Cambridge, Mass., 1973), especially, chs. 7 and 9; A. C. Bhuyan, *The Quit India Movement: The Second World War and Indian Nationalism* (Delhi, 1975), especially pp. 93–102; Narain, 'The Colonial Army in India', ch. 6; M. Harcourt, 'Kisan Populism and Revolution in Rural India: The 1942 Disturbances in Bihar and East United Provinces', in D. A. Low (ed.), *Congress and the Raj: Facets of the Indian Struggle, 1917–1947* (London, 1977), pp. 315–48; G. Pandey (ed.), *The Indian Nation in 1942* (Calcutta, 1988).

most directly served these global interests. The pattern of collaboration which allowed the British to build up a formidable armoury of repressive force in India also prevented them from using it indiscriminately against their political opponents. Moreover, these patterns of collaboration were sufficiently varied and complex that their apparatus of repression could not simply be laced at the disposal of Indian magnates. If the British were to leave themselves free to deploy Indian resources to their global and imperial purposes, they could not afford to become the prisoners of their collaborators. The Quit India movement represented the most potent threat to British rule, at least since 1857. But the British in 1942 commanded sufficient military force in the subcontinent to snuff out the movement in a month. It might appear that the British were at the zenith of their power in India and their armed forces could be decisively used to secure their rule. However, the prospect of a replay under the changed conditions after the second world war led the British to the conclusion that they would have to fundamentally alter the basis of their rule, and adjustments to their position in India after 1945 pointed them in the direction of dismantling their empire.

So here lay one of the abiding contradictions of the colonial state. In the late nineteenth century, the British had recognized that the only solution to the problem of order was to leave it to the disciplinary mechanisms of local structures of power. Increasingly, after the 1920s, this technique of rule seemed constantly on the verge of breakdown. Colonial rulers who witnessed the growth of popular politics as the disorderly effusions of the ignorant and the fanatical, easily roused by disaffected publicists, were increasingly driven by the imperative to restore public order at the earliest opportunity, indeed with immediate and moral effect. Under the weight of this imperative, the distinction between the use of minimum and maximum force was obliterated. Yet the survival of Britain's autocratic rule in India and the fulfilment of its imperial purposes imposed upon its guardians a forbidding economy of repression, which was somewhat more likely to be observed in the breach.

7   Plague panic and epidemic politics in India, 1896–1914

Between 1896 and 1914, bubonic plague killed over eight million people,[1] a modest estimate which does not allow for cases which were concealed, misdiagnosed or wrongly classified. Of all the various epidemics which afflicted India in the late nineteenth and early twentieth centuries, a Kaliyuga, a period of very high mortality, stagnant, even falling population and declining life expectancy,[2] the plague was not the most destructive. Malaria and tuberculosis killed more than twice as many people over a similar period;[3] in barely four months, the influenza epidemic of 1918–19 accounted for twice as many;[4] smallpox and cholera counted their death toll in millions.[5] Yet no other epidemic evoked the fear and panic generated by the plague.

The plague epidemic prompted massive state intervention to control its spread. It also sometimes provoked fierce resistance, riots, occasionally mob attacks on Europeans and even the assassination of British officials. The vigorous and energetic intervention of the state, in itself prompted by the general panic, bore no direct relation to the virulence of the epidemic. The focus of the state's most vigorous measures was Bombay city and its

---

[1] *Annual Reports on Sanitary Measures in India*, PP, *passim*; R. Pollitzer, *Plague* (Geneva, 1954), p. 26; L. Fabian Hirst, *The Conquest of Plague. A Study of the Evolution of Epidemiology* (Oxford, 1953), pp. 296–301.

[2] The population of Bombay Presidency declined in three of the five decennial periods between 1871 and 1921. See L. Visaria and P. Visaria, 'Population, 1757–1947', in D. Kumar (ed.), *CEHI*, vol. XI: *1757–1970* (Cambridge, 1982), pp. 463–532, especially Tables 5.7 and 5.12; Kingsley Davis, *The Population of India and Pakistan* (Princeton, N.J., 1951), pp. 33–66, especially, on life expectancy, Tables 16 and 17, p. 63.

[3] I. Klein, 'Death in India', *JAS*, 32:4 (1973), 642–3; I. Klein, 'Malaria and Mortality in Bengal', *IESHR*, 9:2 (1972), 132–60; Davis, *Population*, pp. 53–7.

[4] I. D. Mills, 'Influenza in India during 1918–19', *IESHR*, 23:1 (1986), 1–40; Davis, *Population*, Appendix B, p. 237.

[5] D. Arnold, 'Smallpox and Colonial Medicine in Nineteenth Century India', in D. Arnold (ed.), *Imperial Medicine and Indigenous Societies* (Manchester, 1988), pp. 45–65; D. Arnold, 'Cholera Mortality in British India, 1817–1947', in T. Dyson (ed.), *India's Historical Demography. Studies in Famine, Disease and Society* (London, 1989), pp. 261–84; D. Arnold, 'Cholera and Colonialism in British India', *Past and Present*, 113 (1986), 118–51.

Presidency between 1896 and about 1902. But plague mortality continued to rise thereafter, reached its peak between 1903 and 1907, exceeding the levels of the late 1890s by twelvefold, and proved far more lethal in the Punjab. Yet neither plague policy nor plague riots in the Punjab appear to have displayed the zeal or acquired the political prominence they achieved in Bombay.[6]

Underlying the nature of this response is a further paradox. The late nineteenth century was a period of enormous self-confidence in medical science and, particularly, in its newly founded and burgeoning branch of tropical medicine.[7] The plague epidemic in India became the occasion for the most intensive international research on bubonic plague and its eventual findings largely laid the foundations for, indeed established much of, what is now known about the disease.[8] Yet the measures adopted by the colonial state at the turn of the twentieth century remained highly reminiscent of the Black Death or the epidemic in seventeenth-century England.[9]

The intensity of the panic which gripped colonial officials and humble subjects alike suggests the need to examine how the epidemic came to be constructed. Studies of epidemics in India have ranged widely, examining their demographic implications, or tracing their course and their attendant social and political effects. They have examined the administrative problems posed by epidemics,[10] the conflicts and rivalries which they opened up within government,[11] how the state and elites exploited the chaos they caused to extend their control,[12] how political factions within

[6] Over 354,000 died of the plague between 1896 and 1900. This figure rose to slightly under 4.5 million for the period 1903–7. Between 1903 and 1907, Punjab alone accounted for between one quarter and one half of the plague deaths each year. *Annual Reports on Sanitary Measures in India, PP, passim.*

[7] M. Warboys, 'The Emergence of Tropical Medicine: A Study in the Establishment of a Scientific Specialty', in G. Lemaine, R. Macleod, M. Mulkay and P. Weigart (eds.), *Perspectives on the Emergence of Scientific Disciplines* (The Hague, 1976), pp. 75–98; H. H. Scott, *A History of Tropical Medicine*, 2 vols. (London, 1939).

[8] Hirst, *Conquest of Plague*; I. J. Catanach, 'Plague and the Tensions of Empire, 1896–1918', in Arnold (ed.), *Imperial Medicine*, pp. 149–71; Scott, *Tropical Medicine*, vol. II, pp. 702–67.

[9] P. Slack, 'The Response to Plague in Early Modern England: Public Policies and their Consequences', in J. Walter and R. Schofield (eds.), *Famine, Disease and the Social Order in Early Modern Society* (Cambridge, 1989), pp. 167–87.

[10] Arnold, 'Cholera and Colonialism'; Arnold, 'Smallpox and Colonial Medicine'; D. Arnold, 'Touching the Body: Perspectives on the Indian Plague, 1896–1900', in R. Guha (ed.), *Subaltern Studies*, vol. V, pp. 55–90; I. J. Catanach, 'Plague and the Indian Village, 1896–1914', in P. Robb (ed.), *Rural India. Land, Power and Society under British Rule* (London, 1983), pp. 216–43; Catanach, 'Plague and the Tensions of Empire'; I. Klein, 'Urban Development and Death: Bombay City, 1870–1914', *MAS*, 20:4 (1986), 725–54; Klein, 'Plague, Policy and Popular Unrest in British India', *MAS*, 22:4 (1988), 723–55.   [11] See, especially, Catanach, 'Plague and the Tensions of Empire'.

[12] Arnold, 'Touching the Body': Arnold, 'Cholera and Colonialism'.

the Congress arranged themselves around the event[13] and even the 'indigenous' cultural response to Western science and colonial policies.[14] These studies have been illuminating but they have often proceeded piecemeal. This chapter is predicated on the assumption that epidemics do not represent a single, integrated phenomenon but signify different things to different people. It argues that their inherent interest lies less in the discrete events which occur in their wake, than in the manner of their construction. The historical process of their construction not only illuminates wider relationships between social groups and between state and society, but it can also be argued that the constituent events of an epidemic upon which historians focus might be grasped most firmly when they are acknowledged to be, separately and discretely, a function of the very process of its construction. This chapter will, therefore, try to explore how the plague epidemic was put together and the interplay between some of the numerous elements which made it up: colonial perceptions of Indian society, medical and scientific rivalries, the interaction between the plague administrators and the people upon whom their attentions focused. These perceptions, ideologies and political processes were not created for the first time by the plague epidemic; they were indeed endemic to colonial India. However, the significance of these relationships, and of the tensions and antagonisms they generated during the epidemic, lies in the ways in which their interplay helped to construct the panic of the late 1890s.

The policies of the state and the popular response to them have been frequently portrayed in terms of the inexorable conflict between 'Western anti-plague measures and popular culture',[15] the unavoidable clash of 'two different, often antagonistic value-systems, the one Indian, the other European'.[16] Indian responses, it is suggested, served as 'a reminder of the great cultural gulf which divided the colonizers and the colonized'.[17] There was, we are told, an 'Indian view of disease and its treatment' which called for 'family involvement and religious ministration, not secular segregation'.[18] I will be arguing, however, that there was neither a uniform nor a homogeneous, culturally specific Indian response, and further that the response of the populace, like that of the state, was integral to, and the product of, the generalized panic from which none escaped. While antipathy to the plague measures was often shared by disparate social groups who might have nothing else in common, it arose

---

[13] I. J. Catanach, 'Poona Politicians and the Plague', in J. Masselos (ed.), *Struggling and Ruling. The Indian National Congress, 1885–1985* (New Delhi, 1987), pp. 198–215.
[14] Arnold, 'Touching the Body'; Arnold, 'Cholera and Colonialism'; and Klein, 'Plague, Policy and Popular Unrest'.   [15] Klein, 'Plague, Policy and Popular Unrest', 739.
[16] Arnold, 'Cholera and Colonialism', 119.   [17] *Ibid.*, 134.   [18] *Ibid.*, 137.

less from the stirrings of an autonomous realm of popular culture than from the political conjuncture in which the plague was constructed.

I

On 23 September 1896, Dr A. C. Viegas, medical practitioner and local politician, declared before the Bombay Municipal Corporation, and thereby to the world, that bubonic plague had broken out in the city.[19] Thus, the plague acquired the character of an epidemic. The colonial state was, at first, reluctant to lend its authority to a panic which might cripple trade and threaten the social order. The Health Officer conceded that 'the peculiar type of fever referred to by Dr Viegas . . . was of a suspicious character' and 'appeared to be in some respects of a bubonic character'.[20] In the following weeks, as the death toll mounted, officials referred to the disease as the 'fever plague' or 'bubonic fever' but never 'bubonic plague'.[21] It was only in early October when the Viceroy provided London with confirmation of 'true bubonic plague'[22] that the epidemic finally received official sanction.

But the mere suspicion of the plague was always likely to wrest the situation out of their control. Viegas's announcement had set the alarm bells ringing across the world. The Calcutta Corporation, fearing that Bombay's fate today might be Bengal's tomorrow, began to discuss precautionary measures on the following day.[23] By early October, ports in South-East Asia, the Persian Gulf and East Africa had applied plague regulations to all vessels arriving from Bombay.[24] The French feared the prospect of riots at Marseilles[25] and pressures mounted for 'restrictive measures to prevent passage of [sic] plague to Europe'.[26]

Once the colonial state was compelled to act, it initiated a vigorous, indeed draconian, programme of measures. The plague measures, as W. C. Rand described them from Poona, 'were perhaps the most drastic that had ever been taken to stamp out an epidemic'.[27] They were, indeed, to

[19] *Times of India*, 24 September 1896, pp. 4, 5.   [20] *Ibid.*, p. 5.
[21] Hirst, *Conquest of Plague*, p. 77.
[22] Viceroy to Secretary of State for India, 2 October 1896, 'Papers Relating to the Outbreak of Bubonic Plague in India with Statement Showing the Quarantine and Other Restrictions Recently Placed upon Indian Trade, up to March 1897', p. 3, *PP*, 1897, vol. LXIII.
[23] *Times of India*, 25 September 1896, 5.
[24] GOB, General, vol. 131, Compilation no. 178, Part I, and vol. 132, Compilation no. 178, Part II, MSA.
[25] Catanach, 'Plague and the Tensions of Empire', pp. 151–2.
[26] Secretary of State for India to GOB, 18 January 1897, 'Papers Relating to the Outbreak of Bubonic Plague', *PP*, 1897, vol. LXIII, p. 55.
[27] *Draft of Report to Government of Bombay by the Late Mr W. C. Rand, I.C.S., Chairman, Poona Plague Committee* (n.p., n.d [1897?]), p. 3, MSA.

cost Rand his life. Their primary objective was to identify and isolate the sick, remove them swiftly to hospital and segregate their contacts in 'health camps'. Their houses were to be disinfected, their floors dug up, for they were believed to harbour the offending microbes, and their personal effects fumigated and sometimes burnt. Physicians and families were required by law to notify all cases of sickness and 'all cases of fever were treated as "suspects".'[28] The sick were to be isolated in hospitals, where most died, and their relatives segregated in special camps. Corpses had to be compulsorily inspected before disposal and the procedures for the registration of deaths were tightened. Vigorous steps were taken to disinfect the whole environment. Houses and gullies 'under any suspicion were at once flushed and disinfected'; buildings were limewashed or cleansed, usually at the owners' expense; and the drains and sewers were flushed every day with 3 million gallons of a dilution of carbolic acid and sea water. The city was literally drenched in disinfectant solution. Hankin, a bacteriologist with the Plague Research Committee, reported that he 'had to put up an umbrella before entering some plague houses in order to protect himself against the deluge of carbolic acid solution descending from the upper stories into which the disinfectant was pumped by a fire engine for spraying on the walls and floors of the premises'.[29] In addition, a system of surveillance was instituted to examine cargo and passengers at the ports,[30] and inspection checkpoints and detention camps became a common feature of the railway system as the movement of people into or out of the city was severely restricted. As plague began to spread, similar measures were extended across a wider area and were sometimes enforced by British soldiers.

This forceful and aggressive intrusion of the colonial state into the private domain was not simply dramatic and brutal but also novel and unprecedented. Its effect was often to intensify and quicken the panic occasioned by the disease. As the epidemic spread across the subcontinent, the severity of the plague measures was matched only by their desperation and it is not surprising that they met with fierce, if sporadic, resistance.

Then, almost as suddenly as the disease had appeared, the stringency of the plague measures was relaxed. In October 1906, the *Times of India* observed that no notice was taken of the revival and increase of plague in Poona, 'whereas a few years ago it would have caused a panic'.[31] This was

[28] *The Bombay Plague, Being A History of the Progress of Plague in the Bombay Presidency from September 1896 to June 1899*, compiled by Capt. J. K. Condon (Bombay, 1900), p. 125.
[29] Hirst, *Conquest of Plague*, p. 117.
[30] Port Health Officer quoted in Condon, *The Bombay Plague*, p. 136.
[31] *Times of India*, 13 October 1906, quoted in Catanach, 'Plague and the Tensions of Empire', p. 169 fn. 82.

not simply a reaction to popular hostility and violence. Although plague riots had often been heeded by the state as a warning that it should proceed with caution, the recrudescence of the epidemic frequently 'compelled us to attempt more drastic and comprehensive measures'.[32] Nor can this change of heart be attributed to the decreasing virulence of the epidemic since plague mortality rose as the panic subsided.

It was perhaps more important to the changing direction of plague policy that the disease had begun to acquire a specific social character. If, at the outset, Viegas had failed to find any poor people among the afflicted, it became increasingly obvious, as the epidemic worked its way through the subcontinent, that 'the poorer classes suffered most severely'.[33] In the memorable phrase of Surgeon-General Harvey, Director-General of the Indian Medical Department, bubonic plague was 'a disease of filth, a disease of dirt, and a disease of poverty'.[34] As the disease took on the character of a plague of the poor, it came to be seen as endemic. 'We Europeans are indifferent', declared one of their number as the plague revived yet again, in its annual cycle, in March 1902: 'for the statistics show that fewer Europeans have died from plague than die each year from cholera, so we can chance plague as we chance cholera.'[35] Bubonic plague had become simply another disease in the formidable pantheon of plagues which flourished in India's malignant climate and integral to the burden which the white man carried dutifully.

II

The pattern of state intervention in the plague epidemic was unique in the history of colonial India. It cannot be taken to exemplify 'the interventionist ambitions and capacity of India's mature colonial state'.[36] The scale and consistency of state intervention, as it entered homes, meddled with caste and religious practices, regulated the disposal of the dead and restricted the free movement of people, was unprecedented. And the colonial state would never again orchestrate such a penetrative programme of government, intrude so remorselessly upon the private domain, or attempt to exert such ambitious and extensive measures of social control. The frenzied zeal with which the colonial state launched itself at

---

[32] Lord Sandhurst and others, GOB, Judicial, to Her Majesty's Principal Private Secretary of State for India in Council, London, 9 April 1898, in GOB, General (Plague), vol. 389, Compilation no. 298, 1898, MSA.
[33] Condon, *The Bombay Plague*, p. 132.
[34] Quoted in the *Report of the Indian Plague Commission, 1898–99, with Appendices and Summary*, vol. V, p. 170, *PP*, 1902, vol. LXXII.
[35] *Pioneer*, 15 March, 1902, quoted in Catanach, 'Plague and the Tensions of Empire', p. 159.   [36] Arnold, 'Touching the Body', p. 56.

its subject was integral, as both symptom and cause, to the panic which accompanied the epidemic. It played a determining, perhaps creative, role in the political construction of the plague epidemic.

The severity and desperation of the government's response may be explained partly in terms of folk memories of the Black Death and partly in terms of the possible imperial consequences of the plague. An international embargo on Indian shipping not only threatened to close an important market and source of raw materials for Britain but also disturb the intricate system for the multilateral settlement of its balance of payments, in which India played a large and vital part.[37] The extensive commercial and financial connections centred on Bombay made it seem highly improbable that the epidemic could be contained within the city.[38] If it spread through the subcontinent, it might devastate India's social order and economic base, flatten the pivot of empire and undermine the foundation of Britain's influence between the Yellow and the Red Seas.

These were powerful pressures but they do not provide a sufficient explanation. The European powers were quickly impressed by the stringency of the plague measures and by 1897 there was little evidence that the scourge was about to engulf the West. Nor was the threat to trade insuperable. The International Sanitary Convention which met at Venice in 1897 to discuss the plague favoured the medical inspection of people and their personal effects over embargoes on the import or movement of merchandise.[39] Moreover, plague mortality in the first three years of the epidemic did not distort the ordinary death rate for the subcontinent. Although the threat to trade and empire seemed less grave in the late 1890s, the vigour of the plague administration did not slacken.

So the immoderate, perhaps irrational, severity of the state's response requires that we dig at a deeper level. The official construction of the plague epidemic was shaped by its assumptions about its own statecraft as well as its perceptions of the governed. In the course of the epidemic, colonial officials not only expressed these assumptions with unusual freedom, but also developed them to their logical extreme and further were able to manifest them in practice. The plague, it would appear, became the focus of the most terrible anxieties which India evoked in the British imagination. India appeared to be a land of potential, sometimes hidden, dangers, political and corporeal, moral and cultural. The defence of the 'thin red line' could not be left to the redcoats alone. The struggle

[37] S. B. Saul, *Studies in British Overseas Trade* (Liverpool, 1960), pp. 188–207; Tomlinson, 'India and the British Empire'.
[38] For an account of Bombay's relationship with its hinterland and its role in the Indian economy, see Chandavarkar, *The Origins of Industrial Capitalism*, ch. 1.
[39] Hirst, *Conquest of Plague*, pp. 389–90.

to maintain it had to be waged individually against moral and physical sickness, collectively against intrigue, conspiracy and rebellion.

Among the most awesome and compelling dangers represented by India, because it was both intimate and insidious, was the threat of disease. If, in the British perception, India was a repository of infectious diseases, there were two possible remedies. Since most diseases were caused by filth, one obvious solution lay in a massive programme of sanitary measures undertaken by the state. Alternatively, a minimalist answer might be found in segregation and the rigorous maintenance of a substantial social distance from the native town and its inhabitants.

Neither proved to be practicable. The British in India, as the Sanitary Commissioner reported in 1894, would 'never be safe so long as the native population and its towns and villages are left uncleansed to act as a reservoir of dirt and disease'.[40] But the task of cleaning the subcontinent was too gigantic to contemplate. Despite the prominence of the threat of disease in British perceptions of India, sanitation and sewers, town planning and public health occupied a low place in the imperial order of priorities. The colonial state was unwilling to incur the cost and averse to bearing the political risks of sanitizing India. For such a project would require the British to meddle deeply and dangerously in the habits and customs of the natives. Yet, as they knew only too well, the key to the enjoyment of their political kingdom lay not in social engineering but in salutary neglect. If the problem of public health was thus conceived in terms which could not possibly allow its resolution, the insanitary and unhygienic conditions of India's towns and villages, however dangerous, were increasingly portrayed as innate and natural to the subcontinent. Colonial officials, as the Sanitary Commissioner for the North-Western Provinces observed in 1885, did not hold themselves 'to blame for this condition of things. Plainly, indeed, the view was expressed that if the natives chose to live amidst such insanitary surroundings, it was their own concern. And how they managed to do it without greater penalty of death than seemed apparent, was a frequent cause of expressed surprise.'[41]

It was no more viable for the British to segregate themselves in hygienic, native-free, sanitary enclaves. Indian society was too complex and too turbulent to be managed from afar. It was unrealistic to expect that the army, which employed the overwhelming majority of British residents in India, would function effectively if it was segregated along racial lines. Segregation in India remained more a conceptual than a physical reality. Thus, army cantonments were inhabited predominantly by poor, low-

[40] *Annual Report of the Sanitary Commissioner with the Government of India, 1894* (Calcutta, 1896), p. 27.

[41] *Eighteenth Annual Report of the Sanitary Commissioner of the North-Western Provinces, 1885* (Allahabad, 1886), p. 60.

caste Indians – prostitutes, hawkers and halalkhores – whose proximity the British so feared and whose habits they so deeply deplored.[42] Similarly, in the larger urban settlements of Europeans, segregation was even more fervently imagined and even more ineffectually maintained. At various times in the nineteenth century, town planners in Bombay city envisaged residential segregation as an integral part of its future development. But as an architect told one such committee: 'A good many middle class Europeans live in Tarwadi and Byculla. Poor Europeans live in the same class of houses as poor Natives.' Moreover, he added, 'the rich and poor have always lived together – the former in the principal, the latter in the back streets – and always will'.[43]

As the possibility of treating the cause of their anxieties grew more remote, so these anxieties grew more entrenched and their social and political implications seemed more menacing. Increasingly, the British became fatalistic, though never sanguine, about the threat of disease. The outbreak of bubonic plague challenged this fatalism. The plague represented the apotheosis of the threat of disease. Moreover, its threat was highly personalized; it attacked scores of Europeans in the first few months.[44] Immediate and summary action now seemed imperative. Policy initiatives which had once seemed impolitic now seemed indispensable; those which seemed to lie beyond the capacity of the state suddenly fell within its grasp and no effort or expense was to be spared. Intervention in a style which was considered unthinkable before was now seriously pursued.

Bombay city had grown prodigiously in the second half of the nineteenth century, but it had lacked the most basic infrastructure to accommodate this growth. Its most densely populated areas in 1900 had only decades earlier been lying beneath the sea. Health Officers in the city had regularly predicted impending doom and devastating epidemics. In 1875, T. S. Weir, observing 'the low standard of living and the insufficient diet of the majority of the people' and 'their weak and puny constitutions', predicted the periodic and recurrent 'outbreak of one or other of the epidemic diseases; it may not be Cholera; it may not be Small Pox, but

[42] *Report of the Sanitary Commissioner for Bombay, 1867* (Bombay, 1868), Report on Colaba, Inspection Report, no. 1, pp. 10–11. See also the excellent article by J. W. Cell, 'Anglo-Indian Medical Theory and the Origins of Segregation in West Africa', *American Historical Review*, 91:2 (1986), 307–35.

[43] Proceedings of the Committee on the Extension of the City of Bombay, 1887, Evidence, Mr D. Gostling, p. 2. GOB, PWD (General), vol. 1162, Compilation no. 4133 W, 1868–89, MSA.

[44] Report by T. S. Weir, Executive Health Officer, Bombay Municipality, in P. C. H. Snow, *Report on the Outbreak of Bubonic Plague in Bombay, 1896–97* (Bombay, 1897), pp. 144–5. Eighty-eight Europeans died of the plague between September 1896 and May 1897; many others were attacked by the disease.

some disease will arise, and sweep off the most effete of the population'.[45] In the early 1890s, the inadequacy of the city's drainage system suggested that 'there will surely come a time when the population of each district will not be able to live in health'.[46] With the plague, it seemed that the time had come. The apocalypse which the Health Officers had long anticipated was now firmly in their midst. To many colonial officials, the plague appeared not simply the product of ineffectual or misconceived policies, but, more especially, divine retribution for sanitary neglect.

III

It was from this psychology of guilt and terror that the official mind formulated its strategy to combat the plague. Public health policies had been often conceived as the application of modern, scientific knowledge among people who were not only ignorant of the principles of hygiene but whose traditions and modes of life were violated by them. The British in India sought to tame the dangers of the subcontinent and impose order upon its chaos with justice, rationality and science. It was their privileged access to reason, the superiority of their knowledge and their ability to implement it with an incorruptible justice which legitimized their harshest, most vigorous measures. Thus, W. L. Reade, who took over the plague administration in Poona after Rand's assassination, proclaimed, 'I consider that plague operations properly undertaken present some of the best opportunities for riveting our rule in India' and 'also for showing the superiority of our Western science and thoroughness'.[47]

Sanitary and medical science was as integral and critical to the official perception of their statecraft as education and justice. Yet the formulation of an effective plague policy was seriously hindered by general ignorance about the causes and transmission of the disease as well as about possible methods of treatment. At the start of the epidemic, plague authorities still favoured the view that its cause lay in a localized miasma, which could nonetheless be caught through contact with infected persons.[48] The identification of the plague bacillus simultaneously by Yersin

[45] Tenth Annual Report of the Health Officer, in *Annual Report of the Municipal Commissioner of Bombay for the Year 1875* (Bombay, 1876), pp. 148–9.

[46] Report of the Health Officer in *Administrative Report of the Municipal Commissioner for the City of Bombay for the Year 1892–3* (Bombay, 1893), p. 383.

[47] W. L. Reade to Arthur Godley, 3 March 1898, quoted in Catanach, 'Plague and the Tensions of Empire', p. 154.

[48] Hirst, *Conquest of Plague*, p. 41. According to Hirst, this 'miasmatico-contagious point of view' was 'favoured until the end of the nineteenth century by many writers on plague' and indeed, as late as the 1920s, there was 'a vigorous reaction on the part of an influential group of British epidemiologists against current conceptions of the role of microbes in the causation of disease': *ibid.*, p. 89.

and Kitasato in 1894 had not resolved the problem of causation when the epidemic took root in Bombay two years later. Unless the aetiology of the disease was known, it was unclear whether the bacillus was indeed its cause or simply its consequence. Thus, with the advent of plague in Bombay, several official teams of scientists, sponsored by their national governments, 'hastened to the affected city, charged with the task of studying the disease. Probably never before or since has such an imposing array of epidemiological talent assembled in one place for research into a specific disease.'[49] Their findings were to throw as much darkness as light on the subject while thousands continued to die. At times, their investigations proceeded along lines determined less by scientific evidence than by social assumptions.

The initial consensus which had emerged out of the Hong Kong epidemic was that the plague bacilli entered the body through the alimentary canal. This hypothesis had been developed by analogy with cholera and other food- and water-borne infections, which had recently occupied the attention of bacteriologists and sanitary commissioners in India. It was swiftly replaced, following feeding experiments in Bombay which produced negative results, by the suggestion that human beings became infected when cuts and abrasions on their bare feet came into contact with bacilli in excreta of rats, who it was still assumed acquired it through ingestion. This notion coincided with the recognition that 'patients mostly belonged to the lower classes who commonly go bare-footed and bare-legged'.[50] Circumstantial evidence that 'halalcores who remove the night-soil from the houses, and who form probably the dirtiest portion of the population, were notably free from plague' cast some doubt on this hypothesis. But this difficulty was briskly overcome with the suggestion that 'they are a strong, well-nourished class, of whom only the fittest have survived, and they are highly paid and live well'.[51] Tests on plague patients showed only a tiny proportion of cases in which the bacillus was found in skin abrasions. By 1898, the studies of Hankin and Simond demonstrated that the plague bacillus survived only briefly outside the body and was only rarely, if ever, recovered from supposedly infected objects, including the surface of the soil, foodstuffs, the floors of houses or other articles in areas of infection.[52]

The major breakthrough in the aetiology of bubonic plague occurred when the French bacteriologist, P. L. Simond, published a paper in 1898 identifying it as a rat disease and postulating that its transmission to man occurred through rat fleas. The case was not experimentally proven to the

[49] Ibid., p. 105.
[50] Condon, The Bombay Plague, p. 104; Hirst, Conquest of Plague, pp. 111–19.
[51] Condon, The Bombay Plague, p. 70.   [52] Hirst, Conquest of Plague, p. 117.

satisfaction of his fellow bacteriologists and least of all the Indian Plague Commission. To them, it seemed to rely too heavily upon the imagination. The Plague Commission preferred the theory of bare-foot Indians. It was convinced that if rats were involved in the initial outbreak of the disease, the infection was primarily spread through human agency. It poured scorn on Simond's hypothesis that transmission was effected by a blood-sucking insect and although it acknowledged that plague bacilli in rat corpses rapidly died, it adhered to the notion of infection through microbes on the surface of the ground.[53] The rat flea theory provoked such vigorous scepticism primarily because it undermined the assumptions, connecting hypotheses about the nature of the disease to notions of social behaviour and cultural characteristics in India, upon which epidemiological research had been proceeding. Significantly, it was from Sydney, where the cholera analogy and the bare-foot theory were somewhat less obviously sustained, and where images of proliferating microbes and metaphors of contagion strained credulity, that some of the early confirmation of Simond's hypothesis came forth.[54]

In India, medical and official opinion adhered to the view, attractive in this repository of disease, that the plague was spread by contact between human beings. Consequently, the emphasis of policy was placed primarily on early detection and diagnosis, segregation, hospitalization, disinfection and the close inspection of travellers and merchandise in transit. These policies had been frequently implemented to control infectious diseases. But in the case of the plague they were carried to their extreme. Since the 1860s, the response to outbreaks of cholera in the army was to move soldiers out of their barracks and house them in temporary camps;[55] now whole villages and even small towns were evacuated. Isolation in a contagious diseases hospital might appear a reasonable precaution; now it was effected under an armed military guard. Disinfection was another common recourse in times of smallpox or diphtheria; now cities were flooded and incessantly sprayed with mercuric chloride solution. Fantasies about cleaning up the subcontinent now took on a new and substantive meaning. No form of executive action, it seemed, was too extravagant in the frenzy and panic of the epidemic.

The medical and scientific experts did not always privilege the claims of evidence over their own preconceptions about Indian society and they were eventually ensnared within them. Sometimes they overlooked or

---

[53] *Report of the Indian Plague Commission, 1898–99*, vol. V, pp. 68–71, 75–7, 101–2, 108–11, 122–7, *PP*, 1902, vol. LXXII; Cell, 'Anglo-Indian Medical Theory', 326–7; Catanach, 'Plague and the Tensions of Empire', pp. 158–9.
[54] Hirst, *Conquest of Plague*, pp. 160–9, 144–8; Cell, 'Anglo-Indian Medical Theory', 325–8; Catanach, 'Plague and the Tensions of Empire', pp. 162–3.
[55] Cell, 'Anglo-Indian Medical Theory', 322.

neglected the evidence; sometimes, they simply could not read its signs. Thus, it was clear, at the outset of the epidemic, that 'the contagion of the prevailing fever is very slight',[56] and it was soon demonstrated that 'the quickest possible isolation of the sick had no effect on the march of the malady'.[57] As early as 1897, 'discerning observers in Bombay' knew, as Hirst pointed out, that bubonic plague was not 'infectious in the ordinary sense'.[58]

Nonetheless, policies, formulated on the assumption that the plague was a virulently infectious disease, proved at best oppressive and at worst fatal. Thus, the stringent inspections along the railway lines and at ports yielded a minute number of plague cases, although many tens of thousands were detained under 'suspicion'.[59] When roofs were removed, floors dug up, houses flooded with disinfectant, the rats simply moved away and spread the infection. By pumping the sewers with disinfectants, rats were driven into houses and carried the fleas with them to infect the inhabitants.[60] Had the scientists and medical experts given the rat flea theory more serious consideration, they may have resolved some of the conundrums – for instance, the erratic and spasmodic pattern of its dissemination – posed at the time by the epidemiology of the plague. Moreover, its implications for changing the direction of plague policy, swiftly seen as ineffectual, were substantial. For it suggested the need to switch the emphasis from the inspection and control of human beings to that of merchandise and from disinfection to disinfestation. As it was, plague policies put forward as rational measures to control the epidemic among traditional, ignorant people fell prey to the superstitions of science, derived from preconceptions about Indian society and generated by a wider discourse in which the experts shared.

IV

From the onset of the epidemic, officials readily acknowledged that plague measures were likely to have 'undesirable consequences' but the only alternative was to endure a growing incidence of sickness and a rising death toll. To them, it seemed imperative to do whatever was necessary to stamp out the plague. Yet it was by no means clear how far they could go in asserting the virtues of science over the traditional sentiments and religious susceptibilities of the people. The riots which occurred at the

---

[56] *Times of India*, 25 September, 1896, p. 4.   [57] Hirst, *Conquest of Plague*, p. 116.
[58] *Ibid.*, p. 119.   [59] Condon, *The Bombay Plague*, p. 146.
[60] *A Monograph on Evacuation as a Protective and Combative Plague Measure, Compiled Under the Orders of Sir A. Wingate, KCIE, Acting Chief Secretary to Government by Lt. J. K. Condon, Under-Secretary to Government (Plague Department) for the Use of the Indian Plague Commission, 30 March 1899* (Bombay, 1899), p. 1.

Arthur Road Hospital in Bombay as early as October 1896 suggested to the provincial government 'that it was extremely doubtful whether we could enforce in Bombay City all the measures which high medical authority commended to us as desirable to combat the epidemic'.[61] The annual revival of the plague and its dissemination came increasingly to be explained not in terms of misconceived and misdirected policies but of 'the failure of the people to comprehend its characteristics and the value of the measures'.[62] Popular resistance was perceived as irrational and dysfunctional, a product of the pre-scientific attitudes, the sacred traditions and customary prejudices of the Indian people, a view which later historians have sometimes unwittingly endorsed.

Contemporary officials tended to homogenize the Indian response to the epidemic. In fact, it was extremely uneven. Resistance was not the only response to the plague measures and collaboration was by no means confined to the elites. When the Government of Bombay drew up a list of the city's inhabitants who merited rewards and commendations for their assistance in carrying out plague measures, Demos was strongly represented, including street corner bosses like Hashim Dada of Nagpada.[63] 'In every street row', British officials were relieved to discover, 'some were found to stand beside the executive and calm the mob.'[64] The epidemic yielded neither a homogeneous popular response to the epidemic nor a simple and consistent opposition between the colonial state and the Indian people as a whole. Nor should we postulate a natural affinity between the colonial state and the 'Indian elites', to be neatly distinguished from the mass of the population. To W. C. Rand in Poona, it appeared, 'some of the most influential men in the City . . . were more likely than not to work against any operations that might be set on foot by Government'.[65] In Hubli, where the local Muslim population had 'given trouble ever since Plague operations began', the Collector of Dharwar reported, 'the list of ringleaders' included 'a prominent Kazi and an ex-Municipal Commissioner', who, he believed, had thereby betrayed a pact he had made with the town's elites.[66]

Forms of resistance also varied. Perhaps the most common response to the frenzied plague measures, and indeed the scourge itself, was flight.

---

[61] Lord Sandhurst, Governor of Bombay and Others, GOB, Judicial, to Her Majesty's Principal Private Secretary of State for India in Council, London, 9 April 1898, GOB, General (Plague), vol. 389, Compilation no. 298, MSA.

[62] Condon, *The Bombay Plague*, p. 11.

[63] GOB, General (Plague), vol. 8, Compilation no. 712 P/11 Confidential, 1899, MSA.

[64] Snow, *Report on the Outbreak of Bubonic Plague*, p. 19.

[65] *Draft of Report . . . by the Late Mr W. C. Rand*, p. 4, MSA.

[66] Collector, Dharwar, to Commissioner, Southern Division, 13 March 1898, GOB, General (Plague), vol. 389 of 1898, Compilation no. 298, MSA.

From most large towns, a substantial proportion of the population simply ran away. This was why the evacuation of whole settlements met with the least resistance and in some places, like Bassein, it was 'in high favour with the people'.[67] Concealment and evasion were also extensively practised. 'Incredible shifts were resorted to', reported Rand from Poona, 'to prevent the authorities from becoming aware of the occurrence of cases. Plague patients were hidden in lofts, cupboards and gardens – anywhere in fact, where their presence was least likely to be suspected.'[68] In Surat city, where 'the virulence of the disease was never great' in 1897 and 1898, patients were moved from house to house to avoid search parties with the effect it was erroneously supposed, of spreading the germs more quickly.[69] Various stratagems were adopted by travellers to avoid the inspection at ports and along railway lines.[70]

Popular violence and riot provided the least frequent manifestation of such resistance, but they were also, of course, the most dramatic. In view of the zeal with which the plague administrators invaded the homes and the physical and social privacy of the people, riots appear to be remarkably rare occurrences. But the colonial state often took careful note of local skirmishes which it might otherwise have simply overlooked. In part, this was because these 'riots' did sometimes exercise a check on what the official mind grasped with certitude as necessary measures. In addition, these moments of collective action often exposed the weakness and vulnerability of local administrations, at a time when they were parading their power and exerting control and in an atmosphere governed by perceptions of physical danger. Finally, these riots often displayed what colonial officials charmingly described as 'racial characteristics and innate prejudices'.[71] Thus, in the Bombay riots of March 1898, the 'mob' chased Inspector Coady shouting 'Mardalo goreku, mardalo goreku' or 'kill the white man'. At the statue of the Standing Parsi, 'it was impossible for any European to pass with safety. No distinction was made . . . the principle the rioters acted upon was to hit a solah topee wherever they saw it and it mattered not whether the victim had ever had any participation in the plague administration.'[72] Numerous Europeans were attacked in the streets and at least two soldiers were lynched. The only shop to remain open on Abdul Rahman Street sold revolvers and 'the owner of this establishment was much sought after by Europeans during the afternoon'.[73]

It might be supposed that to understand popular hostility to the plague

[67] Condon, *The Bombay Plague*, p. 192.
[68] *Draft of Report . . . by the Late Mr W. C. Rand*, p. 7, MSA.
[69] Condon, *The Bombay Plague*, p. 177.   [70] Ibid., pp. 138, 146.   [71] *Ibid.*, p. 131.
[72] 'An Account of the Riots in Bombay on 9 March 1898', in GOB, Judicial, 1898, vol. 217, Compilation no. 669, Part I, MSA.   [73] *Ibid.*

measures we need to look no further than their character and the style of their implementation. If the plague measures were harsh, it might appear that popular resistance to them was wholly rational. It would be tempting to suggest that while the most extravagant fantasy seemed credible and the wildest speculation highly plausible to the boffins of the government bacteriological laboratories and the learned practitioners of the medical sciences, Demos alone took a steady view. This is a useful corrective to the supposition that the idiom of popular thinking was based on rumour and religion rather than fact or reason. But, of course, nobody was exempt from the 'unreasoning panic'. Popular responses, no less than elite reactions, the frenzied exertions of the state or the brittle and sometimes destructive certainties of medical and scientific experts, were shaped by the political conjuncture of the plague.

The most prominent feature of the plague operations, because of the stress laid on 'detection', was the search parties. In Poona, but less intensively elsewhere, the chosen agents for search were British soldiers and the searches were conducted like a military operation. The locality was surrounded by cavalry which paraded the streets, while soldiers moved from house to house, accompanied ideally by 'a native gentleman' and at least a hospital assistant to adjudicate upon suspicious cases. But inevitably resources were overstretched. There were too few doctors to accompany every search party[74] and while there was no shortage of 'native gentlemen', they were not always willing to assist: some, according to Rand, 'worked steadily and well . . . others irregularly, others not at all'.[75]

The 'detection' of sickness was a sensitive and intimate operation. 'To eliminate the suspicious cases', as one official report put it, 'a careful individual examination of each native was necessary' which involved in particular 'a careful exploration of his body for glandular enlargement'.[76] Not surprisingly, there were complaints that 'all the females are compelled to come out of their houses and stand before the public gaze in the open street and be there subjected to inspection by soldiers'.[77] Soldiers were said to 'behave disgracefully with native ladies'[78] and the tenor of the official response that they had merely 'joked with a Marathi woman' suggests that sexual harassment probably did occur.[79] Shripat Gopal

[74] In Bombay, in 1898–9, only five doctors were available for 'plague duty'. See Condon, *The Bombay Plague*, pp. 131–2.

[75] Note by Chairman, Poona Plague Committee, 7 July 1897, in GOB, General (Plague), vol. I, Compilation no. 70/P, 1897, p. 157, MSA.

[76] Condon, *The Bombay Plague*, p. 136.

[77] V. M. Bhide *et al.* to Chairman, Poona Plague Committee, 7 April 1897, in GOB, General (Plague), vol. I, Compilation no. 70/P, 1897, p. 8, MSA.

[78] Bhide *et al.* to chairman, Poona Plague Committee, 20 April 1897, *ibid.*, p. 15, MSA.

[79] Chairman, Poona Plague Committee, to Secretary, GOB, General, 20 July 1897, *ibid.*, p. 179, MSA.

Kulkarni, an octogenarian, complained that ten or twelve soldiers had burst into his house, forced him to undress, 'felt . . . the whole of my body and then made me sit and rise [several times] and, sitting around me, went on clapping their hands and dancing'.[80] In addition, there were complaints that while conducting their house searches, soldiers 'put into their mouths whatever eatables they find', 'insist upon being supplied with milk and other drinks' or 'put into their pockets such things as come into their fancy'.[81] Petitioners were often aggrieved that there was a wanton and indiscriminate destruction of property during searches. Officials knew only too well that the 'concealment of cases is also practised in order to avoid the inconvenience and petty expenses of disinfection, destruction of clothing etc.'.[82]

Those who had the misfortune of being placed under suspicion, however wrongly, by any one plague agency, it was said, could suffer the attention of several others. The suspicion of the search party brought in its train the disinfection gangs and limewashing parties. It could also result in the hospitalization of suspects, the segregation of their relatives, the loss of their property, perhaps the destruction of their homes.[83] Sometimes, it was said, 'their neighbours and in many cases even the passers by are indiscriminately seized and sent to segregation camp'.[84]

The most common complaint concerned false diagnosis which resulted in 'perfectly healthy persons' being 'seized and forcibly taken away by the search parties'.[85] There was some considerable uncertainty in the diagnosis of the plague, particularly by the search parties. The chairman of the Poona Plague Committee conceded that the Medical Officer in charge of the Plague Hospital had been 'complaining of the excessive number of cases sent to him which were not plague'.[86] It is probable that before September 1896 bubonic plague had long gone undiagnosed[87] but once the panic gathered force, doctors as well as the lay search parties found plague everywhere.[88]

---

[80] Petition by Shripat Gopal Kulkarni, *ibid.*, pp. 306–7, MSA.
[81] V. M. Bhide, Chairman, Deccan Sabha, Poona, to Chairman, Poona Plague Committee, 20 April 1897, *ibid.*, p. 15, MSA.   [82] Condon, *The Bombay Plague*, pp. 51–2.
[83] Petition of Bhiku-bin-Tatya Shimpi to President, Deccan Sabha, 1 August 1897, GOB, General (Plague), vol. I, Compilation no. 70/P, 1897, pp. 245–7, MSA.
[84] V. M. Bhide, Deccan Sabha, *et al.*, to chairman, Poona Plague Committee, 20 April 1897, *ibid.*, p. 13, MSA.   [85] *Ibid*, MSA.
[86] Note by Chairman, Poona Plague Committee, 7 July 1897, *ibid.*, pp. 154–5, MSA.
[87] Snow, *Report on the Outbreak of Bubonic Plague*, pp. 1–3; see also, Condon, *The Bombay Plague*, p. 68.
[88] A dispute over the misplaced suspicions of a search party culminated in the Bombay riot of March 1898. See GOB, Judicial, vol. 217, Compilation no. 669, Part I, MSA. On Dr W. J. Simpson's diagnosis of a case of syphilis as the plague, which caused a panic in Calcutta in 1896, see 'Papers Relating to the Outbreak of Bubonic Plague in India . . . up to March 1897', *PP*, 1897, vol. LXIII, pp. 41–2; Catanach, 'Plague and the Indian Village', p. 241 fn. 107.

The Government of Bombay vociferously denied the allegations made by petitioners and the press and few of them could be proved. Sometimes, the author of the petition could not be traced which in the prevailing terror is neither surprising nor significant. Of course, the truth of these allegations matters less than the fact that, as their collector was subsequently to point out, 'they were rife in the City'.[89] It is unlikely that the truth would dramatically alter the significance of their narratives.

Historians of India have recently paid considerable attention to rumours about epidemics and especially the plague. In particular, David Arnold has characterized them 'as a form of popular discourse'[90] which shows 'a significant divergence of outlook between the middle classes and the subordinate population'.[91] There are several problems with this argument. First, the historical source of rumours lies most frequently in official reports, the memoirs of civil servants and newspapers, which created as much as they reported them, and which were compiled largely by the middle classes. Rumours may also be taken, therefore, as an elite discourse about popular attitudes.

Second, the British in India were highly susceptible to rumours. This susceptibility reflected their isolation from, imperfect knowledge of and vulnerability to Indian society. Falsehoods put about in the bazaar might spread discontent and provoke rebellion, which they might not always be in a position to control. In part, this was why colonial officials compiled and reported 'rumours' with such exasperation and dread as they occurred, such bemusement, curiosity and fascination after the event. After the 1898 riots in Bombay, the Commissioner of Police reported, 'Rumours, of course, are flying about in plenty, but I think it is a pity that people are so very anxious to credit even the most absurd stories, the origins of which it is almost impossible to trace.'[92] Sometimes, however, it was his own officers who appeared most anxious to credit them. In the immediate aftermath of the riot, the Plague Committee peon at Bandra, to the north of the island, reported that some Mohammedan 'roughs' were throwing stones at his shed near Mahim causeway and the superintendent on duty saw 'a large gang of Mahammedan roughs . . . to be collecting near the Railway in the vicinity of the [Bandra Observation] camp'. Superintendent A. H. Bingley telegraphed for reinforcements, as he later explained, because 'I was aware that a persistent rumour had been spread abroad for the last few days that a disturbance might be expected on Friday.'[93] The

[89] Statement by V. M. Bhide, Chairman, Poona Plague Committee, 1 August 1897, GOB, General (Plague), vol. I, Compilation no. 70/P, 1897, p. 108, MSA.
[90] Arnold, 'Touching the Body', p. 76.   [91] Ibid., p. 68.
[92] Commissioner of Police, Bombay, to Secretary, GOB, Judicial, 1 April 1898, in GOB, General (Plague), vol. 389, Compilation no. 298, 1898, MSA.
[93] Superintendent of Police, Bandra Observation Camp, to Plague Commissioner, Bombay, 25 March 1898, ibid, MSA.

police reinforcements were rushed from Thana districts only to discover that 'no stone throwing had taken place at the camp and that there was not the slightest cause of alarm'.[94]

Moreover, Indian elites subscribed to rumours about the plague as much as the poor. For instance, one rumour, quoted by Arnold,[95] was recorded when 'a well-disposed Brahmin' asked the epidemiologist Hankin, 'in all seriousness . . . whether it was true that an English sahib had put snake-venom into the Bombay water-supply and thus produced the great epidemic in the city'.[96] Similarly, P. C. Snow, the Municipal Commissioner for Bombay, reported, in 1896, that of all the plague measures, segregation and hospitalization 'caused the most alarm' and 'reports were freely circulated that the authorities merely took them there to make a speedy end of them'.[97] But these were measures which 'the whole people, high and low, viewed with the wildest hostility'. Similarly, diverse social groups subscribed, as we have seen, to the 'stories' about soldiers and segregation, search parties and disinfection gangs, medical diagnoses and hospital treatments contained in the petitions to the Poona Plague Committee and found them highly convincing.

Finally, there can be only the most slender distinction between the rumours of the populace and the superstitions of science. To attribute the causes of the plague, against the evidence, to microbes harboured in the earth seemed to many officials and experts to constitute 'in all seriousness' an immutable fact: real knowledge sanctified by scientific learning. But this was not very far removed from the 'well-disposed Brahmin's' theory of snake-venom.

Rumours about the plague need not be understood in terms which are specific to Indian culture alone. They may be profitably read as the expression of a pervasive mood of unreality and mortal danger, shared by many across divisions of class, caste and creed, as the plague raged and retreated around them. Rumours were an earthy, accessible and, in a sense, even tangible way of sustaining hope, expressing anger, of paradoxically keeping in touch with reality. Rumours provided a magical idiom for discussing the most horrible and menacing realities while sometimes providing a means of liberation from them. Rumours cited by Arnold anticipating the collapse of British rule or predicting impending doom are examples of the latter. Moreover, sometimes ordinary, daily anxieties could find an exaggerated and exotic focus. Thus, perhaps, stories of being 'kidnapped' by soldiers, and kept segregated, only to return to discover relatives had died, articulated a deepseated fear of

---

[94] District Superintendent of Police, Thana to Secretary, GOB, General (Plague), 27 March 1898, *ibid*, MSA.   [95] Arnold, 'Touching the Body', p. 70.
[96] Hirst, *Conquest of Plague*, p. 21.
[97] Snow, *Report on the Outbreak of Bubonic Plague*, p. 6.

separation and loss, at a time when both abounded. Stories about the behaviour of soldiers may have borne a considerable measure of truth but they also reflected the nightmarish invasion and violation of privacy – even god-rooms and kitchens – by the most frightening, powerful, uniformed and foreign agent of public authority. Sexual harassment by the soldiers and their 'disgraceful behaviour towards native ladies' almost certainly occurred – and, indeed, physical examination, 'the exploration of the native's body' in the streets or at railway checkpoints may themselves be regarded precisely as that – but reports of them also served as a metaphor for the violent eruption of the state into the privacy of people's lives. Rumours about poisoning and snake-venom which attributed the plague to the conspiracy of officials did not simply represent a popular appreciation of the 'undivided malevolence'[98] of the state. It was rather that by blaming official conspirators it was possible to evade one's own irredeemable vulnerability to the epidemic. For the British, too, it was preferable to blame the spread of the plague on the incomprehension and obscurantism of the native, rather than on the failure of their hopelessly misconceived policies, or to attribute their own continued danger from the disease as well as physical assault by riotous mobs to the currency of rumours propagated by trouble-makers in the bazaars and the credulity of the simple and illiterate, if sullen and resentful, poor.

Rumours during the plague, or indeed at other times, should not be interpreted literally, either for their foundation in reality or as a text, to 'discern' the 'preoccupations'[99] of the popular mind. Rather, rumours, and stories, even when they circulated fictions more terrifying than the facts, were a means of mediating the unremitting horrors entailed in the actual circumstances of the plague. Nor can rumours be regarded as the exclusive, or even primary, idiom of the poor. Men of science and letters, physicians with formidable reputations, the 'most imposing array of epidemiological talent' in the world, and the hand-picked brilliance of Oxford and Cambridge who filled the ranks of the Indian Civil Service, were all similarly susceptible. If the plague epidemic facilitated the expression of the deepest popular anxieties, it had also become the focus of British anxieties about their inability to control India and their vulnerability to the numerous epidemics, medical as well as political, which it harboured.

V

While the prospect of receiving the attention of the search parties, with their military-style campaigns of detection, filled people with dread and

[98] Arnold, 'Touching the Body', p. 76.   [99] *Ibid.*, pp. 72, 75–7.

provoked them to anger, the threat of hospitalization loomed alarmingly large in public anxiety. Indeed, at times it culminated in riots and mob attacks upon hospitals. But this should not be taken to signify an innate, indiscriminate and implacable antipathy to Western medicine. Of course, it is not intended to suggest that the Indian people embraced Western medicine enthusiastically at the first opportunity, but rather that popular attitudes were too complex and too diverse to be reduced to a simple choice between acceptance and rejection. Indeed, this complexity stemmed precisely from the fact that popular attitudes were not simply and reflexively drawn as frequently assumed from a reservoir of religious and cultural traditions, but were shaped by historical and political contingencies and, in particular, by the experience of various medical cures.

In late nineteenth-century India, the 'Western' medical presence was extremely thin on the ground. In Bombay city, where its density was greatest, the census returned 555 qualified practitioners in 1901,[100] while in the countryside, outside the district towns, there was generally 'no skilled medical assistance of any kind'.[101] To obtain medical attention, most people had to travel considerable distances, suffer a loss of work and incur considerable expense. Nonetheless, where they existed, rural dispensaries were extensively used.[102] In Bombay city, too, there is little evidence that 'Western' medical practitioners were abjured. On the contrary, at the very start of the epidemic, Dr Thomas Blainey, visiting the afflicted district of Mandvi with Dr Viegas, found people eager for medical attention. 'The people around me', he wrote,

urged me to go and see other similar cases at varying distances and said that many persons in their locality were similarly attacked. Several of them informed their friends that I was a municipal representative deputed to inquire into the present fever outbreak and that every facility should be afforded me to make the inquiry complete. I have no doubt that Dr. Viegas corrected their mistake on my official identity . . . The people, though ignorant, are quite alive to the dangerous character of the prevailing fever.[103]

Many of them were, of course, shortly to die. But their response to Dr Blainey was far removed from the response evinced by the plague authorities as the epidemic wore on.

Like the colonial officials before them, historians have sometimes too

---

[100] *Census of India, 1901*, vol. XIA, *Bombay Town and Island*, Part VI, tables, compiled by S. M. Edwardes (Bombay, 1901), Table XV, p. 138. These were listed as 'practitioners with diploma'. Another 398 'practitioners without a diploma' were also returned by the census.

[101] J. K. N. Kabraji, Second Assistant Collector, to R. B. Stewart, Ag. Collector, Nasik, 16 August 1897, in GOB, Revenue, vol. 19, Compilation no. 67, Part IV, 1898, MSA.

[102] R. B. Stewart, Collector, Nasik, to Commissioner, Central Division, 25 September 1897, *ibid*, MSA.   [103] *Times of India*, 25 September 1896, p. 4.

readily taken for granted that 'Western medicine outstripped popular disease comprehension'.[104] In fact, 'Western' medicine knew little about the disease and its ability to learn more was inhibited precisely by its perceptions of Indian culture and society. To the extent that policies were shaped by its wisdom, their effect was often to intensify and disseminate the epidemic. The plague was notoriously difficult to diagnose. As a result, 'numbers of cases had to be segregated . . . not because the patients had plague but because they had suspicious symptoms'.[105] Depending upon which symptoms predominated in a given case, bubonic plague could resemble relapsing fever, severe cases of malaria, typhoid, typhus, glandular fever and even drunkenness. Physicians sometimes misread its symptoms for another disease or treated rather more benign illnesses as if they were the plague. The official history of the plague cited the case of Govind Jeeva who, treated for alcoholic poisoning by the doctor, was thus speeded on his way to death from bubonic plague.[106]

Nor were there any known remedies for the disease.[107] By 1900, 'Western' medical practitioners had discovered 'no specific remedy' for the plague and none of those which they tried had influenced 'favourably the mortality among those attacked'. The plague hospitals could offer nothing more than 'hygienic and symptomatic treatment'. Not knowing what else to do, they tried to tide 'the patient over a certain period' and trusted to 'the natural tendency to recover'.[108] Medical practice, especially in the 'Western' tradition, was seen to be experimental in its procedure and ineffective in its results. The descriptions of their own activities by plague officials suggest that this perception was on the whole justified. To Bombay's Municipal Commissioner, 'The outbreak of plague in the House of Correction afforded a particularly good opportunity of watching the effect of M. Haffkine's prophylactic treatment.'[109] When Haffkine took a medical team to inoculate the villagers of Undhera, a village near Baroda, in February 1897, they were able to report their satisfaction that 'the conditions approached very nearly the strictness of a laboratory experiment'.[110] It is doubtful whether the subjects of their experiments shared their satisfaction as the threat of death loomed over them and it is scarcely surprising, in the

---

[104] Klein, 'Plague, Policy and Popular Unrest', p. 739.
[105] Snow, *Report on the Outbreak of Bubonic Plague*, p. 3.
[106] Condon, *The Bombay Plague*, pp. 78–9.
[107] For a description of some remedies tried at the start of the epidemic, see *Times of India*, 25 September 1896, 4.   [108] Condon, *The Bombay Plague*, p. 81.
[109] Snow, *Report on the Outbreak of Bubonic Plague*, p. 17.
[110] Condon, *The Bombay Plague*, pp. 43–4; W. M. Haffkine, *Experiment on the Effect of Protective Inoculation in the Epidemic of Plague at Undhera Taluka, Baroda, February and March, 1898* (Bombay, 1898).

256   Imperial power and popular politics

light of these attitudes, that medical officers found it hard to win public confidence.

The widespread hostility to hospitalization, shared by diverse social groups, was not simply a function of caste and religious sensibilities. Indeed, it extended 'even to hospitals established and managed by Hindoos for their own caste fellows'.[111] Hospitalization represented the culmination of all plague measures, perhaps the most coercive manifestation of a brutally intrusive state, and the end of a terrifying chain of events which began with the search parties. The case mortality rate of plague patients entering hospital averaged over 80 per cent at the height of the first epidemic in Bombay.[112] The overwhelming majority who were admitted to hospital did not return alive. The arrival of the ambulance must, therefore, have seemed like the state's death sign on the patient or the suspect. 'People who thought the poor . . . ought to be happy because they had been born to it', reported T. S. Weir from Bombay, 'almost wept when they saw one of the same poor ill from Bubonic Plague, lifted into a municipal ambulance.'[113] 'Peals of screams' from plague patients in the Contagious Diseases Hospital in Bombay 'not only pervaded the whole hospital, but even attracted the notice of passers-by on the road', one of the major thoroughfares through the mill districts.[114] Not surprisingly, hospitals came to be perceived in the public imagination less as a refuge from the ravages of the plague, than as a potent and destructive instrument of terror, as 'places of torture and places intended to provide material for experiments'.[115]

If to the Indian mind, as one historian has recently suggested, hospitals were 'a place of pollution, contaminated by blood and faeces', this was often less because they appeared 'inimical to caste, religion and *purdah*',[116] than because these were the real conditions to be found there.[117]

---

[111] Condon, *The Bombay Plague*, p. 126; Snow, *Report on the Outbreak of Bubonic Plague*, p. 16.
[112] Snow, *Report on the Outbreak of Bubonic Plague*, p. 17; Condon, *The Bombay Plague*, pp. 132–3.
[113] Report by Executive Health Officer, Bombay, in Snow, *Report on the Outbreak of Bubonic Plague*, p. 81.
[114] 'Report on Bubonic Plague Cases Treated at the Arthur Road Hospital from September 24, 1896 to February 28, 1897', by Khan Bahadur N. H. Choksi, Extra Assistant Health Officer, in charge of the Arthur Road Hospital, *ibid.*, p. 237.
[115] Report by Executive Health Officer, Bombay, *ibid.*, pp. 73–4.
[116] Arnold, 'Touching the Body', p. 62.
[117] For a description of the plague hospital in Poona by one who was taken there on suspicion and later released, see the letter from Sodaji Pundlik More to *Dynanprakash* in GOB, General (Plague), vol. I, Compilation no. 70/P, 1897, pp. 197–238, MSA. On conditions in the Arthur Road Hospital in Bombay, see 'Report on Bubonic Plague Cases Treated at . . .' by N. H. Choksi, in Snow, *Report on the Outbreak of Bubonic Plague*, pp. 210–12, 237.

But this was not simply an 'indigenous' perception. When his daughter contracted the plague in Poona, Surgeon Major Barry, a British officer of the Indian Medical Service, recognized that she would have a better chance of recovery at home. Rather than entrust her to what should have appeared to his 'Western eyes' as 'the sanitized and healing environment of the hospital',[118] he conspired with his colleague, Surgeon Major Baker, who examined the patient, to conceal the fact and break the regulations they were working so vigorously to enforce upon others.[119]

Nonetheless, popular attitudes to the plague hospitals, and to Western medicine in general, were by no means inflexible. Some caste and communal hospitals, having created an environment which people felt more able to use, found general favour.[120] As Bombay's inhabitants fled the plague in 1897, the Petit Mills, facing an acute shortage of labour, 'promised to erect a temporary plague hospital' where their workers, 'would be looked after instead of being sent away to the Municipal hospitals'. As a result, it was said, they 'abandoned the idea of going away'.[121] If hospitals were not always hospitable places, they were particularly forbidding to the poor.[122]

By contrast, the occasional glimpses that we have into the domestic treatment of the sick during the epidemic suggest the enormous care often taken by friends and relatives. W. D. Shepherd, the Collector of Poona, complained that 'the inability of the family to refrain from attending on sick relatives ensured that a large number should die where many might have lived'. While they were 'generally very keen to keep plague out of their villages', they refused to allow their own 'separation from their sick relatives'.[123] The official historian of the plague expressed his frustration at those who, sharing rooms with plague patients, contracted the infection from being in constant attendance upon them. 'The poor and ignorant' were said to be more vulnerable to infection than, for instance, nursing staff, because of 'the common custom which exists of friends receiving the sputa of the sick in their hands, and using their hands and clothing to wipe away discharges from the patients'

[118] Arnold, 'Touching the Body', p. 62.
[119] W. L. Harvey, Municipal Commissioner, Bombay, to Plague Commissioner, Bombay, 14 March 1900, in GOB, General (Plague), vol. 16, Compilation no. 15, 1900, pp. 129–31, MSA.
[120] *Report of the Municipal Commissioner on the Plague in Bombay in the Year Ending 31st May, 1899* (Bombay, 1899), p. 318.   [121] *Ibid.*, pp. 354–6.
[122] This is also suggested by some evidence from the 1920s and 1930s. See, for instance, RCLI, *Evidence, Bombay Presidency, 1929–31*, Mr Dattatraya Ramchand Mayekar and Mr Narayanrao Kulkarni representing the Girni Kamgar Mahamandal, vol. I, part ii, p. 387. See also Proceedings of the TLIC, 1938–40, Main Inquiry, Evidence, Cotton Mill Workers, Spinning Side, File 60 A, pp. 1020–2, MSA.
[123] Report from Poona District in Condon, *The Bombay Plague*, pp. 234–5.

mouth'.[124] It would be folly to idealize the Indian family; not even among kin might we find a single and undifferentiated response. From Surat district, for instance, it was reported that 'the relatives and caste fellows of the Hindu patients often shrank from performing the last offices for their own dead', while those who contracted the disease in private segregation camps 'crawled back to their empty houses to die' and neighbours threw their corpses into the streets before officials marked their houses for special attention.[125]

At the height of the panic, Western medicine must have often appeared as nothing less than the theological carapace of an intrusive and oppressive state, and the hospital its most terrifying institutional embodiment. We might under these circumstances expect most people to have turned their backs upon the whole apparatus of Western medicine. In fact, the public response to Western medicine – if indeed an 'Indian' response may be inferred from the evidence at all – was more nuanced and flexible and many showed a willingness to use both doctors and hospitals. During the epidemic, some people strained to hear the 'Western' physician's mantra; others read the shaman's lips; still others turned to the hakims and vaidyas or the folk remedies which the most wizened village elders could recall. Each was as likely to be as effective as the other. There is nothing to suggest that those who sought the intercession of Sitaladevi did not also seek the help of the government-approved physician. In fact, popular attitudes to Western medicine in the 1890s, as perhaps more recently, were determined by its efficacy, its accessibility and its cost.[126] Popular resistance to medical intervention and hospitalization during the plague epidemic is more plausibly explained by the terms on which it was offered to those stricken or threatened by the disease than by some primordial sentiment or cultural essence embedded in the Indian mind.

VI

The plague epidemic did not give rise to a single, homogeneous Indian response. Neither is it possible to identify in it any consistent pattern of social differentiation. The diverse responses to the epidemic reflected in part the various ways in which it was perceived and experienced. People found themselves pitted against each other in the panic more often than they were gathered into large social solidarities. Social tension, competi-

[124] Condon, *The Bombay Plague*, p. 72.
[125] Report from Surat District, *ibid.*, pp. 178–9.
[126] Cf. A. R. Beals, 'Strategies of Resort to Curers in South India', in Charles Leslie (ed.), *Asian Medical Systems: A Comparative Study* (Berkeley and Los Angeles, 1976), pp. 195, 192–4, 198.

tion and antagonisms were heightened not only between but also within classes. The fragile facade of social order was cracked open and whole towns and villages appeared to be on the edge of chaos. In virtually every town, the outbreak of plague paralysed trade and put its inhabitants to flight. From Karad, it was reported, typically, in June 1897, 'The utter disorganization that prevailed in the town could hardly be imagined by one who had not seen it.'[127] In Poona, it was said, 'The state of the city was one of panic.'[128] By February 1897, nearly half the inhabitants of Bombay city had fled, there was 'open bidding for labour at the street corners',[129] and the city's officials grew increasingly apprehensive that the social and political fabric of the city was about to disintegrate.[130]

At anarchy's edge, the panic created fresh opportunities for profit and power for those with the temerity and ruthlessness to seize them. Shortly after the first outbreak of the disease in 1896, the Municipal Commissioner in Bombay reported: 'A gang of scoundrels took to blackmailing by personating the Police and Municipal servants, and increased the general terror, extorting money as they did under threats of removal to hospital.'[131] The evacuation of towns and villages, which it was believed had a salutary effect on public health, was accompanied by an increased incidence, and fear, of crime. At the model segregation camp at Anand in Kaira district in Gujarat, the banias having set up general provisions stores, were said to be 'in league with the *badmashes* in the town' to rob the detainees.[132] During the epidemic, the police, whose detectives 'gave us the fullest information',[133] may also have found opportunities for gain.[134] The implementation of the plague measures left much to the discretion of the search parties and in the course of their activities, large informal powers accrued to their 'detectives'. Once a household or a neighbourhood became the object of the search party's suspicion, its members were inextricably pulled into the vortex of the plague's terror. Their only means of escape was to negotiate and bargain these suspicions to rest. Sometimes the official status of the search parties was difficult to ascertain, and some behaved no differently from 'scoundrels'. The Government of Bombay became sufficiently anxious about their conduct to

[127] Report from Satara District, in Condon, *The Bombay Plague*, p. 243.
[128] *Draft of Report . . . by the Late Mr W. C. Rand*, p. 4, MSA.
[129] S. M. Edwardes, *The Rise of Bombay – A Retrospect* (Bombay, 1902), p. 330.
[130] Snow, *Report on the Outbreak of Bubonic Plague*, pp. 4–5, 7–9; Report by Executive Health Officer, *ibid.*, pp. 70–8.
[131] Snow, *Report on the Outbreak of Bubonic Plague*, p. 6.
[132] Report from Kaira District, in Condon, *The Bombay Plague*, pp. 160–3.
[133] Report from Executive Health Officer, Bombay, in Snow, *Report on the Outbreak of Bubonic Plague*, p. 80.
[134] For a general comment on such opportunities for the police during times of disturbances, see S. M. Edwardes, *The Bombay City Police*, p. 183. See also ch. 6 above.

instruct its officers that 'The closest supervision is especially necessary over subordinates and they should be taught to treat people civilly.'[135] If search parties fuelled public anxieties, enterprising spirits exploited the uncertainty they created.

The uncertainties which shrouded medical opinion about the plague and the desperation with which people sought cures wherever they might be found cleared the way for the proliferation of quacks. They were drawn from diverse social groups. As the Bombay Health Officer reported,

> Many good men were spoiled by aspiring to the honours of being Plague Doctors. Mallees and Mahars, and even men employed in the service of the Tramway Company and in the service of the city, persuaded themselves and encouraged others to believe that they had a cure for plague . . . Once a man became a Plague Doctor, he was seldom happy or contented in any regular work. If he did not save his followers, he ruined himself for honest toil.[136]

Healing and curing, blackmail and extortion did not exhaust the commercial opportunities created by the panic. Evacuation and segregation camps opened up new fields in trade. The collapse of the labour market offered marginal groups the chance to entrench themselves in particular occupations. Those who wielded enough influence in a neighbourhood or a village could try to oust their rivals and establish themselves as jobbers and procurers and suppliers of labour. The growing intervention of the state and its feverish search for collaborators enlivened the factions of the neighbourhood and as existing structures of power were subjected to unprecedented stress, political rivalries were more freely pursued.

The style and method of the plague administration also enabled, indeed invited, people to prey on each other. It assumed that they would spy on their neighbours. It expected that caste elders and local magnates would report suspicious cases and act as enforcers of the plague regulations. It hoped that, when detainees escaped from segregation camps, the inhabitants of uninfected areas would 'refuse to harbour such fugitives'.[137] These hopes were sometimes fulfilled and at other times frustrated. Some people responded with an enthusiasm which could be readily mistaken for public-spiritedness. If suspicion was the defining characteristic of the plague operations, it was also the hallmark of the panic.

The burden of this suspicion fell primarily upon those who could be defined as marginal and isolated as outsiders. With its vocabulary of

---

[135] Circular from GOB, General (Plague), no. 2551 P-43 Confidential, 6 April 1898, Home, Judicial, June 1898, 228–9 (B), NAI. I am grateful to Gordon Johnson for this reference.

[136] Report from Executive Health Officer, Bombay, in Snow, *Report on the Outbreak of Bubonic Plague*, p. 80.   [137] Condon, *The Bombay Plague*, pp. 28–9.

'detection' and 'search', 'surveillance' and 'informants', 'suspects' and 'fugitives', the plague administration served to criminalize the disease and its victims. At one level, officials identifying the disease with filth, directed their gaze naturally and primarily towards the poor. In October 1898, the 'Surveillance System' introduced on the railways focused especially upon 'travellers who . . . were suspicious whether by reason of their appearance or symptoms, or the daily conditions of their clothes or effects'.[138] In what can only be assumed to be an extraordinary slip of the pen, the Bombay Health Officer boasted in 1897: 'From the beginning the greatest attention was paid to the disinfection of houses and to the segregation of the poor.'[139] The Anand detention camp in Kaira district was transformed in May 1898 to 'a Disinfection Camp for dirty persons arriving from infected localities'.[140] But, of course, the whole body of the poor could scarcely be stigmatized with the plague or uniformly defined as criminal or marginal.

While plague officials may have worked with rather crude definitions of marginality, dominant groups and local majorities tried to deflect the impact of the plague measures onto weaker and more peripheral groups. Certainly, those whose rights in the village or the neighbourhood appeared the most tenuous, or who could otherwise be defined as out of the 'community', were the most likely to be reported for 'suspicion' of sickness. It was among untouchables, 'deviants' and outsiders that the disease was first identified in previously unaffected localities. The ill-fated search party which visited the village of Ghori in Nasik district in September 1897 was immediately directed by the village schoolmaster to the 'suspicious cases' in the Teli's quarter.[141] The plague in Ankleshwar was said in August 1898 to have 'originated among the Ghanchis, a very dirty class'.[142] In Rajapur in Ahmednagar district, it was first registered among the Mahars and Chambars, but it was nonetheless concealed by the village officers for over a fortnight. Its origin was attributed locally to an outsider: 'the brother of a Marwari from Sirur, who died of the plague, presented the clothing of the deceased to a family of Mahars, of whom five caught the plague'.[143] The 'infection', in Sirur taluka, Poona district, was said to have been imported 'from prostitutes in the town'.[144] The disease was introduced to Broach, it was claimed, not by rats but by

---

[138] *Ibid.*, p. 143.
[139] Report by Executive Health Officer, Bombay, in Snow, *Report on the Outbreak of Bubonic Plague*, p. 87.
[140] Report from Kaira District, in Condon, *The Bombay Plague*, p. 160.
[141] J. K. Kabraji, Assistant Collector, to Collector, Nasik, 26 November 1897, GOB, General (Plague), vol. 389, Compilation no. 298, 1898, MSA.
[142] Report from Broach District in Condon, *The Bombay Plague*, p. 155.
[143] Report from Ahmednagar District, *ibid.*, pp. 201–2.
[144] Report from Poona District, *ibid.*, p. 227.

butchers and the quarter 'mostly inhabited by Mohammedans' was 'deeply infected with plague'.[145] In Hubli, too, it was associated with 'the Mussalman community'. They were regarded as 'turbulent',[146] particularly hostile to the plague measures,[147] and as Fakrudin Budansab, in charge of the local police and himself a Muslim, advised, 'being arrogant and daring, it cannot be known what they would do in course of time'.[148]

In view of the havoc which could be wrought upon a locality or even a whole town, once it fell prey to official suspicion, it is not surprising that a common reflex was simply to keep the plague administration at bay. Even local elites preferred to avert the official gaze altogether. This was in part why those who became suspects simply denied that they were sick while the afflicted refused to believe that it was the plague that had struck. The proximity of the disease, let alone its arrival in the locality, was also so terrifying to contemplate that people often refused to countenance the very idea of it. The progress of the search party in Ghori, for instance, was intercepted by a large crowd armed with sticks whose spokesman was reported to have said that 'they did not want a doctor nor was there any sickness in the village' and added that 'we shall not allow men of other creeds into our houses'.[149] Buboes found on two patients in Jalgaon, as mortality rates rose, seemed to suggest that 'it is plague the people are dying of'. But 'the opinion of the town is that it is not plague, and that the mortality is due to ordinary fever acting on constitutions undermined by fever'.[150] As 10 per cent of Karad's population was 'swept away' in three months, in 1897, the Hospital Assistant insisted that the disease was 'not plague but remittent fever'.[151]

At the start of the epidemic in Bombay, an initial and spontaneous search for medical and official help was swiftly replaced by a general refusal of state intervention. The municipal authorities and the provincial government, who had for decades done next to nothing to alleviate the social and sanitary conditions of the city, found it impossible to persuade its inhabitants that the cause of the epidemic lay in 'the hopeless condition of their own dark, damp, filthy, overcrowded houses'. Instead, they 'raved about the sewers' and 'looked to everything except the buildings and the rooms in which they lived for the cause of the disease'.[152] It was

[145] Report from Broach District, *ibid.*, p. 156.
[146] Collector, Dharwar, to Commissioner, Southern Division, 13 March 1898, in GOB, General (Plague), vol. 389, Compilation no. 298, 1898, MSA.
[147] District Magistrate, Dharwar to General Officer Commanding, Belgaum, 13 March 1898, *ibid*, MSA.
[148] First Deputy Head Constable, in charge of the town of Hubli, to Assistant Superintendent of Police, Dharwar, 11 March 1898, *ibid*, MSA.
[149] J. K. Kabraji, Assistant Collector, to Collector, Nasik, 26 November 1897, *ibid*, MSA.
[150] Report from Khandesh District, in Condon, *The Bombay Plague*, p. 208.
[151] Report from Satara District, *ibid.*, pp. 243–4.
[152] Snow, *Report on the Outbreak of Bubonic Plague*, p. 18.

preferable by far to flee the city or even simply pray that the plague would pass them by than to place their trust in a government which had shown little real or sustained interest in their welfare, and now intervened in an arbitrary and brutal manner. The Municipal Commissioner found that 'the people refused all medical aid or to listen to any advice'.[153] To the official mind, the popular response sometimes appeared indiscriminately hostile. 'Nearly every hand was against the Municipal Officers', complained the Health Officer.[154] 'Such a pass had we come to, that picking up a few sick pigeons . . . nearly led to a riot, and peaceful Bunnias, for 10 sick pigeons threatened to raze the city.'[155] It was almost as if to combat the disease and reorganize their lives around the epidemic people felt it imperative to resist the wise and rational men who came bearing the officially prescribed remedies, like so many satanic gifts.

VII

It is perhaps easier to explain why panics begin than why they end and the plague epidemic in India was no exception. Bubonic plague was after all, *the* plague; it was devastatingly and unremittingly deadly in its effects; it was a new and unfamiliar disease which no one fully comprehended and for which no remedies were known. Official frenzy acted as the catalyst of the panic and the public response. This frenzy was informed by colonial perceptions of the threat which the epidemic posed to Britain's empire and its international trade. It was conditioned and its expression inflected by colonial assumptions about Indian society and its cultural characteristics. In the panic, such economy as may have guided the techniques of colonial rule was quickly spent and these assumptions were expressed with an unusually uninhibited freedom. The excesses and desperation of official policies fed upon and fattened the terror which the epidemic unleashed upon those exposed to the disease. Many responded to the desperation of official measures with an equally desperate resistance to and refusal of official, even medical, intervention. What colonial officials saw as an irrational and obscurantist resistance to the dictates of science and reason only incited them to further, yet more ferocious and despairing executive action. In this way, panic, terror and guilt engorged each other in a seemingly unending spiral.

The spiral was broken only when the frenzied temper of the plague measures relaxed. In part, this was a consequence of the identification of the plague as a disease of the poor. At the same time, while the plague continued to flourish, it was impossible to escape the conclusion that the

---

[153] *Ibid.*, p. 5.   [154] Report from the Executive Health Officer, Bombay, *ibid.*, p. 71.
[155] *Ibid.*, p. 70.

vigorously enforced policies of the state had achieved very little.[156] They
had failed to control the spread of the disease, protect the people or save
the lives of the afflicted. Rather, as the plague extended its sway, officials
perceived more starkly the political risks inherent in these colonial policies. As early as July 1897, the Lieutenant-Governor of the North-Western Provinces had observed, 'If the plague regulations had been enforced
in any city of these provinces in the way in which . . . they were . . .
enforced in Poona, there would certainly have been bloodshed here.'[157]
The formulation and implementation of the plague measures, indeed the
official construction of the panic, had been facilitated in the late 1890s, in
two respects, by the prevailing political circumstances. First, in Bombay
Presidency, British rule was more firmly anchored and British government more developed than in the old Mughal heartland or the outlying
frontier regions of the Punjab. In Bombay, the British often fondly
perceived the embodiment of the success of their technique of rule
through collaboration. The Punjab, vital to the defence of the Indian
empire and the recruiting ground of the Indian Army, was, however, the
home of the 'martial races' rather than the 'scribal classes'. At the height
of the panic in 1897, the Bombay Government had felt able to strike
decisively at the apparently formidable political base which the 'extremist' Tilak had been building, through his famine campaigns, Ganpati and
Shivaji festivals and the recently captured Poona Sarvajanik Sabha.[158] By
contrast, to officials in the Punjab, it seemed extravagant to antagonize
merely in the name of science or in the interests of public health. It was
here that the British rediscovered the fatalism with which they had long
regarded questions of public health and social conditions before the
outbreak of plague. Second, colonial plague policies had also been facilitated by the decline of the Congress as an all-India focus of political
opposition. By the mid-1890s, the Indian National Congress had settled
into torpor. It was only after 1903, while the plague continued unabated
and even reached its peak, that the Congress coincidentally began to
revive and in this revival the contribution of Punjab and the North-
Western Provinces was to be substantial.[159] As they emerged from the
whirligig of the plague panic, the British could reassure themselves about

[156] The first shifts of official thinking in this direction can be seen in *Report of the Indian Plague Commission, 1898–99*, vol. V, pp. 400–4, *PP*, 1902, vol. LXII.
[157] Macdonnell to Elgin, 16 July 1897, Keep-With 5, Home Public A, May 1898, 329–44, NAI, cited by Johnson, *Provincial Politics and Indian Nationalism*, p. 97 fn. 1.
[158] Cashman, *The Myth of the Lokamanya*; Johnson, *Provincial Politics and Indian National-ism*, especially, chs. 2 and 3; Catanach, 'Poona Politicians and the Plague'.
[159] N. G. Barrier, 'The Punjab Disturbances of 1907: The Response of the British Govern-ment in India to Agrarian Unrest', *MAS*, 1:4 (1967), 353–83; N. G. Barrier, 'The Arya Samaj and Congress Politics in Punjab, 1894–1908', *JAS*, 26:3 (1967), 363–79; C. A. Bayly, *The Local Roots of Indian Politics: Allahabad, 1870–1920* (Oxford, 1973).

the resilience of their systems of collaboration in Bombay; but, more crucially, they had relearnt an old lesson: that the price of political intervention was liable to be the destruction of these systems and, with it, the brittle and unsteady foundations of their rule.

The plague epidemic of the late 1890s in India carries many resonances of the AIDS epidemic of the 1980s in the United States. In the case of AIDS, state intervention and public interest were limited by the belief that only marginal, deviant groups were likely to be affected. But this was not a function of calm. It was accompanied by anxiety that this was Armageddon and rumours circulated about catching the virus from toilet seats, tea cups and toothbrushes. Vested interests, from the homosexual bathhouse-owners to the blood banks, at times impeded and deflected measures to control its spread. Rumours, rife at every stage of the epidemic, explained its causes in terms of African initiation rites, the use of 'poppers' and a creation of germ warfare experiments gone wrong. A San Diego coroner, undoubtedly trained at the best American medical schools, argued that the virus was in fact 'King Tut's curse', 'placed in the tomb to punish those who might later defile his grave'. The legendary 'Orange County Connection' alone was widely believed to be responsible for the first hundred cases in the United States. He visited sex palaces specially to spread the virus as an act of revenge but was so irresistible that the person who went to confront him about his behaviour finished up having sex with him. In May 1985, *Burke's Peerage*, compiled, of course, by literate and rational people, announced that to preserve 'the purity of the human race', it would omit all families in which somebody was known to have AIDS. Their reason, they declared, was that 'AIDS may not be a simple infection, even if conveyed in an unusual way, but an indication of a genetic defect'. American gays, often prosperous professionals, secular and modern in their outlook and highly educated, rather than pre-scientific, superstitious and illiterate, showed at numerous points an antipathy to medical and policy initiatives as possible infringements on their civil liberties, when 'objectively' they might have been seen as necessary and non-threatening, and developed a whole vocabulary of euphemisms to maintain this position. As Randy Shilts, from whose excellent book these instances are quoted, observed: 'Humans who have been subjected to a life-time of irrational bigotry on the part of mainstream society can be excused for harbouring unreasonable fears.'[160] Perhaps this may provide a better clue to popular resistance to the plague measures in India than sacred traditions or religious susceptibilities.

[160] Randy Shilts, *And the Band Played On*, pp. 541–3 and *passim*.

8 Indian nationalism, 1914–1947: Gandhian rhetoric, the Congress and the working classes

I

The period between 1914 and 1947 has frequently been characterized as the phase of mass nationalism. The Congress appeared in this period to be transformed from the annual tamasha of a bombinating, mendicant elite to an irresistible mass movement inspired by a more radical leadership. Gandhi, it seemed, had marshalled the Indian people behind the banner of the Congress and led them struggling rightfully and unitedly to be free. Yet on closer scrutiny the attitude of the Congress leadership to the involvement of the working classes in this age of mass nationalism was suspicious and defensive. At one level, the working classes could no longer simply be ignored: their own militancy, the impetus of political reform and the extension of the franchise, and the Congress claim to represent the nation as a whole pushed them to the forefront of Indian politics. Moreover, while revolt in the countryside was what the British feared most, the great Congress agitations were largely urban affairs. So for the Congress there was much to be gained by establishing their presence in the back streets and neighbourhoods of the towns.

On the other hand, no sooner was the Congress drawn into the sphere of working-class politics than its leaders disclaimed or denounced their newly acquired connections. Tilak, in whom Lenin's hopes for the future of the Indian proletariat were invested,[1] exhorted the millworkers of Bombay to sink their differences with the millowners and intoned sonor-

---

[1] After the strike which followed the arrest and sentencing of Tilak in Bombay in 1908, Lenin observed that the Tilakites had 'introduced to the Bombay working class certain socialist ideas they had drawn primarily from the experience of the Russian working class' and were thus 'instrumental in awakening the class consciousness of the Indian proletariat'. Now that the Indian 'proletariat had developed to conscious political mass struggle . . . the Russian-style British regime was doomed'. V. I. Lenin, *The National-Liberation Movement in the East*, pp. 14–15, cited by Cashman, *The Myth of the Lokamanya*, p. 182 and A. I. Chicherov, 'Tilak's Trial and the Bombay Political Strike of 1908', in I. M. Reisner and N. M. Goldberg (eds.), *Tilak and the Struggle for Indian Freedom* (New Delhi, 1966), p. 545.

ously 'Bolshevism as it is preached in the West cannot succeed in India. Let us stick to our Vedanta and all our desires shall be fulfilled.'[2] 'It does not require much effort of the intellect', Gandhi declared in the early 1920s, 'to perceive that it is most dangerous to make political use of labour until labourers understand the political condition of the country and are prepared to work for the common good'.[3] During the Assam tea-coolies' strike of 1921, at the height of the non-cooperation campaign, Gandhi defined his objectives thus:

In India, we want no political strikes . . . We do not need an atmosphere of unsettled unrest . . . We must gain control over all the unruly and disturbing elements or isolate them even as we isolate government . . . We seek not to destroy capital or capitalists but to regulate the relations between capital and labour. We want to harness capital to our side.[4]

When he was elected the President of the All-India Trade Union Congress for 1929, Nehru confessed to the disappointed candidate, D. B. Kulkarni, a communist railwayman, that he did not want the job, that he had been elected in a fit of absence of mind and that he would have certainly withdrawn in favour of his opponent, if only he had been present at the session which elected him.[5] In the year of his presidency, he had hoped to bring the 'National Congress' and the Trade Union Congress 'closer to each other', encouraging the former 'to become more socialistic' and 'organised labour to join the national struggle'. But in retrospect, he noted ruefully in his *Autobiography* , this had been 'a vain hope, for nationalism can only go far in a socialistic or proletarian direction by ceasing to be nationalism'.[6] In the mid-1930s, the Congress Socialist Party professed a more direct interest in the working class and played a more active role in trade union organization. But the Congress leadership took the offensive against those whom Vallabhai Patel dismissed as 'young men with brain fever'[7] and the Working Committee considered banning 'any Congressman "who preaches class war" from membership of any executive committee'.[8] In the late 1930s, the provincial Congress ministries, having taken office under the 1935

[2] Quoted in Cashman, *The Myth of the Lokamanya*, p. 187.
[3] *Young India*, 16 February 1921, *CWMG*, vol. XIX, p. 366.
[4] *Young India*, 15 June 1921, *CWMG*, vol. XX, p. 228.
[5] J. Nehru to D. B. Kulkarni, 10 September 1929, AICC Papers, File 16, 1929, NMML. See ch. 3 above.
[6] J. Nehru, *An Autobiography: With Musings on Recent Events in India* (London, 1936), pp. 197–8.
[7] Cited by B. R. Tomlinson, *The Indian National Congress and the Raj: The Penultimate Phase, 1929–1942* (London, 1976), p. 52.
[8] *Ibid.*, p. 169, n. 103; Jamnalal Bajaj to Uma Nehru, 21 June 1934, AICC Papers, File G-29, 1934, NMML, cited by Tomlinson, *The Indian National Congress and the Raj*, p. 52.

Act, set about bashing trade unions and repressing strikes seemingly with more enthusiasm than the preceding colonial administration.[9]

Popular support for the Congress has usually been measured in relation to its great agitational campaigns. However, the timing of the major Congress campaigns was determined not by the groundswell of popular political action but rather by imperial and constitutional considerations. Non-cooperation was the Gandhian alternative to council entry; civil disobedience was the Congress response to the Round Table Conference, the Quit India movement its answer to Cripps's offer of a 'post-dated cheque on a crashing bank'. Popular participation in these campaigns was rooted in local grievances and social conflicts, which pre-dated the national campaigns and did not cease when the Congress agitations were called off.[10]

This discordance in the timing and objectives of the Congress agitations and the particular struggles which constituted them manifested itself in the uneven and variable response of peasants and workers to the Congress. Not surprisingly, perhaps, workers who were drawn readily into non-cooperation sometimes remained aloof from civil disobedience; towns which appeared insurrectionary in the early 1930s remained relatively quiescent in the early 1940s. Non-cooperation flourished among various working-class groups in Bengal[11] but civil disobedience drew a more muted response, while labour, it appears, 'remained largely irrelevant to the Congress strategy'.[12] The strikes of 1920–22 in Jamshedpur fed conveniently into the non-cooperation campaign, but civil disobedience failed as workers ignored the satyagrahis and achieved record levels of production,[13] but the Quit India

[9] The policies of the Congress Ministry in Bombay towards labour are extensively documented in the papers of the Government of Bombay's Home (Special) Department. See especially, GOB, Home (Special), Files 550 (25) IV A of 1938, 550 (25) III-A of 1938 and 550 (25)-B of 1938, MSA; see also AICC Papers, File PL-2 of 1938, especially J. Nehru to B. G. Kher, 5 August 1937, p. 583, NMML. For the case of Ahmedabad, see ATLA Papers, File 3, part 2, microfilm copy, reel 9, NMML; and also, Patel, *The Making of Industrial Relations*, pp. 126–36. For the Madras Presidency, see Murphy, *Unions in Conflict*, pp. 148–219; Ramaswamy, *The Worker and His Union*, ch. 1; on Bihar, see D. Simeon, *The Politics of Labour under Late Colonialism: Workers, Unions and the State in Chota Nagpur, 1928–1939* (New Delhi, 1995), chs. 7–9.
[10] This commonplace of the 'Cambridge school' in the 1970s has become a shibboleth of the 'subaltern school' in the 1990s.
[11] Rajat K. Ray, 'Masses in Politics: The Non-Cooperation Movement in Bengal, 1920–22', *IESHR*, 11:4 (1974), 370 ff. See also, Basu, 'Workers' Politics in Bengal', ch. 5; S. Gourlay, 'Nationalists, Outsiders and the Labour Movement in Bengal During the Non-Cooperation Movement, 1919–1921', in Kapil Kumar (ed.), *Congress and Classes: Nationalism, Workers and Peasants* (Delhi, 1988), pp. 34–57.
[12] T. Sarkar, 'The First Phase of Civil Disobedience in Bengal, 1930–31', *Indian Historical Review*, 4:1 (1977), 94.
[13] Vinay Bahl, 'TISCO Workers' Struggle, 1920–28', *Social Scientist*, 10:8 (1982), 44, fn. 34.

campaign registered an impressive and dramatic response from the town's industrial workers.[14]

The relationship between the Congress and its popular following was as problematic at the time as it has later proved elusive to historians. Despite the scholarly attention paid to the subject, the past two decades have represented an interpretative Dark Age in the historiography of Indian nationalism. Although there have been numerous interesting and illuminating studies, they have been characterized by a reluctance to address the relationship between the Congress and its fluctuating and intermittent popular following, and, therefore, an inability to adequately explain its popular appeal. The protean character of the Congress and the plurality and diversity of its followings, and the complex social formations which constituted them, has made it difficult to define and analyse this relationship. But in part its elusiveness has also owed something to the ways in which it has been conceptualized.

The question first posed by Tilak in a newspaper column in 1895: 'Whose is the Congress? Of the Classes or of the Masses?' [15] has, thus, led inexorably to a historiographical stalemate. It is neither satisfactory to assume that nationalism was a reflexive response to, and natural outcome of, colonial exploitation nor to attribute the growth of popular support for the Congress to a mass awakening from traditional passivity. Not only are the working classes thus perceived as a natural constituency for the Congress, but this diffusionist approach also takes the political initiative out of the hands of the actors whose behaviour it seeks to explain. In a Marxist variant, the nationalist movement was seen as serving a particular mix of class interests. While broadly appearing to work in coalition, their final shape was invariably determined by the 'real' bourgeois character of the movement. The masses were preparing, and being prepared, for their own betrayal.

The 'mass awakening' thesis could now be extended into a 'betrayal' thesis. The ambivalence of the Congress towards its popular following has sometimes been interpreted as an affirmation of its bourgeois character. The object of the Congress, in this view, was to control the masses and to divert them from their revolutionary goals. But it is scarcely satisfactory to inveigh against the Congress for failing to lead a mass movement in a final assault against the colonial state. For if its leadership proved inadequate to the task, and such an outcome was a realizable

---

[14] N. Mansergh (ed.), *The Transfer of Power, 1942–47*, vol. II: *Quit India, 30 April–21 September 1942* (London, 1971), especially Documents nos. 600–2, 612, 636, 650 and 672.

[15] *Mahratta*, 27 October 1895, cited by Johnson, *Provincial Politics and Indian Nationalism*, p. 120.

possibility, it is perhaps more pertinent to ask why the Congress was not replaced by a more effective popular agency of revolt.[16] If 'workers, peasants and the urban petty bourgeoisie' simply 'waited in vain' for the emergence of a 'revolutionary leadership',[17] we might usefully ask why they did not manifest a greater impatience.

In reaction to the emphasis of the Cambridge school on factions competing for power and the squabbles for spoils, its critics sought to offer in its place the ideological and cultural dimension of nationalism. But the old paradigm of 'mobilization', with all its limitations, continued to haunt their enquiries into the nature of popular movements. Historians sought to reach the masses primarily through nationalist propaganda and the class interests of the peasantry. They focused on the divergence between the latter and the bourgeois character of the Congress. The peasants were allowed to make their own history – if only when they rejected the importunities of the Congress. But, for the most part, historians were concerned with how the Congress brought 'the people' into its orbit and the masses remained precisely what the term described – a shadowy, undifferentiated lump which was faded into the background, and only intermittently brought to the fore by political activists.

For all their (sometimes acrimonious) differences, what all these approaches share in common is the attempt to comprehend the relationship between the Congress and the masses as a process of mobilization. Indeed, this paradigm of mobilization has severely limited the interpretative scope of the historiography of Indian nationalism. Arguments about political mobilization have perhaps been overly concerned with how parties spread their message and propagate their ideas and rather less with how they were received or re-interpreted. Even those historians who are concerned with the latter have tended to measure the success of political mobilization by trying to assess how directly it spoke to specific class interests or how literally it was lodged in an innate cultural idiom. But there is a certain circularity in such reasoning: political mobilization is seen to have been successful when it attracted widespread support; the fact that it attracted widespread support is then taken as proof that its rhetoric was appropriate whether in terms of class or culture.

[16] For instance, Pandey, *The Ascendancy of the Congress in Uttar Pradesh*; D. Hardiman, *Peasant Nationalists of Gujarat: Kheda District, 1917–1934* (Delhi, 1981). By the late 1930s, according to Pandey, 'there was, however, no longer any question of [the Congress] assigning a primacy . . . to political struggle for the advancement of consciousness and the achievement of radical change in society, within which the nationalist leadership had been caught up for a short time'. G. Pandey, 'Congress and the Nation, 1917–1947', in R. Sisson and S. Wolpert (eds.), *Congress and Indian Nationalism: The Pre-Independence Phase* (Berkeley, 1988), pp. 130–1.

[17] Ranajit Guha, 'On the Historiography of Colonial India', in Ranajit Guha (ed.), *Subaltern Studies*, vol. I, pp. 6–7.

Faced with the 'elitist' bias of the historiography, whether intended or not, some historians set out in search of 'the relatively autonomous culture or mind' of the subaltern.[18] The notion of popular culture was now deployed to rescue the subaltern from the condescension of the historian. But, given the provenance of the notion itself, it was more likely to mire her more deeply in it. In view of the diversity of the conditions and contexts in which the 'subordinated' operated, let alone the indeterminacy of the boundary which separated them off from the 'dominant', this search for the collective 'mind' of the subaltern classes was bound to prove as elusive as the Holy Grail. For where, after all, was the historian to find the common denominator by which these diverse elements could be identified collectively as a 'popular culture', except in his own bag of tricks? Its definition was characterized by its arbitrariness, which in turn was liable to introduce an inherently circular analytic procedure. Once the assumption was made that a 'popular culture', at one level, subsumed differences of class and occupation, age and gender, caste and religion, language and region, it became possible to hold various and conflicting forms of social action within it. As soon as it was assumed that the 'subaltern mind' operated primarily in a religious idiom, for instance, historians privileged metaphors and practices of religion in their accounts of the resistance of the subordinated.[19]

For an insight into the 'subaltern mind', moreover, historians have had to depend largely on the discourse of the dominant classes, in which, of course, the characteristics of those whom they seek to control are delineated; and it need hardly be said that their perceptions of the 'subalterns' was an integral part of the conditions of their domination.[20] Studies of local responses to the Congress, rooted in their 'popular culture', have often found themselves resorting to rather traditional

[18] S. Sarkar, 'The Conditions and Nature of Subaltern Militancy: Bengal from Swadeshi to Non-Cooperation, c. 1905–1922', in Guha (ed.), *Subaltern Studies*, vol. III, p. 277.

[19] See, for instance, David Hardiman's account of how Kunvarji Mehta mobilized the adivasis in the Bardoli and Valod talukas of Surat district. After his initial efforts failed, Kunvarji hit upon 'a new strategy'. He sought the name of the adivasis' most revered god, Simariyo Dev. In fact, 'he appears to have obtained the information in a rather confused form' – that is, he got the wrong name and in any case thought Simariyo Dev was two gods. He began to tell the adivasis that Gandhi had been chosen by Simadiya Dev and Shiliya Dev as their replacement, and that he was an avatar of Ram and Krishna. Although Kunvarji mistook the god's name, the religious adivasis believed him, and as a consequence began to shout 'Mahatma-Gandhi-ni-jai'. D. Hardiman, *The Coming of the Devi* (Delhi, 1987), pp. 168–9; see also S. Amin, 'Gandhi as Mahatma: Gorakhpur District, Eastern UP, 1921–2', in Guha (ed.), *Subaltern Studies*, vol. III, pp. 1–61.

[20] Thus, rumours and stories which indicate how the peasants perceived Gandhi and invested him with a magical status and divine powers are drawn from local newspapers, official accounts, sometimes even the memoirs of Lord Ronaldshay. See Amin, 'Gandhi as Mahatma', pp. 1–57; Hardiman, *The Coming of the Devi*; Sarkar, 'The Conditions and Nature of Subaltern Militancy'.

counters of explanation – material discontent, class and colonial oppression and the diffusion of nationalist ideas by political agents – when they have had to explain the political appeal of Gandhi and the Congress.[21] What popular culture provides in these accounts is often the religious idiom in which these supposedly simple, unsophisticated folk are said to interpret and express their political preferences and, thus, the appeal of their leaders.[22] But in view of the prior assumption that 'the consciousness of the subordinated' embraces, as Amin puts it, 'the complex relationship between popular culture, religiosity and inchoate political consciousness',[23] this is less remarkable than it is tautological. Moreover, to the extent that they insist upon the autonomy of subaltern politics, these accounts would tend to marginalize the role of the Congress and its leadership. Yet the subject they define and the evidence they present on popular responses to the nationalist movement demonstrates the apparently dominating influence of Gandhi and the Congress in local political discourse.

This emphasis on popular culture and the vigorous search for the 'subaltern mind' which it has unleashed has also served to stultify our understanding of popular political responses to the nationalist movement. If in the 'animal politics' of the Cambridge school,[24] there was little scope for grasping the terms on which the Congress engaged with the working classes or the rural poor, the subaltern insistence on 'the autonomy of peasant insurgency'[25] can scarcely allow for the systematic investigation of the relationship between the Congress and its popular follow-

---

[21] Amin, 'Gandhi as Mahatma'; Hardiman, *The Coming of the Devi.* However, Amin's most recent and impressive work appears successfully to overcome the limitations imposed by the notion of 'popular culture' upon 'Gandhi as Mahatma': see S. Amin, *Event, Metaphor, Memory: Chauri Chaura, 1922–1992* (Berkeley, 1995).

[22] Thus, according to Hardiman, the reason why the Patidars of Kheda, unlike their counterparts in Surat did not see visions of Gandhi at the bottom of their wells, was because they were 'generally more sophisticated than those of South Gujarat'. Hardiman, *The Coming of the Devi*, pp. 50–1, n. 92. Significantly, it is at this point of his argument that Hardiman seeks to set his findings beside those of Amin, 'Gandhi as Mahatma'.

[23] S. Amin, 'Agrarian Bases of Nationalist Agitations in India: An Historiographical Survey', in D. A. Low (ed.), *The Indian National Congress: Centenary Hindsights* (Delhi, 1988), p. 105. The religiosity of the 'masses' was, of course, a recurrent theme in colonial discourse. It could serve conveniently to explain both the fanaticism of the mob as well as the appeal of nationalist movements directed against the British. 'Those who wish to rouse the unpolitical masses', explained the Government of India in 1930, 'are able to play upon their feelings by appealing to the interests which are intense and vivid in their lives. First among these interests must be placed the power of religion.' *Government of India's Despatch on Proposals for Constitutional Reform, dated 20th September 1930*, PP, 1930–1, vol. XXIII, p. 695.

[24] T. Raychaudhuri, 'Indian Nationalism as Animal Politics', *Historical Journal*, 22:3 (1979), 747–63.

[25] R. Guha (ed.), *Subaltern Studies*, 6 vols. This notion of 'autonomy' has sometimes been combined with the contradictory thesis of betrayal.

ing.[26] In some versions, this relationship is not even problematized and its investigation is postponed or ruled out altogether. Thus, Amin exhorts historians to pursue the 'investigation of peasant political activity *within* nationalist activity', rather than 'concentrate on the relationship between the two'.[27] However, since peasant politics 'within' nationalism entails a relationship, it is difficult to see why historians should, or, indeed, how they could, avoid the latter. The interpretative costs of the failure to address this relationship is reflected in the historiographical and conceptual stagnation of the past two decades.

This chapter explores the relationship between the Congress and its popular following, in particular among the working classes. It will proceed by abjuring the notion (or more accurately, the assumption) of 'popular culture'. No inherent solidarity will be attributed to the 'subordinate classes' for the conditions of their subordination divided them more fundamentally than it united them. Rather, it will be argued that perceptions of mutuality among them, indeed the political vocabulary in which it was expressed, was produced by the specificities of a particular intellectual and political context. Their solidarities, their coming together, should be observed and analysed; they cannot be assumed. They merit investigation and demand explanation.

II

The success of political movements, their ability to attract widespread support, would depend to a large extent upon how far their rhetoric and programme could penetrate the assumptions and ideologies of their putative followers, not simply how far their rhetoric spoke to specific and given social interests or political cultures.[28] To achieve this fully, their political programme would have to do far more than express or reflect the specific interests of the working classes or find a resonance in the daily struggles of workplace and neighbourhood. It would have to offer workers a means of comprehending and contextualizing their immediate situations, which were necessarily diverse, while also indicating how they might be realistically transformed. Their programme would have to encapsulate and offer a social and political alternative and enunciate a method by which it might be realized. In other words, their programmatic

---

[26] Some recent work has, on the other hand, focused upon nationalist discourse while it has tended to neglect the wider social response to its programmes. See P. Chatterjee, *Nationalist Thought and the Colonial World: A Derivative Discourse* (London, 1986); and P. Chatterjee, *The Nation and Its Fragments: Colonial and Post-Colonial Histories* (Delhi, 1994).   [27] Amin, 'Agrarian Bases of Indian Nationalism', p. 100.

[28] See the seminal essay by G. Stedman Jones, 'Rethinking Chartism', in Stedman Jones, *The Languages of Class*, pp. 90–178.

framework would have to be sufficiently flexible to be meaningful within particular and diverse contexts, while at the same time enabling workers to interpret and develop this ideology in new directions and to forge fresh political strategies from within its parameters. Political ideologies rarely teach or convert, even if political activists are fond of confessing to Pauline conversions. The effectiveness of political programmes is perhaps best judged, not in terms of how far they can squeeze themselves into what their protagonists may perceive as an appropriate class or cultural idiom, but in terms of their dynamic and creative potential in the hands of their adherents. In practice, the Congress was faced with the task of doing nothing less than defining the nation in terms which would find a continuing echo in the daily struggles of the working classes.

These desiderata, never easy to achieve over any length of time, were to prove particularly difficult for the Congress in its relationship with the working classes. The Congress neither became nor sought to become a party of the working class. This is not because, as was often implied in contemporary discourse and subsequently too readily accepted by later historians, it was a bourgeois party. Conversely, it should not be taken for granted that a political programme for the working classes could only be formulated within the language of socialism as if there was an organic – rather than a historical or a contingent – connection between them. It would be misleading to assume that a political ideology – whether nationalism or socialism – has a given social embodiment or yet more metaphysically, that it expresses the 'consciousness' of a particular class.

In any case, the working classes represented less a single, coherent social category than a kaleidoscope of social groups. 'Factory' or 'industrial workers' composed a small minority of the Indian workforce. But they were recruited largely from the smallholding peasantry. Frequently, they retained over several generations close connections with their village base and drew upon its resources.[29] Nor did they form a homogeneous social group. Industrialization often exacerbated the differences between them.[30] Labour for the coal mines and the tea gardens was recruited not only from the impoverished peasantry but also from groups of 'tribals',[31]

[29] Chandavarkar, *The Origins of Industrial Capitalism*, ch. 4.
[30] *Ibid., passim*; see ch. 3 above.
[31] R. P. Behal and P. P. Mohapatra, 'Tea and Money Versus Human Life: The Rise and Fall of the Indenture System in the Assam Tea Plantations', in E. Valentine Daniel, H. Bernstein and T. Brass (eds.), *Plantations, Proletarians and Peasants in Colonial Asia* (London, 1992), pp. 142–72; Simmons, 'Recruiting and Organising an Industrial Labour Force in Colonial India'; R. Das Gupta, 'Plantation Labour in Colonial India', in Daniel *et al.* (eds.), *Plantations, Proletarians and Peasants*, pp. 172–98; P. P. Mohapatra, 'Coolies and Colliers: A Study of the Agrarian Context of Labour Migration from Chotanagpur, 1880–1920', *Studies in History*, new series, 1:2 (1985), special issue, *Essays in Agrarian History: India, 1850 to 1940*, edited by S. Bhattacharya, 13–42; C. Bates and

and they were sometimes indentured to serve in the British plantation colonies overseas.[32] By the early twentieth century, a growing number of rural households required off-farm earnings in order to maintain themselves, but most sought employment on the land, some travelled for the harvest season to the neighbouring district or sought wage employment in nearby towns. It was a relatively small proportion who became long-distance migrants to industrial labour in the large cities.[33] The population of most small towns, local market or administrative centres, was drawn from the neighbouring villages. Here, the working classes were employed in manual labour, in service occupations, small workshops or petty trade.[34] Such people were identified in the large cities as the 'casual poor' or, more recently, lumped together in the 'informal sector'. In fact, casual and permanent factory labour described overlapping social spheres. They did not constitute separate labour markets distinguished by special social characteristics peculiar to each.[35] Similar, certainly overlapping, social processes by which 'tribals' or 'artisans' were turned into 'peasants', or each of them into 'workers', had been operating in Indian society for over two centuries. Significantly, the processes by which these working classes were constituted intermeshed. As they did so, they traversed a wide expanse of Indian society and diverse social forms. Their diversity greatly complicated the task of developing a rhetoric or a political programme with a significance for the working class.

It is interesting to speculate that the Congress might most readily have

M. Carter, 'Tribal Migration in India and Beyond', in G. Prakash (ed.), *The World of the Rural Labourer in Colonial India* (Delhi, 1992), pp. 205–47; R. Das Gupta, 'Migrants in Coal Mines: Peasants or Proletarians, 1850s–1947', *Social Scientist*, 151 (December 1985), 18–43; R. Ghosh, 'A Study of the Labour Movement in the Jharia Coalfield, 1900–1977', unpublished Ph.D. thesis, Calcutta University, 1992.

[32] H. Tinker, *A New System of Slavery: The Export of Indian Labour Overseas 1830–1920* (London, 1974); J. Breman, *Taming the Coolie Beast: Plantation Society and the Colonial Order in Southeast Asia* (Delhi, 1989); Marina Carter, *Servants, Sirdars and Settlers: Indians in Mauritius, 1834–1874* (Delhi, 1995).

[33] G. Omvedt, 'Migration in Colonial India: The Articulation of Feudalism and Capitalism by the Colonial State', *Journal of Peasant Studies*, 7:2 (1980), 185–212; Mohapatra, 'Coolies and Colliers'; Brahma Nand, 'Agricultural Labourers in Western India: A Study of the Central Division Districts of the Bombay Presidency During the Late Nineteenth and Early Twentieth Century' *Studies in History*, new series, 1:2 (1985), 221–46; Pradipta Chaudhury, 'Labour Migration from the United Provinces, 1881–1911' *Studies in History*, 8:1 (1992), 13–42; J. Pouchepadass, 'The Market for Agricultural Labour in Colonial North Bihar, 1860–1920', in M. Holmstrom (ed.), *Work for Wages in South Asia* (Delhi, 1990), pp. 11–27; Chandavarkar, *The Origins of Industrial Capitalism*, ch. 4; Das Gupta, 'Migrants in Coal Mines'; Sen, 'Women Workers in the Bengal Jute Industry', especially chs. 1–3.

[34] N. Gooptu, 'The Political Culture of the Urban Poor in North India, 1920–47', unpublished Ph.D. dissertation, University of Cambridge, 1991; Vijay Prashad, 'Chuhras and Colonialism', unpublished paper.

[35] Chandavarkar, *The Origins of Industrial Capitalism*, especially ch. 3.

been able to move a massive broadly based and inclusive political alliance against British rule in the 1870s and 1880s, before or immediately after its foundation. In this period, Indians were most completely excluded and distanced from the political structure of colonial rule.[36] At the same time, the bankrupt colonial state was driving deeper into Indian society in its feverish search for revenues, seeking new sources of taxation, bearing down upon social groups which had previously been allowed a relatively free hand. To hypothesize the existence of conditions conducive to such a broad-based nationalist movement in the 1870s and 1880s is not to suggest that it was imminent or even practicable. Certainly, the early nationalists were 'indifferent or hostile to the efforts being made to ameliorate the conditions of work of the factory workers' and even the radicals among them, including Tilak, are found to have been 'insensitive and even opposed to the cause of labour'.[37] Subsequently, the changing policies of the state made this impossible. From the 1880s onwards, the policies of the state served to fragment what earlier might have provided the basis for a broad front organized around a political programme, both radical and inclusive. Political and bureaucratic reform not only began to remedy the narrow and exclusive character of the political system but it also worked in favour of some and to the disadvantage of others. It helped to bring caste and communal differences emphatically into the political arena. At the same time, the social and economic policies of the state, while claiming to encourage the social transformation of the economy, served to protect the agrarian base from the forces of capital, and contributed increasingly to the disintegration of the broad alliance that might hypothetically have been put together and moved laboriously against the structure of colonial rule. In the twentieth century, the difficulties inherent in seeking to reconcile class conflict within the framework of a representative nationalist movement were increasingly intensified.

From the late nineteenth century onwards, a whole range of frustrated 'bourgeois' interests were being driven into the Congress. But they were a disparate lot, from large merchant shroffs and millowners to liquor distillers in South India and stultified rural capital of diverse sorts. Most of these interests were divided in their response to Congress campaigns. Nonetheless, between the two world wars, the Congress came to establish closer links with Indian capitalists and derived both power and resources from these connections.[38] At the same time, after 1918, the working

[36] D. Washbrook, *The Emergence of Provincial Politics: Madras Presidency, 1870–1920* (Cambridge, 1976), ch. 2.

[37] Bipan Chandra, *The Rise and Growth of Economic Nationalism in India: Economic Policies of the Indian National Leadership, 1880–1905* (New Delhi, 1966), p. 330.

[38] C. Markovits, *Indian Business and Nationalist Politics, 1931–39: The Indigenous Capitalist Class and the Rise of the Congress Party* (Cambridge, 1985); A. D. D. Gordon, *Businessmen and Politics: Rising Nationalism and a Modernising Economy, 1918–1933* (New Delhi,

classes established an increasingly prominent presence in the political arena. Strikes became more frequent, involved more workers and occurred on a larger scale than ever before. In any case, at the level of local and secondary leadership, there were a growing number of Congressmen who were drawn, sometimes by conviction, sometimes by expediency, into acting as spokesmen for labour in industrial disputes. At times, national leaders stepped forward as champions of labour in specific cases, notably those of Gandhi in Ahmedabad in 1918–20[39] and Bose in Jamshedpur in the late 1920s.[40] Indeed, the extension of the franchise made it increasingly important for politicians to pay closer attention to this constituency. Above all, it was imperative for the Congress to demonstrate its representative character and this depended in part upon its ability to bring the working classes into the nationalist fold. As labour registered an increasingly prominent presence in the political arena, the Congress developed closer links with a variety of commercial interests and especially with industrial capital. Fresh life was breathed into dilemmas and contradictions which had been with the Congress since 1885: how was it to attract working-class support without dividing its own ranks? How could it champion labour's cause without becoming the prisoner of the working classes?

At every stage of its development, the effectiveness of the Congress as a bargaining agent with the colonial state and, therefore, its ability to attach significant local interests, rested on its claim to represent the nation as a whole. To fortify this claim, the Congress leadership recognized that the party would have to speak with one voice. To demonstrate its representative character, it was essential for the Congress to expand and diversify its social base. But to speak with one voice, it had to ride the range on its socially diverse constituents and marshal them behind an inevitably thin facade of unity. This was always liable to narrow the range of options before the Congress as a movement of opposition to colonial rule. Since it orchestrated a complex and fragile network of alliances between disparate

1979); A. Mukherjee, 'The Indian Capitalist Class and Foreign Capital, 1927–47', *Studies in History*, 1:1 (1979), 105–48; Bipan Chandra, 'The Indian Capitalist Class and Imperialism before 1947', *Journal of Contemporary Asia*, 5:3 (1974), 309–26; Bipan Chandra, 'Jawaharlal Nehru and the Indian Capitalist Class in 1936', *Economic and Political Weekly*, 10:33–5 (1975), 1307–24; S. Sarkar, 'The Logic of Gandhian Nationalism: Civil Disobedience and the Gandhi–Irwin Pact (1930–31)', *Indian Historical Review*, 3:1 (1976), 114–46; B. Chatterji, *Trade, Tariffs and Empire: Lancashire and British Policy in India, 1919–1939* (Delhi, 1992).

[39] M. Desai, *A Righteous Struggle: A Chronicle of the Ahmedabad Textile Labourers' Fight for Justice* (Ahmedabad, 1951); E. Erikson, *Gandhi's Truth: On the Origins of Militant Non-Violence* (London, 1969); S. Patel, *The Making of Industrial Relations: The Ahmedabad Textile Industry, 1918–1939* (Delhi. 1987), ch. 3.

[40] Simeon, *The Politics of Labour under Late Colonialism*, chs. 2–3; V. Bahl, 'TISCO Workers' Struggle, 1920–28'; V. Bahl, *The Making of the Indian Working Class: The Case of the Tata Iron and Steel Company* (Delhi, 1995).

social groups and conflicting political interests negotiated on terms of limited advantage to each, it was committed to a strategy of glossing over what might divide and concentrating upon what was sure to unite its followers.[41] Programmes, propaganda and policies designed to 'harness capital to our side' were unlikely to attract labour and, further, they could lead the Congress to act antagonistically to the interests of the working classes. The constraint of speaking with one voice to London reduced the Congress to a babel of tongues when it spoke to the working classes. The price of accommodation at the top was often proliferating confusion at the base.

Moreover, there were several and persistent attempts to challenge the Congress's attempts to define or indeed represent the nation. Most obviously, the British repeatedly questioned the Congress claim to speak for the nation as a whole. Indeed imperial ideologues frequently went one step further and denied that there was, or ever had been, or indeed ever could be an Indian nation. In the 1880s, John Strachey had enunciated the doctrine that 'the first and most essential thing to learn about India – [is] that there is not, and never was an India . . . possessing . . . any sort of unity'.[42] If the subcontinent was teeming with countless distinct nationalities, it followed that the Congress could not possibly represent them all, let alone weld them into a single harmonious whole. Whereas, in the 1880s, colonial ideologues had dismissed the Congress as merely a clerisy of the Western-educated, who represented no one other than themselves, by the 1920s, they portrayed it as the instrument of the political agitator, seeking to manipulate the illiterate and the innocent, if contented, masses for their own selfish purposes. The Congress was unrepresentative, not only because 'the politically-minded class' was divorced from the 'real people', but also because it had failed to win and retain the confidence of the Muslims.[43] In this apparent failure to represent the Muslims, colonial discourse fixed on one of its perennial, indeed defining, themes. For colonial rulers feared above all that where the forces of darkness and superstition reigned, the masses, 'when captured by those who wilfully or

[41] A. Seal, *The Emergence of Indian Nationalism: Competition and Collaboration in the Later Nineteenth Century* (Cambridge, 1968); Johnson, *Provincial Politics and Indian Nationalism*, ch. 1.

[42] John Strachey, *India* (London, 1888), p. 5. See also Sir Auckland Colvin, *Audi Alterem Partem: Being Two Letters on Certain Aspects of the Indian National Congress Movement* (Simla, 1888); Richard Temple, *India in 1880* (London, 1880); Valentine Chirol, *Indian Unrest* (London, 1910); Sir Verney Lovett, *A History of the Indian Nationalist Movement* (London, 1920); P. C. Bamford, *Histories of the Non-Co-operation and Khilafat Movements* (Delhi, 1925; reprinted Delhi, 1974).

[43] For an excellent, recent account of colonial views of the Congress, see W. H. Morris-Jones, 'If It Be Real, What Does It Mean?': British Perceptions of the Indian National Congress', in Sisson and Wolpert (eds.), *Congress and Indian Nationalism*, pp. 90–118.

recklessly pour jars of paraffin upon their ignorance and credulity, can break into fanatical fury'.[44] Not only did colonial ideologues take it for granted that this fanaticism sprang from sources which lay outside the universe of reason and, therefore, beyond their grasp, but they were also apprehensive that the fury which it unleashed would exceed their power to control. This innate unreasonableness, this inherent fanaticism made it imperative for the British to rule India. But it could also swiftly render India ungovernable. That India might be granted independence at all could be nothing other than a tribute to the British achievement in forging a nation from such unpromising and fissiparous material; for some, it would constitute the 'fulfilment' of British rule.

The oldest apology for British rule, which, indeed, has outlasted it, was that in a land with a thousand definitions of the word, only the Collector could rule impartially and was therefore indispensable. Colonial suspicions were then enshrined in the principle of special and communal representation. Similarly when Ambedkar declaimed against what Gandhi and the Congress had done to the untouchables, he was interrogating the credibility and content of swaraj.[45] The 'two-nations theory', one Hindu, the other Muslim, proved to be the most devastating blow to the definition of a single nation, although there was no innate reason why this should have been the case.[46]

Within the fold of the Congress, too, there were ambiguities about the character of the nation which could only be resolved by refusing to define. Congress rhetoric in the UP acquired a Hindu idiom and a revivalist tone which alienated Muslims.[47] Brahmins and 'non-Brahmins' in the Deccan were agreed that the untouchables must be kept firmly in their place.[48] The association of the Congress with locally dominant peasants or urban capitalists often suggested that class divisions might obtrude upon equal rights in the nation. Thus, during the non-cooperation and civil disobedience campaigns, numerous businessmen grew anxious that the Congress agitations would 'create a feeling of disregard for authority' far beyond

[44] Sir Verney Lovett, *A History of the Indian Nationalist Movement*, pp. 247–8, cited by Morris-Jones, 'British Perceptions', p. 104.

[45] B. R. Ambedkar, *What Congress and Gandhi Have Done to the Untouchables* (Bombay, 1945).

[46] F. C. R. Robinson, *Separatism among Indian Muslims: The Politics of the United Provinces' Muslims, 1860–1923* (Cambridge, 1974); D. Page, *Prelude to Partition: The Indian Muslims and the Imperial System of Control* (Delhi, 1982); A. Jalal, *The Sole Spokesman: Jinnah, the Muslim League and the Demand for Pakistan* (Cambridge, 1985); G. Pandey, *The Construction of Communalism in Colonial North India* (Delhi, 1990); J. Chatterji, *Bengal Divided: Hindu Communalism and Partition, 1932–1947* (Cambridge, 1994).

[47] C. A. Bayly, 'Patrons and Politics in Northern India', in J. Gallagher, G. Johnson and A. Seal (eds.), *Locality, Province and Nation: Essays on Indian Politics* (Cambridge, 1973), pp. 29–68; Pandey, *The Ascendancy of the Congress*, ch. 5.

[48] GOB, Home (Special), File 363 (5) of 1928, MSA.

the capacity of even a swaraj government to remedy[49] and, in 1930, even the normally astute Ambalal Sarabhai predicted in panic that 'Bolshevik propaganda will find fertile soil in India', if things continued as they were.[50]

It was in this context of ambiguity, contradiction and conflict that the rhetoric and programme of the Congress began to take shape. Crucially, the very object or slogan of swaraj, self-rule, was re-defined and used by Gandhi to mean all things to all men: from dominion status to independent parliamentary government, from an expression of the grievances of Khilafat Muslims to the promise of a golden age, from devotion to the charkha to self-discipline and inner self-realization. The meanings of swaraj could range from the personal to the political, from the spiritual to the constitutional, from millenarian promise to immediate and concrete objectives. It offered flexibility but remained far too opaque to establish realizable connections between the sphere of daily social conflict and the sense of a programmatic politics. Its strength was that it offered a receptacle into which the aggrieved might pour whatever they chose. Its persistent weakness, however, was that it seemed to offer a great deal in general and nothing very much in particular. It offered a programme which was not so much flexible as formless, and highly vulnerable to competing programmes and ideologies.

Although Congress was not, as Nehru once pointed out, 'a labour organization and to expect it to act as a pure labour organization is a mistake',[51] the terms which Congress offered in its attempt to pull the working classes into a nationalist alliance were not fashioned to consistently encourage them. Indeed, for the Congress, the imperative of placing its representative credentials before the colonial state was always likely to narrow its freedom of manoeuvre in developing a programme and rhetoric which might embed itself within the political assumptions and vocabulary of the working classes. Since the Congress was always less a political party than a field of political action and an arena for the brokerage of particular interests, there was a bewildering variety of publicists who spoke in its name. The audiences which they addressed were similarly diverse and the interests which they represented, and which the Congress, whether at the local, provincial or the all-India level, sought to coalesce, were heterogeneous and divided. As a result, it is impossible to capture the rhetoric of nationalism in a single voice or a consistent and coherent social message. Indeed, its rhetoric was often cacophonous. But it is not merely by generalization of sweeping and magisterial simplicity

[49] Lalji Naranji to Thakurdas, 28 March 1930, Thakurdas Papers, File 91, NMML.
[50] Ambalal Sarabhai to Thakurdas, 28 March 1930, *ibid*, NMML.
[51] J. Nehru to D. B. Kulkarni, 10 September 1929, AICC Papers, File 16, 1929, NMML.

that we might identify its dominant forms. It is possible to discern the broad parameters within which the Congress sought to address and lead the working classes. Gandhi's rhetoric came increasingly to inflect nationalist discourse and to provide it with its distinct vocabulary. Gandhi's political rhetoric will, thus, be used here as a point of entry to the examination of the relationship between the Congress and the working classes.

The rhetoric of nationalism rarely sought, least of all before its heterogeneous audiences, to define a particular working-class interest, or to speak, even within a given context, exclusively to its immediate objectives. Of course, the Congress did not readily admit the distinction between the interests and aspirations of the working classes and those of the nation, and when it did so, it was usually not in order to represent the former but to control and constrain them in the name of the latter. From a perspective which assumed the coherence of a working-class interest or insisted on distinguishing it from national aspirations, the Congress appeared as the purveyors of the doctrine of class conciliation.

Moreover, the relationship of these politicians and publicists to their popular base, as well as their influence within the Congress as a whole, was often determined by local circumstances and, especially, their own place within local structures of power. Yet, while many publicists addressed the working classes in the name of the Congress, the latter engaged or distanced itself from these local movements and publicists, according to its perception and evaluation of their social and political character. In the 1930s, as the Congress became increasingly centralized, and the unitary structure of its formal organization was strengthened, only those could champion the particular interests of the working classes who had nothing to lose by alienating local party bosses and propertied and commercial magnates.

There were, in particular, two recurrent themes in nationalist rhetoric in relation to the working classes. First, considerable emphasis was laid upon the partnership between labour and especially Indian capital. This theme had a long history. Tilak, who had once opposed factory legislation, on the grounds that the millworkers of Bombay preferred to work long hours, advised the latter in 1919, in the midst of a wave of strikes, and on a rare occasion when he addressed a workers' meeting, that they should sink their differences with their employers and combine against the British.[52] Lala Lajpat Rai, in his presidential address to the All-India Trade Union Congress, added a plea for equity to this doctrine of class harmony. 'Labour and capital', he declared 'must meet on equal ground

---

[52] Cashman, *The Myth of the Lokamanya*, p. 185.

and join hands to develop Indian industries . . . at present neither the
government nor the capitalist is disposed to treat the worker fairly and
equally.'[53] Similarly, Joseph Baptista, once a Fabian in Cambridge and
later a Tilakite in India, in his welcoming address, looked forward to 'the
higher ideal of partnership', without which 'the well-being of workers will
never be secured'. For workers and capitalists, he observed, were 'partners and co-workers, and not buyers and sellers of labour. They are all
engaged in promoting the well-being of society.' But this ideal of partnership, he argued, would only be realized 'by the power of unions, strikes
and boycotts'.[54]

To Gandhi, of course, partnership was scarcely a novel idea and it was a
theme to which he was repeatedly to return. 'When mill-hands learn to
identify themselves with the rest of the mill-owners', Gandhi told the
Ahmedabad millworkers in 1920, 'they will rise and with them will rise
the industries of our country.'[55] While suggesting thereby that the interests of labour and capital were intimately linked, Gandhi also eschewed
the notion that strikes may be used as a threat, or as an instrument of
coercion. But it would be misleading to conclude that Gandhi was merely
offering a mystical rendition of the truisms and dogma of the capitalist
classes. In this instance, as in many others, Gandhi intervened in political
discourse to transform it and, indeed, he developed and deployed the
existing discussion in a strikingly fresh direction.

During the 1918 strike, Gandhi developed a code of ethics, a philosophy of practice, to govern industrial relations and he elaborated it over
the next two decades. It was founded on a supposition of the interdependence of labour and capital. In 1918, Gandhi sometimes lamented the
strike, rather whimsically, as a family dispute. In so doing, he referred at
the same time to the interdependence of the interests of labour and
capital, rich and poor, majur and seth, as well as to the fact that Ambalal
Sarabhai, the President of the Millowners' Association, was the brother of
the workers' leader, Anasuyabehn. Earlier, when, in December 1917 Seth
Ambalal had first sought his advice about how to deal with the weavers'
demand for higher wages, Gandhi had told him to 'remove their discontent' by 'binding them with the silken thread of love'.[56] In February 1918,
in the midst of the strike, even the Collector of Ahmedabad was led to
report to his less sanguine and less credulous superiors in Bombay that 'a

[53] *AITUC – Fifty Years On: Documents,* vol. I (AITUC, New Delhi, 1973), p. 29.
[54] *Ibid.,* p. 12.   [55] *Young India,* 6 October 1920.
[56] Gandhi to Ambalal Sarabhai, 21 December 1917, *CWMG,* vol. XIV, p. 115. Indeed,
Gandhi went so far as to read him the lesson that he 'should satisfy the weavers for the
sake of Shrimati Anasuyabehn' who 'has a soul which is absolutely pure', thereby placing
Ambalal, as he pointed out, 'under a double obligation: to please the workers and earn a
sister's blessings'.

piquant feature of the whole affair' was that the dispute 'partakes of the nature of a family one and unlike many family disputes is conducted with a complete lack of acerbity'.[57] Many years later, in 1925, Gandhi re-stated his 'ideal' that 'capital and labour . . . should be a great family living in unity and harmony' with the capitalists serving as 'the trustees' for the moral and material 'welfare of the labouring classes'.[58]

In seeking to reconcile the interests of labour and capital within the figurative framework of the family, Gandhi argued that workers had a right to their needs but these could only be properly assessed in terms of the economic condition of the industry or the employers. But he did not dwell too long or define too carefully the criteria by which the workers' needs or the financial condition of industry might be assessed. Gandhi did insist, however, that the workers' demands, like their means of securing them, should be 'just'. Thus, workers should 'ask only for what is our right'[59] and not seek 'merely to take advantage of the capitalist's position'.[60] They were to refrain, therefore, from making demands 'at will', 'irrespective of the employer's financial condition'.[61] In this light, it may be supposed that it was the self-control of the workers which would set the limit on their demands. But he was 'aware', he wrote in 1921, 'that the labouring classes in India has not yet become enlightened enough to have the ability to regulate the relations between labour and capital on a just basis'.[62] Until that time came, labour was in need of 'disinterested friendship'.[63] To such potential friends of labour, his advice was that they should aim

to elevate the workmen by creating between the two parties a family relationship . . . And to secure this end there is no path like Truth. Mere increase in wages should not satisfy you; you must also watch by what means they get it and how they spend it.[64]

It was also, then, the duty of the workers' adviser, in the case of Ahmedabad in 1918 happily himself, to curb his followers, if this became necessary, and to ensure that their demands were just. The workers' adviser, in Gandhi's view, should also seek to effect a consensus, and persuade the employers of the justice of the workers' demands. If the employers rejected a 'just' demand, then the claim would have to be submitted to a neutral 'umpire' or even a 'panch' for arbitration, whose

[57] Collector of Ahmedabad to Secretary, GOB, Judicial, 25 February 1918, Bombay Confidential Proceedings, Judicial Department, for March 1918, vol. 36, p. 33, OIOC.   [58] *Young India*, 20 August 1925.
[59] Ahmedabad Millhands' Strike, Leaflet no. 7, 4 March 1918, *CWMG*, vol. XIV, p. 236.
[60] *Young India*, 6 October 1920.
[61] Desai, *A Righteous Struggle*, p. 49; *CWMG*, vol. XIV, p. 233.
[62] *Young India*, 8 June 1921.   [63] *Ibid.*, 1 June 1921.   [64] *Ibid.*

decision would be binding on both sides.[65] Employers who refused to consider the just needs of the workers or, in the case of disagreement, countenance arbitration, had succumbed to 'the Western or modern devilish kind of justice' in which 'each thus thinks only of himself and is bound not to think of the other'.[66] If the workers had no option but to embark upon a strike, they should act as satyagrahis. 'The workers' struggle', he wrote in 1918, 'depends solely on the justice of their demand and the rightness of their action'.[67] By using just and non-coercive means to struggle for just demands, the workers would ensure that the employers would 'rectify their mistake'.[68] In fact, the satisfaction of a 'just' demand 'will not harm the employers' interests but will do them good'.[69] Thus, during the 1918 strike, Gandhi had insisted: 'We can never wish or do ill to the employer, and in every action of ours the idea of their good is also always present. We want to secure the good of the workers while safeguarding the good of the employers.'[70]

Gandhi's ruminations on industrial relations may be interpreted as simply an arcane expression of capitalist interests. It is possible to argue – indeed, it has frequently been suggested – that once Gandhi's rhetoric is stripped of reference to the principles of satyagraha and ahimsa, truth and non-violence, little remains to distinguish it from the case which employers throughout the world had argued for over a hundred years. Certainly, employers in various industries in India in the 1920s and 1930s had sought to defuse workers' grievances – whether wage demands or protests against job losses – by resolutely placing them in the context of the trade conditions, or what the market could bear. They would warmly welcome the argument that wage demands ought to be governed strictly by the financial condition of the employer and of the industry as a whole, which in any case was difficult to ascertain without their fullest co-operation. Employers were by no means enthusiastic, not even in Ahmedabad, about subjecting their business practices and their labour relations to the scrutiny and the judgement of outsiders. At the same time, arbitration proceedings, which appeared equitable in theory, were quite the opposite in practice, for they tended to favour the stronger side in any dispute – which for the most part meant the employers. Otherwise, arbitration tribunals, established to effect an agreed and viable settlement, were liable to find that their recommendations were set aside or simply ignored and their objectives subverted. It has even been suggested that, as the colonial state elaborated arbitration and conciliation procedures in trade disputes legislation after 1929, they proceeded along lines which were not fundamentally different from those which Gandhi

[65] *Ibid.*   [66] Desai, *A Righteous Struggle*, p. 49.   [67] *Ibid.*, p. 61.   [68] *Ibid.* p. 42.
[69] *Ibid.*, p. 46.   [70] *Ibid.*, p. 45.

had elaborated in Ahmedabad a whole decade earlier.[71] In fact, this body of legislation, including the Trade Disputes Act which was introduced in Bombay by the Congress provincial ministry in 1938, had its origins perhaps rather more clearly in the Whitley Councils and the legislation being formulated in Britain than in Gandhi's thought. Each of these arguments employed by capitalists, however, can be said to have found a resonance in Gandhi's precepts only by ignoring other parts of his strictures and obligations represented in his ideal state of capital–labour relations. It is significant that while some traders and industrialists, notably G. D. Birla, became devoted followers or at least grasped that Gandhi's influence served as a force for conservatism, there were many capitalists in the 1920s and 1930s who viewed satyagraha with suspicion and feared that civil disobedience would lead to chaos and anarchy.

If it is implausible to portray Gandhi as a capitalist ideologue, it is, conversely, misleading to suppose that his rhetoric was devised to appeal to the class interests of workers while at the same time somehow compromising or undermining them. To suggest that Gandhi simply wrapped a message of class conciliation in a vocabulary of resistance and opposition is to take an overly simplistic and instrumental view of his rhetoric. Nor can it begin to explain why his rhetoric exercised any attraction for the working classes. The discourse of class was alien to Gandhi's intellectual and political idiom. When he addressed the issue, it was within terms whose scope and reach were wider and more expansive. It would be highly reductivist to measure his precepts and practice, and their appeal to workers, strictly by the ideology of class. On the other hand, it is important to recognize that the 'class interests' of the working classes, far from being uniform and homogeneous, were themselves fractured by relations of power, emanating from village and neighbourhood, caste and religion, gender and, indeed, the very process of production.

To grasp why (say) the working classes were sometimes able to find a resonance in his rhetoric, it is essential to appreciate Gandhi's ability to develop the blandest metaphor and the most platitudinous axiom in a distinctly subversive direction. This, for instance, is how Gandhi extrapolated his notion of the industrial 'family' and of the role of capitalists as 'trustees' for the workers. 'Speaking as a labourer, like you', he told the workers of the Maharaja Mills in Bangalore in August 1927,

I do not think there need be any clash between capital and labour. Each is dependent on the other. What is essential today is that the capitalist should not lord it over the labourer. In my opinion, the mill-hands are as much the proprietors of their mills as the shareholders, and when the mill-owners realise that the

[71] Patel, *The Making of Industrial Relations.*

mill-hands are as much mill-owners as they, there will be no quarrel between them . . . When you know that the mill is as much yours as of the mill-owners, you will never damage your property, you will never angrily destroy cloth or machinery with a view to squaring your quarrel with the mill-owners.[72]

The notion of the interdependence of capital and labour could now be read as something akin to a syndicalist argument for workers' control. Several months later, he returned to a similar theme while elaborating his fond metaphor of the family. 'The relation between mill-agents and mill-hands', he declared in May 1928 (while the communist general strike in Bombay was in full swing), 'ought to be one of father and children, or as between blood-brothers.' He deplored the tendency of the Ahmedabad millowners to describe themselves sometimes as 'masters' and their employees as their 'servants' as 'a negation of ahimsa'. Thus, he told the millowners:

What I expect of you, therefore, is that you should hold all your riches as a trust to be used solely in the interests of those who sweat for you, and to whose industry and labour you owe all your position and prosperity. I want you to make your labourers co-partners of your wealth.

Indeed, he advised them to respect 'the mutual obligations of love' as they exist between father and son, for thereby they would be able to bring about 'an end to all labour disputes' and render trade unions redundant. But this ideal could not be realized, he warned, so long as 'there is a single mill-hand who does not regard the mill in which he works as his own'.[73]

For the millhand to 'regard' the mill as his own was not, of course, for him to own it. If the millowners, presumably all capitalists, owed 'all [their] position and prosperity' to the 'industry and labour' 'of those who sweat' for them, it did not necessarily follow that the workers could ask for control and ownership as theirs by right. For workers to seek control, let alone ownership, would in 1918, for instance, have amounted to a negation of ahimsa, to the extent that it sought to usurp and undermine the capitalist. But there is no reason to suppose that the working classes were, for Gandhi, precluded from justly making such demands under changed circumstances as relations between capital and labour changed, and especially as his social and economic ideal of a world of self-sufficient producers came to be realized. Nor did the notion that the workers should be encouraged to regard the mill as their own imply that Gandhi was seeking to destroy the distinction between labour and capital. On the contrary, by seeking to ensure 'harmony' and mutual trust between them, he appeared, if anything, to affirm it. It is true that he sometimes appeared to espouse a labour theory of value, for which he owed something to

[72] *Young India*, 4 August 1927.   [73] *Ibid.*, 10 May 1928.

Ruskin. Labour, he insisted, represented a form of capital.[74] Without labour, capital would not 'fructify', just as the very existence of labour depended upon capital. What capital offered to complement the skill and strength of labour was not wealth alone, but also, as Gandhi was sometimes led to observe, 'intelligence and tact'; and 'labour will never attain to that intelligence', for if it did, 'labour will cease to be labour and become itself the master'.[75] If it was incumbent upon the capitalist to act as the 'trustee' for the moral and material welfare of the labouring classes, to act as the father of his workers, it was obviously not for the son to damage, hurt or replace, let alone destroy the father. Yet, this relationship did impose upon both sides a 'mutual obligation of love', which would enable workers to come to see the capitalist's property as their own.

So Gandhi was no advocate of workers' control or theorist of the dissolution of capitalism. But there is room within his account to imagine a time when 'labour will cease to be labour', when the son, to develop Gandhi's metaphor, might inherit his father's wealth, 'intelligence and tact', and when it could be wholly appropriate and just, rather than coercive, for workers to demand to own the capital they had helped to create as no more than 'what is our right'. In the meanwhile, what Gandhi offered the working classes, and insisted upon in their name, was their greater empowerment. For as he was to write in the late 1930s, when labour and capital recognize the true nature of their interdependence, they will learn 'to respect and appreciate each other as equal partners in a common enterprise' and realize that 'they need not regard each other as inherently irreconcilable antagonists'. The working man, he lamented, was insufficiently organized, which

prevented him from realizing the power and full dignity of his status. He has been taught to believe that his wages have to be dictated by capitalists instead of demanding his own terms . . . It is the grossest of superstitions for the working man to believe that he is helpless before the employers.[76]

There is so little correspondence between the language of class and Gandhi's own inimitable vocabulary that it will always be misleading to seek to measure the specific gravity of 'classness' in his rhetoric and extremely narrow to ask if he served in this context to encourage class conciliation or class solidarity. At the same time, once it is recognized that for all the ambiguities and contradictions of his pronouncements, he sometimes developed his ideas, and they could similarly be interpreted and extended by his audience, in more radical and subversive directions, it becomes far less plausible to cast him in the role of a capitalist ideologue or damn him as the agent of working-class betrayal.

[74] *Harijan*, 23 March 1934.   [75] *Young India*, 1 June 1921.   [76] *Harijan*, 3 July 1937.

The second theme in Congress rhetoric relating to labour and industrial relations was the notion that workers should sacrifice current needs for future bliss. Present grievances which could not be resolved under British rule would be redressed by swaraj, the ultimate goal for which the masses should rally behind the Congress banner. Strikes in Indian-owned industries only served, it was argued, to exacerbate foreign domination. It was considered incumbent upon labour to refrain from industrial action, but it was also imperative that Indian capitalists fulfil their obligation to satisfy the basic needs of the workforce. Thus when Subhas Chandra Bose intervened in the TISCO strike in 1929, Sir Ibrahim Rahimtoola was able to reassure Birla that the workers' champion would seek an early settlement because he took the view that, 'if as a result of the strike, the industry is forced into other than Indian hands, it would be highly detrimental to national progress'.[77] This doctrine could serve not only to alienate workers, especially those in the midst of a strike, but it also placed a weapon in the hands of the employers to wield against trade unions and their leaders, not infrequently Congressmen, who attempted to intervene in industrial disputes. It was an argument which might have seemed plausible when predominantly Indian employers in Bombay, Ahmedabad or Jamshedpur sought to retrench their labour force or increase workloads or cut wages in the interests of national progress. But the situation could become infinitely more complex when, for instance, the expatriate British owners of the Calcutta jute mills justified their own rationalization schemes during the 1929 general strike by arguing that any alternative to reducing jobs and wages, and increasing workloads, would simply surrender a share of their market to Dundee and foreign competitors in general.[78] Certainly, a doctrine which invited workers to reconcile themselves to job losses, lower wages and higher workloads in the national interest was likely to have limited sectional appeal. Furthermore, it was a doctrine which employers could turn against trade unions in general, and those Congressmen in particular, who attempted to intervene in industrial disputes. The recurrent themes of Congress rhetoric on the labour question, it might seem, were so unlikely to attract working-class support that it may reasonably be asked whether this was ever their intention.

In the rhetoric of the Congress, social conflicts and class struggles were frequently subordinated to its political objectives. Sometimes, the con-

---

[77] Sir Ibrahim Rahimtoola to G. D. Birla, 9 July 1929, Thakurdas Papers, File 42 (II), NMML.
[78] *Bengal Legislative Proceedings, 5–9 August 1929* (Calcutta, 1930), p. 302, quoted by B. Chakrabarty, *Subhas Chandra Bose and Middle Class Radicalism: A Study in Indian Nationalism, 1928–1940* (London, 1990), p. 72; P. Saha, *History of the Working Class Movement in Bengal* (New Delhi, 1978), pp. 114–31; Goswami, 'Multiple Images: Jute Mill Strikes of 1929 and 1937', 560–3.

sideration of the former was postponed in favour of the realization of the latter. But the interpretation of this rhetoric as conclusive proof of the social character of the Congress as a 'bourgeois party' would be misleading. The Congress did not represent a conspiracy to dupe or betray the working classes and the peasantry or to deflect their natural propensity to revolutionary action. It was not, indeed, the agency of a 'passive revolution'. Nationalism was primarily a discourse of political exclusion, not of social conflict or economic grievance. The social evils of British India were perceived and portrayed as the outcome of the political injustice of foreign, imperial rule. To end this political injustice would not, as Gandhi frequently warned, necessarily lead to the correction or the resolution of the society's wrongs. But without independence, Indians could not emancipate themselves from its thraldom. On the contrary, independence from British rule would merely constitute a 'formal' freedom, if Indians did not effect 'reform from within', achieve 'inward freedom' or attain individual 'self-realization'. But even this would not suffice. 'I am afraid I must repeat the gospel to you and remind you', Gandhi told a meeting of village workers at Nagpur in March 1935, 'that when you demand swaraj, you do not want swaraj for yourself alone, but for your neighbour too'.[79] When the Congress advised the postponement of social struggle until the achievement of independence, this was not simply an expression of its determination to subordinate the class interests of the poor to its own long-term political goals – indeed, this would be a rather mechanistic and narrow interpretation. Rather, it reflected its diagnosis of the underlying cause of existing social evils in terms of the larger system of colonial oppression, political coercion and tyrannical power.

Of course, from the earliest days of their rule, the British had drawn Indians into the structure of governance at its various levels. As the British began to associate more Indians with their rule, the differential access to power, which Indians thus gained, began to divide them. Increasingly, in the nineteenth century, the British were drawn into reconciling two contradictory aims in their government of India. On the one hand, they sought to unify and centralize their government in order to enable them to appropriate and deploy Indian resources more effectively for imperial purposes. On the other hand, they had to offset the consequences of an increasingly meddlesome government and to secure the acquiescence of their subjects by allowing them larger areas of influence and control within the colonial system, preferably at points which would not limit their freedom to work their dominion in their own larger, global imperial interests. It was a persistent, perhaps defining, theme of colonial dis-

---

[79] *Harijan*, 1 March 1935, in *The Moral and Political Writings of Mahatma Gandhi*, vol. III: *Non-Violent Resistance and Social Transformation*, ed. R. Iyer (Oxford, 1987), p. 262.

course that India was a museum of tribes, castes, races, religions and even languages, each of which needed to be classified and represented. It is not surprising, therefore, that as the British searched for a principle of differentiation and classification, they should have found these categories of ethnicity, language, caste and religion, however fictive the unities they presumed, to be the most compelling. Indeed, it became essential for Indians to define themselves along these communal lines to seek representation within, and to widen their access to, the structure, and the resources, of British government. Ethnicity thus became a basic principle of social and political competition. In this way, the British imparted to the protean languages of Indian politics a fresh vocabulary of sectarianism, a political language of social and communal interests within which competition of diverse sorts and a wide range of conflicts were likely to be expressed.

To the extent that its protagonists may have appeared to be in quest of a larger share of political power, nationalism might be seen as the political programme of Indian elites with limited social interest or appeal. But its significance was widened by two factors. First, the terms on which Indians might extend their place within the representative system and bureaucratic structure of British rule was of considerable interest to those groups who were unlikely to benefit personally from it. As some social groups obtained and consolidated their position within the structure of governance, or the educational system, it made their protection and patronage accessible to their friends and villagers, caste-fellows and co-religionists, and created among them at least the promise and opportunity for social mobility. Substantial interests, however defined, which were seemingly backward in gaining access to English education, government employment or political office, might receive official encouragement to advance or be offered special representation. The demand for a greater share of power, especially when it was couched in terms of the representation of caste, religious and ethnic groupings, could discover an appeal among those who gained nothing directly from it.

Second, Gandhian ideology, which increasingly inflected the rhetoric of the Congress, could be stretched to include those whom the electoral system did not reach and who were unlikely to wield any influence within the bureaucracy. Significantly, Gandhians abjured power and their influence derived in part from their dissociation from the structure of power. Some non-cooperators became Swarajists; many satyagrahis wished to accept office. But Gandhi and his followers were not tainted by the unseemly rush for a limited share of power to wield against those who had none. Their rhetoric of self-denial and self-sacrifice, and their ennobling of 'garibi' identified them with the 'deprived' and 'downtrodden'. 'Swaraj for me', Gandhi had written in 1924, 'means the freedom for the meanest of our countrymen . . . I am not interested in freeing India from merely the English yoke. I am bent upon freeing India from any yoke whatsoever.'[80] To be realized, swaraj would have to extend beyond independence. It would have to encompass universal adult suffrage and require the transcendence of the coercion, manipulation and exploitation of the powerless. It could bring about a society 'in which every man and woman knows . . . that no one should want anything that others cannot have with equal labour'.[81] In a speech to the Ahmedabad millworkers, who were on the point of taking industrial action in response to a threatened wage cut of 20 per cent in 1936, Gandhi told them that the 'key to Swaraj' lay in the villages which were 'in a worse plight' than even those who lived in the city: 'When I succeed in ridding the villages of their poverty, I have won Swaraj for you and the whole of India . . . Their deliverance is also yours.'[82]

III

Political programmes are not wafted on rhetoric alone. How the working classes interpreted the rhetoric of the Congress, as well as the nature of their response to its programme, was also influenced by the role which the party played in working-class life and working-class politics. Indeed, popular perceptions of the political interventions of the Congress could also shape how its rhetoric was interpreted. As government policies, at any level from district and municipality to the centre, increasingly impinged upon the working classes, the scope for politicians to act as mediators between them and the state increased. How they performed this role would determine how they were perceived by the working classes. From the 1890s, in the aftermath of the plague epidemic, urban improvement and town planning, housing and public provision, slum clearance and sanitation, acquired a growing significance on local political agendas and in the public domain. They were matters of immediate concern to the working classes. The response of local politicians to such issues, in addition to their role in labour disputes, became important criteria by which they were assessed.

As Indian politicians exercised greater power in municipal and provincial politics, so workers came to assess them and their political associates by the initiatives they took to ameliorate the social conditions of their neighbourhoods and to improve their access to housing and employment.

[80] *Young India*, 12 June 1924.
[81] *Harijan*, 28 July 1946, in Iyer (ed.), *The Moral and Political Writings*, vol. III, p. 232.
[82] *Harijan*, 7 November 1936.

Thus, the Ahmedabad Textile Labour Association's role in municipal politics played an important part in enabling it to rebuild its organization, regain its credibility and revive its fortunes after the mill strike of 1923. In addition, following Gandhi into 'constructive work', the ATLA's activities now focused upon education, social reform, housing and flood relief. By the mid-1920s, its membership exceeded a quarter of the workforce and between 1928 and 1930, it doubled yet again.[83] Similarly, in the mid-1920s, the working classes in Madras 'became disillusioned' with, and turned against, the Swarajists because they 'had shown little real interest in the industrial divisions of the city in such pressing needs as drainage, lighting and adequate housing'.[84] Similar issues dominated the political responses of the North Indian urban poor and shaped their political identity. Indeed, the success of the Congress Socialists in the mid-1930s in attracting the support of the urban poor hinged on their ability and willingness to write these needs into their political agendas.[85]

Working-class responses to the Congress were also informed by the role which the latter played in the sphere of industrial relations. What the Congress as a national institution could offer the working classes was a wider focus for specific disputes. Its influence with the state and the access of its politicians to the councils of government sometimes made the Congress a powerful ally. This influence enabled it, for instance, to secure the position of the Ahmedabad Textile Labour Association as the sole bargaining agent in the city's textile industry. With the exception of the Ahmedabad Textile Labour Association, the Congress eschewed any direct connection with the trade unions. Nevertheless, numerous Congressmen intervened in industrial disputes and offered themselves as publicists of labour's cause. They often acted in this context in their individual capacities and not as agents of the Congress. Some, like Gandhi and Subhas Chandra Bose, boasted a national prominence; most were drawn from the secondary leadership or local-level publicists of the Congress. The growing rewards for representing labour in the formal institutions of the state attracted such men to this field of political activity. Their calculations were not entirely misplaced. Many of these publicists rose to prominence within the Congress itself or came to dominate local or provincial politics. Gulzarilal Nanda, the main force of the Ahmedabad Textile Labour Association, and V. V. Giri, the railway trade unionist of South India, became Labour Ministers in the provincial Congress governments of 1937–39 and occupied important central cabinet offices in the 1950s and 1960s. Nanda was twice a caretaker Prime

[83] Patel, *The Making of Industrial Relations*, pp. 81–92.
[84] Murphy, *Unions in Conflict*, p. 103.
[85] Gooptu, 'The Political Culture of the Urban Poor in North India', ch. 5.

Minister in the 1960s while Giri was to become the President of India in the 1970s.[86]

The increasing interest of a growing number of publicists in the conditions of the working classes, which first became fully evident in labour politics in the immediate aftermath of the first world war, is perhaps most clearly grasped in relation to two developments. First, between 1900 and 1920, famines and epidemics, the debate about the causes of Indian poverty and the destruction of Indian industry, had directed attention to the social conditions of the urban poor. In the context of the swadeshi campaign of 1905–8 and anxieties about the social consequences of industrialization, it is not surprising that humanitarian sentiment should have drawn middle-class youth, many of them lawyers and doctors, into 'social service', the amelioration of the conditions of the poor and necessarily into the representation of their interests to the state and the mediation of their disputes with their employers. N. M. Joshi's involvement with labour's cause developed from his activities on behalf of the Social Service League, which was inextricably linked with the Bombay Textile Labour Union.[87] S. K. Bole and H. A. Talcherkar were social workers who organized the Kamgar Hitwardhak Sabha, which played a prominent role in the general strike of 1919 in Bombay, and they were subsequently to carry their connections into the Bombay Textile Labour Union in 1925.[88] Anasuyabehn Sarabhai had been engaged in setting up schools for the children of millworkers when they approached her to represent them in their disputes with their employers.[89] Chelvapathy Chetty and Ramanujulu Naidu, who led the Binny's strike in 1918, were primarily associated with a religious association to moralize the working classes.[90] B. P. Wadia, the founder of the Madras Labour Union, N. S. Ramaswamy Iyengar, protagonist of the Coimbatore Labour Union, and B. Shiva Rao, labour leader, public servant and the outstanding writer on Indian industrial workers, came to the labour movement through the Theosophical Society, while the charismatic Tiru Vi Kalyansundaram Mudaliar discovered his interest in working-class politics through Saiva Siddhanta philosophy.[91] Social work and a humanitarian, even philanthropic, concern for the plight of the working classes did not necessarily precede – it could sometimes follow – the interest and engagement of these publicists with trade unions. The self-proclaimed mother of the

[86] V. V. Giri, *My Life and Times*, vol. I (Delhi, 1976).
[87] V. B. Karnik, *N. M. Joshi – Servant of India* (Bombay, 1972).
[88] 'The Kamgar Hitwardhak Sabha: A Brief Sketch', *Indian Textile Journal*, 29 (July 1919), 177–9 and *ibid.*, 29 (August 1919), 209–10.
[89] Desai, *A Righteous Struggle*, p. 4; Erikson, *Gandhi's Truth*, pp. 300–2; Patel, *The Making of Industrial Relations*, p. 38.   [90] Murphy, *Unions in Conflict*, pp. 64–5.
[91] *Ibid.*, p. 90.

Bengal jute workers, Santosh Kumari Devi, recalled how she 'started the labour movement' in the early 1920s:

> I went to almost all the jute mills at Naihati, Garifa, Halisahar, Bhatpara, Sodepur to organize the labourers. Over and above making the labourers members of the jute workers' union, we set up night schools and even health centres for working women and children in some centres . . . Unfortunately the national leaders of that time gave little or no thought for the toiling masses. Of course, I worked there in the name of the Congress and hence some of the more conscious [sic] workers were attracted towards the Congress. My concept was that the Congress should come forward to organize the working class, so that the workers in their turn realised the importance of the Congress.[92]

Second, in the first two decades of the twentieth century, political reform, the extension of the franchise and the proliferation of new municipal councils created fresh opportunities in public life. Not only did it allow politicians a certain autonomy from their patrons in the mofussil, but it granted those with weaker access to power the opportunity to shake the grip of established politicians and their networks on the existing political institutions, by widening their base of support.[93] Some publicists attempted to develop this following by representing the new 'backward caste' or 'communal' constituencies which were being brought into existence. Others presented themselves as protectors of the poor and guardians of the deprived, and stepped forward readily as spokesmen for the workers during industrial disputes.

Congress publicists who thus styled themselves as advocates of the workers' cause often had an ambiguous relationship with the party. In the 1910s and 1920s, the character of the Congress changed quickly, its ideological and political identity appeared constantly in flux and its fortunes flowed and ebbed dramatically. Its organizational machinery, first fashioned during the early 1920s – possibly the most enduring legacy of non-cooperation – fell into disuse later in the decade and was revived as an effective force only in the mid-1930s.[94] It was only then – and then, too, not very consistently – that the freedom with which publicists moved into or out of the Congress, and sometimes just as readily into or out of other political groupings, was curtailed. As the Congress geared itself to

---

[92] Santosh Kumari Devi, 'How I Started The Labour Movement', unpublished memoir, cited by M. Chattopadhyay, 'Santosh Kumari Devi: A Pioneering Labour Leader', *Social Scientist*, 128 (January 1984), 65; Sen, 'Women Workers in the Bengal Jute Industry', esp. ch. 6.

[93] Washbrook, *The Emergence of Provincial Politics*; Bayly, *The Local Roots of Indian Politics*; Rajat Ray, *Social Conflict and Political Unrest in Bengal, 1875–1927* (Delhi, 1986); Robinson, *Separatism Among Indian Muslims*; Cashman, *The Myth of the Lokamanya*.

[94] Gopal Krishna, 'The Development of the Congress as a Mass Organization, 1918–1923', *JAS*, 25:3 (1966), 413–30; Tomlinson, *The Indian National Congress and the Raj*, pp. 33–5.

contest the 1937 elections, the incentive to move into other groupings, less likely to triumph at the polls, declined. Membership of the Congress, or the adoption of its nomenclature, does not provide a ready or reliable guide to the political and ideological identity of the individual publicist.

Between 1914 and 1922, a wide range of politicians identified themselves with working-class causes. For instance, we are told, in Madras Presidency, 'most of the labour leaders in the immediate post-war period were either supporters or members of . . . the Indian National Congress'.[95] 'Non-cooperators', who are said to have formed 15 per cent of all trade union office holders in Bengal between 1918 and 1921, made up the largest single group of 'outsiders' among labour leaders, while more than a further 10 per cent styled themselves simply as 'nationalists'.[96] Some of these 'outsiders' in Bengal, notably S. N. Haldar and Byomkesh Chakrabarti, were invited by the steelworkers of Jamshedpur to represent them during the strikes of 1920.[97] Local publicists of the Home Rule League in Bombay intervened in labour disputes and sought to establish their presence in the mill districts after 1917 and played a prominent role in the early stages of the general strike of 1919.[98]

It should not be supposed, however, that by virtue of their intervention, these publicists determined the shape of workers' politics. On the contrary, their role was more usually governed by the momentum of workers' industrial and political action. Although a majority of trade union posts were held by 'outsiders' in Bengal, they were involved in less than one-fifth of the strikes which occurred between January 1918 and December 1921.[99] Similarly, 'almost all the strikes between 1918 and 1922 and later on' in Madras Presidency were initiated by the workers 'very often without knowledge of the outside leaders'. Since these leaders were generally 'extremely nervous and cautious about initiating strikes', they were frequently 'embarrassed' by workers' actions.[100] Similarly, in Ahmedabad, the aftermath of the 1918 dispute witnessed numerous strikes in individual mills in which the local Gandhians played only the most minimal role. The non-cooperation movement provided a further spur to industrial action. Strikes now continued to occur without the direction of

[95] Murphy, *Unions in Conflict*, p. 63.
[96] Gourlay, 'Nationalists, Outsiders and the Labour Movement in Bengal', p. 39.
[97] Bahl, 'TISCO Workers' Struggle', 37–40.
[98] 'A Report from the Commissioner of Police, Bombay, to Government of Bombay, Concerning Political Developments before and during 1919', Curry Papers, Box IV, nos. 54 and 55, Centre of South Asian Studies, Cambridge.
[99] Gourlay, 'Nationalists, Outsiders and the Labour Movement', pp. 36–7.
[100] Murphy, *Unions in Conflict*, pp. 86–7. For an account of a strike in Coimbatore which thus embarrassed Shiva Rao so that 'he returned to Madras in a huff', see *ibid.*, pp. 120–4.

the ATLA leadership, sometimes in flat contradiction to their wishes. The union, officially formed in February 1920, could scarcely claim to control the workers, let alone exert any influence over its increasingly militant members, especially when it was seeking to restrain them.[101] It was a characteristic feature of the development of working-class politics in Bombay, as elsewhere, that trade unions usually formed only after a strike began and collapsed soon after it had ended. Frequently, as the Home Rule League as well as Bole's Kamgar Hitwardhak Sabha discovered during the 1919 general strike, they were swept aside by the workers' refusal to accept a settlement on the terms they obtained, or even simply by the groundswell of popular action.[102] Until at least the late 1920s, when it became easier for officials, millowners and political observers to point an accusing finger at communist trouble-makers, they were frequently bemused by and hard pressed to explain the ability of workers to sustain lengthy strikes with at best only the most rudimentary formal organization.[103]

Since the Gandhians represented a dissident faction within the Congress between 1915 and 1920, and the non-cooperation movement was explicitly oppositional to the state, it is scarcely surprising that they provided a refuge for irreconcilables and brought into the nationalist fold varied and often conflicting political aspirations. While Congress in its agitational mode became a party of all-comers, and a wide range of publicists sought to represent workers' grievances, it should not be supposed that all labour leaders lent their weight to the non-cooperation movement. Prominent trade union leaders, like N. M. Joshi , S. K. Bole and B. Shiva Rao, opposed the movement. Others, like C. R. Das, doyen of the Bengal Congress, 'broker between irreconcilables' and the political guide of Santosh Kumari Devi, were drawn into labour disputes as part of the non-cooperation movement but rejected the path of the 'no-changers' after 1922, successfully contested the council elections of 1923 and swiftly lost interest in the proletariat.[104]

The non-cooperation movement did not rupture the old linkages which had constituted the political system before 1920. Nor did it radically transform the character of the Congress. As the movement stut-

---

[101] Patel, *The Making of Industrial Relations*, pp. 51–63, 126–36.

[102] For an account of the 1919 strike in Bombay, see Newman, *Workers and Unions*, pp. 120–9; Kumar, 'The Bombay Textile Strike, 1919'.

[103] Secretary, GOB, Home to Secretary GOI, Home, 7/15 February 1919 in Bombay Confidential Proceedings, vol. 46, 1919, OIOC; *Report of the Industrial Disputes Committee, 1922*, in *Labour Gazette*, 1:8 (April 1922), 24; *Bombay Chronicle*, 21 February 1924.

[104] J. A. Gallagher, 'Congress in Decline: Bengal, 1930–39', in Gallagher, Johnson and Seal (eds.), *Locality, Province and Nation*, pp. 269–325; Ray, *Social Conflict and Political Unrest*, ch. 5; Basu, 'Workers Politics', ch. 6.

tered violently to a close, provincial politicians and local bosses began to desert it. The 'no-changers' failed to prevent the Swarajists from contesting the 1923 elections or the Cocanada Congress from ratifying their decision. In most provinces, there were enough politicians willing to work the Montford constitution to make dyarchy effective. By allowing Indian elected representatives a real, if modest, share of power in the provinces, the Montford reforms rendered the linkages of all-India politics redundant and all-India parties gradually became moribund. By contrast, provincial politics were in ferment, animated by deepening factional rivalries and by unstable ministerial coalitions, whose meddling served inevitably to disappoint more clients than their patronage could satisfy. During the 1920s, the Congress divided between several parties and disintegrated into numerous factions. Political interests did not necessarily retain the same identity at local and provincial levels. Thus, the Ahmedabad Textile Labour Association, seemingly the creature of the Congress, joined forces in the municipal corporation with the Independent Party of the millowners and acted increasingly in opposition to the Congress.[105] Trade union leaders who may have been non-cooperators in the early 1920s now found that their connections with the Congress were becoming more attenuated. As more Indian elected politicians acquired provincial power under dyarchy, and exercised it under various, often changing, party labels, so these publicists of labour's cause had less need to operate under the banner of the Congress. The alliances which they forged with the ministerial coalitions which governed the province could be deployed to widen their base among the workers or to strengthen their negotiating status with the employers.

Furthermore, in the 1920s, labour began to be absorbed into the representative system of colonial rule. Spokesmen for labour, notably, in 1920, K. C. Roy Chowdhury from Bengal and N. M. Joshi from Bombay, were nominated to the central legislative assembly, and both of them initiated important pieces of legislation during the decade. More crucially, perhaps, the extension of the franchise meant that workers and their unions exerted a growing, sometimes a decisive influence, on elections, especially to the municipal councils, but also to the provincial legislatures. In the early 1920s, in Bombay, over 11 per cent of the residents of the predominantly working-class municipal Ward F were entitled to vote, although only about one-eighth of them actually did. In Wards E and G, which were also predominantly working class , the turn-out was much higher – roughly one-third of the electorate – but the proportion of the residents who were eligible to vote was about 3 per cent and 5 per

[105] Patel, *The Making of Industrial Relations*, pp. 86–92.

cent respectively.[106] Although working-class voters generally formed as yet a small proportion of the electorate, they sometimes exercised a disproportionate influence on the result. In the Madras municipal elections of 1924, it was said, 'they largely determined the outcome of the elections in the industrial wards as the union was able to mobilise them as a bloc'.[107] When the Madras Labour Union contested the 1927 election to the provincial legislature, they were able, together with their allies, to defeat the Swarajists in each constituency 'where the vote of the industrial workers was most effective'.[108] By 1936, when the Madras Labour Union supported the Congress, the working-class vote was shown to be influential not only in the constituencies which they won but also in those which they lost because of the local influence of a rival trade union clique.[109]

During the 1930s, however, this fluid and flexible relationship between labour leaders, on the one hand, and the Congress, on the other, underwent fundamental change. The Congress imparted to its organization a greater formality and tightened and centralized its control through its 'High Command'. Increasingly, it defined the criteria of party membership and it became less tolerant of divided loyalties within its ranks. In the unseemly rush for Congress 'tickets' which gathered force after 1934, it acquired the opportunity and the power to discriminate between its followers. By the mid-1930s, it was becoming increasingly clear that there were important electoral gains to be made by organizing labour and forming trade unions, while, at the same time, labour leaders, no less than other publicists, recognized that the route to electoral success and ministerial power lay through the Congress. In the 1920s, local circumstances had largely determined the attitude of labour leaders to the Congress. Where hostile elements held sway over the local Congress (or the Swarajists), it was sometimes preferable to seek leverage upon the political system through a rival political grouping. On the other hand, if their access to the Congress remained open, and where, for instance, antagonistic local bosses remained suspicious of the party, they might prefer to operate beneath the nationalist banner. The possible permutations seemed numerous and complex. In the 1930s the options narrowed. Publicists who stepped forward as champions of the urban poor had already, in the 1910s and 1920s, been most commonly drawn from among politicians with relatively little access to power and few firm and powerful alliances to put at risk. But in the 1930s, as landlords, merchants and even some industrial capitalists, acquired greater influence

[106] K. T. Shah and G. J. Bahadurji, *Constitutions, Functions and Finance of Indian Municipalities* (Bombay, 1925), pp. 31–2.   [107] Murphy, *Unions in Conflict*, p. 102.
[108] *Ibid.*, p. 105.   [109] *Ibid.*, pp. 130–1.

and control within the Congress, so labour publicists in the party, especially the more radical among them, came increasingly to be marginalized. The Congress was no longer a party of all-comers, even less a refuge for irreconcilables. If, in the early 1920s, publicists on the margins of the political system were able to forge wider political alliances and achieve a greater political prominence by organizing and representing labour, by the mid-1930s it was becoming far more difficult to build such careers within the Congress. Increasingly, the Congress representatives of labour and working-class interests, with wider political ambitions, had to act in ways which did not offend their other political constituents. Whereas, in the 1920s, labour was only one of a range of political concerns for the publicist, and often a rather marginal concern, more labour leaders emerged in the following decade who were concerned exclusively with labour matters. At the same time, these labour leaders, if they chose to operate within the fold of the Congress, were more effectively subordinated to the High Command and they were often precluded from rising to greater prominence within the movement. The outcome, in Bengal and Madras, in Kanpur and Ahmedabad, in Sholapur and Coimbatore, was the growth of socialist and communist organizations within the labour movement.[110] The 'rise' of the left was not limited to working-class movements alone in the 1930s.[111] In part, it reflected the sharpening and proliferation of class conflicts in Indian society during the depression. It also reflected the changing character of the Congress and its relationship with its social base, which in itself was affected by changes in the nature of the relationship between the Congress and the colonial state and, in particular, its structure of governance. Finally, the growth of socialist organization was stimulated by the hopes raised and expectations generated among the working classes, and the followers of the Congress more generally, by its electoral victories in

[110] On Bengal, see Chakrabarty, *Re-thinking Working Class History*; Basu, 'Workers' Politics in Bengal'; on Madras, see C. J. Baker, *The Politics of South India, 1920–37*, (Cambridge, 1976), pp. 190–2; Baker, *An Indian Rural Economy*, ch. 5; Murphy, *Unions in Conflict*; Ramaswamy, *The Worker and His Union*, ch. 1; on Kanpur, see Joshi, 'Bonds of Caste, Ties of Religion'; Pandey, 'Ideological Conflict in the Kanpur Trade Union Movement'; Gooptu, 'Political Culture of the Urban Poor in North India'; on Ahmedabad, see Patel, *The Making of Industrial Relations*; GOB, Home (Special), File 550 (25) III-A of 1938, MSA; on Sholapur, see GOB, Home (Special), File 550 (14) of 1933, File 543 (53) A of 1934 and File 550 (25) IV-A of 1938, MSA.

[111] Rajnarayan Chandavarkar, 'From Communism to Social Democracy: The Rise and Resilience of Communist Parties in India, 1920–1995', *Science and Society*, 61:1 (1997), 99–106; D. N. Dhanagare, *Peasant Movements in India, 1920–1950* (Delhi, 1983); A. Cooper, *Sharecropping and Sharecroppers' Struggles in Bengal, 1930–1950* (Calcutta, 1988); K. Damodaran, 'Memoir of an Indian Communist', *New Left Review*, 93 (1975), 35–59; D. Menon, *Caste, Nationalism and Communism in South India: Malabar 1900–1948* (Cambridge, 1994).

1937. To some, it appeared, in their enthusiasm, that the elections had brought the irreconcilables to office.

IV

It should not be supposed, however, that these interventions in labour disputes and attempts at labour organization always worked in favour of the Congress inevitably securing its place within the diverse political cultures of the working class. As labour organizers, these publicists had to act within the constraints imposed upon them by the structure of industrial relations. They were always liable to be ground between the irreconcilable grievances of labour and the implacable resistance of capital. Historians have perhaps too readily assumed that the formation of trade unions reflected the level of industrialization in the economy or a particular stage of working-class consciousness. But this is to minimize the extent to which the growth of trade unions depends upon the tolerance of the state and the acquiescence of employers.[112] In India, the employers as well as the state disclosed a low threshold of tolerance for workers' combinations. Workers' grievances, when they could not be resolved within the apparatus of labour discipline at the workplace, were rarely given serious consideration, unless they went on strike. But if a strike did not result in a complete closure, workers ordinarily risked dismissal. By dismissing the irreconcilable, locking out the implacable, cajoling the sullen, bullying the waverers, discriminating against those whom they could not dismiss, and choosing whom they would negotiate with, the employers could decisively influence the complex, if fragile, alliances both within and outside the workplace, upon which trade unions rested. Most commonly, they could undermine and destroy workers' combinations at the point of production.

Under these adverse circumstances, politicians seeking to organize labour could follow two courses of action. First, they could try to persuade the employers and the state to accept their credentials and negotiate with them as representative, responsible and legitimate spokesmen for the workers. Certainly, the political influence of some Congressmen gave them a certain leverage upon employers when seeking recognition as bargaining agents on behalf of the workforce. They could deploy their wider connections or their positions in the councils of state to the advantage of their followers or the embarrassment of the employers and the government. Their influence at these levels might encourage employers to invite them to settle disputes while the confidence they commanded

[112] See ch. 3 above.

with employers or the state could allow them to build up a significant following at the workplace. In a sense, the effectiveness of trade union leaders in these circumstances depended on their skill not in putting the workers' grievances to the employers but in representing the employers to the workforce. Their success and their survival depended upon their ability to please both masters and frequently they were to find themselves ground between the upper and the nether millstone.

On the other hand, trade unions whose existence was not safeguarded by the relative tolerance of the employers and the state often had to impose themselves forcibly upon industrial politics, by adopting a strategy of direct action and confrontation: meddling in the daily disputes of the workplace, taking up minor grievances, demonstrating their ability to secure favourable settlements, attempting to generate sufficient momentum for large-scale action. By intervening energetically in minor disputes and assiduously airing workers' grievances, they attempted to generate sufficient momentum for large-scale action. Necessarily, they established themselves most successfully during general strikes. Excluded from the workplace, these unions often paid closer attention to building up connections in the neighbourhood. They were sometimes able to deploy these connections, conversely, to forge closer linkages with the workplace as well as to generate and sustain industrial action, whether by combating blacklegs or cajoling landlords and grain merchants to extend credit to their members.[113]

Of course, this distinction between unions committed to strategies of confrontation and conciliation is too starkly drawn. There were many who moved adroitly between both styles of trade unionism and some who wholly embraced neither. Trade unions which flourished on their accreditation by the employers and the state could not for long ignore those who cut a figure on the street corner. Strategies of confrontation were futile if they never yielded concessions. At some point or other, 'company unions' had to lead strikes and yet protect their favoured status, while the most radical unions had to face the dilemma of how to reflect the militancy of their followers without permitting it to go too far. But the confrontational style is most readily associated with the communist trade unions which operated in Bombay in the late 1920s and 1930s, in Sholapur in the 1930s and in Kanpur in the late 1930s and early 1940s. This style of trade unionism was aptly captured by the jute workers of Calcutta who during the strikes of 1929 began to refer to the communist trade union leaders as 'the strike babus'.[114] Congress politicians could not always follow the path of confrontation. They often brought to trade

---

[113] See ch. 4 above.
[114] Mitra, 'Growth of Trade Union Consciousness among Jute Mill Workers', p. 1841.

union organization wider and more secure political connections which were jeopardized by the pursuit of any highly adventurist strategy of confrontation. By allowing labour militancy its head, they could alienate capital when they were seeking to harness it to their side and put at risk their own local political alliances. This meant that they frequently found themselves trying to move against the tide of working-class opinion. It often required them to restrain their followers from industrial action or to advise them to return when they wanted to prolong the strike or indeed to negotiate an early settlement even at the expense of accepting terms less favourable than their original demands. In such circumstances, these spokesmen for labour could rapidly discover that they had nobody to speak for. Even when leaders of national prominence, like Gandhi or Bose, intervened in labour disputes, able to deploy their reputations and their extensive political connections to the advantage of the workers and to command, however reluctantly it was given, the confidence of the employers, they could emerge with little to show for their efforts.

Despite all his bluster, Bose, involved in the closing stages of the Jamshedpur strike of 1928, obtained a deal from the employers which, in the interests of a quick settlement, studiously ignored the most vital demands behind the strike.[115] Thus, when Bose returned to Jamshedpur in the following year, as the champion of the Golmuri tinplate workers, Birla, a Calcutta industrialist, assured his Bombay counterpart, Thakurdas, that the tiger of Bengal might roar but he certainly would not spring. 'Mr Bose', he wrote, 'can be relied upon to help Tata Iron and Steel Works whenever necessary.' For 'Mr Bose', he went on to explain,

is a very sincere and scrupulous man and appreciates the necessity of co-operation with reasonable and advanced type of capitalists. He himself belongs to the aristocratic class, although he voluntarily renounced many luxuries. His main object in labour matters no doubt is service to the labour but not necessarily inimical to the capitalist.[116]

This style of intervention in labour disputes often served to alienate working-class support. It is scarcely surprising that the Jamshedpur workers simply ignored the Congress satyagrahis during the civil disobedience campaign in 1930.[117]

In Ahmedabad, the relationship between the Congress and the working classes followed a different pattern, even if the outcome was in fact all too familiar. The Congress, as we have seen, developed an uniquely intimate relationship with the Ahmedabad Textile Labour Association, and while it did not seek to forge similar links with other trade unions, it guarded its

[115] Simeon, *The Politics of Labour under Late Colonialism*, chs. 2–3; Bahl, 'TISCO Workers' Struggle, 1920–28'; Bahl, *The Making of the Indian Working Class*.
[116] Birla to Thakurdas, 16 July 1929, Thakurdas Papers, File 42 (I), NMML.
[117] Bahl, 'TISCO Workers' Struggle', p. 44, n. 34.

connections with the ATLA closely.[118] Gandhi's involvement with the city's textile workers began with the satyagraha of 1918, before he was firmly established as a dominant figure within the Congress. Although Gandhi withdrew from active involvement with the union after 1920, he continued to keep a watchful eye on the conduct of its affairs, which were left in the charge of his loyal and talented followers, Anasuyabehn Sarabhai and, increasingly, Gulzarilal Nanda. Perhaps in part as a consequence, the textile workers developed after 1918 a closer affinity and loyalty to Gandhi than the ATLA was able to evince. The national standing of the Congress and the wider political influence of Gandhi encouraged the millowners and the colonial state to raise the threshold of their tolerance of workers' combinations in this instance. The leverage which Gandhi and the Congress exercised on the colonial state and their potential for mobilizing mass support enabled them to lodge the ATLA as the principal bargaining agent on behalf of the textile workers. The commercial possibilities which the swadeshi campaign opened up for the millowners in the domestic market must have also entered their calculations. Moreover, the millowners, like local officials, recognized as early as 1918 that Gandhi's charisma might serve to restrain the working classes and pose a lesser threat to the public order than any imagined, or available, alternative. While Gandhi's advice to the workers in 1918 'was all in the direction of sobriety and conciliation', the fact remained that 'a few of the wilder spirits' among the workers 'question what he can do'.[119] Clearly, if for the millowners it was preferable to deal with Gandhi than with 'the wilder spirits', it was essential for them to strengthen his hand. Of course, neither the millowners nor the colonial state were unwavering in this belief. Indeed, the Ahmedabad Millowners' Association was often engulfed by bitter and acrimonious disputes over the formulation of a labour policy, which not only threatened at times to destroy their own organization but led them periodically to severely undermine the ATLA to the point of virtually wrecking it.[120]

For nearly a decade after the 1923 strike the millowners entertained the existence of something remotely resembling a system of collective bargaining, and roughly along the lines envisaged by Gandhi in 1918 – where industrial relations were conducted through the ATLA and, if necessary, a board of arbitration. It was facilitated by the relative prosperity of the Ahmedabad mills, by the ATLA's own stance of 'collaboration' in its 'indigenous experiment in trade unionism' and the millowners' recognition that it was best to deal with the devil they knew. If they were to destroy the ATLA, as they very nearly did in 1923, who knew what

[118] See ch. 3 above.   [119] *BPP, SAI, 1918*, p. 164, para 235.
[120] G. L. Nanda to S. G. Banker, 23 March 1933, in File 40, pp. 77–83, ATLA Papers, microfilm copy, reel no. 1, NMML.

manner of beast might be raised up from the deep? Thus, the ATLA dedicated itself 'purely to promote the moral and social welfare of the workers and to raise their value as citizens'.[121] Seth Maganlal Girdhardas, no friend of the trade union, had warned the Millowners' Association, over which he presided, that 'we should not commit the error of taking all labour organizations as inimical to our interests' but rather support and strengthen the hand of those unions which sought 'to evolve order out of chaos and deal with rough illiterate masses'.[122]

Once the depression which had afflicted other centres of the cotton textile industry several years earlier now began to affect the Ahmedabad mills, however, and their markets slumped in the early 1930s, the millowners showed that they preferred the freedom to make 'private settlements' with their workers to the rigours of collective bargaining and arbitration, which lumped them all together even as local rivalries grew sharper and more antagonistic. The millowners began once more to deal with the ATLA as often as they ignored or side-stepped it, followed the rules of arbitration more often in the breach than in the observance and submitted, if they were forced, to agreements over wages and conditions, only to steadfastly evade their implementation. It was only the growing threat of the communist Mill Mazdoor Sangh in the mid-1930s, drawing upon the support of the mainly Muslim weavers,[123] which led the millowners to close ranks and to seek to blunt the red menace by consolidating the position of the ATLA, while the latter, apprehensive of the pressure of their communist rivals on their flank, and the Congress, now in office, and anxious about the possibility of a socialist challenge to the control of the local party, were only too willing to collaborate.[124] It was the pressure of this rivalry within the labour movement in Ahmedabad, rather than, for instance, the power of capitalist interests within the Congress, which drove the highly repressive policies towards labour – including the formulation and passage of the Bombay Trade Disputes Act of 1938, and directed primarily against the communist unions – adopted by the provincial Congress ministry in Bombay between 1937 and 1939.[125] Significantly, it was the threat of labour militancy which persuaded the millowners to accept in 1939 the

---

[121] 'Memorandum on the Reorganization of the Administration of the Textile Labour Association, 1933–34', File 47, ATLA Papers, *ibid.*

[122] *Annual Report of the Ahmedabad Millowners' Association, 1923*, pp. 32–3, cited by Salim Lakha, *Capitalism and Class in Colonial India: The Case of Ahmedabad* (New Delhi, 1988), pp. 111–12.

[123] GOB, Home (Special), File 550 (25) III-A of 1938, MSA.

[124] ATLA Papers, File 3, Part 2, microfilm copy, reel no. 9, NMML.

[125] GOB, Home (Special), Files 550(24) of 1938, 550(25) III A, MSA; AITUC Papers, File 59, NMML; Markovits, *Indian Business and Nationalist Politics*, especially pp. 150–78; see also ch. 3 below.

principles over which the 1918 and 1920 strikes had, in part, been fought: that, under the terms of the Industrial Disputes Act, the ATLA would be the exclusive representative of the workers and that arbitration would be mandatory.[126]

Large claims have been made for the Ahmedabad Textile Labour Association and many of them should be treated with scepticism. It is true that the ATLA, quite unlike most other unions in India, achieved a certain permanence and boasted an impressive longevity. But it benefited from the local and national standing of Gandhi and from its own early entrenchment, through its alliance with the Congress, within the wider structure of politics. It was also blessed at times by the favour and tolerance of officials and employers. The readiness of the employers to deal with workers' grievances only when they were routed through the machinery of the union was a privilege enjoyed by few other effective trade unions. In the quotidian context of the workplace, it was difficult for most workers, except, perhaps, the most skilled, to operate consistently outside its framework, let alone in opposition to it. This fact helped to lodge the ATLA as an agent of collective bargaining in the industry. It is not intended to suggest, however, that the ATLA was merely the stooge of the millowners. Despite the continued impression that industrial conflict in Ahmedabad 'partakes the nature of a family [dispute] and unlike many family disputes is conducted with a complete lack of acerbity',[127] the ATLA was not simply a company union. The tensions which its presence generated, after all, served to divide the Ahmedabad Millowners' Association for twenty years.

In the long view, however, its record is far less impressive. Its appeal appears to have been rather sectional, manifesting itself most strongly among Harijan spinners. Weavers, and especially the Muslims, initially remained sceptical of Gandhi in 1918, joined the union subsequently and then left it in large numbers in 1923, were increasingly alienated from it in the 1930s, when less than one-tenth of their numbers counted among the members, and formed what was effectively their own union in the Mill Mazdoor Sangh under communist leadership.[128] Despite its acceptance as the workers' representative, and for all the influence it appeared to command in the wider political sphere, employers were able to dismiss strikers with greater regularity and in larger numbers in Ahmedabad than was ever possible in Bombay. Similarly, the ATLA was

---

[126] Patel, *The Making of Industrial Relations*, pp. 134–6.

[127] Collector of Ahmedabad to Secretary, Government of Bombay, Judicial, 25 February 1918, Bombay Confidential Proceedings, Judicial Department, for March 1918, vol. 36, p. 33, OIOC.

[128] GOB, Home (Special), File 550 (25) III-A of 1938, MSA.

unable to defend the wage levels of its members. In 1918, the general strike was settled with some reference to the existing wage levels in Bombay. For the next two decades, the Bombay millowners watched with envy, and with regret, as their Ahmedabad rivals were able to cut wages without always paying the price of the bitter and protracted general strikes on the scale which they had endured. Fred Stones, managing director of the E. D. Sassoon group of mills in Bombay, observed somewhat ruefully in 1939, 'Had we Gandhiji in Bombay I say our firm would have saved lakhs and lakhs of rupees.'[129] It is doubtful that Gandhi would have denied the charge. 'You have given me the credit', he told the Ahmedabad millowners, a whole decade earlier, in 1928, 'for keeping the city of Ahmedabad free from a labour upheaval such as Bombay is at present passing through. Well, I cannot quite disclaim that credit.'[130] Indeed, the ATLA often found itself following the lead of the workers with some embarrassment or alternatively distancing itself from the strikes of its members. Although the arbitration machinery established the ATLA as the main and most effective channel through which the workers could express their grievances, the millowners frequently ignored this machinery to make their own private settlements outside the formal institutions so elaborately designed for the industry as a whole. While labour policy became the cause of open schism in the Millowners' Association, Gulzarilal Nanda had begun to complain vociferously by 1933 that the arbitration machinery was on the point of collapse and threatened to take much of the union's organization away with it. So for all the longevity and institutionalization of the ATLA, this is what the 'indigenous experiment in trade unionism' had come to. 'The difficulty', as he put it, was rather 'fundamental':

It is the mental reservations on the side of the employer in accepting the Union and the procedure of negotiations and arbitration. As long as it is a question of tolerating the organization as a necessary nuisance when it is too strong for them and constantly trying to undermine its strength and influence, the conditions for successful cooperation do not exist.[131]

The fact that political linkages with the Congress could bring various working-class groups tangible benefits whether in the workplace or the neighbourhood may help to explain why the Congress could attract a significant working-class following. But the limitations of Congress interventions in the problems and politics of the working classes, combined

---

[129] Proceedings of the TLIC, Main Inquiry, Oral Evidence, Mr. F. Stones, Director, Messrs. E. D. Sassoon and Co., File 72, p. 3624, MSA.
[130] *Young India*, 10 May 1928.
[131] Gulzarilal Nanda to Shankarlal Banker, 23 March 1933, ATLA Papers, File 40, 'Papers Relating to the Depression, 1933', pp. 77–83, microfilm copy, reel no. 1, NMML.

with the ambivalence towards labour which was inherent in its rhetoric and programme, may also help to explain why working-class support for the Congress was so often sporadic and intermittent. At certain times and some places, the Congress was able to win the adherence of specific groups of workers.

V

The hybridity and sectionalism of the working class and its fragmentary and uneven response to the Congress has complicated the task of identifying the content and character of working-class nationalism. Clearly, this nationalism did not arise out of a universal commitment to a territorial principle. To some extent, working-class participation in the nationalist campaigns invited the Congress to redefine its own varied, sometimes unformulated concept of the nation. Working-class support for the Congress did not stem from a general concern that the interests of the Indian people were homogeneous and indeed it occurred despite the persistent and often painful recognition that they were not. Moreover, the work experiences of different groups of workers in the same industry and the same town, let alone in the same industry in different centres or different occupations in different towns, varied considerably. But these experiences and conditions of work clearly inflected the response of particular groups of workers to the rhetoric, programme and ideology of the Congress.

Nationalist ideologies were likely to disclose a more accessible and immediate social meaning on the railways. Racist and discriminatory practices pervaded the operations and organization of work in the railways. Railway colonies, inhabited by 'European' and 'Eurasian' officers and supervisors, fostered conditions of apartheid. 'Europeans' enjoyed a virtual monopoly of the higher paid jobs and the vital operations. Indian workers, or 'coolies', were employed in the lowest-paid 'native grades'. Structures of pay, promotion and apprenticeship were highly discriminatory. The jobs and promotion prospects of most Indian employees, even in the more skilled occupations or in the intermediate wage categories, often depended on the whim or the good will of their 'European' or 'Anglo-Indian' supervisors, who were sometimes less skilled, if better paid. Considerable violence and brutality, we are told, were used in the discipline and 'management' of labour[132] – although whether there was

---

[132] *Proceedings of the MCC*, Defence Statement, K. N. Joglekar, pp. 1768–76; Jagga, 'Colonial Railwaymen and British Rule', pp. 106–14; *BPP SAI*, 1916, no. 29, 22 July, para 958; Arnold, 'Industrial Violence', pp. 249–54; I. J. Kerr, *Building the Railways of the Raj, 1850–1900* (Delhi, 1995).

308   Imperial power and popular politics

anything specifically 'colonial' about this is a more problematic and vastly underrated question.[133]

Work on the railways was characterized by a complex division of labour and intricately devised structure of grades and functions, finely drawn hierarchies and fiercely maintained demarcations of status, all of which was overlaid by patterns of racial exclusion and segregation. Railwaymen, even in the native grades, were notoriously fond of their uniforms and, like university bureaucrats, revelled in the pomp of office, however lowly. This 'petty bourgeois sentimentalism', as K. N. Joglekar, the Bombay communist, once described it, was often deemed to be an obstacle to the unity of workers across the various grades, ranks and departments. The service and clerical occupations looked down upon the workshop hands and both groups held those who worked 'on the line' in the deepest contempt. Nonetheless, their resentment of the privileges of European and Anglo-Indian workers could override these prejudices and sometimes created the possibility of alliances across entrenched, customary divisions among Indian railwaymen. The nationalism of railway workers was nourished by racial conflicts between European and Eurasian foremen and Indian workers.[134]

It is not intended to suggest that the frequency of strikes on the railways between 1917 and 1922 and, indeed, between 1928 and 1931, demonstrated the submission of workers to the nationalist programme. Of course, several hartals and stoppages did occur on various railways in 1921–22 explicitly in response to the Khilafat and non-cooperation movements. Most strikes, however, focused on issues directly related to wages and the conditions of work, and not infrequently to the abuse and violence meted out by supervisors and managers. Nonetheless, their occurrence was not unrelated to the rhetoric and objectives of the anti-colonial agitations. Occasionally, as in the case of the North Western Railwaymen's Association, the conduct of a strike threatened to effect an alliance across the racial divide. The North Western Railwaymen's strikes in 1919 and 1920 were inextricably bound up with the Rowlatt satyagraha, the Khilafat movement and the non-cooperation agitation. In May 1920, however, a strike which began in response to the dismissal of seven fitters of the Moghulpura workshop in Lahore turned into a battle for the recognition of the union. The support which this action secured from the European engine drivers, briefly appearing to knit together the whole workforce, forced the employers to accede to the union's demands. The inspiration behind the union's campaign was the charismatic John 'the Mahatma' Miller, formerly an engine driver himself and a 'European',

---

[133] See ch. 5 above.
[134] *Proceedings of the MCC*, Defence Statement, K. N. Joglekar, pp. 1770 ff.

who had since 1907 been dismissed by at least three railway companies for his role in organizing strikes.[135] But this solidarity was both too difficult to sustain and too good to last. In the early 1920s, 'Mahatma' Miller crumbled under the pressures of his own charisma. Following its triumphs of 1919–20, 'corruption set in' and the union was said to have became 'a grazing ground' for its leadership. In 1925, a campaign of passive resistance in the Rawalpindi workshop against retrenchment on the North West Railway led to a lock-out and the strike spread along the line from Karachi to Delhi. The union, led by Miller, now opposed the strike; the workers sustained it for four months. By the time the strike collapsed, the union had become moribund and 'Mahatma' Miller was 'rewarded . . . with a kushi job on the North West Railway'.[136]

Where 'Europeans' were found in profusion and dominated the structure of supervision, discipline and, indeed, ownership, it was for workers far easier to identify nationalist sentiments with their everyday experiences or, conversely, to develop a social interpretation of the nationalist question. But it would be simplistic and misleading to conclude that workers' nationalism arose only from, or directly in relation to, their personal experience of 'European' capitalists, managers and overseers. The Congress found its most devoted, loyal and strongest working-class following in Ahmedabad, where owners, managers and jobbers were not only Indian but predominantly Gujarati.[137] In Bombay, the millworkers manifested a greater enthusiasm for the nationalist cause even as the ranks of supervisors and mill managers became increasingly Indianized – although the situation was complicated by the fact that they frequently identified Parsi supervisors, managers and millowners with the colonial regime.[138] In fact, it is one of the least observed peculiarities of Indian nationalism that its rhetoric was largely free of racism – or at least that it saved its racism primarily for other Indians. However, it was when the lines of antagonism, which marked their social relations both within and beyond the workplace, could be readily traced to the wider context of the colonial state that the protean languages of nationalism most obviously provided the working classes with an explanation, and a remedy, for the social and political conditions in which they found themselves.

[135] Jagga, 'Colonial Railwaymen and British Rule', pp. 120–7, esp. p. 120, n. 51.
[136] *Proceedings of the MCC*, Defence Statement, K. N. Joglekar, pp. 1781–4.
[137] Mehta, *The Ahmedabad Cotton Textile Industry*; Gillion, *Ahmedabad*; Patel, *The Making of Industrial Relations*.
[138] Chandavarkar, *The Origins of Industrial Capitalism*, pp. 411–20; S. Bhattacharya, 'Swaraj and the Kamgar: The Indian National Congress and the Bombay Working Class, 1919–1931', in Sisson and Wolpert (eds.), *Congress and Indian Nationalism*, pp. 223–49; R. Kumar, 'From Swaraj to Purna Swaraj: Nationalist Politics in the City of Bombay 1920–32', in D. A. Low (ed.), *Congress and the Raj: Facets of the Indian Struggle* (London, 1977), pp. 77–107.

It might be supposed that in Bengal, where capital was overwhelmingly dominated by 'Europeans', where the jute mills were both owned and managed by them, where expatriates observed and maintained the finest caste distinctions among themselves as well as in relation to Indian merchants, the working classes would more readily, indeed naturally, identify themselves with the Indian nation. In fact, working-class nationalism owed as much to the social relations of the workplace as to the political conflicts of the milltowns. Here, subordinated bhadralok elites sought to wrest control of the town municipalities from the Scottish mill managers and their Indian allies by drawing on working-class support. They developed this working-class following partly by their willingness to intervene in the disputes of the workplace but, more especially, by the promise that placed in power they might act to improve conditions of housing and sanitation and restrain the police.[139]

The formation of a labour force in the plantations and mines was as deeply marked by colonial precept and practice as it was on the railways. It was a function of the generic weakness of expatriate capital in South Asia that it had sought its fortune on the margins of agrarian settlement since the early nineteenth century. The rough-and-ready capitalism which expatriate entrepreneurs created so cheaply was particularly exploitative and oppressive of labour. The discourse of labour deployment and discipline, primarily, perhaps even quintessentially, *the* colonial discourse, and one which served, and continues to serve, the interests of Indian capital so handsomely, was fashioned in the coal mines, plantations and in systems of labour indenture. In the Jharia coalfields, the support for non-cooperation was driven in part by an alliance between the Indian owners of the small, surface mines and motley interests drawn from the largely 'European'-owned sector of large, deep mines – Bengali clerks and literate service groups, raising contractors and migrant labour from UP (the 'paschimas' to be distinguished from the local 'dehati' and 'jungli' labour of Santhals, Bauris and other tribal and low-caste groups employed under particularly harsh conditions in the Indian sector). It did not take long for this alliance to come unravelled in the 1930s. But it was motivated as much by the search of Indian capital for a larger stake in the industry as by the often economic grievances of the Indian employees of the larger European mine-owners.[140]

In Madurai, by contrast, similar motives on the part of Indian merchants who dominated the local Congress led them first to seek an alliance with local labour and then repudiate it. In 1931, the Madurai Congress Committee decided to take on the redoubtable Harvey industrial empire

[139] Basu, 'Workers' Politics in Bengal', ch. 3.
[140] Ghosh, 'The Labour Movement in the Jharia Coalfield'.

during the civil disobedience movement. They named the Harvey mills as importers of foreign yarn, boycotted their products and, with the help of 'the tough, unscrupulous union boss', Varadarajulu Naidu, they effectively disrupted production. They demanded that Harveys should appoint more Indians to their board of directors, employ more Indians as mill executives and allow Indians to buy a larger stake in their mills. In fact, the local Congress committee was dominated by the town's leading merchants, some of whom, including its leading figure, N. M. R. Subbaraman, had already invested in the mills. The prospect that the boycott, and the financial pressures which it could generate during the depression, could create an opportunity for them to acquire a larger share and extend their control of the mill would not have been lost on these entrepreneurs, and leading protagonists of the satyagraha. The struggle for truth might yield handsome dividends. On the other hand, liberating Indian capital from the dominance of British businessmen did not necessarily mean that they should embrace the rights of labour. Certainly, Varadarajulu Naidu for his part had entertained the hope that by supporting civil disobedience he might extract the employers' recognition of his union and thus secure its position as the principal bargaining agent in the local industry. However, the leading lights of the Congress campaign approached Varadarajulu Naidu with the utmost caution. They were reluctant to allow the mill-workers to participate in the civil disobedience campaigns for fear that such mass participation might threaten their own control over the movement. Moreover, as cloth merchants and industrialists themselves, they had little wish to aggravate the problems of labour control in the town. Having now acquired a larger stake in the mill, they could scarcely countenance Varadarajulu Naidu's suggestion that the authority of his union to represent the workers be recognized. The larger their financial stake in the industry, the less they could afford to risk the entrenchment of trade unions within its structure of management and control.[141]

In the labour unrest witnessed in Assam between 1920 and 1922, the strikes, violence and desertions of the tea garden labourers arose out of disputes about wages and working conditions. Although the planters insisted on explaining these conflicts in terms of the machinations of the Congress agitators, local officials found, as the Deputy Commissioner of Lakhimpur told the Assam Labour Enquiry Committee, 'little or no evidence that the strikes were due to the influence of the Congress agitators', while his counterpart at Darrang was willing only to go so far as to say that the non-cooperators 'had created an atmosphere which was favourable to the occurrence of strikes and outbreaks among the ignorant

[141] Murphy, *Unions in Conflict*, pp. 139–41.

coolies'.[142] On the other hand, the so-called sympathetic strike on the Assam–Bengal Railway, which followed the Chargola exodus and the Chandpur incident, does not appear on detailed scrutiny to have been particularly sympathetic. The railwaymen who went on strike wished to register their protest, not primarily against the violence which the troops visited upon the tea garden labourers at Chandpur railway station, but especially against the Gurkhas who, while attacking the fleeing tea garden labourers, had been sufficiently indiscriminate to assault them as well. Once the strike began, both railwaymen and steamer crews focused upon their wages and working conditions – including racially discriminatory wage rates – and the union, led by the then non-cooperator, J. M. Sen Gupta, quickly distanced itself from the nationalist agitation.[143] Ironically, at the same time, C. R. Das, the Bengal Congress leader, was busy declaring that 'if it had been a labour strike, a mere question between the employer and the employed, I should certainly have discouraged it from the Congress point of view'.[144]

The response of workers to specific forms of political action adopted in the various Congress agitations also varied considerably. Thus, in Bombay, the picketing of liquor shops found the most enthusiastic response during the non-cooperation campaign while the boycott of foreign cloth was received most readily in the early 1930s. The reasons are not far to seek. First, in the initial stages of non-cooperation, picketing concentrated primarily on foreign liquor shops. Foreign liquor symbolized wealth and was readily identified with the customs and habits of the colonial rulers. Second, in the context of the Khilafat wrongs, the theme of colonial injustice was also infused with religious prohibitions on the consumption of liquor, and, indeed, although both Hindus and Muslims participated in the picketing, the excise administration claimed that 'where picketing is done by Hindus, it is done in a less objectionable way than where it is done by Mahomedans'.[145] Cross-communal picketing did not diminish the use of communalist abuse to customers, who when they emerged from the shops were greeted with 'such choice language as . . . if the customer is a Hindoo whether he had been there to drink cow's blood or in case of a Mahomedan, pig's blood'.[146] Theorists of popular culture

---

[142] *Report of the Assam Labour Enquiry Committee, 1921–22*, p. 19; cited by R. P. Behal, 'Forms of Labour Protest in Assam Valley Tea Plantations, 1900–1930', *Economic and Political Weekly*, 20:4 (26 January 1985), *Review of Political Economy*, pp. PE-21 to PE-22.

[143] Gourlay, 'Nationalists, Outsiders and the Labour Movement in Bengal', pp. 49–53.

[144] *Mussalman*, 17 June 1921, cited by Sarkar, 'The Conditions of Subaltern Militancy', p. 295, fn 97.

[145] Chief Excise Inspector, Bombay, to Superintendent of Salt and Excise, Bombay, 7 November 1921, in GOB, Home (Special), File 355 (21) F of 1921, p. 15, MSA.

[146] *Ibid.*

might have discovered a syncretism on the picket lines which overrode the effects of a language, often taken at other times and places to explain the occurrence of communal riots. Third, the bulk of liquor shops were owned by Parsis, from whose ranks were also drawn the most prominent and the most loyal millowners, a significant proportion of mill managers and officials and a large number of skilled workers and supervisors in the cotton mills and the railway workshops. These were the 'Biryaniwallahs' of Willingdon Club' who supported the Willingdon Memorial in 1918 and seemingly refused to observe the hartal which greeted the Prince of Wales on his visit to Bombay in November 1921. In fact, despite the opposition of K. F. Nariman, Burjorji Bharucha and the nationalists of the *Bombay Chronicle* office, the Parsi Panchayat had insisted on presenting an address to the Prince and in the midst of the general observance of the hartal, extending to him 'an enthusiastic welcome'.[147] The fact that communal riots in Bombay in the nineteenth century had primarily occurred between Parsis and Muslims – arising out of commercial rivalries in the shipping and export trades – added a further dimension to these tensions. What were commonly described at the time as the Prince of Wales riots in November 1921 at times acquired the character of a communal riot in which Parsis became the target of the violence of mainly, but not exclusively, Muslim crowds enthusiastically assisted by Hindu 'satyagrahis'. In the case of the boycott campaigns in the early 1930s, the connections between the imports of foreign cloth and the economic troubles of the industry were easily made. Indeed, the millowners in their excise duty, rupee ratio and tariff campaigns as well as the Currency League had repeatedly made them. Foreign competition, it was said, had resulted in wage cuts in 1923 and 1925 and it was also supposed by millworkers to lie at the root of the retrenchment and rationalization schemes which were central to the strikes of 1928–29.[148]

Attempts by the Congress to attract a working-class following could serve to accentuate the sectionalism of the labour force, not solely to bind its solidarities. In the 1920s, as labour became increasingly peripheral to the concerns of the Congress, labour leaders who styled themselves as Congressmen often found themselves in conflict with the local Congress party, with Swarajist ministries or local mercantile and propertied interests which espoused and constituted the Congress. Conversely, as its own organizational machinery disintegrated, the Congress exercised less direct control over its local publicists, including those who acted as labour

---

[147] Note by Deputy Commissioner of Police, CID, Bombay, 1 December 1921, enclosed in Commissioner of Police, Bombay to Secretary, GOB, Home, 1 December 1921, in Bombay Confidential Proceedings, Home Department, December 1921, vol. 62, p. 777, OIOC.   [148] Chandavarkar, *The Origins of Industrial Capitalism*, chs. 8 and 9.

leaders. This situation was to change in the 1930s, when the High Command tightened its control over the rank and file and when leading labour became a rather more specialized profession within the fold of the Congress. Although one consequence of this changed context in the 1930s was the growth of socialist and communist agitations, Bombay city had witnessed the left rising on the crest of a wave of working-class militancy much earlier in the late 1920s. The decay and decline of the city's Congress was manifested in the growing prominence of communist activists in the ward and district Congress committees.[149] During the civil disobedience movement, and in its immediate aftermath, the Congress, in seeking to revive its local organization, tried also to extend its linkages with working-class politics. But since the general strike of 1928, the mill districts of Bombay had been dominated by the communists of the Girni Kamgar Union. As the conduct and the collapse of the strike in 1929 laid bare the divisions within the working classes, and the Meerut arrests by removing the more prominent leadership created new opportunities for, and sharpened old rivalries among, those who had been left behind, the Congress sought to develop a more extensive working-class following. At first, they cultivated those who had long harboured an antagonism against the communists, notably Mayekar and Keshav dada Borkar. But it soon became apparent that it was essential to break into the domain of the Girni Kamgar Union. Thus, S. K. Patil, the doyen of the city's Congress, with the assistance of Vallabhai Patel, courted the Kandalkar faction of the Girni Kamgar Union.[150] During the 1930s, as unemployment and repression combined to undermine the solidarities forged by the Girni Kamgar Union, the Congress became an alternative source of support for those labour leaders who were disappointed and disgruntled with the dominant factions within the labour movement. Of course, it was not unusual for labour leaders driven by conflicting ideological commitments or diverse political connections to compete with each other to develop a following. Nor is it surprising that this competition could extend into workplace and neighbourhood and attach itself to deeper and more fiercely contested rivalries in the daily social relations of the working classes. In Bombay, however, its significance lay in the fact that it was the Congress which by trying to acquire a stake in this seemingly volatile political constituency fed the rivalries, deepened the antagonisms and accentuated the sectionalism of the working classes. Its effect was to further weaken the solidarities which had been forged in the strikes of 1928–29.

The sectionalism of the working class could sometimes take caste and

---

[149] GOB, Home (Special), File 143 (K) Part IV (a) of 1928; File 143 (K) VII of 1928; and File 543 (18) C of 1928, MSA.

[150] GOB Home (Special), File 750 (39) – II of 1930, MSA.

'communal' forms. Since competition for jobs (as well as housing and credit) could follow lines of caste and communal difference, trade union rivalries, sometimes promoted by the Congress, could acquire a communal edge. Employers frequently sought to diversify the caste and communal composition of their labour force to extend their control over it.[151] When, during strikes, they tried to recruit workers of a different religious, caste or regional identity from those who had struck, their attempts to manipulate the social composition of the workforce could deepen rivalries, provoke violent conflict and lead – as it did in Bombay in February and May 1929 and again in May 1932 – to communal riots.[152]

Congress agitations, especially the picketing of liquor and cloth shops could provoke communal antagonisms and sometimes led to large-scale violence. Young men, collected together in large groups, intoxicated by the carnivalesque spirit which prevailed on these occasions, sometimes puffed up by their righteousness, were unlikely to proceed with sensitivity and care or attend the disciplines of non-violence, and they readily and frequently gave offence. It has already been shown how the picketing of liquor shops and the hartal organized for the Prince of Wales's visit to Bombay in November 1921 led to a communal riot between Parsis and Muslims.[153] Similarly, picketing generated resentment and led to communal violence in Banaras in 1931.[154] In 1932, the picketing of piece-goods shops in Bombay which sold foreign cloth exacerbated rivalries in the trade and, because Muslim traders were largely, though not exclusively, involved in the import trade, it intensified communal antagonisms and fed into the riots which engulfed the city in May.[155]

---

[151] Examples may be found in Bengal in the 1890s, Madras in the early 1920s, and in Kanpur in the late 1930s. For Bengal, see Das Gupta, 'Factory Labour in Eastern India', pp. 289–303; Chakrabarty, 'Communal Riots and Labour', pp. 150–4; Basu, 'Workers' Politics in Bengal', ch. 4; on Kanpur, see Joshi, 'Bonds of Caste, Ties of Religion', and Joshi, 'Kanpur Textile Labour', p. 1827; on Madras, see E. D. Murphy, 'Class and Community in India: The Madras Labour Union, 1918–21', *IESHR*, 14:3 (1977), 292–321.

[152] For the 1929 strike, see G. D. Birla to P. Thakurdas, 4 May 1929, Thakurdas Papers, File 81 (II) of 1929, pp. 287–85; G. D. Birla to P. Thakurdas, 4 May 1929, Thakurdas Papers, File 42 (II), of 1923–34, NMML. See also, GOB, Home (Special), File 348 Part II of 1929 and GOB, Home (Poll), File 344 of 1929, MSA. On the 1932 riots, see Commissioner of Police, Bombay to Secretary, GOB, Home (Special), 4 April 1932 in GOB, Home (Special), File 792 of 1932, MSA. Of course, explanations for communal antagonisms and communal riots, to be plausible and to be adequate, will have to extend beyond the social and economic conflicts which informed them. Crucially, the hiring of Muslims and Pathans to break strikes was not the only cause of these three Bombay riots.

[153] Bombay Confidential Proceedings, Home, December 1921, vol. 62, pp. 771–81, OIOC.

[154] Pandey, *The Ascendancy of the Congress in UP*, pp. 129–30 ff.; Gooptu, 'Political Culture of the Urban Poor in North India', ch. 5.

[155] GOB, Home (Special), Files 792 of 1932, 793 (1) of 1932 and 793 (1), Parts I –III of 1932, MSA.

The attempt by Congress 'volunteers' to enforce a hartal in Kanpur on the day of Bhagat Singh's execution led to a ferocious communal riot which left 400 people dead and 1,200 injured in three days of violence.[156] Such riots are detonated on long fuses and many of these had been working their way through the region for over a decade. The reluctance of Muslim traders, shopkeepers, artisans and the urban poor to participate in the hartal grew in part out of their resentment about Gandhi's withdrawal of non-cooperation, which many perceived as a betrayal of the Khilafat cause. The intensification of communal tensions in the 1920s found expression in the revivalist shuddhi and tanzeem movements. The decline of the trades which Muslims had once dominated, the rapid rise of some Hindu traders on the back of local economic expansion during the first world war and in its immediate aftermath, and the increasingly fierce competition for jobs, housing and credit as the flow of migrants to the city gathered pace, each contributed to the entrenchment of communal antagonisms. More generally, political discourse in the early twentieth century was fashioned increasingly by a sectarian vocabulary, as political groupings defined themselves in caste or communal terms to gain access to the structure of colonial power and its system of representation. Thus Harijans and backward castes sought to define their own 'communities' by inventing past glories, which, it was inevitably said, had been flattened by Muslim invaders, thus explaining their current lowly status in communal terms.[157] Factional rivalries within the provincial Congress often led their protagonists to cultivate a wider constituency by espousing an increasingly explicit Hindu rhetoric.[158] In a sense, the policies of government and the politics of the provincial Congress sanctioned the increasingly free expression of communal antagonisms in public discourse.

It has been a central contention of this book that relations of power which constituted the working classes cannot be understood in terms of class alone. The formation of the working classes also encompassed relations of power described by caste and kinship, village and neighbourhood, skill and occupation, age and gender, religion and nation. None of these signified a permanent and unchanging, or a compelling and necessary social and cultural identity or a state of 'consciousness'. How and why workers identified with one or other of these affinities was determined by

[156] Report of the Congress Cawnpore Riots Enquiry Committee in N. G. Barrier (ed.), *Roots of Communal Violence* (Delhi, 1976); *Report of the Commission of Inquiry into the Cawnpore Riots and Resolution of the Government of the United Provinces, PP, 1930–1*, vol. XII, Cmd. 3891; Pandey, *The Ascendancy of the Congress in UP*, pp. 129–42; Joshi, 'Bonds of Community, Ties of Religion', pp. 269–73 and *passim*; Gooptu, 'Political Culture of the Urban Poor in North India', ch. 5.
[157] Gooptu, 'Political Culture of the Urban Poor in North India', ch. 4.
[158] Pandey, *The Ascendancy of the Congress*, pp. 115–27.

the specificities of a particular political conjuncture. Furthermore, it should be apparent that the efforts of the Congress to 'mobilize the masses' could serve to divide them; the latter possessed no inherent or natural propensity to unite, let alone behind the Congress. The rhetoric of nationalism yielded competing images of the nation. This competition rested on the claim made by some groups that they represented the nation more fully and effectively than their rivals. Thus, the rhetoric of a Hindu nationalism might claim to distil the essence of the Indian nation, to represent the 'real people' better than their non-communal variants; and it is clear that to some sections of the working classes this rhetoric appeared plausibly to explain their circumstances and hold out the promise of redress. While the Congress claim to represent the nation as a whole precluded, or at least set firm limits to, its espousal of a particular class or religious identity, it also declared an intent to transcend and subsume communal difference, even if the rhetoric of some Congressmen was suffused by an increasingly strident Hindu idiom. In the 1920s and 1930s, the Congress, in the mainstream, sought to place their nation on a firmly popular footing, not only through mass mobilization, but by representing the nation in terms which made it interchangeable with 'the real people', 'the common man' and 'the meanest of our countrymen'. But here lay the rub. For, in nationalist, as in colonial discourse, 'communalism' was also explained as the product of ignorance and superstition and its symptoms were thought to be most commonly displayed by simple and ordinary people. It followed, therefore, that they needed to be protected from themselves, not simply from the machinations of bigots and reactionaries or from colonial pro-consuls seeking to divide and rule. In this way, one of the many contradictions of Congress rhetoric was elaborated. For nationalism was called upon to transcend the people and, at the same time, to represent them, to protect them from themselves and yet become of them. 'The Congress', as Jawaharlal Nehru had told the Lucknow Congress in his famous presidential address, 'must be not only *for* the masses, as it claims but *of* the masses'.[159]

VI

However, there was one important theme of Congress rhetoric which had significant implications for the development of working-class politics. But its consequences were unintended and unforeseen. In the 1920s and 1930s, the colonial state was subject to increasingly stringent political criticism. The rhetoric of the Congress became more explicitly anti-

[159] *The Selected Works of Jawaharlal Nehru*, vol. VII, p. 178.

colonial. It no longer spoke of the un-Britishness of British rule in India, but questioned the morality of the colonial state. It challenged the justice of its laws; it withheld its cooperation from the Government; it elevated civil disobedience into an act of heroism. Although some Congressmen entered the councils in 1923, council entry could only be justified by the objective of wrecking the legislatures from within. Of course, this had a greater symbolic or rhetorical value than any consistent practical effect.

In the domain of working-class politics, its benefits accrued not to conciliatory Congress trade union organizers but to political groups who, seeking to represent labour, were marginalized by employers as well as the state. These publicists, notably communists, were forced by their own marginality in industrial politics, by their exclusion from the workplace, not only to adopt a stance of continuous opposition to the employers and the state but also, through their repeated interventions in the disputes of workplace and neighbourhood, to realize this rhetoric in political action. In the 1920s and 1930s, one of the most significant factors in working-class politics was the growing presence of the state. Attempts to recruit workers for a distant and irrelevant war caused considerable disquiet in 1917. The economic dislocations of the war and its immediate aftermath were widely perceived as a failure of government. The grain riots in Madras in 1918 were the result, we are told, of 'popular resentment . . . against the government [which] seemed to be exercising no control to ensure supplies and keep prices down'.[160] The tariff, excise and monetary policies of the state impinged directly upon working conditions, employment and wages, and sharpened the lines of antagonism between workers and the state. The Bombay millowners frequently justified their wage cuts or rationalization schemes as the necessary, though undesirable, consequences of the government's tariff and exchange policies. Lower wages, higher workloads and greater unemployment lay at the heart of the communist-led general strikes of 1928–29 in Bombay.[161] Large-scale, sometimes industry-wide, strikes, frequently prolonged and bitter disputes, stoked official anxieties about the public order. Strikers were more closely policed. The intervention of the state to settle disputes worked more often to defeat their objectives and to negate their demands than to secure them. In the 1930s, the effect of trade union legislation was largely to narrow the already limited freedom of manoeuvre which workers and their representatives had previously possessed.

The political experience of the working classes was constituted in relation to the state. In the late 1920s and 1930s, in Bombay and

[160] D. Arnold, 'Looting, Grain Riots and Government Policy in South India, 1918', *Past and Present*, 84 (1979), 145.
[161] Chandavarkar, *The Origins of Industrial Capitalism*, ch. 9.

Sholapur, and later in the decade in Coimbatore, Kanpur and Calcutta, communist trade unions gained considerably from their stance of consistent opposition to the state. The anti-colonial rhetoric of the Congress, by challenging the legitimacy of the state, paid handsome dividends to trade unions and political groups which pursued an active strategy of confrontation. Opposition to the state provided a focus around which a fragmented and sectionalized working class could at times coalesce, though not necessarily behind the banner of the Congress – indeed often under the hammer and sickle of various socialist and communist groupings.

VII

In the 1940s, however, this situation was reversed. It became much harder for the working classes to perceive the left, and especially the communists, in this oppositional role. After 1941, the communists abandoned their oppositional stance altogether and adopted an increasingly conciliatory method in industrial disputes. They sought actively to prevent strikes, to encourage greater productivity, even to dissuade workers from participation in nationalist agitations and tried to convince their once enthusiastic followers that they were fighting the people's war.[162] On the other hand, the Congress now appeared to be the only party which was willing to move against the state. Having accepted office in 1937, they had spurned it after 1939. The Quit India movement was a far more impressive campaign than civil disobedience had been and it attracted widespread support in Bombay and Gujarat, UP and Bihar, Bengal and Orissa.[163] According to the Viceroy, it was 'by far the most serious rebellion since that of 1857'. The immediate future, he feared, would bring 'a formidable attempt to renew this widespread sabotage of our war effort', which could if successful 'damage India irretrievably as a base for future allied operations'.[164] In 1942, however, the British commanded

---

[162] The fate of the communists in Bombay during the second world war can be followed in GOB Home (Special), File 543 (13) – B (4) of 1941–3 and File 543 (13) – B (5) of 1943–5, MSA.

[163] A. C. Bhuyan, *The Quit India Movement: The Second World War and Indian Nationalism* (Delhi, 1975); F. G. Hutchins, *Spontaneous Revolution: The Quit India Movement* (New Delhi, 1971); F. G. Hutchins, *India's Revolution: Gandhi and the Quit India Movement* (Cambridge, Mass., 1973); Y. B. Mathur, *Quit India Movement* (Delhi, 1979); S. Henningham, 'Quit India in Bihar and the Eastern United Provinces: The Dual Revolt', in R. Guha (ed.), *Subaltern Studies*, vol. II, pp. 130–79; P. Greenhough, 'Political Mobilization and the Underground Literature of the Quit India Movement, 1942–44', *MAS*, 17:3 (1983), 353–86; P. N. Chopra (ed.), *Quit India Movement: British Secret Report* (Faridabad, 1976); G. Pandey (ed.), *The Indian Nation in 1942* (Calcutta, 1988).

[164] Linlithgow to Churchill, 31 August 1942 in P. N. Mansergh (ed.) *The Transfer of Power, 1942–47*, vol. II: *'Quit India', 30 April–21 September 1942* (HMSO, London, 1942), Document no. 662, pp. 853–4.

greater military force than at any time in the history of their rule. This was no time for 'rough-housing Indian rioters' with *'bandobast* and bluff'[165] – the habitual role of the Indian Army in the 1920s and 1930s. The British moved their artillery and their aeroplanes swiftly into action and the Quit India movement was suppressed, rather ruthlessly, within a month. In parts of Bihar and east UP it rumbled on for months and even years.[166]

Between 1942 and 1945, Congressmen were imprisoned in droves, while the communists, standing shoulder to shoulder with the British to fight the people's war, were ironically able to operate openly and legally. During this period, communist labour leaders entrenched themselves effectively in political institutions, and especially in the trade union movement. Where the communists had been relatively marginal to the labour movement in the 1930s, for instance in Bengal, they took their opportunity to capture the provincial Trade Union Congress gleefully. But in the 1946 elections in Bengal, the Congress swept the polls in the labour constituencies, with only two exceptions, one of them being Jyoti Basu, the future leader of the CPI (M) and the chief minister of West Bengal.[167] In Bombay, however, where the communists had dominated the labour movement, they knew only too well that dominating the committees of evanescent trade unions did not ensure influence and control at the level of the workplace and the neighbourhood. It was in the 1940s that their fortunes began to wane. But the loyalty which the communists could inspire among the working classes in Bombay, especially in the cotton textile industry, was not wholly eroded until the 1960s and 1970s. The People's War was to cast a lengthening shadow over its strategists as well as its foot soldiers.

It has already been argued that Indian nationalism, as it was represented by the Congress, was primarily a discourse of political exclusion. As the second world war ended, and swaraj seemed realizable, political liberation brought with it for many in India the promise of social renewal and transformation as well. Now that the political aims of swaraj were about to be achieved, the social questions which had been subordinated to it would be more explicitly addressed. Between 1945 and 1947, the

[165] J. Gallagher, *The Decline, Revival and Fall of the British Empire*, ed. Anil Seal (Cambridge, 1982), p. 137.
[166] M. Harcourt, 'Kisan Populism and Revolution in Rural India: The 1942 Disturbances in Bihar and East United Provinces', in Low (ed.), *Congress and the Raj*; G. Omvedt, 'The Satara Prati Sarkar' in Pandey (ed.), *The Indian Nation*, pp. 223–62; G. Pandey, 'The Revolt of August 1942 in Eastern UP and Bihar', in *ibid.*, pp. 123–64; and C. Mitra, 'Popular Uprising in 1942: The Case of Ballia', in *ibid.*, pp. 165–84.
[167] Singh, *Life is a Struggle*, p. 63; N. Basu, *Political Parties and Labour Politics, 1937–1947* (Calcutta, 1992) especially ch. 5.

working classes could more closely identify the Congress with a political programme which appeared most consistently and effectively to encompass their interests. Ironically, at the same time, the objectives of the Congress now focused less on mobilizing these aspirations than, increasingly, on curbing them.[168] In 1946–47, however, as independence took shape before their eyes, it seemed to many, including large sections of the working classes, that there was room for all in the nation of the future. Nothing suggested this more strongly than the fact that despite the comprehensive failure of Ambedkar's Scheduled Caste Federation in the 1946 elections, this inveterate champion of separate electorates for the untouchables was first brought into the Constituent Assembly, and then appointed to chair the committee which drafted the constitution, by the Congress, whom he had in the previous year made the subject of his coruscating invective. Article 17 of the constitution briskly abolished untouchability. Even some of the temples which had most stubbornly resisted the entry of untouchables opened their doors to them on the eve of independence.[169] Nobody, it seemed, was to be excluded from India's 'tryst with destiny' – nobody that is, except the Muslims of Bengal and Punjab and of the remote Muslim-majority provinces of the north-west.

Those who remained in India could now be embraced by an inclusive concept of the nation. Significantly, the constitution adopted the principle of universal adult suffrage and it abolished special and communal electorates. As the Congress drew closer to inheriting the Raj, its social base was dominated by propertied, mercantile and scribal elites whose interests would ostensibly have been better served by limited electorates than by universal franchise. The adoption of universal adult suffrage, therefore, requires explanation. It cannot, of course, be explained as the culminating triumph of a 'mass' nationalism. Nor, in view of the many Gandhian precepts which the Congress flouted, can the decision be understood as deferential to Gandhi's enunciation of universal suffrage as one of the essential pre-conditions of swaraj in its most comprehensive sense. Nor can it simply be explained as the logical expression of the inherently democratic impulse of Indian nationalism. There is little to justify quite such a romantic view. On the contrary, shrewd observers of Indian politics in the 1940s noted with disquiet and apprehension the undemocratic tendency of the Congress to seek to substitute itself for the apparatus of the colonial state. In the last decades of British rule, the

[168] S. Sarkar, 'Popular Movements and National Leadership, 1945–47', *Economic and Political Weekly*, 17:14, 15 and 16 (annual number, April 1982), 677–89.
[169] E. Zelliot, 'Congress and the Untouchables, 1917–1950', in Sisson and Wolpert (eds.) *Congress and Indian Nationalism*, pp. 193–4.

Congress had presented itself not merely as a party of nationalist opposition to the colonial state, but as a parallel government, even a state-in-waiting.[170]

The commitment to universal suffrage in 1950 owed something to the lessons which the Congress had learnt in 1937. When the British extended the franchise in 1935, their aim was to secure their rule on a firmer foundation by creating a political system which would reward their collaborators, like the zamindars of Bengal and Bihar and the taluqdars of the UP, the big capitalists and moribund Liberals like Tej Bahadur Sapru. They calculated that by extending the vote beyond the thirty million who were enfranchised by the Government of India Act of 1935, they would favour the Congress and that by excluding the masses, they would favour the Liberals and their other allies. In fact, they made the mistake of wishing to attach their rule to men whose future lay behind them and whose collaboration would not secure their position; and they compounded it by assuming that the Congress was the party of the masses. Plainly, it was not. If the British persuaded themselves that they knew their India, the Congress sometimes took its own rhetoric too literally. As much to the surprise of the British as to the Congress, the latter was elected to power in seven out of eleven provinces. By limiting the electorate to thirty million, the British had, in fact, enfranchised precisely those intermediate castes and substantial peasants who in the 1930s had entrusted their hopes and their interests to the safekeeping of the Congress and excluded those who might from deference or dependence, or even antagonism against dominant peasants, have voted for the taluqdars and zamindars.[171] By the late 1940s, it must have been clear to any discerning Congressman that it was imperative to avoid the mistakes which the British had made in the previous decade.

This imperative was made more, rather than less, urgent by the extent to which the Congress benefited from the settlement of 1947. As the constitutional negotiations were deadlocked in 1946, and the Congress had pressed for the partition of India, it emerged with a centralized political structure and strong unitary powers. In the light of its experience of the 1920s, which had demonstrated beyond doubt that it would not

---

[170] R. Coupland, *India – A Restatement* (London, 1945), esp. pp. 173–6; R. Coupland, *A Report on the Constitutional Problem in India*, 3 vols. (London, 1942–3); George E. Schuster and Guy Wint, *India and Democracy* (London, 1941).

[171] *Government of India Despatch on Proposals for Constitutional Reform, dated 20th September 1930, PP, 1930–31*, vol. XXIII, pp. 71–14, Cmd. 3700; *Report of the Indian Franchise Committee, 1932*, vol. I, *PP, 1931–32*, vol. VIII, Cmd. 4086; Coupland, *India*, pp. 127–54; Tomlinson, *The Indian National Congress and the Raj*, pp. 65–85; Baker, *The Politics of South India*, chs. 3 and 4; R. J. Moore, *The Crisis of Indian Unity, 1917–1940* (Oxford, 1974).

flourish in a federation of strong provinces, these were major assets. The sheer size of the electoral system also worked in favour of the Congress. None of its rivals – now that the Muslim League was removed from the scene – had the resources, experience and political networks to compete on an equal footing for the support of such a massive, dispersed and heterogeneous electorate. The Congress leadership learned from the experience of 1937 that no political party or social interest with a firm grip on a strong centre could hope, especially in the context of the 1950s, to long survive a narrowly restricted franchise. To thus leave a significant section of the population out of the political nation was for the Congress in power to offer its rivals an opportunity to unleash a popular movement against them.

If nationalism had been primarily a discourse of political exclusion before 1947, its main protagonist, having inherited the state, now continued to accommodate the citizens of independent India within its political domain. The rhetoric of planning and economic development, national integration and nation-building offered a stake in the nation for each of its citizens; and as it came to be embellished more explicitly with the idioms of socialism and the slogan of garibi hatao, it held out the promise that each might eventually have an equal share. Having been nurtured on the claim that it represented the nation as a whole, the Congress was reluctant radically to alter its character in the 1950s and 1960s. In 1957, the general secretary of the Congress, stressing the need for ideological clarity, and 'for bringing about the socialist order through the democratic process', described it as the party of the

landlords as well as the tenant class; there are businessmen as well as representatives of the working class. When natural differences arise as a result of existing conflict of class interests we try to strike a balance in order to satisfy both sections. We must recognize that there do exist class conflicts and it is necessary to resolve them not through hatred and violence but through persuasion and democratic legislation. The Congress stands for the ultimate welfare of all sections of the population and desires to hate none.[172]

It was only in the late 1960s, as foreign exchange and balance of payments crises, and then industrial stagnation began to take effect, that this rhetoric lost its force and it became increasingly difficult for the Congress to sustain its all-embracing definition of nation.[173] As deeper and more

[172] Shriman Narayan, 'Need for Ideological Clarity', *AICC Economic Review*, 15 June 1957, cited by F. Frankel, *India's Political Economy, 1947–1977: The Gradual Revolution* (Princeton, 1978), p. 160.
[173] On the crisis of the 1960s, see P. Patnaik, 'Imperialism and the Growth of Indian Capitalism', in R. Owen and R. Sutcliffe (eds.), *Studies in the Theory of Imperialism* (London, 1972), pp. 210–29.

ferocious social conflicts revealed how difficult it would be to manage the Indian state on the old terms, the definition of the Indian nation was to be debated within a new, narrower and more sectarian idiom.

VII

Despite the proliferation of local studies of the Congress, and of nationalist agitations, explanatory frameworks for understanding the relationship between the Congress and its fluctuating and intermittent 'mass following' have been not only scarce but also rudimentary. Circumstances have made cases. And as circumstances have been infinitely varied, cases have proliferated. It has been the intention of this chapter to propose that a way out of this historiographical stagnation is to address the relationship between the Congress and its following specifically as a relationship, or as a 'problematic' in its own right. Studies of 'mass mobilization', by their diffusionist assumption that ideas and a consciousness of resistance trickled down from the leaders to their followers, have taken the initiative out of the hands of those whose behaviour needs to be explained, and have thus cast more darkness than light upon the nature of popular politics. Studies of 'popular culture', by seeking polemically to dissociate the politics of nationalism from 'peasant' or 'subaltern' action, have undermined the very notion of a relationship between them.

In examining this relationship between the Congress and its popular following, this chapter has proceeded on the assumption that popular nationalism was more than the sum of their diverse class interests or their particular and varied social relations. Thus, it will not be enough to conclude that popular discontent found 'articulation' in nationalist campaigns – although at specific moments this may indeed have happened.[174] Moreover, popular responses to the Congress were not always contained within the ideological parameters or discursive framework of an Indian nationalism. It could develop a more specific affinity to caste or religious community, or it might be extended in a more explicitly anti-colonial direction, seeking to register its hostility to the colonial state. To suggest that popular support for the Congress could amount to more than the sum of its social and sectional parts should not invite the assumption that there was a latent nationalism in Indian society waiting to be picked up and developed by an appropriate leadership, rhetoric or political programme.

The argument that nationalism proved attractive to the class interests which it served is not our concern, not least because class interests were

---

[174] Or, for that matter, they might have found expression in communal conflicts.

not naturally solidaristic but inherently fragmented and sectionalized by the diverse relations of power through which they were constituted. The investigation of the relationship between the Congress and its popular following should begin with a scepticism of the axiom that social groups can be ascribed a single common interest derived from their relationship to the means of production. Not only the supposedly objective interests of given social groups but even their defining identities were subject to the flux of changing historical circumstances. Their recognition of the mutuality of their interests, no less than the language in which they were described, were contingent upon particular and shifting intellectual and political contexts. Theoretical assumptions about the nature and effects of production relations, which have yielded such abstractions of common interest, have been repeatedly and often rudely brought to ground by the subversive play of politics.

To challenge the assumption of a solidaristic working class is not, of course, to foreclose the possibility that workers might perceive the mutuality of their interests within a particular historical conjuncture, but rather to reject the notion that its permanence was inscribed in the relations of production and that its permanence transcended its formation in, and re-shaping by, changing historical circumstances. There is no reason to suppose that industrial workers had a natural propensity to grasp their social situation consistently, or exclusively, in the language of class. If the working classes sometimes perceived their common interests in the language of class, they could individually and severally under different circumstances grasp their identity in the language of caste, religion or nation. The working classes did not constitute a natural, if underutilized, resource for nationalism. On the contrary, the ideology of nationalism, like the organization of the Congress, had to be socially constituted and reproduced. The nationalism of the working classes, perhaps any nationalism, could take diverse forms and find a variety of contradictory expressions. Its development did not necessarily work to the benefit of the Congress but in some cases and at certain times profited the communists. Similarly, the definitions of nation produced by these developments could serve to divide a fragmented working class yet further, accentuating differences between Hindus and Muslims, untouchables and caste Hindus, sometimes between occupations, though probably mediating and temporizing those between the sexes.

The appeal of the Congress depended largely on how it represented its followers to themselves both in its rhetoric and its political action. Whether workers identified themselves with the Congress, or the nation, was contingent upon the plausibility of its political language, upon whether the working classes could explain their social and political circumstances in terms of its rhetoric and find within its programmatic framework both a convincing diagnosis of their ills and a realizable charter for the redressal of their grievances, the resolution of their problems and the transformation of their conditions. No conception of nationalist discourse, however, would be sufficient if it excluded what its protagonists did. The political stratagems and campaigns of the Congress influenced the ways in which workers interpreted their rhetoric. After the first world war, the rhetoric of the Congress, never univocal even at its most harmonious, came increasingly to be inflected by Gandhi. For all the inspirational quality of his rhetorical message, Gandhi's popularity among the Ahmedabad millworkers during the 1918 strike was rapidly slipping until he turned the tables on the millowners and the workers with his fast. In addition, during the strike, his rhetoric was grasped and interpreted in the light of his own imaginative conduct of the dispute: his accessibility (and that of his lieutenants) to the workers, his attention to detail, his willingness to associate with the needs of the workers and to intervene on behalf of individual workers on any matter however insignificant, his daily leaflets, his evening meetings on the banks of the Sabarmati.[175] In the early 1920s, Gandhian rhetoric represented the masses more persuasively than, for instance, the nationalism of the preceding decade. Its significance lay in its ability to offer materials from which its followers could not only grasp their situation with greater clarity but also forge strategies to ameliorate, remedy and alter its conditions. This in itself was not a permanent, or even necessarily an enduring condition. On the other hand, the ability of the Congress to generalize disputes beyond the locality enabled it to attach itself to specific and localized struggles and at the same time made it worthwhile for working-class groups to recruit the Congress at particular moments. The limitations of the rhetoric of the Congress, and its political context, were sometimes to be cruelly exposed in the following decades and sometimes, as conditions changed, to make fresh political strategies and opportunities available to its constituents. Political mobilization should be considered, therefore, not as a process of the diffusion of ideas and beliefs from leaders to followers, from the literate to the ignorant, from the sophisticated to the simple, which stimulates the masses into action, but as a process of empowerment in which the latter are able to interpret a political discourse not only for an explanation of their present situation but also for a realizable method of changing it.

[175] Desai, *A Righteous Struggle.*

9   South Asia and world capitalism: towards a social history of labour

I

In the past three decades, the work of dependency theorists and 'world systems' analysts has ensured that it is no longer tenable to study the history of any region, whether in the West or the Third World, in isolation from the world economy.[1] But it is also becoming something of a commonplace that a perspective centred upon the 'metropole' or the 'core' has tended to peripheralize the history of large parts of the world. The view from the periphery has sometimes suggested that the leading question is misdirected:[2] while it is impossible to deny that the world economy has impinged upon social relations and economic development in India, it is also important to ask how Indian society shaped and channelled the impact of the West. This chapter will seek to situate the development of

---

An earlier version of this chapter was presented to a conference at Tufts University in December 1986 on the theme of South Asia and World Capitalism. Some of the papers presented at the conference were published in S. Bose (ed.), *South Asia and World Capitalism* (Delhi, 1990). The conference focused upon the work of Immanuel Wallerstein, which is reflected in the particular emphasis placed in this chapter upon his treatment of world capitalism.

[1] I. Wallerstein, 'The Rise and Future Demise of the World System: Concepts for Comparative Analysis', *Comparative Studies in Society and History*, 16 (1974), 387–415; I. Wallerstein, *The Capitalist World Economy* (Cambridge, 1979). For Wallerstein's attempt to place the history of India in relation to the world system, see I. Wallerstein, 'Incorporation of the Indian Sub-continent into the Capitalist World Economy', *Economic and Political Weekly*, 21:4 (25 January 1986), *Review of Political Economy*, PE-28 to PE-39. For useful surveys of dependency theories, see A. Brewer, *Marxist Theories of Imperialism: A Critical Survey* (London, 1980), especially, Part III; K. Griffin and J. Gurley, 'Radical Analyses of Imperialism, the Third World and the Transition to Socialism', *Journal of Economic Literature*, 23 (1985), 1089–143. For an interesting and important critique, see R. Brenner, 'The Origins of Capitalist Development: A Critique of Neo-Smithian Marxism', *New Left Review*, 104 (1977), 25–94.
[2] Wallerstein, 'Incorporation of the Indian Sub-continent into the Capitalist World Economy'. For a detailed critique of Wallerstein, see D. Washbrook, 'South Asia, the World System and World Capitalism', *JAS*, 49:3 (1990), 479–508. For a different perspective, see A. K. Bagchi, 'Colonialism and the Nature of "Capitalist" Enterprise in India', *Economic and Political Weekly*, 23:31 (30 July 1988), *Review of Political Economy*, PE-38 to PE-58.

327

capital–labour relations in South Asian industry within the context of world capitalism as well as the subcontinent's economic history. In seeking to examine how the formation of an industrial labour force shaped the nature of capitalist development in India, it will also attempt to pull together some of the leading themes which this book has investigated.

II

How to classify social change or grasp the meaning of capitalism in South Asia, however, is a vexed question. Marx defined and elaborated the concept of the capitalist mode of production specifically in the context of the industrial revolution. Its defining feature was its inherent tendency to reproduce itself on an increasing scale. This was most fully realized with the commoditization of labour power, facilitating its progressive subsumption by capital. Production for the market, and the increasing commoditization of labour power, propelled the development of capitalism when it was accompanied by a complementary process of industrialization.

To a large extent, Marx inferred the characteristics of pre-capitalist modes of production from his more systematic exposition of capitalism. Few subsequent theorists have matched his range and historical insight and pre-capitalist modes of production have remained weakly formulated. Most studies of the rise of capitalism and the dissolution of earlier modes of production in the Third World identify elements of 'commercialization' as markers towards capitalist development, but usually these processes are observed without a corresponding growth of industry and its effects are unlikely, although they are often assumed, to be the same. As Wallerstein illustrates effectively, historians of capitalism in the West have also found it especially difficult to conceptualize social relations in transitional periods characterized by the absence of significant industrialization.[3] Another response to the problem of transition and the task of identifying the emergence of the capitalist mode of production has been to acknowledge the existence of diverse forms of production relations in pre-capitalist societies and to focus upon their articulation within a given social formation. But these modes of production have often appeared so diverse and varied and their articulation so remote, complex and abstract that this has proved a difficult method to apply in concrete empirical or historical analysis.[4]

[3] Wallerstein, The *Capitalist World Economy*, pp. 15–17.
[4] G. Arrighi, 'Labour Supplies in Historical Perspective: A Study of the Proletarianization of the African Peasantry in Rhodesia', *Journal of Development Studies*, 6:3 (1970), 197–234; Brewer, *Marxist Theories of Imperialism*, ch. 8. For the mode of production debate conducted in relation to India, see Utsa Patnaik (ed.), *Agrarian Relations and Accumulation: The 'Mode of Production' Debate in India* (Bombay, 1990).

The roots of this problem may well lie in a rather absolutist application of definitions of capitalism in terms of 'free' wage labour. Such an application may be facilitated by cases where all the processes of commercialization in Marx's model were working simultaneously and together. But these were special cases. Where these processes occurred partially, historians may be better served by a looser and more flexible understanding of capitalism. The readiness of the world systems approach to accept that capitalist exploitation could occur through several forms of labour use should facilitate a broader definition of both capital and labour in South Asian history. With the emergence of world capitalism, a wide range of production relations manifested in large parts of the world could no longer simply be taken to reflect pre-capitalist modes for they were being constituted in relation to, and were indeed passing under the hegemony of capitalism. Paradoxically, by relaxing the rigidities of the concept, the world systems approach may offer South Asianists most usefully, not so much a method of investigating its incorporation into the world economy, as a means of recovering the subcontinental context and history of capitalist development.

While the world systems approach may have directed our attention to 'the problems incurred by using the pervasiveness of *wage* labour as a defining characteristic of capitalism',[5] it has generated problems of its own. The capitalist mode of production was conceived as an abstract model, which nowhere manifested itself in real circumstances, but provided a key to understanding a wide variety of cases. The world systems approach while inveighing against the reification of its parts has tended to reify capitalism as a whole. Its explanatory value seems to lie in its claim that the world system constituted a real observable totality, for which it provided the most suitable generalizing description. The world system is offered as the only real 'totality' since no other categories are self-sustaining units of analysis or able to provide an adequate basis for comparison. But the notion of totality is, of course, beset with epistemological problems, for its integrity lies most securely in the eyes of its beholder.

Furthermore, the world system, it would appear, is created primarily through the expansion of networks of exchange. But the mechanism of capitalist expansion for Marx was not simply the driving force of production for sale and profit but the appropriation of surplus value as it was shaped by class conflict between labour and capital at the point of production. In its steady diffusion of market relations, world capitalism often appears to be an inexorable force hammering ceaselessly upon passive, traditional societies, moulding them according to its needs. On the other hand, class struggle and contradiction were integral and indis-

---

[5] Wallerstein, *The Capitalist World Economy*, p. 17.

pensable to Marx's conception of capitalist development. To recognize that their outcome would determine the nature and characteristics of capitalism in particular cases appears also to promise a more specifically historical approach to the investigation of social change.

III

Industrialization within the periphery raises a special problem for the analysis of the modern world system. If the expansion of the European world economy in its phase of industrial capitalism, driven forward by its thirst for markets and raw materials, created a single division of labour within the capitalist world economy, and progressively appropriated and transferred the surplus to the core, it is easier to conceptualize the incorporation within the world economy of an agrarian periphery than an industrializing one. Already, by the early twentieth century, India had a substantial industrial sector and one of the ten largest labour forces in the world.[6]

The conventional explanation of the origins of industrialization in India has been that it formed part of a steady process of technological diffusion working gradually outwards from eighteenth-century Western Europe.[7] Seen as a process of technological diffusion, industrialization in India can be understood as a function of the expansion of networks of exchange throughout the world and the incorporation of new regions into a world economy centred upon Western Europe. Some strength is lent to this argument by the fact that the capital for industry was raised predominantly from the profits of trade, and in the case of the Bombay textile industry in the China trade, where peddling cotton and pushing opium were integral to the mechanisms by which Western European capitalism penetrated the periphery and undermined pre-existing 'world empires'.[8] Similarly, expatriate British capital which sponsored industrialization in eastern India had been fattened on the gains of the private trade and nurtured by the Company's mercantilism. Moreover, expatriate capital engaged primarily in the extraction, processing and export of raw materials, enabled the incorporation of the subcontinent into the capitalist world economy, and helped to foster the division of labour

[6] B. R. Tomlinson, *The Political Economy of the Raj: The Economics of Decolonization in India* (London, 1979), p. 31. See ch. 2 above.   [7] See ch. 2 above.

[8] Chandavarkar, *The Origins of Industrial Capitalism*, pp. 44–67; Siddiqi, 'The Business World of Jamsetjee Jejeebhoy'; A. M. Vicziany, 'The Cotton Trade and the Commercial Development of Bombay, 1853–1875', unpublished Ph.D. thesis, University of London, 1975; A. K. Bagchi, 'Reflections on Patterns of Regional Growth in India During the Period of British Rule', *Bengal Past and Present*, 95:1 (1976), 247–89; on the China trade, see M. Greenberg, *British Trade and the Opening of China, 1800–1842* (Cambridge, 1951).

based upon it.[9] That the domination of European capital was nurtured by the mercantilist Company state, acting as an agency for the incorporation of the Indian economy, only serves to strengthen the argument that the rise of industry was integral to the incorporation of the subcontinent to the world economy.

But the logic of the notion that industrialization was part of a Eurocentric diffusion of technology is tied to social theories of modernization, tends to remove the growth of factory industry from larger patterns of social and economic change and understands attenuated and incomplete processes of industrialization in terms of a teleology derived from what we think we know about its final outcome, which in turn has usually emerged from special or even unique cases.[10] Historical evidence, both in South Asia and Western Europe, suggests a different view: it points to an understanding of industrialization, not in terms of the forces of production, of technological advance sustained by its own inner logic, but in terms of the social relations of production, as an outcome of class conflict.[11] In this perspective, industrialization was not simply the consequence of the widening flows of exchange and their effects upon the development of the forces of production. On the contrary, its emphasis upon production relations and class conflict suggested that the history of industrialization would most fruitfully be returned to its South Asian context, albeit one which was influenced by its relationship to the capitalist world economy.

It is not intended to suggest either that industrial development in India was the natural or inevitable outcome of the relationships between capital and labour or that the South Asian context of class formation and class conflict was somehow autonomous of world capitalism. But it is doubtful that the expansion of the capitalist world economy may be adequately explained in terms of 'sources . . . internal to the European world-economy', irrespective of its interaction with the regional economies and polities which it sought to pull into its orbit.[12] We might, indeed, accept,

---

[9] Bagchi, 'Reflections on Patterns of Regional Growth in India'; S. Bhattacharya, 'Regional Economy (1757–1857): Eastern India, Part I', and B. B. Chowdhury, 'Regional Economy (1757–1857): Eastern India, Part II', in Kumar (ed.), *CEHI*, vol. II, pp. 270–95, 295–332; Wallerstein, 'Incorporation of the Indian Subcontinent'; C. Fisher, 'Planters and Peasants: The Ecological Context of Agrarian Unrest on Indigo Plantations of North Bihar, 1820–1920', in C. J. Dewey and A. G. Hopkins (eds.), *The Imperial Impact: Studies in the Economic History of Africa and India* (London, 1978), pp. 114–31; Sir P. Griffiths, *The History of the Indian Tea Industry* (London, 1967); J. Richards, 'The Indian Empire and Peasant Production of Opium in the Nineteenth Century', *MAS*, 15:1 (1981), 59–82.
[10] See ch. 2 above.
[11] See, especially, the highly suggestive essay by Stephen Marglin, 'What Do Bosses Do?' *Review of Radical Political Economy*, 6 (1974), 60–112.
[12] Wallerstein, 'The Incorporation of the Indian Subcontinent', PE-30.

as Wallerstein has advised, that 'we should not look too far for reasons peculiar to the Indian subcontinent' to explain its 'incorporation' into the world economy. Yet it was precisely these reasons of specific, historical context which determined the manner and pattern of its 'incorporation'. Indeed, they led Wallerstein to admit, in contradiction, that in the manner of its incorporation India was 'the exception and exceptions need to be accounted for'.[13] Recent research has increasingly directed attention to the domestic origins of Indian capitalism.[14] In the late eighteenth and early nineteenth centuries, diverse social groups, with some command of capital, were able to exploit the mechanisms of local state systems and growing commercial opportunities to consolidate their position and accumulate capital while chipping away at communal reciprocities and social obligations upon it, and eroding labour's customary rights to its share of the product.[15] The expansion of British power in India picked up these tendencies, was even facilitated by their workings, and indeed developed them further. Its effects, which only became apparent in the 1830s and 1840s, were manifested in the subordination of Indian capital to the interests of the colonial state and metropolitan capitalism.[16] The economic function of mercantile capital was progressively reduced to petty trade and usury. The relative acquiescence of local elites, or their lack of resistance to the expansion of British power, has been attributed to the increasing control which capital gained over labour.[17] The development of Indian capital thus came to be predicated upon the more intensive exploitation of labour.

The nature and contradictions of indigenous capitalist subordination may not have become fully apparent until the long depression of the 1820s–50s[18] began to lift and rising prices, a buoyant and expanding

---

[13] *Ibid.*, PE-32.

[14] See the seminal article by Irfan Habib, 'The Potentialities of Capitalistic Development in the Economy of Mughal India', *Journal of Economic History*, 29:1 (1969), 32–78.

[15] These arguments are most clearly stated in D. Washbrook, 'Progress and Problems: South Asian Social and Economic History, *c.* 1720–1860', *MAS*, 22:1 (1988), 57–96. See also C. A. Bayly, *Rulers, Townsmen and Bazaars: North Indian Society in the Age of British Expansion, 1770–1870* (Cambridge, 1983), chs. 5 and 6; E. T. Stokes, *The Peasant and the Raj: Studies in Agrarian Society and Peasant Rebellion in Colonial India* (Cambridge, 1978), chs. 1–3; Perlin, 'Proto-Industrialization in Pre-Colonial South Asia'.

[16] Bayly, *Rulers, Townsmen and Bazaars*, ch. 7; Washbrook, 'Progress and Problems'; Bagchi, 'Reflections on Patterns of Regional Growth'; Siddiqi, 'Jamsetjee Jejeebhoy'; D. A. Washbrook, 'Land and Labour in Late Eighteenth Century South India: The Golden Age of the Pariah', in P. Robb (ed.), *Dalit Movements and the Meanings of Labour* (Delhi, 1993), pp. 68–86. See also Wallerstein, 'The Incorporation of the Indian Subcontinent', which takes a longer view of this process of subordination.

[17] Washbrook, 'Progress and Problems'.

[18] *Ibid.*; Bayly, *Rulers, Townsmen and Bazaars*, chs. 6 and 7; A. Siddiqi, *Agrarian Change in a Northern Indian State: Uttar Pradesh, 1819–1833* (Oxford, 1973); S. Guha, *The Agrarian Economy of the Bombay Deccan, 1818–1941* (Delhi, 1986), ch. 2.

export demand and favourable exchange rates held out fresh opportunities for capitalist development at the very moment when an unfavourable
legal system and political initiatives to prevent land alienation, protect the
debtor and define tenants' rights served to restrict the possibilities of its
development and limit its scope.[19] The rapidity with which the agrarian
buoyancy of the later nineteenth century collapsed in the late 1890s
exposed most clearly the contradictions inherent in the development of
Indian capital.[20] The growth of nationalism, particularly among a wide
range of 'bourgeois' groups in the 1880s, may perhaps be seen as a
political manifestation of this contradiction.

The consequence of limited capitalist development in the countryside
was the stagnation of the agrarian structure. The limitations of capitalist
development signified its weakness as an agent of fundamental or far-
reaching changes in the structure of the agrarian economy. On the other
hand, economic buoyancy served to shore up the fragile smallholding
agrarian base. Agrarian stagnation increased the risks of investment and
left the rural economy vulnerable to demographic pressures, the vagaries
of the weather and international price fluctuations.[21]

Of course, some of the impulses which served to subordinate indigenous capital and subsume labour to it originated in the capitalist world
economy or stemmed from the colonial state. Bullion inflows had been
crucial to the consolidation of indigenous capital while their contraction
in the 1830s conversely weakened its position. In any case, bullion began
to be replaced by land revenue as the driving force of commercialization.[22] De-industrialization undermined the interests of mercantile capitalists but it also forced artisans onto the land and thus swelled the supply

---

[19] Stokes, *The Peasant and the Raj*, chs. 9–12; Washbrook, 'Law, State and Agrarian Society
in Colonial India'; Baker, *An Indian Rural Economy*; on the Punjab, see N. G. Barrier,
The Punjab Land Alienation Bill of 1900 (Duke University, 1966); N. Bhattacharya, 'The
Logic of Tenancy Cultivation: Central and South-East Punjab, 1870–1935', *IESHR*,
20:2 (1983), 121–70; Bhattacharya, 'Lenders and Debtors'; on the Deccan, see
N. Charlesworth, *Peasants and Imperial Rule: Agriculture and Agrarian Society in the
Bombay Presidency, 1850–1935* (Cambridge, 1985), pp. 95–203; J. Banaji, 'Capitalist
Domination and the Small Peasantry: Deccan Districts in the Late Nineteenth Century',
Economic and Political Weekly, 12:33–4 (1977), special number, 1375–404; Guha, *The
Agrarian Economy of the Bombay Deccan*, chs. 3–6.

[20] Stokes, *The Peasant and the Raj*, ch. 12; Washbrook, 'Law, State and Agrarian Society',
681–94; Banaji, 'Capitalist Domination and the Small Peasantry'; Guha, *The Agrarian
Economy of the Bombay Deccan*, esp. ch. 5; S. C. Mishra, 'Agricultural Trends in the
Bombay Presidency, 1900–1920: The Illusion of Growth', *MAS*, 19: 4 (1985), 733–59.

[21] Stokes, *The Peasant and the Raj*, ch. 12; Washbrook, 'Law, State and Agrarian Society';
Banaji, 'Capitalist Domination and the Small Peasantry'; Guha, *The Agrarian Economy of
the Bombay Deccan*, ch. 5; S. C. Mishra, 'Commercialization, Peasant Differentiation and
Merchant Capital in Late Nineteenth Century Bombay and Punjab', *Journal of Peasant
Studies*, 10:1 (1982), 3–51.   [22] Bayly, *Rulers, Townsmen and Bazaars*, chs. 6–7.

of labour.[23] Land revenue became the main engine for the appropriation and remittance of the surplus to England.[24] While the colonial bureaucracy destroyed the revenue farming function of mercantile capital and reduced its function within the state and agrarian society, the weight of the revenue demand increased the demand for credit from cultivators especially when prices began to fall in the 1830s, and thus facilitated their subordination to merchant capital. While productive investment declined, rising population, the settlement of mobile peasants, pastoralists, 'tribals' and forest dwellers under the twin imperatives of policing and taxation, and the effects of de-industrialization meant that competition of labour for the land increased and while the economy became less diversified and more dependent upon agriculture, so poorer and marginal lands were brought under the plough.[25]

These were scarcely promising beginnings for capital to embark upon industrialization. Yet on a comparative time-scale, modern factory industry appeared in India before it came to be established in Japan or Russia. In the face of the steady transfer of surplus to the core, industrial development in the periphery might be explained as a consequence of capitalist interests 'seeking to distort [a single world] market for their benefit by organizing to exert influence on states'.[26] Yet this argument would be difficult to sustain in the case of the colonial state whose aim was to act as the instrument of incorporation into the capitalist world economy on particular terms of advantage to Britain. Of course, the imperatives of political stability within India made the colonial state vulnerable to some Indian pressures. But in fact industrialization in India was driven forward by responses to the general subordination of indigenous capital rather than its development.[27] Those fractions of capital which invested in industry were usually marginal groups, often distanced from the institutions of the colonial state or even facing decline in valuable areas of the

---

[23] On the 'de-industrialization' debate, see the literature cited in ch. 2, fn 56, above. See also T. Roy (ed.), *Cloth and Commerce: Textiles in Colonial India* (New Delhi, 1996); for a recent general survey, see B. R. Tomlinson, *The New Cambridge History of India*, vol. III, part 3: *The Economy of Modern India, 1860–1970*, (Cambridge, 1993), pp. 101–9.

[24] A. Siddiqi, 'Money and Prices in the Earlier Stages of Empire', *Indian Economic and Social History Review*, 18:3 and 4 (1981), 231–62; Bagchi, 'Reflections on Patterns of Regional Growth'.

[25] C. A. Bayly, *The New Cambridge History of India*, vol. II, part 1: *Indian Society and the Making of the British Empire* (Cambridge, 1988), pp. 138–50; Washbrook, 'Problems and Progress'; M. Gadgil and R. Guha, 'State Forestry and Social Conflict in British India', *Past and Present*, 123 (1989), 141–77; M. Rangarajan, 'Imperial Agendas and India's Forests: The Early History of Indian Forestry, 1800–1878', *IESHR*, 31:2 (1994), 147–67.

[26] Wallerstein, *The Capitalist World Economy*, p. 25.

[27] See ch. 2 above; and Chandavarkar, *The Origins of Industrial Capitalism*, pp. 44–71, 239–77, 335–96.

export trade. For the risks of industrial investment were high and the returns uncertain. Parsi and Bhatia entrepreneurs invested in the first cotton mills in Bombay when they had been undermined in the export trade in raw cotton.[28] Marwaris provided the major Indian competitors within the jute industry.[29] Expatriate capital appears to have been rather timid and, in particular, slow to introduce mill production of jute textiles, which in any case were eventually able to compete effectively with the handloom sector largely because of their control over the export outlets and carrying trade and their access to the Presidency banks, the capital of the agency houses and the ear of the government.[30] Moreover, expatriate capital was invested in plantation industries, like indigo and tea, in the hope of generating raw material supplies and primary products within the British empire, seeking, in other words, to define an autarkic union within the capitalist world economy.[31]

The subordination of Indian capital and the structural constraints within which it developed conditioned the circumstances in which it might be drawn forward for industrial investment. Under-capitalization was a general characteristic and indeed constraint upon the development of Indian industry. Capital was characteristically mobilized in small pools, specifically for enterprises whose risks were known, whose viability was proven and whose directors were trusted. As a result investment tended to be imitative. Successful lines of production could attract a flood of investment until they became over-subscribed and unprofitable. At or preferably before this point, entrepreneurs would seek to diversify their investment, thus perpetuating the instability inherent in conditions where investment was so susceptible to fashion and believed to be so exposed to risk. The low ratio of fixed capital, the intensity of competition and the general tendency to under-capitalization called for a rapid turnover to

[28] Marika Vicziany, 'Bombay Merchants and Structural Changes in the Export Community, 1850 to 1880'; see ch. 2 above; and Chandavarkar, *The Origins of Industrial Capitalism*, ch. 6. Rutnagur (ed.), *Bombay Industries: The Cotton Mills*.

[29] Bagchi, *Private Investment in India*, chs. 6 and 8; T. A. Timberg, *The Marwaris: From Traders to Industrialists* (New Delhi, 1978); Goswami, 'Then Came the Marwaris'; Goswami, 'Collaboration and Conflict'; Goswami, '*Sahibs, Babus* and *Banias*'; Chakrabarty, *Rethinking Working Class History*, ch. 1.

[30] Bagchi, *Private Investment in India*, ch. 6; A. K. Sen, 'The Commodity Pattern of British Enterprise in Early Indian Industrialization, 1854–1914', in *The Second International Conference of Economic History, Aix-en-Provence, 1962*, vol. II: *Middle Ages and Modern Times* (Paris, 1962), pp. 781–808; Tomlinson, 'Colonial Firms and the Decline of Colonialism in Eastern India'; B. R. Tomlinson, 'British Business in India, 1860–1970', in R. P. T. Davenport-Hines and Geoffrey Jones (eds.), *British Business in Asia since 1860* (Cambridge, 1989), pp. 92–116; Goswami, '*Sahibs, Babus* and *Banias*'.

[31] Indigo, raw silk, opium and cotton accounted for nearly two-thirds of the total value of exports between 1814 and 1850. K. N. Chaudhuri, 'Foreign Trade and Balance of Payments (1757–1947)', in Kumar (ed.), *CEHI*, vol. II, p. 844; Wallerstein, 'The Incorporation of the Indian Subcontinent', PE-30 to PE-31.

finance debts, and production strategies sufficiently flexible to adapt to unpredictable markets. This pattern of investment also committed entrepreneurs to operate on narrow margins, tailoring production to short-term fluctuations of demand, minimizing their overheads and varying their labour force according to need.[32]

How far capital operated in this way varied according to the nature of the industry, its labour supply and labour relations, and its markets. But even in the case of the iron and steel or the coal industry, there were periodic crises of under-capitalization and the manipulation of working capital often held the key to the organization and deployment of labour.[33] The cotton textile industry operated on a larger scale in Bombay than anywhere else in the subcontinent; yet here too the millowners forsook the advantage of realizing the full value of their machinery costs and other fixed investments through the maintenance of steady levels of production. Despite an apparently oligopolistic structure of ownership in Bombay, the industry was rarely able to impose its wishes on individual entrepreneurs and attempts to fix price or output levels, or even to reach agreement on production conditions, seemed doomed to failure.[34] More surprisingly, in view of the relative weakness of foreign competition, attempts to introduce short-time working and curtail production in Bengal proved similarly problematic in the late 1920s and early 1930s.[35]

The causes of these production strategies were varied and complex ranging from the nature and institutions of industrial finance to the effects of foreign and to a lesser extent domestic competition in the home market. They reflected the interplay between structural constraints within the internal economy and the effects of the world economy upon the accumulation and reproduction of capital in India. Their consequence was a fluctuating demand for labour and the extensive use of casual hiring. Cumulatively these conditions, characterized by flexible patterns of labour use and the extensive deployment of casual labour, tended to produce a labour supply in excess of the usual needs of local industry in

[32] See ch. 2 above; Chandavarkar, The *Origins of Industrial Capitalism*, pp. 67–71, chs. 6–8. The evidence for the jute industry may be read in a similar fashion, even if it has been interpreted rather differently, for instance, in Chakrabarty, *Rethinking Working Class History*, ch. 1.

[33] Simmons, 'Indigenous Enterprise in the Indian Coal Mining Industry', 189–218; C. P. Simmons, 'Vertical Integration and the Indian Steel Industry', *MAS*, 11:1 (1977), 127–48; V. Bahl, 'The Emergence of Large-Scale Steel Industry in India under British Colonial Rule, 1880–1947', *IESHR*, 31:4 (1994), 413–60; S. B. Datta, *Capital Accumulation and Workers' Struggle in Indian Industrialization: The Case of the Tata Iron and Steel Company, 1910–1970* (Stockholm, 1986); Simeon, *The Politics of Labour Under Late Colonialism*; Bahl, *The Making of the Indian Working Class*.

[34] Chandavarkar, The *Origins of Industrial Capitalism*, chs. 6–8.

[35] Goswami, *Industry, Trade and Peasant Society*; Goswami, 'Collaboration and Conflict'; Chakrabarty, *Rethinking Working Class History*, ch. 1.

order to meet the peak periods of production. In turn, this situation of excess supply perpetuated the labour-intensive strategies of employers, for if labour appeared to be abundant they had little incentive to maintain steady levels of employment in the face of volatile markets.[36] The extensive use of casual labour is sometimes attributed to the lack of dynamism in the industrial sector, a case of inefficient entrepreneurs following anachronistic pre-industrial methods seeking and obtaining an equally inefficient and tradition-bound labour supply.[37] But a more plausible view would be that these stratagems were adaptations to a given economic context and, judged within these terms, they may have yielded a reasonably efficient pattern of labour deployment.

It is perhaps more significant, in understanding the nature of class formation, that the overwhelming majority of the industrial labour force experienced uncertain conditions of employment. Employers and experts alike preferred to distinguish between permanent and casual labour in Indian industry. But these were categories of employer policies; they did not reflect accurately either attitudes to work or the nature of the labour supply. For the demand for labour itself was scarcely permanent: it fluctuated substantially as employers took workers on or laid them off as the market for their products required. Permanent workers could easily and often arbitrarily lose their jobs and thus be thrown on to the casual labour market, whether for reasons of trade or because they were attempting to defend their position at work through industrial action. Neither considerations of 'mentalities' and consciousness nor those of wage differentials and skill provide the basis for a tenable distinction between industrial workers and the casual poor.[38]

If the effects of the structural stagnation of the Indian economy by the late nineteenth century shaped the options before industrial capital, they also influenced the formation of an industrial labour force. Demographic and commercial pressures, playing upon the fragile smallholding agrarian base, served to swell the supply of labour to the towns. Rural migration constituted the most important source of labour supply for urban industry. The purpose of migration was to earn cash to pay off debts or buy seed or simply to relieve, however temporarily, the subsistence pressures on shrinking family holdings in the village base.[39] This was sometimes achieved by moving to neighbouring districts or even further afield for

[36] Chandavarkar, The Origins of Industrial Capitalism, ch. 3.
[37] Most recently, for instance, in Chakrabarty, Rethinking Working-class History, ch. 1.
[38] Chandavarkar, The Origins of Industrial Capitalism, ch. 3. This finding informs the arguments of chs. 2, 4, 5 and 8 above.
[39] Ibid., ch. 4; for an account of how this pattern of migration and the rural connections of workers were shaped by, and in turn influenced, gender relations, see Sen, 'Women Workers in the Bengal Jute Industry', esp. chs. 1–3.

agricultural work. Long-distance migration accounted for a small proportion of the movement of people within the subcontinent.[40]

Among migrants in search of wage labour, the majority were male. This male bias was greater in the case of long-distance migration, urban and industrial employment and indentured labour especially in its early phase. Consequently, the struggle of smallholding peasant households to retain their land depended increasingly upon the more intensive exploitation of female and child labour. Whole families migrated in search of work only in periods of distress or in a fit of prosperity. Family migration may have been more common in the case of seasonal agricultural labour seeking employment in neighbouring districts. A higher proportion of women migrated to the towns among dalits and low castes, who had a lower rate of migration overall until the 1920s, and among higher-status artisan castes. The effect of factory legislation, which regulated the conditions of women's work after 1881, was to deprive them of any staple, large-scale employers. In the 1870s, for instance, women, including migrants, had formed a growing proportion of the labour force in the Bombay cotton mills.[41] Female labour was limited to the casual, manual, unskilled and poorly paid occupations. If women's work was confined to the domestic sphere in the peasant household and thus devalued, their alternative employment opportunities carried low status, considerable uncertainty and meagre rewards. However central women's work may have been to the reproduction of the household economy of the working classes, it was increasingly perceived and treated as marginal.

As the status of women's work diminished, more substantial peasant households sought to withdraw their labour when they could. On the other hand, women workers in the cotton and jute mills counted a substantial proportion of single, 'deserted' and widowed among them. They entered public discourse with the stigma and the threat of existing beyond the control of the family or, implicitly, of men. Confined to the low-status and low-wage sectors of the urban economy, women often withdrew from the labour market precisely when conditions were buoyant and the demand for labour was growing, and sought to enter it when conditions were depressed and jobs were scarce. The fact that the supply of female labour was determined in this sense by the demand for male labour ensured that women commanded little bargaining power and

[40] Omvedt, 'Migration in Colonial India', p. 188; Chandavarkar, *The Origins of Industrial Capitalism*, ch. 4; Sen, 'Women Workers in the Bengal Jute Industry', esp. chs. 1–3; Das Gupta, 'Migrants in Coal Mines'; Mohapatra, 'Coolies and Colliers'; Brahma Nand, 'Agricultural Labourers in Western India'; Chaudhury, 'Labour Migration from the United Provinces'; Pouchepadass, 'The Market for Agricultural Labour in Colonial North Bihar'; Bhattacharya, 'Agricultural Labour and Production'.
[41] Chandavarkar, The *Origins of Industrial Capitalism*, pp. 94–5.

found it difficult to entrench themselves in more favourable positions within the labour market. The identification of women's work with low status had significant social consequences. Respectability became the exclusive attribute of households which were able to withdraw the labour of women. If women's work was confined to their home, their public presence degraded them. Women workers in Bombay as well as Bengal were labelled as sexually promiscuous and they were not infrequently associated with prostitution. The domestication of female labour and its withdrawal from the public domain influenced the shift from bride price to dowry. Similarly, it facilitated the moralizing discourse of philanthropists and social reformers and set up the spectacle of notables lecturing unselfconsciously to the poor about the secrets of household management and healthy diets, ideals of motherhood and child-rearing.[42]

Throughout the colonial period, it remained predominantly the case that the industrial labour force was composed largely of male migrants, most of whom had spent their childhood in their villages and moved to the cities in their adolescence. They left their families behind and when their wives migrated with them they sometimes returned to the village to have their children. In retirement or old age they returned to the land. While they worked in the factories they maintained their rural connections: returning to the village to help with the harvest or to recover their health or to participate in family and village celebrations or religious observances; and remitting money to their relatives to supplement their incomes and liquidate their debts.[43]

The relationship between their rural base and their industrial employment varied according to region and industry. Some important industrial centres recruited workers from adjacent villages;[44] but workers migrated over long distances to Bombay, Calcutta and Jamshedpur, where the labour force poorly represented their contiguous districts.[45] The railways were the largest single employers of 'industrial' labour in India; yet line

[42] *Ibid.*, pp. 94–9; Sen, 'Women Workers in the Bengal Jute Industry'.
[43] Chandavarkar, *The Origins of Industrial Capitalism*, ch. 4; Sen, 'Women Workers in the Bengal Jute Industry', esp. chs. 1–3.
[44] For instance, two-thirds of the mill labour force in Ahmedabad were recruited within the district; one-fifth were exclusively dependent upon urban, industrial employment, had no rural connections and were permanently resident in the city. See *RCLI, Evidence, Bombay Presidency*, Memorandum of the Government of Bombay, vol. I, part i, p. 4.
[45] On Bengal, see Das Gupta, 'Factory Labour in Eastern India'; and Sen, 'Women Workers in the Bengal Jute Industry', esp. chs. 1–3; on Jamshedpur, where unskilled labour was recruited locally, see M. D. Morris, 'The Labor Market in India', in W. E. Moore and A. S. Feldman (eds.), *Labor Commitment and Social Change in Developing Areas* (New York, 1960), pp. 173–200; Bahl, *The Making of the Indian Working Class*; Simeon, *The Politics of Labour*, ch. 1; on Bombay, see *RCLI, Evidence, Bombay Presidency*, vol. I, part. i, Memorandum of the Government of Bombay, p. 4; Morris, *Industrial Labour Force*, pp. 62–5; Chandavarkar, *The Origins of Industrial Capitalism*, ch. 4.

workers were often recruited from and remained in the villages along the tracks.[46] Migration to the tea plantations involved movement to a rural setting and involved for many what was perceived as primarily 'agricultural' work.[47] In the coal industry, attempts were made to induce tribals from the neighbouring areas to work underground by offering them allotments of cultivable land near the mines.[48] The Raniganj and Jharia coalfields experienced their worst labour shortages in the harvest season when workers were drawn away by higher agricultural wages.[49] There was an even more intimate connection between agricultural and industrial work in the seasonal industries which were concerned primarily with the processing of raw agricultural products and offered employment as soon as the harvest ended.[50]

While the major motivation behind migration was to supplement the rural resources of the family, their ability to fulfil these intentions registered differences between workers. Labour in the tea plantations was recruited from the tribal areas of Chota Nagpur and Bihar frequently as whole families, and once in the gardens they were governed by draconian laws of contract and the general system of indenture.[51] Labour contractors also secured workers for the coal mines by buying out their debts and simply renewing their obligations within a changed context.[52] Casual work and general labouring in the towns did not yield either a regular or sufficient income for workers to supply the rural base, and in periods of sickness and unemployment they would be forced back upon their rural connections.[53] Large numbers of industrial workers found themselves in a similar situation. In the early 1920s, 64 per cent of the adult male labour force in the Bombay mills earned less than the daily wage rate for skilled rural labour in the Konkan, the major supplier of

[46] *Proceedings of the MCC*, Defence Statement, K. N. Joglekar, pp. 1766–965; Jagga, 'Colonial Railwaymen and British Rule'; Kerr, *Building the Railways of the Raj*.

[47] Behal, 'Forms of Labour Protest in Assam Valley Tea Plantations'; Griffiths, *The Indian Tea Industry*, pp. 267–420.

[48] See Simmons, 'Recruiting and Organising an Industrial Labour Force in Colonial India'; Das Gupta, 'Migrants in Coal Mines'.

[49] *Report of the RCLI*, pp. 115–17.

[50] S. Amin, *Sugarcane and Sugar in Gorakhpur: An Inquiry into Peasant Production for Capitalist Enterprise in Colonial India* (Delhi, 1984); J. Breman, *Of Peasants, Migrants and Paupers: Rural Labour Circulation and Capitalist Production in West India* (Delhi, 1985).

[51] Behal and Mohapatra, '"Tea and Money Versus Human Life"'; Das Gupta, 'Plantation Labour in Colonial India'; Mohapatra, 'Coolies and Colliers'; Bates and Carter, 'Tribal Migration in India and Beyond'; Carter, *Servants, Sirdars and Settlers*.

[52] For evidence of similar practices followed in the coal mines, see *Report of the RCLI*, p. 15; Simmons, 'Recruiting and Organising an Industrial Labour Force', p. 473–5; Das Gupta, 'Migrants in Coal Mines'; Omvedt, 'Migration in Colonial India', 193–4.

[53] Chandavarkar, *The Origins of Industrial Capitalism*, ch. 4.

labour to the city.[54] Low wages, irregular employment and intolerable housing conditions characterized the urban experience of most migrant workers.[55] Millworkers in the large industrial centres may have been in closer touch with, and better placed to supply, their rural base than plantation labour, but the conditions of urban life required them to repeatedly seek the support of their village base, both because their social connections, based upon village and kinship, might help them to find work, credit and housing in the towns and relief and support in periods of unemployment, sickness and old age, and because their ability to maintain and renew their rural ties improved their access to rural resources. Town and country should be seen as mutually supportive spheres in the family economy of the working class. Remittances from industrial earnings may have enabled some working-class families to extend their holdings or invest in the education of their (male) children; but, for most, remittances simply enabled them to stay where they were, to roll their debts and to hold on to their stake in the village. This symbiosis between the urban resources and rural base of the family economy of the working class was sometimes perpetuated and reproduced over several generations. Underlying this continuity was the instability of the urban economy, characterized by the fluctuations in the flows of capital and the demand for labour.[56]

The difficulties of maintaining an adequate supply in the face of the fluctuating demand for labour posed special problems of recruitment and discipline.[57] Employers had to devise methods of recruitment which would enable them to employ additional workers at short notice or lay them off as the market required and, in discharging them, still hold them within the urban economy or the industry's pool of labour supply. To this end, employers in a large number of industries delegated responsibility for the hiring and firing of workers to intermediaries known variously as jobbers and sirdars, muccadams, mistries and serangs and by sundry other names. This practice, apparently pervasive throughout the subcontinent, has often been understood as a culturally specific phenomenon. Yet the term 'jobber' came from Lancashire, where it was associated with

---

[54] Labour Office, Bombay, *Report on an Enquiry into the Wages and Hours of Labour in the Cotton Mill Industry, May 1921* (Bombay, 1923), pp. 6–7. For a different view, see Mazumdar, 'Labour Supply in Early Industrialisation'.

[55] Chandavarkar, *The Origins of Industrial Capitalism*, ch. 4; Basu, 'Workers' Politics in Bengal'; Sen, 'Women Workers in the Bengal Jute Industry'.

[56] See ch. 2 above. These issues are examined more extensively in Chandavarkar, *The Origins of Industrial Capitalism*, ch. 4.

[57] See ch. 2 above; and Chandavarkar, *The Origins of Industrial Capitalism*, pp. 99–110, 195–200, 295–307.

a technical function, and involved no stated recruiting or supervisory duties. In fact, foremen in British industry were frequently involved in recruiting labour and similar agents of recruitment and discipline were to be found in the world beyond South Asia.[58] Indeed, Sikh foremen were employed in the Shanghai cotton mills because they were believed to be particularly good at disciplining the workforce.[59]

It is frequently assumed that the jobber system was a function of an early stage of industrialization reflecting the immaturity of both entrepreneurs and workers, their insufficient adaptation to the industrial setting and their general and mutually deserved inefficiency. This is a harsh view, somewhat distanced from the daily politics of the workplace. The prevalence and pervasiveness of the jobber is also attributed to the need felt by urbane managers and supervisory staff for an intermediate cadre to mediate the linguistic and cultural chasm that divided them from the labour force. Doubts about one of these views undermine the plausibility of the other.

If cultural factors shaped methods of recruitment, it is probable that the 'colonial' perceptions of employers were more important than the rural connections of the workforce. Their social distance and isolation from the working-class life and their apprehension of labour's social threat may have led them to suppose that the maintenance of discipline and control hinged upon factors inward and specific to South Asian culture, calling for mediation through selected individuals deemed to be the leaders or 'headmen' of the working classes.[60] Employers may have supposed that the diversity of South Asian culture implied that workers from the same village or kinship group would be more compatible and perhaps more efficient. One historian, who took it for granted that these systems of recruitment were adaptations to a migrant labour force, nonetheless adduced evidence to show to the contrary that plantation owners held romantic notions of labour contracting as a patriarchal system particularly suited to the culturally specific needs of Indian workers.[61]

On the other hand, employers profited more extensively from the fact that these systems of recruitment accentuated the sectionalism of the workforce than that the jobber mediated its cultural heterogeneity. In fact, entrepreneurs in most industries attempted to diversify the ethnic composition of their workforce and sought to maintain its heterogeneity.

---

[58] P. Joyce, *Work, Society and Politics: The Culture of the Factory in Late Victorian England* (London, 1980); J. Melling, 'Non-Commissioned Officers: British Employers and their Supervisory Workers, 1880–1920', *Social History*, 5:2 (1980), 183–221; R. Gray, *The Aristocracy of Labour in Nineteenth Century Britain, c. 1850–1900* (London, 1981).

[59] J. Chesneaux, *The Chinese Labour Movement, 1919–1927* (Stanford, 1974).

[60] On the character of this colonial discourse, see ch. 1 above.

[61] Omvedt, 'Migration in Colonial India', 185–212.

The jobber was valued more for his managerial than his cultural functions: to maintain an adequate labour supply at low wage levels in the face of a fluctuating demand for labour. He also fulfilled certain pace-making and disciplinary tasks. These roles were intimately linked. Thus, absenteeism was not simply a problem of labour supply, but it could also be a challenge to the discipline of a jobber's team, and in either case was related to the maintenance of production levels. Most crucially, these functions of discipline and control, recruitment and diversification enabled employers to see the jobber as an invaluable bulwark against industrial action. Even when they complained of being locked out of the management of their own workforce or considered the possibility that the abolition of this supposedly anachronistic, dysfunctional institution might permit the development of a perfectly responsive labour market, they remained respectful of the political functions of the jobber system. Significantly, it was the momentum of working-class politics in Bombay which most clearly revealed the weaknesses of the jobber system and led millowners to contemplate its reform and the modification of their methods of labour control.[62]

Historians, following contemporary observers, have almost universally exaggerated the strengths and overlooked the weaknesses of the jobber system. The jobber has been repeatedly cast as a figure of awesome power but his dominance has more often been assumed than demonstrated.[63] Indeed, assessments of whether the jobber system was functional to industry simply took it for granted that the jobber could deliver what was expected of him or, alternatively, that he could consistently impede the realization of the common good. But the jobber system was by no means homogeneous. Its form varied according to industry and region. Its diversities were shaped by the nature of the industry, the character of the labour process and the wider political context.

The power of the jobber within a single industry varied according to occupation and the skill and bargaining position of the workers he supervised. Labour for the tea plantations and the coal mines was recruited either through sardars, who were employees, or contractors.[64] Most factory industries in the cities were able to recruit their labour force from

---

[62] Chandavarkar, *The Origins of Industrial Capitalism*, pp. 99–110, 295–307.
[63] Most recently, for instance, in Chakrabarty, *Rethinking Working Class History*.
[64] High rates of mortality in transit as well as on the plantations led to the passing of legislation which required that these contractors were licensed. See Griffiths, *The Indian Tea Industry*, pp. 267–96; for coal mining, see Simmons, 'Recruiting and Organising an Industrial Labour Force', 473–4; R. Shlomowitz and L. Brennan, 'Mortality and Migrant Labour in Assam, 1865–1921', *IESHR*, 27:1 (1990), 85–110; R. Shlomowitz and L. Brennan, 'Mortality and Migrant Labour en route to Assam, 1863–1924', *ibid.*, 27:3 (1990), 313–30.

those who had already migrated to the town and did not need to scour the countryside for workers.[65] Jobbers were, thus, often selected for their influence in the workplace rather than their patronage in the village, and, for migrant workers, jobbers formed only the most decorative thread in the warp and woof of the social connections through which they found work.[66]

How wages were paid was also crucial in determining the power of the jobber. The sardars who recruited for the tea plantations were often responsible for distributing wages; at times, they 'procured' labour by relieving men of their debt bonds to moneylenders or landlords and, by appropriating a proportion of their wages, held them firmly in relationships of subordination.[67] In addition, the position of the sardar was strengthened by the attenuated nature of workers' rural connections, their dependence upon plantation housing and draconian legislation governing breach of contract widely construed.[68] Coal mines at Raniganj and Jharia hired raising contractors, who in return for an agreed rate per tonnage, recruited, disciplined and paid labour.[69] Jobbers in the cotton mills and sardars in the jute industry may have often accepted bribes and commissions for hiring workers and retained some power to influence wages by choosing how to allocate tasks, machines and raw materials, but in not having direct responsibility for calculating and distributing wages, lacked a vital instrument of control. Jobbers often acted as moneylenders or petty landlords or their agents. But for most workers in the industrial centres there were competing sources of credit and patronage, so that migrants did not simply move from one form of debt bondage to another form of personal dependence. In these contexts, too, the jobber's authority and influence varied with his position in the division of labour. He was subject to the competition of rivals and was often squeezed between the workers' demands and managerial expectations. Moreover, the role assigned to jobbers was not fulfilled exclusively by them. Some workers were

[65] By 1918 the Buckingham and Carnatic Mill in Madras relied largely on their school where the children of their employees were being educated for a lifetime in the mills. Murphy, 'Class and Community in India'.

[66] *RCLI, Evidence, Bombay Presidency*, Seth Ambalal Sarabhai, Ahmedabad Manufacturing and Calico Printing Co. Ltd, vol. I, part. i, p. 277.

[67] *Report of the RCLI*, p. 15; Omvedt, 'Migration in Colonial India', 193–4; Behal and Mohapatra, '"Tea and Money Versus Human Life"'; Mohapatra, 'Coolies and Colliers'; Bates and Carter, 'Tribal Migration'.

[68] It was not until 1926, following the recommendations of the Assam Labour Enquiry Committee (1921–2) and N. M. Joshi's persistent efforts in the Legislative Assembly that this Act was repealed. But the specificity of the Assam case needs at least slightly to be modified. As V. B. Karnik observed, in the view of officials and employers, 'a strike was regarded as an act of insubordination and indiscipline, an illegal breach of contract'; see Karnik, *Strikes in India*, pp. 24–5.

[69] Simmons, 'Recruiting and Organising an Industrial Labour Force', 473–5.

recruited by friends and caste-fellows in the industry; managers and lesser supervisory personnel were also often involved in recruiting labour and sometimes developed similar relationships with workers both in the workplace and the neighbourhood. To the extent that the jobber was required to build up a following outside the workplace, he was forced to remain responsive to the needs and satisfy the expectation of the working-class neighbourhood. The wider his range of intervention in the material structure of the neighbourhood, the greater would be the competition to which he was subjected.[70]

The nature of the industrial labour force, and its relationship with capital, formed around the fitful and spasmodic patterns of investment and an inherently volatile urban and industrial sector. By the early twentieth century, price fluctuations in the world economy were registering their impact on an internal economy which had already been frozen into stagnation.[71] The depression of the 1930s was symptomatic of the incorporation of the Indian subcontinent into the capitalist world economy, though this process was mediated to a significant degree by the class structure, the social and economic institutions of the internal economy and the character of local production relations. In the depression, the tightening of money supply, dramatically falling prices and the difficulties of recovering dues in the countryside combined with the effects of tariff protection, the disruption of international trade and the flow of cheap labour to attract capital increasingly to the towns. At the same time, scarce credit and rising interest rates only made it more important for smallholders, trapped within a stagnant agrarian economy subject to unprecedented pressures and finding their rural base shrinking, to find wage-employment in the towns.[72]

It was not so much that the demand for labour in large-scale industry expanded rapidly to absorb this migration, but that the large cities offered the widest range of economic opportunities. For migrant workers, contraction in one area of the urban economy could still leave them the possibility of finding work in another.[73] In the 1930s, the population of the largest towns increased by three-quarters while the total urban population rose by less than a third. In the 1940s, grain rationing, public distribution systems in the largest towns, most seriously affected by the disruption of food supplies, inflation and wartime scarcities, made these

[70] Chandavarkar, *The Origins of Industrial Capitalism*, pp. 99–110, 195–204, 295–307.
[71] Baker, *An Indian Rural Economy*, esp. ch. 2; Tomlinson, *The Economy of Modern India, 1860–1970*, ch. 2.
[72] Baker, *An Indian Rural Economy;* Tomlinson, *The Political Economy of the Raj*.
[73] Baker, *An Indian Rural Economy*, ch. 5; Chandavarkar, The *Origins of Industrial Capitalism*, ch. 3.

particularly attractive to migrants from the countryside.[74] From the 1930s onwards, the largest cities recorded the fastest growth rates, some of the smaller or middling towns entered decline or stagnated. Until the 1930s, the fluctuations of the urban economy had often led to the movement of labour, especially those in casual employment, between town and country. Subsequently, expanding urban opportunities have drawn in the slack of the countryside while their contraction has often left labour stranded in the towns. This does not mean that migrant workers became progressively urbanized or proleterianized. On the contrary, most migrants still attempted to maintain their village connections, but those who were most securely employed were now most likely to succeed whereas the loss of rural ties was generally the result of distress. The rapid growth of India's largest cities over the last half-century is symptomatic of agrarian decline and rural deprivation rather than a function of economic growth.

At one level, we might suppose that there is nothing very surprising about this pattern of labour force formation. It could be understood simply as a labour force in an early stage of industrial development. But then we would also have to acknowledge that in this case its development remained at an early stage for considerably over a century. This line of argument could be carried a stage further: perhaps the formation of the labour force was a function of inefficient entrepreneurs engaging an inefficient, unskilled, unstable supply of migrant labour, of capitalists trying to scamper up backward-sloping curves. But it has often been misleading to measure entrepreneurial behaviour against some ideal of neo-classical or Marxist theory and highly problematic to arrive at a meaningful comparative standard of skill or labour efficiency. Such an argument, moreover, can be so completely circular as to be happily self-sustaining. Thus, for instance, when metropolitan and expatriate capitalists entering Kenya or Rhodesia in the 1920s continued the systems of migrant labour utilized by inefficient settlers, they are said to have brought their methods of labour management intact with them from South Africa or India.[75] Within a given economic and political context, it is possible that capitalists as well as migrant workers were making optimal choices in India.

[74] Christopher Baker, 'Colonial Rule and the Internal Economy in Twentieth Century Madras' in Baker, Johnson and Seal, *Power, Profit and Politics*, pp. 575–602.
[75] For instance, J. Forbes Munro observed that 'Metropolitan and expatriate firms coming in during the 1920s, to mine copper in Northern Rhodesia or plant tea in Kenya . . . had needs for large amounts of unskilled labour and brought with them, from South Africa and India, methods which were compatible with migrant labour'. See J. Forbes Munro, *Britain in Tropical Africa, 1880–1960: Economic Relationships and Impact* (London, 1984), p. 56.

Finally, the pattern of labour force formation in India may be explained in terms of the inadequate penetration of the world economy. The incorporation of the Indian subcontinent into the world economy may be variously dated in its origins but it had progressed substantially by 1900. The logic of further incorporation and the progressive transfer of surplus to the core would suggest the prevention rather than the expansion of capitalist development. On the other hand, Wallerstein has also argued that the 'further development of the world-economy' advances class formation in the periphery, so that class consciousness becomes 'a more relevant political tool', although 'a class conscious proletariat cannot emerge before in fact it represents a larger sector of the population'.[76]

Such arguments build upon evolutionary assumptions which can only be justified by the prognosis that the Indian economy was always becoming more like the capitalist West. Frequently, the ensuing question is counter-factual: why did it not increasingly approximate to the capitalist West? In India, however, a migrant working class, retaining its rural connections, operating within an overstocked labour market, apparently divided by caste and religion, lacking the support of trade union organization, showed a remarkable propensity for collective industrial action on a considerable scale.[77] The nature of their political action cannot readily be deduced from the characteristics of labour force formation. Nor is it usefully illuminated by the common theories, or expectations, of working-class political behaviour. Migrant workers were, for instance, often the most militant strikers. They migrated to the town with the aim of preserving their stake in rural society and, consequently, they were deeply committed to the defence of their wages, their jobs and their position at work. The importance of their urban, industrial interests combined with their access to an alternative base, however fragile, made migrant workers often the most resilient in the course of industrial action. Their political consciousness can only be flattened and distorted by notions of their 'rural mentalities'.

Similarly, there was no clear divide between the unskilled and skilled labour, the casual poor and industrial workers, but rather numerous gradations between them, complicating the attribution of a specific mentality to any given economic or social status within the working class. Caste, kinship and communal ties could facilitate association and solidarity: they did not work simply, permanently or irretrievably to divide the working class along predictable lines. On the other hand, the rise of a manufacturing sector by aggregating workers did not simply forge solidarities among them; on the contrary, its development often acted to

[76] Wallerstein, *The Capitalist World Economy*, p. 199.
[77] See chs. 3, 4, 5 and 8 above.

349 Imperial power and popular politics

divide workers and intensify the competition between them. There is no reason to suppose that an increase in their numbers, or more generally the progress of manufacturing industry, would lead inevitably to class consciousness.

The absence of trade unions did not reflect a lack of consciousness among workers but suggested rather that they could not easily be sustained in the face of hostility from employers and the state, which in turn was facilitated or circumscribed by the wider political context.[78] The fact that most working-class struggles arose out of or focused upon the issues of the workplace should not lead us to conclude, as Wallerstein suggests, that they were economistic. For the obstacles to industrial action sometimes appeared so awesome, from the manipulation of the wage relationship to the legal framework in which it operated and the repression by the agencies of the state, that to resist the initiatives of employers often entailed stark political and moral choices, and the conduct of and participation in industrial action was a powerful driving force in the development of class consciousness. Indeed, the scale of some strikes in India, most notably the 1928–29 strikes in Bombay organized in the teeth of such opposition and sustained more or less continuously for eighteen months,[79] was unprecedented and scarcely repeated in the history of the Western working class, in cases where the development of capitalism had ostensibly met Wallerstein's desiderata – a proletariat of significant proportions and conditions which facilitated its awareness of its class identity.

Working-class resistance in India cannot be contained within the limitations imposed upon it by the categories of Wallerstein's analysis. The strikes of Indian workers may have amounted to nothing more than 'the political struggles of . . . segments of classes within national boundaries', but they cannot be defined reductively as 'the daily bread and butter of local politics'.[80] Nor did they represent the crystallization of class consciousness as the discovery of 'the clearest route to the acquisition of power within a given state structure'.[81] Indeed, the Indian working classes could scarcely be said to represent a 'syndical interest group' at the national level, bound together by their 'collective relationship to the world economy'.[82] Of course, the momentum of working-class action exerted an influence upon the policies of the colonial state. But working-class politics in early twentieth-century India was characteristically local-

[78] See ch. 3 above.
[79] See ch. 4 above; for an account of these strikes, see Newman, *Workers and Unions*, pp. 168–250; see also S. Bhattacharya, 'Capital and Labour in Bombay City, 1928–29', *Economic and Political Weekly*, 16:42 and 43 (17–24 October 1981), *Review of Political Economy*, PE-36 to PE-44.
[80] Wallerstein, *The Capitalist World Economy*, p. 25.   [81] *Ibid.*, p. 226.   [82] *Ibid.*, p. 24.

ized and the formal or indeed informal connections across industrial centres were invariably weak. Industrial action centred upon the workplace and extended outwards into the urban neighbourhood. The conduct of industrial action frequently generalized the scope of working-class politics: when the state appeared to intervene on the side of the employer in an industrial dispute it tended to nurture the growth of political consciousness. If class consciousness was not national in scope, the working classes scarcely organized to act at the level of the 'national' state and bend its workings to safeguard working-class interests within the world economy.

In the context of these localized struggles, the world economy did not weigh very heavily in the formation of working-class consciousness. Of course, there were moments when it was prominent. The Bombay millworkers appreciated that the excise duty impinged upon their wage cuts of 1925 and that the tariff and rupee questions had an important bearing upon the redefinition of work, increased workloads and wage reductions that passed under the sobriquet of rationalization in 1928 and 1929.[83] But their battle was waged in each case against the initiatives of the employers. There was some suspicion that the employers and the state, while passing the responsibility onto each other, were in equal measure undermining the social and economic position of the workforce. However, their attitude to the state was conditioned largely by its role in the development or settlement of their conflicts with their employers.[84]

Since class consciousness did not emerge in terms of a clear awareness of how the working class was situated within the world economy and since their struggles were informed principally by the tensions and antagonisms of the local, rather than the national, context, it is difficult to credit Wallerstein's assertion that in 'peripheral areas of the world-economy', 'the primary contradiction is between the interests organized and located in the core countries and their local allies on the one hand, and the majority of the population on the other'.[85] The periphery was scarcely a nest of singing birds. And such an argument subsumes beneath 'the primary contradiction' the fundamental class differences and conflicts which divided the majority of the population, let alone the fact that the local allies of core interests were often interchangeable with their local opponents, unless, of course, we understand class as an ontological thing, so that this primary contradiction was always immanent in social relations, even if it was never fully realized.

Historians have often approached the question of class consciousness rather negatively. The expectation that class consciousness flowed nat-

[83] Chandavarkar, *The Origins of Industrial Capitalism*, pp. 397–411, 419–20, 335–96.
[84] See ch. 4 above.   [85] Wallerstein, *The Capitalist World Economy*, p. 200.

urally from the development of large-scale production and advanced
industrial capitalism has frequently obliged historians to explain its absence. Conversely, in India, it has been something of a commonplace to
dismiss class and class consciousness altogether as a possible outcome of
social conflict. Thus, in an argument which sought to situate capital–labour relations at the heart of an analysis of the development of
'world capitalism', one historian has recently observed, 'Of the many
forces which have threatened South Asian society's political stability over
the last one hundred and fifty years, that represented by the *fur sich* class
power of the deeply impoverished masses would not rank as the most
significant.'[86] If historians have approached the question of class so
defensively, it is not because of the economic deficiencies in class formation in India or even its political weakness, but rather because of the
conceptual difficulties inherent in the term. Class and class consciousness, categories grounded in a historical theory, have given rise to ahistorical approaches to the subject. For it has frequently led historians
either to conceive of political behaviour, *a priori*, in terms of assumed
social collectivities, or to measure a given set of conditions against an
ideal construct of class and then to seek to explain the gap between them
as well as the shortcomings of the latter. If class formation could not occur
simply within the nation-state, historical enquiry has focused upon determining the functions of class and class conflict within the capitalist world
economy. A certain functionalism underlies Wallerstein's definition of
'ethno-national consciousness' as 'the constant resort of all those for
whom class organization offers the risk of a loss of relative advantage
through the normal workings of the market and class dominated political
bargaining'.[87] Class and ethnicity are perhaps more fruitfully conceived as
discursive categories. The principal historical questions which their
analysis raises are then why at particular moments diverse groups with
often conflicting interests and varied cultures came together in often
fragile political coalition, why these apparently common interests are
perceived in class terms, and why in particular contexts social and political conflicts appear to be illuminated by ethnic, religious or national
identities. It would follow, therefore, that nationality itself entailed a
discursive reality, so that its definition could exclude groups among 'the
majority of the population' from the boundaries of national or ethnic
identity or include them on strictly unequal terms.

[86] Washbrook, 'South Asia, the World System and World Capitalism', 486–87.
[87] Wallerstein, *The Capitalist World Economy*, p. 228.

Bibliography

MANUSCRIPT SOURCES

Proceedings of the Secretary of State for India, in the Public and Judicial, and the Economic and Overseas Departments; the Private Office Papers; the Proceedings of the Government of India; and Proceedings of the Government of Bombay. Oriental and India Office Collections, British Library, London.

Records of the Government of India, Home, Commerce and Industries, Industries and Labour Departments. National Archives of India, New Delhi.

Records of the Government of Bombay, Judicial, Home (Political), Home (Special), Finance, Revenue Development, General, General (Plague), Public Works Departments. Maharashtra State Archives, Bombay.

Records of the Commissioner of Police, Bombay. Office of the Commissioner of Police, Bombay.

Records of the Deputy Inspector-General of Police, Criminal Investigation Department, Maharashtra, Secret Abstracts of Intelligence, Bombay Presidency Police, Office of the Deputy Inspector General of Police, Criminal Investigations Department, Maharashtra, Bombay.

UNPUBLISHED PROCEEDINGS OF COMMITTEES OF ENQUIRY

The Extension of the City of Bombay, 1887, GOB, Public Works Department (General), Vol. 1162, Compilation no. 4133 W, 1868–89. Maharashtra State Archives, Bombay.

Bombay Strike Enquiry Committee, 1928. Maharashtra State Archives, Bombay.

Bombay Riots Inquiry Committee, 1929. Maharashtra State Archives, Bombay.

Court of Enquiry into a Trade Dispute between Several Textile Mills and their Workmen, 1929. Maharashtra State Archives, Bombay.

Bombay Provincial Banking Enquiry Committee, 1929. Maharashtra State Archives, Bombay.

Meerut Conspiracy Case, Statements and Exhibits, 1929–33. National Archives of India, New Delhi.

Bombay Disturbances Enquiry Committee, 1938. Government of Bombay, Home (Special) Files. Maharashtra State Archives, Bombay.

Textile Labour Inquiry Committee, Interim and Main Inquiry, 1937–40. Maharashtra State Archives, Bombay.

PRIVATE PAPERS

Papers of J. C. Curry, Centre of South Asian Studies, Cambridge.
Papers of N. M. Joshi, Nehru Memorial Museum and Library, New Delhi.
Papers of Sir P. Thakurdas, Nehru Memorial Museum and Library, New Delhi.

PAPERS OF ORGANIZATIONS

Ahmedabad Textile Labour Association, Microfilm copy. Nehru Memorial Museum and Library, New Delhi.
Minute Books of the Committee of the Bombay Millowners' Association. Office of the Bombay Millowners' Association.
All India Congress Committee. Nehru Memorial Museum and Library, New Delhi.
All-India Trade Union Congress. Nehru Memorial Museum and Library, New Delhi.

OFFICIAL PUBLICATIONS

PARLIAMENTARY PAPERS

Annual Report on Sanitary Measures in India.
Royal Commission on Labour, Foreign Reports, vol. II, The Colonies and the Indian Empire with an Appendix on the Migration of Labour, 1892, vol. XXXVI, Cmd. 6795-XI.
'Papers Relating to the Outbreak of Bubonic Plague in India with Statement Showing the Quarantine and Other Restrictions Recently Placed Upon Indian Trade, up to March 1897', 1897, vol. LXIII, Cmd. C-8386.
Report of the Indian Plague Commission, 1898–99, with Appendices and Summary, vol. V, 1902, vol. LXXII, Cmd. 810.
Report of the Select Committee on the Employment of the Military in Cases of Disturbances, Parliamentary Papers, 1908, vol. VII, Cmd. 236.
Report of the Committee Appointed by the Government of India to Investigate the Disturbances in the Punjab etc. vol. XIV, 1920, Cmd. 681.
Reports on the Punjab Disturbances, April 1919. vol. XIV, 1920, Cmd. 534.
Disturbances in the Punjab, Statement by Brigadier-General R. E. H. Dyer. vol. XXXIV, 1920, Cmd. 771.
Report of the Commission of Inquiry into the Cawnpore Riots and Resolution of the Government of the United Provinces. vol. XII, 1930–1, Cmd. 3891.
Government of India's Despatch on Proposals for Constitutional Reform, dated 20th September 1930, vol. XXIII, 1930–31, Cmd. 3700.
Report of the Indian Franchise Committee, 1932, vol. 1, vol. VIII, 1931–32, Cmd. 4086.

HIS MAJESTY'S STATIONERY OFFICE (HMSO)

Report of the Indian Statutory Commission, vol. I, *Survey.* London, 1930.
Report of the Royal Commission on Labour in India, and *Evidence* (11 vols.). London, 1931.

GOVERNMENT OF INDIA

Report of the Indian Factory Commission, Appointed in September 1890, under the Orders of His Excellency, the Governor-General-in-Council, with Proceedings and Appendices. Calcutta, 1890.
Census of India, 1891–1941.
Report of the Indian Factory Labour Commission 1908, 2 vols. Simla, 1908.
Indian Industrial Commission, Vol. I – Report, vols. II–V – Evidence. Calcutta, 1918.
The Indian Tariff Board (Cotton Textile Industry Enquiry), 1927. Vol. I – Report, vols. II–IV – Evidence. Bombay, 1927.
Indian Central Banking Enquiry Committee. Vol. I – Reports, vols. II–III – Evidence. Calcutta, 1930–32.
Report of the Indian Tariff Board Regarding the Grant of Protection to the Cotton Textile Industry. Calcutta, 1932.
Report of the Indian Tariff Board Regarding the Grant of Additional Protection to the Cotton Textile Industry. Calcutta, 1932.
Report of the Special Tariff Board on the Enquiry Regarding the Level of Duties Necessary to Afford Adequate Protection to the Indian Cotton Textile Industry Against Imports from the United Kingdom of Cotton Piecegoods and Yarn, Artificial Silk Fabrics and Mixture Fabrics of Cotton and Artificial Silk. Delhi, 1936.
Government of India, *Terrorism in India, 1917–1936.* Simla, 1937.
Main Report of the Labour Investigation Committee. Delhi, 1946.

GOVERNMENT OF BOMBAY

Coneybeare, H. *Report on the Sanitary State and Requirements of Bombay, Selections from the Records of the Bombay Government,* new series, vol. XI. Bombay, 1855.
Report of the Commissioner Appointed by the Governor of Bombay in Council to Inquire into the Conditions of the Operatives in the Bombay Presidency, 1875. Bombay, 1875.
Report by W. O. Meade King on the Working of the Indian Factories Act in Bombay together with Certain Suggestions and Proposals. Bombay, 1882.
Report of the Commission Appointed to Consider the Working of Factories in the Bombay Presidency, 1888. Bombay, 1888.
Fawcett, C. G. H. *A Monograph on Dyes and Dyeing in the Bombay Presidency.* Bombay, 1896.
Enthoven, R. E. *The Cotton Fabrics of the Bombay Presidency.* Bombay, 1897.
Snow, P. C. H. *Report on the Outbreak of Bubonic Plague in Bombay, 1896–97.* Bombay, 1897.
Haffkine, Mons. W. M. *Experiment on the Effect of Protective Inoculation in the Epidemic of Plague at Undhera Taluka, Baroda, February and March, 1898.* Bombay, 1898.
A Monograph on Evacuation as a Protective and Combative Plague Measure, Compiled Under the Orders of Sir A. Wingate, KCIE, Acting Chief Secretary to Government by Lt. J. K. Condon, Under-Secretary to Government (Plague

Department) for the use of the Indian Plague Commission, 30 March 1899. Bombay, 1899.

Report of the Municipal Commissioner on the Plague in Bombay in the Year Ending 31st May, 1899. Bombay, 1899.

Condon, Capt. J. K. *The Bombay Plague, Being A History of the Progress of Plague in the Bombay Presidency from September 1896 to June 1899.* Bombay, 1900.

Gazetteer of Bombay City and Island, 3 vols. Bombay, 1909.

Report of the Bombay Development Committee. Bombay, 1914.

Report of the Industrial Disputes Committee. Bombay, 1922.

Report of the Bombay Strike Enquiry Committee, vol. I. Bombay, 1929.

Report of the Bombay Riot Inquiry Committee. Bombay, 1929.

Report of the Court of Inquiry into a Trade Dispute Between Several Textile Mills and their Workmen. Bombay, 1929.

Report of the Bombay Provincial Banking Enquiry Committee. Vol. I – Report, vols. II–IV – Evidence. Bombay, 1930.

Report of the Rent Enquiry Committee, with Evidence. Bombay, 1939.

Report of the Textile Labour Inquiry Committee 1937–38. Vol. I – *Interim Report.* Bombay, 1938.

Report of the Textile Labour Inquiry Committee. Vol. II – *Final Report.* Bombay, 1953.

LABOUR OFFICE, BOMBAY

Labour Gazette (monthly).

Report on an Enquiry into the Wages and Hours of Labour in the Cotton Mill Industry, May, 1921 by G. Findlay Shirras. Bombay, 1923.

Report on an Enquiry into Working Class Family Budgets in Bombay by G.Findlay Shirras. Bombay, 1923.

Report on an Enquiry into the Deductions from Wages or Payments in Respects of Fines. Bombay, 1928.

Wages and Unemployment in the Bombay Cotton Textile Industry. Bombay, 1934.

Report on Wages, Hours of Work and Conditions of Employment in the Textile Industries (Cotton, Silk, Wool and Hosiery) in the Bombay Presidency (excluding Sind), May 1934. General Wage Census, Part I – Perennial Factories. Third Report. Bombay, 1937.

ANNUAL REPORTS

Administration Report of the City of Bombay Improvement Trust.

Administration Report of the Government of Bombay.

Administration Report of the Municipal Commissioner for the City of Bombay.

Bombay Presidency Police, Secret Abstracts of Intelligence.

Factory Report for the Bombay Presidency.

Report of the Department of Industries in the Bombay Presidency.

Report on the Native Newspapers Published in the Bombay Presidency.

Report on the Police in the Town and Island of Bombay for 1884–1912.

Report on the Police in the City of Bombay, 1913–47.

Prices and Wages in India. Calcutta.
Report of the Sanitary Commissioner for Bombay.
Report of the Sanitary Commissioner with the Government of India,
Report of the Sanitary Commissioner for the North-Western Provinces.
Report on the Working of the Development Department in Bombay.
Report on the Working of the Indian Factories Act.

NON-OFFICIAL REPORTS

Annual Reports of the Bombay Millowners' Association.
Manchester Chamber of Commerce. *Bombay and Lancashire Cotton Spinning Inquiry: Minutes and Evidence.* Manchester, 1888.
Great Indian Peninsular Railway, *Report for the Royal Commission on Labour in India.* Bombay, 1929.

NEWSPAPERS

Bombay Chronicle
Bombay Sentinel
Congress Socialist
Harijan
Indian National Herald
Kranti (Marathi)
Nava Kal (Marathi)
Times of India
Young India

PUBLISHED SOURCES

AITUC – Fifty Years On: Documents, Introduction by S. A. Dange, vol. I. AITUC, New Delhi, 1973.
Chopra, P. N. (ed.). *Quit India Movement: British Secret Report.* Faridabad, 1976.
The Collected Works of M. K. Gandhi, 90 vols. Delhi, 1958–84.
Desai, M. *A Righteous Struggle: A Chronicle of the Ahmedabad Textile Labourers' Fight For Justice.* Ahmedabad, 1951.
Mansergh, P. N. S. (ed.). *The Transfer of Power, 1942–47,* vol. II: *Quit India, 30 April–21 September 1942.* HMSO, London, 1971.
The Moral and Political Writings of Mahatma Gandhi, 3 vols., ed. R. Iyer. Oxford, 1987.
Punjab Disturbances, 1919–20, 2 vols., *Report of the Commissioners Appointed by the Punjab Sub-Committee of the Indian National Congress to Look into the Jallian-walla Bagh Massacre.* Delhi, 1976.
Report of the Congress Cawnpore Riots Enquiry Committee in N. G. Barrier (ed.), *Roots of Communal Violence* Delhi, 1976.
The Selected Works of Jawaharlal Nehru, 15 vols., ed. S. Gopal. New Delhi, 1972–82.
Source Material for a History of the Freedom Movement in India, vol II, *1885–1920.* Bombay, 1958.

Source Material for a History of the Freedom Movement in India, vol VI, *Non-Co-operation Movement, Bombay City, 1920–1925*, ed. B. G. Kunte. Bombay, 1978.

BOOKS, PAMPHLETS AND ARTICLES

Abrams, P. *Historical Sociology*. London, 1983.

Ambedkar, B. R. *What Congress and Gandhi Have Done to the Untouchables*. Bombay, 1945.

Amin, S. *Sugarcane and Sugar in Gorakhpur: An Inquiry into Peasant Production for Capitalist Enterprise in Colonial India*. Delhi, 1984.

   'Gandhi as Mahatma, Gorakhpur District, Eastern UP, 1921–22', in R. Guha (ed.), *Subaltern Studies*, vol. III, pp. 1–57.

   'Agrarian Bases of Nationalist Agitations in India: An Historiographical Survey', in D. A. Low (ed.), *The Indian National Congress: Centenary Hindsights*, pp. 98–128. Delhi, 1988.

   Event, Metaphor, Memory: Chauri Chaura, 1922–1992. Berkeley, 1995.

Amin, S. and D. Chakrabarty (eds.). *Subaltern Studies*, vol. IX. Delhi, 1996.

Arnold, D. 'The Armed Police and Colonial Rule in South India, 1914–1947', *Modern Asian Studies*, 11:1 (1977), 101–25.

   'Labour Relations in a South India Sugar Factory 1937–39' *Social Scientist*, 65 (December 1977), 16–33.

   'Dacoity and Rural Crime in Madras, 1860–1940', *Journal of Peasant Studies*, 6:2 (1979), 140–67.

   'Industrial Violence in Colonial India', *Comparative Studies in Society and History*, 22:2 (1980), 234–55.

   'Cholera and Colonialism in British India', *Past and Present*, 113 (1986), 118–51.

   Police Power and Colonial Rule: Madras, 1859–1947. Delhi, 1986.

   'Touching the Body: Perspectives on the Indian Plague, 1896–1900', in R. Guha (ed.), *Subaltern Studies*, vol. V, pp. 55–90.

   'Smallpox and Colonial Medicine in Nineteenth Century India', in D. Arnold (ed.), *Imperial Medicine and Indigeneous Societies*, pp. 45–65. Manchester, 1988.

   'Cholera Mortality in British India, 1817–1947', in T. Dyson (ed.), *India's Historical Demography: Studies in Famine, Disease and Society*, pp. 261–84. London, 1989.

   Colonizing the Body: State Medicine and Epidemic Disease in Nineteenth Century India. Berkeley and Los Angeles, 1993.

Arnold, D. and D. Hardiman (eds.), *Subaltern Studies*, vol. VIII. Delhi, 1994.

Arrighi, G. 'Labour Supplies in Historical Perspective: A Study of the Proletarianization of the African Peasantry in Rhodesia', *Journal of Development Studies*, 6:3 (1970), 197–234.

Baden-Powell, B. H. *The Indian Village Community*. London, 1896.

Bagchi, A. K. *Private Investment in India 1900–1939*. Cambridge, 1972.

   'Foreign Capital and Economic Development in India: A Schematic View', in K. Gough and H. P. Sharma (eds.), *Imperialism and Revolution in South Asia*, pp. 43–76. London, 1973.

'De-Industrialisation in Gangetic Bihar, 1809–1901', in B. De (ed.), *Essays in Honour of Professor S. C. Sarkar,* pp. 499–522. Delhi, 1976.

'De-Industrialisation in India in the Nineteenth Century: Some Theoretical Implications', *Journal of Development Studies,* 12:2 (1976), 135–64.

'Reflections on Patterns of Regional Growth in India During the Period of British Rule', *Bengal Past and Present,* 95:1 (1976), pp. 247–89.

'A Reply', *Indian Economic and Social History Review,* 16:2 (1979), 147–61.

'Colonialism and the Nature of "Capitalist" Enterprise in India', *Economic and Political Weekly,* 23:31 (30 July 1988), *Review of Political Economy,* PE-38 to PE-58.

Bahl, V. 'Attitude of the Indian National Congress Towards the Working Class Struggle in India, 1918–1947', in Kapil Kumar (ed.), *Congress and Classes: Nationalism, Workers and Peasants,* pp. 1–33.

'TISCO Workers' Struggle, 1920–28', *Social Scientist,* 10:8 (1982), 32–44.

'The Emergence of Large-Scale Steel Industry in India under British Colonial Rule, 1880–1947', *Indian Economic and Social History Review,* 31:4 (1994), 413–60.

The Making of the Indian Working Class: The Case of the Tata Iron and Steel Company. Delhi, 1995.

Bairoch, P. 'International Industrialization Levels from 1750 to 1980', *Journal of European Economic History,* 11:2 (1982), 269–333.

Baker, C. J. *The Politics of South India 1920–37.* Cambridge, 1976.

'Debt and Depression in Madras, 1929–1936', in C. J. Dewey and A. G. Hopkins (eds.), *The Imperial Impact: Studies in the Economic History of Africa and India,* pp. 233–42.

'Colonial Rule and the Internal Economy in Twentieth Century Madras', *Modern Asian Studies,* 15:3 (1981), special issue, *Power, Profit and Politics: Essays on Imperialism, Nationalism and Change in Twentieth Century India, 1870–1940,* ed. C. Baker, G Johnson and A. Seal, 575–602.

'Economic Reorganization and the Slump in South and South-East Asia', *Comparative Studies in Society and History,* 23:3 (July 1981), 325–49.

An Indian Rural Economy: The Tamil Nad Countryside, 1880–1950. Oxford, 1984.

Balibar, E. 'Basic Concepts of Historical Materialism', in L. Althusser and E. Balibar (eds.), *Reading Capital,* pp. 199–308. London, 1970.

Bamford, P. C. *Histories of the Non-Co-operation and Khilafat Movements.* Delhi, 1925; reprinted Delhi, 1974.

Banaji, J. 'Capitalist Domination and the Small Peasantry: Deccan Districts in the Late Nineteenth Century', *Economic and Political Weekly,* 12:33–4 (1977), special number, 1375–404.

Baran, P. *The Political Economy of Growth.* New York, 1957.

Barrier, N. G. *The Punjab Land Alienation Bill of 1900.* Duke University, Program in Comparative Studies in Southern Asia, Monograph and Occasional Papers Series, no. 2, 1966.

'The Arya Samaj and Congress Politics in Punjab, 1894–1908', *Journal of Asian Sudies,* 26:3 (1967), 363–79.

'The Punjab Disturbances of 1907: The Response of the British Government in India to Agrarian Unrest', *Modern Asian Studies,* 1:4 (1967), 353–83.

Bates, C. N. 'The Nature of Social Change: The Kheda District, 1818–1918', *Modern Asian Studies*, 15:4 (1981), 771–821.

Bates, C. and M. Carter. 'Tribal Migration in India and Beyond', in G. Prakash (ed.), *The World of the Rural Labourer in Colonial India*, pp. 205–47. Delhi, 1992.

Bayly, C. A. 'Patrons and Politics in Northern India' in J. Gallagher, G. Johnson and A. Seal (eds.), *Locality, Province and Nation: Essays on Indian Politics*, pp. 29–68.

The Local Roots of Indian Politics: Allahabad, 1870–1920. Oxford, 1975.

'Indian Merchants in a "Traditional" Setting: Benares, 1780–1830', in C. J. Dewey and A. G. Hopkins (eds.), *The Imperial Impact: Studies in the Economic History of Africa and India*, pp. 171–93.

Rulers, Townsmen and Bazaars: North Indian Society in the Age of British Expansion, 1770–1870. Cambridge, 1983.

'The Pre-History of "Communalism"? Religious Conflict in India, 1700–1860', *Modern Asian Studies*, 19:2 (1985), 177–203.

The New Cambridge History of India, vol. II:1 *Indian Society and the Making of the British Empire*. Cambridge, 1988.

Beals, A. R. 'Strategies of Resort to Curers in South India', in Charles Leslie (ed.), *Asian Medical Systems: A Comparative Study*, pp. 184–200. Berkeley and Los Angeles, 1976.

Beattie, J. M. *Crime and the Courts in England, 1660–1800*. Oxford, 1986.

Behal, R. P. 'Forms of Labour Protest in Assam Valley Tea Plantations, 1900–1930', *Economic and Political Weekly*, 20:4 (26 January 1985), *Review of Political Economy* PE-19 to PE-26.

Behal, R. P. and P. P. Mohapatra. '"Tea and Money Versus Human Life": The Rise and Fall of the Indenture System in the Assam Tea Plantations, 1840–1908', in E. V. Daniel, H. Bernstein and T. Brass (eds.), *Plantations, Proletarians and Peasants in Colonial Asia*, pp. 142–72.

Bhattacharya, N. 'The Logic of Tenancy Cultivation: Central and South-East Punjab, 1870–1935', *Indian Economic and Social History Review*, 20:2 (1983), 121–70.

'Agricultural Labour and Production: Central and South-East Punjab, 1870–1940', in K. N. Raj, N. Bhattacharya, S. Guha and S. Padhi (eds.), *Essays on the Commercialization of Indian Agriculture*, pp. 105–62. Delhi, 1985.

'Lenders and Debtors: Punjab Countryside, 1880–1940', *Studies in History*, 1:2 (1985), 305–42.

Bhattacharya, S. 'Cotton Mills and Spinning Wheels: Swadeshi and the Indian Capitalist Class, 1920–22', *Economic and Political Weekly*, 11:47 (1976), 1828–34.

'Capital and Labour in Bombay City, 1928–29', *Economic and Political Weekly*, 16:42 and 43 (17–24 October 1981), *Review of Political Economy*, PE36 to PE44.

'Regional Economy (1757–1857): Eastern India, Part I', in D. Kumar (ed.), *The Cambridge Economic History of India*, vol. II: *C. 1757–c. 1970*, pp. 270–331.

'Swaraj and the Kamgar: The Indian National Congress and the Bombay Working Class, 1919–1931', in R. Sisson and S. Wolpert (eds.), *Congress and Indian Nationalism: The Pre-Independence Phase*, pp. 223–49. Berkeley and Los Angeles, 1988.

Bhuyan, A. C. *The Quit India Movement: The Second World War and Indian Nationalism*. Delhi, 1975.

Bose, Sanat. '"Industrial Unrest" and the Growth of Labour Unions in Bengal, 1920–1924', *Economic and Political Weekly*, 16:44–6 (November 1981), special number, 1849–60.

Bose, S. (ed.) *South Asia and World Capitalism*. Delhi, 1990.

Brahma Nand. 'Agricultural Labourers in Western India: A Study of the Central Division Districts of the Bombay Presidency During the Late Nineteenth and Early Twentieth Century', *Studies in History*, new series, 1:2 (1985), special issue, *Essays in Agrarian History: India, 1850 to 1940*, ed. S. Bhattacharya, pp. 221–46.

Breman, J. *Of Peasants, Migrants and Paupers: Rural Labour Circulation and Capitalist Production in West India*. Delhi, 1985.

Taming the Coolie Beast: Plantation Society and the Colonial Order in Southeast Asia. Delhi, 1989.

Beyond Patronage and Exploitation: Changing Agrarian Relations in South Gujarat. Delhi, 1993.

Breman, J. and E. Valentine Daniel. 'Conclusion: The Making of a Coolie', in E. V. Daniel, H. Bernstein and T. Brass (eds.), *Plantations, Proletarians and Peasants in Colonial Asia*, pp. 268–95.

Brenner, R. 'The Origins of Capitalist Development: A Critique of Neo-Smithian Marxism', *New Left Review*, 104 (July–August 1977), 25–94.

Brewer, A. *Marxist Theories of Imperialism: A Critical Survey*. London, 1980.

Brogden, M. The Emergence of the Police: The Colonial Dimension', *British Journal of Criminology*, 27:1 (1987), 4–14.

Burnett-Hurst, A. R. *Labour and Housing in Bombay: A Study in the Economic Condition of the Wage-Earning Classes of Bombay*. London, 1925.

Cannadine, D. 'The Present and the Past in the English Industrial Revolution, 1880–1980', *Past and Present*, 103 (May 1984), pp. 131–71.

Carter, M. 'Strategies of Labour Mobilisation in Colonial India: The Recruitment of Indentured Workers for Mauritius', in E. V. Daniel, H. Bernstein and T. Brass (eds.), *Plantations, Proletarians and Peasants in Colonial Asia*, pp. 228–45.

Servants, Sirdars and Settlers: Indians in Mauritius, 1834–1874. Delhi, 1995.

Cashman, R. I. *The Myth of the Lokamanya: Tilak and Mass Politics in Maharashtra*. Berkeley and Los Angeles, 1975.

Catanach, I. J. 'Plague and the Indian Village, 1896–1914', in P. Robb (ed.), *Rural India: Land, Power and Society under British Rule*, pp. 216–43. London, 1983.

'Poona Politicians and the Plague', in J. Masselos (ed.), *Struggling and Ruling: The Indian National Congress, 1885–1985*, pp. 198–215. New Delhi, 1987.

'Plague and the Tensions of Empire, 1896–1918', in D. Arnold (ed.), *Imperial Medicine and Indigeneous Societies*, pp. 149–71. Manchester, 1988.

Cell, J. W. 'Anglo-Indian Medical Theory and the Origins of Segregation in West Africa', *American Historical Review*, 91:2 (1986), 307–35.

Chakrabarty, B. *Subhas Chandra Bose and Middle Class Radicalism: A Study in Indian Nationalism, 1928–1940*. London, 1990.

Chakrabarty, D. 'Sasipada Bannerjee: A Study in the Nature of the First Contact of the Bengal Bhadralok with the Working Class of Bengal', *Indian Historical Review*, 2:2 (1976), 339–64.

'Communal Riots and Labour: Bengal's Jute Mill Hands in the 1890s', *Past and Present*, 91 (May 1981), 140–69.

'Conditions for Knowledge of Working-Class Conditions: Employers, Government and the Jute Workers of Calcutta', in R. Guha (ed.), *Subaltern Studies*, vol. II, pp. 259–310.

'On Deifying and Defying Authority: Managers and Workers in the Jute Mills of Bengal, circa 1890–1940', *Past and Present*, 100 (August 1983), 124–46.

Rethinking Working-Class History: Bengal, 1890–1940. Delhi, 1989.

Chandavarkar, R. 'Workers' Politics in the Mill Districts of Bombay Between the Wars', *Modern Asian Studies*, 15:3 (1981), special issue, *Power, Profit and Politics: Essays on Imperialism, Nationalism and Change in Twentieth Century India, 1870–1940*, ed. C. Baker, G. Johnson and A. Seal, 603–47.

'Workers' Resistance and the Rationalization of Work in Bombay between the Wars', in D. Haynes and G. Prakash (eds.), *Contesting Power: Resistance and Everyday Social Relations in South Asia*, pp. 109–44. Berkeley and Los Angeles, 1991.

The Origins of Industrial Capitalism in India: Business Strategies and the Working Classes in Bombay, 1900–1940. Cambridge, 1994.

'From Communism to "Social Democracy": The Rise and Resilience of Communist Parties in India, 1920–1995', *Science and Society*, 61:1 (1997), 99–106.

Chandra, B. *The Rise and Growth of Economic Nationalism in India: Economic Policies of Indian National Leadership 1880–1905*. New Delhi, 1966.

Charlesworth, N. 'Rich Peasants and Poor Peasants in Late Nineteenth Century Maharashtra', in C. J. Dewey and A. G. Hopkins (ed.), *The Imperial Impact: Studies in the Economic History of Africa and India*, pp. 97–114.

British Rule and the Indian Economy, 1800–1914. London, 1983.

Peasants and Imperial Rule: Agriculture and Agrarian Society in the Bombay Presidency, 1850–1935. Cambridge, 1985.

Chatterjee, P. *Nationalist Thought and the Colonial World: A Derivative Discourse*. London, 1986.

The Nation and Its Fragments: Colonial and Post-Colonial Histories. Delhi, 1994.

Chatterjee, P. and G. Pandey (eds.), *Subaltern Studies*, vol. VII. Delhi, 1992.

Chatterji, B. 'Business and Politics in the 1930s: Lancashire and the Making of the Indo-British Trade Agreement', *Modern Asian Studies*, 15:3 (1981), special issue, *Power, Profit and Politics: Essays on Imperialism, Nationalism and Change in Twentieth Century India, 1870–1940*, ed. C. Baker, G Johnson and A. Seal, 527–73.

'The Political Economy of "Discriminating Protection": The Case of Textiles in the 1920s', *Indian Economic and Social History*, 20:3 (1983), 239–75.

Trade, Tariffs and Empire: Lancashire and British Policy in India, 1919–1939. Delhi, 1992.

Chatterji, J. *Bengal Divided: Hindu Communalism and Partition, 1932–1947.* Cambridge, 1994.

Chattopadhyay, M. 'Santosh Kumari Devi: A Pioneering Labour Leader', *Social Scientist*, 128 (January 1984), 62–73.

Chaudhuri, K. N. 'The Structure of the Indian Textile Industries in the Seventeenth and Eighteenth Centuries', *Indian Economic and Social History Review*, 11:2–3 (1974), 127–82.

The Trading World of Asia and the English East India Company, 1660–1760. London, 1978.

'Foreign Trade and Balance of Payments (1757–1947)', in D. Kumar (ed.), *The Cambridge Economic History of India*, vol. II: *C. 1757–c. 1970*, pp. 804–77.

Chaudhuri, K. N. and C. J. Dewey (eds.). *Economy and Society: Essays in Indian Economic and Social History.* Delhi, 1979.

Chaudhury, P. 'Labour Migration from the United Provinces, 1881–1911', *Studies in History*, new series, 8:1 (1992), pp. 13–42.

Chesneaux, J. *The Chinese Labour Movement, 1919–1927.* Stanford, 1974.

Chicherov, A. I. 'Tilak's Trial and the Bombay Political Strike of 1908', in I. M. Reisner and N. M. Goldberg (eds.), *Tilak and the Struggle for Indian Freedom*, pp. 545–626.

Chirol, V. *Indian Unrest.* London, 1910.

Cholia, R. P. *Dock Labourers in Bombay.* Bombay, 1941.

Chowdhury, B. B. 'Regional Economy (1757–1857): Eastern India, Part II', in D. Kumar (ed.), *The Cambridge Economic History of India*, vol. II: *C. 1757–c. 1970*, pp. 270–331.

Cobb, R. *The Police and the People: French Popular Protest, 1789–1820.* Oxford, 1970.

Cockburn, J. S. 'Patterns of Violence in English Society: Homicide in Kent, 1560–1985', *Past and Present*, 130 (February 1991), 70–106.

Cohen, S. P. *The Indian Army: Its Contribution to the Development of the Indian Nation.* Berkeley, 1971.

Colvin, Sir Auckland. *Audi Alterem Partem: Being Two Letters on Certain Aspects of the Indian National Congress Movement.* Simla, 1888.

Cooper, A. *Sharecropping and Sharecroppers' Struggles in Bengal, 1930–1950.* Calcutta, 1988.

Coupland, R. *A Report on the Constitutional Problem in India*, 3 vols. London, 1942–3.

India – A Restatement. London, 1945.

Cox, E. C. *Police and Crime in India.* London, 1910.

Crouzet, F. *Capital Formation in the Industrial Revolution.* London, 1972.

Curry, J. C. *The Indian Police.* London, 1932.

Dale, S. F. *Islamic Society on the South Asian Frontier: The Mappilas of Malabar, 1498–1922.* Oxford, 1980.

Damodaran, K. 'Memoir of an Indian Communist', *New Left Review*, 93 (1975), 35–59.

Daniel, E. V., H. Bernstein and T. Brass (eds.). *Plantations, Proletarians and Peasants in Colonial Asia*. London, 1992.

Das, S. *Communal Riots in Bengal in the Twentieth Century*. Delhi, 1992.

'The "Goondas": Towards a Reconstruction of the Calcutta Underworlds through Police Records', *Economic and Political Weekly*, 29:44 (29 October 1994), 2877–83.

Das, V. 'Introduction: Communities, Riots and Survivors: The South Asian Experience', in Das (ed.), *Mirrors of Violence: Communities, Riots and Survivors in South Asia*.

Das V. (ed.), *Mirrors of Violence: Communities, Riots and Survivors in South Asia*. Delhi, 1990.

Das Gupta, R. 'Factory Labour in Eastern India: Sources of Supply, 1855–1946: Some Preliminary Findings', *Indian Economic and Social History Review*, 13:3 (1976), 277–328.

'Migrants in Coal Mines: Peasants or Proletarians, 1850s–1947', *Social Scientist*, 151 (December 1985), 18–43.

'Plantation Labour in Colonial India', in E. V. Daniel, H. Bernstein and T. Brass (eds.), *Plantations, Proletarians and Peasants in Colonial Asia*, pp. 173–98.

Datta, P. 'Strikes in the Greater Calcutta Region, 1918–1924' *Indian Economic and Social History Review*, 30:1 (1993), 57–84.

Datta, S. B. *Capital Accumulation and Workers' Struggle in Indian Industrialization: The Case of the Tata Iron and Steel Company, 1910–1970*. Stockholm, 1986.

Datta, V. N. *Jallianwalla Bagh*. Ludhiana, 1969.

Davis, J. 'The London Garotting Panic of 1862: A Moral Panic and the Creation of a Criminal Class in mid-Victorian England', in V. A. C. Gatrell, B. Lenman and G. Parker (eds.), *Crime and the Law: The Social History of Crime in Western Europe since 1500*, pp. 190–213. London, 1980.

'From "Rookeries" to "Communities": Race, Poverty and Policing in London, 1850–1985', *History Workshop Journal*, 27 (Spring 1989), 66–85.

'Jennings' Buildings and the Royal Borough: The Construction of an Underclass in mid-Victorian England', in D. Feldman and G. Stedman Jones (eds.), *Metropolis – London: Histories and Representations since 1800*, pp. 11–39. London, 1989.

Davis, K. *The Population of India and Pakistan*. Princeton, N.J., 1951.

Desai, A. V. 'The Origins of Parsi Enterprise', *Indian Economic and Social History Review*, 5:4 (1968), 307–17.

Dewey, C. 'Images of the Village Community: A Study in Anglo-Indian Ideology', *Modern Asian Studies*, 6:3 (1972), 291–328.

'Some Consequences of Military Expenditure in British India: The Case of the Upper Sind Sagar Doab, 1849–1947', in C. Dewey (ed.), *Arrested Development in India: The Historical Dimension*, pp. 93–169. Delhi, 1988.

'The End of the Imperialism of Free Trade: The Eclipse of the Lancashire Lobby and the Concession of Fiscal Autonomy to India', in C. J. Dewey and A. G. Hopkins (eds.), *The Imperial Impact: Studies in the Economic History of Africa and India*, pp. 35–67.

Dewey, C. J. and A. G. Hopkins (eds.). *The Imperial Impact: Studies in the Economic History of Africa and Asia*. London, 1978.

Dhanagare, D. N. *Peasant Movements in India, 1920–1950.* Delhi, 1983.

Dirks, N. *The Hollow Crown: Ethnohistory of an Indian Little Kingdom.* Cambridge, 1987.

Ditton, J. *Controlology: Beyond the New Criminology.* London, 1979.

Drummond, I. *British Economic Policy and the Empire, 1919–1939.* London, 1972.

Dumont, Louis 'The "Village Community" from Munro to Maine', *Contributions to Indian Sociology,* 9 (December 1965), 67–89.

Edwardes, S. M. *The Rise of Bombay – A Retrospect.* Bombay, 1902.

The By-Ways of Bombay. Bombay, 1912.

Memoir of Rao Bahadur Ranchodlal Chotalal. Exeter, 1920.

The Bombay City Police – 1672–1916. A Historical Sketch. London, 1923.

Emsley, C. *Policing and Its Context, 1750–1870.* London, 1983.

Erikson, E. *Gandhi's Truth: On the Origins of Militant Non-Violence.* London, 1969.

Fabian, J. *Time and the Other: How Anthropology Makes Its Object.* New York, 1983.

Farnie, D. A. *The English Cotton Industry and the World Market, 1815–96.* Oxford, 1979.

Fisher, C. 'Planters and Peasants: The Ecological Context of Agrarian Unrest on Indigo Plantations of North Bihar, 1820–1920', in C. J. Dewey and A. G. Hopkins (eds.), *The Imperial Impact: Studies in the Economic History of Africa and India,* pp. 114–31.

Frank, A. G. *Capitalism and Underdevelopment in Latin America: Historical Studies of Chile and Brazil.* New York, 1967.

Frankel, F. *India's Political Economy, 1947–1977: The Gradual Revolution.* Princeton, 1978.

Freitag, S. 'Collective Crime and Authority in North India', in A. Yang (ed.), *Crime and Criminality in British India,* pp. 140–63.

'Crime in the Social Order of Colonial North India', *Modern Asian Studies,* 25:2 (1991), 227–61.

Gadgil, M. and R. Guha. 'State Forestry and Social Conflict in British India', *Past and Present,* 123 (1989), 141–77.

Gallagher, J. 'Congress in Decline: Bengal, 1930–39', in J. Gallagher, G. Johnson and A. Seal (eds.), *Locality, Province and Nation: Essays on Indian Politics,* pp. 269–325.

The Decline, Revival and Fall of the British Empire, ed. A. Seal. Cambridge, 1982.

Gallagher, J. and A. Seal. 'Britain and India Between the Wars', *Modern Asian Studies,* 15:3 (1981), special issue, *Power, Profit and Politics: Essays on Imperialism, Nationalism and Change in Twentieth Century India, 1870–1940,* ed. C. Baker, G. Johnson and A. Seal, 387–414.

Gallagher, J., G. Johnson and A. Seal (eds.). *Locality, Province and Nation: Essays on Indian Politics.* Cambridge, 1973.

Gatrell, V. A. C. 'Crime, Authority and the Policeman State, 1750–1950', in F. M. L. Thompson (ed.), *The Cambridge Social History of Britain, 1750–1950,* vol. III, pp. 243–310. Cambridge, 1990.

Geary, R. *European Labour Protest, 1848–1918.* London, 1981.

Gillion, K. *Ahmedabad: A Study in Indian Urban History.* Berkeley and Los Angeles, 1968.

Giri, V. V. *My Life and Times,* vol. I. Delhi, 1976.

Gopal Krishna. 'The Development of the Congress as a Mass Organization, 1918–1923', *Journal of Asian Studies,* 25:3 (1966), 413–30.

Gordon, A. D. 'Businessmen and Politics in a Developing Colonial Economy: Bombay City, 1918–1933', in C. J. Dewey and A. G. Hopkins (eds.), *The Imperial Impact: Studies in the Economic History of Africa and India,* pp. 194–215.
Businessmen and Politics: Rising Nationalism and a Modernising Economy in Bombay, 1918–1933. New Delhi, 1978.

Gordon, S. 'Scarf and Sword: Thugs, Marauders and State Formation in 18th Century Malwa', *Indian Economic and Social History Review,* 6:4 (1969), 403–29.

Goswami, O. 'Collaboration and Conflict: European and Indian Capitalists and the Jute Economy of Bengal, 1919–1939', *Indian Economic and Social History Review,* 19:2 (1982), 141–79.
'Then Came the Marwaris: Some Aspects of the Changes in the Pattern of Industrial Control in Eastern India', *Indian Economic and Social History Review,* 22:3 (1985), 225–49.
'Multiple Images: Jute Mill Strikes of 1929 and 1937 Seen Through Other's Eyes', *Modern Asian Studies,* 21:3 (1987), 547–83.
'*Sahibs, Babus* and *Banias*: Changes in Industrial Control in Eastern India, 1918–1950', *Journal of Asian Studies,* 48:2 (1989), 289–309.
Industry, Trade and Peasant Society: The Jute Economy of Eastern India, 1900–1947. Delhi, 1991.

Gourlay, S. 'Nationalists, Outsiders and the Labour Movement in Bengal During the Non-Cooperation Movement, 1919–1921', in Kapil Kumar (ed.), *Congress and Classes: Nationalism, Workers and Peasants,* pp. 34–57.

Gray, R. *The Aristocracy of Labour in Nineteenth Century Britain, c. 1850–1900.* London, 1981.

Greenberg, M. *British Trade and the Opening of China, 1800–1842.* Cambridge, 1951.

Greenhough, P. 'Political Mobilization and the Underground Literature of the Quit India Movement, 1942–44', *Modern Asian Studies,* 17:3 (1983), 353–86.

Griffin, K. and J. Gurley. 'Radical Analyses of Imperialism, the Third World and the Transition to Socialism', *Journal of Economic Literature,* 23 (1985), 1089–143.

Griffiths, P. *To Guard My People: The History of the Indian Police.* London, 1971.

Griffiths, Sir Percival. *The History of the Indian Tea Industry.* London, 1967.

Guha, R. 'On Some Aspects of the Historiography of Colonial India', in R. Guha (ed.), *Subaltern Studies,* vol. I, pp. 1–8.

Guha, R. (ed.), *Subaltern Studies,* 6 vols. Delhi, 1982–89.

Guha, S. *The Agrarian Economy of the Bombay Deccan, 1818–1941.* Delhi, 1986.

Guha Ray, S. 'Tramworkers of Calcutta: Some Reflections on their Unionisation and Political Experience', *Social Scientist,* 156 (May 1986), 15–32.

Gupta, A. *The Police in British India, 1861–1947.* Delhi, 1979.

Gupta, P. S. 'Notes on the Origin and Structuring of the Industrial Labour Force in India – 1880 to 1920', in R. S. Sharma (ed. with V. Jha), *Indian Society: Historical Probings: In Memory of D. D. Kosambi*, pp. 414–34. New Delhi, 1979.

Gurr, T. R. 'Historical Trends in Violent Crime: A Critical Review of the Evidence', *Crime and Justice: An Annual Review of Research*, 3 (1981), 295–353.

Habakkuk, H. J. 'The Historical Experience of Economic Development', in E. A. G. Robinson (ed.), *Problems in Economic Development*, pp. 112–38. London, 1965.

Habib, I. 'The Potentialities of Capitalistic Development in Mughal India', *Journal of Economic History*, 39:1 (1969), 32–78.
'The Technology and Economy of Mughal India', *Indian Economic and Social History Review*, 17:1 (1980), 1–34.
'Monetary Systems and Prices', in T. Raychaudhuri and I. Habib (eds.), *Cambridge Economic History of India*, vol. I, pp. 360–81. Cambridge 1982.

Hall, S., C. Critcher, T. Jefferson, J. Clarke and B. Roberts. *Policing the Crisis: Mugging, the State and Law and Order*. London, 1978.

Harcourt, M. 'Kisan Populism and Revolution in Rural India: The 1942 Disturbances in Bihar and East United Provinces', in D. A. Low (ed.), *Congress and the Raj: Facets of the Indian Struggle, 1917–1947*, pp. 315–48.

Hardiman, D. *Peasant Nationalists of Gujarat: Kheda District, 1917–1934*. Delhi, 1981.
The Coming of the Devi. Delhi, 1987.

Hasan, A. 'The Silver Currency Output of the Mughal Empire and Prices in India in Sixteenth and Seventeenth Centuries', *Indian Economic and Social History Review*, 6:1 (1969), 85–116.

Haynes, D. 'The Dynamics of Continuity in Indian Domestic Industry: *Jari* Manufacture in Surat, 1900–1947', *Indian Economic and Social History Review*, 23:2 (1986), 128–49.

Henningham, S. 'The Contribution of "Limited Violence" to the Bihar Civil Disobedience Movement', *South Asia*, new series, 2:1 and 2 (1979), 60–77.
'Quit India in Bihar and the Eastern United Provinces: The Dual Revolt' in R. Guha (ed.), *Subaltern Studies*, vol. II, pp. 130–79.

Heston, A. and R. Summers. 'Comparative Indian Economic Growth: 1870 to 1970', *American Economic Review*, 70:2 (1980), 96–101.

Hirst, L. Fabian. *The Conquest of Plague. A Study of the Evolution of Epidemiology*. Oxford, 1953.

Hobsbawm, E. J. *Primitive Rebels: Studies in Archaic Forms of Social Movement in the 19th and 20th Centuries*. Manchester, 1959.
Labouring Men: Studies in the History of Labour. London, 1964.
Industry and Empire. London, 1968.

Hoselitz, B. E. and W. E. Moore (eds.). *Industrialisation and Society*. Paris, 1963.

Hunter, Sir W. W. *Bombay, 1885 to 1890: A Study in Indian Administration*. London, [1892?].

Hutchins, F. G. *Spontaneous Revolution: The Quit India Movement*. New Delhi, 1971.

India's Revolution: Gandhi and the Quit India Movement. Cambridge, Mass., 1973.

Inden, R. *Imagining India.* Oxford, 1991.

Jagga, L. 'Colonial Railwaymen and British Rule: A Probe into Railway Labour Agitation in India, 1919–1922', in B. Chandra (ed.), *The Indian Left: Critical Appraisals,* pp. 103–45. New Delhi, 1983.

Jalal, A. *The Sole Spokesman: Jinnah, the Muslim League and the Demand for Pakistan.* Cambridge, 1985.

James, R. C. 'Trade Union Democracy: Indian Textiles', *The Western Political Quarterly,* 11:3 (1958), 566–72.

'The Casual Labour Problem in Indian Manufacturing', *The Quarterly Journal of Economics,* 74:1 (February 1960), 100–16.

Jeffrey, K. and P. Hennessey. *States of Emergency: British Governments and Strike-breaking since 1919.* London, 1983.

Jeffrey, R. *The Decline of Nayar Dominance.* Brighton, 1976.

Johnson, G. *Provincial Politics and Indian Nationalism: Bombay and the Indian National Congress, 1880–1915.* Cambridge, 1973.

Jones, E. L. (ed.). *Agricultural and Economic Growth in England, 1650–1815.* London, 1967.

Joshi, C. 'Kanpur Textile Labour: Some Structural Features of Formative Years', *Economic and Political Weekly,* 16:44–6 (November 1981), special issue, 1823–38.

'Bonds of Community, Ties of Religion: Kanpur Textile Workers in the Early Twentieth Century', *Indian Economic and Social History Review,* 22:3 (1985), pp. 251–80.

'Worker Protest, Managerial Authority and Labour Organization: Kanpur Textile Industry', Nehru Memorial Musem and Library, Occasional Papers on History and Society, no. 27. Delhi, 1985.

Joshi, H. and V. Joshi, *Surplus Labour and the City: A Study of Bombay.* Delhi, 1976.

Joshi, N. M. *The Trade Union Movement in India.* Poona, 1927.

Urban Handicrafts of the Bombay Deccan. Poona, 1936.

Joshi, P. C. (ed.). *Rebellion –1857: A Symposium.* Delhi, 1957.

Joyce, P. *Work, Society and Politics: The Culture of the Factory in Late Victorian England.* London, 1980.

Kadam, Manohar. *Narayan Meghaji Lokhande: Bharatiya Kamgar Calvalliche Janak.* Bombay, 1995.

Karnik, V. B. *Strikes in India.* Bombay, 1967.

N. M. Joshi: Servant of India. Bombay, 1972.

Kaye, J. W. *A History of the Sepoy War in India,* 3 vols. London, 1864, 1870 and 1876.

Keer, D. *Dr Ambedkar: Life and Mission.* Bombay, 1954.

Kelly, J. D. '"Coolie" as a Labour Commodity: Race, Sex and European Dignity in Colonial Fiji', in E. V. Daniel, H. Bernstein and T. Brass (eds.), *Plantations, Proletarians and Peasants in Colonial Asia,* pp. 246–67.

Kennedy, M. *Notes on the Criminal Classes in the Bombay Presidency.* Bombay, 1909.

Kerr, C. 'Changing Social Structures', in W. E. Moore, and A. S. Feldman (eds.), *Labour Commitment and Social Change in Developing Areas*, pp. 348–59.

Kerr, C. and A. Siegel. 'The Structuring of the Labour Force in Industrial Society', *Industrial and Labour Relations Review*, 8:2 (1955), 151–68.

Kerr, C., F. H. Harbison, J. T. Dunlop and C. A. Myers. 'Industrialism and Industrial Man', *International Labour Review*, 82:3 (1960), 236–50.

Industrialism and Industrial Man: The Problems of Labour and Management in Economic Growth. London, 1962.

Kerr, I. J. *Building the Railways of the Raj, 1850–1900*. Delhi, 1995.

Kirk, R. and C. P. Simmons. 'Lancashire and the Equipping of Indian Cotton Mills: A Study of Textile Machinery and Supply, 1854–1939', in K. Ballhatchet and D. Taylor (eds.), *Changing South Asia: Economy and Society*, pp. 169–81. London, 1984.

Klein, I. 'Malaria and Mortality in Bengal', *Indian Economic and Social History Review*, 9:2 (1972), 132–60.

'Death in India', *Journal of Asian Studies*, 32:4 (1973), 639–59.

'Urban Development and Death: Bombay City, 1870–1914', *Modern Asian Studies*, 20:4 (1986), 725–54.

'Plague, Policy and Popular Unrest in British India', *Modern Asian Studies*, 22:4 (1988), 723–55.

Kling, B. B. *Partner in Empire: Dwarkanath Tagore and the Age of Enterprise in Eastern India*. Calcutta, 1981.

Kooiman, D., 'Jobbers and the Emergence of Trade Unions in Bombay City', *International Review of Social History*, 22:3 (1977), 313–28.

Krishnamurty, J. 'De-industrialization in Gangetic Bihar during the Nineteenth Century: Another Look at the Evidence', *Indian Economic and Social History Review*, 22:4 (1985), 399–416.

Kumar, D. (ed.). *The Cambridge Economic History of India*, vol. II: *C. 1757–c. 1970*. Cambridge, 1982.

Kumar, D. and J. Krishnamurthy. 'Regional and International Economic Disparities since the Industrial Revolution: The Indian Evidence', in P. Bairoch and M. Levy-Leboyer (eds.), *Disparities in Economic Development since the Industrial Revolution*, pp. 361–72. London, 1981.

Kumar, Kapil (ed.). *Congress and Classes: Nationalism, Workers and Peasants* New Delhi, 1988.

Kumar, Radha. 'Family and Factory: Women in the Bombay Cotton Textile Industry, 1919–1939', *Indian Economic and Social History Review*, 20:1 (1983), 81–110.

Kumar, R. 'The Bombay Textile Strike, 1919', *Indian Economic and Social History Review*, 8:1 (1971), 1–29.

'From Swaraj to Purna Swaraj: Nationalist Politics in the City of Bombay 1920–32', in D. A. Low (ed.), *Congress and the Raj: Facets of the Indian Struggle*, pp. 77–107.

Lakha, Salim. *Capitalism and Class in Colonial India: The Case of Ahmedabad*. New Delhi, 1988.

Lakshman, P. P. *Congress and the Labour Movement in India*. Congress Economic and Political Studies, no. 3, Economic and Political Research Department, All-India Congress Committee, Allahabad, 1947.

Lal, B. 'Kunti's Cry: Indentured Women on Fiji's Plantations', *Indian Economic and Social History Review*, 22:2 (1985), 55–71.

Landes, D. S. *The Unbound Prometheus: Technological Change and Industrial Development in Western Europe from 1750 to the Present*. Cambridge, 1969.

Lewis, W. A. 'Economic Development with Unlimited Supplies of Labour', *The Manchester School of Economic and Social Studies*, 22:2 (1954), 139–91.

Lovett, V. *A History of the Indian Nationalist Movement*. London, 1920.

Low, D. A. (ed.). *Congress and the Raj: Facets of the Indian Struggle*. London, 1977.

Macfarlane, A. *The Justice and the Mare's Ale: Law and Disorder in Seventeenth Century England*. Oxford, 1981.

Maine, H. S. *Village Communities in the East and West*. London, 1871.

Marglin, Stephen. 'What Do Bosses Do?' *Review of Radical Political Economy*, 6 (1974), 60–112.

Markovits, C. *Indian Business and Nationalist Politics, 1931–39: The Indigenous Capitalist Class and the Rise of the Congress Party*. Cambridge, 1985.

Masani, R. P. *The Evolution of Local Self-Government in Bombay*. Oxford, 1929.

Masselos, J. C. 'Power in the Bombay "Moholla" 1904–15: An Initial Exploration into the World of the Indian Urban Muslim', *South Asia*, 6 (1976), 75–95.

'Change and Custom in the Format of the Bombay Mohurram During the Nineteenth and Twentieth Centuries', *South Asia*, new series, 5:2 (1982), 47–67.

Mathur, Y. B. *Quit India Movement*. Delhi, 1979.

Mazumdar, D. 'Labour Supply in Early Industrialization: The Case of the Bombay Textile Industry', *Economic History Review*, second series, 26:3 (1973), 477–96.

Mehta, M. J. *The Ahmedabad Cotton Textile Industry: Genesis and Growth*. Ahmedabad, 1982.

Mehta, M. M. *Structure of Indian Industries*. Bombay, 1955.

Mehta, S. D. *The Cotton Mills of India, 1854–1954*. Bombay, 1954.

Melling, J. 'Non-Commissioned Officers: British Employers and their Supervisory Workers, 1880–1920', *Social History*, 5:2 (1980), 183–221.

Menon, D. *Caste, Nationalism and Communism in South India: Malabar 1900–1948*. Cambridge, 1994.

Metcalf, T. R. *Land, Landlords and the British Raj: Northern India in the Nineteenth Century*. Berkeley and Los Angeles, 1979.

Mills, I. D. 'Influenza in India During 1918–19', *Indian Economic and Social History Review*, 23:1 (1986), 1–40.

Mishra, S. C. 'Commercialization, Peasant Differentiation and Merchant Capital in Late Nineteenth Century Bombay and Punjab', *Journal of Peasant Studies*, 10:1 (1982), 3–51.

'Agricultural Trends in the Bombay Presidency, 1900–1920: The Illusion of Growth', *Modern Asian Studies*, 19:4 (1985), 733–59.

Misra, B. 'Factory Labour During the Early Years of Industrialisation: An Appraisal in the Light of the Indian Factory Commission 1890', *Indian Economic and Social History Review*, 12:3 (1975), 203–28

Mitra, C. 'Popular Uprising in 1942: The Case of Ballia' in G. Pandey (ed.), *The Indian Nation in 1942*, pp. 165–84.

Mitra, Ira. 'Growth of Trade Union Consciousness among Jute Mill Workers, 1920–40', *Economic and Political Weekly*, 16:44–6 (November 1981), special number, 1839–48.

Mohapatra, P. P. 'Coolies and Colliers: A Study of the Agrarian Context of Labour Migration from Chotanagpur, 1880–1920', *Studies in History*, new series, 1:2 (1985), special issue, *Essays in Agrarian History: India, 1850 to 1940*, ed. S. Bhattacharya, 13–42.

Moore, R. J. *The Crisis of Indian Unity, 1917–1940*. Oxford, 1974.

Moore, W. E. and A. S. Feldman (eds.). *Labour Commitment and Social Change in Developing Areas*. New York, 1960.

Morgan, Jane. *Conflict and Order: The Police and Labour Disputes in England and Wales, 1900–1939*. Oxford, 1987.

Morris, M. D. 'The Labour Market in India', in W. E. Moore and A. S. Feldman (eds.), *Labour Commitment and Social Change in Developing Areas*, pp. 173–200.

   The Emergence of an Industrial Labour Force in India: A Study of the Bombay Cotton Mills, 1854–1947. Berkeley and Los Angeles, 1965.

   'The Growth of Large Scale Industry to 1947', in D. Kumar (ed.), *The Cambridge Economic History of India*, vol. II: *C. 1757–c. 1970*, pp. 553–676.

Morris-Jones, W. H. ' "If It Be Real, What Does It Mean?": British Perceptions of the Indian National Congress', in R. Sisson and S. Wolpert (eds.), *Congress and Indian Nationalism: The Pre-Independence Phase*, pp. 90–118. Berkeley, 1988.

Mukherjee, A. 'Crime and Criminals in Nineteenth Century Bengal (1861–1904)', *Indian Economic and Social History Review*, 21:2 (1984), 153–83.

Munro, J. Forbes. *Britain in Tropical Africa, 1880–1960: Economic Relationships and Impact*. London, 1984.

Murphy, E. D. 'Class and Community in India: The Madras Labour Union, 1918–21', *Indian Economic and Social History Review*, 14:3 (1977), 292–321.

   Unions in Conflict: A Comparative Study of Four South Indian Textile Centres, 1918–1939. New Delhi, 1981.

Myers, C. A. *Labour Problems in the Industrialization of India*. Cambridge, Mass., 1958.

Nehru, J. *An Autobiography: With Musings on Recent Events in India*. London, 1936.

Newman, R. 'Social Factors in the Recruitment of the Bombay Millhands', in K. N. Chaudhuri and C. J. Dewey (eds.), *Economy and Society: Essays in Indian Economic and Social History*, pp. 277–95.

   Workers and Unions in Bombay, 1918–29: A Study of Organisation in the Cotton Mills. Canberra, 1981.

Nigam, S. 'Disciplining and Policing the "Criminals by Birth", Part I: The Making of a Colonial Stereotype – the Criminal Tribes and Castes of North India', *Indian Economic and Social History Review*, 27:2 (1990), 131–64.

Nigam, S. 'Disciplining and Policing the "Criminals by Birth", Part II: The Development of a Disciplinary System, 1871–1900', *Indian Economic and Social History Review*, 27:3 (1990), 257–87.

Omvedt, G. 'Migration in Colonial India: The Articulation of Feudalism and Capitalism by the Colonial State', *Journal of Peasant Studies*, 7:2 (1980), 185–212.

'The Satara Prati Sarkar', in G. Pandey (ed.), *The Indian Nation in 1942*, pp. 223–62.

Omissi, D. *The Sepoy and the Raj: The Indian Army, 1860–1940*. London, 1994.

Page, D. *Prelude to Partition: The Indian Muslims and the Imperial System of Control*. Delhi, 1982.

Pandey, G. *The Ascendancy of the Congress in Uttar Pradesh, 1926–1934: A Study in Imperfect Mobilization*. Delhi, 1978.

'Economic Dislocation in Nineteenth-Century Eastern Uttar Pradesh: Some Implications of the Decline of Artisanal Industry in Colonial India', in P. Robb (ed.), *Rural South Asia: Linkages, Change and Development*, pp. 89–129. London, 1983.

'Congress and the Nation, 1917–1947', in R. Sisson and S. Wolpert (eds.), *Congress and Indian Nationalism: The Pre-Independence Phase*, pp. 121–33. Berkeley, 1988.

'The Revolt of August 1942 in Eastern UP and Bihar', in G. Pandey (ed.), *The Indian Nation in 1942*, pp. 123–64.

The Construction of Communalism in Colonial North India. Delhi, 1992.

Pandey, G. (ed.). *The Indian Nation in 1942*. Calcutta, 1988.

Pandey, S. M. 'Ideological Conflict in the Kanpur Trade Union Movement: 1934–1945', *Indian Journal of Industrial Relations*, 3:2 (1967), 243–68.

As Labour Organises: A Study of Unionism in the Kanpur Cotton Textile Industry. New Delhi, 1970.

Panikkar, K. N. *Against Lord and State: Religion and Peasant Uprisings in Malabar, 1836–1921*. Delhi, 1989.

Parvatibai Bhor. *Eka Rannaraginichi Hakikat*, as told to Padmakar Chitale. Bombay, 1977.

Patel, K. *Rural Labour in Industrial Bombay*. Bombay, 1963.

Patel, S. *The Making of Industrial Relations: The Ahmedabad Textile Industry, 1918–1939*. Delhi. 1987.

Patnaik, P. 'Imperialism and the Growth of Indian Capitalism', in R. Owen and R. Sutcliffe (eds.), *Studies in the Theory of Imperialism*, pp. 210–29. London, 1972.

Patnaik, Utsa (ed.). *Agrarian Relations and Accumulation: The 'Mode of Production' Debate in India*. Bombay, 1990.

Pearse, A. *The Cotton Industry of India: Being the Report of a Journey to India*. Manchester, 1930.

Perlin, E. 'Eyes Without Sight: Education and Millworkers in South India, 1939–1976', *Indian Economic and Social History*, 18:3 and 4 (1981), 263–86.

Perlin, F. 'Proto-industrialization and Pre-colonial South Asia' *Past and Present*, 97 (February 1983), 30–95.

Pollard, S. *Peaceful Conquest: The Industrialization of Europe, 1760–1970*. Oxford, 1981.

Pollitzer, R. *Plague*. Geneva, 1954.

Pouchepadass, J. 'The Market for Agricultural Labour in Colonial North Bihar, 1860–1920', in M. Holmstrom (ed.), *Work for Wages in South Asia*, pp. 11–27. Delhi, 1990.

Prakash, G. *Bonded Histories: Genealogies of Labor Servitude in Colonial India*. Cambridge, 1990.

Pryde, A. W. 'The Work of the Labour Officer', in C. Manshardt (ed.), *Some Social Services of the Government of Bombay*. Bombay, 1937.

Radhakrishna, M. 'The Criminal Tribes Act in the Madras Presidency: Implications for the Itinerant Trading Communities', *Indian Economic and Social History Review*, 26:3 (1989), 269–95.

'Surveillance and Settlements under the Criminal Tribes Act in Madras', *Indian Economic and Social History Review*, 29:2 (1992), 171–98.

Raghunathji, K. *The Hindu Temples of Bombay*. Bombay, 1900.

Ramasamy, P. *Plantation Labour, Unions, Capital and the State in Peninsular Malaysia*. Kuala Lumpur, 1994.

Ramaswamy, E. A. *The Worker and His Union: A Study in South India*. New Delhi, 1977.

Rangarajan, M. 'Imperial Agendas and India's Forests: The Early History of Indian Forestry, 1800–1878', *Indian Economic and Social History Review*, 31:2 (1994), 147–67.

Ray, R. K. 'Masses in Politics: The Non-Cooperation Movement in Bengal, 1920–22', *Indian Economic and Social History Review*, 11:4 (1974), 343–410.

Industrialization in India: Growth and Conflict in the Private Corporate Sector, 1914–47. Delhi, 1979.

Urban Roots of Indian Nationalism: Pressure Groups and Conflict of Interests in Calcutta City Politics, 1875–1939. New Delhi, 1979.

'Pedhis and Mills: The Historical Integration of the Formal and Informal Sectors in the Economy of Ahmedabad, *Indian Economic and Social History Review*, 19:3 and 4 (1982), 387–96.

Social Conflict and Political Unrest in Bengal, 1875–1927. Delhi, 1986.

Reiner, R. *The Politics of the Police*. Brighton, 1985.

Reisner, I. M. and N. M. Goldberg (eds.), *Tilak and the Struggle for Indian Freedom*. New Delhi, 1966.

Revri, C. *The Indian Trade Union Movement: An Outline History, 1880–1947*. New Delhi, 1972.

Richards, J. F. 'The Indian Empire and Peasant Production of Opium in the Nineteenth Century', *Modern Asian Studies*, 15:1 (1981), 59–82.

Richards, J. F. 'Mughal State Finance and the Premodern World Economy', *Comparative Studies in Society and History*, 23:2 (1981), 285–308.

Robb, P. 'The Ordering of Rural India: The Policing of Nineteenth Century Bengal and Bihar', in D. M. Anderson and D. Killingray (eds.), *Policing the Empire: Government, Authority and Control, 1830–1940*, pp. 126–50. Manchester, 1991.

Robinson, F. C. R. *Separatism Among Indian Muslims: The Politics of the United Provinces' Muslims, 1860–1923*. Cambridge, 1974.

Robinson, R. 'Oxford in Imperial Historiography', in F. Madden and D. K. Fieldhouse (eds.), *Oxford and the Idea of the Commonwealth: Essays Presented to Sir Edgar Williams*, pp. 30–48. London, 1982.

Rostow, W. W. *The Stages of Economic Growth: A Non-Communist Manifesto*. Cambridge, 1960.

Rowe, W. D. 'Caste, Kinship and Association in Urban India', in A. Southall (ed.), *Urban Anthropology: Cross Cultural Studies of Urbanization*, pp. 211–49. New York, 1973.

Roy, T. *Artisans and Industrialization: Indian Weaving in the Twentieth Century*. Delhi, 1993.

Roy, T. (ed.). *Cloth and Commerce: Textiles in Colonial India*. New Delhi, 1996.

Russell, W. H. *My Diary in India in the Year 1858–59*, 2 vols. London, 1860.

Rutnagur, M. C. *The Indian Textile Journal Directory of Indian Manufactories, 1894*. Bombay, 1894.

Rutnagur, S. M. (ed.). *Bombay Industries: The Cotton Mills – A Review of the Progress of the Textile Industry in Bombay from 1850 to 1926 and the Present Constitution, Management and Financial Position of Spinning and Weaving Factories*. Bombay, 1927.

Saha, P. *History of the Working Class Movement in Bengal*. New Delhi, 1978.

Said, E. *Orientalism*. New York, 1978.

Sandilands, J. 'The Health of the Bombay Worker', *Labour Gazette*, 1:2 (October 1921), 14–16.

Sarkar, S. 'Popular Movements and National Leadership, 1945–47', *Economic and Political Weekly*, 17:14, 15 and 16 (April 1982), annual number, 677–89.

   'The Conditions and Nature of Subaltern Militancy: Bengal from Swadeshi to Non-Cooperation, *c.* 1905–1922', in R. Guha (ed.), *Subaltern Studies*, vol. III, pp. 271–320.

Sarkar, T. 'The First Phase of Civil Disobedience in Bengal, 1930–31', *Indian Historical Review*, 4:1 (1977), 75–95.

   Bengal, 1928–34: The Politics of Protest. Delhi, 1987.

Saul, S. B. *Studies in British Overseas Trade*. Liverpool, 1960.

Sayer, D. 'British Reactions to the Amritsar Massacre, 1919–1920', *Past and Present*, 131 (May 1991), 130–64.

Schuster, George E. and Guy Wint. *India and Democracy*. London, 1941.

Scott, H. H. *A History of Tropical Medicine*, 2 vols. London, 1939.

Scott, J. C. *Weapons of the Weak: Everyday Forms of Peasant Resistance*. New Haven, 1985.

   'Everyday Forms of Peasant Resistance' in J. C. Scott and B. J. T. Kerkvliet (eds.), *Everyday Forms of Peasant Resistance in South-east Asia*, pp. 5–35.

Scott, J. C. and B. J. T. Kerkvliet (eds.). *Everyday Forms of Peasant Resistance in South-East Asia*. London, 1986.

Seal, A. *The Emergence of Indian Nationalism: Competition and Collaboration in the Later Nineteenth Century*. Cambridge, 1968.

Seers, D. 'The Birth, Life and Death of Development Economics', *Development and Change*, 10:4 (1979), 707–19.

Sen, A. K. 'The Commodity Pattern of British Enterprise in Early Indian Industrialization, 1854–1914', in *The Second International Conference of Economic History, Aix-en-Provence, 1962*, vol. II: *Middle Ages and Modern Times*, pp. 781–808. Paris, 1962.

Sen, S. N. *Eighteen Fifty Seven*. New Delhi, 1957.

Seth, B. R. *Labour in the Indian Coal Industry*. Bombay, 1940.

Shah, K. T. and G. J. Bahadurji. *Constitutions, Functions and Finance of Indian Municipalities*. Bombay, 1925.

Sharpe, J. A. 'The History of Violence in England: Some Observations', *Past and Present*, 108 (1985), 206–15.

Shilts, Randy. *And the Band Played On. Politics, People and the Aids Epidemic*. London, 1988.

Shiva Rao, B. *The Industrial Worker in India*. London, 1939.

Shlomowitz, R. and L. Brennan. 'Mortality and Migrant Labour in Assam, 1865–1921', *Indian Economic and Social History Review*, 27:1 (1990), 85–110.

'Mortality and Migrant Labour en route to Assam, 1863–1924', *Indian Economic and Social History Review*, 27:3 (1990), 313–30.

Siddiqi, A. 'Money and Prices in the Earlier Stages of Empire', *Indian Economic and Social History Review*, 18:3 and 4 (1981), 231–62.

'The Business World of Jamsetjee Jejeebhoy', *Indian Economic and Social History Review*, 19:3 and 4 (1982), 301–24.

Simeon, D. *The Politics of Labour under Late Colonialism: Workers, Unions and the State in Chota Nagpur, 1928–1939*. New Delhi, 1995.

Simmons, C. P. 'Indigenous Enterprise in the Indian Coal Mining Industry, c. 1835–1939', *Indian Economic and Social History Review*, 13:2 (1976), 189–218.

'Recruiting and Organizing an Industrial Labour Force in Colonial India: The Case of the Coal Mining Industry c. 1880–1939', *Indian Economic and Social History Review*, 13:4 (1976), 455–85.

'Vertical Integration and the Indian Steel Industry', *Modern Asian Studies*, 11:1 (1977), 127–48.

Singh, Moni. *Life is a Struggle*, trans. Mrs Karuna Banerjee. New Delhi, 1988.

Singha, Radhika. '"Providential" Circumstances: The Thuggee Campaign of the 1830s and Legal Innovation', *Modern Asian Studies*, 27:1 (1993), 83–146.

Slack, P. 'The Response to Plague in Early Modern England: Public Policies and Their Consequences', in J. Walter and R. Schofield (eds.), *Famine, Disease and the Social Order in Early Modern Society*, pp. 167–87. Cambridge, 1989.

Smelser, N. J. *Social Change and the Industrial Revolution*. London, 1959.

Stedman Jones, G. *Languages of Class: Studies in English Working Class History, 1832–1982*. Cambridge, 1983.

Stokes, E. *The English Utilitarians and India*. Cambridge, 1959.

The Peasant and the Raj: Studies in Agrarian Society and Peasant Rebellion in Colonial India. Cambridge, 1978.

Stone, L. 'Interpersonal Violence in English Society, 1300–1980', *Past and Present*, 101 (1983), 22–33.

'A Rejoinder', *Past and Present*, 108 (1985), 206–15.

Strachey, J. *India*. London, 1888.

Sutcliffe, R. 'Imperialism and Industrialisation in the Third World', in R. Owen and R. Sutcliffe (eds.), *Studies in the Theory of Imperialism*, pp. 171–92. London, 1972.

Temple, Richard. *India in 1880*. London, 1880.

Thomas, P. J. *The Growth of Federal Finance in India*. London, 1939.

Thorner, D. and A. Thorner. *Land and Labour in India*. Bombay, 1962.

Tilly, C. 'The Changing Place of Collective Violence', in M. Richter (ed.), *Essays in Theory and History: Approaches to the Social Sciences*, pp. 139–64. Cambridge, Mass., 1970.

Tilly, C., Louise Tilly and Richard Tilly. *The Rebellious Century, 1830–1930*. London, 1975.

Timberg, T. A. *The Marwaris: From Traders to Industrialists*. New Delhi, 1978.

Tinker, H. *A New System of Slavery: The Export of Indian Labour Overseas, 1830–1920*. Oxford, 1974.

Tomlinson, B. R. 'India and the British Empire, 1880–1935', *Indian Economic and Social History Review*, 12:4 (1975), 339–80.

'India and the British Empire, 1935–1947', *Indian Economic and Social History Review*, 13:3 (1976), 331–52.

The Indian National Congress and the Raj: The Penultimate Phase, 1929–1942. London, 1977.

The Political Economy of the Raj: The Economics of Decolonization in India. London, 1979.

'Colonial Firms and the Decline of Colonialism in Eastern India, 1914–1947', *Modern Asian Studies*, 15:3 (1981) special issue, *Power, Profit and Politics: Essays on Imperialism, Nationalism and Change in Twentieth Century India, 1870–1940*, ed. C. Baker, G. Johnson and A Seal, 455–86.

'Writing History Sideways: Lessons for Indian Economic Historians From Meiji Japan', *Modern Asian Studies*, 19:3 (1985), 669–98.

'British Business in India, 1860–1970', in R. P. T. Davenport-Hines and Geoffrey Jones (eds.), *British Business in Asia since 1860*. Cambridge, 1989.

The New Cambridge History of India, vol III:3: *The Economy of Modern India, 1860–1970*. Cambridge, 1993.

Townshend, P. *The British Campaign in Ireland, 1919–1921: The Development of Political and Military Policies*. Oxford, 1975.

Trebilcock, R. C. *The Industrialization of the Continental Powers, 1750–1914*. New York, 1981.

Tripathi, D. *The Dynamics of a Tradition: Kasturbhai Lalbhai and His Entrepreneurship*. New Delhi, 1981.

Tripathi, D. and M. J. Mehta. 'The Nagarsheth of Ahmedabad: The History of an Urban Institution in a Gujarati City', *Proceedings of the Indian History Congress* (1978?), 481–96.

Twomey, M. 'Employment in Nineteenth Century Indian Textiles', *Explorations in Economic History*, 20:1 (1983), 37–57.

Vicziany, A. M. 'Bombay Merchants and Structural Changes in the Export Community, 1850 to 1880', in K. N. Chaudhuri and C. J. Dewey (eds.), *Economy and Society: Essays in Indian Economic and Social History*, pp. 163–96.

'The De-Industrialization of India in the Nineteenth Century: A Methological Critique of Amiya Kumar Bagchi', *Indian Economic and Social History Review*, 16:2 (1979), 105–46.

Visaria L. and P. Visaria, 'Population, 1757–1947' in D. Kumar (ed.), *The Cambridge Economic History of India*, vol. II: *1757–1970*, pp. 463–532.

Wagle, D. M. 'Imperial Preference and the Indian Steel Industry', *Economic History Review*, 34:1 (1981), 120–31.

Wallace, D. R. *The Romance of Jute*. Calcutta, 1909.

Wallerstein, I. 'The Rise and Future Demise of the World System: Concepts for Comparative Analysis', *Comparative Studies in Society and History*, 16:4 (1974), 387–415.

The Capitalist World Economy. Cambridge, 1979.

'Incorporation of the Indian Sub-continent into the Capitalist World Economy', *Economic and Political Weekly*, 21:4 (25 January 1986), *Review of Political Economy*, PE-28 to PE-39.

Warboys, M. 'The Emergence of Tropical Medicine: A Study in the Establishment of a Scientific Speciality', in G. Lemaine, R. Macleod, M. Mulkay and P. Weingart (eds.), *Perspectives on the Emergence of Scientific Disciplines*, pp. 75–98. The Hague, 1976.

Warren, Bill, *Imperialism – The Pioneer of Capitalism*. London, 1980.

Washbrook, D. A. *The Emergence of Provincial Politics: Madras Presidency, 1870–1920*. Cambridge, 1976.

'Law, State and Agrarian Society in Colonial India', *Modern Asian Studies*, 15:3 (1981), special issue, *Power, Profit and Politics: Essays on Imperialism, Nationalism and Change in Twentieth Century India, 1870–1940*, ed. C. Baker, G Johnson and A. Seal, 649–721.

'Progress and Problems: South Asian Economic and Social History, *c.* 1720–1860', *Modern Asian Studies*, 22:1 (1988), 57–96.

'South Asia, the World System and World Capitalism', *Journal of Asian Studies*, 49:3 (1990), 479–508.

'Land and Labour in Late Eighteenth Century South India: The Golden Age of the Pariah', in P. Robb (ed.), *Dalit Movements and the Meanings of Labour*, pp. 68–86. Delhi, 1993.

Weber, Max. *The Religion of India*, trans. H. H. Gerth and D. Martindale. Glencoe, Ill., 1958.

Williams, R. *Keywords: A Vocabulary of Culture and Society*. London, 1976.

Wood, C. 'Peasant Revolt: An Interpretation of Moplah Violence in the Nineteenth and Twentieth Centuries', in C. J. Dewey and A. G. Hopkins (eds.), *The Imperial Impact: Studies in the Economic History of Africa and India*, pp. 132–51.

Yang, A. 'The Agrarian Origins of Crime: A Study of Riots in Saran District, India, 1886–1920', *Journal of Social History*, 13:2 (1979), 289–306.

Yang, A. (ed.). *Crime and Criminality in British India*. Arizona, 1985.

Yolland, Z. *Boxwallahs: The British in Cawnpore, 1857–1901*. Norwich, 1994.

Zelliot, E. 'Congress and the Untouchables', in R. Sisson and S. Wolpert (eds.), *Congress and Indian Nationalism. The Pre-Independence Phase*, pp. 182–97. Berkeley and Los Angeles, 1988.

UNPUBLISHED PAPERS AND DISSERTATIONS

Basu, S. 'Workers' Politics in Bengal, 1890–1929: Mill-Towns, Strikes and Nationalist Agitations'. Unpublished Ph.D. thesis, University of Cambridge, 1994.

Dewey, C. J. 'The Agricultural Output of an Indian Province: The Punjab, 1870–1940'. Paper read to the Economic History Seminar, Institute of Commonwealth Studies, 30 April 1973. Centre of South Asian Studies Library, Cambridge.

Ghosh, R. K. 'A Study of the Labour Movement in the Jharia Coal Field, 1900–1977'. Unpublished Ph.D. thesis, University of Calcutta, 1992.

Gooptu, N. 'The Political Culture of the Urban Poor in North India, 1920–47'. Unpublished Ph.D. thesis, University of Cambridge, 1991.

Haynes, D. 'From Merchant Capital to Weavers' Capital: The Slow Transformation of Artisanal Production in the Bombay Presidency, 1900–1950'.

Narain, N. 'Co-option and Control: The Role of the Colonial Army in India, 1918–1947'. Unpublished Ph.D. thesis, University of Cambridge, 1993.

Pradhan, G. R. 'The Untouchable Workers of Bombay City'. Unpublished M.A. thesis, University of Bombay, 1936.

Sen, Samita. 'Women Workers in the Bengal Jute Industry, 1890–1940: Migration, Motherhood and Militancy'. Unpublished Ph.D. thesis, University of Cambridge, 1992.

Vicziany, A. M. 'The Cotton Trade and the Commercial Development of Bombay, 1853–1875'. Unpublished Ph.D. thesis, University of London, 1975.

Index

trade unions   12–13, 74–99
  and Bombay working-class
    neighbourhoods   117–42, 192
  and the colonial state   92–4
  and the Congress   19, 77–8, 91, 96–7,
    267–8, 292, 297, 301–2, 306, 320
  and employers   80–4, 85, 88, 89–90,
    98, 99
  and industrialization   35, 74–5, 79–80,
    97–8
  and jobbers   79, 80, 82, 83, 126, 128,
    129
  leadership   84–9
  legislation   93, 285, 304, 318
  and neighbourhood leaders   194
  neighbourhood recruitment   104
  organization   74, 97–8, 101–2
  and the police   211
  studies of   5
  and violence   148
  weakness of   143–4
  and working-class nationalism   315
  see also Bombay Girni Kamgar Union;
    communist trade unions; strikes
tribes, and criminalization   226, 228, 229
Tuticorin, trade unions   82

unemployment
  cotton textile industry   63, 133
  and neighbourhood connections   107
  and working-class violence   160–1
United States, AIDS epidemic of the
    1980s   18, 265
urban poor, and colonial discourse on
    violence   15

Varerkar, Mama, Dhavta Dhota   159
Vicziany, M.   53
Viegas, Dr A. C.   237, 239, 254
village community, in colonial discourse
    23, 24, 25
village connections
  and Bombay working-class
    neighbourhoods   107, 108
  and jobbers   106
  and neighbourhood leaders   195
  and policing   16
  and the workforce   77, 274
villages
  and the plague epidemic   259, 261
  and the police   184–5
  rural migrants from   7
  and swaraj   291
Vincent, Fatty   198–9, 202
violence   2, 143–79

and 'bad characters'/hooligans   160–3,
    174–5
and collective action   155–6
and colonial discourse   14–15, 28
crowd control and the police   212–16
discourse of   14, 150, 176–7
historians' conceptualization of
    147–50, 152, 176
industrial   155, 177
Marxist theories of   148
mass, and colonial discourse   216
reporting of   150, 152–3
and 'the other'   174
threat of   151
and trade unions   98, 144–5
in workers' politics   9
see also riots

Wadia, B. P.   293
wages
  adult male labour force   340–1
  in colonial discourse   26, 27
  entrepreneurs and industrialization   40
  and the jobber system   344
  policemen   185, 188
  and strikes   92, 100
Wallerstein, I.   328, 332, 347, 348, 349,
    350
Washbrook, David   145
Watts, T.   158
weavers, in the Bombay workforce   141
Weber, Max, The Religion of India   27
Weir, T. S.   242, 256
Western Europe, and industrialization
    30, 31, 32–4, 38, 40, 42, 79
Whig historiography of industrialization
    42, 44
women
  and police violence   214
  sexual harassment by soldiers   249,
    253
  in the workforce   338–9
workforce
  absenteeism   343
  and the Congress   274–5
  and jobbers   67–8, 76, 105–6, 341–5
  labour market collapse, and the plague
    epidemic   260
  labour market segmentation, and
    neighbourhood   9
  labour patterns, and large-scale
    industries   44
  migrant workers   337–8, 339–41,
    345–6, 347
  pre-industrial character   79, 101